REGIMES

AND

OPPOSITIONS

edited by

ROBERT A. DAHL

New Haven and London

Yale University Press

1973

Library of Congress catalog card number: 79–151571
International standard book number: 0–300–01390–6

Set in Janson type and
printed in the United States of America by
The Colonial Press Inc., Clinton, Massachusetts.

Published in Great Britain, Europe, and Africa by
Yale University Press, Ltd., London.
Distributed in Canada by McGill-Queen's University
Press, Montreal; in Latin America by Kaiman & Polon,
Inc., New York City; in Australasia and Southeast
Asia by John Wiley & Sons Australasia Pty. Ltd.,
Sydney; in India by UBS Publishers' Distributors Pvt.,
Ltd., Delhi; in Japan by John Weatherhill, Inc., Tokyo.

CONTENTS

CONTENTS

1

INTRODUCTION

Robert A. Dahl

The Argument

1. Let me begin with an elementary proposition about politics that I think no one seriously questions. No government receives indefinitely the total support of the people over whom it asserts its jurisdiction. Certainly the government of a large collection of people, such as the government of a country, is never completely supported in all that it does by all the people whom it claims to govern. In no country, in short, does everyone have the same preferences as to the conduct of the government, using the term *conduct* in its broadest sense. So much is, I believe, obvious.

2. It is an equally well-grounded observation, I believe — though one more often denied, even in highly influential theories of politics — that differences in what people think they want from the government that rules over them tend toward diversity and multiplicity rather than toward bipolarity: to many groupings rather than merely two. Let me call what people think they want the government to be, or to do, their *political preferences*, or, if you prefer, their *political interests*. Whenever the barriers to the expression and organization of political preferences are low, one should expect (as the usual thing) the emergence of a multiplicity of camps, whereas polarization into two internally cohesive and unified camps would be rare.

Although the second proposition may be more debatable than the first, the experiences of the countries described in the chapters of this book lend great weight to it, as I hope to show in a moment.

3. Because people are not in perfect accord as to their political preferences, every political system, if it is to endure, must provide ways for determining which (or whose) political preferences the government responds to. It will be useful to consider two extreme possibilities. At one extreme, a government might respond to the political preferences of only one person (or perhaps to a tiny and wholly unified minority); it would ignore or override all other preferences. A system of this kind might be

1

called a pure *hegemony*. At the other extreme, the political preferences of everyone might be weighted equally, and the government would respond always to the preferences of the greatest number. A system of this kind might be called a pure *egalitarian democracy*.

4. All political systems in some respects constrain the expression, organization, representation, and satisfaction of political preferences. Given the existence of disagreements as to what the government should do (that is to say, given the human condition, if my first assumption is valid), even an egalitarian democracy cannot respond fully to the preferences of both the greatest number and the smaller number who disagree with them. During any given period, therefore, a political system will contain some people who, if there were no barriers or costs to their doing so, would be opposed to the conduct of the government.

5. Political systems vary a great deal, however, in the barriers or opportunities they provide for the expression, organization, and representation of political preferences and thus in the opportunities available to potential oppositions.

To cope adequately with these variations among different political systems poses some difficulties. For example, a moment ago I offered two extreme types, hegemony and egalitarian democracy; yet both are purely theoretical types. Although neither exists in pure form, they do hint at a possible continuum, running from one to the other. However, it is more accurate for our purposes to think not just of one but of two dimensions. One is the dimension of *liberalization* or *public contestation:* the extent to which institutions are openly available, publicly employed, and guaranteed to at least some members of the political system who wish to contest the conduct of the government. The other is the dimension of *participation* or *inclusiveness:* the proportion of the population (or of adults) who are entitled to participate on a more or less equal basis in controlling and contesting the conduct of the government — that is, who are entitled to participate in the system of public contestation.

In practice, political systems (particularly if we include historical ones) seem to vary over most of the space enclosed by these two hypothetical dimensions, except perhaps for space near the edges. Although the space can be carved up and labeled in many different ways, for the purposes of this essay it seems to me preferable to run the risk of oversimplification by distinguishing no more than three very general categories (see figure 1.1).

One: Regimes that impose the most severe limits on the expression, organization, and representation of political preferences and on the opportunities available to opponents of the government. In these systems, individuals are prohibited from expressing public opposition to the incumbent leaders, to their policies and ideology, and to the major social, eco-

Figure 1.1 Types of Regimes

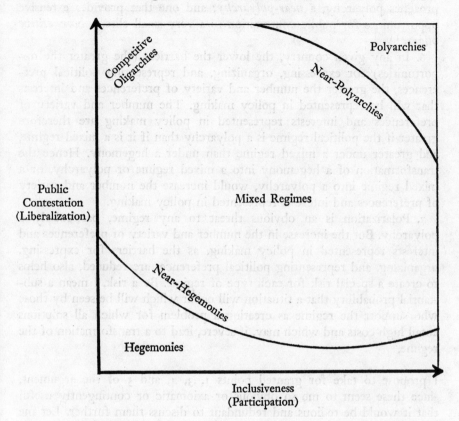

Public
Contestation
(Liberalization)

Competitive
Oligarchies

Polyarchies

Near-Polyarchies

Mixed Regimes

Near-Hegemonies

Hegemonies

Inclusiveness
(Participation)

nomic, and political structures. Organized dissent and opposition are prohibited in any form. I shall call such systems *hegemonies*.

Two: Regimes that impose the fewest restraints on the expression, organization, and representation of political preferences and on the opportunities available to opponents of government. Most individuals are effectively protected in their right to express, privately or publicly, their opposition to the government, to organize, to form parties, and to compete in elections where voting is secret, unintimidated, and honestly counted and where the results of elections are binding according to well-established rules. Ordinarily, the use of violent means is forbidden, and in some cases it is punishable to advocate the use of violence for political purposes. I shall call such systems *polyarchies*.

Three: Mixed regimes, which in various ways approach hegemonies or polyarchies. Among the countries of the world, these are the most numerous. I shall sometimes call an intermediate regime that more closely approaches a hegemony a *near-hegemony;* one that more closely approaches polyarchy, a *near-polyarchy;* and one that provides extensive opportunities for public contestation to a very small elite, a *competitive oligarchy.*

6. In any given country, the lower the barriers (the greater the opportunities) for expressing, organizing, and representing political preferences, the greater the number and variety of preferences and interests that will be represented in policy making. The number and variety of preferences and interests represented in policy making are therefore greater if the political regime is a polyarchy than if it is a mixed regime, and greater under a mixed regime than under a hegemony. Hence the transformation of a hegemony into a mixed regime or polyarchy, or a mixed regime into a polyarchy, would increase the number and variety of preferences and interests represented in policy making.

7. Polarization is an obvious threat to any regime, particularly a polyarchy. But the increase in the number and variety of preferences and interests represented in policy making, as the barriers for expressing, organizing, and representing political preferences are reduced, also helps to create a special risk for each type of regime. By a risk, I mean a substantial probability that a situation will occur which will be seen by those who support the regime as creating a problem for which all solutions entail high costs and which may, if severe, lead to a transformation of the regime.

I propose to take for granted points 1, 3, 4, and 5 of the argument, since these seem to me so obvious or axiomatic or contingently useful that it would be tedious and redundant to discuss them further. Let me then concentrate briefly on points 2, 6, and 7 and in so doing draw upon the later chapters of this volume by way of evidence and illustration.

Polarization and Plurality

That the forces of conflict in society are polarizing, in the sense that they exhibit an irresistible tendency toward a cleavage into two enduring sets of antagonists, is a view that seems to have a powerful attraction. Although it is perhaps best set out in Marxist thought, its reach extends far beyond any particular political philosophy or ideology.

Usually this current of thought stresses the strictly economic or purely socioeconomic axis of conflict; thus societies tend to be bipolar along a socioeconomic line of cleavage. The fact is, however, that the great bulk of experience in the past century — whether in traditional, modernizing, industrial, or postindustrial societies — seems to run counter to this hypothesis. It is rare for a country to divide into two camps along socioeconomic lines; it is rare, indeed, for a country to divide into only two camps along any lines. But it is commonplace for countries to display *more* than two sets of conflicting interests.

The explanation seems to be that most countries have some conflicts based at least in part on differences in language, religion, race, or ethnic group. Frequently these conflicts cut, wholly or partly, across one another and across differences of status, function, or reward based on economic activity. And they do not disappear or become attenuated with modernization. It is, rather, the conflicts derived from economic differences that often become attenuated, leaving more room, so to speak, for the other conflicts to occur. What is more, different political preferences or interests stimulated by differences in economic function, status, or reward seldom divide a people into only two groups, each with more or less identical preferences. Much more often, it seems, when people respond to economic factors, they divide into more than two groups — frequently, in fact, into a bewildering multiplicity of contesting interests.

What seems to vary most from one country to another is, not so much this tendency toward diversity rather than polarization, but rather the extent to which the societal cloth is cut up into separate pieces by a succession of cuts or, alternatively, is woven with strong strands that hold one part to another. In language more familiar to social scientists (but which reverses the metaphor I have just used) I am of course speaking of the extent to which cleavages "reinforce" one another and hence produce "segmentation" or "fragmentation," or instead "crosscut" one another and thus produce a greater tendency toward cohesion.

The important — and, one would have supposed, by now obvious — point is the comparative rarity of strongly bipolar social conflicts, particularly along an economic axis, and the comparative frequency of conflict involving more than two sets of contestants.

Thus in describing the social basis for opposition in the single-party states of tropical Africa, Foltz refers to the impact of a half-dozen kinds of differences. Language and ethnic group reinforce each other to make tribal differences perhaps the dominant source of conflict; yet differences in region, mode of livelihood, religion, caste, modernity, urban-rural residence, and education reduce the cohesiveness of the tribe and enable politicians to build intertribal coalitions. As elsewhere in the world — India, Canada, Belgium, or Spain, for instance — the most serious conflicts are likely to arise where regional differences coincide with some of the other differences, most notably in language and ethnic groups. It is this kind of combination, in fact, that seems much more likely to lead to polarization or segmentation than any purely socioeconomic difference alone has ever succeeded in doing. Throughout the world, the overt or latent forces of nationalism continue to be the most powerful sources of political antagonisms.

Segmentation and pluralism are central themes in Indian society, as Kothari shows in his essay. In India there has not yet been any clear polarization of conflict, either between the dominant Congress party and its opponents or among the incredible variety of castes, subcastes, and ethnic, linguistic, and regional groups. Although the differences between the preponderant Hindu population and the Muslim minority are an ever present source of danger, these do not form a principal line of cleavage in political conflicts; most political conflicts occur among Hindus, not between Hindus and Muslims. As to socioeconomic cleavages, the peasantry is of course numerically overwhelming, but it is not a unified force; and conflict between the urban working class and employers is simply one cleavage among many. As Kothari says, "India is still far from becoming a mass society; its pluralism also is of a different kind from that in Western democracies. It is less a confrontation between aggregated subsystems and more a coexistence between historically autonomous diversities and identities. Hence the great variety and diffusion of oppositions and their lack of clear-cut boundaries."

Tropical Africa and India are, of course, areas where traditional society and its differences exert an extraordinarily powerful pull, and it would not be unreasonable to argue that as they undergo the changes that come with modernization, traditional societies would be most prone to a diversity of cleavages. Latin America is hardly a region of traditionalism in quite the same sense as India or Africa, though it is an area where the forces of modernization are nearly everywhere bringing about rapid changes in previous patterns of social, economic, and political life. As Dix points out, in the early decades of this century economic growth and urbanization in a number of Latin American countries, stimulating the expansion of new social sectors — "the industrialists, the middle sectors, and urban and mining proletariats" — helped make traditional political coalitions less effectual and increased the political importance of "categorical groupings based on occupation and economic interest." Yet these bases of conflict and coalition have "far from overwhelmed the past. Modern institutions and orientations often coexist with others that are traditional, sometimes in surprisingly compatible ways." Wealthy industrial entrepreneurs do not see eye to eye with upper-class landowners. The middle classes are at best a nominal category, not cohesive social classes; they are divided in their attitudes toward public policy, in ideology, in their commitment to Catholicism or anticlericalism, and in their personal and party loyalties. The lower, or "popular," classes, to use Dix's term, are divided by more than an urban-rural cleavage; in the countryside, traditional agriculture vies with modern agriculture, and in the city the skilled worker or the worker employed in a modern industry feels little or no solidarity with the unskilled, with the newly arriving peasant from the countryside, or with the "marginals living in the jerry-built slums that surround many of the large urban centers." As in many Catholic societies, women are more likely to support the church than men, while anticlericals are predominantly male. And of course the generation gap (or gaps) is (or are) as marked in Latin America as anywhere else.

Despite palpable evidence of this kind in Latin America as elsewhere in the world, many political activists and intellectuals continue to interpret politics as a struggle between classes. Certainly socioeconomic differences are sufficiently important as bases of cleavage and conflict in Latin America (as elsewhere) to give considerable credibility to their interpretations. The fact is, however, that other lines of cleavage, and the plurality of cleavages based on socioeconomic differences, so complicate political life in these countries that when political movements base their strategies on a pure class interpretation, they suffer grievous political defeat. Despite the presence of poverty, revolutionary rhetoric, and severe conflict, the Marxist parties of Latin America have failed to acquire a leading role except in Chile, Cuba, and Guatemala, where, in Dix's words, they were "tails to the kites of non-Communist nationalistic revolutions." In the rare cases where a Communist party has acquired a substantial electoral following, as in Chile, or where it is relatively small and hopes to expand its mass following in order to compete effectively in elections, as in Venezuela, party leaders seem to have recognized the failure of the classic strategy based on hopes of polarization. Like Communist leaders in Italy and France, they now seek alliances that would lead to a broad and heterogeneous collection of interests capable of winning an electoral majority.

Many people who cling to the belief that politics in evil and still unredeemed societies must embody an inherent motion toward socioeconomic polarization, apocalypse, and redemption can protect their vision from doubts, which evidence of the kind I have just discussed might otherwise create, by pointing to the persistence of rich and poor, the divergence in their "real interests," the obvious economic origins of many conflicts, and, above all, the expectation that the process of polarization will occur in some indefinite future. None of these arguments can be proved false; in particular, locating apocalypse and redemption in the future surely helps to preserve this faith, as it has others.

It would seem reasonable that as the United States lurched recklessly through the process of becoming an advanced industrial society and then went on to become a postindustrial society, the processes of polarization, apocalypse, and redemption, if they were ever to occur anywhere, would surely have occurred there first of all. But even the Civil War does not fit the schema. The inconvenient experience of the United States has been dealt with by ignoring it, by treating it as a unique case, or by postponing the American apocalypse (and redemption) to a yet more distant future.

An alternative test is provided by Japan, which like Russia has in less than a century traveled the path from an agrarian-based feudal society to a highly industrial economy and society — and soon, no doubt, to a post-industrial economy and society. As in Western Europe in the second half of the nineteenth century, so too in Japan during the first third of the twentieth century, industrialization created some of the familiar conditions for the exacerbation of twentieth-century class conflict. As Leiserson describes Taishō Democracy, it appears to have consisted of a competitive oligarchy undergoing a measure of liberalization and democratization; but before this evolutionary process was completed and consolidated, it was interrupted by Showa Fascism, which repressed the public expression of many latent conflicts. It is conceivable, certainly, that Taishō Democracy would ultimately have seen the emergence of political conflict highly polarized along clear-cut socioeconomic lines, but no such development seems to have occurred by the time Showa Fascism took over.

Japanese politics since World War II appears to be more polarized than American politics. At the level of electoral conflicts, the Liberal-Democrats and conservative independents gain the preponderant support of large business, farmers, and the national bureaucracy, while their opponents gain more supporters among labor, youth, intellectuals, and the lower middle classes. But as Leiserson's analysis makes clear, not only is this too simple a description, but the results have hardly been a polarization of political conflict along clear-cut socioeconomic lines. Voting patterns are a tangle of socioeconomic interests, party loyalties, personal loyalties, variations in organizational effectiveness, and deference to immediate or remote authority figures. The parties themselves are collections of factions. And some of the most important lines of cleavage, as Leiserson shows, are differences in ideological perspectives that are, it appears, only loosely related to socioeconomic position.

In Soviet Russia and in the socialist countries of Eastern Europe, except Yugoslavia, the barriers to the public expression of political preferences are comparatively high. Yet, like other countries, these socialist countries contain within their boundaries people who differ in language, religion, ethnic group, status, economic position, policy views, ideology, personal loyalty, organizational loyalties, and the like. The widespread defection among certain nationality groups in the Soviet Union during World War II may reveal something of the persistence of ethnic and national identities. One of the most powerful arguments against introducing a plural party system in Yugoslavia is the danger that parties would form around ethnic groups and intensify ethnic conflicts.

Where the barriers to the public expression of preferences are high, as in the Soviet Union, one can only guess at the patterns that conflict would take were the differences allowed to express themselves. In Yugoslavia, where the barriers have been very much reduced, the variety of interests claiming attention is remarkable. And during the brief period when the barriers were dropped in Czechoslovakia, diversity flourished like long-dormant flowers in a desert after a rain. Thus it is a reasonable conjecture that whenever the barriers to the public expression of preferences are reduced in Communist countries, in the long run (should they get through the short-run period of turmoil that may ensue) they will face a problem not so much of polarization as of diversity and possible segmentation.

The experiences of the countries described in this volume seem to support what I referred to at the beginning of this chapter as a well-grounded observation: differences in political preferences among the people of a country tend toward diversity and multiplicity rather than bipolarity. To many readers, the proposition, which is hardly a novel one, will seem so nearly self-evident that any appeal to experience of the kind I have just made is an exercise in demonstrating the obvious. Yet some readers, I am sure, will remain unconvinced.

Admittedly I have done no more than assert the existence of a very general and ubiquitous tendency, and a statement of a general tendency is a long way from a precise proposition in a comprehensive theory. At a minimum, a satisfactory theory would say something about the variations in the strength and characteristics of this tendency, the conditions under which polarization, even if an infrequent process, would be likely to occur, the causes and consequences of crosscutting rather than reinforcing cleavages, and doubtless many other matters. But perhaps it is enough here simply to give some substance to the assertion that the general tendency exists over long periods and in a great many countries at different stages of socioeconomic development and with different political regimes and economic systems.

A hasty reader might be tempted at this point to jump to some unwarranted conclusions. To say that polarization, like the plague, is rare is obviously not to say that it presents no dangers. And because polarization, though rare, is dangerous, one should not leap to the conclusion that a multiplicity of political interests, though more common, inevitably produces cohesion and stability. For diversity, like polarization, can also create problems, even for polyarchies. In what follows it is the problems which seem to stem from diversity rather than from polarization that I want to stress. But first let me emphasize one further part of the argument.

Regimes and Interests

One part of the argument I offered at the beginning was that the lower the barriers to, or the greater the opportunities for, expressing, organizing, and representing political preferences, the greater the number and variety of preferences that would be represented in policy making. Hence the number and variety of interests represented in policy making would be greater under a polyarchy than under a mixed regime and greater under a mixed regime than under a hegemony. Therefore the transformation of a hegemony into a mixed regime or polyarchy, or of a mixed regime into a polyarchy, would increase the number and variety of preferences and interests in policy making.

If one were not careful about definitions, the argument could of course become circular. Even if a meticulous concern for definitions will enable us to avoid the latent circularity, the hypothesis is not easy to test. Yet changes in regime occur, and the results do seem to bear out the argument. When hegemonic regimes are suddenly displaced by regimes that provide greater opportunities for opposition — as in Spain after the flight of the king in 1931 and the establishment of the republic, or in Italy and Germany with the fall of their dictatorships, or more recently in Ghana with the fall of Nkrumah — political preferences and latent oppositions that have dammed up spout forth like water through a collapsing dam. Thus Leiserson mentions how, after the military dictatorship was defeated in Japan, "the profusion of political groups which burst into the open as soon as the wartime straitjacket had been removed showed that the eclipse of oppositions had been only temporary."

During its "interrupted revolution," as Skilling calls it, Czechoslovakia provided an even more dramatic example of the abrupt surfacing of hitherto submerged interests and preferences. Ideological cleavages became visible as opponents of all change clashed with those who were ready to accept limited reforms, and moderate reformers differed not only with conservatives but with advocates of more radical, even revolutionary, alterations. Organized groups and associations flourished, pressed for advantage, demanded changes. Long-dormant or merely formal associations took on life; pre-Communist organizations like the Boy Scouts were revived. The cleavage between Czechs and Slovaks appeared as a basic organizational principle. With the virtual suspension of censorship, existing journals became controversial, new papers sprang into existence, and conflicting views were heard on radio and television. Then, almost as abruptly as the revolution had begun, with the Russian occupation these processes were reversed, and hegemony was gradually restored.

Yet, like Khrushchev's famous speech, the brief Czech revolution opened a window deep into the interior of a hegemonic system and made clear how illusory is the tranquillity of hegemony, for contained within it are pent-up forces ready to burst forth whenever the barriers to expression and organization are lowered.

Inadequate as the institutions of polyarchy may be, the variety of political preferences or interests that are taken into account in policy making appears to be much greater than in hegemonic or mixed regimes. After reading Kothari's description of India, one could readily imagine how a hegemonic regime in India might give decisive weight to certain kinds of preferences by overriding many interests that now assert themselves in the complex and endless negotiations, bargaining, demonstrations, and formation and dissolution of coalitions that characterize Indian politics. But it is difficult to imagine how any Indian regime, unless it were another polyarchy, could give representation to a greater variety of interests.

Yet it is this very tendency for political interests to crowd against the barriers to expression and to participate in policy making in increasing number and variety as the barriers are lowered that sometimes generates threats to regimes.

Threats to Regimes

HEGEMONIES: SELF-FULFILLING PROPHECY   Hegemonies by definition are regimes that impose the most severe limits on the opportunities available to opponents of the government. They forbid the organization of all political parties, like the dictatorship in Argentina, or they establish a uniquely privileged party organization, like the Movimiento Nacional in Spain or the Communist party in the USSR and Eastern Europe.

Fully hegemonic regimes not only suppress all rival parties or convert them into mere appendages of the dominant party; they suppress factions within the dominant party as well. Internal party democracy, then, provides no alternative channel for expressing dissent. Thus in Spain, as Linz has pointed out elsewhere, "the internal organization of the Movimiento has not been ideologically, legally, or in practice democratic, nor have recent changes in its statutes changed this even on paper, nor is there much prospect that changes in that direction would in practice lead to any broad and decisive changes in participation through the party." [1] In the USSR within a few years after the October Revolution all rival

1. Juan J. Linz, "The Inauguration of Democratic Government and Its Prospects in Spain" (unpublished ms., n.d.), p. 3.

parties had been suppressed; and as Barghoorn points out, in 1921 the Tenth Party Congress adopted a resolution prohibiting "further activity within the party by 'fractions,' based on 'special platforms,' with their own 'group discipline.' . . . its final provision . . . empowered the party's Central Committee to expel from the party anyone engaged in such activity." Skilling summarizes the situation in Eastern Europe:

> In Eastern Europe [in the fifteen years after Stalin's death] even peaceful advocacy of basic opposition to the regime and its policies was not tolerated and could usually express itself only through sub-terranean channels. In none of the countries was genuine opposition inside the ruling party permitted. Even in Yugoslavia, where the position and role of the party were significantly modified, the idea of a multiparty system or of an opposition party was explicitly rejected. The Yugoslav party's internal structure was amended, and widespread debate often occurred, but dissidence on basic issues among party members was not tolerated.

Nor are interest organizations permitted to function autonomously. The official organizations tend to be transmission belts for the regime — so much so that, as in Spain, the official trade unions have come to be displaced by illegal workers' councils.

Yet even in highly hegemonic regimes, opposition continues. Perhaps in all regimes, no matter how representative they may be, conflicts are bound to occur among the most powerful. These conflicts may be no more than surreptitious, lethal struggles by men who seek to win the dictator's favor and avoid his wrath. But beyond these struggles for power and place among the courtiers, there may also be, to quote Barghoorn, "efforts by members of the highest party and governmental decision-making bodies to change the personnel or policies of the party-state." As he and Skilling show, this kind of factional opposition has persisted in Communist countries, and it is clear from Linz's essay that factional opposition has also been a salient characteristic of Franco's dictatorship. Factionalism may spread beyond the inner circle as allies are sought in lower echelons of the party, the bureaucracy, the controlled press, or among intellectuals. In addition to the struggles among factions, there is the seemingly unavoidable maneuvering among leaders who wish to protect or improve the position of specific segments and institutions of the society: the military, heavy industry, consumer goods, education, sciences, the arts. Factional and interest-based opposition by leaders essentially loyal to the regime verges on a more fundamental opposition to basic policies or institutions — for example, by nationality groups who feel themselves unfairly treated, by intellectuals to whom a thaw following a harsh winter of repression is but a prelude to a libertarian regime, to economists who believe that a decentralized price-system economy must replace rigidly centralized planning. Beyond these oppositions, there are opponents who wish to subvert the regime and who are prepared to participate, if need be and if the opportunity arises, in conspiracies, violence, and revolution.

From the perspective of those who uphold a hegemonic regime, factional opposition may seem less dangerous than the others, while the kind of opposition that Barghoorn calls "subversive" and Skilling "integral" will no doubt seem most dangerous of all. Yet each shades off imperceptibly into the other. How can a line be drawn between "safe" and dangerous oppositions? The hegemonic regime, in fact, creates a self-fulfilling prophecy:

> *Since all opposition is potentially dangerous, no distinction can be made between acceptable and unacceptable opposition, between loyal and disloyal opposition, between opposition that is protected and opposition that must be repressed. Yet if all oppositions are treated as dangerous and subject to repression, opposition that would be loyal if it were tolerated becomes disloyal because it is not tolerated. Since all opposition is likely to be disloyal, all opposition must be repressed.*

I may have overdrawn the point. Yet highly hegemonic regimes seem unable wholly to escape the force of this self-fulfilling prophecy, particularly if they are endowed with an official ideology that claims a kind of divine right to rule based upon the exclusive possession of political truth and virtue. They move within a small orbit of toleration and repression: as toleration begins to set free the latent forces of opposition, the regime's leaders become fearful and clamp down. Their fear is not necessarily irrational, for the hitherto repressed opposition *might* surge out of control. Thus, because toleration may sow the seeds of the regime's destruction, it contains the seeds of its own destruction.

The self-fulfilling prophecy, then, holds so long as the basic premise is accepted that all opposition imperils the regime. Suppose, however, that leaders in a hegemony were to abandon this premise and try to establish a protected area within which opposition would be tolerated. If they could tolerate *some* opposition, could they indefinitely enforce *any* limits to toleration — short of the wide limits set in polyarchies?

This, in fact, is the dilemma of the mixed regime.

THE DILEMMA OF MIXED REGIMES: REPRESSION OR EXPLOSION? Although there are a substantial number of polyarchies and full hegemonies among the national regimes that govern various countries, mixed regimes are more numerous. The frequency of mixed regimes partly reflects the fact that they make up a rather undiscriminating residual category in my classification. They vary from highly competitive oligarchies where public contestation, including party organizations, is well protected but restricted to a small elite (as in Britain by the end of the eighteenth century) to systems like that of Tanzania, where in 1965, under universal suffrage and the dominance of a single party, two candidates ran against one another in every parliamentary district, apparently in honestly conducted elections. During the late Meiji period and even under the Taishō Democracy, Japan was evidently ruled by a mixed regime. Yugoslavia should probably be classed as a mixed regime. During its brief revolution Czechoslovakia was rapidly being transformed from a full hegemony into a mixed regime.

In mixed regimes, some oppositions can engage in at least some forms of public contestation, "loyal" oppositions are tolerated, and (as in late eighteenth-century Britain or a century later in Japan) their leaders may even succeed from time to time in peacefully displacing some of the incumbents in the highest political offices.

If the barriers are, by definition, lower in mixed regimes than in hegemonies, and if as a result a greater variety of interests engage in public contestation, it is also true that by definition in mixed regimes the barriers are higher than in polyarchies. For example, even if opposition is well protected, the whole political game may be legally restricted to a tiny segment of the people, as in eighteenth-century Britain or in Japan until after World War II; and even if everyone is allowed to participate in the game (at least nominally), the rules of the game impose certain marked limits on the right to form political organizations, to contest elections, and so on. In Czechoslovakia under Dubček, the Action Program of the Central Committee called for democratization of the party but rejected the more radical argument that socialist democracy would be impossible without a plural party system. Of Tanzania, probably the most liberal of the one-party African states, Foltz writes:

> Because of the safeguards against coordination between different candidates, and because the party moved after the [1965] election to tighten restrictions against party members speaking publicly out of turn, the elections do not seem to have materially changed the conditions under which Tanzanian factions operate nor opened up acceptable means for party members to discuss major differences publicly.

Under mixed regimes, political preferences are repressed that would make themselves felt if the barriers to public contestation or participation were lower. In competitive oligarchies, the preferences of great mass segments — peasants, rural laborers, artisans, middle strata, and some commercial or industrial segments — are largely unorganized, unexpressed, and unrepresented. Only the extension of effective political rights to these excluded segments enables them to enter into the existing system of public contestation. This was the familiar historical process by which more and more strata of society were brought into the oligarchical but already somewhat liberalized systems in a number of European countries in the nineteenth century.

Today, however, highly exclusive regimes — competitive oligarchies in the historical sense — are comparatively rare. More typical is the mixed regime with a broad citizenship but limits on public contestation, particularly on the right to form opposition parties. Where one party is privileged and others are prohibited, intraparty democracy is sometimes offered as an alternative to plural parties. Foltz quotes Nyerere's statement in 1963: "A National Movement which is open to all — which is identified with the whole nation — has nothing to fear from the discontent of any excluded section of society, for there is no such section." Yet when this alternative is examined theoretically or tested against practice, it proves to be, I believe, a rather romantic exaggeration of the possibilities.

If one makes reasonable assumptions about political motives and behavior and tries to specify carefully the kinds of guarantees and institutions that would be required for intraparty democracy in a one-party state to serve as effectively for the expression of political preferences as a plural party system in a polyarchy, the institutions and guarantees one must specify turn out to be remarkably like those of a plural party system in a polyarchy. (The theoretical exercise is highly illuminating; if the reader is unconvinced, he may wish to try it for himself.)

The catch in the theory of intraparty democracy in a one-party state is that the kinds of guarantees that would fully protect the expression, organization, and representation of interests within a party would also allow the formation of de facto parties, even if these masqueraded as factions in the single party. Conversely, if opponents of government are not protected in their right to form opposition parties in order to challenge the conduct of the government in elections, it is difficult to see how opposition within the dominant party can be fully protected.

In practice, it is probably not accidental, then, that organized party factions do not seem to exist in anything like the same degree in one-party states as they do in some countries where oppositions can express themselves not only in party factions but also in opposition parties. The highly organized factions in the Liberal-Democratic party of Japan, or the Christian Democratic party in Italy, seem to have no counterpart in one-party countries. As Foltz points out, since the time Nyerere made the statement quoted above,

> Tanzania's case itself has shown . . . that, as the regime comes to be beset with more and more problems, the old emphasis on upward communication of grievances that was useful to the party in the na-

tionalist period is sharply reversed. Downward communication from
the top party leadership becomes the rule and is reinforced by the
leadership's right to approve nominations to lower party offices and
particularly by the president's ability to give his personal investiture.

Thus in mixed regimes as in hegemonies, when the barriers are lowered,
oppositions, interests, and political preferences previously repressed or
inhibited spring forth to engage in public contestation. Leaders in these
countries of course know this perfectly well — whatever they may say
in public. And the presence of these repressed forces creates a genuine
danger to the regime for which it can find no easy solution.

Since at least limited opportunities are available to oppositions, some
oppositional elements will almost certainly use their opportunities to press
for a further lowering of the barriers. In the competitive oligarchies of
the nineteenth century it was inevitable that the restricted suffrage should
come under attack; in one country after another, leaders were faced with
the alternative of either yielding peacefully to demands for broadening
suffrage or else repressing the organizations that arose first among the
middle classes and later among the workers. Today the question of
suffrage is less controversial; attempts to deny suffrage to a special group,
such as the discrimination against Negro voting in the southern United
States (now ending), are comparatively rare. Unlike their predecessors in
liberal regimes, therefore, oppositions in mixed regimes today do not
usually need to force their way into already existing systems of public
contestation. An opposition in a mixed regime is less likely to be seeking
inclusion in the system or effective citizenship and more likely to be
seeking greater liberalization, more opportunities for public contestation.
And just as it was possible for social strata excluded from citizenship or
suffrage to find ways of exploiting the opportunities available for contestation in order to press their demands for suffrage, so in mixed regimes
today oppositions can doubtless find ways of using the limited system of
public contestation in order to press their demands for liberalization.

Viewed from the perspective of those who want to maintain a mixed
regime and avoid both hegemony and polyarchy, the danger is that by
yielding to the demands of oppositions for liberalization they will trigger
a runaway explosion out of which polyarchy will emerge or, if repression is needed to bring liberalization to a halt, hegemony.

Just as it took only moderate foresight in the nineteenth century to see
that it would be difficult to limit inclusion short of universality, so it is
reasonable now to conclude that in a mixed regime some oppositions will
not rest content with liberalization until the threshold to polyarchy has
been crossed. In mixed regimes with a privileged party, a crucial step
toward or even across that threshold will take place when an opposition

is permitted to organize a rival party to challenge the hitherto dominant party in fairly conducted elections; for once this step is taken, the opposition might then be able to win an election, displace incumbents, and alter their most treasured policies and institutions. Leaders of a regime who do not regard this as a fearful danger to be avoided at all costs scarcely require the limitations of a mixed regime.

Can oppositions in a liberalized regime be expected to refrain from pressing demands for an opposition party and from mobilizing behind it those who feel inadequately represented? As we have seen, the doctrine of intraparty democracy is unlikely to provide enough representation in practice to satisfy all the major interests of a country. Some interests will therefore hope to organize a party more immediately responsive to their particular views. Democratic ideology also continues to exert a powerful force for plural parties. After all, the institutions of polyarchy were developed partly as a response to democratic ideas. Since the institutions of polyarchy now exist and do not need to be invented anew, the idea of plural parties as an integral part of democracy is hardly unfamiliar, nor can it easily be dismissed as ridiculous or unwarranted.

Can the process of liberalization be launched and then checked just short of this critical threshold? Neither the Yugoslavian example nor the case of Czechoslovakia's interrupted revolution provides a clear-cut answer. The process of liberalization has gone much further in Yugoslavia than in any other Communist country (if we except the brief Czech interlude). The regime has definitely established the principle, however, that it will not tolerate public demands for an opposition party, much less the actual existence of a rival party. To pass over this last threshold to polyarchy is seen as perilous, not merely because "antisocialist" forces might gain strength, but perhaps even more because of the conviction, which seems to be widely held, that each of the different nationalities would soon have its own party and that plural parties would thus sharpen ethnic conflict and seriously endanger national cohesion. In short, some Yugoslavs argue, polyarchy means national fragmentation — and their fears can hardly be written off as simply a rationalization for the status quo. Yet as liberalization proceeds further in Yugoslavia, can the regime remain poised indefinitely on the last threshold to polyarchy? There is the risk that the demand for plural parties will grow so strong that the regime must yield, with all the dangers this transformation is thought to carry with it, or else step back firmly from the threshold and in no uncertain terms suppress demands for further liberalization.

Because the revolution in Czechoslovakia was terminated by the Russian occupation, no one can know how far it would have gone. The Action Program indicates clearly that Dubček and the Central Committee intended to stop short of polyarchy and opposition parties. Yet the process of liberalization was gathering such great speed and momentum before the Soviets moved in that one wonders whether it could have been brought to a skidding halt at the crucial threshold.

In view of the danger inherent in arriving at this threshold and then trying to restrain the forces that would pull the country across it, it will often seem wiser — from the perspective of those who support a mixed regime — to confine public contestation to fairly narrow limits. Yet if repression is needed to maintain these boundaries, as it probably will be, the mixed regime confronts a painful and inescapable dilemma: by increasing discontent and disloyalty, repression also increases the chance for a runaway explosion — and so the need for even more repression.

Thus mixed regimes are prone to oscillate between liberalization and repression. By suitable dosages of each, skilled leadership may successfully avoid both full hegemony and polyarchy. Yet the moment of truth will arrive for any mixed regime if, in the process of liberalization, it should ever reach the threshold to polyarchy and a substantial group of spokesmen should begin to make a public demand for an opposition party.

TWO SOURCES OF DISCONTENT IN POLYARCHIES   By definition polyarchies are systems that offer the lowest barriers to the expression, organization, and representation of political preferences and hence provide the widest array of opportunities for oppositions to contest the conduct of the government. But polyarchal regimes are not immune to discontent.[2] For even in polyarchies, the political preferences of some people — perhaps of many people — remain unsatisfied. Let me focus here on two reasons why this happens.

1. *Inequalities.* In the first place, even in polyarchies some people have grounds for believing that their interests are inadequately expressed, organized, and represented. For one thing, there are no generally accepted, objective criteria for deciding when an interest is fairly or adequately taken into account in political processes. Everyone is prone to emphasize the importance of his own preferences; but even if one were content with mere equality, it is by no means clear what equality among preferences would require. Since political philosophers have not been able to agree on whether individuals or interests should be equal — or on whether *majority rule* means an absolute majority of people, or of interests, or both, or a qualified majority of one or the other — one should scarcely expect ordinary citizens to agree on criteria for fair representation of interests. In any case, one scarcely needs a sophisticated view of politics to be aware

2. William Gamson's *Power and Discontent* (Homewood, Ill.: Dorsey Press, 1968) has been helpful for the following discussion, though I have not followed his theoretical scheme.

that even when a polyarchy meets some such rough criterion as "one man, one vote," there remain great inequalities in the effective representation of different individuals and groups. The fact is too familiar to require documentation here.

One obvious source of political inequalities is the massive differences in the political resources of different individuals and groups. In extreme cases, within the confines of the same state, one stratum of the population may govern itself through a polyarchy and at the same time impose a hegemony on other strata. The political regime of Athens may have been a direct "democracy" among adult male citizens (I use quotes because I do not know how much inequality of power existed even among citizens), but it was a hegemony vis-à-vis the slaves. The aristocratic republic of Venice was perhaps a kind of constitutional "democracy" among the fifteen hundred to two thousand families who were privileged to participate in making the laws and electing the doge, but it was a hegemony (even though a constitutional one) vis-à-vis the people of Venice. Before the abolition of slavery — and for a century afterward in the South — the United States was a polyarchy for whites but a hegemony for most blacks.

These are anomalies, however, and not the main source of inequalities in polyarchies. Indeed, it is reasonable to argue that these anomalous cases do not indicate defects in polyarchy per se but simply demonstrate the existence of dual political systems in which hegemony is partly substituted for polyarchy. But even disregarding these cases, no polyarchy has ever eradicated large differences in the political resources of its citizens. In every polyarchy, therefore, these differences help to generate inequalities in the effective representation of individuals and groups. Again, this fact is so widely known that it needs no supporting evidence here.

In addition to these ancient and well-known causes of political inequalities, representation itself presents technical problems in ensuring equality that have never been satisfactorily solved. The size of the nation-state, even if it happens to be as small as most new countries in Africa or the smaller polyarchies of Europe, puts a great distance between ordinary citizens and national policy makers, complicates communication, and makes for distortions in the representation of interests. Moreover, in many polyarchies the systems of representation — for example, the single-member district with a winner-take-all principle — have built-in biases, such as marked exaggeration in the proportion of representatives going to the largest party or to regional majorities. Even the ideal schemes proposed by legal pluralists and advocates of functional representation (such as the Guild Socialists) and the various methods of proportional representation do not, so far as I am aware, guarantee perfect equality in representation. It should be remembered too that in the absence of perfect consensus, no system of representation and decision making can produce solutions perfectly satisfactory to everyone. Even in a society of political equals there might be a permanent minority whose preferences always ran counter to those of the majority.

Finally, the more a polyarchy represents the full variety of preferences in a country, the more laborious becomes the task of aggregating and then resolving or reconciling all these preferences in order to arrive at decisions. Since many citizens prefer that their government not be immobilized by conflict, a regime may, in order to satisfy this particular preference, have to find ways to ignore many interests that would otherwise lead to deadlock.

To be sure, over a fairly extended period so many people might be at least partly satisfied in so many of their most salient political preferences (even though they might be dissatisfied in particular cases) that discontent would not be high. This result sometimes seems to be considered inherent in democratic procedures, but obviously it is not. I have already suggested the hypothetical case of the permanent minority for which no democratic rules provide a satisfactory solution. This of course represents an extreme form of persistent polarization, which, as I have argued earlier is comparatively rare. In practice, discontent is less likely to be associated with polarization between a permanent majority and a permanent minority than with fragmentation or segmentation in political conflicts.

2. *Polarization and Segmentation.* This last consideration points directly to a second reason why the greater opportunities that polyarchies provide for the expression, organization, and representation of interests do not protect them from serious discontent — and why they would not necessarily be immune from severe dissatisfaction even if they were considerably more democratic than in fact they are. For even if decisions were arrived at among political equals according to exact rules of democratic procedure, the outcome of decisions, in a country with a great diversity of political preferences, could rarely satisfy everyone.

To facilitate discussion, it will be helpful at this point to call attention to several aspects of political conflict: One is the level of anatagonism. Although antagonism is admittedly difficult to measure, particularly across countries or cultures, as a theoretical (and potentially operational) concept it seems indispensable. The number of sets of antagonists involved in a single conflict is a second aspect. To simplify the discussion, I intend to consider only the distinction between conflicts involving two sets of antagonists (bipolarity) and those involving more than two (multipolarity). A third aspect of conflict is the extent to which the composition of the sets of antagonists in one conflict is identical with the composition of the sets involved in other conflicts. If they are substantially the same, the conflicts are reinforcing or cumulative; if substantially different, the conflicts are crosscutting.[3] A fourth aspect is the duration of any particular pattern, that is, the extent to which all of these aspects persist unchanged over time. In what follows, for the sake of simplicity I usually ignore the question of duration by assuming a more or less persistent pattern over a fairly substantial period of time. Although the possible patterns are innumerable, table 1.1 shows some important possibilities.

Table 1.1 Some Patterns of Conflict

Conflicts	Sets of Antagonists	Levels of Antagonism Low	High
Reinforcing {	Constant		
	Bipolar	Moderate bipolarity	Polarization
	Multipolar	Moderate multipolarity	Severe segmentation
Crosscutting {	Changing	Moderate crosscutting conflicts	Moderate segmentation

Obviously, conflicts are relatively easy to handle as long as the level of antagonism remains low. They become dangerous to a regime when the level of antagonism is too high. Persistently high levels of antagonism seem to be less associated with purely socioeconomic differences than with differences in language, religion, ethnic or racial identity, and ideology. Japan offers an interesting confirmation of the hypothesis that while the harsh injustices of the early stages of industrialization and urbanization do generate bitter conflicts (it was these that Marx witnessed in nineteenth-century Europe), the severity of strictly economic conflict tapers off during the stage of late industrialization, while purely ideological differences, such as those that tend to surround foreign affairs or ideas of the good society, may become sharper. Leiserson observes that:

> A new initiative by the government along the "reverse course" [i.e., to reverse the reforms introduced by the Occupation] or in foreign policy will produce a major political crisis — refusals to participate in investigatory commissions; demonstrations and strikes; physical violence in the Diet — but bread-and-butter policies are disposed of fairly calmly.

3. I refrain from introducing other aspects that would unnecessarily complicate the discussion here. Over a series of conflicts, for example, the number of sets of antagonists is a function of the third variable and two others that I do not present here: (a) the number of characteristics, each of which forms a single, separate dimension of conflict, such as class, religion, region, and language; and (b) the number of antagonistic groups formed along a particular dimension of cleavage.

As table 1.1 indicates, depending on whether cleavages reinforce or cut across one another, high antagonism may result either in polarization or in segmentation.

That polarization is a profound threat to any regime seems so little open to doubt as to need no demonstration here. Polarization seems particularly dangerous for polyarchies, since they lack the coercive forces and the willingness to repress severe antagonisms. If polarization occurs along regional lines, the best that can be hoped for as a solution consistent with polyarchy is peaceful separation, as between Norway and Sweden in 1905. But if separation is a threat to the prevailing concept of the nation, as the threat of secession was to the idea of the Union in the United States in the late 1850s, or as it would be in India today, the result is likely to be an attempt to coerce the separatists. Indeed, the most likely short-run consequence of polarization in a polyarchy seems to be civil war, as in the United States in 1861, in Austria in 1934, and in Spain in 1936. If polarization persists, a hegemony is likely to emerge as a kind of permanent means of coercion and, perhaps, of long-run pacification.

Yet if my earlier argument is roughly correct, segmentation is a good deal more likely than polarization. Like polarization, segmentation also carries with it a threat to polyarchy. For, like polarization, segmentation can also endanger nationhood whenever regional conflicts are reinforced by antagonisms arising from such differences as those of language, religion, or socioeconomic condition. Language and region do often coincide, as in much of India; if these differences are reinforced by still others, such as socioeconomic condition, regions may seek not only autonomy but separation. If Spain and Yugoslavia, for example, were to become polyarchies, they might be threatened by segmentation along regional lines, for in both countries differences of region, language, tradition, and economic status tend to reinforce one another.

Even where this is not the case and segmentation carries no threat to nationhood, it is likely to foster a form and style of politics that will produce discontent and cynicism about polyarchy. Such an enormous effort must be invested in building easily fragmented coalitions that the game of politics is reduced to — or at least is widely thought to be — little more than a narrow struggle for partisan advantage. Moreover, without some system of mutual guarantees, every major segment must live in perpetual fear lest a coalition from which it is excluded should override its most important interests. If, on the contrary, every major segment manages to win a veto over policy, no coalition can ever deal firmly with any pressing problem. Immobilism is the classic lot of the segmented polity. And immobilism combined with a total transformation of politics into the art of maneuvering for partisan advantage is likely to breed discontent, political cynicism, and, in time, demands for a new political order more suited to decisive action.

The level of antagonism in political conflicts might decline if politics and government were to become less salient, less important as a source of advantages and disadvantages. Thus one reason for what the late Otto Kirchheimer called the waning of oppositions in Western Europe after World War II was thought to be the rapid and widespread rise in personal incomes, which made conflicts over governmental policies seem less important. Or, as in the case of fiscal and monetary policies, the actions of government may become more technical and remote — arcane matters for specialists who can be left in charge as long as the machine functions satisfactorily and incomes keep increasing. But the decline in political antagonisms in some polyarchies after World War II appears to have been temporary. When economic controversies became less salient, ideological differences involving foreign affairs and the distribution of power and opportunity began to manifest themselves. After twenty years of rising incomes in France, fierce antagonisms among Frenchmen were revealed during the uprising of May 1968. And in many countries below the high levels of affluence reached by the late- or postindustrial countries, conflicts over economic policy still carry a considerable freight of antagonism. Moreover, some countries, like Argentina, may find themselves locked into a system in which segmentation makes it nearly impossible for a polyarchal government to solve major economic difficulties; the government's failure then perpetuates the antagonisms that help produce segmentation.

Obviously, polyarchy is able to cope better with the dangers of segmentation if it can find more effective ways of reconciling the antagonistic groups. Reconciliation requires the investment of more energy and talent in the search for mutually satisfactory solutions to the issues in conflict. One system for mobilizing energy and talent in such a search is the large, catchall party that stands a good chance of putting together enough of the segments to win control of the government. In this situation, crass political incentives are mobilized in a search for solutions which, by being acceptable to a wide range of voters and interest groups, insure the dominance of the big, catchall party. The Congress party in India may be the world's leading example, as Kothari's description makes clear, and the Liberal-Democrats in Japan may well run a close second.

Unfortunately for the social engineer who opts for this solution, the large, catchall, integrating government party is more likely to be a product of historical accident than design. Nonetheless the extent to which a country's system of political parties is itself segmented seems to be influenced in some measure by the method of election. If on independence India had adopted a system of proportional representation in national elections, the

Congress party could never have won a majority in the Lok Sabha; the
fragmentation that befell the oppositions would have wrecked the Congress party as well; and that extraordinary institution for expressing,
representing, and reconciling an enormous variety of interests could not
have carried out its task of national integration—a task for which no other
institution in India seems to have been so well suited.

Another kind of incentive for mobilizing energy and talent in the search
for mutually satisfactory solutions is provided by a system in which all the
major segments have, de jure or de facto, a veto on the government's
policies, as in Lebanon or the Netherlands; for the threat of a veto com-
pels the leaders of all segments to throw themselves into the search for
conciliatory solutions. Conceivably a country endangered by nationality
conflicts, such as Yugoslavia, might be able to manage the transition to
polyarchy if it were to develop some system of mutual veto among the
nationalities.

Yet a system of mutual veto reduces one danger only to create another:
immobilism. For often the only solution acceptable to everyone is the
status quo; and even if this results in satisfactory short-run outcomes, the
long-run outcome may be massive dissatisfaction with a system unable to
confront and solve pressing problems of poverty, economic growth, welfare, redistribution, housing, and the like.

A special case of this system of mutual vetoes for reconciling antagonistic groups in a segmented polity requires a willingness to decen-
tralize — investing a great deal of authority in the various cohesive segments — and at the same time to permit the settlement of the remaining
major issues by the leaders of the various segments. In a broad sense, to
be sure, this formula might be read as no more than a standard description of polyarchy; but what I have in mind is the system in the Netherlands as it has been described by Daalder and Lijphart.[4] A system like this
does not, of course, spring up overnight, and probably not every segmented society could successfully engineer it. It requires a commitment
all round, but particularly among the leaders, to maintain the nation
intact, to the seriousness of politics, to the importance of discovering
mutually acceptable solutions, and to a process in which leaders are often
allowed to negotiate solutions in secret, outside the usual contentions of
politics, that are then willingly accepted by their followers.

The Dutch system suggests a more general kind of solution or partial
solution: the development of a specialized set of institutions or arrangements for searching for mutually satisfactory solutions and ensuring their

---

4. See particularly Hans Daalder, "The Netherlands: Opposition in a Segmented
Society," in *Political Oppositions in Western Democracies*, ed. Robert A. Dahl (New
Haven: Yale University Press, 1967), and Arend Lijphart, *The Politics of Accommo-
dation* (Berkeley: University of California Press, 1968).

adoption. The classic site of this process was the national parliament and its network of personal, bloc, and party activities. But parliaments have not been able to handle the job by themselves, and their inability to overcome fragmentation and immobilism doubtless has often contributed to dissatisfaction with parliamentary democracy itself. Hence in practically every polyarchy, other institutions have emerged to take over a share — usually a very large share — of the task. These institutions are typically more hierarchical than legislative bodies, their top leaders are endowed with more political resources, they have greater legitimacy, they usually have more technical skills, and they are better able to operate in secret.

In some countries these institutions are the executive and bureaucracy, operating with very considerable independence of the legislature. In the Scandinavian countries, for example, the dangers of socioeconomic segmentation implicit in a very comprehensive organization of all the major economic interests in nationwide associations of workers, farmers, employers, and consumers is overcome by the periodic negotiating sessions at which contracts and policies are arrived at for the ensuing term under the aegis of the government. Despite the fact that the future of the economy depends on the results of these negotiations, the parliament can do little more than stand to one side until it can ratify the agreements that have been reached by the interest organizations themselves.

There may well be still other and better solutions to the dangers that segmented pluralism creates for polyarchies. Surely the invention of new institutions for political reconciliation — institutions consistent with democratic goals — should have a high place on the agenda of social scientists. For the prospect that existing polyarchies can do a better job of satisfying the claims of citizens, and that countries with hegemonic or mixed polities can in time be democratized, depends in no small measure on the creation of institutions for reconciling diversities.

2

FACTIONAL, SECTORAL, AND SUBVERSIVE OPPOSITION IN SOVIET POLITICS

Frederick C. Barghoorn

Historical and Theoretical Contexts

Concepts such as opposition, dissent, and resistance, it is assumed in this study, are applicable not only to pluralistic political systems but also to "hegemonic," "monist," or "monocratic" systems.[1] Fruitful comparison of types of political systems requires due attention to both similarities and differences. Certainly the USSR is not and never has been free of dissent from official policy or to conflicts of judgment and purpose among politically influential men. Lenin sought to limit its damaging effects by prohibiting "factionalism" within the ruling party, and Stalin, when it interfered with his objectives, branded and punished it as machinations of "enemies of the people." These attitudes toward opposition and their reflections in official Soviet practices and doctrines differ enormously from the long-established patterns of political life in countries whose history fostered the development of legitimate, organized, loyal oppositions, with functions defined by informal or formal customs, laws, and constitutional provisions. Of course we should not expect to find equivalents of such accepted — and system-acceptive — oppositions in Soviet Russia.

1. The category "hegemonic" has been suggested by the Polish political sociologist Jerzy Wiatr and has been used also by Robert A. Dahl in *Polyarchy: Participation and Opposition*. Ghiţa Ionescu, in his study *The Politics of the European Communist States* (London: Praeger, 1967), employs similar terminology; but while devoting much attention to dissent, he describes Communist polities as "oppositionless," at least in conventional Western terms. George Fischer, in *The Soviet System and Modern Society* (New York: Atherton Press, 1969), develops a "monist model." Frederic J. Fleron, Jr., in his article "Toward a Reconceptualization of Political Change in the Soviet Union" (*Comparative Politics*, January 1969, pp. 228–44) usefully discusses "monocracy" and "co-optation" as explanatory concepts for analysis of Soviet politics. However, Fleron stipulates his own somewhat unusual meaning for the term co-optation.

27

Russian political experience, under the rule of the tsars, and still more so under Communist *apparatchiki*, has not permitted development of the broad consensus and responsible participation which, fostered by relatively favorable conditions, characterizes the "civic culture" in polyarchies.

To be sure, the death of Stalin was followed by a perceptible reduction in the uses of coercion and the threat thereof as instruments of political and social control in Soviet Russia. Concomitant with a change in compliance patterns came increased, if reluctant, tolerance for efforts by individuals and small ad hoc groups — and, to a degree, by subcommunities and subcultures, or at least segments thereof — to lobby for emerging group interests, to demand increased professional autonomy, and to articulate long-cherished but hitherto suppressed traditional values, such as freedom of information and expression. The risks involved in factional strife and the costs of defeat in political combat at or near the summit of power diminished substantially. These new trends were registered and partially legitimated by numerous official statements and actions, particularly at the "de-Stalinizing" Twentieth and Twenty-second CPSU Congresses.

In the still very oppressive but relatively freer conditions that have prevailed since about 1956, a political opposition of sorts has emerged. As one writer has defined it:

> If by opposition one means a more or less organized body of people . . . who make propaganda for their own opinions through meetings, newspapers, radio and television, etc., then one cannot speak of the existence of a political opposition in the USSR. If, however, one means by opposition a very loose group of people who are in some way or other known to be opposed to their government and who sometimes know of each other's existence, and some of whom sometimes manage to ventilate some of their opinions—then one can say that there is a political opposition in the Soviet Union.[2]

It would not be very incorrect to assert that a plateau of tolerance for dissent has persisted since 1956, but it is clear that progress toward the development of a more responsive, less coercive regime faltered after the overthrow of Khrushchev in October 1964. Indeed, a retrogression set in after Khrushchev's ouster. Particularly after the at best quasi-legal trial of the writers Andrei Sinyavski and Yuli Daniel in 1966 for allegedly slandering the Soviet state in works of fiction, sent abroad for publication and not approved by the Soviet censors, there has been a partial reversion to the Stalinist practice of equating dissent with treason. At the same time, censorship, intimidation, blackmail, physical coercion, and the other

2. Karel van het Reve, *Dear Comrade: Pavel Litvinov and the Voices of Soviet Citizens in Dissent* (New York: Pitman, 1969), p. vii.

methods traditionally utilized by police states have been resorted to with some increase in frequency, although it should be emphasized that the Russia of Brezhnev is still significantly freer and more humane than that of Stalin. This partial reversion to Stalinist practices was — presumably not by accident — accompanied by a limited, secretive, selective, tortuous, largely covert, and perhaps somewhat shamefaced rehabilitation of Stalin and his policies and pronouncements.

Lest this be taken as a forecast of a probable Soviet relapse into something resembling full-blown Stalinism, let us offer two qualifying observations. First, we suggest that the repression and suppression inflicted upon a relatively small number of the most defiant and outspoken Soviet dissenters and rebels in recent years has resulted in part from their response to the more favorable conditions for articulating diverse interests and values available in the post-Stalin era. The regime — in which militant "conservatives," such as Brezhnev's protégé, Sergei Trapeznikov, gradually increased their influence after Khrushchev's ouster — felt compelled to counterattack whenever extreme dissenters pressed (in their view) too hard to widen the limits of freedom. Since 1967, the regime-opposition confrontation has sharpened; regime exasperation and oppositional resistance waxed as frustrated reform impulses clashed with Moscow's determination to still demands for further liberalization.

Second, it should be noted that, although the post-Khrushchev leadership has treated writers and artists, for example, with less understanding and greater harshness than was displayed by Khrushchev, it has on the whole pursued a more enlightened policy than did Khrushchev toward natural scientists, at least until 1968, when a policy of selective harassment and repression of politically dissident natural scientists was instituted. The most striking evidence of this now-threatened improvement was the dramatic decline in the fortunes of T. D. Lysenko and the energetic effort to repair the damage done by this favorite of both Stalin and Khrushchev to several branches of the agricultural and biological sciences. However, in 1968–69 propaganda pressures and some cautious, limited administrative measures were applied by the authorities against a few natural scientists who ventured to criticize official political and ideological, as distinct from scientific, decisions and doctrines.

The present Soviet regime's methods of social and legal control are generally much more rational and consistent, as well as somewhat less harsh, than they were under Stalin. An attempt is made to provide a rationale of formal legality for suppressive actions instituted by the authorities against oppositional utterances and activities. This legalistic style differs substantially from the crudely terroristic, capricious practices of the Stalin era. Nevertheless, some eighteen years after Stalin's death the USSR is still far from being as tolerant of dissent as an authoritarian-pluralistic polity of the type of Franco Spain, although it has the great advantage over Spain, or perhaps even Mexico, of still possessing some of the ideological dynamism and, to a degree, legitimacy derived from its proclaimed adherence to a revolutionary ideology.

SOME FORMATIVE FACTORS   The primary purpose of this study is to categorize and illustrate the phenomena of politically significant dissent, resistance, and opposition in the USSR and to do this, insofar as possible, in a fashion that facilitates comparison with similar phenomena in other states. We are more concerned with analysis and description than with explanation; to account for the attitudes and behaviors herein described would require another study. However, it may be useful to attempt, in this introductory section, to identify some of the factors that appear to have shaped the warped and skewed structure of dissent and opposition in Soviet Russia. Only a very brief discussion of the nature of, and relations among, these factors can, unfortunately, be attempted.

In studying any major aspect of Soviet politics, especially those treated here, it is necessary to take into account the existence in the USSR of an official, established ideology and the fusion, at the apex of the political leadership structure, of the functions of national policy formation and authoritative interpretation of the official ideology. While it would be inappropriate here to refer extensively to the content of Leninist doctrine, it is necessary to bear in mind Lenin's insistence upon the mutual exclusiveness and utter incompatibility of "bourgeois" and "socialist" values. Both as prescription and as rationalization, this dichotomy inhibits and constricts critical or dissenting thought, for it tends to confront dissenters with only three choices — remaining silent, speaking out and then recanting their "heresies," or persisting in defiance of the ideologically consecrated authorities and being branded as "agents of the international bourgeoisie," perhaps even as political criminals subject to prosecution. It is striking that more than fifty years after the "Great October Socialist Revolution" a resolution of the CPSU Central Committee reiterated, in bold-face type, Lenin's statement that "any neglect of socialist ideology . . . signifies . . . the strengthening of bourgeois ideology." [3]

3. *Pravda*, 6 October 1968. In a long, hard-hitting article in *Sovetskaya Rossiya*, 29 May 1969, Kh. Sabirov, invoking Lenin's authority on the necessity of firm party control over intellectuals, attacked "freedom of criticism" as a bourgeois weapon in the class struggle and interpreted the events of 1968 in Czechoslovakia as Western bourgeois exploitation of the "oppositional tendencies" of "pseudoradical" and "demagogic" elements hostile to socialism. While he regarded the instability and insufficient indoctrination of East European intellectuals as an especially serious problem, Sabirov also expressed indignation regarding the attitudes of some Soviet intellectuals. He noted among their shortcomings a preoccupation with the consequences of Stalinism (he employed the euphemism, "the cult of the individual"), which,

Repeated invocations of Lenin's intolerant and fanatical warnings about the dangers of ideological backsliding point, of course, to vulnerabilities in the Soviet system. We know that some of the best minds in Russia despise the tyranny justified by such injunctions. However, the regime of intellectual tutelage is probably still accepted, at least passively, by most Soviet citizens. It is sustained by habit and inertia, as well as by police power and by the vested interests of an army of bureaucrats. Freedom-loving intellectuals still fight an unequal battle against it. As long as the unrestricted sovereignty of the party and the unquestioned authority of Marxism-Leninism prevail, opposition and dissent will be but shadows of the force that a free and critical public opinion can exert in the Western democracies.

Many students of Soviet politics, particularly those who have a sub-stantial knowledge of Russian history, are inclined to find in Russian tradition or political culture certain factors or traits that help to explain the absence of rights and freedoms taken for granted in Western Europe — by Communists, incidentally, as well as by non-Communists — and in the Anglo-American polities. When one compares the vigor of the thrust for freedom in "socialist" Czechoslovakia, Yugoslavia, Hungary, and Poland, or even in the other European, Communist-ruled lands, with the relative feebleness of political protest in Soviet Russia, one can scarcely fail to perceive that, for whatever reason, dictatorship seems more ac-ceptable to a majority of the Russians and other peoples of the USSR than it does to those of the European "socialist" states.

Certain experiences in the course of Russian political development seem to have instilled in the Russian political mind an exceptionally high level of appreciation for stern, autocratic, overwhelmingly powerful authority. It appears that the liberal reforms that accompanied and followed the emancipation of the serfs in the 1860s did not strike deep roots in popular culture, with the main features of which they were not compatible. It is interesting, in this connection, that in referring to the traditional Russian reliance on autocracy as a safeguard against threats to the state, Nikolai Chernyshevski, most venerated of the nineteenth-century radical demo-crats, wrote that "among us the consciousness of national unity has al-ways had a decisive preponderance over provincial strivings." Cherny-shevski's statement was included in an anthology of patriotic sentiments which appeared during World War II, when Stalin caused historians to publish works glorifying Tsar Ivan the Terrible.[4] With, one fears, little

according to Sabirov, distracts them from "contributing to the solution of the great creative tasks of communism."

4. On the dictator's revival of the cult of Ivan the Terrible, see Frederick C. Barghoorn, "Stalinism and the Russian Cultural Heritage," *Review of Politics* 14, no. 4 (April 1952): 178–203. For Chernyshevski's statement see *Rodina* (Moscow, 1942), p. 88.

exaggeration a thoughtful emigré Russian historian of religion wrote in 1945:

> Yet Russia's past does not seem to warrant much optimism. For centuries Russia was the most despotic monarchy in Europe. Her rather frail constitutional regime lasted only eleven years; her democracy, which was an enunciation of principles rather than their materialization, lived seven months. Having just rid themselves of the Tsar, the people, though against their will and after some struggle, submitted to a new tyranny, compared with which Tsarist Russia seems the incarnation of liberty.[5]

A British historian writing in the liberal, constitutional tradition has recently reemphasized that Russia never developed a modern, "Western" middle class, or bourgeoisie. He observes, with respect to the situation of the late nineteenth-century Russian empire:

> Yet it was still unrealistic to apply West European categories to Russia and to speak of a *bourgeoisie,* or of a single homogeneous middle class. Russian bureaucrats, businessmen, and intelligentsia did not share a common ethos. . . . The capitalists of Russia were drawing nearer in outlook to their European or North American counterparts . . . but they mostly retained their indifference to political rights. . . . Finally, the intelligentsia remained . . . rebellious, rejecting . . . the values of the European *bourgeoisie.* For the most part they . . . believed themselves resolutely opposed to autocracy in principle, yet in many cases the objection was to an autocracy which served the existing social system rather than to autocracy as such.[6]

Perhaps if Russia had escaped the traumatic and disintegrating pressures of World War I — which it, of all the great powers involved, was least prepared to withstand — the autocratic principle might have gradually given way to the values of the civic culture. However, when the Soviet dictatorship, lacking at first even the legitimacy conferred by tradition and the workings of the kinship system of hereditary monarchy, took power in a wartorn country, the dictatorial, coercive elements in the Russian political culture took on added force. The Bolsheviks, in their exercise of coercion, were even less — in fact, far less — constrained by custom or by international public opinion than the tsars had been.

In part, this reinforcement and magnification of the coercive and ter-

---

5. Quoted from G. P. Fedotov, "Russia and Freedom," *Review of Politics* 8, no. 1 (January 1946), reprinted in Hans Kohn, ed., *The Mind of Modern Russia* (New York: Harper, 1962), p. 258.

6. Hugh Seton-Watson, *The Russian Empire* (London: Oxford University Press, 1967), p. 538.

roristic impulse in Russian government resulted from the relationship that always tends to exist between revolutionary dictatorships and their citizenry.[7]

Such dictatorships are, not without reason, obsessed by fears of counter-revolutionary conspiracies, abetted by foreign powers. Moreover, in the modern era, at least in such a relatively underdeveloped country as Russia still was in 1917, the political leadership may resort to economic development policies that exact heavy, resentment-generating sacrifices from a population parts of which are indifferent or hostile to the leadership goals. This tension between the values of the revolutionary elite — particularly those of the dictator Stalin — and those of the majority of the population helped impel Stalin to embark upon a program that can be characterized as coercive modernization, which in turn further heightened tensions and served to justify terroristic political controls.

This writer considers a number of other factors also relevant to the nature of opposition and dissent in the USSR, among them the despotic, Jacobin elements introduced into the Russianized Marxism of Lenin and Stalin, the hostility toward the capitalist social system and international order inherent in Marxism but intensified in Lenin's interpretation, and the premium on toughness, guile, suspiciousness, and vigilance which the life of the Bolshevik revolutionaries in prison and exile clearly engendered. Finally, he would stress the negative factors in the international environment in which the Soviet political leadership has functioned during almost its entire history. Tsarist and especially Soviet Russia were impelled by circumstances to compete for influence against rival nations which enjoyed the advantages of superiority not only in science and technology but in general economic and social development.[8]

When a government, a party leadership, or a political elite feels compelled to give priority to national and international power and influence, rather than to the wide distribution of goods, services, and individual freedoms which might win it the willing support of its citizens, it is likely also to feel constrained to create — and give some measure of autonomy to — a powerful agency of coercion, such as the tsarist Okhrana or the Soviet KGB. An exceptionally coercive pattern of social and political

7. Alexander Gerschenkron has in many of his writings—including a brilliant review of Robert Conquest's *The Great Terror* in *The New York Review of Books*, 19 June 1969—set forth the "stability conditions" of modern dictatorships, which include, in his view, "maintenance of a permanent condition of stress," "creation of a charismatic image of the dictator," and (most relevant for this study) "proscription of any deviating values, supported by threats and acts of repression."

8. Theodore H. von Laue, in his stimulating study *Why Lenin? Why Stalin?* (New York: Lippincott, 1964), propounds the thesis that regimentation and oppression can be traced ultimately to the "pressures of global politics" on Russian governments, both tsarist and Soviet, caught up in a difficult struggle against richer, more secure, and more advanced rivals.

controls seems likely to develop when a social revolution occurs in an economically underdeveloped society with an authoritarian political culture. Especially in such a context, a revolutionary regime confronts, within a relatively short span of time, the grievous crises of identity, legitimacy, participation, distribution, and penetration.[9] In its effort to cope with what must seem like an endless series of threats, a revolutionary regime of the Soviet type tends overly to develop its coercive capabilities, thus adversely affecting its capacity to gain the affection and voluntary support of the citizenry. Beset with fears of counterrevolution, which Communists perceive as the danger of the "restoration of capitalism," leaders of Soviet-type states seek to impress upon their party cohorts and upon the population generally the need for vigilance.

THE EVOLUTION OF COMMUNIST AUTOCRACY   Before entering upon a detailed description of the forms of dissent and opposition in the USSR, it will be useful to consider briefly the origins and growth of what Leonard Schapiro has termed the Communist autocracy. Lenin's Bolsheviks, their ideological convictions confirmed and reinforced by victory, early evinced an almost obsessive sensitivity to and aversion from even potential opposition to their rule. This is not surprising; for although, unlike previous social revolutionaries, they had succeeded in holding on to power, they found themselves ruling a hostile or at best indifferent population, whose way of life they were determined to alter fundamentally, rapidly, and, if need be, ruthlessly. Isolation from the mass of the Russian citizenry, together with the hostility of foreign powers, spurred their efforts to suppress or eliminate all potentialities for internal resistance. Lenin's party very early (in Ulam's vivid words) "choked every other political organization and force in Russia." [10]

Suppression of dissent and opposition within the single ruling party was also early achieved. In 1921 the Tenth Communist Party Congress adopted a resolution, entitled "Concerning the Unity of the Party," which forbade further activity within the party by "fractions," based on "special platforms," with their own "group discipline." In its final provision, not published until 1924, it empowered the party's Central Committee to expel from the party anyone engaged in such activity. Needless to say, the revolutionary Bolsheviks displayed no mercy toward "bourgeois" or monarchist political groupings or movements. What is striking is that the situation even of other socialist parties, after a few months of relative liberalism, became so precarious that (as Schapiro points out) their relationship to the Bolsheviks, "at any rate after 1918, was not opposition

9. On the general nature of these crises see Lucian W. Pye, *Aspects of Political Development* (Boston: Little, Brown, 1966), pp. 62–67.
10. Adam B. Ulam, *The Bolsheviks* (New York: Macmillan, 1965), p. 462.

in the ordinary, Western political sense of that term at all; it was a struggle for survival." [11]

Lenin demanded unquestioning obedience to and enthusiastic support of party decisions once they had been taken. However, decisions were usually preceded, in Lenin's time, by extensive and frank discussion. Stalin, in a few years, created a regime of personal dictatorship and terror, effected through the political police, which he controlled and which became one of the main instruments of government, at least after December 1934. The murder at that time of the popular leader of the Leningrad party committee, Sergei Kirov — instigated or at any rate not interfered with by Stalin, as Khrushchev broadly hinted in a speech to the Twenty-second CPSU Congress in 1961 — provided the pretext for ferreting out and destroying all elements dangerous or even merely inconvenient to him, an operation which reached its orgiastic culmination in the Great Purge of 1936–38 (or Ezhovshchina, so named for Nikolai Ezhov, head of Stalin's political police during the height of the terror). Under Stalin, of course, not even the heads of the political police enjoyed personal security. Stalin destroyed Yagoda and Ezhov after each had outlived his usefulness, and the available evidence strongly indicates that shortly before his death in March 1953 he was preparing to liquidate Lavrenti Beria, who had presided since 1938 over a vast police and forced labor empire. Not even the most skillful conspirators could mount a successful opposition to Stalin's regime, although suspicion has been expressed that his death was, at least indirectly, hastened by the machinations of his lieutenants.

Stalinist terror and the dire poverty that was the other major deprivation inflicted by his rule engendered much hatred of the dictator. These conditions also tended to reduce perhaps to a dangerously low level, support for the political system. Stalin's successors were to feel that some relaxation of regime pressures on the citizenry was necessary. Life under Stalin had been nasty, brutish, and all too often short, even for those who had climbed to the highest rungs of the social and political ladder. There was apparently a very broad elite consensus that in the interests of everyone's personal security, as well as of national morale and international respectability, control of the machinery of repression created by Stalin must be subjected to the collective leadership of the party and its operations cleansed of elements of caprice and brutality.[12]

11. Leonard Schapiro, *The Origin of the Communist Autocracy* (Cambridge, Mass.: Harvard University Press, 1955), p. xiii.
12. Such works as Khrushchev's famous "secret speech"—still not published in the USSR—and as Svetlana Allilueva, *Twenty Letters to a Friend* (New York: Harper and Row, 1967) and Milovan Djilas, *Conversations with Stalin* (New York: Harcourt, Brace and World, 1962), convey a vivid sense of the terrifying insecurity and uncertainty in which even Stalin's closest personal associates lived.

Some of the most important features of the policies of Stalin's successors — not only the criticism of "the cult of personality of J. V. Stalin," but also the dismantling of much of Stalin's terror machine, the restoration of party control over the police, and the partial replacement of Stalinist arbitrariness in the sphere of law enforcement by "socialist legality" — were undoubtedly motivated by their desire to gain the willing and enthusiastic support for the Soviet system of the formerly cowed masses and especially of the administrators and specialists on whose effective performance depended the continued vitality of the economy and society. However, it is by no means certain that this effort achieved the success that Khrushchev, in particular, appears to have hoped it would. Criticism of Stalin and at least partial revelations of his crimes shook the faith of many Soviet citizens, especially youths, in the legitimacy of the political system that had produced him and even in the Marxist-Leninist ideology of which he had claimed to be the outstanding exponent. Of course, if de-Stalinization, limited though it was, gave rise to ferment, confusion, and reexamination of values, this was largely because repressed memories and sentiments of moral indignation against the injustices and brutalities committed by Stalin, especially during the Great Purge, were released by Khrushchev's revelations of Stalin's crimes and his deviations from Leninism. Thus the infallible "genius" Stalin, once fulsomely extolled by those who later denounced him, created an ideological and moral vacuum which left his successors faced by what may, in the long run, prove to have been an insoluble crisis of legitimacy.

It is, of course, sheer speculation to say this, but Stalin, in liquidating his opponents, may also have fatally undermined the moral authority of Soviet communism. By mid-1957 a perceptive young Russian-speaking American, with wide experience in the Soviet Union, was reporting that "some young Russians . . . are passionately dedicated to the communist system. Some advocate violent and immediate change. But the majority are simply bewildered and pitifully disturbed." [13]

Khrushchev did not carry the process of de-Stalinization nearly far enough to satisfy many critical Soviet citizens. However, he carried it too far for the liking of many conservative party executives, official propagandists, and secret police officials. His successors, in particular Brezhnev, probably prodded by the powerful and orthodox party leader, Mikhail Suslov, saw to it that such aspects of the Khrushchev presentation of Stalin's record as the linking of Stalin with the murder of Kirov disappeared from the Soviet press. Indeed, Brezhnev and other party leaders even went so far as to make cautious moves toward the rehabilitation of Stalin.

13. Marvin L. Kalb, "Soviet Youth: The 'Bewildered Generation,'" *New York Times Magazine*, 28 July 1957.

Incensed perhaps by these evidences of the greater disinclination of the post-Khrushchev party leadership to draw what seemed to many to be the logical conclusions of the critique of Stalin and Stalinism and to permit the full disclosure and discussion of domestic and foreign reality increasingly demanded by critical Soviet intellectuals, some dissident young intellectuals, such as Vladimir Bukovski and Aleksandr Ginzburg, organized illegal demonstrations and engaged in other actions to express their indignation against such official acts as the 1966 trial and sentencing to long terms in forced labor camps of the writers Andrei Sinyavski and Yuli Daniel. These acts of defiance may have marked a new stage in the development of resistance to authority in the Soviet Union.[14] A new aspect of the protest actions in recent years by young Soviet intellectuals, many of them, like the young scientist Pavel Litvinov, of impeccable revolutionary family background, has been their willingness to take the awesome risks involved in defying the security police.[15]

Such resistance to authority and demands for freedom of expression and respect for individual human dignity, personal security, and civil liberties (voiced by Sinyavski and Daniel; by the young rebel Bukovski; by Ginzburg and his colleagues and codefendants in a January 1968 trial, Yuri Galanskov, Alexei Dobrovolski, and Vera Lashkova; by Pavel Litvinov, the historians A. M. Nekrich and Petr Yakir, and many other intellectuals and professionals) reflect the existence in the USSR of a crisis of legitimacy. However, there is little reason to expect any reduction in the near future in the capability of the Soviet political authorities — when faced with demands for what, in countries with less despotic traditions and deeper, wider voluntary support for the political system, would be regarded as elementary civil liberties — to respond with arrests, one-sided propaganda and public defamation of critics of official policy, police interrogations without participation of defense counsel, and carefully managed, secret or near secret judicial proceedings.

A novel feature of Soviet intellectual dissent, especially since the Sinyavski-Daniel and Ginzburg-Galanskov trials, has been the demand that the provisions of the Soviet Constitution guaranteeing freedom of speech and assembly be honored in practice. Undoubtedly this "subversive constitutionalism" is feared by neo-Stalinists, but both Soviet citizens and foreigners who perceive freedom as indivisible in an increasingly interdependent world can justifiably regard it as not only shrewd strategy but the expression of a legitimate aspiration.

14. Timothy McClure, "The Politics of Soviet Culture, 1964–1967," *Problems of Communism* 16, no. 2 (March–April 1967): 26–43. For a bibliography of the works of Sinyavski and Daniel published abroad, see Leopold Labedz and Max Hayward, *On Trial* (London: Collins and Harvill Press, 1967).
15. On the pressures exerted by the KGB on Pavel Litvinov and his resistance thereto, see van het Reve, *Dear Comrade*, pp. 3–17.

Contemporary Patterns and Conditions of Opposition

Opposition activity, in the USSR as elsewhere, can seek to replace or change the composition of the national political leadership.[16] It can involve, or perhaps only imply, criticism of or resistance to decisions or policies of the central political authorities on matters of national and international importance. In most cases it is doubtless limited in scope, seeking to promote or defend values and preferences of subcultures, professional and occupational groups, and other segments of the citizenry which either the central authorities or members of various establishment-supporting lobbies and cliques hold to be incompatible with regime-established policy. It may, in the most extreme forms, involve efforts to tinker with, even to alter drastically or perhaps abolish, fundamental institutions or structures. In the late 1960s, for the first time since the 1920s and early 1930s, wide-ranging systemic or programmatic dissent, demanding radical changes in political thought and practice, surfaced. Moreover, the opposition began to acquire rudimentary organization, channels of communication, and means of conveying its demands to its

16. Of the scholarly literature on or relevant to political opposition in the USSR, the fundamental works are Leonard Schapiro, *The Origin of the Communist Autocracy*, and Robert V. Daniels, *The Conscience of the Revolution* (Cambridge, Mass.: Harvard University Press, 1960). Schapiro deals with the period 1917–22; Daniels covers in detail the period 1917–29 and provides brief treatment of the 1930s, 1940s, and 1950s. James Bunyan, *The Origin of Forced Labor in the Soviet State* (Baltimore: Johns Hopkins Press, 1967), adds to our knowledge of labor opposition to the Lenin-Trotski policies of labor militarization in 1917–21. Boris Nicolaevsky, *Power and the Soviet Elite* (New York: Praeger, 1965), based partly on the author's conversations with Nikolai Bukharin in Paris in 1936, is extremely valuable, especially on the resistance in high party circles to Stalin's main policies in the early 1930s. See also the very useful study prepared at the request of the late Senator Thomas J. Dodd by Sergius Yakobson and Robert Allen, Legislative Reference Service, Library of Congress, "Aspects of Intellectual Ferment in the Soviet Union," 89th Cong., 2d sess., 1966, Document no. 130. On ideological aspects of the Lenin-Stalin and more particularly the Khrushchev attitude toward opposition, see Frederick C. Barghoorn, "Soviet Political Doctrine and the Problem of Opposition," *Bucknell Review* 12, no. 2 (May 1964): 1–29. The major studies of Soviet politics by Merle Fainsod, Barrington Moore, Jr., Robert Conquest, and others contain much that is relevant to our subject. Data on disaffection from Soviet communism, obtained by interviewing wartime "nonreturners" and some post–World War II defectors, is analyzed in parts of Alex Inkeles and Raymond A. Bauer, *The Soviet Citizen* (Cambridge, Mass.: Harvard University Press, 1959), and intensively and ingeniously in Bauer's article, "Some Trends in Sources of Alienation from the Soviet System," *Public Opinion Quarterly* (Fall 1955), pp. 279–91. *The Program of the Democratic Movement* is discussed by Albert Boiter in a Radio Liberty Research study, "A Program for Soviet Democrats" (Munich, 6 April 1970); it and other programmatic documents are the subject of an editorial article, "Budushchee rossii opredelit nravstvennoe nachalo," *Posev*, no. 7 (Frankfurt, July 1970), pp. 2–10.

domestic supporters and foreign well-wishers. Perhaps the most comprehensive such program was entitled *Program of the Democratic Movement of the Soviet Union,* issued in 1969 in the name of the "Democrats of Russia, the Ukraine and the Baltic Region." Unlike much previous dissenting opinion, including that articulated by men like Academician Andrei Sakharov, the *Program* did not envisage the realization of democracy in the USSR as the result of evolution within the CPSU; it ignored this possibility and, in its negative criticism, emphasized the necessity for the elimination of party controls over social and political life; however, it shared, but more vigorously stressed, Sakharov's view that socialism was compatible with a multiparty political system. With the appearance of the *Program,* following on that of other radical protest documents — some of them dating back to 1967 or earlier — a considerable range both of reformist, within-system political dissent and of radical, maximalist, and even revolutionary thought had been articulated. Perhaps as the 1960s gave way to another decade a new stage was beginning in the development of political consciousness in the USSR — a stage of systematic elaboration of alternatives to the still dominant but increasingly ossified political culture of Russianized Marxism inherited from the Stalin era.

The patterns of oppositional thought and activity which will be the major foci of this study can be briefly designated as factional, sectoral, and subversive. Generally the first two terms refer to within-system opposition; the third, however, refers to efforts to fundamentally restructure or destroy the established order. By *factional opposition* we refer to efforts by members of the highest party and governmental decision-making bodies to change the personnel or policies of the party-state. Most factional opposition, at least in terms of what can be known of the perspectives of the oppositionists, might be described as within-system, system-acceptive, loyal opposition. Those who engage in what is here termed *sectoral opposition* — it might also be called interest-group politicking — are also, as a rule, basically loyal to or at least acceptive of the structure of the Soviet system, but not necessarily of policies pursued by incumbent leaders. They usually seek, within relatively circumscribed limits, to maximize the values and promote the interests of their particular professional or institutional groups — or, as is often the case, of innovating, liberalizing, nonconformist subsections of their groups, the majority of whose members may be passive conformists or even willing supporters of the regime. *Subversive opposition,* in contrast, is system-rejective. Its advocates desire the drastic alteration or even the total abolition of the established order. They have little opportunity, under Soviet conditions, to formulate precise alternatives to existing structures and policies. Their behavior, fueled by frustration, is often anomic, irrational, or even desperate and self-defeating.[17]

Some attributes of the tightly centralized, ideologically rationalized Soviet pattern of rule which significantly affect opposition today should be recalled to mind. Fundamental is the single, more or less monolithic ruling party's ability to penetrate or envelop social structures and interest groups and largely to isolate them from one another. The pervasive, often intimidating presence of agents of the central authority shapes a situation in which not only competitive political parties but all sorts of interactions, linkages, and communications exchanges between the various oppositional factions and groups, which might flourish if they were not inhibited or suppressed, are — if not entirely lacking — weak, limited, illegitimate or only semilegitimate, impermanent, and often almost invisible. Here, however, as in the area of exchanges of ideas and of persons and the establishment of personal relationships between Russia and the West, significant changes have occurred in recent years. Interactions and intellectual communion among individuals and among members of various professions are easier and less dangerous than they were. One might even say that the rudiments of an independent and critical, though — in Kremlin eyes — not yet fully legitimate, public opinion are now at hand. In connection with these developments, it is perhaps appropriate to offer some speculative observations.

The fact that dissent blossoms whenever controls over intellectual life are relaxed, as happened during World War II and after Stalin's death, points to a general weakness — one might say, to opposition-generating properties — of revolutionary ideological dictatorships, at least of the Soviet type. The utopian pretensions of such regimes, while inspiring to their supporters and beneficiaries, at least in the early stages of development when ideological fervor runs high, also provide a justification for harsh, terroristic, suppressive policies. Utopian visions, pretensions, and promises seem inevitably to clash with the capabilities of leaders and led alike to fulfill them. Certainly the utopian vision serves to rationalize the cruelty and injustice of the sanctions to which the more fanatical of

17. The extremely complex political implications of party–armed forces relationships cannot be dealt with briefly and have hence been almost entirely omitted from this study, but the writer is aware of their importance. Like other institutional interest groups, the military are not homogeneous. Military elements—as represented by Marshal Georgi Zhukov's temporary, ill-fated alliance with Khrushchev—sometimes have played an important role in factional politics. Military opposition is usually sectoral (concerned with resource allocation, etc.), but it has, of course, a subversive potential. Military resentment over Khrushchev's fiasco in Cuba in 1962, for example, undoubtedly played some part in his ouster. The best and most recent study on the political roles and potential of the Soviet military establishment is Roman Kolkowicz, *The Soviet Military and the Communist Party* (Princeton: Princeton University Press, 1967).

its hard-pressed adherents resort. It also seems to generate cynicism and moral fatigue, as the gulf grows between professed ideals and a reality pervaded by expediency.

The organizational aspects of the Marxist-Leninist formula can also produce negative, opposition-generating predispositions. Party controls can be frustrating and irritating, not only to creative writers and scientists, but also to military officers, industrial managers, and jurists — indeed, to professionals generally. Party and police snooping and intimidation generate resentments. However, the overwhelming dominance of professional politicians in all spheres of policy formation might be more acceptable than it apparently is to Soviet civil servants and experts if the latter had more than their present, very nominal representation in the Central Committee — and almost none in the Politburo — of the ruling party. Of course, the highly centralized, though by no means monolithic party apparatus can, to a considerable extent, fight its battles with various autonomy-seeking challengers on something like its own terms. Should a powerful enough faction someday arise, however, in the party apparatus, or perhaps even outside it, to create a broad coalition of elite elements with a cohesive organization and an appealing ideological platform, the power of a "combat party" better suited to conducting a revolutionary struggle than to governing a complex modern society may rapidly crumble. When and if this comes to pass, Russia will cease to be a cause and will be once again a country. The patterns and techniques of suppression of opposition, to which so much attention is devoted in these pages, will then be unrecognizably altered, and the world will hopefully be enabled to turn to the tasks of international cooperation and order.

The highly organized, party-directed political socialization and education program which still performs with considerable success the function of shaping the opinions of Soviet citizens helps to render difficult the crystallization of oppositional predispositions into alternatives to official doctrines. Censorship plays an even more obvious role. If alternatives are perceived, they must be disguised, or rationalized, and then articulated within a context which can easily distort or cripple them. It is all too easy for the authorities, in such a context, to brand reformers as unpatriotic or even as treasonable. The effects of positive indoctrination are reinforced by censorship and other methods of shielding the citizenry from "alien" influences. Within this pattern, it is relatively difficult for even the deeply disaffected to perceive or formulate alternatives to the points of view, programs, and ideologies sponsored and imposed by the political authorities.

However, the replacement of Stalin's terror-based cult by a somewhat more permissive pattern of controls, affording increased though by no means unfettered access both to foreign cultural influences and ideas and

to hitherto forbidden aspects of Russia's prerevolutionary cultural heritage, has made it easier for rebels and dissenters to inform themselves about
— and, to some degree, to discuss and even disseminate — alternative
models of thought and action. In this somewhat freer atmosphere the
latent, half-forgotten, liberal, humanitarian, and cosmopolitan elements in
the tradition and mentality of the Soviet intelligentsia were rediscovered,
reactivated, and reinforced. With this background in mind we can better
understand the attitudes and behavior of the oppositional groupings which
have been active within many segments of the Soviet scientific, artistic,
and scholarly intelligentsia since the death of Stalin.

Despite official disapproval, harassment, and in some instances administrative and penal sanctions, the Soviet "free speech movement" grew
in numbers and ideological scope from its first dramatic manifestations in
1965–66 to early 1972. However, dissenters who engaged in activities
such as street demonstrations, or whose writings, published abroad, especially affronted or alarmed the authorities, were likely to be tried and
sentenced to corrective labor camps for "political" crimes or to be committed to psychiatric hospitals. The latter technique of repression apparently came into increasing use in 1969–71 as a method of getting rid
of troublesome dissidents without the embarrassing publicity of a regular
court trial. Some particularly talented dissenting professionals, such as
the writer Solzhenitsyn and the physicists Andrei Sakharov and Valeri
Chalidze, because of their world and professional stature and their
scrupulous avoidance of words or deeds remotely resembling illegality or
conspiracy, were able to exert quiet pressure on the authorities in aid of
victims of arbitrary police power. Indeed, beginning in November 1970,
Sakharov, Chalidze, and a few associates conducted their campaign for
the protection of the legal and constitutional rights of Soviet citizens
through the medium of a Human Rights Committee chaired by Chalidze.[18]

18. Paul Smith, in "Protest in Moscow," *Foreign Affairs* 47, no. 1 (October 1968):
151–63, analyzing "protest documents" against the treatment of Ginsburg and his
associates, expressed the opinion that the some four hundred persons who up to that
time had signed protest petitions were motivated, not only by a desire to ward off
a possible return to Stalinist police methods, but also by a feeling that "the ideological
orthodoxy of the post-Khrushchev leadership" had "become irrelevant," and that
"there must either be a revival of earlier national values or a formulation of new
values" to fill the gap left by the loss of Stalin's tyrannical but effective rule. Smith
perceived the thinking of Soviet dissenters to be "reformist," "constitutional," and
strongly nationalistic. Andrei Amabik, in *Will the Soviet Union Survive until 1984?*
(New York: Harper and Row, 1970), pp. 13–15, referred to "several dozen active
participants" of the "Democratic Movement" and to 738 signers of protests against
the Ginzburg-Galanskov trial. As of early 1972, it seems certain that the number of
persons who have in some way contributed to the "Movement" is well in excess of a
thousand, and, if religious protesters such as Baptists and members of such ethnic
groups as Jews and Crimean Tatars and Ukrainians are included, the number might
be as high as ten thousand. On the Chalidze-Sakharov Human Rights Committee,
see Donald S. Harrington, "Four Brave Men and the Rights of Man in Russia,"

To a degree which is probably increasing, though it is very difficult to measure, the Soviet intelligentsia, especially its scientific-technical components, shares the professional values, but probably not the ideological outlooks, of its "bourgeois" counterparts. Indeed, the advocacy by Sakharov, a leading atomic physicist, of Soviet–United States cooperation and his predictions, not only of socioeconomic "convergence" between "socialist" and "capitalist" nations, but also of multiparty political systems in the former, indicate that at least some Soviet scientists share a broad range of values and beliefs with Western colleagues.[19] As the Soviet scientific-technical revolution (which is, incidentally, a subject of increasing attention in the general Soviet press and in scholarly journals) proceeds further, these similarities of outlook — including, probably, similar feelings of alienation from many aspects of modern industrial society — may be expected, over a period of time, to foster a sense of identity of interests and standards of judgment between Soviet intellectuals and professionals and their "bourgeois" counterparts. To a certain extent, in fact, the latter probably serve as reference groups for their Soviet colleagues, especially in the literary, artistic, and scientific fields. Some recent protest documents, such as the *Program of the Democratic Movement*, referred to earlier, have sharply condemned dogmatic anticapitalism. Nevertheless, some basic attitudes, such as a deep revulsion, often expressed in terms of overt moral condemnation, against "capitalist" society (on the current state of which even well-educated Russians are badly misinformed) and aversion to what is probably rather generally regarded, even by the disaffected Soviet "liberals," as an "imperialist" American foreign policy — especially, in recent years, in Vietnam — constitute formidable ideological and cultural barriers to mutual understanding between the Soviet and American intelligentsia.

The intense hostility displayed in Soviet doctrine and in the political culture generally toward all forms of "deviation" and even toward failure to render full, wholehearted support to party policy, let alone resistance or overt, organized opposition — a hostility which is still strong, though less intense and irrational than in the past, when the Soviet citizenry had not yet been socialized into the new order — indicates that party leaders and perhaps the political elite generally, especially in the apparatuses of

New York Times, 11 November 1971. Zhores and Roy Medvedev, in *A Question of Madness* (New York: Knopf, 1971), describe and explore the significance of Zhores's commitment to a mental institution in 1970 and the successful campaign to free him, to which scores of scientists, writers, and other professionals contributed.

19. Andrei D. Sakharov, *Progress, Coexistence and Intellectual Freedom*, with Introduction, Afterword, and Notes by Harrison E. Salisbury (New York: Norton, 1968). There is evidence, in the form of reports known to this writer of conversations between American and Soviet scientists, that Sakharov's views are widely known in the Soviet scientific community and are generally supported by many members of that community.

party, state, and economic administration, regard it as deeply harmful, dangerous, and indeed evil.

Curiously enough, however, even from the point of view of the health of the party as a political organism, it is possible that the party leaders and official theorists exaggerate the damaging effects of opposition. Opposition, one can speculate, may even in an autocratic or oligarchical system serve the useful purpose of alerting the leadership to social pressures to which it is expedient, even if distasteful, to respond; and it may, together with purges, play a role in the process of weeding out incompetents from the leadership. Implicit admissions that opposition is not always or completely dysfunctional in the Soviet system were made by Khrushchev, especially in his very frank official report to the Twenty-second CPSU Congress in 1961, and by the much more cautious post-Khrushchev oligarchs shortly after they seized power.[20] However, esoteric and guarded implications that within-system opposition can be useful are almost inaudible in a pattern of political discourse which thunderously demands eager acceptance of official values.

The non-Communist analyst of the Soviet political process can scarcely fail to be struck by the rigidities and proneness to stagnation of a system which has always lacked the sifting and testing capabilities of democratic elections and, since Stalin, has also lacked the partial, if crude, substitute for regular elections provided by blood purges. The only major supplement to the tradition of co-optation in the selection of leaders would now appear to be conspiracies, such as the one that ousted Khrushchev, and the possibility of further succession crises. It must be kept in mind, however, that Stalin's successors have maintained reasonably high rates of economic growth and have instituted some sensible if modest, administrative reforms. Soviet society seems at present to be relatively stable; the policies of Khrushchev's heirs have thus far produced reasonably satisfactory results. All of this, and in particular the fact that the Stalin and Khrushchev succession crises were surmounted without great difficulty, indicate a degree of competence in the quality of Soviet leadership that should make us wary about diagnosing Moscow's situation today as one of incurable political decay.

---

20. Khrushchev's analysis of the failings and defects of his colleagues and rivals, contained in his secret speech and in the above-mentioned report, reads almost like an unwitting, or implicit, recommendation of some form of regular political competition. It may, one surmises, have been so construed by some Soviet citizens. It is interesting, in this connection, that Khrushchev introduced into the party statutes a provision for regular replacement of fixed proportions of members of party decision-making bodies and that Brezhnev and his colleagues repealed this reform in 1966. However, it is important to remember that Khrushchev did not make any overt, explicit concessions to the principle of the legitimacy of opposition in a "socialist" state, though he did sharply distinguish between Lenin's "magnanimity" and rationality in dealing with "mistaken" opponents and Stalin's destructive brutality.

Factional Opposition

In spite of their utopian ideological pretensions, Soviet leaders from Lenin through Brezhnev have perforce pursued rather realistic and pragmatic policies. Revolutionaries, if they are to cling to power, must sooner or later learn that the exigencies of administration and the struggle to preserve their power interfere with early or easy achievement of utopian goals. Revolutionary ideologies tend, sooner rather than later, to be interpreted by practically minded leaders in a spirit likely to alienate many whose support was attracted by a more romantic vision during the struggle for power.

Lenin and his successors have of course been sterner, more demanding, and far more effective rulers than the tsars. They have imposed stern discipline upon their subjects, rewarding loyalty and efficiency, severely punishing disloyalty and inefficiency. It is not surprising that many associates of Lenin in the struggle to win power and of Stalin in the consolidation of the new order were dissatisfied, disillusioned, or morally outraged by the harsh realities of Soviet politics. As members of a ruling political party which forbade political competition even within its hierarchical organization, those who disapproved of official policy were forced either to conform silently or to risk the dangerous, guilt-ridden path of intrigue and conspiracy. Those who resisted, those who sought to alter the conduct of — or, worse yet, to unseat — the leaders of the monolithic party, and those who in desperation plotted the violent overthrow or death of its chiefs were, of course, diverse in motivation and perspective; but they shared a situation imposed by the exigencies of the monocratic pattern of politics.

As early as 1926, a young party member named Ossovsky pointed out that the party could not be both united and unique. If it chose to exercise power uniquely, it would inevitably become an arena of struggle among representatives of different interests. To be truly united, according to Ossovsky, it must permit other parties, representing various strata of society, to compete for power.[21] Ossovsky pointed to diverse sources of factional strife, but for our purposes it is convenient to divide what he correctly regarded as normal, inevitable factional oppositions into two broad and loose categories: *utopian*, or idealistic, and *liberal*, or revisionist. These categories correspond roughly to the more familiar terminology of left and right, with the realistic-expediential Lenin-Stalin line in the center.

The various utopian oppositions flourished mainly while Lenin was still the party leader and to a lesser degree during the first few years after

21. Nicolaevsky, *Power and the Soviet Elite*, pp. 132–33.

his death. Under Lenin, and to some extent during the years before
Stalin achieved tight control over the party leadership, it was possible to
debate political issues, mainly within party deliberative bodies but to a
certain extent even in the Soviet press. Typical of the various early
utopian opposition were the Bukharin and Preobrazhenski groups and,
to some extent, Trotski and his followers. Located also within this broad
tendency was the so-called Workers' Opposition, which unsuccessfully
advocated that Soviet factories be managed by the workers rather than
by party-controlled professional managers and party-controlled trade
unions.

In contrast to the liberal oppositions — which have, as Daniels notes,
tended to develop whenever the party leadership seems ready to relax
ideological and political controls[22] — the principled, doctrinaire, and
sometimes fanatical utopians have sought to maximize the achievement of
ideological goals. They have been exceptionally future-oriented. They
have often demanded a militant, expansionist foreign policy. During the
debates over Soviet foreign policy in 1918, when they opposed Lenin's
willingness to accept the harsh Brest-Litovsk peace with imperial Germany, the utopians seemed to come close to readiness to sacrifice Soviet
state interests to the interests of "world revolution." The relatively
pragmatic but despotic Stalin was in due course to accuse not only the
Bukharinites but also the followers of Trotski of having covertly plotted,
at the time of the frank and open debates within the party prior to the
conclusion of the onerous Brest-Litovsk peace, to permit the destruction
of the fledgling Soviet republic at the hands of a German imperialism
which, so the Stalin propaganda retrospectively charged, could have
utilized Soviet refusal to sign the treaty as a pretext for crushing Soviet
Russia.

In distinction from the utopian oppositional programs and attitudes, the
liberal oppositional views have tended to be responsive to the aspirations
not only of rank-and-file party members but even of the "broad masses"
of the non-party citizenry, who craved respite from the pressures imposed by the "Bolshevik tempo." In their preferences regarding allocation
of resources, Communist rightists have always favored a greater input into
agriculture, consumer goods, and services than the Stalinist centrists, the
neo-Stalinists, or the leftists of the early 1920s. In cultural policy liberal
Communists are relatively permissive and experimental. In foreign policy
they are disposed to seek some degree of accommodation with the
capitalist world and to be relatively permissive regarding exchanges of
persons and other aspects of cultural relations with the West.

There are, to be sure, substantial differences in the atmosphere and
style of government, especially in the relations between the Kremlin and

22. Daniels, *The Conscience of the Revolution,* pp. 382–85.

the citizenry, which distinguish the period of Stalin's terroristic autocracy both from the earlier period (1917 to the early 1930s) and from the period since 1953. The patterns sketched above still seem useful, however, in sorting out the goals of various kinds of oppositional tendencies and currents which have existed throughout the history of Soviet Russia.[23]

The sharpness and clarity of this utopian-liberal, or left-right, distinction should not be exaggerated. A particular leader may at any given time pursue policies that represent an eclectic combination of formally conflicting orientations. Moreover, a leader may shift from one orientation to another, either because he has rethought his position or simply because changing circumstances make it expedient for him to do so. Stalin, for example, allied himself for a time with the relatively moderate elements in the party leadership against the leftist policies of Trotski; then he appropriated Trotski's policies in his struggle against Bukharin, who had earlier been a radical utopian but later became a moderate liberal. During the first few months after Stalin's death, police chief Beria, who had for years been the dictator's enforcer and executioner, turned, in a struggle for survival and perhaps in a bid for supreme power, to relatively liberal policies.[24] Khrushchev and his supporters, in their struggle to oust G. M. Malenkov as head of the Soviet government, defended some of Stalin's major policies, attacking as "right deviations" Malenkov's tendency to approve at least verbally of accommodative, responsive foreign and domestic options. Later, of course, Khrushchev chose an "empiricist," "populist" line for which — and for his "harebrained schemes" in administration — he was anonymously taken to task after his ouster in October 1964. He had at long last aroused the collective alarm and anger of his erstwhile moderate supporters, inducing them to join with his older, more conservative factional opponents.[25]

The events just mentioned suggest other interesting aspects of factional opposition in the USSR and presumably in other Communist — and perhaps non-Communist dictatorial — systems as well. First, men like Khrushchev and Brezhnev, who, when they are in power, devote much of their effort to nipping in the bud attempts to organize effective oppositions, themselves came to power as leaders of, or at least as allies of, oppositional forces. Second, leadership groups and oppositions tend to be

23. T. H. Rigby, in "The Extent and Limits of Authority," *Problems of Communism* 12, no. 5 (September–October 1963): 36–41, identifies twelve sets of competitive or antagonistic relationships.

24. Robert Conquest, *Power and Policy in the USSR* (New York: St. Martin's Press, 1961), chap. 9.

25. Sidney Ploss, in *Conflict and Decision-Making in Soviet Russia* (Princeton: Princeton University Press, 1965), correctly, in this author's opinion, characterizes Khrushchev and his supporters as "reformists" and the anti-Khrushchev faction as "conservatives."

coalitions.[26] Third, an innovative and renovative leader, in the Soviet situation, seems inevitably to arouse anxiety, antagonism, hostility, or even hatred within the Soviet establishment.

Soviet intolerance of opposition is, like other basic traits of Soviet political behavior, the product of a political culture and an ideology antipathetic to pluralism. Such legitimacy as the leaders enjoy is not derived from the freely given consent of the governed, in elections or otherwise, or from laws stipulating a process of selection, or from custom. It tends to be based, rather, on the leader's skill in political manipulation and in the use of political violence. The Stalin-Vyshinski formula for rule was summed up in the formula "coercion and persuasion" (*primuzhdenie i ubezhdenie*). Authoritative statements published toward the end of the Khrushchev era, when frankness about Stalin was still permitted, indicated that at the Seventeenth CPSU Congress in 1934, Sergei Mironovich Kirov and his supporters represented the majority opinion in the party, while Stalin led a minority faction opposed to "Leninist" policies.[27] Stalin, of course, created his own consensus. There was no real factional opposition once his rule was firmly established. There was, however, a pattern of court politics, in which the leader's lieutenants vied for his favor. As Khrushchev partially revealed in his secret speech, rivalry among Stalin's courtiers not only affected the making of crucial decisions but sometimes cost the lives of men against whom the dictator's suspicion had been aroused.

Khrushchev, in contrast to Stalin, had to take account of the opinions and interests of his colleagues in the Presidium and the Secretariat — and even, at times, of the members of the Central Committee of the party. Sometimes his opponents were able at least partially to frustrate his plans and programs. Although he usually had his way, in the main, his policies aroused a cumulative and bitter resentment which helped to topple him from power.[28] Of course, Khrushchev fell, not only because

26. The "antiparty group" defeated and ousted by Khrushchev, in 1957 and subsequently, was clearly a coalition of disparate elements. It included, for example, Kaganovich and Molotov, both categorized correctly by Khrushchev as among the chief lieutenants of Stalin in his purges, and Malenkov, denounced with less justification for his post-Stalin "revisionist" policies in industry and agriculture.

27. See, for example, *Istoriya kommunisticheskoi partii sovetskoga soyuza* (Moscow, 1963), p. 46, and especially the article by L. Shaumyan in *Pravda*, 7 February 1964. After the ouster of Khrushchev, articles on Kirov, Vlas Chubar, and other victims of Stalin's "cult of personality" omitted accusations that Stalin had been responsible for their deaths. The toning down of de-Stalinization by Khrushchev's successors probably indicates concern about damage done to the legitimacy of rule by the CPSU as a result of Khrushchev's ideological indiscretions.

28. Much pertinent information on partly successful opposition to various Khrushchev policies is contained in Ploss, *Conflict and Decision-Making*, and in the valuable study edited and partly written by Peter H. Juviler and Henry W. Morton, *Soviet Policy Making* (New York: Praeger, 1967). See especially Morton's introductory

of opposition on the part of other leaders toward his policies, but also because bad luck and bungling had led to fiascoes such as the Cuban missile crisis of 1962 and the crop failure of 1963. During the months before his fall he was, it seems clear, getting ready to embark upon drastic new ventures, especially in agriculture and industry, which, his colleagues apparently feared, could undermine the Soviet system.[29]

Shortly after his removal, the authoritative Central Committee organizational journal stated editorially that any leader, no matter how high his rank or position, must "answer for the results of his activity" and must take the consequences of his mistakes.[30] In such dicta the new leadership expressed its repudiation of the style, if not the content of Khrushchevism. It also registered the determination of the new oligarchs to preserve the consensus which had enabled them to overthrow Khrushchev. Implicitly, such statements constituted at least a retrospective justification of opposition — very similar, it should be noted, to that implied by statements Khrushchev himself had made when he expelled the antiparty group in 1957.

The origins and outlook of the cautious and hesitant Brezhnev-Kosygin leadership were to help it preserve a remarkable degree of unity for a surprisingly long time. Brezhnev soon instituted a style of leadership which might be described as one of shared authority, although he himself, judging by the pattern of officially reported activities, was *primus inter pares* in the new collective leadership. Well into the sixth year after it had skillfully pulled the rug from under Khrushchev, the collective which replaced him was working, under Brezhnev's chairmanship, with quiet efficiency and relative harmony. Consensus within the post-Khrushchev leadership, however, as in earlier Soviet leadership groups, was threatened by impulses of rivalry and competition. The fact that harmony was by no means complete was indicated, for example, by the fashion in which, in 1965 and again in 1967, the able, ambitious Shelepin was deprived of some of his functions.[31] It was revealed also by criticisms on the part

article, "The Structure of Decision Making in the USSR," and the contribution by Robert M. Slusser, "America, China, and the Hydra-headed Opposition: The Dynamics of Soviet Foreign Policy." The best study of Khrushchev's decline and fall is Michel Tatu, *Le pouvoir en URSS* (Paris: B. Grasset, 1967), which contains a wealth of information on the attitudes of leading Soviet political figures and of major segments of the apparatus in general toward Khrushchev's policies. See also William Hyland and Richard W. Shryock, *The Fall of Khrushchev* (New York: Funk and Wagnalls, 1968).

29. See especially *Pravda*, 11 August, 2 October, and 3 October 1964.
30. *Partiinaya zhizn*, no. 20 (October 1964).
31. In December 1965 the Party-State Control Committee, headed by Shelepin, was abolished without apparent participation in the action by Shelepin himself. In 1967 he lost his membership in the Central Committee Secretariat, which he had held since 1962, and was appointed to leadership of the All-Union Central Council of Trade Unions, a post which in the past had never led to the political summit.

of Dmitri Polyanski, presumably one of Brezhnev's principal supporters, of "some comrades" who allegedly were not sufficiently concerned about agricultural policy and the welfare of the Soviet farmer.[32] In this connection, it is interesting that Brezhnev, like Khrushchev before him, apparently had to contend with opposition to his efforts to increase somewhat the share of the long-neglected collective farm peasantry in the national income. There is evidence, relevant to the question of top-level unity or disunity, of differences of opinion in the Politburo regarding the invasion of Czechoslovakia. Also, in 1969–70, Brezhnev's criticisms of the economy's performance seemed to indicate friction between him and Kosygin, the latter having been the leader responsible for supervising this sphere of policy.

The main sites of factional struggle are the Central Committee Presidium (renamed the Politburo at the Twenty-third CPSU Congress in 1966), its Secretariat, and to a lesser degree the Central Committee itself, which since the death of Stalin has met with relative regularity in Moscow, a requirement of the party statutes to which Stalin had been impressively indifferent. In addition, ministries and state committees — especially such powerful, sensitive ones as those of defense and state security — the editorial boards of important newspapers and magazines, and institutions such as the Academy of Sciences of the USSR can form elements of the power bases of coalitional factions with representation in a number of party and government organizations. Although the centralized, hierarchical structure of the party and state organization gives the incument leader or leaders great advantages vis-à-vis those who would seek to oppose their policies or remove them from office, these advantages are not necessarily overwhleming, as the fall of Khrushchev demonstrated.

We should here mention certain socioeconomic trends which in recent years have increasingly affected the environment in which factional politics unfolds. With the increasing complexity of the Soviet economy, the influence, status, and personal security of scientific, technical, administrative, legal, educational, and other specialists has increased. Specialization and professionalization have brought into elite recruitment — especially in state and industrial administration, the staffing of research laboratories, the military, and, increasingly so it appears, in all branches of law enforcement — selection and staffing practices similar to those applied in other advanced industrial nations. The bureaucratization of Soviet society and the steadily increasing role of both the creative and

32. Of several statements by Polyanski criticizing "conservative" opposition to increased investment in agriculture, the fullest and perhaps the most important was his long signed article in *Kommunist*, no. 10 (October 1967). Various indications, including the increased prominence of the industrially oriented Politburo member A. P. Kirilenko, and the diminished prominence of Polyanski, seem to point to a decline in the influence of agriculturally oriented elements after 1968–69.

the technical intelligentsia have been reflected also in the increasingly bureaucratic operations and ethos of the ruling Communist party itself.[33]

In a bureaucratic, differentiated, and "rational" Soviet society — with increasingly exacting skill criteria for status advancement, even in the various party and police hierarchies — power and influence have come to be somewhat more widely distributed and diffuse than they were in the cruder, more primitive society over which Stalin ruled. Not only in the policy-forming and decision-making agencies of the party and state, but also in relationships between political decision makers and the military, scientific, legal, literary, and other communities, autocratic and even oligarchical rule has been to a certain extent replaced by consensual and consultative patterns. This shift began under Khrushchev and has continued to develop under his successors.[34]

Given these social trends — which are in part this writer's own impressionistic views of the emerging social reality in the USSR — one would logically expect the nature of oppositional tendencies and activities to have changed over the last ten or fifteen years. Indeed, as strivings for autonomy have become more widely diffused, there does seem to have been a change toward less emotional intensity in the thinking of even the political elite regarding the dangers of opposition, and the frontier posts at the boundary between state and society have come to be somewhat less closely guarded. Although Soviet society still lacks anything like a flexible, highly differentiated, sensitive network of communications and opinion channels between the government and various interest groups, such as exists in advanced Western industrial nations, it is much easier than it was under Stalin for political groups and factions and for the representatives of the major professional communities to present their views to the top leaders. Khrushchev with demagogic fanfare and his successors with quiet practicality have, in fact, encouraged experts to present their views, at least in a consultative capacity, on a wide range

33. Our understanding of these trends has been assisted by such émigré scholars as Boris Nicolaevski, David Dallin, and other contributors to the extremely valuable but unfortunately now defunct journal, *Sotsialisticheski vestnik;* later by Barrington Moore, Jr., in his major studies *Soviet Politics: The Dilemma of Power* (Cambridge, Mass.: Harvard University Press, 1950) and *Terror and Progress* (Cambridge, Mass.: Harvard University Press, 1954); and by Zbigniew Brzezinski, especially in his perceptive article, "Evolution in the USSR: Two Paths," *Problems of Communism* 15 (January–February 1966): 1–15. George Fischer's study, *The Soviet System and Modern Society* (New York: Atherton Press, 1969), and other recent works have explored the implications of the emergence, within the party apparatus, of a new type of executive with experience in and connections with the world of industrial management.
34. On the increasing influence of Soviet scientists on policy formation in recent years, at least in the spheres of their own professional concerns, see, in particular, Loren R. Graham, "Reorganization of the U.S.S.R. Academy of Sciences," in Juviler and Morton, eds., *Soviet Policy Making.*

of policy issues, sometimes in the press, especially the specialist press, and probably more often — and more effectively — in the privacy of party and government offices and in conferences of scholars and experts. At least some elements of the feedback well known in modern Western systems have been introduced into the Soviet decision-making process. The pattern which has been developing during the last ten or fifteen years offers an increasing range of sites for oppositional activity, or at least for lobbying.[35]

Very seldom, however, and then usually after years of delay, do Soviet sources provide readers with more than guarded hints of the extent and on occasion the ferocity of domestic factional strife. A notable, if partial, exception to this pattern of secrecy was the startling version presented by some leaders, then supporters of Khrushchev, to the Twenty-second CPSU Congress in 1961 of the alleged misdeeds of the antiparty group. In his speech at this congress A. N. Shelepin, for example, stated that in June 1957, "when the factionalists went over to an open attack against the Central Committee," N. A. Bulganin, then chairman of the Council of Ministers, had placed his guard in the Kremlin in such a manner that without his permission nobody could obtain access to "the government building where the session of the Presidium of the Central Committee of the CPSU was taking place." Shelepin charged that "the conspirators" had thus indicated their readiness "to take the most extreme measures to achieve their base ends." [36] Khrushchev and Frol R. Kozlov, in speeches at the same congress, asserted that if the antiparty group had been successful, they would have done away with "the honest leaders" of the party.[37] Later, in 1964, Khrushchev himself was removed from office by a conspiracy in which the KGB must have played at least a benevolently neutral role.

What we know about such events — together with continued Soviet secrecy, which indeed was considerably tightened after the garrulous Khrushchev was pushed off the political stage — warns us that despite tendencies and pressures for wider participation in public life and for a more open and regular pattern of interest articulation, the dominant patterns of Soviet politics, including those which determine the nature of political opposition, remain closed, concentrated, tight, and rife with semiconspiratorial rivalries, which seem everywhere to be produced by

35. That the growth of dissent and of willingness on the part of the top party leadership — or perhaps of only some elements thereof — to engage in a dialogue with loyal dissenters was not entirely aborted by Khrushchev's fall, at least for some time, is indicated by the observations of a young American political scientist and former exchange student at Moscow University, William Taubman, in his *The View from Lenin Hills* (New York: Coward-McCann, 1967), especially chaps. 1 and 20.
36. *Pravda*, 27 October 1961.
37. *Materialy XX sezda KPSS* (Moscow, 1962), p. 282.

a bureaucratic structure but which assume special intensity in a Soviet-type system.

In contrast with both the Stalin and the Khrushchev leadership, that of Brezhnev and Kosygin, at least during its first six years, was remarkably free of outward indications of irreconcilable inner conflict. There was, however, the gradual whittling down of the Shelepin group (A. N. Shelepin, V. Semichastny, and others) and the removal of N. G. Egorychev as head of the Moscow party organization, apparently for excessive hawkishness in connection with the 1967 Arab-Israeli war. There was the controversy over agricultural policy, which has already been mentioned. Finally, there is strong, though inconclusive, evidence of difference of opinion regarding policy toward Czechoslovakia in 1968. Well-informed Western newspaper correspondents reported that such leaders as Suslov and Kosygin, for rather different reasons, were less disposed than the majority of their colleagues toward the military solution adopted in August 1968 to deal with Czechoslovak "revisionism." While Kosygin asserted that the Politburo's decision was unanimous, available evidence — both in Soviet published sources, according to which Suslov was not present at the CPSU plenum of 15 July 1968, at which the decision to intervene was probably made, and in presumably reliable statements made by Western Communists present in Moscow when intervention began — casts doubt on Kosygin's statement, though it may be formally correct.[38]

Sectoral Opposition

What is here termed sectoral opposition takes its impetus from the aspirations, wants, and demands of specialized professional, occupational, and functional groups, such as natural and social scientists, jurists, writers and artists, and industrial executives, for what seems to at least some members of these communities (as they are often called in Soviet sources) a just and necessary degree of freedom from prescriptions, controls, and intervention by party functionaries in the performance of their professional functions and in their personal lives.

Only a small minority of Soviet specialists and professionals have so far overtly expressed demands for radical reform of the political and social order; in particular, few have indicated a desire to alter such basic structural features of Soviet society as the socialist, planned economy. As

38. For a perceptive analysis of the confusing, and perhaps confused, pattern of decision making — and indecision — in the post-Khrushchev era, see Leonard Schapiro, "Collective Lack of Leadership," *Survey*, Winter-Spring 1969, pp. 193–99. See also Frederick C. Barghoorn, "Trends in Top Political Leadership in the U.S.S.R." in R. Barry Farrell, ed., *Political Leadership in Eastern Europe and the Soviet Union* (Evanston, Ill.: Northwestern University Press, 1970), pp. 61–87.

a rule — doubtless partly for tactical reasons — they advocate within-system changes, when they advocate institutional changes of any kind. It is possible, of course, that materialization of aspirations for professional autonomy will indirectly lead to fundamental changes; and it may be significant that the party press has occasionally accused unnamed persons of wanting to establish, on foreign "bourgeois" instigation, opposition parties financed from abroad. Although there is still relatively little solid evidence of broadly supported, aggressive demands for basic structural changes in any major sphere, such charges may bespeak regime concern about real and persistent demands for such changes, which as we have indicated began to be articulated with increasing frequency in the late 1960s.

Moreover, it is often difficult for all concerned, including non-Soviet analysts, to distinguish clearly between within-system and subversive opposition. Subversive opposition (which is discussed in the next section of this chapter) is defined here as efforts to interfere seriously with, or to undermine or drastically alter, regime practices and their ideological rationalizations. Acts of evasion or passive resistance can, especially if they occur on a large scale, fall into this category. System-acceptive dissent or opposition differs from antisystem opposition, in part, in the content and intensity of its aspirations; but it must be emphasized that in a polity as allergic to all forms of contestation and resistance as is the USSR, what has for a time been regarded by the authorities as loyal or orthodox criticism has often, without notice, been reclassified as heretical or subversive. For example, much that Khrushchev tolerated or even encouraged as salutary criticism of the "cult of personality" of Stalin came to be regarded during the Brezhnev era as harmful or dangerous.

The two kinds, or degrees, of dissent have much in common, even though dissenters and authorities, at least in the post-Stalin era, seem usually able to distinguish between them without great difficulty. The distinction is presumably based on perceptions of the compatibility of the given attitudes and demands with established practices and structures. However, both kinds of dissent and opposition undoubtedly stem from disillusionment, disaffection, and resentment — motives which are common to all cultures but differ among and within cultures in respect to specific origin, form, and intensity.[39]

Our definition assumes that interest group or sectoral oppositionists such as Sakharov are normally willing (provided the authorities make

39. For a broad typology of varieties of dissent in a context of acceptance or rejection of "innovation," which contains insights applicable with discrimination to the Soviet type of society. See H. G. Barnett, *Innovation: The Basis of Cultural Change* (New York: McGraw-Hill, 1953), chap. 14.

it possible) to work within the basic framework of Communist rule, such as recognition of the leading role of the party in economic, political, and even, broadly speaking, cultural spheres. It further assumes that they do not reject Marxist ideology, if it is interpreted in a flexible and sophisticated manner. However, there is a real question whether a symbiotic relationship between the party apparatus and a burgeoning array of increasingly independent, well-informed, and confident professional groups will prove to be viable over the long term. It is possible, nevertheless, that the top party leaders regard moderate sectoral opposition as a less serious threat to the Soviet system than some forms of factional opposition. Some of them, sometimes, may even regard it as useful insofar as it helps, by improving morale, to elicit support from professionals, experts, and intellectuals for the political order.

Sectoral opposition — operating, as it usually does, at relatively low levels of the political system and thus affecting, at any given time, only limited aspects of policy — has as a rule been relatively easy for the authorities to contain and control. In coping with it, the leadership normally enjoys the advantages of unity of command and organizational initiative. Not only are specialists compartmentalized in terms of their occupational interests, values, and wants; most sectors seem also to be divided within their own ranks into liberal and conservative factions, which the Kremlin can set against one another. The ability of the party leadership to deal effectively with sectoral opposition is further enhanced, not only by the compartmentalization of the Soviet occupational structure and administration, but also by the penetration of all occupational structures and organizations by the highly comprehensive and ramified party organization. However, this penetration and coverage is counterbalanced by the increasing specialization of function within the party apparatus itself. This tends increasingly to transform the middle and upper echelons of the party bureaucracy into an aggregation, or "tent," within which party specialists, linked to functional groupings in the economy, lobby for their own particular special interests.[40]

The widespread but compartmentalized phenomenon of sectoral opposition could turn out to be a potent factor in the transformation of Soviet society. It will be particularly influential as the various professional, bureaucratic, and occupational groups and strata involved in it become

40. There has in recent years been considerable discussion, some of it relatively frank, on the problems posed by tendencies toward the development of what might tentatively be termed functional interest articulation at various levels of the party structure. See, for example, F. Petrenko, "The Collective Principle and Responsibility," *Pravda*, 20 July 1966, partly translated in *Current Digest of the Soviet Press* 18, no. 29 (1966), and his long article in *Kommunist*, no. 18 (December 1965). Khrushchev's successors seem to be more hostile to pluralistic tendencies within the party than was Khrushchev. However, both leaderships were concerned by this problem.

increasingly conscious of common interests transcending narrow occupational or organizational lines and move toward unity of perspectives and strategies. Since 1968, with the growth of the underground press, and particularly with the appearance of the underground organ *Chronicle of Current Events*, various currents of dissenting opinion have tended to merge into something resembling a single stream. Perhaps even more ominous, from the point of view of those in the party determined to preserve the present system virtually unchanged, is the possibility that linkages will develop between factional leaders and the moving spirits in important sectoral oppositions.

The sites of sectoral oppositions seem to be quite varied. With the relaxation of police controls following the death of Stalin, they developed within a wide range of official professional organizations, scientific academies, and literary and artistic unions, such as the Union of Soviet Writers. Although intended to be agencies of mobilization and party control over the various professional groups, these organizations also facilitate a measure of genuine professional communication, and through the very party units charged with controlling them they provide some degree of access for their members to high-level policy-making bodies.

Nonsubversive lobbyists for improvement in the environment of professional life, like the more completely alienated dissenters, make use not only of formal and legitimate channels for the articulation and transmission of their views but also of informal and sometimes of underground, illegitimate channels. There seems to be a gray area of informal patterns of interaction and relations among dissident intellectuals, lying somewhere between regime-approved behavior and subversive activity. Although it is of course difficult to obtain information on such matters, one is told by knowledgeable foreigners with extensive experience in the USSR that members of various intellectual groupings commune freely and frequently at their professional clubs, that they often express orally opinions which they cannot publish, and that the more unorthodox, "underground" intellectuals keep in touch with one another in semiclandestine fashion — in brief encounters, for example, in the lobbies of theaters.

Since Stalin, some rudiments of an independent public opinion appear to have emerged, at least among the intellectuals and students of a few major cities and scientific research centers. However, communication even among the intelligentsia remains somewhat clandestine. The high priests of ideology and the practitioners of political coercion can still force men and women who, in the opinion of their Western colleagues, are worthy of the highest esteem to skirt or violate arbitrarily imposed laws and regulations if they seek to communicate their opinions beyond a narrow circle of close friends and professional associates. They cannot legally publish them in uncensored form to the citizenry as a whole or to foreign audiences. In this connection, one thinks first of all of the physicist Sakharov and the novelist Solzhenitsyn, both of whom are far better known abroad than in their homeland.[41] But these outstanding men are apparently representative of scores, hundreds, or even thousands of others.

However, this situation has changed considerably in recent years with the emergence of a substantial *samizdat,* or self-published, literature, uncleared by censorship and distributed in typed or handwritten copies among persons sharing unauthorized views and a belief in freedom of opinion and information. By February 1971, 558 *samizdat* works had been identified by foreign experts.[42] Much, but not all, of this underground opinion was being regularly reported and commented on in the already mentioned *Chronicle of Current Events* and reprinted both in emigré Russian periodicals such as *Posev* (Frankfurt), *Novoe russkoe slovo* (New York) and in major world newspapers.

The Soviet authorities have firmly and consistently refrained from making any concessions in principle to the idea that professional and other groups of citizens should be permitted to organize open, formal interest groups or instruments of interest articulation of the type so common in the West. The official policy regarding professional and other associational groups is, as a rule, either to prohibit completely the establishment of an organization or to set up an organization of the transmission belt variety within the framework of the unified party-state bureaucracy.

For certain purposes, such as facilitation of official contacts between Soviet professionals and their "bourgeois" foreign counterparts, dummy, or paper, organizations such as the Soviet Political Science Association may be established. It is significant that Soviet political scientists — who are not, save by the existence of this shadow organization, formally recognized as a discipline — do not have their own professional journal or the other facilities and attributes of group activity possessed by their colleagues in many countries.[43] Soviet historians, in contrast, have several professional journals, but despite a number of proposals made by members of the profession, they have still not been granted the right to set up a professional association. Neither have a number of other professions, such

41. On manipulation, distortion, and suppression of information by the party, police, and censorship agencies, which many Soviet intellectuals find frustrating and demeaning, see Zhores Medvedev, *The Medvedev Papers* (London: Macmillan, 1971), and *The Soviet Censorship,* Studies on the Soviet Union (New Series), 11, no. 2 (Munich: Institute for the Study of the U.S.S.R., 1971).
42. *Register of Samizdat,* comp. Albert Boiter and Peter Dornan (New York: Research Department of Radio Liberty, February 1971).
43. David Powell and Paul Shoup, *American Political Science Review* 64 (June 1970): 572–88, contains "The Emergence of Political Science in Communist Countries," data on both the organization and the achievements of the discipline in an unfavorable environment.

as lawyers, although legal scholars dominate the Soviet Political Science Association. Of course, writers, musicians, journalists, and many other professionals do belong to organizations, but these are bureaucratic institutions over which the CPSU has usually succeeded in maintaining tight control.

It is rather frequently acknowledged in official statements, however, that informal groups which articulate independent points of view exist and indeed sometimes flourish. Since such admissions, often couched in accusatory language, have been appearing for at least ten years, it seems safe to assume that the existence of the relationships and attitudes to which they refer has become a more or less permanent and accepted feature of Soviet life. Of course, professional aspirations toward autonomy and rudimentary, fragmentary interest groups existed even during the Stalin era, as is indicated by the 1949 attack on the "antipatriotic" group of theater critics; but latent tendencies to crystallization and articulation of group attitudes were stimulated by the more favorable conditions created by Stalin's successors. In particular, Khrushchev's denunciations of Stalin at the Twentieth CPSU Congress encouraged Soviet intellectuals, especially Soviet creative writers and literary critics, to demand increased freedom of expression. Khrushchev himself admitted as much when, in 1957, he told a gathering of party leaders and intellectuals:

> When the party unleashed its criticism of the cult of personality and of Stalin's mistakes, some writers seemed to think that almost all of their past creative work was incorrect. Among some writers there developed a tendency to assume that all of their books should be rewritten. It must also be admitted that among the intelligentsia there were people, who had not taken an active part in our cause previously, who began to vilify and smear workers in literature and the arts who had glorified the successes our people achieved under the leadership of the party. They invented and launched the abusive label of "prettifier," pinning it on all who wrote the truth about our reality and about the creative labor and great victories of the Soviet people.[44]

In one of his 1957 admonitions to intellectuals Khrushchev praised N. M. Gribachev, a leading writer of the officially sponsored school of socialist realism, who asserted four years later, in a speech to the Twenty-second CPSU Congress, that some Soviet literary critics were still going about "with the stone of group prejudices in their bosom."[45] These statements convey, of course, only the harsh side of Khrushchev's attitude toward creative freedom. The moody and contradictory Khrushchev actually performed some important services to the development of freedom in

44. *Kommunist,* no. 12 (August 1957), p. 21.
45. *Pravda,* 28 October 1961.

Russia, especially in literature. Perhaps the most important was his assumption in 1962 of responsibility for authorizing the publication in the magazine *Novy mir* of Aleksandr Solzhenitsyn's short novel, *One Day in the Life of Ivan Denisovich*, which was the first account of life in Stalin's slave labor camps to be published in the USSR.[46] However, the above statements by Khrushchev and Gribachev indicate how limited and grudging has been the willingness of the party leadership and its conservative supporters, even in the Soviet intelligentsia, to grant anything approaching the right of free expression of the aspirations of even the most informal groups of creative intellectuals for intellectual autonomy. Both during and since the Khrushchev era, the Russian words equivalent to *group* and to something that might be rendered in English as *groupiness*, or *groupism*, have been used pejoratively by party leaders and by highly placed functionaries charged with administrative supervision or ideological guidance of intellectuals.

In a very important article published in 1965, A. M. Rumyantsev, then editor of *Pravda*, stated, among other things, that the party would continue to conduct an "open, principled struggle against manifestations of bourgeois ideology and also against manifestations of 'groupiness' (*gruppovshchina*), which is incompatible with the spirit of creative competition in science and art." [47] It was significant that Rumyantsev, who is characterized by an exceptionally well-informed specialist on Soviet cultural life, Timothy McClure, as a "moderate conservative," considered it necessary once again to reiterate the party's opposition to sectoral factionalism. Another among many manifestations of such concern was the criticism in a *Pravda* editorial of January 1967 of "noisy and importunate group wrangling" between the liberal magazine *Novy mir* and the conservative review *Oktyabr*.[48]

Over the years, the tone of such criticisms seems to have changed from outrage to something approaching weary resignation. While the party leadership did not become more lenient toward intellectuals whose words or actions indicated that they rejected the leadership's right to proclaim and apply the principles that should govern intellectual activity, it gradually, albeit in zigzag fashion, permitted an expansion of the spheres within which sectoral oppositions could operate. The leadership allowed and even abetted a situation which the British scholar Ronald Hingley has

---

46. On the significance of the "Solzhenitsyn affair," see Priscilla Johnson, *Khrushchev and the Arts* (Cambridge, Mass.: M.I.T. Press, 1965), pp. 4–6, 10, 70–78, 270–78. For later developments in Solzhenitsyn's career, see Leopold Labedz, ed., *Solzhenitsyn* (London: Allen Lane, 1971).

47. *Pravda*, 21 February 1965.

48. *Pravda*, 27 January 1967. In *Izvestiya*, 20 September 1968, Georgi Markov complained that there were "still" appearing in literary journals "unobjective" articles that were, in fact, "repercussions of group passions."

characterized as an "officially tolerated feud." By June 1967, Victor Zorza could observe, with only slight exaggeration, that the Union of Soviet Writers, the official organization set up by the party in 1932 to politically supervise writers, actually contained within its membership an "unofficial opposition." Zorza added that Soviet writers were "divided into a Right and a Left Wing, each with its own press organs, its own ideology, and its own supporters at the centre of political power and throughout the country." [49]

Some of the best and most courageous Soviet writers, such as Solzhenitsyn and the poet Andrei Voznesenski, have not been satisfied with the limited degree of intellectual freedom and professional autonomy that the Kremlin was willing to grant. Such men have kept pressing for more and more freedom, utilizing every legitimate avenue of access to the authorities and the interested public in their stubborn and ingenious struggle. For some time after Khrushchev's fall Moscow continued the former's policy of permitting such spokesmen of limited dissent as Voznesenski and Evtushenko to travel abroad. Since 1967, however, this and other channels of access to foreign colleagues and foreign support have been progressively restricted, and measures of heavy, persistent, and sometimes threatening social and psychological pressure, or worse, against, for example, Solzhenitsyn and scientists such as Zhores Medvedev, who in 1970 was placed in a mental institution but released after some of his colleagues brought his plight to the attention of the Western press, have been resorted to with increasing frequency. It seems that in recent years a tacit bargaining situation has developed between the regime and the writers, but the rules of the game are not clearly defined and are violated from time to time by both sides. Of course, most of the advantages in this relationship are on the side of the regime, which, after all, controls access to the market for the output of writers and artists and which numbers among its many other powers the ultimate weapon of violence.

Immediately after the May 1967 congress of the Union of Soviet Writers, which was so unexciting and uneventful that it seemed to some outside observers as though all parties concerned had agreed upon an ideological truce, the world learned that Solzhenitsyn had demanded — in a letter addressed to the presidium and delegates of the congress, as well as to the membership of the union and to the editorial boards of Soviet literary magazines and newspapers — that censorship over literature and the arts be abolished in the USSR.[50] He had originally sought to present his views on censorship from the floor, but as he presumably expected permission was not granted. Like several other leading writers, in-

49. Victor Zorza, "The Unofficial Opposition," *Manchester Guardian Weekly*, 1 June 1967.
50. For the text of Solzhenitsyn's letter, see Labedz, *Solzhenitsyn*, pp. 64–69.

cluding Voznesenski and the late Ilya Ehrenburg, he did not attend the congress. His letter, about four thousand words in length, is a moving, emotionally charged criticism of censorship, repression, persecution, arrest, interrogation, imprisonment, exile, and the moral and physical destruction of Soviet writers at the hands of the Soviet authorities. To it he appended an account of his own persecution by the KGB, which had seized and held for two years the manuscript of his novel *The First Circle*. He also pointed out that in spite of his military service at the front throughout World War II and his eleven years of imprisonment and exile for criticism of Stalin, he had been subjected to slander, which had been organized in pursuit of secret instructions and supervised by officials. All of his efforts to reply to the accusations against him — these even included statements to the effect that he had betrayed his country and had served the Germans — had been ignored and frustrated.

Solzhenitsyn thus lent the prestige of his name to the case for the constitutionality of nonsubversive dissent. He argued that the practices exerted against him and, in a far more aggravated form, against many other writers were completely incompatible with the Constitution of the USSR and with other Soviet legal instruments and principles. Justification of freedom of expression by reference to constitutional rights has been resorted to in recent years not only by writers recognized by the Soviet establishment but also by persecuted writers, teachers, scientists, and other unorthodox intellectuals — among them the Ukrainian group whose plight was disclosed, without authorization, by the radio journalist Vyacheslav Chornovil, (who suffered imprisonment, now reportedly terminated, for his pains). There is much evidence that Solzhenitsyn's stand on censorship as well as his unsuccessful efforts to publish his novels *The First Circle* and *Cancer Ward* was supported by the "majority of the most talented Soviet writers," [51] but it was bitterly opposed by such orthodox writers as Gribachev and Kochetov and by a powerful faction in the Politburo and the highest echelons of the party. Although Solzhenitsyn's letter was not published or even mentioned in the official Soviet communications media, some of his papers, which had been seized by the police, were reportedly returned to him. His protest thus apparently produced some effect, perhaps because the Soviet authorities were alarmed by its impact in the West, especially among some prominent Western Communist intellectuals, particularly in Italy, who have often been sharply critical of Soviet treatment of writers and artists.

In their struggle for freedom of expression, dissenting Soviet writers and other intellectuals have resorted in recent years to a strategy of seeking support for their views and aspirations and exerting pressure on the authorities by unauthorized disclosure of their dissenting opinions. Be-

51. See Labedz, *Solzhenitsyn*, pp. 43, 69-70.

yond an uncertain, shifting line, disclosure or dissemination of dissenting opinions or even of unorthodox works of art is likely to be regarded by the authorities as subversive behavior. This is especially true when, as in the case of various works by Sinyavski and Daniel, the impact on Soviet or foreign public opinion of such disclosure is, in the opinion of the incumbent leaders, harmful. It is not surprising that in a state in which articles of the criminal code have been interpreted so as to make it a crime to publish works of fiction which "slander" the authorities or the official ideology — a state in which control over access to typewriters, mimeograph machines, and other document reproduction devices is exercised by the secret police — the government has sometimes severely punished those who have deliberately infringed upon what it regards as its rightful monopoly of opinion formation. What is surprising is that in spite of these controls and penalties, there has been in the post-Stalin era a great deal of unauthorized expression and dissemination of critical opinion.

This struggle of "liberal" Soviet writers for freedom of expression, like that of Soviet artists, is potentially of exceptional import. Not only is there a tradition in Russia, as in many other countries which until recently were economically underdeveloped, of looking to writers and artists as custodians of the community conscience; but literary and artistic professionals, far more than other intellectuals, possess the capability of projecting their influence to relatively wide circles of public opinion. Moreover, the weapon of creative imagination that they wield has a singularly powerful impact on the shaping and inculcation of social values.

Particularly interesting and perhaps potentially very significant has been the tendency toward the formation in the post-Stalin era of a kind of partnership or alliance between some experimental and innovative writers and artists, on the one hand, and some leading natural scientists and mathematicians, on the other. On a number of occasions, leading scientists such as Petr Kapitsa, as well as lesser members of the natural science community, have rendered moral and even limited organizational support to artists and writers when the latter were under severe political pressure.[52] In this connection, the fact that Pavel Litvinov is a natural scientist by profession is most interesting.

Despite the special situation of writers and artists, one can discern among other segments of the Soviet intelligentsia a similar pattern of relationships between them and the authorities — a pattern which might be described as one of contained diversity. As has already been indicated, this pattern is the product, not only of insistent demands made by crea-

52. For some interesting data on links among abstract artists, innovative writers, and natural scientists, see, for example, Albert Parry, *The New Class Divided* (New York: Macmillan 1966), chap. 19.

tive, ingenious, energetic, and courageous intellectuals and professionals, but also of the need of the Soviet leadership to stimulate productivity and achievement in all fields of endeavor. As part of their effort to find incentives more positive than the Stalinist police methods, his successors have permitted, encouraged, and even organized public discussions of a wide range of issues. Indeed, there are very few fields of public policy in which such semifree discussions have not taken place.

Some of these discussions have been quite sharp in tone and have involved the expression of ideologically unorthodox views. For example, the factory economist O. Volkov, in an article published in 1964, in effect advocated bargaining by Soviet manufacturing and trade organizations in the sale of their products and in the determination of prices.[53] Like many other Soviet specialists who advocate bold measures, Volkov sought to legitimate his proposal by couching it in respectable ideological terms. He asserted that in the socialist economy there existed a market — cleansed, to be sure, of the imperfections of the capitalist market — which could perform, much better than the capitalist market, the functions of controlling the quantity, quality, and variety of goods. The economic reform of September 1965 did not, of course, go nearly as far toward the adoption of decentralization, profit and market principles, and other fundamental economic reforms as the Volkovs, the Libermans, the Aganbegians, the Birmans, and other advocates of the predominance of "economic" over "administrative" factors desired.[54]

An extremely significant focus of struggle between liberalizing innovators, on the one hand, and both the regime and the neo-Stalinist conservatives, on the other, is the area of reform of the principles of jurisprudence and legal procedure. Symbolic of and central in this conflict of ideas and policy was M. S. Strogovich, a dedicated Communist and the most influential critic of the abuses of justice perpetrated by Stalin and his major collaborator in their effort to cloak the "show trials" of 1936–38 in legal forms and rituals. The complex and contradictory nature of this aspect of sectoral opposition — waged not only by Strogovich and other liberal legal scholars but also by some highly placed legal officials — is suggested by the fact that A. N. Shelepin, while he was the top party leader charged with overall supervision of legal and police administration, apparently supported Strogovich, at least up to a point short of the latter's full program but beyond that palatable to the standpat conservatives in

53. *Pravda*, 23 August 1964.
54. A. Birman's article in *Novy mir*, no. 12 (December 1965), presents an illuminating analysis of the groups and issues involved in the discussions prior to the 1965 economic reform. Among other things, Birman strongly indicates that the partial victory achieved by the opponents of extremely centralized administrative controls over economic policy and administration can be credited largely to the support or at least the approval of Kosygin.

the legal profession, in the party, and, presumably, in particular in the secret police.

Even during the Stalin era Strogovich courageously opposed the Vyshinski view that in Soviet court trials the proper role of counsel for the defense is as an aide to the court, rather than as advocate of the defendant's interests. After Stalin's death the Strogoviches, Rakhunovs, and other legal liberals sought, although with only partial success, to persuade the party to come out in support of such principles as presumption of innocence in criminal trials, the thesis that the only criterion of truth in judicial proceedings is the inner conviction of the judge, and other foundations of the rule of law. [55] As Harold J. Berman has pointed out, the interest of Soviet lawyers in consistency and stability of expectations in law has significance beyond their narrowly professional concerns. "It is the lawyers who understand best of all, perhaps, the integrity of law, the universality of legal standards — in other words the threat to legality *in general* which is posed by any *particular* infringement of legality." [56]

The struggle between relatively liberal jurists and a party leadership unwilling or unable to go beyond partial satisfaction of their demands reached a standoff in the late 1950s and early 1960s. Since then the liberals have continued their fight for further reform, but they seem constrained to wage it largely by esoteric, Aesopian discussions of ostensibly theoretical — but, in their implications, highly practical — policy-oriented issues. For its part, the national political leadership has adopted a non-committal, equivocal attitude toward the reformist aspirations of liberal lawyers, law enforcement officers, and legal scholars. The party leaders as a general rule refuse to commit themselves to positions which would restrict their future freedom of political action. Presumably they are also influenced by concern that an unequivocal commitment to legal reform might cost them a loss of support from conservative elements in the bureaucracy, the professions, and Soviet society generally. More fundamental, perhaps, is the bedrock ideological conflict between the rationality of a rule-of-law position and Leninist ideological principles.

Above all, the party leaders must be concerned about the potential difficulties inherent in any foreclosure of their recourse to increased coercion if future circumstances should, in the interests of the regime, require its

55. The reference to the judge's "inner conviction" is on p. 72 of George Ginsburg, "Objective Truth and the Judicial Process in Post-Stalinist Soviet Jurisprudence," *American Journal of Comparative Law* 10 (1961): 53–75, cited in an unpublished study by Eugene Leff, "Soviet Lawyers as an Interest Group." This writer's discussion of sectoral opposition by and among Soviet lawyers is based in part on Mr. Leff's study.

56. Harold J. Berman, "The Role of Soviet Jurists in the Struggle to Prevent a Return to Stalinist Terror," *Harvard Law School Bulletin* 14, no. 3 (December 1962): 4.

exercise. It is likely that any future Soviet leadership (barring a radical transformation of the political system to a democratic, constitutional order) will be similarly compelled, to heed the desires of powerful forces, especially those manning the control posts of police and army, for the maintenance of a level and machinery of coercion adequate to safeguard the status, morale, and privileges of the watchdog agencies and to prevent disintegration of social and political discipline.

Certainly the party leadership, both of Khrushchev and of his successors, has acted as if it believed that the USSR needs very powerful "punitive organs," as the police and security agencies are often called. Indeed, despite the subordination of these agencies to party control, their political, propaganda, intelligence and counterintelligence, and judicial-investigatory functions remain formidable. In matters involving state security and the prevention, investigation, and punishment of "crimes against the state" — a category that includes not only such acts as treason and espionage but also "anti-Soviet agitation and propaganda," "slander" of the party and state, "ideological espionage," and other broad, vaguely defined offenses — the KGB remains above and outside the regular system of law enforcement. It has actually increased its ideological and "thought police" functions in recent years,[57] and since 1958 its merits and services to Soviet society have been extolled in a vast and growing body of journalistic and fictional output. It seems clear that as long as the KGB, which serves as the Kremlin's anti-interest-group interest group and as the extremely formidable last line of defense of party apparatus interests, continues to exercise so pervasive an influence and wield as much power as it still does, neither legal reform nor the rule of law nor the full unshackling of interest groups can occur.[58]

Of course, the existence of a huge police establishment is not the only aspect of the Soviet system inimical to realization of the legal liberals' aspirations. Another serious obstacle is the regime's attempts to "popularize" justice by such devices as the "comradely courts," the "antiparasite assemblies," and the "people's guards." The liberal lawyers have unsuccessfully opposed — and the party has supported — these experiments, which impeded progress toward the rule of law and partly undercut the gains scored by the reform-minded jurists in the post-Stalin years.

57. Evidence of this increase may be found in the speech by KGB chief Yuri Andropov on the fiftieth anniversary of the founding of the Cheka, the original Soviet secret police and state security agency, published in *Izvestiya,* 21 December 1967.

58. Considerable material on the functions of the security agencies is contained in Frederick C. Barghoorn, *Politics in the USSR* (Boston: Little, Brown, 1966), chap. 9. A much fuller treatment of the interest-group aspects of the Soviet security agencies is in this writer's contribution to H. Gordon Skilling and Franklyn Griffiths, eds., *Interest Groups in Soviet Politics* (Princeton: Princeton University Press, 1971), pp. 93–130.

Khrushchev's successors, while they strengthened the legal and police defenses against "political" crimes, played down these quasi-legal institutions, especially the antiparasite assemblies.

Partly because Western scholars have only recently begun to analyze patterns of interest articulation in Soviet politics and partly because they must work with heavily censored Soviet sources, very little information is available on linkages between factional and sectoral oppositions. However, some faint light was shed on such linkages by accusations in 1957 against Dimitri Shepilov, former foreign minister and member of the CPSU Secretariat who, in Khrushchev's criticisms of the defeated antiparty group, was charged with having made inappropriate statements at meetings of the Union of Soviet Writers and the Union of Soviet Artists. He was accused of "flirting with demagogues" and offering an ideological platform "broader" than that authorized by the party. Shepilov was reportedly popular in Moscow intellectual circles. Khrushchev or influential elements in his entourage seem to have felt that Shepilov had come under the influence of "revisionist" intellectuals, and perhaps it was thought that he sought to use their support to promote personal interests inimical to those of the party.[59] For a while, in the early post-Khrushchev days, there were indications that A. M. Rumyantsev, while editor of *Pravda*, was seeking, though with only limited and transient success, to persuade the dominant faction of the party leadership to display a measure of sophistication and consideration for individual and professional values in its relations with the Soviet intelligentsia.[60]

While we cannot here examine the sectoral opposition in each of the many professions, it is important to take note of the dissenting attitudes among historians and within the highly privileged stratum of the natural scientists. Historians have traditionally been among the most strictly controlled of Soviet scholars. Their craft is politically significant to an exceptional degree — and they are, in consequence, extremely vulnerable to political reprisal — in a state ruled by politicians whose legitimacy is at least partially based upon the "inevitable" unfolding of a prophecy that the CPSU asserts is grounded in the "laws of social development." Political leaders in such a tradition dare not make mistakes, still less admit them, lest the faith of followers wane while the confidence of enemies waxes.

It is easy to understand, in this context, why de-Stalinization and even de-Khrushchevization are such ticklish issues. Mistakes can either be admitted or suppressed; but if admitted, they must be explained, and any effort at explanation invites the growth of a pattern that at least implicitly tolerates alternative opinions. This in turn admits prospects of

59. See the speech by Shvernik printed in *Pravda*, 7 July 1957, and some details in Barghoorn, "Soviet Political Doctrine" (note 16), pp. 6–8.
60. McClure, "Politics of Soviet Culture," pp. 30–34.

open discussion and debate that could shake faith in the basic legitimizing creed itself.

Criticism of Stalin therefore, even under Khrushchev, had to be circumspect, and under his successors it was attenuated. However, many Soviet intellectuals, including some professional historians, and perhaps also many ordinary citizens felt that the interests of truth and justice — and the prevention of the rise of a new Stalin — required not the end of de-Stalinization but its resolute continuation and completion. Among the historians who courageously championed this cause, perhaps the most notable are Yakir, Nekrich, and the more cautious E. M. Burdzhalov. Particularly important is Nekrich's book, *22 June 1941*, published in 1966 — the first Soviet work of historical scholarship systematically to describe the ineptitude and blindness of Stalin's diplomacy during the fateful period of the Nazi-Soviet pact. But Nekrich went too far in his critique of the quality of Stalin's leadership for the cautiously conservative post-Khrushchev team. He was subjected to scathing public attack and given no opportunity to defend himself.[61]

Natural scientists are the most privileged of Soviet professionals. They enjoy enormous prestige among their fellow intellectuals, even in the CPSU cadres, and probably among ordinary people, as well as a high standard of living and considerable access to the policy-making process. They are permitted to influence the decisions regarding the organization and conduct of their own professional activity, and some politically trusted scientists are consulted in the making of decisions of national and international import.[62] However, as the Sakharov memorandum and other evidence has reminded us in recent years, there are conflicts of values and interest between some natural scientists and the party officials who supervise them. One major source of tensions is the clash of values between the pseudoscientists, such as Sergei Trapeznikov, who assist the CPSU in exercising political control over the scientific community, and professional scientists, who share with their colleagues throughout the world a commitment to internationally accepted criteria of research and verification. It seems increasingly clear that many scientists regard party control of science as detrimental and that they despise, or look with condescension upon, overseers whom they regard as their intellectual inferiors.

61. Vilification of Nekrich appeared, for example, in *Voprosy istorii KPSS*, no. 9 (September 1967). One of the best discussions of the attack on Nekrich is Christian Duevel's study, "Stalinist Blow to Soviet Historiography," Radio Liberty Dispatch (New York, 1967).
62. A good description of the situation of natural scientists in Stalinist Russia and the official doctrine on their functions and role is contained in Barrington Moore, Jr., *Terror and Progress*, chaps. 4 and 5. A valuable recent analysis is Loren R. Graham, "Reorganization of the U.S.S.R. Academy of Sciences."

While Soviet scientists have gained a reasonably satisfactory degree of professional autonomy, they have by no means completely thrown off the fetters of party tutelage, surveillance, and influence over the recruitment and career opportunities of members of their profession.[63] In the post-Stalin era they have not been content with the relatively high degree of professional autonomy they have achieved, since it is certainly inferior to that of their colleagues in the United States, with whom they naturally compare themselves. Some of the most outstanding among them, at least, have with increasing frequency and urgency thrown their influence into the struggle of other elements of the Soviet intelligentsia for freedom of inquiry and expression. Following publication in the West of Sakharov's plea for abolition of crude political controls over scientific research and for intellectual freedom generally at home and Soviet-American cooperation abroad, for example, a group of Soviet scientists in the Estonian Republic reportedly drew up demands for scientific and also political reforms which went considerably beyond those posed by Sakharov.[64] Later, in 1970, Sakharov and his fellow physicist Turchin, together with the historian Roy Medvedev, addressed a reform program to the political authorities (which we discuss subsequently) that also went far beyond the political objectives contained in the 1968 Sakharov memorandum.

Cautiously and gingerly, the authorities began in 1968 to strike back against natural scientists who made political demands.[65] Reports reaching this country through the international scientific grapevine indicate that Sakharov was denied access to a number of laboratories, was called in for admonition by officials, and may have been assigned — in a sense, exiled — to a scientific installation in a remote part of the USSR. Some Western colleagues saw and communicated with him in Tbilisi in September 1968. Yet Soviet delegates to the fall 1968 Pugwash Conference reportedly referred to his views in a manner indicating that they were widely known and approved in the higher levels of the Soviet scientific community.[66]

63. On this point see, for example, Sakharov, *Progress, Coexistence and Intellectual Freedom*, pp. 57, 88, 125. See also the study by Peter Dornan, " 'Three Protestors' Nominated to Membership in Academy of Sciences," Radio Liberty Research no. 83/69 (Munich, 5 March 1969).

64. See article entitled "Sowjetische Wissenschaftler fordern Democratisierung," *Frankfurter Allgemeine Zeitung*, 18 December 1968. Some experts are dubious about the authenticity of the Estonian manifesto, but it has been accepted by some of the most reliable West German newspapers.

65. See, for example, Victor Zorza, "Rebel Scientists Shake the Kremlin," *Manchester Guardian Weekly*, 6 February 1969, and Paul Smith, "Protest in Moscow."

66. On the early consequences to Sakharov of the distribution of his memorandum, see Bryce Nelson, "A. D. Sakharov: Soviet Physicist Believed to Have Been Punished," *Science*, 30 May 1969, pp. 1043-44. On his role in the Human Rights Committee, see Harrington's article cited in footnote 18 above. For Sakharov's active role in the campaign to free Zhores Medvedev from "psychiatric blackmail" in 1970, see Zhores and Roy Medvedev, *A Question of Madness*, pp. 69-71, 115-17.

Important recent overt evidences of regime concern and irritation specifically directed at Soviet scientists include an article in *Partiinaya zhizn* by Obninsk City Committee Party Secretary V. Lesnichy and a more authoritative article in *Kommunist* by N. Sviridov, a top-level propaganda official, both criticizing political apathy and "naïveté" among scientists at the atomic research center of Obninsk, near Moscow. Dismissals of a number of scientists either from their jobs or from party membership because of political attitudes or activities have been reported; in October 1970 the *New York Times* carried an article which mirrored vividly the clash between the values of libertarian scientists and the Brezhnev-led party apparatus. It reported a conversation between Revolt I. Pimenov, a mathematician, and a secretary of the Leningrad party organization, in which the former defended freedom of information and of political expression and vigorously denied any subversive intent, while the latter asserted that there could "never be any compromise on the ideological question," and no one could publish "whatever comes into his head" — since that would do harm to the state. Pimenov was subsequently arrested and charged with slandering the Soviet state. Academician Sakharov took it upon himself to mobilize opinion on behalf of Pimenov, as he had on behalf of other scientists harassed by the authorities. His protest petition, signed by himself and four other scientists, defended Pimenov's innocence, expressed concern over the likelihood of violation of his legal rights, and proclaimed the determination of its signers to be present in the courtroom in Kaluga, where the trial was to be held, to determine whether or not legality was observed.[67]

This episode in the now chronic confrontation between the regime and the scientific sector — or a subsector — of the still nominally loyal oppositional intelligentsia raises questions ominous for both sides. If there is to be no compromise regarding "ideology" — which, realistically defined, means the party leadership's pretensions to infallibility — can there be cooperation between the party and a large enough proportion of the scientific community to maintain scientific performance at a level adequate for the regime's political and economic needs? How much coercion may

---

67. *Partiinaya zhizn*, no. 19 (October 1968); *Kommunist*, no. 24 (December 1968), pp. 55–60. On the Obninsk situation, see also the illuminating study by Peter Dornan, "Who Are the Passive Scientists of Obninsk?" Radio Liberty Research Paper (New York: n.d., probably 1968). The above-cited Zorza article (note 65), as well as an unsigned *New York Times* dispatch dated 24 April 1968 reported the dismissals. For reports on the Pimenov case, see the *New York Times*, 8 and 12 October 1970. It should be noted that, in addition to the above items, several other indications of official concern over the ideological-political posture of scientists — including those at Akademgorodok in Siberia and at the Lebedev Physics Institute in Moscow — appeared in 1969 and 1970. It is also significant that the Twenty-fourth CPSU Congress in 1971 restored the "right of control" over scientific and educational institutions to the primary party organizations within the institutions. On the latter point, see A. Boitsov, "Dolg politicheskogo boitsa," *Pravda*, 22 July 1971.

be required to contain or deter the impulses and actions of men like Pimenov? How far into the future will it be possible to differentiate, as we have tried to do in this essay, between within-system sectoral dissent and antisystem subversive dissent?

Subversive Opposition

By *subversive opposition,* some aspects of which might also be denoted by Robert Dahl's term *structural opposition,* we mean both (a) acts and patterns of behavior which would be regarded as treasonable or criminal by most if not all governments and (b) actions and the expression of attitudes which are regarded as subversive and criminal only in dictatorships, particularly Communist dictatorships, and perhaps especially that of the USSR with its despotic, centralistic Russian heritage. A loose application of, for example, article 70 of the criminal code of the RSFSR adopted in 1960, which deals with anti-Soviet agitation — or the more recent and even vaguer 1966 statute, article 190–1, which provides severe penalties for offenses similar to those covered by article 70 but does not require proof of malicious intent — can lead to criminal punishment for the mere expression of opinions currently disapproved of by the authorities.[68] (Incidentally, one might be able to classify political leaderships or "administrations" in the USSR, or stages in the development of leaderships, in terms of the severity with which they apply laws, administrative rules, and ideological canons to dissent and opposition. This suggestion is prompted by the increase in severity and suppression under the post-Khrushchev, as compared with the Khrushchev, administration.)

In applying the label of political crime, close attention is paid to the still frequently proclaimed danger that Soviet citizens who enter into unauthorized relationships with "bourgeois" foreigners may be tricked or tempted into committing offenses against the state. But actions devoid of such contacts may also be suspect. Thus the Soviet criminal codes contain provisions regarding crimes against social and state property, and

68. Article 70 deals with agitation or propaganda "carried on for the purpose of subverting or weakening Soviet authority," "defaming the Soviet state and social system," and "circulating . . . slanderous fabrications," or keeping literature with such content. An English translation of the full text is available on p. 180 of Harold J. Berman and James W. Spindler, eds., *Soviet Criminal Law and Procedure* (Cambridge, Mass.: Harvard University Press, 1966).

An addition (article 190–1) to article 190 of the RSFSR criminal code, enacted in September 1966, provides penalties up to three years' deprivation of liberty for "organizing or participating in group actions which grossly violate public order, involve clear disobedience to the lawful demands of representatives of authority," etc. Reports of arrests of Soviet dissenters in 1969 and 1970 seem to indicate that article 190–1 is applied somewhat more frequently than article 70. They may be found in *Ugolovny kodeks, RSFSR,* 1957, p. 65, and in *Vedomosti verkhovnogo soveta RSFSR,* 1966, no. 12, pp. 219–20; No. 38, p. 910.

although ordinary crimes such as burglary and robbery are not classified as political, the struggle against such crimes — particularly against "hooliganism" — has political overtones. Prior to the 1958–59 and subsequent legal reforms — in the period when designedly vague legal codes, in particular the notorious article 58 of the criminal code, and unrestrained arbitrariness, reflecting both Stalin's suspicious nature and real international and internal tensions, determined the pattern of Soviet justice — it was easier, of course, for a Soviet citizen to be regarded as subversive and treated accordingly by the authorities, even though he had committed no crime by normal standards applicable in most societies.[69] Even today, and in fact increasingly since 1967, the line dividing legitimate criticism or opposition from subversion is far from clear.

Court action that is apparently ideologically or politically motivated, though not taken under expressly political provisions of the law, may also be applied against eccentric or deviant individuals. The young poet Iosif Brodski, for example, was exiled to the Far North in 1964 under a provision of the "antiparasite" law, technically because he had no regular employment, but probably in fact because he rejected the official literary theory of socialist realism. Fortunately, Brodski was released. Whether his release was motivated by the Kremlin's effort to respond to protests by Soviet intellectuals, or by concern regarding unfavorable publicity abroad (especially among European intellectuals, including some Communists), or by pragmatic calculation that Brodski was politically harmless anyway, or, least likely, by a concern for justice, it is impossible to know. A more recent illustration of this problem of classification is the case of Pimenov, referred to earlier. Generally, whether unorthodox opinions will be regarded by the authorities as subversive or not is problematical and unpredictable. However, in the post-Stalin era the authorities seem to have drawn a line between the "loyal oppositions" (represented by the Victor Nekrasovs, Evtushenkos, Voznesenskis, Kapitsas, Tamms, and Sakharovs), on the one hand, and the Brodskis, Sinyavskis, Daniels, Pavel Litvinovs, Grigorenkos, and Ukrainian and Crimean Tatar dissenters who refuse to be silenced, on the other. It should perhaps be noted that Sakharov and Solzhenitsyn are exceptionally close to the borderline dividing the two categories.

A series of events in 1967 cast doubt on the probability that the Soviet authorities, or the dominant ruling faction, would continue indefinitely

69. Broad and sharp criticism of vague, unconstitutional legal provisions and their arbitrary, brutal misapplication by Stalin and his henchmen is contained in M. S. Strogovich, *Osnovnye voprosy sovetskoi sotsialisticheskoi zakonnosti* (Moscow, 1966). On the unconstitutionality of some of Stalin's "laws," see especially pp. 22–23. Particularly deadly was article 58 of the RSFSR criminal code, which was so worded as to enable the political police and the prosecutors, who were dominated by the former, to label as political crimes anything that the authorities wanted so designated.

to differentiate clearly between "loyal" and "subversive" dissent, a doubt which seems increasingly justifiable. This doubt was perhaps raised by *Pravda* editor Zimyanin's threat to "grind to dust" the highly respected poet Andrei Voznesenski if the latter again defied the authorities, as he had by making public a letter criticizing the leadership of the Writers Union for canceling his long-planned trip to America in June 1967. It was intensified by the flimsiness of the charges and the secrecy of the trials of a number of young intellectual dissenters, as well as by KGB threats to bring others to trial if they refused to stifle their protests. As recently as June 1969 the *New York Times* reported from Moscow that "the cultural scene [continues] to be dominated by an officially sanctioned balance between conservatives, apparently favored by the communist party, and liberals, on whom the party seems unwilling to crack down." The same article noted that while most literary journals were edited by conservatives, "regular party publications often criticize both the conservative and liberal journals." [70] Here again, the forced resignation in 1970 of *Novy mir* editor Tvardovski and several of his deputies raised troubling questions.

In 1967–69 information became available about secret trials of Ukrainian writers and other intellectuals, including some natural scientists. This may have reflected regime determination to suppress the particularly dangerous type of dissent represented by an intersection of ideological dissidence with efforts to attain a level of cultural autonomy regarded as intolerable by Moscow.[71]

Another national minority, the Crimean Tatars, struggling to defend their threatened group interests and constituting perhaps the largest single group of active oppositionists, organized an at least partly successful national pressure group, which was particularly active in 1968 and 1969. Probably nothing quite like the campaign of petitions, mass street demonstrations, and other protest actions — led by members of the Tatars' intellectual upper stratum, in particular by such individuals as the nuclear physicist Kadiev, and supported, it seems, by tens of thousands of his

70. Excerpts from Zimyanin's attack on Voznesenski and other liberal intellectuals were published in the *New York Times*, 25 February 1968. The secrecy of the handling of the cases of the young dissident Vladimir Bukovski — reported, and in a very brief and misleading fashion, in only one newspaper, *Vechernyaya Moskva* — and of Aleksandr Ginzburg and their associates stirred widespread alarm and concern in the Soviet intelligentsia generally, according to Paul Wohl, *Christian Science Monitor*, 6 March 1968. For evidence that toleration of a measure of dissent and aesthetic debate, which under Soviet conditions inevitably has political implications, continued well into 1969, see Bernard Gwertzman, "Soviet Party Sanctions Balance of Views on the Cultural Scene," *New York Times*, 27 June 1969.
71. On dissent in the Ukraine and the illegal, secret trials of Ukrainian historians, writers, philologists, engineers, and others, see in particular *The Chornovil Papers*, with a foreword by Z. K. Brzezinski and introduction by Frederick C. Barghoorn (Toronto: McGraw-Hill, 1968)

countrymen — had been seen in the USSR since the 1920s. The entire Crimean Tartar nation, numbering some 250,000, had been deported at Stalin's order in 1943 to Central Asia, mainly to Uzbekistan, for allegedly giving aid and comfort to the Nazi invaders of the USSR. In 1967 an official decree, apparently published only in the Uzbek press, absolved the Crimean Tatars of the blanket charges made during the war. However, the Crimean Tatar Autonomous Republic was not reestablished, and only a handful of Crimean Tatars were permitted to return to their ancestral homes, which had, it seems, been assigned to Ukrainians and Russians living in the Crimea.

When the Crimean Tatars in 1968–69 persisted in petitioning and demonstrating dozens of times for redress of their varied grievances, which reportedly included difficulty in obtaining employment, the authorities responded with harsh and increasing severity. According to one account, more than two hundred had been sentenced to prison camps and hundreds more had received short jail terms for "hooliganism" as of the end of April 1969. In late June eleven, mainly young intellectuals, were awaiting trial in Tashkent, charged apparently with slandering the Soviet state. In 1968 some prominent Moscow dissidents — among them Pavel Litvinov, Larisa Daniel, and former Major General Petr Grigorenko — began to include among the causes they championed that of the Crimean Tatars. Although the arrests and trials of this trio were doubtless occasioned by a number of factors (Litvinov and Mrs. Daniel were sentenced to camps after they had publicly protested the Soviet invasion of Czechoslovakia), that of Grigorenko came immediately after he defied an official order not to go to Tashkent, where he continued his agitation against the Crimean Tatars' arrest. Subsequently six Crimean Tatars were manhandled and arrested in Moscow for demonstrating against Grigorenko's arrest.[72]

The Crimean Tatar question was only one of many pretexts used by the KGB during 1968–69 for harassments, searches, beatings, arrests, and trials of active oppositionists. This must be seen in the context of the mushrooming, since the February 1966 Sinyavski-Daniel trial, of what the Kremlin and the KGB obviously regarded as subversive intellectual dissent, which they appeared determined to eliminate — if need be, by jailing all Soviet dissenters who refused to be silenced. One well-informed authority refers, in fact, to "the arrests of hundreds of intellectuals, for offenses ranging from the distribution of anti-Soviet propaganda to

72. For background on the Crimean Tatars see Robert Conquest, *Soviet Nationalities Policy in Practice* (London: Praeger, 1967), especially pp. 104–07, and a number of *New York Times* dispatches, especially that by Henry Kamm on 3 May 1969 and an unsigned item dated June 6. See also the material on "ethnic resistance" in the USSR reprinted from West German and British publications in *Atlas*, June 1969, pp. 32–40.

armed conspiracy." She also perceived a tendency toward the development of what may prove to be a highly significant alliance and unity of action between hitherto "distinct and antithetical groups," namely, the "loyal opposition" and the "underground" dissidents.[73]

The foregoing, it must be admitted, is not fully consistent with the piecemeal, limited revision and mellowing of official Soviet theory regarding opposition in the post-Stalin era. The framework of the post-Stalin perspective on the nature and dangers of dissent and contestation — which, in spite of the negative trends of recent years, seems still to be formally intact — was provided by Khrushchev's repudiation in 1956 of Stalin's terrible, purge-justifying doctrine that (in Khrushchev's words) "the closer we are to socialism, the more enemies we will have." [74] The new, more sensible doctrine was reflected in the change adopted by the Twenty-second CPSU Congress in the section of the party statutes dealing with the possibility of "attempts by an insignificant minority to impose their will upon the majority of the party . . . or attempts to cause splits, which may shake the strength and stability of the socialist system." [75] Although the Twenty-second Congress's version of the statutes also contained a provision against activities which might be detrimental to party unity, it omitted the warning that factions and "splits" might "shake the . . . stability of the socialist system." [76]

A major post-Stalin tenet is that there are no social or class bases for organized "anti-Soviet activity." (The term *opposition* and its cognates are very seldom used in Soviet discussions of potential or actual "anti-Soviet" behavior, presumably to avoid even implying the legitimacy of behavior which is still branded, at worst as treasonable, at best as pathological.) However, security chief Andropov has said that "there are still cases of commission of antistate crimes and individual cases of hostile, anti-Soviet actions, which not infrequently are committed under the influence of hostile foreign influence." [77]

Especially since the efflorescence of "revisionism" in Czechoslovakia, particular concern has been expressed in major Soviet evaluations of public

73. Patricia Blake, "This Is the Winter of Moscow's Dissent," *New York Times Magazine*, 24 March 1968, p. 129. See also Paul Smith, "Protest in Moscow"; his approach to some events discussed by Blake is more cautious than hers.
74. Quoted from the text of Khrushchev's speech in *Current Soviet Policies II* (New York, 1957), p. 177. See also Strogovich, *Osnovnye voprosy*, p. 139, citing Shelepin's speech at the Twenty-second CPSU Congress.
75. *KPSS v resolyutsiyakh i resheniyakh sezdov, konferentsii i plenumov tsk*, 7th ed., part I (Moscow, 1963), pp. 527–30. The above is the language of the statutes as amended in 1952, while Stalin was alive.
76. For further detail on the situation through 1961 see Barghoorn, "Soviet Political Doctrine," especially pp. 11–18. A search of the stenographic report of the Twenty-third Congress (1966) indicated that this issue was not raised there. Hence we can assume that the doctrine adopted in 1961 was then still in force.
77. *Izvestiya*, 21 December 1967.

opinion and political attitudes in the USSR and Eastern Europe over the alleged susceptibility of some intellectuals to moods and opinions that "imperialist propaganda" can exploit. What is particularly interesting in some of these evaluations is their authors' admissions, more than fifty years after the Bolshevik seizure of power, that, not only "survivals" of the "presocialist" culture, but also the conditions of life of the "socialist" intelligentsia help to foster the survival of "individualism," a "semi-anarchistic, haughty attitude toward discipline," and other deplorable attitudes. Kh. Sabirov in 1969 explained these "survivals" by the fact that "many kinds of intellectual labor are individual and are carried on without direct contact with the group." [78]

Writing in the same year and undoubtedly in support of the same central directive, Aleksandr Chakovski, hard-line editor of *Literaturnaya gazeta,* included in a long article entitled "The Ideological Struggle and the Intelligentsia" the statement that such traits of intellectuals as "a tendency toward individualism, receptivity to illusions of classlessness, to overestimation of their social role," and the like can survive for a long time after the victory of socialism. He added that as long as a socialist intelligentsia, "or more precisely a part of it," preserves such "bourgeois traits, typical of the intelligentsia," anti-Communists would seek to exploit the situation for their own "imperialist" purposes. Interestingly enough, Chakovski, among other things, undertook to defend spiritual values against what he depicted as the anti-Communist "legend of the hegemony of physicists." Perhaps here he was striking indirectly (and unfairly) at Soviet scientists who share or sympathize with the views of men like Andrei Sakharov.[79]

In connection with Chakovski's unfavorable reference to physicists, it is worth noting that there is evidence tending to identify as perhaps the largest group of dissenting intellectuals a collection of influential members of the Soviet scientific and technical professions — although members of this group tend to be more moderate in their views than do some other groups of dissenters — as indicated by the letter reportedly addressed to Brezhnev, Kosygin, and Podgorny in March 1970 by Sakharov, his fellow physicist V. B. Turchin, and the historian Roy Medvedev advocating a fourteen-point program of democratic reforms to be carried out "under party control." They apparently still hope that the existing system can peacefully evolve in a democratic direction.[80]

78. Sabirov, *Sovetskaya Rossiya,* 29 May 1969.
79. Aleksandr Chakovski, "Ideologicheskaya borba i intelligentsiya," *Smena* (a magazine published by the Komsomol central committee), no. 6 (March 1969), pp. 11–13.
80. Albert Boiter, "A Program for Soviet Democrats," p. 5, expresses the opinion referred to above, in commenting on the Sakharov-Turchin-Medvedev letter. The earlier cited editorial in *Posev,* no. 7 (1970), expresses on p. 2 the view that the Sakharov group is spearheading a reformist movement backed not only by prominent

Sabirov's and Chakovski's articles not only reflect Kremlin concern over the state of mind of intellectuals but also provide rationalizations for the application of whatever measures may be regarded as necessary to cope with infection of Soviet intellectuals by "bourgeois" ideas. It should be noted that the emphasis in these articles is on persuasion. They do not prescribe the use of police methods in the ideological struggle, nor do they advocate the Stalin-Vyshinski formula of "coercion and persuasion." However, the Sabirov-Chakovski line presumably would not be violated by the use of such measures as the placing of dissenters like the poet-mathematician Esenin-Volpin in psychiatric hospitals; the refusal of permission to travel abroad to scientists who sign petitions protesting against the arrests of writers such as Sinyavski and Daniel; the denial of the right of peaceful demonstration to representatives of the Crimean Tatars; the refusal of the Union of Soviet Writers to consider Solzhenitsyn's request for the abolition of censorship, a request that is presumably regarded as reflecting "bourgeois" influence; and the imprisonment of scores of persons under the more and more frequently applied articles 70 and 190–1 of the RSFSR criminal code. The former article permits the authorities to prosecute persons who express objectionable opinions or even hold objectionable meetings in their homes; the latter can be used against persons who lobby or demonstrate for objectionable causes.

Given the still very great coerciveness of the Soviet political system, the cleavages of the society, and the suspiciousness and vigilance of the leaders, it would be surprising if there were not many Soviet citizens who have been suspected of inclination to act, or even merely of being capable of acting, in such fashion as to be regarded by the party leadership and its law enforcement agencies as subversive. Especially suspect have been those belonging to disadvantaged occupational, class, ethnic, religious, and cultural categories, such as peasants, children of "bourgeois" parents, and, to a considerable degree, persons of non-Russian and especially non-Slavic culture. (The dominant Great Russians, after all, constitute only about half the total Soviet population and the Slavs only about three-quarters.) Also highly suspect are churchgoers — such as the actively proselyting segment of the Russian Baptists, the members of sects such as Jehovah's Witnesses, and Jews, especially if they have relatives in Israel or the United States — with perspectives, interests, and traditions sharply at variance with the Bolshevik demand for unquestioning conformity to a materialistic ideology.

members of the scientific-technical intelligentsia but by a faction of the party apparatus; the objective of this movement is to liberalize the Soviet system by a process of peaceful change that will prevent the stagnation or disintegration which, in the opinion of the reformers, will occur if adequate reforms are not effected within the next few years.

Particularly affected by the centralist economic and cultural policies have been the peasants and intellectuals of non-Russian linguistic and cultural background. As Robert Conquest has observed, "Allegiance to one's nation requires no counter-organization, no overt propaganda of its own. It resides in the simple realities of language, culture, land and history." [81] These "simple realities," however, can interpose barriers to a centralized regime's efforts to achieve ideological homogeneity. The difficulties which industrialization, urbanization, and modernization generally involve in a multinational society are exacerbated in the Soviet case by Marxist contempt for traditional, especially peasant, religiously oriented culture and also by Great Russian ethnocentrism. [82]

During most of its fifty years of existence the Soviet Union has, moreover, existed in an atmosphere of tension and under controls similar to, or even more rigorous than, those that prevail in non-Communist societies during full-scale wars. Soviet Russia, of course, experienced the rigors of revolution and the expropriation of the "exploiting" classes, including millions of "kulaks" (many of whom were in fact quite poor peasants), as well as a bitter civil war and a bungling, half-hearted, but destructive and infuriating military intervention by Britain, France, Japan, the United States, and other "imperialist" powers in 1918–22. After the uneasy respite of NEP in the 1920s came forced-draft industrialization, collectivization and dekulakization, and the tense years of preparation for World War II. Victory, achieved at the cost of some 25 million Soviet lives, was followed, not by the era of international good feeling and friendly relations with the West which many Soviet citizens had hoped for during the war — hopes which had been subtly encouraged by the Kremlin while the outcome of the war seemed to hang in the balance — but by cold war, the nuclear arms race with the United States, and, since about 1960, increasing tension between the Soviet Union and Communist China.

The "building of socialism" under Stalin's auspices and the "full-scale construction of communism" inaugurated by Khrushchev and his successors made Russia a world power and brought industrial, technological, and scientific achievements which generated deep patriotic pride among many, perhaps most Soviet citizens. However, the methods of coercive mobilization, police surveillance and terror, and starving of the consumer sector of the economy — and sometimes of the consumer himself — generated tensions, anxieties, resentments, jealousies, and perhaps class

81. Conquest, *Soviet Nationalities Policy*, p. 7.
82. On non-Russian resistance over the years to Moscow's centralist, Russifying pressures, see Frederick C. Barghoon, *Soviet Russian Nationalism* (New York: Oxford University Press, 1956), and Conquest, *Soviet Nationalities Policy*. The best recent general treatment of the nationality problem in the USSR is Vernon V. Aspaturian, "The Non-Russian Nationalities," in Allen Kassof, ed., *Prospects for Soviet Society* (New York: Praeger, 1968), pp. 143–200.

antagonisms. In reflecting on this record, one is reminded of the expression coined by the sociologist Alex Inkeles: "Stalin's errors and others' trials."

It must be remembered that the intellectual heritage of Soviet Russia is complex and diverse. Marxism, even Leninism, and of course the Russian culture of the nineteenth century — not to mention those aspects of classical "bourgeois" culture which Lenin, like Marx and Engels before him, regarded as suitable ingredients of "socialist humanism" — contain not merely punitive and coercive, materialistic and technocratic, but also utopian-anarchistic, egalitarian, humanistic, and idealistic elements. Stalin was able to suppress but not to extirpate completely from the consciousness of at least some Soviet citizens aspects of the Russian cultural heritage which clashed with the dominant values of his coercive, despotic, and mind-benumbing system. Even without consciousness of a gulf between Soviet reality and socialist ideals, there would have been severe tensions in the Soviet Union, resulting both from the unequal distribution of scarce goods, services, and status which industrialization, particularly rapid, coercive industrialization, seems inevitably to involve and from the destruction of traditional culture patterns, especially among the non-Russian peoples of the USSR.

Inequality, deprivation, and coercion do not, of course, necessarily lead to extreme and desperate dissent, still less to rebellion, subversion, conspiracy, or revolutionary activities. The negative effects of deprivation were and are offset, in part, by tremendous achievements in economic and social development, education, public health, and social security; by a sense of onward and upward progress, especially in the natural sciences; by pride in belonging to the "vanguard of world revolution"; and, perhaps most of all, by a dynamic upward social mobility which has given millions of citizens, Russians and non-Russians alike, a deeply satisfying sense of individual and group self-enhancement. Moreover, skillful socialization and propaganda techniques — backed, when necessary, by coercion — have, together with these achievements, generated the impressive degree of solidarity, patriotism, and willingness to sacrifice which were demonstrated by the Soviet Union during World War II.

Yet during that same war millions of Soviet soldiers, both Russians and non-Russians, surrendered to the German armies, and many served in the military forces organized by the Germans and headed by their appointee, the captured General Vlasov. George Fischer, who made a thorough study of the "Vlasov movement," came to the conclusion that the behavior of the vast majority of its leaders and followers can be attributed not so much to ideological conviction as to a massive passivity, or "inertness." [83] Many Soviet citizens in the territory occupied by the

83. George Fischer, *Soviet Opposition to Stalin* (Cambridge, Mass.: Harvard University Press, 1952).

German or Axis forces collaborated in various ways with the enemy. Six entire small nations, including the Chechens and Kalmyks, were uprooted from their native lands and exiled for alleged collaboration with the German invaders.[84] As the Soviet armies reconquered lost territory, many collaborators were tried, and some of them were publicly executed, as at Kharkov in 1943. The Soviet authorities found it necessary during the war to establish a special counterintelligence service, known as SMERSH ("Death to Spies"), to combat such actions as circulation of harmful rumors. SMERSH was headed by Victor Abakumov, later head of the state security forces, who was executed after the death of Stalin for alleged complicity in crimes committed by Beria. Even in recent years there have been occasional executions of Soviet citizens who had succeeded in concealing from the authorities their wartime collaboration with the enemy. When the German armies retreated from Soviet territory, millions of Soviet citizens retreated with them, and hundreds of thousands never returned to the USSR. There is no doubt that many others would have behaved as did the nonreturners had the Allied armies not turned them back to the Soviet authorities.

The massive defections and related activities made possible by the military situation during World War II may have constituted one of the most significant episodes in the history of subversive opposition to the Soviet authorities. Defection can be regarded as subversive, not only because it is illegal to emigrate from the USSR without permission, which until 1971 was seldom granted, but because it strikes a blow at the official myth of the monolithic solidarity of Soviet society. There had been earlier — and there were to be later — significant episodes of this kind. The mutiny of Soviet sailors and other members of the armed forces at Kronstadt in 1921 shocked Lenin and his colleagues. Consternation and anger resulting from Kronstadt helped to inspire the official legend, which was to be greatly elaborated by Stalin, that any resistance to Soviet power was by its very nature the result of foreign instigation. In 1953, shortly after Stalin's death, there were mutinies of forced laborers at Vorkuta and other labor camps.[85] During the East German and Hungarian uprisings of 1953 and 1956, respectively, the Soviet troops sent to suppress the uprisings sympathized in some cases with the rebels, and apparently a number of them defected.

Throughout the history of the USSR some discontented citizens who, by virtue of service abroad in the merchant marine or on diplomatic, intelligence, or military assignments, had the opportunity to defect did

84. On the background and overall treatment of the "deported peoples" see Robert Conquest, *The Soviet Deportation of Nations* (New York: St. Martin's Press, 1960). It is worth noting that Khrushchev in his secret speech asserted that Stalin would have deported the Ukrainians also, if there had not been too many of them.
85. On the Vorkuta uprising see, for example, Joseph Scholmer, *Vorkuta* (London: Weiderfeld and Nicolson, 1954).

so. In the period since World War II the principal source of defections has been Soviet military and civilian personnel assigned to service in East Germany. However, there were many defections before World War II, and many postwar defectors have escaped by other routes. Probably most defectors fade inconspicuously into some facet of life in the country in which they defect; some are brought by American authorities to the United States, there to live in quiet but anxious obscurity. However, many Soviet defectors have become well known throughout the world — but not, as a rule, in the USSR itself, where, although defection is widely regarded as a loathsome, indecent act, information regarding individual defections is usually kept from the public, presumably because the authorities regard it as unsettling. One thinks, for example, of the Soviet intelligence officer General Walter Krivitski, or the high-ranking secret police officer Aleksandr Ouralov, or Victor Kravchenko, or Igor Gouzenko. By far the most famous of all living refugees from Soviet authority, of course, is Stalin's daughter, Svetlana. In her case, the Soviet authorities displayed more sophistication than they have traditionally mustered in dealing with the unfavorable publicity attendant upon flights of important Soviet citizens.

A special, perhaps unclassifiable, violent act — apparently, but not certainly, one of purely individual rebellion — was the firing of shots on 23 January 1969 at an auto caravan carrying Soviet cosmonauts on Red Square in Moscow, possibly with the intention of assassinating top leaders of the CPSU. No details of the official investigation of this "provocative" act, as it was characterized in the briefest of newspaper items, have been divulged; but a report in the French Communist newspaper *L'Humanité*, apparently leaked by Soviet authorities, claimed that its perpetrator was a "demented" military officer.

Subversive behavior need not involve either armed resistance or the supplying of highly significant military, economic, and political information to foreign intelligence services, as seems to have happened in the case of Colonel Oleg Penkovski, convicted of treason in May 1963. Work stoppages and strikes, for example, are among the types of behavior that have traditionally been regarded as subversive in the Soviet Union and have been very severely punished.[86] There is no doubt that defiance of management and the state-controlled trade unions by workers,

---

86. The best discussion of strikes and work stoppages is Boiter, "When the Kettle Boils Over," pp. 33-43. Additional information and analysis is available in Emily Clark Brown, *Soviet Trade Unions and Labor Relations* (Cambridge, Mass.: Harvard University Press, 1966), especially pp. 234-37, 370; and some relevant background is contained in Robert Conquest, ed., *Industrial Workers in the USSR* (London: Praeger, 1967). Maurice Hindus, in *The Kremlin's Human Dilemma* (New York: Doubleday, 1967), provides vivid reportage — based on travel in Russia and partly on personal experience — on labor attitudes and on some illegal strikes.

especially in the form of riots or work stoppages, alarms and angers the Soviet authorities. This writer caught a sense of the wrath that the mere mention of labor strikes can kindle in the Soviet official mind when, in the course of a discussion in Moscow, a *Pravda* editor asked with asperity, "Are you advocating that workers strike against the state?"

There is general agreement among scholars that the most disadvantaged — and potentially, if not actually, discontented — social stratum, except for prisoners and forced laborers, is the collective farm peasantry. Indeed, Bauer, Inkeles, and Kluckhohn — in their important, although now perhaps somewhat outdated, study based on interviews with Soviet refugees — referred to the peasant as the "angry man" of Soviet society.[87] However, because of restrictions imposed upon foreign observers in the Soviet Union, nothing very specific or detailed is available in Western publications on the degree to which the subversive potential of peasant attitudes is actually manifested in behavior.

The goals of subversive opposition can range from relatively petty individual objectives, through constructive or drastic reforms, all the way to the overthrow of the Soviet state. On the basis of the defective information available, it would appear that most of the hostility toward authorities, regime, or ideology which could lead to subversive behavior probably remains in the realm of unarticulated predispositions, although, as has already been pointed out, there is reason to believe that some Soviet citizens have conscious leanings toward political pluralism and electoral competition. Certainly there are some who favor the rule of law and an independent judiciary, and there are probably many more who would like to see the socialist economy modified in the direction either of a socialist market economy or of a mixed socialist-capitalist system. While it seems clear that such aspirations are regarded as subversive by at least the majority of the present Soviet leadership, this may not be the position of more liberal and flexible future leaders. However, especially since recent events in Czechoslovakia, we should be under no illusions regarding the difficulties of moving from a command to a market-oriented economy, which in this writer's opinion is a prerequisite for a significant growth of freedom in Russia.

The sites and strategies of subversive opposition are extraordinarily varied. Sites range from farm fields through factory workbenches on up to the most sensitive nerve centers of the political, administrative, and military structures. Strategies include almost any that human ingenuity — restrained, however, by fear of reprisal and by the effects of the official

87. Raymond A. Bauer, Alex Inkeles, and Clyde Kluckhohn, *How the Soviet System Works* (Cambridge, Mass.: Harvard University Press, 1957), p. 188. See also some pertinent remarks in Arvid Brodersen, *The Soviet Worker* (New York: Random House, 1966).

system of surveillance — can devise. There can be no doubt that in terms of the number of individuals involved at one time or another, subversive resistance, mutiny, and rebellion bulk larger than factional or sectoral activity. However, given the vigilance and striking power of the Soviet political command — and the amorphous, often anomic properties of subversive opposition, which render it vulnerable to effective counter-measures — such opposition, except when it represents the extremist aspect of what is essentially sectoral within-system dissent, is probably self-defeating. It presumably tends to unite thte privileged strata of Soviet society in defense of what are likely to be perceived as common elite interests against a threat to public order and national security.

Prospects for the Future

It is this writer's tentative hypothesis that during the next few years at least — provided, as seems almost certain, that the Soviet armed forces remain loyal and the KGB vigilant, united, and efficient — there will be no successful, organized subversive opposition to the policies and structures of the Soviet regime. However, factional opposition will probably continue to be an important feature of political life, although less likely than in the past to be accompanied by violence. Finally, it seems highly probable that increasingly sophisticated sectoral oppositions will flourish. Whether or not they will assume a revolutionary character probably depends on the willingness and ability of the political leadership to institute well-timed and thoroughgoing reforms which could generate support among the increasingly alienated intellectuals and specialists upon whose loyalty and effective performance the future of the system so largely depends.

Perhaps some indication of future events is furnished by the fact that as a result of the leadership's callous treatment, first of Sinyavski and Daniel and then of hundreds of other intellectuals — most of whom were probably, subjectively, completely loyal to the Soviet political community — the Kremlin found itself as early as 1968 confronted by what has been called "an alliance between the 'loyal opposition' and the 'underground.' " [88] It is only realistic to recognize, however, that this "alliance" has thus far made little if any progress toward fulfillment of its aspirations. While a few hundred or perhaps a few thousand Soviet citizens have continued to risk their careers and what passes for freedom in the USSR by defying the authorities, the highest-ranking, most prestigious dissenters, such as Evtushenko, Voznesenski, and Kapitsa, have, since 1967 or early 1968, perhaps only too wisely and justifiably refrained from com-

88. Victor Zorza, *Manchester Guardian Weekly*, 18 January 1968. Patricia Blake's *New York Times* article (note 71) provides additional detail.

mitting "slander" against the state and from committing any of the other "political crimes" which might have given the KGB an excuse for removing them from the social body. It remains to be seen whether the more extreme dissenters will be remembered, by those who share their values and admire their courage, as martyrs in a largely hopeless cause or as the Soviet counterparts of the pioneer leaders of reform movements in other countries, which suffered reverses in their early stages but gathered even more adherents with time, as they shook the confidence and destroyed the moral authority of the tyrannies they opposed.

Prospects for the Soviet future, at least in the short run, have been rendered more obscure and less hopeful by the Kremlin's snuffing out of the Czechoslovak experiment in democratic socialism and by Moscow's reactionary cultural policy of the last few years. The deterioration of Sino-Soviet relations may be regarded, like Soviet policy toward Czechoslovakia, as evidence of a reviving encirclement psychology, which can scarcely fail to damage and slow the progress of reform. These are discouraging trends, but they are balanced by pressures for increased flexibility in a maturing economy. We need not rule out the possibility of a regime-controlled "normalization" of the existing pattern of closed politics.

This prognostication is based upon what is known of some central features of post-Stalin political development — in particular, the relative smoothness of both the Stalin and Khrushchev succession crises and, perhaps even more impressive, the relatively high degree of flexibility and adaptiveness displayed by Khrushchev's successors, whose reformist impulses, though not identical in mix and style with those dominant during his evangelistic administration, are clearly vigorous. The highly educated, gray flannel — blue serge would be more accurate — Communist leaders of today have finally begun to tackle, with the aid of survey research and other social science techniques, the problems involved in converting Stalinist austerity communism into what might be called minimum-level welfare communism, if not the "goulash communism" dear to Khrushchev. The range of the support-seeking measures instituted by Khrushchev's businesslike successors is too broad to be described here.[89]

It seems as if every few days an article or editorial appears in a major Soviet newspaper or magazine which reflects awareness of and concern about the rising expectations of Soviet citizens, especially about their rising demands for goods and services. Rising expectations can, of course, create troublesome problems for governments seeking to work the tricky and uneasy passage from a reign of terror to a less coercive, quasi-legal

89. For this writer's forecast of "adaptive evolution" as a possible path of future Soviet development, see his "Prospects for Soviet Political Development: Evolution, Decay or Revolution?" in Kurt L. London, ed., *The Soviet Union: Fifty Years of Communism* (Baltimore: Johns Hopkins Press, 1968).

pattern of rule. It would appear that in recent years the Kremlin has had some success, though not a great deal, in synchronizing reforms with expectations; but it has not succeeded — nor will it succeed in the foreseeable future — in eliminating tensions and instabilities. Until a constitutional regime with institutionalized rules for the selection of party and government leadership by competitive elections is established, factional strife and succession crises will doubtless continue to plague the Soviet body politic.

Political innovation and imagination are not the strong suit of the technobureaucrats now in control of the Kremlin. One indication, however, that some Soviet citizens in relatively high positions think in terms of at least tinkering with the political system was the speech given by N. Arutyunyan, chairman of the Presidium of the Supreme Soviet of the Armenian Soviet Socialist Republic in 1966. Arutyunyan advocated a measure of competition in elections for local governing bodies. However, no attention was paid to his proposal at the Twenty-third CPSU Congress, which convened a few weeks later. Moreover, the commission established in 1962 to propose reforms in the 1936 Constitution (formerly referred to as the Stalin Constitution) and headed since December 1964 by Brezhnev, had not reported by the fall of 1972, despite a number of hopeful references to the expected results of its deliberations in various press organs.

There are some grounds for hope that a regime which originated as a revolutionary dictatorship may eventually — if the international situation is not excessively unfavorable and if it can achieve success in economic development and in providing a decent level of prosperity for its citizens — create a synthesis of its revolutionary ideology with the traditional political culture of the society it governs and a synchronization of the value patterns of that society with the new division of labor it has established. In other words, it is possible that, as bitter memories of struggle and suffering fade, what Chalmers Johnson terms a "moral community" may gradually replace a pattern of order based on "deterrence." [90] Such a transformation — the gradual replacement of political controls, imposed by revolutionaries obsessed with the need for "vigilance," by a compliance pattern of widely shared but loosely defined norms — could produce a freer, less rigidly controlled, but better integrated political community.

In Yugoslavia a Communist regime has already made substantial progress toward permitting more and more individuals and groups to articulate

90. Chalmers Johnson, *Revolutionary Change* (Boston: Little, Brown, 1966). My speculation is based, not only upon observation of Soviet development as revealed in official Soviet sources, but also upon the theoretical structure developed in this thoughtful study.

their interests and aspirations, provided they do not openly attack Marxist ideology or seek to form national organizations that challenge the monopoly of the League of Communists in national political leaderships. Czechoslovakia in 1968 would have gone at least as far toward toleration of dissent as has Yugoslavia, if Moscow had not prevented the Dubček leadership from doing so by military force. Indeed, Czechoslovakia might even have instituted a regime providing for some sort of open, legitimate opposition. The squashing of democracy in Czechoslovakia was a victory for Leninist-Stalinist orthodoxy. The handful of brave Soviet citizens who protested against it have been deprived of their freedom. It remains to be seen, however, if the Kremlin's draconian measures to stamp out the Czechoslovak contagion — measures which, there is evidence to believe, followed a majority, rather than a unanimous politburo decision — may not have hastened, rather than delayed the ultimate decay and collapse of dictatorial rule in Soviet Russia.

One already visible, if not easily measurable cost of crushing Czechoslovakia's democratic experiment is Moscow's failure at the June 1969 International Communist Congress to secure as much support for its general line as it did even at the 1960 congress. In particular, as the *New York Times* stated editorially, "the Soviet press had to inform its readers that unanimity did not exist at this summit. The question must occur to many Soviet minds why dissent is legal at an international communist meeting, but illegal and punishable by prison sentences within the Soviet Union." [91] Even implied and grudging toleration of dissent by foreign Communists must, one would think, tend to erode the authority of a regime whose legitimacy is, in considerable measure, based on a claimed monopoly of doctrinal wisdom.

The impact of Czechoslovakia, the continued independence displayed by Yugoslavia and to a lesser degree by Romania, and the growing independence of the Italian and some other powerful Communist parties may give encouragement to advocates of greater freedom inside the USSR. In the post-Stalin Soviet Union it has at times been possible, if dangerous, for courageous and concerned citizens to propose significant changes in public policy and even, to a lesser degree, in the structure of society. As better-educated young leaders, increasingly free of the ignorance, prejudice, and rigidity nurtured by the traumatic experiences of the Stalinist past, rise in the various chains of command, reformist impulses may wax in strength, even in the political sphere. Of course, whatever the Czechoslovak experiment can contribute to the coming of democracy to Russia may materialize only in the far distant future. The short-term effects of Czechoslovakia were highly detrimental.

91. *New York Times*, 19 June 1969. See also Victor Zorza, "Kremlin Forced to Accept Dissent," *Manchester Guardian Weekly*, 19 June 1969.

Already, however, there has been some modest progress not only toward the rationalization of administration in the USSR but also toward the wider shaping and sharing of values (to borrow a phrase from Harold D. Lasswell). It is perhaps not completely idle to envisage for the longer-term future of the USSR a line of development similar to that which, in the opinion of Robert E. Lane, is gradually bringing into being in the United States a "knowledgeable society." Such a development, of course, would alter and render more rational and civilized Soviet behavior in the difficult and sensitive political relations examined in this essay.

The tentativeness and inconclusiveness of our prognosis for Soviet political development must, unfortunately, be emphasized. The continuation and further development of an adaptive, reformist course in Russian policy depends on conditions difficult to define and perceive, let alone to assure and maintain. Among these is the avoidance not only of all-out international war but also of international tensions or armament costs of a level and magnitude conducive to rigorous, garrison state controls. Responsive and responsible leadership also presupposes a level of courage, skill, and indeed virtuosity among decision makers sufficient to synchronize consensus with dynamism and innovation. Even if all of this and more is forthcoming, rapidly burgeoning expectations — stimulated in part by the authorities' tinkering with the political system, but difficult or perhaps impossible to satisfy — might confront the rulers and the ruled with a series of crises and choices involving, ultimately, a confrontation between repression from above and revolution from below. Such an eventuality would probably be very costly to the USSR and to the world as a whole. Its avoidance depends primarily on the skill of the Soviet leaders in coping with the problems of ideological legitimacy.

Dyadic patterns such as reform–repression and evolution–revolution can only imperfectly suggest the variety and range of possibilities and probabilities, of forks and turnings in Soviet Russia's future path. The continuation and further successful development of the Yugoslav experiment in transforming, by reform from above, what was a unified hegemony into a more and more pluralistic, even a semiconstitutional polity sets an example that provides encouragement and impetus to responsive-reformist tendencies in Soviet politics.

Yugoslav reform from above has thus far been encouraging to those who believe in — or at least do not exclude — the possibility of a peaceful transformation of a regime of extreme concentration of power into a semipluralistic polity. Whether such a development can ever lead, without civil war or at least a coup d'état, all the way to Western-style democracy, it is impossible, in this author's opinion, to predict in the present state of political science; and it may long remain impossible. One is, after all, in such speculation, close to the beginning of a long chain of events, many of them pregnant with contingency. One very real danger, especially for Yugoslavia but perhaps also for the USSR, is strife among the various nationalities composing the populations of these multinational states if the relaxation of central controls proceeds very rapidly, without acceptable guarantees of appropriate political liberties to all concerned.

Lives will be saved, suffering will be minimized, and welfare and enlightenment will be maximized if both leaders and led in the USSR — and of course in the West also — behave with prudence and restraint in managing the transition to the freer society that will probably take shape some decades hence. Change in Russia will probably be built, for some time, largely on the foundations of the established system. Even if subversive structural opposition — employing, at a certain point in time, violent means — leads eventually to a successful democratic-constitutionalist coup d'état (perhaps engineered by a conspiratorial coalition of reformist party leaders, military officers, and intellectuals), this outcome would probably be the culmination of a long, zigzag, crisis-torn process.

Russians who desire constructive, peaceful change will probably do well — to the extent that the regime's response to their demands makes this possible — to press, with determination tempered by prudence, for liberalizing adjustment and change and to utilize all the available channels and loopholes provided by the structure of party, state, and public organizations and by informal interest groups. But it is imperative that they also be keenly aware of the risks to their values inherent in violent, utopian, cataclysmic, or explosive moods and methods. Of course, whether political change will be constructive and peaceful depends on the behavior of all those who are in various ways responsible for shaping the situation in which it occurs. Among these determinants, will be the informed concern of democratic opinion in the United States and elsewhere and the skill, patience, restraint, and sophistication of statesmen, Western as well as Soviet.

3

OPPOSITION IN
COMMUNIST EAST EUROPE

H. Gordon Skilling

To discuss "opposition" in a one-party system, and in particular in a Communist one, might seem on first thought to involve a contradiction in terms. Communist governments have normally been regarded in the West as systems without opposition except in the form of illegal resistance by sections of the population to the very existence of the regimes. Yet Leonard Schapiro, in his foreword as editor to the first issue of *Government and Opposition*, expressed the view that both government and opposition are always and at all times present (or potentially present) in every political order, and he referred to "the tentative process of loyal dissent" becoming apparent in one-party states.[1] A striking feature of many of the Communist states after the death of Stalin was in fact the emergence of political tendencies that can only be called oppositional, in the sense either of resistance to policies enacted or offered by the ruling party or of proposals of alternative courses of action. Observance of these trends by Western scholars and analysis of the experience of non-Communist states in Africa and Asia have led to a reexamination of the nature of one-party states in general and to the recognition that, not only has opposition never been totally absent from Communist systems, but it has assumed more vigorous and varied forms in the years after Stalin.[2]

A revision of an article prepared originally for this volume and published in *Government and Opposition* (1968). The present version was completed in January 1971.

1. *Government and Opposition* 1, no. 1 (October 1965): 1, 3.

2. See the special issue, "The Dead End of the Monolithic Parties," *Government and Opposition* 2, no. 2 (January–April 1967), in particular the symposium, pp. 165–80, and ensuing articles. See also two earlier articles: Jerzy J. Wyatr and Adam Przeworski, "Control without Opposition," ibid., 1, no. 2 (January 1966): 227–39; and Ghita Ionescu, "Control and Contestation in Some One-Party States," ibid., pp. 240–50. In a fuller study, *The Politics of the European Communist States* (London: Weidenfeld and Nicolson, 1967), Ionescu modified some of the concepts and definitions quoted here. Cf. D. J. R. Scott, "Resistance and Opposition," *Survey*,

The process of opposition may be regarded, then, as a universal one, characteristic of all political systems, but its importance and the forms which it takes vary widely from country to country and from period to period. As Robert Dahl's earlier volume, *Political Oppositions in Western Democracies*, clearly demonstrated, even where opposition is an integral and legitimate part of the political system, the patterns differ fundamentally. The contributors to that book concentrated almost exclusively on the legal and formal types of opposition manifested primarily in competing political parties and in parliamentary and electoral procedures. Yet, as the editor observed, political opposition of this orderly and peaceful kind is a rare phenomenon in historical experience, and governments have traditionally sought to suppress or contain opposition.[3] Although in Western democracies opposition usually enjoys constitutional sanction and assumes institutional forms, probably in no country is it exclusively institutionalized and based on constitutional foundations. In nondemocratic countries opposition has normally been forced to assume a variety of nonlegal or illegal forms and to express itself in other than formal and institutional manner.

Communist Theory and Practice

The nature of opposition and the forms of its expression in Eastern Europe have been profoundly affected by the character of Communist politics and have assumed peculiar and unusual forms. The crucial difference between Communist and democratic regimes has been the absence of an institutionalized opposition expressed and guaranteed in constitutional principles or in political custom.[4] In particular, this has been manifested in the absence of two or more major and competing parties and in the limited degree of economic, social, cultural, and political pluralism. The ruling Communist party has possessed a monopoly of political activity and asserted a monolithic unity within itself.

Communist theory and practice have traditionally denied the legitimacy of any form of opposition. The doctrine of the proletarian dictatorship, as developed by Lenin and Stalin, conferred on the so-called party of

no. 64 (July 1967); pp. 34–44. An anthology of opposition texts from Soviet and Eastern European Communist history, with some theoretical analysis, may be seen in Gunther Hillman, *Selbstkritik des Kommunismus: Texte der Opposition* (Reinbek bei Hamburg: Rowohlt, 1967).

3. Robert A. Dahl, ed., *Political Oppositions in Western Democracies* (New Haven: Yale University Press, 1966), especially pp. xi–xii, xiv, 332.

4. Ionescu uses the term *political opposition* to refer to opposition that is "institutionalized, recognized and legitimate." In this sense, Communist states are, in his view, "oppositionless." Nonetheless, there exists "opposition" in a broader sense, signifying "any concerted attitude or action, spontaneous or deliberate, sporadic or continuous, of anomic or associational groups under any circumstances or by any means" (*Politics of the European Communist States*, pp. 2–3).

the working class the exclusive authority to exercise leadership and denied to other parties the right to share this power or to counteract it. At the same time the principle of democratic centralism assigned supreme authority to the top party leaders and required disciplined obedience by all lower officers and members. As interpreted and applied by Lenin, these theories led to the banning, not only of *opposition* in the form of organized groups seeking to replace those in power, but also of *dissent* in the form of criticism of policies adopted or proposed by these leaders.[5] Carried to its extreme conclusion by Stalin, this led eventually to the complete elimination of opposition in almost every form.[6] At the most, passive resistance or revolutionary conspiracy remained as the only vestiges of opposition. In Eastern Europe this Soviet practice was introduced in its full form after 1948, when Communist power was everywhere fully established and the people's democracies were identified as forms of the proletarian dictatorship. Any opposition, inside or outside the party, was regarded as disloyal and impermissible.

In the fifteen years after Stalin's death there were, however, striking changes in the role of opposition in Eastern Europe. Paradoxically, in no country, with the partial exception of Czechoslovakia under Dubček, was there any fundamental doctrinal change in the attitude of the regime toward opposition as such. As in all systems, needless to say, revolutionary or conspiratorial opposition of any kind was strictly curbed by law and by force. In Eastern Europe even peaceful advocacy of basic opposition to the regime and its policies was not tolerated and could usually express itself only through subterranean channels. In none of the countries was genuine opposition inside the ruling party permitted.[7] Even in Yugoslavia, where the position and role of the party were significantly modified, the idea of a multiparty system or of an opposition party was explicitly rejected.[8] The Yugoslav party's internal structure was amended, and

5. See Leonard Schapiro, " 'Putting the Lid on Leninism,' Opposition and Dissent in the Communist One-Party States," *Government and Opposition* 2, no. 2 (January–April 1967): 181–203. See the fuller treatment in his book *The Origin of the Communist Autocracy: Political Opposition in the Soviet State, First Phase, 1917–1922* (London: Bell, 1955). See also Frederick C. Barghoorn, "Soviet Political Doctrine and the Problem of Opposition," *Bucknell Review* 12, no. 2 (May 1964): 1–29.

6. See Robert V. Daniels, *The Conscience of the Revolution: Communist Opposition in Soviet Russia* (Cambridge, Mass.: Harvard University Press, 1960).

7. In Hungary, for instance, the existence of "separate platforms," or "factions," within the party was explicitly rejected by the party daily newspaper, *Népszabadság*, 16 May 1963. Cf. the views of a top Czech leader, J. Hendrych that party members could have "different opinions on different problems" but could not be "representatives of different ideologies" (*Rudé právo*, 10 February 1967).

8. M. Mihajlov, Split University lecturer, was imprisoned in 1966 and again in 1967 for criticizing the one-party system and seeking to establish an opposition journal. Cf. the rejection of the idea of an opposition party by a Czech theorist, V. Mejstřík, "The Concept and Practice of Party Democracy," *Nová mysl* 20, no. 8 (19 April 1966): 29–31.

widespread debate often occurred, but dissidence on basic issues among party members was not tolerated. Yet despite these restrictions, in almost all the countries of Eastern Europe dissent was in actual fact expressed in diverse forms and was tolerated in varying degrees by the regimes.

Types of Opposition

We may distinguish four types of opposition which are characteristic of, although not necessarily peculiar to, the Communist systems of Eastern Europe. First, there may be opposition to the system itself —what we may call *integral opposition*.[9] This involves overt or covert disloyalty; when expressed in action, it may take such forms as violent revolts or revolutionary conspiracies designed to oppose official policies or over-throw the existing regime, or other types of resistance, such as mass demonstrations, underground activity, or political emigration. This kind of antisystem opposition is normally carried on by anti-Communist forces, who may owe allegiance to a democratic faith or to conservative or extreme nationalist beliefs. In certain cases, however, it is the work of dissident Communists acting illegally. It may also manifest itself more inchoately in alienation from the established order and in emotional or intellectual resistance to it — as, for instance, in apolitical attitudes among some of the youth, underground creations of writers and painters, or the hostility of rational and regional subcultures — or, as in the case of the churches, it may involve not so much active resistance as passive rejection of communist doctrine and espousal of an alternative faith.

Second, there may be opposition to the leaders in power, normally by rivals for the topmost positions but sometimes by partners sharing power with those whom they seek to oust. This *factional opposition* is sometimes carried on by individuals or groups within the highest organs of party and government — perhaps even a prime minister, such as Yugov in Bulgaria,[10] or a first secretary, such as Rakosi in Hungary — although support may be sought in broader social and political groupings. Such opposition, although by definition equated with disloyalty to other leaders, does not represent opposition to the Communist system as such and does not

9. This is close to what Robert Dahl refers to as *structural opposition;* see *Political Oppositions in Western Democracies,* p. 342. It is not unlike what Brzezinski and Huntington call *alienation* or *unorthodox dissent;* see *Political Power: USA/USSR* (New York: Viking, 1964), pp. 114, 105. Barghoorn, in his chapter in this volume, uses the term *subversive.* Cf. Ionescu's term *contestation,* which he defines as "the anti-system, basic and permanent postulates of any opposition on the grounds of fundamental dichotomic differences of opinion and ideologies" ("Control and Contestation," p. 241). In *Politics of the European Communist States* he abandons this term and employs the word *dissent,* which, he argues, is not always against the government or the holders of power (pp. 169, 178).

10. Yugov was described by Vice-Premier S. Todorov in 1962 as the only premier who was in opposition to his own government (*Borba,* 10 November 1962).

always involve even basic differences of view concerning public policies. Normally, however, it embodies a fundamental ideological rift, as between nationalist and proletarian internationalist, or liberal and conservative, or leftist and rightist viewpoints.

Third, there may be opposition to, or severe criticism of, a whole series of key policies of the regime, reflecting crucial differences in standards of value but not a rejection of the Communist system itself. This *fundamental opposition* may be, and often is, linked with factional antagonisms among the topmost leaders. It also takes the form, however, of resistance on the part of key groups within or outside the party, who seek not to displace the leaders but to resist or influence the policies pursued by them. As we shall note more fully later, the major occupational groups — for example, party *apparatchiki*, state bureaucrats, police, writers, lawyers, and economists — may divide into opinion groups defending (or opposing) hard or soft, conservative or reformist policies. In some cases a powerful ruling group, such as the state administrators or even the *apparatchiki*, is subject to severe criticism by other governing elements. Such opposition may express the discontent of key nationality groups, such as the Slovaks in Czechoslovakia or the Croats or Slovenes in Yugoslavia, who desire an improved position within the system. Although intraparty opposition of this kind does not necessarily challenge either the system or its leaders, it verges on integral opposition if it is intense enough and embraces a wide range of policy questions.

Finally, there may be opposition to specific policies without a rejection of the regime, its leaders, or its general policies. Such *specific opposition*, or dissent, may be relatively orthodox in general, though quite unorthodox in its particular recommendations.[11] This opposition is normally con-

---

11. Barghoorn, in chapter 2 of this book, uses the term *sectoral opposition*. This is comparable to Alex Nove's term *dissent within consensus* in *Government and Opposition* 2, no. 2 (January–April 1967): 175–76. Cf. the term *orthodox dissent* in Brzezinski and Huntington, *Political Power: USA/USSR*, p. 110. Ionescu and Wjatr use the concept of *control* in this connection. Ionescu defines "political control" as *nonconstitutional, noninstitutional*, direct participation in and influencing of the decision-making processes in a nonparliametary society by forces, groups, and agencies indispensable to the running of that society ("Control and Contestation," p. 240). Wjatr and Przeworski define control in the political sense as "the possibility of influencing those who hold power in such a way that they take into account the interests of groups exerting this control" ("Control without Opposition," p. 231). Ionescu, in *Politics of the European Communist States*, abandons the term *control* (as well as *contestation*) and replaces it with *checks*. He classifies the two major forms of opposition in Communist states as (1) "political checks," or "plural checks," exercised on the party by subordinate apparatuses, such as the state and trade unions, as well as by broader unorganized social groups, such as the workers and peasants, and by certain constitutional bodies, such as the courts, the assemblies, local government organs, and the press; and (2) "dissent," expressed by other groups, such as the churches, the students and universities, and the cultural reviews. Checks give expression to "interests" contradictory to those of the party apparatus; dissent, to "values" contrary to those officially demanded. (Pp. 2–3, 90–95, and parts II and III.)

ducted by Communists, either inside the party — even within the apparatus — or outside the party in officially approved organizations and associations. If opposition of this kind is extreme and deals with crucial issues, it verges on fundamental opposition, at least in the sense of seeking a radically reformed Communism. In some cases, such opposition within the system is a veiled form of integral opposition; in any case it is sometimes treated by the regime as disloyal. In the main, however, it is a loyal opposition, seeking to change or influence public policy by criticizing established policies, offering different measures from those proposed, or suggesting future courses of action. This discussion of policy alternatives is sometimes open and explicit, sometimes veiled and subtle. The party, while at times encouraging this kind of criticism, also seeks to channel and limit it, but it often escapes party control and goes beyond permissible limits.

Not all of these oppositional tendencies are always present in Communist systems. Indeed, it can hardly be sufficiently emphasized that individual Communist systems differ greatly from one another and from one period to another, both in the type of opposition predominant and in the intensity and forms of the various kinds of dissent. Moreover, the several oppositional tendencies present at any time in a given country cannot be sharply marked off from one another; they often overlap or merge. In particular, oppositional attitudes and behavior alter with changing conditions. Specific dissent may gradually develop into fundamental or even integral opposition and may become involved in factional conflicts among leading groups. Integral opposition may recede with leadership changes and policy shifts and with increased opportunities for the expression of specific opposition. As will be discussed below, much depends on the attitude of the ruling group toward oppositions of various types, since intolerance toward specific opposition may generate fundamental or integral opposition.

A simple dichotomy between "orthodox" and "unorthodox" dissent, between "control" and "contestation," or between "opposition" and "dissent," [12] as employed by some analysts of Communism, does not fully bring out the complexity of opposition under Communism. If such a dual classification is used, it should be understood, not as a clear-cut demarcation of two sharply opposed forms, but as defining the extremes of a continuum. The fourfold classification suggested here should reveal more clearly both the spectrum of degrees of opposition and its distinctive forms and methods.

12. Schapiro defines "opposition" as "an organized political group, or groups, of which the aim is to oust the government in power and to replace it by one of its own choosing." "Dissent," on the other hand, seeks "merely to criticize, to exhort, to persuade, and to be listened to." *Government and Opposition* 2, no. 2 (January–April 1967): 182–83.

Phases of Opposition in Eastern Europe

Even before 1948 — when in some countries, such as Czechoslovakia and Hungary, more or less genuine coalitions existed — neither integral nor fundamental opposition was regarded as legitimate. A kind of policy consensus was embodied in the National Fronts on which the governments were based. No doubt there was strong dissent by some sections of the population against the radical disruption of the status quo espoused by the Communists and implemented in part with the consent of the other coalition parties. Integral opposition by those opposed to the National Front itself was, however, banned, as was fundamental opposition to the Front's policies. There were in certain countries competitive electoral struggles and opportunities for the expression of dissent in public discussion. Nonetheless, in the elections there was often a prearranged distribution of seats among the National Front partners, and there were limitations on public discussion, sometimes self-imposed, at other times required by the prevailing atmosphere of conformity.

Even within the coalitions themselves there was, however, opposition by non-Communist members to policies advocated by their Communist partners and reciprocal opposition by the Communists to the actions of their "allies." Although this opposition was normally directed against specific policies, it often — implicitly and covertly, or even openly — involved resistance to the system as such and to the whole range of policies advocated by the opposite party. There was, in fact, a scarcely veiled struggle for power between the competing parties, Communist and non-Communist. Although during these early years the Communists tolerated a certain freedom of discussion and some element of opposition by their coalition partners, their ultimate goal was a complete consensus unmarred by difference of views or opposition to their own ends. By 1948 even the less extreme forms of interparty competition — parliamentary debate, electoral contests, and criticism of specific policies — were eliminated, and the full-blown Leninist doctrine was imposed wherever it had not yet been introduced.[13]

During the period of Stalinism after 1948, the East European states, with the exception of Yugoslavia, assumed the monolithic or totalitarian form which had been established in the Soviet Union in the 1930s. Other parties, where they existed, were required to give full and unconditional support to the ruling Communist party. No opposition parties were permitted to function. Representative assemblies became nothing more than rubber stamps, and societal organizations, such as the trade unions, mere

13. See H. Gordon Skilling, *The Governments of Communist East Europe* (New York: Crowell, 1966), especially pp. 36–39.

transmission belts. Severe coercion was employed to suppress not only integral but also fundamental and specific oppositions. Although "criticism" and "self-criticism" were officially encouraged, this practice in fact allowed little or no room for the open expression of conflicting views or the advancement of alternate policies. Within the party command, as in the Soviet Union in earlier periods, various factional oppositions emerged, but they were dealt with severely by purges and by the strictest penalties, including imprisonment and execution. Nonetheless, the nature of the system and the radical policies introduced generated intense oppositional attitudes among some Communists as well as non-Communists. Coercion did not mean the elimination of oppositions; it simply deprived them of all means of overt expression and forced them to assume underground, antisystem forms. Indeed, since all lesser forms of dissent from specific policies were curbed, opposition inevitably took the more radical form of rejection of the system as a whole and of the leaders and their policies.

SHIFTS IN OPPOSITION IN THE POST-STALIN PERIOD   In the post-Stalin period there was a significant rise in opposition in Eastern Europe and a marked shift in the types of opposition which predominated. Analysis is rendered difficult by the sharp variances in the development in the eight Communist countries, with the special circumstances and the peculiar traditions of each affecting the course of events.[14] At one extreme, in Albania, no basic change in the traditional Stalinist system occurred: factional opposition was stamped out, and coercion and tight control prevented almost any form of dissent. At the other extreme was Yugoslavia, where the Stalinist pattern was modified (after 1948) in fundamental ways: institutional arrangements guaranteed a substantial amount of articulation of diverse interests of nationalities and social groups, and specific opposition on concrete issues was permitted and even encouraged.

Between these extremes, each of the other countries had, by the end of 1967, evolved a particular variant of de-Stalinization, less pronounced in Bulgaria, the German Democratic Republic, and Romania and somewhat more marked in Hungary, Poland, and Czechoslovakia. In Romania independence of outlook in foreign affairs, including her relations with the Soviet Union, was not matched by equally significant domestic changes, although some lessening of police power and some relaxation of intellectual controls gradually occurred. In Bulgaria and East Germany, domestic shifts were less striking; at the most, some degree of specific opposition was tolerated, largely in the forms of government and party

14. See H. Gordon Skilling, *Communism National and International* (Toronto: University of Toronto Press, 1964).

consultation with experts and specialists and of a somewhat freer discussion of basic policy issues.

In the more "liberal" states of Hungary, Poland, and Czechoslovakia there was much greater toleration and even encouragement of specific dissent and sometimes acceptance, to some degree, of fundamental opposition. After the revolution of 1956, the Hungarian regime, without introducing essential changes in the system, eventually made an effort to win public support and, not without some success, to moderate the deep currents of integral and fundamental opposition manifested in 1956. In Czechoslovakia and Poland, in 1967 and 1968, there were open expressions of fundamental opposition and sharp factional conflicts within the top leadership. A vivid contrast was evident, however, in the subsequent evolution of these two states. In Poland, in March 1968, the Gomulka leadership was able to contain the challenges of rival factions and to suppress dissidence by force and compulsion. A few months earlier, in Czechoslovakia, Novotný, on the other hand, was overthrown by a coalition of rivals, with dissident social forces providing the stimulus of these political changes. By mid-1968 Czechoslovakia was in the midst of a remarkable process of change, moving in the direction of a diminution of the power of the party, democratization of political procedures, and freedom of expression and association to a degree not witnessed previously in any Communist state. (See below, pp. 112–19 and chapter 4.) If, as was intended, these tendencies had been embodied in legal and institutional form and had not been reversed by invasion, Czechoslovakia would have surpassed and replaced Yugoslavia at the extreme "liberal" end of the spectrum of Eastern European systems.

The differences among the Communist systems are not always clear-cut, nor are they fixed and changeless. On the contrary, they are smudgy and ever shifting, so that analysis of a single country — and still more, generalization concerning all of them — confronts serious difficulties. As the individuality of each country became more pronounced, Communist East Europe presented a kaleidoscopic picture, with a variety in some degree comparable to that of the democracies. One can, however, draw certain generalizations from these differentiated, zigzag courses of development. By late 1967, integral opposition, after a climactic outburst in 1956 in Hungary, had everywhere declined, or at least did not usually express itself in overt action of serious proportions. Factional opposition, after intense activity in the early years of de-Stalinization, especially in Hungary, Poland, and Bulgaria, also declined, but it reoccurred — for example, in Poland and Czechoslovakia in 1967 and after — in somewhat more moderate forms. Fundamental opposition, after an initial flourishing in the Polish and Hungarian crises, also subsided somewhat but persisted and recurred openly in Czechoslovakia and Poland in the late sixties.

Specific opposition, on the other hand, extending over a whole range of issues, expanded in the more liberal states, where the regimes permitted and encouraged the articulation of conflicting interests and opinions, and various occupational groups seized the opportunity to express themselves vigorously on matters of public policy. On the whole, therefore — and generalizing from very complex, differentiated developments — the characteristic opposition became what we may call loyal opposition, which sought peaceful changes within the system, either in leadership or in policy, but not a replacement of the system as such. Unfortunately for clarity of exposition and soundness of conclusions, there were exceptions to all these propositions, each of which requires more extended consideration.

THE DECLINE OF INTEGRAL OPPOSITION   By the end of 1967 integral opposition had declined in most of the Communist systems of Eastern Europe. Immediately after the death of Stalin and under the impact of de-Stalinization, there was an outburst of such opposition in certain states, leading to violent revolts in East Germany and riots at Pilsen in Czechoslovakia and Poznan in Poland and culminating in the Hungarian revolution and the nonviolent Polish unrest in 1956. The failure of all these efforts at resistance and the maintenance of adequate means of repression by the regimes made resort to violence, as a means of integral opposition, a rare occurrence. Underground resistance therefore appeared futile and became less frequent. From time to time individuals or groups were arrested and tried.[15] The heroic days of revolutionary resistance seemed to be over, however, and were likely to recur only in conditions of extreme crisis.

This decline of integral opposition reflected factors other than the continued presence of coercion. Since 1953 there was, in varying degrees and with interruptions and reversals, a deceleration of the "permanent revolution" imposed from above, the removal of some of the worst causes for grievance created by Stalinism, and a series of partial reforms designed to make the system more palatable and to give satisfaction to the interests of diverse social groups. An important factor, paralleling similar shifts in some Western democracies, was the transition from a predominantly ideological to a more pragmatic and empirical approach on the part of the leaders.[16] These changes, coupled with the futility of integral opposition, brought about significant shifts in opinion and created some willingness to adapt to the requirements of the political system

15. Conspiracy trials were held in Albania in 1961 and in Bulgaria in 1965. Individual arrests and trials for treason or conspiracy occurred in other countries from time to time.
16. Cf. Dahl, *Political Oppositions in Western Democracies*, pp. 354–56.

while seeking to improve it. This was sometimes reinforced by feelings of national solidarity generated by resistance, either, as in Yugoslavia and Romania, to the Soviet Union or, in Poland, to a traditional enemy such as West Germany. Even in East Germany a combination of extreme measures of coercion (such as continuing Soviet occupation and the building of the Berlin wall) and policies designed to improve conditions of life engendered a wider acceptance of the regime by the elite groups and by the population as a whole.[17] In varying measure, almost all the regimes sought to work out a relationship of coexistence with their people and to cease regarding non-Communists as ipso facto enemies or oppositionists. Kadar's slogan, "Whoever is not against us is for us," epitomizes this tendency.[18]

This is not to say, of course, that agreement on fundamentals had been achieved. In the absence of free expression of opinion and a genuine electoral process, there was no way of measuring the degree of consensus or lack of it, or the extent of integral opposition. No doubt there was widespread disaffection and even rejection of the system as such, conveying itself in apathy, in disobedience to the regime and its requirements, and to some degree in passive resistance. From time to time, in various countries, there was evidence of such attitudes by alienated sections of the youth; by parts of the religious communities, such as the Catholics in Poland and the Protestants in East Germany; among the peasants, in devoting their primary effort to their private plots rather than to the collective farms; among workers, in a slowdown or even, in rare cases, ceasing work; or among writers and artists, in creating for private satisfaction rather than for exhibition. Such "opposition in principle," as Otto Kirchheimer has termed it,[19] could not speak out openly through any recognized vehicle of opinion and could manifest itself only in amorphous and anomic forms. At times of acute crisis, as in Poland in 1968 and again in 1970, the continued existence of some degree of integral opposition was revealed in street demonstrations and, in the latter case, violent attacks on party and government buildings, ending, however, in each case, in the forceful restoration of order by the authorities.

The case of the Catholic church in Poland constitutes an outstanding exception to the general rule in Eastern Europe. Its role as an organized oppositional force, capable of counterbalancing party and state by claiming the allegiance of wide sections of the population and by expressing open disagreements with basic policies of the regime, is unique in Com-

17. Jean Smith, "The German Democratic Republic and the West," *International Journal* 22, no. 2 (Spring 1967): 231–52.
18. In defending this policy, Kadar argued that although Hungary had a one-party system, they should work as though there were a twenty-party system and a secret election every day (*New York Times*, 7 March 1962).
19. Dahl, *Political Oppositions in Western Democracies*, p. 237.

munist states. The church has been described by a Polish scholar as "a perpetually competitive ideological force juxtaposed to the party and the state" which "constitutes the political opposition." [20] With Cardinal Wyszynski as the main spokesman and with newspapers, journals, and the churches themselves as media of communication, Polish Catholicism was able to challenge the ruling party not only on matters of religious policy but also on questions of doctrine and education. During the millennial celebrations of church and state in 1966 an extraordinary confrontation of cardinal and first secretary, at separate public meetings held during many months, testified to the political power of the church. True, the latter denied its intention of interfering in political affairs and argued that it confined itself to matters of religious doctrine and policy. Nonetheless, the cardinal's statements on foreign policy and on such questions as atheism and freedom of conscience touched on sensitive political questions[21] and brought accusations from the government that the church was playing a political role in opposition to the regime and the new social order.[22]

THE TEMPERING OF FACTIONAL OPPOSITION   The East European Communist parties have never been as united as propaganda and theory assume. Leaderships have always been divided into factions seeking power and advocating conflicting policies.[23] Such factions are in a sense a surrogate for parties in a one-party state. In the Stalinist past, factional conflict eventuated in radical, violent purges, often dictated from Moscow and with the severest of penalties, including execution, for the defeated. In the initial phase of de-Stalinization, long and bitter struggles were waged between leadership groups in Poland, Hungary, and Bulgaria, leading to the ultimate replacement of existing leaders by more "liberal" or "national" Communist "oppositions." Purges of high-ranking leaders continued to occur in later years, but with less drastic personal consequences for the victims.

Although purges of the old type were not as permanent a feature of Communist rule as was once assumed, an intraparty struggle over leadership and policy was even more likely to occur, since control from

20. Jerzy J. Wjatr, "Elements of the Pluralism in the Polish Political System," *Polish Sociological Bulletin*, no. 1 (1966), p. 25.

21. In a sermon Cardinal Wyszynski was reported to have said, "We have to stand up before the rulers, princes and authorities and calmly and bravely proclaim the Gospel. The people could be without kings, leaders, premiers and ministers, but never without its shepherd. The bishop is the good shepherd who faces the wolves, and although hurt, defends the people against hatred, falsehood and harm" (*New York Times*, 31 January 1966).

22. See Gomulka's speech (*Trybuna ludu*, 15 January 1966) and the editorial in *Nowe drogi*, April 1966.

23. For a discussion of factionalism, see Ionescu's *Politics of the European Communist States*, pp. 227–69.

Moscow was either absent or less decisive and since the outcome was no longer fatal for the losers. Factional opposition, seeking a change in the leadership (either partial or complete), remained therefore an important feature of East European politics.[24] The clash between leaders and opposition usually took place secretly, and within the party, among the high command in the presidium and secretariat. The central committee might in some cases, as in Czechoslovakia in 1967, play a significant part in the transition to a new leadership. There is as yet no evidence that the process of succession is likely to be institutionalized in the form of elections to a representative parliament or even in a more genuine electoral process within the party organs.

THE PERSISTENCE OF FUNDAMENTAL OPPOSITION   The decline of anti-system opposition was accompanied by the persistence of intraparty opposition by individual Communists or groups who were out of sympathy with a whole range of key official policies and with the leadership itself. For example, in 1964 two Polish students, J. Kuron and K. Modzelewski, illegally circulated an open letter which denounced, in Marxist terms, the entire Communist system for its bureaucratic deformations. In 1966 a leading intellectual, Professor Leszek Kolakowski, in a meeting at Warsaw University, severely censured the record of the Polish party in the decade since 1956. In 1967 a prominent Czech writer, Ludvik Vaculík, delivered an eloquent and slashing condemnation of the Prague regime and its policies on the floor of the Writers Union. These instances of individual dissent by Communists were but the foretaste of eventual explosions of fundamental opposition in both countries.

Important social groups sometimes manifested chronic discontent with major policies of the regime. In Yugoslavia and elsewhere, there was resistance to the implementation of economic reforms and to the liberalization of the political climate by the more conservative elements, concentrated especially within the party apparatus.[25] In Poland in March 1968 street demonstrations and mass meetings were held in protest against literary curbs and arrests of students. In Czechoslovakia in the mid-1960s there was widespread criticism, by "progressive" circles among economists, writers, and other intellectuals, of what was deemed the conservative line of the regime in failing to carry through economic reforms and in imposing literary curbs. These currents of dissent, fusing with criticism by Slovaks of Prague's nationality policies and with student demonstrations, produced a major political crisis in 1967. Severe reprisals against dissidents intensified the crisis and led to the replacement of Antonín

24. See Skilling, *Governments of Communist East Europe,* pp. 91–97.
25. See Jan F. Triska, "The Party Apparatchiks at Bay," *East Europe* 16, no. 12 (December 1967): 2–8.

Novotný as party secretary by a new leader, Alexander Dubček. In this way a tidal wave of fundamental opposition, not opposed to the Communist system as such, but in basic disagreement with the party's major policies and leadership, was expressed in successful factional resistance to the established leadership and a major change in the direction of public policy, only later reversed by outside intervention.

The national question is another source of fundamental opposition. Resistance by constitutent national groups of the multinational Yugoslav state to some policies of the federal government in Belgrade was often openly and sharply manifested. The governments of the national republics and the republican parties proved to be effective agencies for articulating the interests of the individual nationalities and regions. In Czechoslovakia, Slovak organs, both party and state, were much weaker and were unable, until the reforms of 1968, to give adequate expression to Slovak discontents. As a result, the articulation of Slovak interests was accomplished through professional groups, including economists, writers, and historians. (The latter, in reassessing crucial events in the past, such as the Slovak uprising in 1944, expressed a distinctive national viewpoint.) The establishment of a new regime in Prague in January 1968, headed by a Slovak, paved the way for the adoption of national policies designed to meet some of Slovakia's grievances and the transformation of Slovak organs into more influential bodies.

THE RISE OF SPECIFIC OPPOSITION   The most striking feature of the post-Stalin scene in the more "liberal" states was the rise of specific opposition, that is, criticism of particular policies which had been adopted or were under consideration. Where it occurred, this development reflected a subtle but significant change in the party's attitude to society and social groups and in its conception of the process of decision making. There was no relaxation of the party's monopoly of political power and no admission of the desirability of political opposition as such, but it was no longer assumed that the party alone, and infallibly, knew the public interest, to which all individual or group interests must be automatically and without question subordinated and sacrificed. There was an increasing recognition that, in a heterogeneous society, some conflicting interests will exist and that there will be clashes between partial individual and group interests and the broader national interest.[26] It was understood that public policy, if it was to be realistic, should take these conflicting interests into account and should represent a reconciliation or synthesis of them. The party would thus perform the role of an aggregator of

26. See, for instance, A. Lantay, *Ekonomický časopis*, no. 6 (1963), and *Pravda* (Slovak), 18 May 1964; and see M. Lakatoš, *Právny óbzor*, no. 1 (1965), pp. 26–36. For fuller discussions of interest groups in politics, see M. Lakatoš, *Občan, právo a demokracie* (Prague, 1966), and Z. Mlynář, *Stát a člověk* (Prague, 1964).

conflicting interests, rather than the exclusive articulator of its own conception of the national interests.[27]

Moreover, public policy, it was increasingly recognized, must be "scientific," in the sense of being based not merely on Marxism-Leninism but also on the findings of scholarship and science. In some cases the party tolerated and indeed deliberately encouraged wide-ranging debates among experts on certain policy issues, such as economic reform or legal revisions.[28] This kind of discussion, permitting the expression of oppositional viewpoints on specific issues, was, needless to say, subject to strict limits. It nonetheless created a new climate of policy making and — without altering the essential forms of political action, in particular the leading role of the party — subtly and significantly modified the actual working of the political system.

The chief exponents of this loyal opposition were the intellectuals — especially economists, lawyers, social scientists generally, natural scientists, writers, and journalists. These *intellectual interest groups*, as they may be called, did not have the official power of *bureaucratic interest groups*, such as the party *apparatchiki*, the state bureaucrats and managers, and the police.[29] However, they possessed knowledge and enjoyed pres-

27. For an elaboration of this theme by the Czech theorist Z. Mlynář, see *Věda a život*, no. 1 (1965). Mlynář described the leading role of the party as involving "the conscious embodiment of the interests of the whole of society in its entirety, but also the deliberate harmonization of these interests." See also his article "Problems of Political Leadership and the New Economic System," *Problemy mira i sotsializma*, no. 12 (December 1965), p. 98. The Polish scholar Jerzy J. Wjatr referred to the party as "the forum of the expression of the non-antagonistic clashes of interests of various socialist strata of the Polish society" and as "the platform where the divergent interests of the socialist society collide." Although the struggle of class interests takes place outside the party, the "resolution of conflicts which harmonize the interests of workers and their allies" takes place within the party and is guaranteed by intraparty democracy ("Elements of the Pluralism," pp. 22–23).
28. Z. Mlynář, in his important article "Problems of Political Leadership," rejected the "effort to solve these problems without discussions and controversies, without democratic deliberation of various possible alternatives, without serious scientific and theoretical elaboration of the perspectives of development" (p. 93). A Hungarian, I. Santa, referred to the "participation of experts," "drawing up and presenting several alternatives or . . . several platforms. This made possible the comparison of differing concepts, a choice among them, their eventual combination, or even their rejection, as well as agreement between the demands of expertise and democracy" ("Debate and Party Unity," *Társadalmi szemle*, June 1967. Cf. M. Soukup, "On the Conception and Tasks of Political Science," *Nová mysl* 20, no. 18 (6 September 1966): 13–15.
29. For a fuller discussion of these concepts see chapters 1 and 2, H. Gordon Skilling and Franklyn Griffiths, eds., *Interest Groups in Soviet Politics* (Princeton: Princeton University Press, 1971). Ionescu is critical of such an interest-group approach, but he himself treats "political checks" and "dissent" as distinct forms of interest-group activity (*Politics of the European Communist States*, pp. 88–95, 226). For a comparative analysis of group conflict in all Communist systems, including China, see H. Gordon Skilling, "Group Conflict and Political Change," in Chalmers Johnson, ed., *Change in Communist Systems* (Stanford: Stanford University Press,

tige which afforded them some possibilities of expressing their views and which gave these views a certain authority and influence. No doubt in some cases such groups were linked with political leaders who sought changes of policy and perhaps of leadership and were thus involved indirectly in the struggle for power among rival factions. They often operated, however, as pressure groups, seeking primarily to influence the actions of the leadership. They were not always organized institutionally and were usually amorphous and informal congeries of individuals of the same occupation or of similar viewpoint on public issues.

Indeed, within each occupational group there was likely to be, not a unanimity of viewpoint, but distinct cleavages between more conservative and more liberal orientations. Such *opinion groups* usually expressed, not an exclusively selfish interest of their occupational group, but a particular conception of the public interest in such matters as economic reform, legal and political changes, or literary freedom. As a result, intellectual groups often articulated the interests of broader social groups which were unable to express their views directly through their own associations. Like-minded opinion groups among intellectuals frequently formed loose, informal alliances with each other, with segments of the bureaucratic interest groups, and with factions in the top leadership, thus creating at least in an amorphous sense a conservative-reformist dichotomy. On the whole, the forces making for change and reform were found primarily outside the party apparatus, among the creative and technical intelligentsia; the party apparatus, although divided, was frequently a conservative force. Yet more conservative groupings also existed in most of the intellectual or bureaucratic groups and in rare cases the party apparatus and certain top leaders espoused reforms opposed by the former.

The Changing Context of Political Action

The paradox of post-Stalin Eastern Europe was that, although the basic structure of the political system changed but little and the leaders did not modify their attitude toward opposition in the abstract, there were significant alterations — in all countries except Albania — in the way the system in fact operated. The making of policy remained exclusively in the hands of the top party leaders, but the style of decision making had undergone striking changes. In almost every country there was a substantial shift in the role of the party and, in particular, in its relations with the other major bureaucratic groups, notably the police, the state apparatus,

1970), pp. 215–35. For an application of this classification scheme to successive phases of Communist Czechoslovakia, see my "Leadership and Group Conflict in Czechoslovakia," in R. Barry Farrell, ed., *Political Leadership in Eastern Europe and the Soviet Union* (Chicago: Aldine, 1970), pp. 276–93.

and the managerial class generally. Where political relaxation occurred — in Poland, Hungary and Czechoslovakia — the diminution of coercion brought with it, not only a decline in the prestige and a reduction in the influence of the police, but also a substantial broadening of the area of permissible discussion. This in turn gave a fillip to the manifesting of loyal opposition in these more "liberal" states, sometimes taking the form of significantly unorthodox specific dissent. Even in these countries, however, the influence of the police continued to be present. In the hard-line states, such as Albania, Bulgaria, East Germany, and Romania, the security forces remained a significant obstacle in the path of liberalization and discouraged the expression of oppositional viewpoints. Even in Yugoslavia the security forces, which as late as 1966 had resisted the course of economic and political reform, were downgraded only after the removal of Ranković in that year and the purge that followed.

Another important development was the broadening of the authority of the state administrators and the inclusion in the state bureaucracy, at least in an advisory capacity, of experts and specialists in the relevant fields.[30] This tendency was most pronounced in Yugoslavia, where the role of the party had ostensibly been reduced to that of a "guiding force,"[31] but it was noticeable in varying degrees in other states where the party's traditional leadership function was maintained. The economic reform which was gradually introduced in several states further reduced the role of the party officials, while increasing the influence of the managers and experts in the running of industry and commerce. This was particularly reinforced in Hungary by the inclusion of non-Communists in important managerial and supervisory posts. Such developments primarily affected the processes of government, or rule making, but they also stimulated the utterance of oppositional views and smudged the dividing line between government and opposition. Consultation with experts, official and nonofficial, and the generally freer atmosphere of discussion encouraged the expression of dissent and proposals of alternative courses of action. The experts were increasingly expected, not merely to advise and consent, but to advise and, if necessary, dissent.

ASSEMBLIES AND ELECTIONS   Changes in the context of decision making were least pronounced in the functioning of the representative system and the mass, or societal, organizations. The representative bodies in nearly all countries (the exception is Yugoslavia) were still deprived of the real power of policy making, which remained in the hands of the

30. Carl Beck, "Bureaucratic Conservatism and Innovation in Eastern Europe," *Comparative Political Studies* 1, no. 2 (July 1968): 275–94.
31. Tito, however, found it necessary on occasion to stress the political role of the League of Communists (*New York Times*, 22 November 1966).

organs of the party. In Bulgaria, Czechoslovakia, Hungary, and Romania there was criticism of the inactivity of the parliaments, and changes were introduced to make the legislature, particularly its committees, places of active, critical discussion. Plenary sessions became longer and more businesslike; committees were more active; a question time was introduced; the parliamentary responsibility of ministers was proclaimed. The assemblies continued, however, to be the scene of unanimous approval of proposed legislation and did not offer a locus of serious opposition or a medium for articulating diverse interests and opinions. In the Polish Sejm, however, the legislative committees played an important role in the discussion of legislation; opposition was sometimes expressed in the plenary session, notably by the Catholic deputies, and negative votes were occasionally recorded.[32] In Yugoslavia the assembly was an even more active arena of debate and opposition, and the defeat of proposed legislation occurred from time to time. In an event unique in the Communist world, the government of the Slovene Republic was on one occasion compelled to resign as a result of an adverse vote, although it resumed office shortly thereafter.[33]

Efforts to invigorate the assemblies were likely to remain abortive as long as the elections simply endorsed the dominant position of the ruling party and excluded competition by opposition parties. In no country of the region were such parties permitted to enter into electoral contests. A minor element of competitiveness was introduced in Hungary and Romania in the form of the legal possibility of multiple candidacies for office, but so far this has not led to frequent electoral conflicts. Where other parties exist, as in Czechoslovakia, Bulgaria, East Germany, and Poland, they were allies and partners of the Communist party and did not compete with it for power.[34] At the most, they might give a modest expression to the interests of certain social or religious groups and seek to influence the ruling party in these spheres. Even in Poland, where the non-Communist parties were more meaningful forces, elections were not competitive but constituted what two Communist theorists called "semi-plebiscitary" or "consent" elections.[35] As a result of the fact that

32. See V. C. Chrypinski, "Legislative Committees in Polish Lawmaking," *Slavic Review* 25, no. 2 (June 1966): 247–58.

33. *East Europe* 16, no. 1 (January 1967): 28; and no. 2 (February 1967): 37.

34. See Jerzy J. Wjatr, "One-Party Systems: The Concept and Issue for Comparative Studies," in *Cleavages, Ideologies and Party Systems: Contributions to Comparative Political Sociology*, Transactions of Westermarck Society, ed. E. Allardt and Y. Littunen, vol. 10 (Helsinki, 1964), pp. 281–90. Wjatr argues that the Polish system is not, strictly speaking, a one-party system but rather a "hegemonical party system" in which other parties coexist with the Communist party but, as in one-party states, there is no real competition for power and no political opposition.

35. Wjatr and Przeworski, "Control without Opposition," pp. 238–39. A fuller analysis of Polish elecions is given by Wjatr in his chapter, "Elections and Voting Behavior in Poland," in A. Ranney, ed., *Essays on the Behavioral Study of Politics* (Urbana:

there were more candidates than seats to be filled and that voters could express preferences for certain candidates and parties, Wjatr argues, the elections provided "an opportunity to criticize government policy by lowering the electoral acceptance of this policy." In this situation "the consent elections do not decide who will rule the country, but they influence the way in which the country will be ruled." [36] In Yugoslavia, no other parties have existed, but a kind of national front, in the form of the Socialist League, has played a significant part. Elections have assumed a somewhat different character in that the number of candidates has considerably exceeded the number of seats to be filled. As a result, a personal competition for office has taken place, although this has not represented opposition in terms of policy.[37]

Traditionally lacking in Communist systems has been an effective system of parliamentary control of the executive power. The danger of uncontrolled power was recognized, however, and the need for a more powerful public opinion as a check on the abuse of power was stressed.[38] As a substitute for parliamentary opposition of a constitutional type, a question time was in some countries introduced in the assembly, and more vigorous criticism of administration by deputies was encouraged, but with minimal results. There were also extraparliamentary checks on official actions, through the newspapers and by so-called "committees of people's control," which were supposed to act as watchdogs of the public interests. Paradoxically, the chief source of criticism of executive arbitrariness or of failures in administrative action was the party itself, especially its leaders and its top agencies, the central committee and the apparatus. This traditional device, used even in Stalinist times, represented a kind of control from above, quite different from the control from below of democratic societies. In Albania, for instance, the Central Committee in an open letter of March 1966 censured the bureaucratic elite

University of Illinois Press, 1962), pp. 237–51, especially p. 239. For further discussion of the Polish system see Wjatr, "One-Party Systems," pp. 287–89, and his "The Electoral System and Elements of Pluralism in a 'One Party' System: Poland," *Transactions of the Fifth World Congress of Sociology* (International Sociological Association, 1962) 4: 381–86.

36. Wjatr, "Elections and Voting Behavior in Poland," p. 239, 251.

37. This has been called Yugoslavia's "1½ party system" (*New York Times*, 29 May 1966). A Yugoslav, M. Popović, used the term "non-party system"; see S. Stanković, "Yugoslavia's Critical Year," *East Europe* 16, no. 4 (April 1967): 16. See also R. V. Burks and S. A. Stanković, "Jugoslawien auf dem Weg zu halbfreien Wahlen," *Osteuropa* 17, no 2/3 (February–March 1967): 131–46. For further discussion of elections in Communist countries of Eastern Europe, see Skilling, *Governments of Communist East Europe*, pp. 130–34.

38. See, for instance, the articles by Miroslav Jodl, a Czech sociologist, in *Literární noviny*, 13 November 1965 and 22 January 1966. The Slovak Lakatoš wrote of the manipulation of the ruled by the rulers and urged genuinely free elections as a means of preventing this (*Právny obzor*, no. 3 [1966], pp. 213–22; translated in *East Europe* 15, no. 6 [June 1966]: 22–23).

of party and state.[39] It is a curious paradox of Communist systems that an important agency of opposition was, in a sense, the ruling party itself, which assumed the functions of supervising and criticizing the actions of the administration and even, in some cases, of leading persons in government and party.[40]

THE WEAKNESS OF ORGANIZED PRESSURE GROUPS   The mass, or societal, organizations, such as the trade unions and the associations of women and youth, have not usually evolved into genuine defenders of the special group interests of their members or the people they claim to represent. In most countries these organizations remained what they had always been, transmission belts employed by the party for imposing on them the party's concepts of group interests and of the general interest of society. In few cases did they emerge as exponents of opposition or serve as arenas for the expression of such views by their members. A novel development, in Bulgaria, Hungary, and Romania, and later in Czechoslovakia, was the establishment of national councils or unions of the collective farms, which have given the peasants a kind of organizational representation comparable in form at least to that of the industrial workers. In Czechoslovakia prior to the reform year, there was outspoken criticism of the mass organizations for their lack of genuine representative character and their failure to act in defense of group interests, and measures were suggested by critics to make them effective.[41] In the case of the Czechoslovak youth movement, an unprecedented claim was made by a radical student spokesman on one occasion that they should be permitted to express views, if necessary, in opposition to those of the party.[42]

Even official statements at the highest level, in some countries, asserted that more vigorous expression of group interests by these organizations was desirable and that the party should consider these special interests in working out public policy in relevant spheres.[43] Special efforts were

39. *Christian Science Monitor*, 31 March 1966.
40. The daily organ of the Hungarian People's Front, *Magyar nemzet*, used this as an argument that an opposition party was not necessary. Criticism, it declared, was "the essence of opposition." In Hungary "the party and the government criticize everything at all times where things are not going as they should and thus supply the checking and criticizing functions of an opposition" (28 August 1966).
41. Z Mlynář (*Rudé právo*, 16 August 1966). The same writer, in the international Communist organ, argued that these organizations should not serve as mere transmission belts operating in one direction only ("Problems of Political Leadership," p. 97). Wjatr wrote of the dual functions of various interest groups, serving not only as "pressure groups" which "represent the interests of their groups vis-à-vis the Party and the government" but also as "mobilizing groups" which mobilize their members to the tasks put forth by party and government ("Elements of the Pluralism," p. 24).
42. *Student*, no. 4 (1966).
43. See for instance, the speech by Kadar, *Nepszabadsag*, 29 November 1966.

made by certain states to broaden the authority of the trade unions in particular and to encourage them both to speak more genuinely for the workers, especially at the local level, and to serve as consultants and advisors of the government and party at the national level.[44] The unions were thus expected to serve as transmission belts operating in two directions, providing information needed by the rulemakers on the attitudes of the workers while funneling policy decisions and directives to the masses. How far these principles would in fact be applied was difficult to estimate, especially as the trade unions remained under the general direction of the party and were not regarded as independent pressure groups.[45] In Yugoslavia, however, the trade unions became somewhat more independent and on occasion exerted a considerable influence on the course of legislation. The national plan for 1965, for instance, was rejected by the trade unions and had to be revised extensively before parliamentary approval. Moreover, strikes occurred from time to time and were treated by the authorities as legitimate forms of action. Apart from Yugoslavia, the most notable action was taken in Hungary in the enactment of a labor code (in October 1967) significantly widening the authority of the trade unions and giving them a veto over managerial actions in certain matters.

THE RISE OF THE INTELLECTUALS   The most impressive development in some East European countries was the emergence of public discussion, either in the mass media (the newspapers and, to a lesser degree, radio and television) or in scholarly periodicals, congresses, and the writers unions. Even novels, plays, poetry, and scholarly works became vehicles for articulating oppositional views or group interests. This activity was in part a product of an official decision to permit freer discussion and to encourage wider consultation outside the party. Official measures of de-Stalinization sometimes encouraged intellectuals to express unanticipated radical criticism of specific facets of the regimes' programs, verging sometimes on fundamental opposition. This in turn often led to official censure and renewed restrictions.

For instance, during the critical early years of de-Stalinization in Hungary and Poland, the writers and journalists emerged as a powerful force seeking an acceleration of the process of liberalization and constituted a radical opposition to the existing regimes. In Hungary the literary community, together with other sectors of the intelligentsia, prepared the ground for the subsequent revolution. Although the revolt was crushed, the liberal writers continued to act as an opposition, at first refusing to

44. M. Gamarnikow, "New Tasks for the Trade Unions," *East Europe* 16, no. 4 (April 1967): 18–26.
45. Cf. M. Pastyřík, "Trade Unions and Participation of the Workers in the Direction of Production," *Nová mysl* 20, no. 22 (3 November 1966): 6–9.

write for publication and later acting as spokesmen for greater freedom of expression. Similarly, the Polish writers and the intellectuals generally, without taking the road of violent revolt, were in large degree responsible for the events of October 1956 and continued to express their own views vigorously thereafter. Even when the Gomulka regime reverted to stricter control of literature and the arts, the writers on more than one occasion defended their interests and protested against government actions.[46]

In Czechoslovakia in the mid-1960s scholars, writers, and journalists became a significant political factor, pressing, in their associations and in their journals, for de-Stalinization and greater freedom of expression and in some cases directly challenging the government and individual leaders.[47] A celebrated case was the courageous attack by the Slovak journalist M. Hysko on Prime Minister Široký. Although Hysko was sharply censured by no less a person than Novotný, president and first secretary, Široký was soon after removed from office. Most significantly, Hysko's speech was published in the organ of the Slovak Communist party, *Pravda*, which thus served as a vehicle of oppositional attitudes. Other literary periodicals, in particular *Literární noviny* and *Kultúrny život*, weekly journals of the writers unions, were for years in effect organs of opposition, publishing critical articles dealing with all aspects of Czech and Slovak life and bringing down on their heads torrents of official disapproval.[48] In 1967 the congress of the Writers Union was the occasion for outspoken criticism of current policies, including the regime's support of the Arab states in the war with Israel and of the practice of censorship. Retaliation in the form of expulsions of three prominent writers from the party and other curbs on the activities of the organization did not eliminate the problems. Instead it contributed to a political crisis which shook the Novotný regime to its foundations.

Social scientists and other scholars also began to play a more important role in the political life of certain countries. Lawyers, economists, sociologists, and even historians and philosophers acted, like the writers, as influential pressure groups. Opinion groups within these professions, conservative as well as liberal, voiced conflicting opinions on public policy and represented oppositions of varying outlook. In particular, the economists played a significant role in criticizing the traditional planning

46. Among these occasions were the letter to the government from thirty-four writers protesting censorship and paper restrictions in 1964 and the mass demonstrations by students in 1968.
47. See Skilling, *Communism National and International*, chap. 7, for a detailed discussion of the 1963 events.
48. See the Central Committee resolution on the cultural periodicals, *Rudé právo*, 4 April 1964. In January 1966 the party organ, *Život strany* referred again to "disquieting tendencies" in these periodicals. In 1967 *Literární noviny* was taken out of the hands of the Writers Union and placed under the Ministry of Culture.

system, in advocating economic reforms, and often in complaining about the slowness of the reforms officially adopted. Sharp cleavages on the nature of the reforms manifested themselves among the economists and between economists and bureaucratic groups.[49] Similar controversies among historians, in attempting a more objective reevaluation of the past, often had direct political relevance. Lawyers were less influential but contributed actively to discussions of legal and political reform. The rise of the discipline of sociology introduced a new element in scholarship capable of serving as an instrument in the formation of policy. A unique feature of certain countries was the part played by philosophers in expressing dissident views and advocating greater freedom of discussion.[50] Indeed, the latter need was the common concern of scholars in all fields, some of whom openly raised demands for unrestricted freedom of expansion.[51]

THE CONTINUING LIMITS ON DISSENT   It should be emphasized that opposition of the kinds we have been discussing differs greatly from what would normally be regarded as legitimate opposition in a democratic political system. Dissent in Communist regimes had perforce to operate within strict limits, although not as strict as was customarily assumed and as was once the case. The party's monopoly of the instruments of coercion could prevent violent revolutionary opposition; and in any case, after the fiasco of Hungary, such a resort to force was not likely to occur except in extraordinary circumstances. Moreover, although the coercive power of the regimes was exercised more lightly than in the past and not usually in the form of ruthless terror, its continuing presence inhibited nonviolent opposition of a fundamental or integral kind. Similarly, the nature of the electoral system and the domination by a single party ruled out effective parliamentary or electoral opposition. The centralized, unified nature of the party set strict limits on factional opposition, although this did not exclude the possibility of conflicts of leadership groups within the politburo. The party's continuing claim to control all facets of society circumscribed the overt, autonomous action of organized interest groups but did not entirely prevent it.

Adherence to a single official theory, Marxism-Leninism, restricted the

49. Note the role, for instance, of Ota Šik, E. Loebl, R. Selucký, and other reform-minded economists in Czechoslovakia. Similar discussions occurred in Bulgaria, Hungary, and Yugoslavia.
50. Note, for instance, the role of Prof. L. Kolakowski, dissident Polish Marxist philosopher, or that of the East German Wolfgang Harich, imprisoned in 1965 for revisionism. Cf. the expression of dissident Marxist views by the Slovene theoretical journal *Praxis*.
51. Such demands were made by the Slovak economist Loebl, the Slovak writer L. Novomeský, the Polish philosopher T. Kotarbinski, and the East German scientist R. Havemann.

expression of oppositional views and compelled dissent to be expressed in orthodox terms, but it did not exclude significant divergence concerning, for instance, economic reform. The party's monopoly of the means of communication also did not rule out the expression of diverse views on sensitive issues such as literary and scholarly freedom or economic and legal reform. While paying homage to the idea of freedom of discussion, however, the party never failed to stress that this freedom was not an absolute one — and that criticism, or dissent, must be conducted within the framework of Marxism-Leninism and the general party line and might not express "bourgeois" or "anti-Communist" views.[52] When necessary, the party could, and did, resort to administrative sanctions, such as the closing down of a periodical, the removal of an editor, public censure of an offending critic, expulsion from the party, dismissal from official posts, and, in extreme cases, arrest and trial.[53] This in turn sometimes led to continued resistance by the person in question and perhaps to protests by his colleagues.[54] It might even, on occasion, prepare the ground for major changes of leadership and policy, as in Czechoslovakia in 1968.

Czechoslovakia: A Special Case

The extraordinary events in Czechoslovakia in 1968 constituted in many respects an exception, at least temporarily, to the general tendencies that had hitherto prevailed in Communist East Europe and opened up the possibility of a fundamental alteration of the role of opposition in that country, and perhaps eventually in other Communist countries. Although fuller treatment of the Czechoslovak exception will be given in the following chapter, certain comments seem desirable on its implications for the general argument of this chapter.

52. The Czech journalist J. Hájek distinguished between "liberalization" and "democratization" and rejected the former because it permitted all kinds of opinion and afforded "equal rights to the opposition" (*Rudé právo*, 1 April 1966).
53. The case of *Literární noviny* in Czechoslovakia has been mentioned (note 48). Earlier, in Poland, the newspapers *Po Prostu* and *Kultura* were closed down; in Yugoslavia in 1964 *Perspektive* and in Czechoslovakia in 1966 *Tvař* were stopped. A prominent case of expulsion was that of the Polish philosopher Kolakowski. In East Germany, Professor Havemann was deprived of his posts in the university but remained at liberty. In 1964–65 in Poland the students Kuron and Modzelewski were imprisoned for their opposition activity. In Yugoslavia, in addition to the well-known case of Djilas, that of Mihajlov has already been referred to (note 8). In Czechoslovakia, three prominent writers were expelled from the party in 1967, and another, L. Mnačko, who left for Israel in protest against the party's pro-Arab policy, was also deprived of his citizenship.
54. A notable case was the resistance to Kolakowski's expulsion (see notes 50, 53) by students and intellectuals. Letters of protest by writers led to further expulsions and resignations from the party. Heated criticism was reportedly expressed at party meetings in Warsaw University, the Academy of Sciences, and the Writers Union.

It should be stressed at the outset that the Action Program of the Dubček regime did not endorse the principle of a formal, institutionalized political opposition. The leading role of the party was in fact to be retained but was to be exercised by persuasion and justified by the winning of public support through the party's deeds. The program expressly excluded the idea of opposition parties and argued instead for a political system based on a National Front representing a partnership of the revitalized political parties and mass associations, based on a common program. The National Front would thus represent "a political platform that would not divide political parties into governing and opposition parties in the sense that an opposition against the line of state policy or the line of the National Front would be created and that a political struggle for state power would be conducted." [55] In the words of one of the more reform-oriented leaders, Čestmír Císař:

> We do not regard as correct isolated opinions concerning the necessity of creating a new political party, with an opposition mission as a massive counterweight to our party. A plurality of political parties competing for power . . . would create the danger of a violent struggle and call forth the need for a violent defense of socialism. The rise of an opposition party with an antisocialist program would mean the end of the Czechoslovak experiment of creating a model of democratic socialism.[56]

In spite of this adamant rejection of a multiparty system involving opposition, the Dubček regime envisaged substantial reforms of political procedures which were described as guaranteeing a genuinely democratic socialism. These reforms, as will be indicated more fully in the next chapter, included guarantees of freedom of expression and of association, an endorsement of independent interest-group activity, a freer system of elections, a federal system of Czech-Slovak relations, the elimination of terror and legal protection of individual rights, and above all, a democratization of the party itself. The implementation of this program would certainly have established an unusual system of institutionalized dissent, unique in the Communist world. This would not involve, it was argued, an opposition in the bourgeois parliamentary sense but rather an *oponentura* (opponent system) in the academic sense,[57]

55. The Action Program was published in *Rudé právo*, 10 April 1968, and in English translation in R. A. Remington, ed., *Winter in Prague, Documents on Czechoslovak Communism in Crisis* (Cambridge, Mass.: M.I.T. Press, 1969), pp. 88–137, especially p. 103.
56. *Rudé právo*, 29 April 1968.
57. This term (equivalent to the German *opponent*) is used in European academic practice to describe the procedure of official criticism of a thesis or a research proposal in an examining board. The *opponent*, something of a "devil's advocate," is assigned the task of offering criticism but is not necessarily obliged to reject the

offering widespread opportunity for the presentation of alternative policies and conflicting viewpoints in policy making.

In actual fact, from March 1968 until the invasion in August, Czechoslovak politics assumed many of the normal features of a democratic system, with open and sharp conflict of rival forces and diverse opinions. There was widespread public debate on specific policies and frequent expression of fundamental opposition by individuals, mass media, and organized groups and associations. There was even some opportunity for the expression of integral opposition by critics of communism, although these so-called "antisocialist forces" were on the whole marginal and much less significant than criticism and opposition "within the system." Moreover, these months were characterized by an intense struggle for power and influence among rival leadership groups, constituting a new form of factional opposition but one carried on more publicly and with democratic procedures for resolving these conflicts within the party. In the absence of elections and serious competing parties, the system remained fundamentally authoritarian but a "democratizing and pluralistic authoritarianism" [58] which contained striking potentialities for further democratic evolution.

In Soviet eyes this situation, with its encouragement of opposition forces and its toleration even of antisocialist trends, was tantamount to "counterrevolution" in the sense of "a political opposition" seeking to restore capitalism.[59] Soviet doctrine was unwilling to approve a political system which permitted "a free play of forces." [60] The trend toward democratization was brought to a halt by military intervention, but, paradoxically, not at once and not without final convulsive struggles of the embryonic pluralistic system. In the seven days immediately following the invasion and preceding the conclusion, under duress, of the Soviet-Czechoslovak agreement in Moscow, the world witnessed dramatic nonviolent resistance to the invasion itself. Less visible, but even more significant, was the secret holding of the Fourteenth Party Congress in a Prague factory and its condemnation of the invasion and reassertion of the goals of reform.

For some seven months thereafter, in spite of the continued massive presence of Soviet armed forces and the subjugation of the restored Dubček regime to constant and direct controls and influences by Moscow,

proposal or thesis. The term was used in Czechoslovak politics to describe what might be called loyal or positive criticism of a measure of public policy as distinct from fundamental disagreement with the party. Cf. J. Smrkovský, Literární noviny, 15 September 1967.
58. This term is used in my classification of Communist systems in Johnson, Change in Communist Systems, pp. 225–27.
59. Pravda, 22 August 1968; in English, Remington, Winter in Prague, p. 317.
60. For example, A. Lukyanov, Pravda, 4 December 1968.

the Czechoslovak political system, although increasingly authoritarian, continued to exhibit many quasi-pluralist features retained from the reform period, including elements of vigorous opposition.[61] Dubček became the focus of massive pressures and counterpressures from below and from above, as well as from outside, some urging a more conciliatory and collaborationist attitude toward Soviet demands and others a firmer and more determined resistance.[62] Many of the reforms were at once reversed, but some continued, in whole or in part. A federal state was established by constitutional law on 28 October as planned, but the corresponding reconstruction of the party was perforce abandoned. The meeting of the Fourteenth Congress was, however, declared illegal and its decisions invalid. Although the more overtly political groups, such as KAN and K-231,[63] were forbidden, many organized interest groups came into existence, and workers' councils were formed in many factories. There continued to be vigorous discussion, in spite of censorship, in the media of communication and in the legislative bodies and the party organizations. Organized pressure groups, such as the trade unions, the students, the Academy of Sciences, and the unions of creative artists, conducted repeated acts of resistance. Examples of open dissent were the three-day student strike, mass demonstrations on Independence Day, the suicide by burning of the student Jan Palach, and the circulation of written protests. This represented specific opposition to the regime on many issues, and sometimes fundamental opposition toward the postoccupation course, and often verged on integral opposition to the entire political system as it was evolving under Soviet control. A fierce factional struggle ensued, as more progressive leaders and forces sought to defend Dubček and to retain as much of the reform program as possible, and conservative forces sought, ultimately with success, to discredit and to oust him and his supporters and to terminate all reforms.

Gustav Husák emerged in the forefront as a key critic of Dubček's policies, both before and after the occupation, and as a major alternative leader. He was especially critical of "pressure groups," acting, as he said, "without the consciousness of the leading Party and state factors and against their intentions." [64] He demanded that an end be put to such

---

61. For a discussion of postinvasion Czechoslovak politics, see Jan Provaznik, "The Politics of Retrenchment," *Problems of Communism* 18, no. 4–5 (July–October 1969): 2–16; Pavel Tigrid, "Czechoslovakia: A Post-Mortem, II," *Survey*, nos. 74–75 (Winter–Spring, 1970), pp. 112–42. See also the book by Tigrid, *La chute irrésistible d'Alexander Dubček* (Paris: Calmann-Lévy, 1969). For a briefer discussion, using the term "quasi-pluralist authoritarianism," see my "Leadership and Group Conflict in Czechoslovakia," in Farrell, *Political Leadership*, pp. 288–93. See also Johnson, *Change in Communist Systems*, pp. 224–25.
62. M. Lakatoš, *Zítřek*, 8 January 1969.
63. See below, chap. 4, pp. 127, 136.
64. Farrell, *Political Leadership*, p. 291.

acts of opposition and to the political crises that resulted. Still another serious crisis was, however, occasioned by mass demonstrations throughout the republic in March 1969 in celebration of the Czechoslovak hockey victory over the Soviet team in Stockholm, accompanied by violent assaults on Soviet military and other installations by the excited crowds. This provided the opportunity for the replacement of Dubček by Husák in April 1969 and cleared the way for the complete ending of the major reforms of 1968 and the repression of all opposition forces. Even this was not immediately accomplished but came only as a result of a step-by-step process of consolidation, including the curbing of the remaining organs of free expression[65] and the purging of oppositional elements from party and state organs. By the spring of 1970, Husák had succeeded in reestablishing the status quo ante, in the form, however, not of the crumbling Stalinism of the sixties but rather of the quasi-totalitarian system of the late fifties, or even, apart from outright terror, of the early fifties.

The Future Outlook

How the process of opposition may develop in Eastern Europe in the future, in the light of these events, is difficult to predict. Prior to the Czechoslovak reform movement, there was speculation in the West on the possibility of the emergence in the Communist system of a kind of political pluralism.[66] Even in the Communist world there has been occasional advocacy of an institutionalized form of opposition as a condition of an enlarged democracy.[67] The most optimistic forecast in the West was that

65. A minor example of the brief continued resistance by the newspapers and journals to the Husák course was the publication, in translation and after slight censorship, of a brief version of this chapter, under the title "Opozice ve východní Evropě," in a Czech monthly journal devoted to popularizing history, *Dějiny a současnost* 11, no. 5 (1969): 13–16. The journal was forced to suspend publication after three further issues.

66. See the discussion on the future of monolithic parties in the special issue of *Government and Opposition* cited above (note 2). Cf. Skilling, *Governments of Communist East Europe*, concluding chapter. See also Ionescu, paper read at the International Conference of Futuribles in Paris, April 1965, mimeographed. In that paper he speculates on the possible emergence of other parties and of a more genuine parliamentarism and a greater role in decision making by specialized bodies and associations. "An a-political pluralism of the future," he suggested, "could replace the political pluralism of the past" (p. 17). See also Jerzy J. Wjatr, "The Future of Political Institutions under Socialism," paper read at the same conference, mimeographed, pp. 22–26. Cf. A. Brown, "Pluralistic Trends in Czechoslovakia," *Soviet Studies* 17, no. 4 (April 1966): 453–72. Carl Beck wrote that "the thrust of the discussion and of institutional reform has been toward a greater degree of participation by a variety of political actors and social forces in the entire political systems (sic)" ("Bureaucratic Conservatism," p. 15).

67. For instance, M. Lakatoš, in a book completed in 1967 but not published until after the invasion, *Úvahy o hodnotách demokracie* (Prague, 1968), chap. 4, argued

made by Ghita Ionescu, who analyzed the growth of checks and dissent in the European Communist states and, citing Yugoslavia as a kind of model, predicted the institutionalization of these tendencies.[68] This he regarded as "an irreversible trend," likely to continue where it had already begun and to spread to other countries where it had not. In his opinion this development reflected the necessities of a rapidly developing industrial society, which, in its concern for "efficiency," must replace "coercion" by "consultation." He also expressed the conviction that in the *European* Communist states (as he called them) this process would be swifter and more marked than in the Soviet Union, due to the relative shortness of the period of Communism and the relative recency of their pre-Communist experience of political pluralism.[69]

The sudden evolution of Czechoslovakia in the direction of an institutionalized pluralism and a legitimized opposition in 1968 seemed at first to confirm these optimistic predictions. Had there been no invasion and had Dubček's program of reforms been fully carried out, a similar process of democratization might have occurred in other Communist systems and a basic transformation of the nature of Communist rule thus accomplished. The Czechoslovak experience, however, went far beyond anything that could legitimately have been expected from previous trends in that country and elsewhere and yet fell short of a fully constitutional order based on an effective multiparty system with recognized opposition parties. Moreover it was clear that the evolution of Czechoslovakia had not been evitable and had resulted from many factors, including not merely the crisis of the economy, important as that was, but also nationality conflicts, the clash of social interests, and the yearning for intellectual freedom. The very nature of the Communist system, in particular its evil features in the fifties and the slowness of their removal in the sixties, contributed to the rising tide of opposition and the ultimate downfall of the regime. It was also clear that the intellectual and political tradition of Czechs and Slovaks, long submerged, became a powerful factor for change in the direction of a more democratic system. In other Communist countries, but for Soviet intervention, the development would have reflected the particular forces and conditions and diversity of traditions of each country.

---

the need for a legal opposition or *oponentura*, since otherwise opposition would exist de facto "outside and against the political system." Distinguishing two types of opposition, he argued that, although the political order did not allow the legal functioning of "basic opposition," which sought a change in the system, it required "an opposition operating on the basis of the social-political system." "For a civil society the possibility of an opposition is the possibility of expressing conflicting interests and of reconciling these conflicts democratically" (p. 87).

68. Ionescu, *Politics of the European Communist States*, pp. 80–85, 166–69, 190, 271–78. See above, note 11, for his definitions of these terms.

69. Ibid., pp. 5–10, 272.

The subsequent invasion and interruption of the Prague reform indicated, however, that the external factor had been minimized or neglected, not only by those directly involved in Czechoslovakia but also by Western observers.[70] The overwhelming influence of the Soviet Union in Eastern Europe and its own backwardness of political development in comparison with most of its smaller Communist neighbors are factors that cannot be ignored in the future. The Soviet condemnation of Czechoslovak evolution and the forceful action taken to interrupt it seemed to rule out the likelihood of any comparable radical reform elsewhere in Eastern Europe and even to threaten the reversal of the moderate progress achieved in the more liberal Communist states. Poland had indeed already embarked on a much more rigorous course of semitotalitarian control of public life after the repression of the protest movement in the spring of 1968.[71] These events in Czechoslovakia and Poland could not but deflate the idea of a common and preordained trend toward greater liberalization of the Communist systems.

Yet one should guard against hasty conclusions, in this case that the doors to reform in Eastern Europe have been irrevocably closed. Forces making for liberalization are still present in most, perhaps all, Eastern European states, even though they are now confronted with powerful counterforces. Hungary has been able, as of the time of writing, to proceed with a drastic economic reform and to continue some relaxations of political and cultural life. And, as always, the unpredictable often disturbs the apparently most valid generalizations about future trends. Massive demonstrations and riots in Poland in late 1970, occasioned by severe price rises and other economic measures, revealed the continued existence in Poland of profound dissent, if not outright disaffection. Whether the spontaneous explosions in the Baltic cities represented resistance merely to specific economic policies or, as was suggested by the attacks on the police and on party and government buildings, a more fundamental or integral opposition to the regime or the system itself was difficult to assess. The regime was able, by ruthless use of force, to crush the revolts and restore order. What was most significant, however, was that, for the second time in Poland (the lesser Pozman revolt in 1956 being the first), spontaneous actions by the working masses had produced a fundamental shift in leadership, this time in the removal of Gomulka, and led to significant changes in policies under the new leaders.

This success of open resistance could hardly fail to have impact on thinking elsewhere in the bloc and suggested the possibility of other

70. See my subsequent discussion of the "external factor" in the process of change under Communism in Johnson, *Political Leadership*, pp. 232–34.
71. See A. Ross Johnson, "Poland: The End of the Post-October Era," *Survey*, no. 68 (July 1968), pp. 87–98, and documents on the Polish events, ibid., pp. 99–117.

tactics of opposition than the peaceful orderly reform movement in Czechoslovakia. Nonetheless, in each country evolution will depend on a subtle balance of human factors, none of them predetermined, including the willingness of dissenters to take the risks of active or open opposition and the readiness of the regime to permit specific or fundamental opposition, an equilibrium difficult to maintain and easily disturbed on either side. The future of opposition therefore continues to depend on conscious acts of human will, the outcome of which cannot be predicted. As always, the towering influence of the Soviet Union remains a conditioning factor likely to discourage far-reaching reforms unless the Soviet regime itself undergoes changes comparable to those of Czechoslovakia in 1968 or Poland in 1970.

4

CZECHOSLOVAKIA'S
INTERRUPTED REVOLUTION

H. Gordon Skilling

The Soviet invasion of Czechoslovakia in August 1968 interrupted a process of far-reaching change which had been under way since the coming into power of Alexander Dubček in January of that year.[1] Although not accompanied by violence and in some respects representing a gradual evolution, the changes in leadership, policy, and political procedures, introduced or planned, were substantial enough to be regarded as revolutionary in the context of a Communist political system. What Dubček was attempting to do was to dismantle the Stalinist system inherited from Klement Gottwald and Antonín Novotný and to rebuild on the ruins of their discredited regime a more stable and more democratic Communist system, more responsive to the wishes and the interests of the people. This process of guided yet spontaneous change, reflecting strong indigenous forces in Czech and Slovak society, had not been completed — was, indeed, in midpassage — when it was rudely interrupted by force from outside. Whatever the ultimate outcome, this brief interlude in Czech and Slovak history deserves careful examination as a unique experiment, never before attempted on such a broad scale, to "democratize" a Communist polity.[2]

A slightly different version of this chapter was originally published in *Canadian Slavonic Papers (Revue canadienne des Slavistes)* 10, no. 4 (1968): 409–29. The author is preparing a full-length book on this subject, tentatively under the same title.

1. For a fuller discussion of the factors leading to the rise of Dubček and of the immediate aftermath, see H. Gordon Skilling "Crisis and Change in Czechoslovakia," *International Journal* 23, no. 3 (1968): 456–65; H. Gordon Skilling, "The Fall of Novotný in Czechoslovakia," *Canadian Slavonic Papers* 13, no. 3 (Fall 1970): 225–42; Pavel Tigrid, "Czechoslovakia, A Post-Mortem," *Survey*, no. 73 (Autumn 1969), pp. 133–64; Pavel Tigrid, *Le printemps de Prague* (Paris: Seuil, 1968); Z. A. Zeman, *Prague Spring: A Report on Czechoslovakia 1968* (Harmondsworth: Penguin, 1968). Cf. also Karel Bartošek, "Revoluce proti byrokratismu?" *Rudé právo*, 18, 24, 26, 30 July and 11 March 1968.

2. The fullest analysis of the Prague spring is given by Rémi Gueyt, *La mutation*

In some respects, the reforms planned in Prague were more modest than analogous efforts in other Communist countries. There was not, at least at the outset, a rejection of Soviet domination, as in the case of Yugoslavia and other later revolts against Moscow; nor were major changes in foreign orientation envisaged, as in the case of Romania and others. There was to be no sharp break in relations with the Communist camp and no defection from Comecon or the Warsaw Pact. Nor was there an immediate, spontaneous rejection of collectivization, as in Hungary and Poland, or a radical reconstruction of the economy, such as followed the initial break by Yugoslavia, although the economic reforms initiated in 1966 would no doubt have been eventually implemented fully and perhaps expanded. In the political realm, however, the changes envisaged and in part introduced were more drastic and more rapid than anything attempted elsewhere: they aimed at nothing less than a "socialist democracy." The political model under construction was more daring and radical than any previous blueprint of reformed Communism. It included freedom of speech, legal institutionalization of democratic procedures, a genuine federalism, and guarantees of free interest-group activity.

To be sure, Prague's de-Stalinization was still in an initial stage at the time of the Soviet invasion, and its ultimate shape and form could only be guessed at. The old order had sunk deep roots and created many vested interests, so that its overthrow was bound to be strongly resisted. The months since January had, in fact, been accompanied by a bitter struggle of opposing forces which was still not finally resolved by August. Moreover, although the initiative for reform came in part from the top — from Dubček and his associates — there were powerful pressures from below, expressing the spontaneous forces of change. The possibility was therefore not excluded of even more far-reaching transformations than those planned from above. These inner tensions of democratization were accentuated by the international context in which outside political forces, especially the Communist ones, openly sided with one side of the struggle or the other and intervened politically and diplomatically to affect the ultimate outcome. There were some in Prague who foresaw a slow, zigzag advance, as in Yugoslavia since 1950; others, a reversal of course, in the Polish style; and still others, a fate similar to that experienced by the Hungarians in 1956, as in fact occurred in a less bloody but equally decisive form. The uniqueness of the conditions of each Communist country,

tchécoslovaque (Paris: Editions ouvrières, 1969). See also Edward Taborsky, "The New Era in Czechoslovakia," East Europe 17, no. 11 (November 1968): 19–29. For the main documents in translation, see R. A. Remington, ed., Winter in Prague: Documents on Czechoslovak Communism in Crisis (Cambridge, Mass.: M.I.T. Press, 1969).

however, warned against facile predictions of the future. Any one of these alternatives seemed a reasonable possibility; so also did a swifter and more complete democratization leading to a genuine democracy.

One must nonetheless guard against sentimentalizing or exaggerating the actual and planned changes in the political sphere. "Democratization" and "democratic socialism" were the watchwords of the Dubček regime, but these were thought to be reconcilable with the maintenance of the "leading role of the party." The Communist party of Czechoslovakia (CPCz) retained its position of political predominance and, in fact, was largely responsible for the direction of reform as set forth in its Action Program.[3] Even the pressures from below, insofar as they were institutionalized, came mainly from Communists in the academic and professional institutions and in the communications media. Dubček had assumed the difficult task of regaining for the party, by its deeds, the confidence of the people and of justifying the continuance of its leading role by persuasion rather than by coercion, as in the past. His purpose was, in essence, to reform the Communist system without abolishing it — or better, to reform it so as to avoid its disintegration. This required drastic changes; the leading role was to be carried out, for example, in a climate of free debate and democratic discussion but without endangering the hegemony of the party. No doubt this move was based on his faith, or hope, that the majority of the people would accept the leadership of the party, but he also recognized the danger that democratization might lead to the undermining of the party's dominant position. This suggested the need for safeguards, which in turn threatened to slow down or even reverse the process of democratization. This recurrent dilemma between attaining the goal of democratization and protecting the party's position was evident in all major aspects of political life from January to August.

There were those in the West who misread the situation in Prague and assumed that a full democracy had already been established or would be achieved in rapid order. It was clear to most Czechs and Slovaks, however, that democratization was not to be equated with democracy but represented only a first step in that direction — and one that was not irreversible. Many, indeed, doubted whether a one-party system could be fully democratized and believed that only a succession of new crises might pave the way for a fundamental restructuring of the political system in a genuinely democratic spirit. What had so far occurred, in their view, was merely a change of guard and minimal changes *in* the system, father than a basic change *of* the system. There were grave dangers of a relapse, some thought, especially if it became apparent that

3. Text published in supplement to *Rudé právo*, 10 April 1968; in English, in Remington, *Winter in Prague*, pp. 88–137.

the Communist party had not been able to secure the support of the decisive majority of the population.

Yet the political changes to be discussed more fully in this article were in fact substantial, even radical in some respects, and would have decisively altered the spirit and procedures of the Communist system. Moreover, they would have shifted the balance of political forces in the direction of reform and opened up possibilities of even more drastic reforms, extending into the economic sphere and affecting the foreign relations of the regime. It was these potentialities which raised the specter of an undermining of the Communist system itself and which aroused the fears of Moscow's ruling circles and, even more, of the less secure leaders in Warsaw and East Berlin. Radical measures which were deemed by the Dubček regime — and by certain other Communist parties, such as the Italian, Romanian, and Yugoslav — as necessary to strengthen and solidify the Communist system were regarded by Moscow and its closest allies as a potential threat to their own security, if not to the very existence of their regimes.

Democratizing the Party

Democratization of public life would be impossible unless the party itself broke with its traditional methods and became more democratic in its operations. Characterized by a highly bureaucratic and centralized organization and by the enforcement of absolute unity and discipline on its members, the party had, in effect, been ruled by its own apparatus and by its topmost leaders in the Presidium and Secretariat. In the eight months after January substantial progress was made in the direction of inner democracy. Vigorous debates occurred within the Central Committee and within the district and regional organizations, and local leaders and congress delegates were elected by nomination at the grassroots and by secret vote, instead of by the cadre section of the apparatus. Old-style monolithic unity gave way to sharp conflicts of varying shades of progressive and conservative opinion, expressed by Communists in the press, on radio and television, and in the National Assembly. An effort was also under way to improve the quality of the apparatus by changes in personnel and to decrease its power by shifting the locus of activity to the party's elected bodies. The apparatus would have become a consultative and administrative arm of the party and would no longer have had the authority to intervene in all spheres of life, including the state organs, mass associations, and journals, laying down the line on all questions and selecting cadres for all positions, public and private. The forthcoming party congress in September would have carried further this process of internal democratization by the selection of new higher bodies. True, this would not have been a purely democratic procedure; the election was to have been based, in the case of the Central Committee and the Control and Revision Commission, on a slate of members selected from over nine hundred nominees proposed by the lower organizations. But the Central Committee, as well as the Presidium, would certainly have been more representative of rank and file opinion and of the progressive tendency of thought among party members, with more conservative spokesmen removed.

The new party statute, published ten days before the invasion, retained the general structure of the party unchanged, from Presidium and Central Committee down to basic organizations, and kept the principles of democratic centralism and discipline characteristic of all Communist parties.[4] In many respects it was sharply criticized by more progressive party members. Yet it was suffused with a new spirit reflecting the actual developments in Czechoslovakia and emphasizing the democratic character of the party. The statute not only provided for the free exchange of opinions and secret election of officers and delegates but also proclaimed the right of a minority to maintain its viewpoint after a decision was made and to request reconsideration at a later date. Although the formation of a "fraction" with a discipline of its own was expressly forbidden, the statute broke with the tradition of monolithic unity and permitted continuing differences of views among party members. Nonetheless, the necessity for discipline and fulfillment of party decisions was, as in the past, underlined. Moreover, the leading role of the party in the political and social system was asserted, as well as its responsibility for elaborating the program for the development of society and for organizing its implementation. The control of state organs by the Central Committee and by corresponding lower organs was not so explicitly formulated as in the past, but it was implicitly recognized in the concept of the party's leading role.

It is difficult to tell whether the party would have continued to move in the direction of inner-party democracy or would have drifted back to a centralized, apparatus-run organization with self-selecting leadership. No political party can be purely democratic and escape the dominant influence of its leaders and its administrative machine. A Communist party would find it difficult to escape from its own tradition, the ingrained patterns of behavior of its members, and the vested interests of its functionaries. Time would have been required for a gradual rejuvenation of party membership and a remolding of the leadership cadres at all levels. The election of more progressive leaders might have encouraged the expansion of democratic procedures, but it would not have guaranteed

4. Text published in supplement to *Rudé právo*, 10 August 1968; in English, in Remington, *Winter in Prague*, pp. 265–87.

that these leaders would abandon arbitrary and self-serving procedures, used not only against the defeated conservatives but also against other, more radical elements within the party. Time would also have been required for an improvement in the personnel of the apparatus and a reduction in its power. No doubt it would have retained substantial authority and important functions, as in any political party, with a key role in policy formation and in running the party machine. Nonetheless, after January, the party had already moved a long way from its past and might have been carried further along this road by the pressure of its own membership and of the more democratic context within which it was operating.

A Multiparty System?

The central dilemma posed for the Communist reformers in their effort to democratize the political system and at the same time to retain the party's leading role was the nature of the electoral system, including the role of other parties. As elections to the National Assembly and to the national committees were postponed until 1969, this crucial problem was not directly faced. The Dubček leadership recognized the necessity of finding ways and means to make the political system more responsive to the wishes and interests of the population, the overwhelming majority of which was not Communist. The discredited National Front, with its several satellite parties, and the meaningless elections of the past had to be replaced by a more realistic representation of varied social interests and viewpoints if the system was to be considered democratic in any sense. Even under Novotný there had been plans for introducing some degree of competition in elections, at least to the extent of having more candidates than seats to be filled. Much more was now required. Since January a vigorous discussion had been taking place in the communications media and in the professional journals about the conditions of genuine democracy, with strong arguments presented in favor of a multiparty system and unlimited electoral competition. In the view of the more radical, reform-minded Communists, eventual elections of this kind would result either in the endorsement of continued Communist rule by a majority vote or in the deserved defeat of the party if it failed to justify itself before the electorate. No doubt many non-Communists entertained the hope that the Communist party would be defeated in such a free election or at least so reduced in strength that non-Communist forces would play an important role in political life. In any case, it was assumed that the possibility of defeat, partial or total, would be an ever-present

5. For example, A. Kliment, *Literární listy*, 14 March 1968; V. Havel, ibid., 4 April 1968.

threat to the party and an effective means of popular control of its policies.

The Dubček leadership, although uncertain about the final solution to this problem, had already made clear its unwillingness to jeopardize the position of the party in free elections. The Action Program and subsequent statements had ruled out the possibility of opposition parties and an electoral struggle for power and had opted for a system of limited competition in which the National Front would play a decisive role.[6] It would act as a screening agency, determining the parties and organizations which would be permitted to take part in political life and requiring a commitment by such parties to the principles of socialism and to the idea of partnership with the leading party. Existing parties, such as the Czechoslovak Socialist and People's parties and the minuscule Slovak Freedom and Renascence parties, along with various associations, such as the trade unions and the youth movement, would have formed the core of a reinvigorated National Front and would have had wide opportunity to compete for representation in the Assembly and other elected bodies. New parties were not excluded, but their participation would be subject to the approval of the National Front. Certainly nonsocialist or anti-Communist parties, such as the pre-1948 parties and still more the pre-1938 parties, would not have been admitted into the political arena. Even a restored Social Democratic party, it was made categorically clear in official statements, would not be permitted to reorganize as an independent party. Whether existing political clubs, in particular the recently formed Club of Committed Non-Party People (KAN), would be permitted to organize as a political party had not yet been made clear.

The balance of forces, therefore, would have been very unequal in an eventual election. The main contestant would undoubtedly have been the Communist party with its large membership, its powerful organizational apparatus, and its almost exclusive opportunity for organizing in the factories and farms. The two main competing parties would have been the Czechoslavak Socialist and Czechoslovak People's parties, which had emerged from the thrall of Communist party control, removed their contaminated leaderships, increased their memberships, and worked out programs and policies of their own. Whether either of them, with their tarnished reputations and their relatively restricted organizing opportunities, would have been able to compete effectively with the Communist party, even in a free election, was doubtful. In Slovakia the two other parties were so tiny that they could be safely disregarded. The future role of a party based on KAN, which at that time was a group of intellectuals mainly in Prague and Brno, with some branches in other parts of the country, was uncertain. Only the revised electoral regulations and the statute of the National Front, neither of which was completed before

6. See above, chap. 3, p. 113.

August, would indicate the manner in which seats would be distributed and the extent to which other parties would be able to compete effectively for representation. There was certainly no likelihood that the dominant position of the Communist party would be seriously affected.

The prospect, therefore, was not of a political system permitting the free formation of political parties, unrestricted candidacy for office, and the possible defeat of the ruling party. For many Czechs and Slovaks, including some Communists, this prospect was highly unsatisfactory. Such a system was a far cry from a fully democratic one; it would have protected the party leadership from the full brunt of public opinion and would have ultimately led to a decline of democracy within the Communist party itself. On the other hand, there were many, including some non-Communists, who were realistic enough to admit the necessity, in the foreseeable future, of the hegemony of the Communist party and to be satisfied with the limited expansion of democracy envisaged by the leadership. The system in prospect, although far from perfect, would have been freer than that in any other Communist country and would have permitted public debate, competition for office, at least among the recognized parties, and some degree of representation of diverse views and interests in the elected organs. Moreover, with the anticipated shift of the political spectrum in the direction of reform after the CPCz party congress in September — and in the context of wide-ranging freedom of public discussion and pressures from existing parties and clubs and from more progressive Communists — the possibility of a future expansion of the democratic features of the system was not excluded.

Reviving the State Organs

A key objective of the Dubček reform was to rescue the institutions of the state, both the administrative organs, and the representative bodies, from the oblivion into which they had sunk under Stalinist rule. With all aspects of policy determined by the party Presidium and with the elections manipulated by the party apparatus, the National Assembly had become nothing more than a propaganda sounding-board, a rubber stamp when legislative action was thought to be required. With the party apparatus interfering in every aspect of day-to-day administration, the executive and public service had degenerated into mere instruments for implementing the will of the party leadership and the apparatus. Even the presidency, a post occupied by the first secretary of the party more or less ex officio, had become a powerless office, discredited further by the incumbency of the much discredited Novotný. The Slovak organs had become even more impotent in view of the concentration of power in the Prague organs of the party.

Separation of party and state and the safeguarding of the autonomy of state organs were set forth as goals of democratization. Complete separation was, of course, unlikely in a Communist system. If the CPCz were to retain its hegemonic role, the broad lines of policy would inevitably continue to be set by the party's leading organs, and key personnel of the government administration and the representative assemblies would continue to be predominantly Communist. Yet subtle and important changes were already occurring in the roles of the government and the National Assembly — and also of the presidency.

The position of the presidency had taken on fresh dimensions after the election of General Svoboda at the end of March. Under Gottwald and Novotný the importance of the office had been submerged by the party rank of the incumbent. The formal powers of the president under the constitution were, in any case, limited and largely ceremonial. Although Svoboda had held high office in the government after 1945 and had played an important role in the Communist coup in 1948, he had never occupied a place in the topmost party echelons. A man of high reputation and distinguished military career, he enjoyed a personal popularity and prestige unusual in a Communist state for any but the highest party leaders. By constant travel throughout the republic and frequent speeches in defense of the democratization program, he served as an important link between the regime and the broad public, generating support for Dubček among both Slovaks and Czechs, non-Communists as well as Communists. In adding luster and distinction to the highest state office, he was reviving and continuing the role of Masaryk and Beneš, although he lacked the constitutional powers and political status of those distinguished predecessors. Moreover, as head of the armed forces and a general himself, he occupied a position of potential significance in the event of a future crisis. In the period of Soviet pressure during the summer, Svoboda did, in fact, begin to play a role of importance above and beyond his party rank, participating in the Čierna and Bratislava conferences and taking decisive action in the Moscow negotiations after the invasion.

The government assumed a new importance under Dubček. Reconstituted in April, with Oldřich Černík as prime minister, it remained almost entirely Communist in composition, with one representative from each of the Socialist and People's parties. Certain key ministries, such as those of defense and the interior, passed from the hands of discredited Novotný supporters into the hands of avowed reformers. The government became an active generator of reforms, with each ministry working out in detail the voluminous legislation and administrative measures necessary to effect the Action Program. Meetings of the full cabinet were frequent and busy, with their decisions fully reported in the daily press. Ministers were more readily available for public comment on the affairs of their departments and were subject to open criticism in parliament and in the press. Although in policy formation the government still remained secondary to the party Presidium, the responsibility for the elaboration of legislation rested with it more than ever before, and the day-to-day intervention of the party apparatus in every sphere was greatly lessened. Most striking, for instance, were the abolition of the apparatus department responsible for army and security affairs and the assertion of the authority of the Ministries of Defense and the Interior to run their own shows, subject to cabinet direction and parliamentary control.

Even more significant was the emergence of the National Assembly as an arena of public discussion and an influential agency of lawmaking. Predominantly Communist in composition and "elected" during the Novotný period, the Assembly developed a remarkable independence and vigor under its newly elected Presidium, headed by a reform-minded Communist, J. Smrkovský. Parliamentary committees became active centers of discussion of government measures. In the plenary session, too, there was sharp debate, open criticism, and divided voting, testifying to the new independence of mind of party members. Eventually, after the election of more progressive deputies, including stronger representation of the non-Communist parties and the main interest groups, these tendencies would presumably have become even more pronounced. True, the party statute provided that Communist deputies would be guided by the party organs and their decisions, but this would not have excluded a certain degree of independence of action. The major principles of policy would continue to be set forth by the leading organs of the party, but the responsibility for their detailed implementation in legislation would pass to the Assembly, in conjunction with the government. At the same time, the Assembly seemed likely to become a place of free discussion of public policy and of the work of individual ministries, and hence a not ineffective organ of control of the executive and of public administration.

Building a Federal System

A major transformation of the political structure was to be effected by the establishment of a federal system, assuring the Slovaks, who comprised approximately one-third of the population, a position of full equality and giving them far-reaching control of their own affairs. A government commission headed by a Slovak, Deputy Prime Minister Gustav Husák, was responsible for coordinating the discussions of a constitutional law on federalism to be approved, it was planned, on 28 October, the fiftieth anniversary of Czechoslovak independence.

Czech opinion was in the main willing to accept the desirability and necessity of federalism, but in Czech areas such as Moravia and even

Silesia there was a strong feeling in favor of a triune or even quadripartite federal system, based on regions rather than on nationality. The Slovaks were utterly opposed to anything other than a dual federalism based on the national equality of Czechs and Slovaks. The sense of urgency which the Slovaks felt about federalism was not matched in the Czech lands, and there was dissatisfaction in Slovakia with the slow pace of advance. There was, moreover, considerable difference of opinion about the distribution of authority under the proposed federal constitution, with some Slovaks arguing for a very narrow range of federal authority (including only foreign affairs, defense, and finance) and others, mainly Czechs, seeking a much stronger central authority. Even more productive of controversy was the Slovak demand for parity of representation in the central organs, both executive and legislative — a demand which most Czechs, in spite of their readiness to adopt provisions protecting vital Slovak interests against outvoting by the Czech majority, were unwilling to accept.

None of these issues had been resolved at the time of the invasion. Discussions were proceeding in the government commission and in the Assembly's Constitutional and Legal Committee, as well as in the mass media. A Czech National Council, a provisional body to articulate Czech views on federal problems and to parallel the existing Slovak National Council, was formed by the National Assembly on the basis of a slate of 150 members prepared by the National Front. The general prospect was for the emergence of a relatively loose federal, or even a confederal or dualist, Czechoslovakia, consisting of two national republics, each with its national council and its own government. The nature of the federal National Assembly was as yet undecided. Each federal government department would include a state secretary who would be of a nationality other than that of his minister.

The federal principle was also to be applied to nongovernmental organizations, as well as to the Communist party itself. Most of the mass associations — including the trade unions, the newly formed collective farm union, the professional organizations such as the writers and journalists unions, and the scientific institutes — were reorganized into separate Czech and Slovak bodies, with coordinating organs of varying degrees of authority. The Communist party, according to the draft statute, was to continue as a "unified international" party; but it was to be composed of two territorial organizations, the Communist party of the Czech lands and the Communist party of Slovakia, each with its own congress, central committee, presidium, and secretariat. In form this would not have altered the position of the Slovak party, but it would have necessitated the creation, for the first time, of a Czech party. Under the proposed rules, joint meetings of the two central committees were to take place, but these meetings would lack the authority to make decisions. Decisions of the CPCz Central Committee on matters affecting sovereignty or national or territorial interests would require a majority vote of the two party organizations, each voting separately. In general, however, each party was to conduct its activities on the basis of the program of the CPCz as a whole.

The party, therefore, was not to be federalized in a manner similar to the state organs and mass associations; it was to remain a relatively unified movement. Whether this would satisfy Slovak Communists and whether they would exploit their special position in order to advance distinctive viewpoints was not as yet clear. The decision of the Slovak party to hold its congress in August, prior to the CPCz Congress — reversing a previous decision to meet afterward — suggested, however, the possibility of independent action.

Assuring Freedom of Expression

A vital aspect of the democratization process was the guarantee of freedom of expression and, in particular, freedom of the press. Under the Novotný regime, repressive measures, especially prior censorship of all publications and intervention by the party apparatus in newspapers and publications of all kinds, had greatly hampered, but not prevented, the rise of public opinion as a factor in political life. After January freedom of expression on a scale hitherto unknown in a Communist country, except briefly in Hungary and Poland prior to 1956, developed and served as a powerful force in pressing the party leadership in the direction of reform. Although this was largely a spontaneous development resulting from the actions of journalists, writers, and radio and television workers, as well as scholars and scientific workers, it received implicit endorsement by the party in the form of a virtual suspension of censorship and the failure of party and state to interfere seriously with the free flow of ideas.

Important journals edited by Communists — such as *Literární listy* and *Kultúrny život*, organs of the Writers Union; *Práce*, the trade union journal; *Mladá fronta*, the youth movement daily; and *Reportér*, the journalists' weekly — as well as the newspapers of the non-Communist parties, *Lidová demokracie* and *Svobodné slovo*, provided channels for the controversial discussion of public issues. New papers sprang into existence, such as the more radical *Student*, published by a group of young intellectuals; and others were planned for the fall, including *Lidové noviny*, a daily newspaper planned by the Writers Union, and *Zítřek*, a weekly review to be published by the Czechoslovak Socialist party. Even *Rudé právo*, the party organ, encouraged the discussion of conflicting views and reported much more objectively on party and state affairs. Its conservative editor-in-chief, Oldřich Švestka, found himself engaged in sharp debates, in the pages of the newspaper, with his own editors and other contributors. Radio and television, although state agencies, also encouraged very free discussion of public issues. This new climate of freedom did not permit the expression of openly anti-Communist views, but it did allow fundamental criticism of past party practice and espousal of radical political reforms for the future.

This freedom of the press was regarded by many as the single greatest achievement of the post-January developments. The progressive forces in the party, in particular the journalists themselves, were determined to secure the institutionalization of this freedom in legislation. This was achieved in June, at least provisionally, by the amendment of the existing press law, subject to a complete revision at a later date. Under this law, censorship prior to publication was abolished, and any intervention by the state against freedom of speech was banned. The editors, however, were themselves to bear responsibility, under law, for the maintenance of state secrets. Citizens were given the opportunity to demand the correction of newspaper reports adversely affecting their rights and, if necessary, to appeal to a court.

Whether freedom of expression could be maintained within a system of one-party dominance was a question few Czechs or Slovaks were ready to answer with assurance. Even the new press law did not exclude party pressures on the newspapers and journals and still more on state agencies such as radio and television. Since most editors and journalists were Communists, party discipline and self-censorship were potentially powerful limiting factors on freedom of expression. Moreover, sharp criticism was expressed in the National Assembly and elsewhere by those who feared that the press, radio, and television had already abused their freedom to the detriment of the party's position and with harmful effects on relations with other Communist states. The strong censure of Czechoslovak developments in the press of the Soviet Union and other neighboring states was not without harmful effect in encouraging caution, especially during the summer months of crisis, although this also had the opposite effect of stimulating sharp rebuttal from those criticized.

Nonetheless, even in the absence of a fully democratic party and electoral system, the continued existence of a free press was an extremely important element of democracy, capable of influencing public opinion, including that of the party rank and file, and serving both to check and prod party and government leaders. It continued to exert, as it had done in the preceding months, a significant influence on the course of public policy. Whatever pressures, subtle or direct, might later be applied, there was bound to be firm resistance by journalists and writers, accustomed to their newfound freedom of expression, to any attempts to limit and control it.

The Abolition of Terror

A crucial element of the democratization process — and a condition of continued advance — was the elimination of terror, the rectification of the legal injustices of the past, and safeguards of the security and rights of the individual in the future. The Action Program promised legal and political guarantees of the political and personal rights of citizens and of legality in proceedings before the courts. It also promised full rehabilitation of victims of illegality and a reduction in the role of the Ministry of the Interior and the security organs. Criticism of the inhuman behavior of these agencies in the past dominated public discussion from January on, with many articles and books revealing the full extent of cruelties and barbarities under the regimes of Gottwald and Novotný. A club, K-231, composed of former victims of injustice under the law for the defense of the republic, no. 231, was formed, with the toleration of the party, to press for the rectification of these wrongs. Rehabilitation was ultimately embodied in a law passed in June, which provided for reconsideration, on individual appeal, of cases tried between October 1948 and July 1965 and for indemnification of those found to have been unjustly sentenced. Persons responsible for miscarriages of justice might be dismissed from their positions under the new law, but they could not be prosecuted, unless their actions resulted in death, because of the statute of limitations. In addition, rehabilitation proceedings were under way in almost every institution, public or private, including government departments, university faculties, research institutes, and the Communist party itself.

A particularly sensitive issue was the responsibility of the highest political personages for the judicial crimes of the 1950s and early 1960s. A party investigation of the role of Novotný and his closest associates (Bacílek, Široký, and others) was under way and might well have led eventually to trials of these former leaders and to revelations of complicity by many others, including Soviet advisors and political leaders. Meanwhile, Rudolf Barák, former Politburo member and Minister of the Interior, who in 1962 had been sentenced to fifteen years in jail for embezzlement and sabotage and who was freed of these charges in a retrial in 1968, charged that Novotný had been personally responsible for his imprisonment, as well as for the trials of Slánský and others in the 1950s, and had acted out of fear that his involvement in the latter would be revealed by Barák.

Guarantees against future injustice would have to wait upon the drafting of a new constitution and judicial reforms scheduled for later consideration. A security police system was to be retained, but avowedly within a system of law and justice that would prevent the concentration of all power in the hands of irresponsible police officials. In particular, the coercive arm of the state was to be subordinated, not, as in the past, to the party apparatus but to the government and the National Assembly. In the meantime, extensive changes were being planned and implemented by the new minister of the interior, Josef Pavel, himself a victim of the terror of the past. The ministry was, of course, a stronghold of Stalinism and included many persons whose jobs — and, in some cases, life or freedom — were involved in the reconsideration of their past. Pavel was confronted with bitter resistance to changes in personnel and was able to secure the removal of several of his deputy ministers only in late June. There was a long road ahead in purifying the lower levels of the security and police apparatuses and later in building up a corps of judges and lawyers capable of rendering independent justice. A related question in the field of public security was the future of the armed People's Militia, which had been active in 1948 during the Communist takeover and had continued to exist in the factories. Although there were calls for the disbanding of this paramilitary force as a possible threat to the democratic order, Dubček. who was in fact its commanding officer, defended it against such charges.

The Rise of Pressure Groups

The Action Program had promised constitutional guarantees of freedom of assembly and association, including the possibility of forming voluntary organizations and interest groups. Even under Novotný there had been criticism of the traditional role of the mass associations as transmission belts controlled by the party apparatus; there had been strong advocacy that these organizations function as independent interest groups. After January there was a dynamic growth of activity by groups and associations. Certain professional associations, such as the Writers Union and the Journalists Union, played political roles of outstanding importance, as they had done before January. Traditional mass associations, such as the trade unions, carried through a change of leadership and proclaimed their intention of becoming active and autonomous "pressure groups." In other cases, such as the Czechoslovak Youth Union, a process of disintegration occurred as specific groups, such as the university students, established their own more or less independent organizations. Similarly, groups of workers in individual industries began to break away from existing trade unions and organize autonomous unions. Pre-Communist associations, such as the Boy Scouts and the Sokols, were revived. Many new interest groups were formed, including a Union of Collective Farms and a League of Women. Other associations of a more political character, such as KAN and the League of Human Rights, also came into existence. As noted earlier, steps were taken in most cases to create Czech and Slovak associations, linked by a common committee or center.

Although this was in large measure a spontaneous development, it was endorsed in principle by the party and, in most cases, accepted in practice. The party strongly urged, however, that interest groups should be unified organizations linking together, perhaps on a federal basis, separate narrower groupings within, say, the youth or the working class. Many of the organizations were provisional in character, lacking a legal basis, until the completion of a law on associations. It was not clear, therefore, how free the right of association would be, especially for the more political groups, and what political role would be permitted for the associations in general. Some of the major associations, such as the trade unions, the farm organization, and the youth and women's leagues, were already constituent parts of the National Front and would presumably be assured representation in the National Assembly. At the same time, like all authorized groups, they would have the right publicly to defend their interests and objectives and to press them upon the party and government authorities.

It was not yet evident to what extent the organizations would become genuine pressure groups, capable of articulating the interests of their constituencies and exerting an influence on the formation of policy. Much would depend on their own internal procedures, in particular the degree to which the members would be able to take an active part and influence the determination of policies and the election of officers. Much would also depend on the extent which non-Communists could participate in leading roles and to which Communists were freed of traditional party control and able to act as spokesmen of the organization rather than the party. Certainly the transmission-belt tradition would not be easy to break in the older bodies, such as the unions, nor would the apathy and indifference of the members — or the bureaucracy of officials — be easily overcome. In the newer organizations, especially those with a political tendency, the likelihood of independent action seemed greater, provided the party and the National Front did not take steps to restrain and limit it. Although the party would no doubt seek to direct the actions of the major groups through its own members in them, a substantial rise of independent activity was likely to affect the spirit and character of public life in a manner not entirely incomparable with that of a more developed pluralist society.

Foreign Policy Unchanged

From the outset, the main focus of the democratization process was on the domestic side, and substantial changes in foreign orientation were not officially envisaged. The Action Program forecast a more active and flexible policy in line with Czechoslovak national interests, but it pledged continuing solidarity with the socialist camp and loyalty to Comecon and the Warsaw Pact. Even diplomatic relations with West Germany were not placed on the immediate agenda of the Prague foreign office. Nonetheless, official statements guardedly indicated that Czechoslovakia would propose changes in Comecon arrangements and even in the Warsaw Pact organization and would seek to expand economic relations with Western countries. None of these intentions was designed to affect seriously Czechoslovakia's continued collaboration with the fellow members of the Warsaw alliance. No doubt, however, the further advance of democratization and the solidification of the position of the regime under more progressive leadership carried with it the potentiality of a more independent course within the framework of this alliance. In the broader Communist world movement also, Czechoslovakia did not fundamentally alter its attitude, but at the Budapest conference in June it adopted a somewhat more independent stance.

As the pressures from the Soviet Union and the neighboring Communist states intensified during the summer, the Czechoslovak party more and more firmly defended its right to conduct its own affairs without outside interference, but it refrained from any action that would sever relations with its allies or break with bloc organizations, such as Comecon or the Warsaw Pact Treaty Organization. Even the refusal to attend the Warsaw conference in mid-July did not exclude the possibility of bilateral discussions.[7] Continued pressures from Moscow strengthened the determination of Czechoslovakia to continue on its chosen path but also forced it to accept as legitimate a substantial degree of influence from its allies, as represented by the Čierna and Bratislava conferences. Closer relations were developed with Yugoslavia and Romania, both of which gave political support to the Czechoslovak course and refrained from participation in bloc pressure against Prague.

The Conflict of Political Tendencies

The process of democratization was accompanied by a continuing and bitter struggle of opposing political forces throughout the eight months

7. For English texts of the Warsaw letter and the Czechoslovak reply and the Čierna and Bratislava communiques, see Remington, *Winter in Prague*, pp. 225-31, 234-43, 255-61.

before the invasion. There were some, who might be termed reactionaries, who would have liked to turn the clock back and restore the Novotný system. There were others, who might be called neoconservatives, unwilling to see a restoration of Novotný and his regime but willing to support only a limited program of change. There were the "progressive" forces, which favored the ousting of the neoconservatives and a substantial, although still moderate, course of reform. And finally there were more radical reformers who proposed far-reaching, in some cases almost revolutionary, changes in the entire structure of Communism.

In the initial struggle to remove Novotný from the first secretaryship, Dubček had secured the support of a majority of the Presidium and the Central Committee, all of whom had been associated with Novotný in the previous period. In the new Presidium formed in January, the most pronounced Novotný supporters were replaced, and a coalition of neoconservatives and moderate reformers was formed. In the months of ferment that followed, spontaneous forces from below exerted increasing influence, thus offering Dubček the support of broader groups favoring more radical reforms and encouraging him to move in that direction. In successive stages he was able, with the continued support of the neoconservatives and the moderates in the top leadership and the more radical reformers outside, to undermine the position of Novotný and his half-dozen closest colleagues and remove them from the Central Committee. Even this body, appointed by Novotný, gave its support to these steps, although a hard core of reactionaries and many neoconservatives remained within its ranks.

The Action Program, adopted in early April, was a relatively moderate program acceptable to the conservative and moderate reformers but not satisfying the more radical ones. Dubček's centrist position, as represented by the Program and the subsequent implementing measures, was designed to weaken both the neoconservatives and the radical progressives, and it naturally awakened fears on both sides. The neoconservatives, still strongly represented in the highest party organs, were alarmed by some features of Dubček's program, especially his more extreme proposals such as freedom of expression. The more radical reformers in the newspapers, journals, and political groups and associations were disturbed by the continued leading role of the party and other conservative aspects of policy.

Preparations and elections for the CPCz Congress in September indicated that a significant shift in the balance of forces was likely to occur at that time, with the elimination of the remaining Novotný supporters and some of the neoconservatives from the Central Committee and the Presidium and their replacement by persons dedicated to the Dubček program or even more radical versions of democratization. As the summer wore on, the fears of the more conservative elements were intensified by this prospect of impending defeat. The doubts and worries of the more radical reformers were also mounting because of their suspicions of Dubček's relative moderation and the continuing bitter resistance of the neoconservatives. When Soviet pressure began to intensify, the fears of the radical and even of the moderate reformers rose, as did the hopes of the more conservative forces. In the Two Thousand Words statement published at the end of June,[8] the fear was expressed that the advance of democratization had come to a halt, and an appeal was made for popular actions of all kinds, within the law, to secure the removal from office of more conservative persons remaining from the Novotný period. The intense feelings on both sides were clearly delineated by the declaration, which provoked angry reactions among conservatives and even some moderates. A significant divergence between Czechs and Slovaks was also manifesting itself, the political spectrum among the Czechs having moved more in the direction of reform than it had among the Slovaks. At the same time, controversy between Czechs and Slovaks over the question of the future of federalism was sharpening.

As pressures from other Communist countries increased during July and August, the position of Dubček was greatly strengthened, partly by the weakening of both the conservative and the more radical forces and partly by mounting national unity and growing solidarity of Czechs and Slovaks against outside interference. Dubček began to emerge as a national leader enjoying very wide popular support, except among a handful of neoconservatives who were inclined to share the Soviet viewpoint. The crucial turning point would have been the congresses, first of the Slovak party in August, then of the Czechoslovak party in September, both of which would probably have documented the high degree of unity within the party on a political line representing substantial progressive reform. Whether this in turn would have produced an acceleration in the tempo of reform and increasing pressure from the radicals, or a solidification of Dubček's centrist line of moderate reform and stricter treatment of the radicals, could not be foreseen. The prospect of a relapse to a more conservative or even reactionary course, seemed, apart from Soviet intervention, very unlikely. Even this, however, could not be excluded if increasing radical pressures had pushed Dubček in the direction of a harder line comparable to that followed by Gomulka in Poland after 1957.

The Revolution Interrupted

This extraordinary and complicated course of events reached an unexpected climax with the military intervention of the USSR and four of

8. *Literární listy*, 27 June 1968.

its allies. It is clear that the Soviet leadership feared that the developments in Czechoslovakia after January might lead eventually, not only to an undermining of the Communist system in Czechoslovakia, but also to a serious weakening or even to the destruction of the Soviet military and political position in Eastern Europe. It was this cumulative effect of the assumed weakening of the domestic order in Czechoslovakia *and* of the Soviet security system in Eastern Europe, accentuating the dangers already created by Romania's and Yugoslavia's independence, that led the Soviet Union to action of a kind not taken in the case of Romania and Yugoslavia and comparable only to that against Hungary in 1956.

The Polish regime, endangered by the serious domestic crisis of March 1968, was even more fearful. The German Democratic Republic was also alarmed by the prospect of its possible isolation, were Czechoslovakia to follow an independent course vis-à-vis West Germany. For these two countries, the dangers seemed a matter of life and death — for the regimes, for their leaderships, and even for communism itself, reinforcing Soviet fears of the eventual spread of political infection to the Soviet Union. The concern of these countries and, to a much lesser extent, of Hungary was evident at the Dresden Conference in March and manifested itself in the intense political and diplomatic pressures in the series of conferences in Moscow, Warsaw, Čierna, and Bratislava. The purpose was clear: to persuade the Czechoslovak leaders to change course or, if necessary, to achieve the replacement of Dubček by other more pliable and conservative leaders. When, in the opinions of the leaders in Moscow, Warsaw, and East Berlin, these exhaustive political efforts had failed to produce the desired results, the fateful decision was made to resort to military intervention.[9]

There was, as can be seen, a certain logic in the actions of Moscow and its allies. Yet it was, in effect, a reactionary rather than even a reasoned conservative response to the dangers present in the Czechoslovak situation; and in some degree it was based on a misreading or an exaggerated interpretation of the developments in Prague. The evils of the Novotný era had been so great that only drastic reform could restore the credit of the Communist party and stabilize its rule in Czechoslovakia. In many ways the reform program being implemented by Dubček, far-reaching as it was, was nonetheless a moderate one, designed to regenerate the Communist system and preserve the leading role of the party. Certain aspects of the program, such as freedom of the press, were indeed more radical and dangerous from the Soviet point of view. In particular, free-

9. For the international aspects of the Czechoslovak crisis, see Philip Windsor and Adam Roberts, *Czechoslovakia, 1968: Reform, Repression and Resistance* (London: Chatto and Windus, 1969); Robert Rhodes James, ed., *The Czechoslovak Crisis, 1968* (London: Weidenfeld and Nicolson, 1969).

dom of expression made possible the frank exposure of much dirty linen from the terror of the 1950s, including the involvement of Soviet security police and political leaders and a reassessment of Czechoslovak party history under Gottwald and Novotný, revealing the constant interference of the Comintern and the Soviet party. However, openly antisocialist or anti-Soviet forces, although they existed, were greatly exaggerated by Soviet analysts and did not, in fact, represent a serious, present danger.

Much more important than the actualities of Dubček's reform were the potentialities of future development as assessed by Soviet analysis, in particular the possible expansion of democracy and the elimination of Communist power in Prague — and, short of that, the growing independence of action of Czechoslovakia in foreign and defense policy and in relations with the Communist bloc. Certainly such potentialities existed, and the forthcoming party congresses would have brought them closer to actuality. Yet even these were not certainties or even probabilities; they were simply possibilities which existed along with other alternatives, such as the eventual stabilization of a reformed Communist system and a relatively independent course by a loyal ally.

More moderate Communists such as the Italians, Yugoslavs, Romanians, and even the Hungarians, considered the Dubček course desirable in itself and designed to make Communism more stable and more popular. Unfortunately, the reactionary views dominant in Warsaw and East Berlin were predominant in Moscow too and triumphed over any more moderate attitudes that may have been present. Although the military intervention warded off the assumed dangers, actual and potential, of "counter-revolution," the ultimate consequence of this action, by excluding the possibility of urgently needed reform, might well be an even graver threat to the Communist system in the Soviet Union as well as in Czechoslovakia and Eastern Europe.

5

POLITICAL OPPOSITION IN
SINGLE-PARTY STATES
OF TROPICAL AFRICA

William J. Foltz

Dislike of government policies and personnel must be as old and wide-spread as the institution of government itself, and in all but the most primitive or depraved political systems people from time to time co-ordinate their activities in hopes of changing the men who rule them or the rules they are called on to obey. We may take this conscious attempt at coordinating actions — "organization" in its simplest form — as the threshold of opposition. Action below this threshold — excepting only the drastic act of a solitary assassin — can have political effect only if it is exploited by a group able to coordinate action toward some goal, however vague. Beyond the threshold, opposition groups vary in com-plexity, action, and intent from the palace clique or party faction inter-ested only in better jobs for its members, to the revolutionary guerrilla band, to the established, legal opposition enjoying full rights of access to some legitimate means for achieving its ends.

We will be concerned here with analyzing the kinds of oppositions that develop when this last form of opposition is ruled out by the de jure or de facto reservation of political rights to a single political party and the ways in which single-party dominance was established.[1] Under single-party rule opposition groups operate close to the organizational threshold, and most achieve even this level of organization for political purposes only by gaining control over some part of the single-party organization

1. The generalizations in this paper are drawn principally from the following present or past single-party regimes: Ghana, Senegal, Mali, Guinea, Upper Volta, Niger, Ivory Coast, and Tanzania. Such limited information as I have on the French-speak-ing areas of Central Africa, Kenya, and Malawi does not contradict the points made here, but I must stress how limited that information is. I am grateful to my colleague Anthony Oberschall for helpful comments.

itself. As I shall argue, the effectiveness and utility of most such political opposition are very limited, primarily because of their inability to achieve a cohesive organizational form, and where effective opposition does develop it is usually by the politicization of an established bureaucratic structure outside the formal arena of partisan politics.

The Social Basis for Opposition

It is commonly argued that African societies are plural — rather than pluralistic — societies in which widely differing groups lead self-contained lives side by side and in which social cleavages tend to reinforce rather than cut across one another.[2] This distinction is clearly an important one for some purposes, but if accepted uncritically it may greatly overstate the case. The great cleavages in tropical African societies are, of course, along the ethnic and linguistic lines that separate the groups commonly called "tribes." At least as important, however, are the cleavages within each ethnic group and the links between the groups. Were it not for these internal cleavages and intergroup links, the single parties which have ruled so many African countries could never have come into existence.

The principal categoric links between different ethnic groups are region, mode of livelihood, religion, and caste. Of these region is probably now the most important, and it is where region coincides most clearly with the territory inhabited by a single large ethnic group, as is the case in Nigeria and part of the Congo, that ethnic conflict is likely to pose the most serious problems. Where a distinctive region, like the North of Ghana or the forest belt of the Ivory Coast, contains numerous ethnic groups competing for advantage against other regions of the same country, this competition is likely to produce increasing regional solidarity, whatever may have been the legacy of conflict between these same groups in the precolonial or colonial periods. It is not unusual for Africans from minority tribes of a given rural area to adopt the identity of a large ethnic group of that same area when they migrate to a city or to another region.[3] Mode of livelihood, particularly the classic distinction between cattlemen and farmers, is another way of forming interethnic bonds. Like region, mode of livelihood becomes a more salient factor mitigating ethnic strife the more economic development continues and the more fractionated the ethnic groups are. A universalistic religion, whether Islam or

2. See, for example, W. Arthur Lewis, *Politics in West Africa* (London: Allen and Unwin, 1965), pp. 64–90. The subject is discussed at great length in Leo Kuper and M. G. Smith, eds., *Pluralism in Africa* (Berkeley: University of California Press, 1969).

3. See the discussion of "supertribalization" in Jean Rouch, "Migrations au Ghana," *Journal des Africanistes* 26 (1956): 33–196.

Christianity, likewise will link different ethnic groups, although the political relevance of religious distinctions varies greatly among the tropical African countries and in most is probably less than it has been in American or European politics. Finally, similar caste, or caste-like, distinctions in social rank and economic specialization cut across ethnic groups in large parts of the Sudanic regions and facilitate interpersonal contact and comparatively high rates of intermarriage among ethnic groups.

Not only may an ethnic group find itself linked with another for particular economic or political purposes, but the ethnic group itself may contain important divisions. Some, like religion or caste, may cut across groups; many more, like divisions into clans, villages, or extended patron-client groups may be contained within a particular tribe, so as materially to affect the sort of solidarity the ethnic group as a whole can manifest. While these intragroup cleavages are primarily aspects of traditional social structure, others, such as the distinction between those who have moved to the big city or to greener pastures and those who have remained in the ancestral homeland, and between the educated young and the illiterate old will continue to grow as economic change proceeds.

For a political party, these various links and cleavages provide the bases on which to build some sort of interethnic political coalition that will guarantee the allegiance of a substantial part of the population by offering at least symbolic representation in its councils. The total population need not be included, since in some of the least economically developed countries the government may benefit from having a substantial part of the population effectively outside the political arena. In an extreme case, Liberia's political system until very recently has effectively included only about one-tenth of the country's population, the so-called Americo-Liberian elite; but even in states as ideologically opposed to Liberia as are Tanzania or Mali perhaps one-quarter of the population still leads a life centered around subsistence agriculture or herding, serenely unconcerned by the political and economic activities of the capital and the major towns. For those who would oppose the government, the various cleavages within the population provide a number of small groups which political entrepreneurs can seize on as popular bases of support for their political activities. The problem of the rulers is to maintain a coalition structured so as to assure at least the passive loyalty of as many as possible of the politically relevant groups, to increase the political importance of loyal groups, and to keep other groups out of the political arena. The problem of any opposition is to split off parts of the rulers' coalition, to increase the political importance of disaffected groups, and to introduce into the political arena new groups whose loyalty to the rulers is doubtful.

The Leaders

The men who have tried to lead both government and opposition co-alitions in tropical African states can be placed in four rough categories: the Notables, or traditional leaders; the Old Bourgeoisie; the Nationalist Middle Class; and the New Intelligentsia. Each of these groups possesses different skills and bases of power, appeals to different groups, and adopts different techniques of political action. Each has also at one time or another constituted an actual or potential source of opposition leadership.

The Notables comprise those individuals with some traditional claim to a leadership position. They are the chiefs, lineage heads, elders, large cattle or landowners, or religious leaders, particularly Muslim, who held political power or high social status before the coming of the colonial powers and in many cases continued to govern in rural areas as auxiliaries of the colonial administration.[4] Their political power is based on social status and sanctioned by tradition. When modern, representative political roles were first created by the colonial regimes, many of these men were pushed into them by the colonial powers, who saw them as responsible and predictable spokesmen for their people and also as amenable to direction from the European administration, which possessed the modern skills the Notables lacked and which could bring bureaucratic or patronage sanctions to bear on them. At first these men had little need for a formal political party organization, since they could rely on tradition and their social position to assure their political position at least in their traditional homeland. When they did form political organizations which extended beyond their traditional bases, these were generally of the loose "congress" type which served only to concert the electoral or parliamentary action of a group of semi-independent leaders, each with his own guaranteed following. In most countries their power has been effectively limited to the rural areas.

The Old Bourgeoisie is in some senses the urban political counterpart of the rural Notables and in the various colonial councils provided the first opposition to the Notables' political leadership. These are the men who acquired modern skills and used them to economic and political advantage under the colonial regime. They are the lawyers, the early African civil servants, the big traders, the Christian divines who formed the first generation of modern African politicians. They were active in

4. Despite their formal centralizing policies, the French in practice ruled through chiefs in most interior areas. See Robert Delavignette, *Freedom and Authority in French West Africa* (London: International African Institute, 1950). The classic statement on rule through Notables on the British side is Lord Lugard, *The Dual Mandate in British Tropical Africa* (Hamden, Conn.: Archon Books, 1965).

the cities, particularly the capitals and major interior trading towns of the most economically advanced colonies, and even in many of the poor interior territories, though they were too small in number there to constitute a significant political group.[5] Their political power was based on their ability to provide complex services for people in the modern realm of life, particularly by manipulating the colonial administration, and also on their command of financial resources, particularly after they moved into positions of prominence in municipal government. Their power was organized in patronage networks extending into cash-crop rural areas. Although the Old Bourgeoisie originally entered politics to oppose the domination of the Notables, they shared with them a basic dependence on the fundamental structures established by colonial rule and later often allied with conservative rural interests to oppose the greater challenge of the Nationalist Middle Class.

The Nationalist Middle Class is the group that everywhere in tropical Africa has dominated the politics of the first years of independence; it is greatly similar to the nationalist groups that have come to power in most of the rest of the underdeveloped world. In stricter terms of class analysis, this is a nonproprietary, petty bourgeoisie dependent on its white-collar skills and training for its status. The group includes lower-level civil servants, primary-school teachers, journalists, veterinarians, male nurses, civil servants, clerks in private businesses, and labor union officials who constituted the new elite that emerged in Africa after the Second World War. In the more economically advanced countries, literate petty traders and market middlemen might also be included. They are usually men with good, but not particularly prestigious educations — at best the products of the William-Ponty Normal School in Dakar that serviced all of French Africa and of secondary schools like Achimota in the Gold Coast and Tabora in Tanganyika, who did not then go on for an Oxbridge or London School of Economics degree. Most of them combined both rural and urban experience; born in rural areas, they came to the city for education or employment and then were usually posted about to several different rural areas in the early course of their careers. Although their standard of living was higher than that of any simple peasant, their life patterns were not so far removed that they were unapproachable. In the course of their daily jobs they came into contact with — and rendered services for — a wide variety of the African population. As the colonial governments came to emphasize rural development and to extend social services to the population in the early postwar years, they did so through the intermediary of the Nationalist

5. An excellent description of such a group is in Dennis Austin's discussion of the Gold Coast "intelligentsia" in *Politics in Ghana* (London: Oxford University Press, 1965), pp. xii, 9–10. For an enlightening memoir of a French African equivalent, see Lamine Guèye, *Itinéraire Africaine* (Paris: Présence Africaine, 1966).

Middle Class. The crucial and frustrating nature of their intermediary position between the foreign ruling elite and the local masses led them into both political activity and a strong sense of their identity as a group. Drake's analysis of Ivory Coast nationalist politicians can be extended continent-wide:

> The more successful among them were those who regarded themselves primarily as members of a generalized modern elite. They treated their identities as . . . educated men as more relevant to most situations than their particular occupations. They considered their political missions more important than their occupational pursuits.[6]

Initially, the Nationalist Middle Class lacked both the status of the Notables and the patronage resources of the Old Bourgeoisie, but it had a freedom of action which these first two groups — whose political status depended on the maintenance of the colonial regime or at the least on the retention of existing political, social, and economic structures — did not possess. Put in its simplest terms, the main thing it had to offer the growing African electorate was the idea of progress, summed up ultimately in terms of African political control.

In addition to satisfying individual or psychic needs, political office provided a schoolteacher or clerk with his only likely opportunity for personal financial advancement. A successful candidate for parliament would easily quintuple his salary and would have access to means for taking care of his extended family's needs and desires. Like most successful politicians anywhere, these men were truly hungry for office.

Unlike the other two groups, the Nationalist Middle Class politicians were obliged to develop coherent and continuing political organizations, since they had neither social nor economic resources to fall back on. The many variants of the mass party form they developed fit the requirements of their situation in the postwar years.[7] They needed votes, since the rules set up by the colonial authorities gave political office to those who won elections, and thus their organizations could not be confined to small groups of like-minded people. They needed money, so the organization had to be set up on a regular enough basis and provide or promise enough services to permit the collection of dues from members and to permit the central party bureaucracy to supervise the collection activities of its local agents, lest all the money remain in local hands. They needed issues with which to prod and upset both the colonial authorities and the older bourgeois and traditional political leaders, so

6. Lyman M. Drake III, "The Anxious Generation: Ivory Coast Youth Look at Work and Politics" (Ph.D. diss., M.I.T., 1968).

7. On African mass parties, see Thomas Hodgkin, *African Political Parties* (London: Penguin, 1963), and Ruth Schachter Morgenthau, *Political Parties in French-speaking West Africa* (London: Oxford University Press, 1965), chap. IX.

good upward communications within the party were necessary to permit it to function as an agency for the collection and amalgamation of grievances. They needed to be able to mobilize people for demonstrations and electoral activities, so leadership had to be coordinated and downward communications had to be maintained. Party-linked organizations for specific categories of people, such as women, youth, veterans, and labor, were set up to increase popular participation and to mobilize target groups. Finally, broad representation of many different social groups had to be assured, so great attention was paid to assuring a balanced ticket in which all major groups could find a spokesman. The genius of the best organized of these parties was to bring about this ethnic balance only on the territorial level, so that people would have to look to the center to find major spokesmen for their ethnic, regional, or other primordial group sentiments.

It is easy to overstate both the strength of these mass parties and the degree to which they differed from other parties competing for electoral advantage in the 1950s.[8] Despite their claims, the mass parties rarely had continually effective organization in rural areas remote from the major lines of communication, and in the days before electoral returns became useless as guides to a party's strength, none was able, though it might defeat any opposition handily, to garner a majority of votes from all eligible voters. Likewise, the commitment demanded of the average member did not go much beyond paying nominal party dues, voting "right," and turning out for an occasional festive party rally or demonstration against the administration's latest iniquity. The mass parties benefited occasionally from the support of leaders drawn from the ranks of the Notables or the Old Bourgeoisie either for ideological reasons, because they recognized a good thing when they saw it, or most often because an opposing party espoused a particularistic claim of some personal rival. The Notables' constant bickering among themselves for patronage and personal prerogatives led several dissatisfied men to throw their support to the Nationalist Middle Class parties at the same time that it weakened the credibility of the Notables' claim as a group to assume positions of political leadership.

The mass parties kept organizational control in the hands of a group of essentially like-minded and primarily Nationalist Middle Class leaders, whatever the heterogeneity of their ethnic backgrounds and whatever small leavening of other sorts of leaders might be present.[9] They also

8. See the balanced presentation in Aristide Zolberg, *Creating Political Order* (Chicago: Rand McNally, 1966).
9. No systematic comparative study of the social backgrounds of African nationalist politicians has as yet been made. Jean-Louis Seurin provides a useful analysis of the social composition of legislators in French-speaking West African countries just before independence in "Élites sociales et partis politiques d'AOF," *Annales*

emphasized nationalism, both in the sense of internal national unity and in the sense of independence from colonial rule. Whatever the limitations of their organization, the mass parties were strong enough to oppose successfully a colonial power that had lost interest in its colonial mission and African competition that remained distant from the expanding electorate and was often tainted by collaboration with the worst aspects of colonial rule.

The final category of elites, the New Intelligentsia, played only a minimal role in preindependence politics. These are the university students and graduates of the postwar era whose numbers attained significant proportions only after the leadership coalitions that were to found the first independent governments were well established. As Victor LeVine has shown, the difference between groups such as those I label New Intelligentsia and Nationalist Middle Class reflects both class and generational cleavages, although three or four years — enough of a delay for a man to have been excluded from membership in the nationalist coalition — may suffice to separate *les jeunes* from *les anciens*.[10] In distinction to the Nationalist Middle Class, the New Intelligentsia possess both real technical skills and high prestige, sanctioned by a university diploma. Both groups have been highly conscious of the difference between them. As LeVine found, "Most of the first generation elite tended to feel that some form of [political] 'activism' was the prime characteristic of [membership in] the elite, while most of those in the second generation stressed the possession of formal education as the main feature of eliteness."[11] Like the Notables and the Old Bourgeois, they have less need for formal political office, because their skills and education guarantee them acceptable employment and social status. During the last years before independence they often served the mass parties as technical ad-

---

africaines (Dakar), 1958, pp. 123–57. See especially the table, p. 154. I compared the background of Malian and Senegalese legislators in *From French West Africa to the Mali Federation* (New Haven: Yale University Press, 1965), pp. 150–51. Data presented by Dennis Austin, *Politics in Ghana*, pp. 195–99; Henry Bienen, *Tanzania: Party Transformation and Economic Development* (Princeton: Princeton University Press, 1967), pp. 46–48, 96–115, 401, and David C. Mulford, *The Northern Rhodesia General Election* (Nairobi: Oxford University Press, 1964), p. 195, indicate that Seurin's conclusion about African nationalist parties — "les mêmes couches sociales détiennent les responsabilités dans tous les partis de façon générale, et . . . la 'classe politique' africaine tend à se recruter dans les mêmes catégories" — can be applied to most English- as well as French-speaking countries. Nigeria demonstrates a different pattern, in which opposition between the Nationalist Middle Class and other social groups was worked out largely within the framework of ethnically homogeneous parties — with disastrous results. See the table in John P. McKintosh, *Nigerian Government and Politics* (Evanston: Northwestern University Press, 1966), pp. 89–91, and the brilliant argument of Richard L. Sklar, "Contradictions in the Nigerian Political System," *Journal of Modern African Studies* 3; no. 2 (1965): 201–13.

10. Victor T. LeVine, *Political Leadership in Africa*, Hoover Institute Studies 18 (Stanford: Hoover Institute, 1967).

11. Ibid., p. 15.

visors and ideologues, but after independence, as political jobs at the top became scarce, many of them left the dominant party. More recent groups of students have tried to maintain their distance from politics as practiced by the ruling party. The extent of their political disengagement is suggested by the responses of African students in British and French universities to questions probing their expectations of future political activity. Only 19.6 percent of those in France queried in 1961 thought they could best serve Africa through political activities, while 59.7 percent thought they would be most useful in professional or private capacities.[12] Africans in British universities were asked in 1963 how politically active they expected to be at age 45; 25 percent responded "very active"; 29 percent "modestly active"; 34 percent predicted that they would be "not at all active." [13] Considering the importance politics had been accorded in their countries, it is surprising to find African responses not too different from those obtained from American undergraduates.

Political participation for most members of the New Intelligentsia has taken two main forms: ideological opposition to the regime or technocratic service in the public or private sector coupled with a refusal to get involved in the "sordid world" of party politics. Where regimes have not applied sanctions, many of the technocrats in high civil service jobs have considered it a badge of honor not to hold a party card. The peaceful integration of this group into a regime dominated by a less-educated and only silghtly older nationalist elite has posed a particularly thorny internal problem for African single-party regimes.

The Elimination of Formal Opposition

Granted that the Nationalist Middle Class possessed the numbers, talents, and motivation necessary for political leadership in the terminal years of the colonial regime, one may still ask why the mass parties were able, and why their leaders sought, to eliminate all legitimate competition. Although there are considerable variations in the cases, the following generalizations seem to hold true.

1. In the particular historical circumstances of the 1950s, when the "winds of change" were starting to blow, however softly, the first competently organized political party to espouse independence openly or at least to appear to be working toward that goal held a considerable advantage. The party that could seize and hold the nationalist initiative quickly developed a popular appeal that was difficult to challenge.

2. For reasons common to most underdeveloped areas, politics tend to

12. Jean-Pierre N'Diaye, *Enquête sur les étudiants noirs en France* (Paris: Réalitiés Africaines, 1962), p. 216.
13. Social Surveys (Gallup Poll) Ltd., "Attitudes on International Affairs among African Students in Britain" (July 1963).

be heavily dominated by personalities, and the party that could first establish a leader as a symbol of national unity and progress, by whatever means, could use his personal investiture as a crucial stamp of approval which, denied to the opposition, could substantially reduce its popular appeal. Whether or not this appeal can usefully be called charisma need not concern us here.[14] The fact remains that TANU (Tanganyika African National Union) is Nyerere's party; Nkrumah was the CPP much more than the CPP ever was Ghana, and in 1960 the writer found some lower-level rural party functionaries in Senegal who recognized the name of the party they worked for only when *le parti de Senghor* was appended to it.

3. The behavior of colonial administrations frequently contributed to the emergence of a single party. After initially denouncing an incipient nationalist movement and perhaps imprisoning its leader, the administrations commonly found themselves obliged, if not by local circumstances then by parliamentary pressure at home, to seek accommodation with some "responsible spokesman" for African opinion. Typically, after a few false starts with Notable or Old Bourgeois leaders, the administration worked out a mutually beneficial modus vivendi with the mass party leader which increased his prestige while leaving most of his anti-colonialist aura intact. The colonial administration was permitted to hand over power with a minimum of unpleasantness, and the mass party, in exchange for some harmless forbearance, helped plan the transitional structures so as to maximize its own powers.

4. All of the single-party states considered here are small-scale societies. The largest, Tanzania, contains some 12 million people, but the median figure is about 3.5 million. The economic scale of the most prosperous is about that of the city of New Haven, Connecticut, and the rate of economic growth is lower. The effective number of political actors in the years just preceding and following independence probably did not exceed 5,000 in most cases, a number well within the range of a gregarious individual's circle of personal acquaintances. In political as well as economic scale, these countries are comparable to Western cities or counties, units which in countries with entrenched national traditions of political opposition are frequently under the control of a single party. In effect, everyone in politics knew everyone else and could probably trace extended family relationships or at least an old school tie in common with a substantial portion of the rest of the political elite. Such ties greatly facilitated building a wide coalition and co-opting leaders of opposition movements into the mass party. This was particularly true right at the

14. David E. Apter uses the term sensibly in "Nkrumah, Charisma, and the Coup," *Daedalus* 97, no. 3 (Summer 1968): 757–92.

time of independence when there were plenty of new jobs to be distributed to the faithful and when it was made clear that anyone outside the political fold would get none. This threat was particularly effective against rival Nationalist Middle Class leaders who rarely had the sort of private economic position which would let them maintain their standard of living without the tolerance of the political authorities.

5. Those interested in such things could easily find ideological legitimation for a single party in the dynamic of nationalism itself.[15] True nationalism, by and large an unquestioned good, required solid national unity in order to fight that great single enemy, "imperialism." Anyone who refused to enter into the great nationalistic movement could easily be portrayed as an enemy of the people, a tool of foreign interests, and not just another political leader. After independence, the diffuse threat of neocolonialism replaced a more concrete imperialism, and the internal goal of economic and social development continued the need for resolute unity behind the nation's leaders. To the degree that the ruling party claimed to be following an integrated and carefully thought-out plan of economic development, even pressure group activity which might distort the plan and thus slow down the pace of national growth could be seen as patently illegitimate and antinational activity. Part of the reason why so many African states have sought to implement balanced growth plans requiring highly centralized decision making considerably beyond their administrative competence is certainly that such plans would seem to require, and thus legitimize, the sort of uniform political control to which the ruling parties aspired. As one perceptive economist said after examining Mali's socialist plan, "These people are Stalinists, but not Marxists."

6. Beyond such ideological concerns, whether advanced in good faith or with a fair component of cynicism, the Nationalist Middle Class leaders of the mass party have had a major concern that any sort of fragmentation into competitive parties could only be along the lines of ethnic attachments. Quite aside from the dangers that such an eventuality might present for national development and tranquility, it might well spell the end of political domination, not just by the party in power, but by the Nationalist Middle Class as a whole, since fragmentation might return leadership to the Notables and to a lesser degree to the Old Bourgeoisie, who could more effectively mobilize local sentiments for political ends.

15. Perhaps the best expression of this is contained in the article by Madeira Keita, "Le parti unique en Afrique," *Présence africaine* 20 (February–March, 1960): 3–24. On the interrelations between nationalism and appeals to unity in Africa see Wilfred H. Whiteley, "Political Concepts and Connotations," *African Affairs No. 1*, St. Antony's Papers, 10 (Carbondale, Ill.: Southern Illinois University Press, 1961), pp. 7–21.

While this fear may well be overemphasized by the men in power, the ethnic violence in such places as the Congo and Nigeria increased such anxieties.

7. Finally, the political and administrative structures that the single-party African states inherited from the colonial era lacked legitimate, modern political substructures within which competing political parties could establish solid regional bases of power from which they could not be ousted. It is significant that the major African states to have maintained multiparty systems for some time after independence were basically federations in which political parties could establish a solid base within one region and, with this support behind them, maintain minority parties in other regions. As in Nigeria, the federal level could see some meaningful competition between regionally secure parties which no majority group could easily destroy. Similarly, the eight states of French West Africa, all of which subsequently developed single-party regimes, functioned under an effective two-party system at the federal level before the federal structure was dismantled in 1958.[16] Whatever constitutional legacy the colonial powers thought they were leaving the African countries, what really counted in the experience of the new African regimes was the administrative legacy, and that was one of centralized authoritarian control. Electoral divisions were very quickly aligned on the administrative divisions, and in most cases as soon as one party achieved a clear majority in the central legislature, it changed the electoral rules into a winner-take-all national slate system, so the majority would be turned into legislative unanimity. Either after or just before this political sleight of hand, most of the legal opposition leaders faced facts and agreed to merge their parties with that of the ruling group or just to retire from active political life.

Opposition Within the Independent State

Independence, of course, has not brought an end to opposition, even where the other parties have been dissolved. The problems a new regime must face are immense. Even where, as in the Ivory Coast, a government is dramatically successful in promoting economic development, some political leaders have been sqeezed out and some areas of the country have felt disadvantaged. In most African countries, the mass party structure is not strong enough and the regime is too limited in top administrative talent to implement its economic goals and too distrustful of the New Intelligentsia returning from the universities to turn out enough of the

16. Foltz, *From French West Africa*, chap. 4. One of the main reasons the federation and its rump successor, the Mali Federation, was abandoned was precisely to assure single-party control in states that felt threatened by the federal-level competition.

old party faithful to give the graduates executive responsibility. In short, once independence turns from a powerful campaign slogan into a long-term responsibility, the single-party regime encounters most of the same problems that rendered the colonial regime unpopular.

The forms opposition may take vary considerably according to the opportunities left available by the regime and the courage and enterprise of the opponents.

1. *Continuing formal opposition.* Not all opposition leaders cross the carpet and dissolve their organization when it is made clear that they will never win another election nor share in the rewards of government, and in only a minority of effective single-party states are other parties legally prohibited. For awhile after independence, remnants of parties, like the United Party of Ghana until 1963, may continue to oppose government policies in parliament, although, as in Ghana, such opposition had no opportunity to affect policies or to bring its case before the public and although members not already jailed were certain to lose their seats in the next election.

Where the regime is squeamish about eliminating formal opposition despite clear intention to reserve all power to itself, small parties may continue to exist even without the protection of parliamentary immunity. Senegal provides a particularly interesting case to examine, since it has permitted a small margin of freedom for opposition parties to organize and present candidates, although only with the tacit proviso that they will under no circumstances be allowed to win any seats. It is thus possible to observe in Senegal the sorts of formal oppositions that might have developed in more stringent single-party states where men who have attempted to activate constitutional provisions guaranteeing freedom to form political parties have been summarily jailed. In Senegal one legal opposition party, the PRA-Sénégal (Parti de Regroupement Africain-Sénégal), though unrepresented in political office, carried over from pre-independence days. This party's leadership was heavily dominated by New Intelligentsia (its three top leaders were all university teachers or researchers), most of whom had for a brief period been active in the ruling Union Progressiste Sénégalaise, but the party also benefited from the support of one perpetually dissatisfied region for an ethnic favorite son. Prevented by government harassment and by its lack of rewards to distribute from acquiring a popular base outside this one region, it found its support almost exclusively in the ranks of the educated elite. At the time of its merger with the UPS in 1966, its active membership, heavily concentrated in the urban areas, was about 7,000.

The Bloc des Masses Sénégalaises, formed two years after independence, brought together a more varied set of opposition leaders whose cohesion was based almost entirely on dislike of the ruling party. The leadership included: a few members of the New Intelligentsia who had played no role in preindependence politics and who did not get along, mostly for reasons of personal rivalry, with the PRA-Sénégal leaders; some members of an Old Bourgeois faction which had caused persistent trouble after being absorbed by the ruling party and which had been expelled shortly after independence; and a few rural Notables who felt that they had been slighted by the government. The latter two groups made their peace with the ruling party after a year and a half of desultory operations, leaving only a rump group of New Intelligentsia supported by one unhappy Muslim religious leader who apparently has found it convenient to maintain the rather remote threat of a revival of the party as a weapon to force greater consideration in the government's distribution of largesse.

Each of the formal opposition leaders has some sort of reasonably secure base in society — whether in an academic sanctuary, in business, or through traditional status — that permits him to receive social deference, to maintain a suitable standard of living, and to support a few loyal helpers even in opposition. Virtually none of the Nationalist Middle Class enjoy such security, and, should they go into opposition, ideological fervor, personal desperation, or simple recklessness are likely to be strong components of their political motivations. It must be recognized that while it could be inconvenient, embarrassing, and perhaps even costly for the government to eliminate the legal opposition, a regime which commanded the army's loyalty could certainly arrange such elimination were it to feel seriously threatened.

In East Africa, both Kenya (in 1969) and Uganda (in 1966) have become de facto single-party regimes on the Senegalese model, and Zambia, under pressure from ethnic dissidence and southern African guerrilla bands quartered on her soil, is moving close to the same position. It seems likely in these three cases that what we now see is the use of central governmental power to force the creation of a broad nationalist-type coalition that sharp ethnic and regional cleavages prevented during the ruling party's early years.

A more widespread pattern of formal opposition is the illegal revolutionary party dedicated to the violent overthrow of the regime. At least three have been active against single-party regimes in the last few years — the Senegalese Parti Africain de l'Indépendance, the Niger Sawaba, and the Front de Libération National Guinéen, which has sought to overthrow the regime of Sékou Touré. The first two started as legitimate parties and were driven into illegality shortly after independence. The PAI, formed under the leadership of African students in France in 1957, from the start considered itself a Marxist-Leninist party and signed a formal pact with the French Communist Party in 1962. Sawaba had been a much more standard competitor for political power during the colonial period (and was defeated only with a strong assist from a particularly reactionary colonial administration), but when forced into exile apparently found it necessary to veer sharply to the left in its ideological pronouncements and in its foreign associations. The PAI has launched guerrilla attacks and Sawaba assassination attempts from friendly African bases, Mali in the case of the PAI and Ghana in the case of Sawaba.[17]

The FLNG has apparently brought together a varied coalition of people opposed to the Touré regime, including several disaffected members of Touré's own party appalled at the economic difficulties the country has experienced. Many of these were once leaders of opposition groups who rallied to Touré's cause only at the time of independence. Others are Notables from ethnic groups that feel slighted in the regime's councils and some recent students influenced by Chinese-style communism who are outraged at Touré's "revisionist" Marxism and at his acceptance of American foreign investment.[18] Like the PAI and Sawaba the FLNG has operated from a friendly African base, first the Ivory Coast and then Portuguese Guinea, and almost certainly has attracted external financing. Unlike them, however, it has something of a ready-made popular base in the two hundred thousand Guineans who have left their country to make a living in Senegal and the Ivory Coast. So far the FLNG has made no apparent attempt to arrive at any program or ideology — even a borrowed one — except to agree that things should be different.

Both foreign financing and a nearby base in a friendly African country appear to be essential to the continued operation of these exile movements. The former seems readily available from African as well as non-African sources that feel they have something to gain from turmoil. The second has become a bit more difficult as leaders have increasingly turned from the millennial schemes for African unity that characterized the first years after independence and under the conservative influence of the Organization of African Unity have come increasingly to accept the territorial status quo. The PAI and Sawaba lost their main exile bases, in 1965 and 1966 respectively, and the Ivory Coast put a damper on open FLNG activities in 1970.

A more common form of exile opposition lacks any organizational base but is led from abroad by a defeated politician who hopes things will get so bad that he will be called back to office. Most of these men were once part of a ruling coalition, but, perhaps because they grew too powerful, were ousted from the leadership. Oscar Kambona (Tanzania);

---

17. On Sawaba's use of Ghana as a base, see the post-Nkrumah government's white paper, "Nkrumah's Deception of Africa" (Accra, 1967?), pp. 5–7 and appendixes. On the PAI's guerrilla activities, see William J. Foltz, "Le Parti Africain de l'Indépendance," *Revue française d'études politiques africaines* 45 (September 1969): 8–35.
18. The arguments of this latter group are developed at length by the pseudonymous B. Ameillon, *La Guinée, bilan d'une indépendance* (Paris: Maspéro, 1964).

Masauko Chipembere (Malawi); the late Kabaka Mutesa (Uganda) and, until 1966, Koffi Busia and Komlah Gbedemah of Ghana are among the most prominent. Few of these men have proposed serious programmatic alternatives, and few stand much chance, through their own efforts, to return to power. Only the last two have returned to political life, and then as the result of a military coup rather than their own initiative.

But more than money and a territorial base are required for any serious attempts to seize power, and so far none of the exile opposition has shown an ability to appeal to wide enough sectors of the domestic population to provoke a general insurrection, nor enough organization or determination to stick with a Cuba-style guerrilla revolt. To judge from events in other African countries, a minimal condition for maintaining an armed revolt would appear to be a sympathetic ethnic base within the country, such as the Union des Populations Camerounaises has enjoyed among the Bamileke, although this raises the possibility that other groups not otherwise strongly involved will rally to the government as a way of settling old scores against the dissident tribe. As Willard Johnson has convincingly argued, the UPC rebellion produced an "integrative backlash" which facilitated the consolidation of government power.[19] Much more promising is a Zanzibar-style revolution in which a small military input led the African majority of the island to rise in bloody revolt against the ruling Arab minority.[20] However, none of the single-party states in Africa is based on such a narrow and distinctive ethnic minority.

2. *Informal domestic opposition.* Most single-party regimes would be delighted if the only opposition they faced came from exiled malcontents. Domestic opposition is harder to combat, and the closer it is to the ruling leadership itself, the more worrisome it becomes and the more it costs the regime to stamp it out. The most obvious sources of opposition are the few structured interest-group organizations that African states inherit at independence, the most common of which are urban ethnic or religious associations, economic organizations such as trade unions and associations of African traders and businessmen, and finally student and youth groups. The regime is likely to be particularly sensitive to the behavior of these organizations because historically it was by gaining control over such organizations that the Nationalist Middle Class was able to begin building the organizational and communications bases for the mass party.

The African single-party regime is singularly ill equipped to deal openly with such interest groups, and the more seriously it takes its role as single

19. Willard Johnson, *The Cameroun Federation* (Princeton: Princeton University Press, 1970), pp. 348–62.
20. On the Zanzibar case, see Michael F. Lofchie, *Zanzibar: Background to Revolution* (Princeton: Princeton University Press, 1965), particularly pp. 69–98, 257–84, and John Okello, *Revolution in Zanzibar* (Nairobi: East African Publishing House, 1967).

spokesman for the masses, the more difficult is the task. The regimes reject the idea of bargaining directly with these specific interests outside the party framework and thus are faced with a choice between incorporating the interest groups into the party (and thus risking a loss of party cohesion and a watering down of purpose) or of simply repressing the organizations and the expression of such interests and thus risking serious loss of information and ultimately popular support. Unfortunately, single-party leaders are often tempted to try to do both, thus turning all expression of interest into a matter involving the structure or personnel of the regime while still creating a disaffected interest group.

The most straightforward cases for single-party regimes are the ethnic and religious associations, which are usually either forbidden altogether or are allowed to exist only in the most anodyne and apolitical form, since their open participation in political affairs would seriously contravene the single-party's claim to be building national unity. Business groups, too, have generally been denied any effective organized political expression, and this is all the easier for the regimes to contemplate if, as is frequently the case, the economic plan implies a diminishing role for African — though not necessarily foreign — private enterprise. Where, as in the Ivory Coast, Kenya, Liberia, and to a lesser extent Senegal, the regime has encouraged local businessmen, they have generally been kept too individually dependent on government loans, import licenses, or quota allotments of primary products for their processing plants to constitute a serious group challenge to the regime.[21]

Labor and youth provide the toughest problems because they involve mostly urban people who are physically close to the seat of political power and because both labor and youth movement members are drawn from the Nationalist Middle Class group that has provided the core support for the regime in the past. Both labor and youth have the smallest stake in the regime and the most to gain from rapid change of the sort that early nationalist rhetoric promised and that few independent regimes have been able to deliver. The issue on which youth and labor are most likely to unite is that of "Africanization" or "localization," the replacement of European, Asian, or even foreign African cadres and advisors by local Africans. Governments which feel they must continue to employ foreigners in visible positions are subject to repeated attack couched in the established rhetoric of nationalism.

While attacks on the position of Europeans may have the strongest logical consistency, they rarely evoke the popular support that accompanies attacks on foreign Africans (seen as competition for low-level

21. For a useful analysis of the dependent position of businessmen in such societies, see Fred W. Riggs, *Administration in Developing Countries* (Boston: Houghton Mifflin, 1964), chap. 3, especially pp. 114–16.

salaried jobs) and Asians (the essential and universally disliked middle-men, moneylenders and shopkeepers). A government under pressure can usually be assured of a short reprieve by expelling at least a symbolic number of Dahomeans, Togolese, Ibos, or Indians.

All of the single-party regimes have moved to bring labor and youth under some form of party control, usually by amalgamating all groups into a party labor or youth movement. Such action, however, has merely displaced the problem from a nominally nonparty to a party setting and furthermore provided an opportunity for frustrated political entrepreneurs within the party to seek to rise as party spokesmen for one of these coordinate groups. As Wallerstein pointed out, this has only made the top leaders more sensitive than ever to the claims of the interest group, which now could speak from an unimpeachable political vantage point and could advance the fortunes of a man, conceivably to the point where he could challenge the top leadership itself.[22] The result, as in Guinea and Mali in 1963, in Ghana in 1964, and in Tanzania and Mali again in 1967, has been discreet but severe repression of the powers of the party spokesmen for these interests. The effects of such crackdowns are varied; most dramatically such events were the prelude to the riots leading to the military overthrow of weak regimes in Dahomey and Upper Volta; and a slightly stronger one in the Congo-Brazzaville was only just barely able to stand off an attack from its Red-Guard-style Jeunesse, which forced the party leaders to barricade themselves in the soccer stadium under the protection of Cuban troops. More usually, such crackdowns have been accepted, at least for the moment, and have turned the more determined members of the interest group into a silent opposition, biding its time.

University student groups in Africa — as elsewhere — tend to oppose their governments, but their opposition is heavily colored both by generational and by educational discrepancies of considerably more moment than those that trouble students in more developed societies. Although opposition to the single-party regimes frequently is cast in ideological form — of the left or of the right, whichever is the opposite of the direction imputed to the regime — student opposition, like that of the earlier members of the New Intelligentsia, generally seeks primarily to establish social distance between themselves and the Nationalist Middle Class regime. Most of the African regimes have ceased getting excited about the student manifestoes and resolutions at international meetings condemning the politicians' various iniquities and have concentrated on working out bases on which individual graduates can go to work for the government. In particular they have sought to establish arrangements by

22. Immanuel Wallerstein, "The Decline of the Party in Single-Party African States" in Joseph LaPalombara and Myron Weiner, eds., *Political Parties and Political Development* (Princeton: Princeton University Press, 1966), pp. 201–14.

which graduates may serve as technocrats, without making more than a cursory commitment to militance in the political party. In essence, the parties hope to buy time and silence from the students, time during which they hope to achieve, with the technocrats' help, enough progress to make them invulnerable to determined opposition from the New Intelligentsia.[23]

As elsewhere, university students are likely to be politically effective only when they can articulate grievances widely held in the population at large and when they do not appear as a remote group interested only in augmenting its own privileges. The Guinea and Tanzania governments successfully isolated and crushed student challenges to their authority by attacking them in simple class-interest terms and by mobilizing labor and urban youth with only primary school education to oppose the university and secondary school elite. Governments faced with joint labor-student revolts have been obliged to rely on military or police force to maintain power, and even if they succeed in putting down the revolt (as for example in Senegal in 1968) they may feel obliged to make substantial concessions to student and labor demands.

3. *Intra-party opposition.* V. O. Key noted in his study of American single-party states, *Southern Politics,* that "Characteristically in one-party politics . . . a strong political combination tends to force rival political elements to associate in an opposition faction. Strong political leadership, be it personal or organized, seems to produce counterorganization." [24] It is the political good fortune of most of the African chiefs of state that intraparty factions have not organized with the primary goal of getting rid of the man who combines both supreme party and governmental leadership. The power and prestige of a chief of state, his control over the means of coercion and publicity, and his essentially lifetime political mandate render nearly worthless and quite hazardous such opposition organization from within. If one goes after the chief, one goes after the regime as a whole, for the party is likely to go down with its boss.[25] Applied to lower levels, however, Key's generalization is apt, and factions grouped along ideological, regional, or personal lines are standard — if inconstant — features of every party level below the very top. One of the most enduring forms is the faction composed primarily of members of an early opposition party that merged at independence with the ruling party, particularly if such a faction has close ties with one or more

---

23. Drake, "The Anxious Generation," pp. 388–427, and Joel D. Barkan, "African University Students and Social Change" (Ph.D. dissertation, U.C.L.A., 1970).
24. V. O. Key, Jr., *Southern Politics* (New York: Vintage Books, 1949), p. 124.
25. The one major case of a party faction trying to unseat a chief of state came in Senegal in 1962, when a faction led by the prime minister came very close to doing so. At the time Senegal was the only single-party state to divide party and government executive responsibility between two men. This constitutional anomaly was quickly abolished after the attempted coup proved unsuccessful.

important regional or ethnic groups whose support the party requires.[26] Such factions are, however, highly visible, and their extraparty links usually limit their effectiveness at the national level. Many factions, particularly those linked with or seeking support from a particular interest group may give themselves a strong cold war ideological coloring, perhaps also in hopes that an interested foreign embassy may care to bankroll their activities. However, far too many of these ideological distinctions turn out to be no more than verbal quibbles or passing opportunistic fancies for one to rank international ideological competition as a significant cause of African factionalism. Rather than causing factionalism in ruling parties, great power competition seems to provide intellectual legitimation and an appropriate vocabulary in which to express reasons for personal, generational, or regional antagonisms.

As Key suggests will be the case in states where the party is organized along lines of personal loyalty, factions tend to be based ultimately on personal loyalty or antipathy rather than on promoting specifically defined policies or interests. This tendency is encouraged by the existence at the top of the regime of a near-untouchable chief whose personal support is the most valuable single asset a lower-level politician can possess. The risk of sycophantism whereby the boss is told only what others think will please him is great, and Kwame Nkrumah's fall is an object lesson of its dangers.[27] Even if a leader avoids such fatal loss of information by listening to as many factions as he can and encouraging them to tell all on their rivals, he will only exacerbate the personal quality of factional feuds. Since the opposition between the New Intelligentsia and the Nationalist Middle Class leaders is based as much on matters of style and social solidarity as on concrete policy issues, this competition, to the degree that is it expressed within the party, also takes a highly personal form.

The most ambitious attempt to structure and control oppositions within a single-party framework is Tanzania's experiment with genuinely competitive elections involving two candidates for parliament running under

26. Examples of such factions are the "PRD" faction of S. M. Apithy, based on Porto Novo in Dahomey, the "Old Socialists" in Senegal, based on support in St. Louis, and the "Forest Bloc" in Guinea.

27. The growing literature on Nkrumah's fall is more noteworthy for its polemical than its analytic power, but most writers would seem to agree with Bretton that as "the result of Nkrumah's tendency to purge his environment of intellectually superior, and most important, independent-minded individuals . . . the learning capacity of Ghana was reduced to the learning capacity of Kwame Nkrumah." Henry Bretton, *The Rise and Fall of Kwame Nkrumah* (New York: Praeger, 1966), p. 142. Nkrumah's admission, "I had for long the gravest doubts about many of those in leading positions in my party," lends credence to Bretton's point. Kwame Nkrumah, *Dark Days in Ghana* (New York: International Publishers, 1968), p. 73.

TANU auspices in each electoral district.[28] The candidates were proposed by their local party organizations and approved by the TANU National Executive Committee. No coordination between candidates in different districts was permitted, and each candidate was required to campaign within the ideological framework the party had set up. Under these circumstances, personality and the most narrowly defined local issues were stressed in the campaign, but equally decisive in the voters' minds may have been their general attitudes toward the regime as expressed through their acceptance or rejection of incumbents. The 1965 elections impressed observers with their honesty, and clearly the party's top leadership learned much from the results, which included the defeat of over half the incumbent MP's running and of 22 out of 31 TANU officials. Since the parliament itself has only advisory functions, and since the president could appoint key defeated men to parliament as national members, however, the regime risked comparatively little in the elections. Because of the safeguards against coordination between different candidates, and because the party moved after the election to tighten restrictions against party members speaking publicly out of turn, the elections do not seem to have materially changed the conditions under which Tanzanian factions operate nor opened up acceptable means for party members to discuss major differences publicly.

What can political oppositions do? The African single-party state limits sharply the range of activities open to the various forms of political opposition and also the utility of these oppositions for the development of the political system as a whole. People who choose an opposition role may seek to promote a specific group interest, attain personal advantage, change the regime, or conceivably just oppose for opposition's sake. As we have seen, promoting a policy interest is the hardest of all goals to implement by itself. The regime is structured so as to deny any opposition, within or outside the party, the use of a meaningful public forum to build support for its case or to explore openly alternative strategies to those proposed by the government. Legislatures, which might serve such a purpose, are too tightly controlled to be effective. Any real discussion takes place in private caucus sessions under party auspices in which party leaders can effectively crack the whip. At most, legislators, local political officials, and civil servants can attempt to affect policy by exercising a limited veto power through legislative foot-dragging and slovenly implementation of policies they dislike. With the means of communication under the con-

28. On the 1965 Tanzanian election, see Bienen, *Tanzania*, pp. 382–405, and Lionel Cliffe, ed., *One Party Democracy: A Study of the 1965 Tanzania General Election* (Nairobi: East African Publishing House, 1967). As yet no adequate account has been published of the 1970 elections.

trol of the top party leadership, public information becomes a matter of rumor or slogan, neither terribly helpful. One standard technique of both intra- and extraparty opposition is the mimeographed tract thrown into the central marketplace or stuffed mysteriously into government mailboxes. However, most tract literature seeks primarily to achieve shock and immediate impact by criticizing some particular abuse, like the corruption of an individual minister, or by indicting the whole regime for "oppressing the people" or for "selling out" to some nefarious foreign interest. Neither form is well adapted for much more than waging a personal vendetta or creating a vague feeling of insecurity within the regime.

The single-party theorists retort that the party itself will provide the forum within which specific interests can be defended. As Nyerere argued in 1963, "A National Movement which is open to all — which is identified with the whole nation — has nothing to fear from the discontent of any excluded section of society, for there is no such section." [29] However, Tanzania's case itself has shown since that speech was made that, as the regime comes to be beset with more and more problems, the old emphasis on upward communication of grievances that was useful to the party in the nationalist period is sharply reversed.[30] Downward communication from the top party leadership becomes the rule and is reinforced by the leadership's right to approve nominations to lower party offices and particularly by the president's ability to give his personal investiture. This means that the most effective means of representing group interests is to put sympathetic men in top party councils where they can themselves influence party politics and also get the ear of the chief. LeVine asked elites in four single-party states what in their opinion was the best tactic for influencing governmental decisions. Thirty-nine mentioned some form of personal contact with top leaders as the best tactic, while only seven preferred acting through the political party.[31]

Opposition for purposes of personal advancement is part and parcel of the factionalism based on personality that dominates the political life of the single-party African regimes. This is true of political opposition outside as well as inside the party. For extraparty opposition the technique is one of making just enough of a fuss — without appearing to be totally subversive — to persuade the regime to admit the opposing leaders into its good graces and into an advantageous position. This has been the principal tactic of most of the aforementioned Senegalese opposition. Two of

29. Julius Nyerere, speech of 14 January 1963, reprinted as "Democracy and the One-Party State" (Dar es Salaam: Tanganyika Standard, 1963).
30. The 1967 "Arusha Declaration" of TANU party principles emphasized ideological conformity to a selective view of the interests of "farmers and workers" who alone are said to comprise the party. For a good analysis of communications within the Tanzanian regime, see Raymond F. Hopkins, "The Role of the M.P. in Tanzania," *American Political Science Review* 64, no. 3 (September 1970): 754–71.
31. LeVine, *Political Leadership in Africa*, pp. 46–47.

the three BMS factions came to terms with the governing party after only a year and a half of issuing manifestoes and tracts, and all of the PRA-Sénégal eventually did, and on very good terms. Even several members of the illegal PAI have now returned to the fold, following the Soviet Union's decision to sacrifice unsuccessful local Communist parties to the more immediate cause of implementing cordial state-to-state relations.[32] For unhappy party factions the same tactic, generally implemented through foot-dragging on developmental projects, may prove useful by obliging the top leaders to buy out a well-entrenched regional faction. Such tactics are of the high risk–high gain sort but have often been successful because they can appeal to the party's tradition of building a broad coalition representative of all aspects of the nation. The usual tactic of the top leadership in such cases is to keep these opponents from building a united opposition front which could command a high political price in terms of offices allotted to it for quieting down and to reduce their bargaining to the coldest cash terms.

The only form of opposition that avoids these pitfalls is systematic opposition for opposition's sake by which a group with some sort of respected position in society simply withholds support from the regime and refuses to cooperate with it. Many Notables and a few of the Old Bourgeoisie have maintained enough power or respect among groups the regimes consider crucial to make their opposition potentially of more than passing interest. More recently this role has fallen principally to the New Intelligentsia, who work either in exile through ideological parties or within the country in some nonpolitical capacity. Their role is to complain, to establish their independence from the regime, and to wait for things to get so bad that popular or military revolt forces a change in the regime.

"Nonpolitical" Oppositions

The lack of formal and legitimate organizations has, then, greatly reduced the utility of most political and extragovernment opposition in single-party African states. Within the governmental establishment, however, two continuing bureaucracies, the civil service and the military, have provided organizational frameworks capable of supporting varying degrees of opposition activity. The fact that these bureaucracies are considered essential either to the day-to-day activities of a political regime or to its long-term survival puts them in a much solider position than that of other social groups. Individual soldiers or civil servants may not, of

---

32. This policy was publicly communicated by Alexander Sobolev to the African "progressive" parties at the October 1966 seminar on Africa arranged by the Soviet-sponsored publication, *World Marxist Review*. A fair summary of Sobolev's speech is contained in *The African Communist*, no. 28 (first quarter 1967), pp. 32–40.

course, have secure personal positions, though there is a limit to the extent
that politicians can interfere with personnel matters without gravely
affecting performance or in the case of the military bringing open rebellion. Those countries with a fairly large educated class can tolerate
more such political intervention without losing effectiveness than can
those with a tiny New Intelligentsia group, but the political risks of
severely alienating such a group may be correspondingly greater.

Of the two bureaucracies, the civil service is in much the better position to perform the ongoing functions of an opposition and can do so
to some extent simply by continuing to exercise some of the powers
bequeathed to it by the colonial regime.[33] Whatever the underlying political realities of later colonial regimes in Africa, the European civil servants
sought consciously — indeed painfully — to project an image of strict adherence to rational-legal bureaucratic norms. And the fact that the power
of these civil servants was challenged by Nationalist Middle Class politicians during the nationalist period reinforced the antipolitical aspects of
their bureaucratic behavior. Few colonial bureaucracies underwent significant structural change following independence, and the young educated Africans who moved into civil service positions were subjected to
strong pressures leading them to accept existing bureaucratic norms. Many
of the New Intelligentsia took courses at the same European institutions
which had previously trained European colonial administrators and where
they were taught by some of the more accomplished and sympathetic
former colonial officers. As one writer has epigrammatically summed up
this continuity, "The colonial service is dead; long live the school of public
administration." [34] In some cases, too, their work was judged by Europeans
manning top "technical" posts in the bureaucracies of the new independent
states. While the African bureaucrats protested, sometimes successfully,
against the continued employment of expatriate technical assistants, they
have had little inducement to challenge the legitimacy or basic norms of
the structures providing their jobs. The feeling against the Nationalist
Middle Class politicians, so evident among university students, could only

33. Richard Symonds, *The British and Their Successors* (Evanston: Northwestern
University Press, 1966), and the issue of *Le mois en Afrique* 2 (February 1966)
provide good general treatments of African bureaucratic functioning. Nelson Kasfir,
"Prismatic Theory and African Administration," *World Politics* 21, no. 2 (January
1969): 295–314, is a particularly useful discussion of the political setting of African
bureaucracies. In a tantalizing article, Last has argued that the Hausaland "civil
service" has continued to perform analogous opposition functions from the time of
the Fulani jihad to the present day. A similar argument could be made for other
bureaucratically organized traditional systems, such as that of Buganda. Murray Last,
"Aspects of Administration and Dissent in Hausaland, 1800–1968," in *Africa* 40, no. 4
(October 1970): 345–57.
34. Martin Staniland, "Colonial Government and Populist Reform: The Case of the
Ivory Coast," *Journal of Administration Overseas* 10, no. 1 (January 1971): 42.

be reinforced by their service in a bureaucracy modeled along colonial lines.

Such feelings of distrust are likely to be amply repaid by the politicians who, in a sense, feel themselves condemned to employ the New Intelligentsia and thereby turn over control of politically important resources to a group of Johnny-come-lately's whose motives and principles are suspect. It is not unusual to see government departments, particularly those dealing with rural expenditures, develop a dual hierarchy: one part filled with New Intelligentsia technocrats, the other with the political faithful whose mission is to watch what the technocrats are up to and whose effect is to paralyze much of their purposive activity.

While it has become fashionable, both in Africa and abroad, to denounce African civil servants for willful corruption, high living, and resistance to innovation, it is usually more helpful to understand their behavior in terms of the conflicting social pressures on them and their often frustrated attempts to render public service toward developmental goals according to a technocratic vision ill adapted to the demands of political leaders and perhaps also to those of a resistant peasant society.[35] If civil servants resist the politicians' imposition of an austerity budget, they do so in part because it is they who will experience the most severe cuts in living standard, not the politicians, at the same time that their programs are cut back. Anyone familiar with the phenomenon of relative deprivation will recognize that it avails little for political leaders or World Bank officials to point out to a man whose professional reference group is European administrators that his cash income is in any case several dozen times that of a poor peasant. Unless a regime is unusually politically effective and wealthy, it will give its bureaucrats ample reasons for dissatisfaction. At the same time, the bureaucrats' technocratic vision may provide a source of stable and development-oriented norms (however imprecise) around which the dissatisfied may organize. The continuing bureaucratic structures offer a framework within which communications for opposition purposes may be carried out as part of the normal round of daily business, while the bureaucrats themselves provide

35. See, for example, Ronald Wraith and Edgar Simpkins, *Corruption in Developing Countries* (London: Allen and Unwin, 1963), and René Dumont, *Afrique noire est mal partie* (Paris: Seuil, 1962). A more balanced perspective is provided by Colin Leys, "What Is the Problem about Corruption?" *Journal of Modern African Studies* 3 (1965): 215–30. D. J. Murray, "The Western Nigerian Civil Service through Political Crises and Military Coups," *Journal of Commonwealth Political Studies* 8, no. 3 (November 1970): 229–40, presents a good case study of the African civil service which made the most serious attempt to adjust to new conditions but which still found itself with an "absence of accord between the principles on which the region's administration is organized and those underlying the social and political organization of the community" (p. 230).

a visible, technically skilled, and socially respectable source of manpower for a new political regime.

The military, even more than the civil service, was kept outside politics under the colonial regime and inherited strong apolitical norms which could become explicitly antipolitical when the issue was one of intervention by politicians in "professional" military decisions. "Keep the army out of politics and politics out of the army," was the farewell message of Ghana's first Chief of Defense Staff. Though he was British, his message rang true to his African successors, who came to blame Nkrumah for politicizing their army.[36] While it is difficult to find reliable information on the social origins of African military officers, few of them seem to have come out of Notable or Old Bourgeois backgrounds. Military training has been their means of social advancement, as university education had been for members of the New Intelligentsia, and the European-type professional norms taught in military academies or in the ranks have given the thinking of most officers a technocratic cast.[37] As Nordlinger has shown, there is considerably less incompatibility between the African military's perception of its corporate interests and a strong commitment to economic development and change than is true for most military establishments in the rest of the underdeveloped world.[38] African military leaders' post-coup affirmations of their commitment to rapid economic development should not be dismissed as mere window dressing, however situations may frustrate their realization. At the very least these technocratic norms, coupled with a tolerance for economic development and a distaste for politicians, are quite enough to facilitate ready understanding between the military and the bureaucratic New Intelligentsia in situations where both feel that economic stagnation and political decay threaten their jobs or professional autonomy as well as the development of the society they are pledged to serve.

The organization of African armies and their coup-making propensities have been well enough described elsewhere not to require elaboration here.[39] Even more than the civil service the military possesses autonomous

36. Major-General H. T. Alexander, *African Tightrope* (London: Pall Mall Press, 1965), pp. 4–5, quoting General Paley. See also the personal accounts of two of Ghana's coup-makers, A. A. Afrifa, *The Ghana Coup* (London: Frank Cass, 1968), and A. K. Ocran, *A Myth Is Broken: An Account of the Ghana Coup d'État* (London, 1968).

37. See Robert M. Price "A Theoretical Approach to Military Rule in New States: Reference-Group Theory and the Ghanaian Case," *World Politics* 23, no. 3 (April 1971): 399–430.

38. Eric A. Nordlinger, "Soldiers in Mufti: The Impact of Military Rule upon Economic and Social Change in the Non-Western States," *American Political Science Review* 64, no. 4 (December 1970): 1131–48.

39. See particularly J. M. Lee, *African Armies and Civil Order* (New York: Praeger, 1969), and William J. Foltz "Psychanalyse des armées sud-sahariennes," *Revue française d'études politiques africaines* 14 (February 1967): 22–29.

organizational structures which facilitate internal communication and trust among at least small groups of like-minded people and the organizational and material resources to bring down any government. The knowledge that civil servants share much of their frustration can lend legitimacy to their armed action against a political regime. Traditions of political reticence and in some cases factionalism within the officer corps have made it difficult for the military establishments to exercise continuing influence over most civilian government policies; the military is no substitute for a loyal opposition. Rather its power is that of a latent threat to overthrow a regime should its policies prove unacceptable to key military leaders.

The military's main opposition function, then, is the extraordinary one of leading the destruction of a political regime. Such coups have led to the installation of authoritarian bureaucratic regimes under the leadership of military and civilian technocrats. From a broad social perspective, military regimes have served the function of bringing leading members of the New Intelligentsia into formal positions of power to replace the Nationalist Middle Class political leaders who dominated the independence regimes. As one would expect, such bureaucratic regimes, structurally reminiscent of colonial regimes, face major problems in trying to penetrate, communicate with, and mobilize most ordinary members of society. These are political tasks which in Africa have most adequately been performed by Nationalist Middle Class individuals, and their exclusion from political life leaves a vacuum that no other social group can easily fill. The Nationalist Middle Class may be ill equipped to rule an African country alone, but no regime is likely to be effective in the long run without the political linkages such a group provides.

Opposition in one form or another will manifest itself in any complex African society not bound up continually in the heady emotions of nationalist triumph. A strict single-party system is no more able to eliminate such opposition than any other regime, including a military one. Under exceptionally favorable circumstances and with exemplary leadership, a strong single-party system like that of Tanzania may be able to channel some carefully limited opposition for creative purposes, but even here the long-term prospect must be judged uncertain. African elites share a widespread fear that any openly competitive political system will disintegrate, and this fear is reinforced by the realistic appraisal of those in power that any fall from their present eminence would be permanent and personally disastrous. Their attempts to hold political control in the hands of personally reliable men must be seen as a rational, if ultimately self-defeating, response to a difficult political environment.

As Wallerstein has argued, "A true party system must await the large-scale entry of the population into the money economy . . . in sufficient numbers, and having sufficient income level, to support combative instruments for their economic interests." [40] In a somewhat shorter perspective, the building of a more secure and prosperous national community at the elite level, freed from the divisive legacies of role and status definitions inherited from the colonial era, and which would permit the expansion of secure modern-sector roles independent of government, could provide conditions under which open opposition activity might be tolerated and kept within socially useful bounds. Such an evolution may well be necessary if widespread popular participation is not to destroy all semblance of a stable political order. The ancient prescriptions of time, economic growth, and human forbearance will be needed for even that short step. So far Africa has been given little enough of them.

40. Immanual Wallerstein, "Class, Tribe, and Party in West African Politics," in S. M. Lipset and Stein Rokkan, eds., *Party Systems and Voter Alignments: Cross National Perspectives* (New York: Free Press, 1957), pp. 512-13.

6

OPPOSITION IN AND UNDER AN AUTHORITARIAN REGIME: THE CASE OF SPAIN

Juan J. Linz

Since a bitter Civil War (1936–39), Spain has been ruled by an authoritarian regime that some would call totalitarian. It refuses any institutionalization of the opposition in the form of political parties[1] and very

A first version of this essay was presented at a Round Table Conference on Opposition and Control organized by the International Political Science Association in Grenoble, 14–15 September 1965. I am most grateful for the comments made at the conference, particularly by Giovanni Sartori. The research was supported by the John Simon Guggenheim Foundation and the Concilium on International and Area Studies of Yale University. It is impossible to acknowledge here all the comments from Spanish colleagues and friends that have contributed toward improving the essay. Edward Malefakis, Robert Dahl, Joan C. Ullman, and Lewis Edinger provided useful criticism and Marian Ash her extraordinary editorial skills.

Intervening events have forced me to revise that first version considerably. A final version was completed before the designation of Prince Juan Carlos de Borbón y Borbón as Prince of Spain and successor to Franco on 22 July 1969. This event forced me to put some sentences in the past tense and to add one paragraph. Unfortunately the Burgos trial of ETA (Euzkadi Ta Azkatasuna) leaders and its political aftermath—the emergence of an extreme right semiopposition, the Matesa scandal and its impact, the more repressive policies that led to the closing of the newspaper *Madrid,* and the recent declaration of the conference of bishops and priests — could not be analyzed in detail. At appropriate places I have added brief references to these events.

1. The attitude toward political parties and toward what we will call limited pluralism can best be seen in Franco's speeches. Presenting the Ley Orgánica to the Cortes in 1966, his formulation gave hope to those who did not want to give up the dream of evolution out of the system from within the system, when he said:

> Dialogue is the basis of politics, but not the anarchic and artificial dialogue of the parties, usurpers of the true national essences, but [dialogue] of the true representatives of those essences. Diversity of thought in politics, as inevitable as it is convenient, has to accept and respect a common denominator, a single arena, and certain rules of the game, without which politics becomes a com-

hesitantly allows, on paper, "associations within the Movimiento" — the
single party — among its supporters.[2] In recent years, however, Spanish
newspapers and magazines have written about different groups in the
opposition and their leaders as well as about the role of a loyal opposition.[3] The pluralism of political tendencies within the regime is openly

> pletely masked state of civil war, of which we had a living example in what
> Spain suffered for more than a hundred years.
> Parties are not an essential and permanent element without which democracy
> cannot be realized. In the course of history there have been many democratic
> experiences without the phenomenon of political parties, which are a relatively
> recent experiment born of the crisis and disintegration of the organic ties of the
> traditional society.
> From the moment that parties become platforms for class conflict and agents
> of disintegration of national unity, they are not a constructive or a tolerable
> way of opening Spanish life to an authentic, ordered, and efficient democracy.
> But the exclusion of political parties in no way implies the exclusion of the
> *legitimate contrast of opinions* [our emphasis; the text, often used since in Aesopian
> political polemics, was: *legítimo contraste de pareceres*], of critical analysis of
> governmental solutions, or of public formulation of programs and measures that
> may contribute toward improving the progress of the community.

However, a speech at Sevilla reinterpreted these thoughts:

> One hears a lot today about the contrast of opinions, but what more contrast
> of opinions is there than the one in the villages, the municipal councils, the as-
> sociations, farmers' organization . . . [etc.]. But if under the excuse of the con-
> trast of opinions what is looked for are political parties, they should know absolutely
> that they never will come [great applause and cheers of "Franco, Franco"]. And
> they cannot come because that would mean the destruction, the dismemberment of
> the fatherland . . . to lose all that has been gained, it would imply treason to
> our dead and our heroes. . . .
> I want to say this clearly and definitively to stop the campaign of pressure groups
> that are always trying to turn back to the old ways.

2. The problem of constitutionalization and institutionalization within the single
party — the Movimiento Nacional — of the limited pluralism in Spanish politics is
discussed in great detail in Juan J. Linz, "From Falange to Movimiento-Organización: The Spanish Single Party and the Franco Regime, 1936–1968," in Samuel P.
Huntington and Clement H. Moore, eds., *Authoritarian Politics in Modern Society:
The Dynamics of Established One-Party Systems* (New York: Basic Books, 1970),
pp. 128–203. In the discussions in the legislature and the press, the constant themes
have been pluralism, dissent, opposition, freedom, democratization, liberalization,
and so forth, but always *without parties;* organizations, associations, yes or perhaps,
but parties, no. Legally there is a basis for such "groups" in the new Estatuto del
Movimiento, but restrictions in the law and other characteristics of the present
Spanish situation make it unlikely that even the main existing factions will choose
legal channels for their action, though perhaps relatively new men in the regime will
use them to create a new power base for themselves. See also "Las asociaciones
políticas," *Dossier Mundo* 1, May–June 1971, a report on the legislative discussions,
bills introduced, platforms of planned associations, newspaper articles, editorials, and
cartoons on the subject. On the conception of the single party and the "contrast of
opinions" within it, see *El Movimiento Nacional: Textos de Franco,* Colección "Nuevo
Horizonte" (Madrid: Ediciones del Movimiento, 1966).

3. Classifications of the opposition, or the forces in the regime, and listings of
groups or factions do not have to be made any longer by foreign journalists alone
but can be found in the Spanish press and magazines, often with not too honest
intentions. As examples we may mention the article entitled "La variedad política

acknowledged in the recruitment of the elite, in legislative debates, in newspaper editorials, and in the official publications of the single party.[4] A foreign visitor to Spain — even when (or particularly when) he speaks with persons close to the ruling groups, not excluding high office holders — may have the impression that almost everyone is opposed to the regime[5] or at least holds opinions that seem incompatible with its

del régimen" in *Pueblo* (1 October 1968), the newspaper of the official Sindicatos, which had pictures under the headings Falangistas, Traditionalists, Demochristians (including with the Minister of Public Works the leader of the collaborationists, Artajo, and one of the "dialoguing opposition," Ruiz-Giménez), Monarchists, and Neo-Catholics (Opus Dei). The definitions given of each group are in themselves an interesting political document. An article by José Antonio Valverde, "Estos son los cerebros de las corrientes políticas" in *Actualidad Española* (no. 854, 16 May 1968), published by the liberal Opus, describes different groups and lists names under each:

Falangists, divided into: Institutionalists; the Left, based on the "Círculo José Antonio"; another Left, based on the "Círculo Medina"; a "third position"
Sindicatos men, led by Solís
Monarchists, divided into: supporters of Don Juan, subdivided into: Institutionalists and Evolved, more democratic; Carlists
Christian Democrats, divided into: the Editorial Católica group; a less conservative but collaborationist group
and then the Opposition, classified as: incommunicado: dynamic; active
"Left Democrats," divided into: the *Cuadernos para el Diálogo* group; the collaborators of the newspaper *Madrid*; intellectuals, not labeled but listed
Socialists: PSOE (Partido Socialista Obrero Español)-UGT (Unión General de Trabajadores) in exile, with some support in the interior; Tierno Galván; illegal opposition — Sindicato Democrático Estudiantil and Comisiones Obreras
Forces of the New Generation: the attempt of Acción Social Democrática; the political clubs — Jovellanos, Centro de Estudios de Problemas Contemporáneos, Horizonte-80

Under the title, "Con libertad y en equipo: La oposición," *Indice* (no. 227, January 1968), an independent intellectual magazine, published six original contributions on opposition and reprinted the article of Aranguren (see footnote 81), an article by the monarchist writer Pemán in *ABC*, the leading conservative newspaper, and one by the editor of *Arriba*, the Movimiento morning newspaper. See also Joaquín Bardavío, "30 nombres para una crisis," *Actualidad Española* (Madrid), no. 849, 11, April 1968.

Interesting examples of daily press discussions of opposition are the editorial in *Madrid*, "Leal oposición" (Loyal opposition), 8 December 1966, and a letter of Gonzalo Fernández de la Mora, a leading conservative intellectual, minister of public works, 29 February 1968 in the same paper.

In "Tres preguntas y tres respuestas sobre la situación política española actual," *Ibérica*, vol. 16, no. 7, 15 July 1968, Raúl Morodo, an opposition leader living in Spain, distinguishes among the exile, intraregime, and extraregime oppositions.

4. See, for example, an article in *Arriba*, "Puntos de vista de la oposición," 4 March 1965 (reprinted in *ABC*, 6 March 1965), which presents an analysis of the functions of an opposition that could be reproduced without change in any democratic newspaper in the United Kingdom or Sweden.

5. This climate of opinion — widespread in many circles — is reflected in a joke about a foreign correspondent who picks up a conversation in a group at a bar and asks, "How about Franco?" One of the participants says, "Let's go outside," and after reaching a lonely park says, "Well, you know I don't think he is so bad, but I did not want to say so among the people in the bar."

avowed ideology. Criticism and discussion of fundamental economic and social policies exist at many levels, from private conversations to public debates in the legislature and even more in the offices of the government. Questioning of basic political institutions is more restrained and can, but does not necessarily, produce unpleasant consequences.

The observer who notes the widespread and often bitter opposition, even at the highest levels, will be right in a sense, but he will also be quite wrong in his perception. Despite the "opposition" of so many people and predictions of its impending doom since the end of World War II, the regime remains stable. Widespread "opposition" has not endangered it in recent years nor have massive force or terror been required to sustain it.[6] The opposition stance of many Spaniards must there-

6. There is no easily available and objective information on the facts of political repression. Stanley G. Payne, *Franco's Spain* (New York: Crowell, 1967), summarizes critically some of the data available for the years 1939-44 (pp. 109-12). For more recent times it would be possible to tabulate the reports of arrests and sentences given in exile opposition publications like *Ibérica* or the volumes published by Ruedo Ibérico, as well as the short reports in the Spanish press.

For a summary of repressive measures over the years from an antiregime point of view, see Elena de la Souchere, *An Explanation of Spain* (New York: Random House, 1964), pp. 249-59. An interesting compilation of facts on the opposition and its persecution in the late fifties is an article by Miguel Sánchez-Mazas, *España Encadenada,* Suplemento de *Combate* (San José, Costa Rica, June 1959). He quotes figures collected by opposition sources for January 1959: 1510 political prisoners, 915 not accused of common crimes, 15 accused of freemasonry, and 480 political criminals also accused of common crimes (p. 17).

Benjamin Welles, in *Spain: The Gentle Anarchy* (New York: Praeger, 1965), p. 188, gives as an official figure 611 persons in jail, for "crimes against the security of the state" in December 1962; in 1964 there were 365, to which one can add 155 in jail for "banditry and treason." He reports non-Spanish estimates of 1300 at that time.

For a long period the only cause célèbre was that of Communist Central Committee member Julián Grimau, who was executed presumably for his activities as a policeman during the Civil War, in spite of the fact that many with identical records on the opposite side have never been prosecuted. The harshness applied to him was not imposed on those who had similar records but were not active in the illegal underground. Apparently the rejection of an appeal even divided the cabinet. An international press campaign, demonstrations, and appeals for clemency by Khrushchev and members of the Catholic hierarchy might well have contributed — indirectly and perhaps, according to some commentators, not unintentionally on the part of some — to his execution on 20 April 1963. The publication by SIE (Servicio Informativo Español), *Crime or Punishment: Unpublished Documents about Julián Grimau García* (Madrid: n.d., 126 pp.) is an interesting document that throws light on the reaction of the Spanish government in such cases. The antiregime version of the Grimau case is presented in Ignacio Fernández de Castro and José Martínez, eds., *España hoy* (Paris: Ruedo Ibérico, 1963), pp. 382-94, and Anonymous, *Julián Grimau: El hombre, El crimen, La protesta,* with a foreword by Santiago Carrillo (Havana: Venceremos, 1965).

On 25 January 1969, a decree law declared that the state of emergency suspending civil liberties was to be continued for two months. This period was used to make arrests of illegal opposition groups and organizations, as well as to harass moderate members of the alegal opposition (and some unexplainable cases) by imposing forced residence in isolated villages. The unexpected scope of this policy, out of propor-

fore be questioned, and we must look for the causes of the ineffectiveness of the true opposition to the system in a country in which, only
thirty-odd years ago, one-half of the population voted for political alternatives completely incompatible with the Franco regime.[7] When
Unamuno reportedly said, "Vencerán pero no convencerán" (They will
win but not convince), was he wrong? The paradox becomes even more
difficult to understand when the visitor discovers that the works of
Marcuse, Che Guevara, and Camilo Torres are in every bookstore[8] and

---

tion to the incidents that provoked it baffled observers of the Spanish scene, particularly in view of the inevitable international reaction and the availability to the
authorities of legal means of repression without this step. It did, however, indicate
the willingness of the regime to defend itself if necessary by repressive measures. A
press communiqué of the Ministry of Interior gives some details on the organizations
dislocated and their locations. The January-February issue (numbers 64–65) of
Cuadernos para el Diálogo reproduces the legal texts enacting the state of emergency and two interesting pastoral letters of the bishops of Bilbao and Pamplona
reflecting on the situation.

Antonio López Pina has compiled a statistical analysis of the government's reactions to regionalist-nationalist, mainly Basque, activities, giving the newspaper source
in Spain, the accusation, place, date, government action, sentence, and jurisdiction
imposing it, as well as the clerical or nonclerical character of the actor, for the
years 1967–68, by months. There were 11 trials in 1966, 31 in 1967, and 37 in 1968.

The issue of the treatment of political prisoners was raised by a number of Spanish
lawyers through the official Madrid bar association and led to interesting press comments during a three-day sit-in of women in the Jesuit churches and one parish as
a protest against the installation of microphones permitting the authorities to over-
hear conversations between visiting families and prisoners in Carabanchel prison.
On legal grounds it was argued that political prisoners should be separate from
other prisoners. See *Cuadernos para el Diálogo*, no. 63, December 1968, pp. 26–29.

7. The February 1936 election results have been seriously contested, but most of
the disagreement is about the allocation of seats, which — as a consequence of the
electoral system — could be drastically changed by a small number of votes. The
data painstakingly collected by Javier Tusell Gómez allow us to count the votes
for candidates of different parties. However, the voter could only vote for the two
great electoral coalitions (the Popular Front and the Right), minor center coalitions or parties, the Basque Nationalists (PNV), and the Fascists. The votes for
parties in the two main coalitions — given the high degree of discipline of their
supporters, particularly of the Left — were largely determined by the slate-makers,
who must have had in mind the tendencies of the electorate in each district (provinces or metropolitan areas). Bearing this in mind, we get the following distribution: Right 8.4%, CEDA (Catholic party) 23.2%, Lliga (right Catalan party) 2.8%,
PNV (Partido Nacionalista Vasco) 1.4%, Center Right and Center 17.6%, Left
Republicans (IR and UR) 19.6%, Catalan Left 4.1%, PSOE (Partido Socialista
Obrero Español) 16.4%, PCE (Partido Comunista Español) 2.5%, other Left 4.0%
Certainly the PNV (with 1.4%), the PSOE and PCE (with approximately 18.9%),
and many of the remaining supporters of the Left Popular Front and some of
those of other parties had identified with the ideals defeated by Franco. See Javier
Tusell Gómez, *Las elecciones del Frente Popular en España* (Madrid: Cuadernos
para el Diálogo, EDICUSA, 1971), vol. 2, app. I, pp. 265–341.

8. Examples of publishing activities that many would not suspect exist in Spain
are the publications of houses like Editorial ZYX, S.A. — Biblioteca Promoción del
Pueblo — and those of houses like Aguilera, Alcón, Ciencia Nueva, and Equipo
Editorial, whose activities were stopped with the state of emergency decree in 1969.

that the country has essentially open borders.[9] But the idea that a break-down of the regime will be inevitable with the death of Franco is being slowly displaced by the reluctant realization that those in power today (or some of them) may assure the continuity of the regime after Franco, at least for some time. The prediction that nothing dramatic will happen with the death of Franco has been reinforced by recent events in Portugal, though obviously one should be cautious about applying to Spain the experience of a very different society.

To account for the widespread tone and mentality of opposition and the simultaneous failure of structural or principled opposition will be one of our tasks. In our attempt to understand it we will have to turn to the history of democratic politics in Spain and the Civil War and its aftermath, as well as to the nature of basic cleavages in Spanish society. However, neither history nor sociology can substitute for an analysis of the political process itself, and therefore our title: opposition in an authoritarian regime,[10] or, perhaps more precisely, in and under such a regime. In my view, it is impossible to understand the problems of the "opposition" to the Franco regime without reference to the distinctive characteristics of the regime, which is neither democratic nor totalitarian, the peculiar forms of semi- and/or pseudo-opposition it produces and the consequences of depoliticization and limited freedom that characterize it in its present phase. (My analysis does not focus on earlier phases.)

THE HERITAGE OF THE PAST   Ever since the Napoleonic invasion disturbed the old order and compromised and divided the forces that had initiated enlightened change in the eighteenth century,[11] Spain's political

9. The openness of the country is reflected in these figures of entries and exits through Spanish borders in 1960 and 1965. To put the figures in perspective, the reader may remember that the population was 30,903,137 in 1960.

	Entries of holders of foreign passports	Exits of Spaniards	
		Resident in Spain	Resident abroad
1960	4,332,363	2,149,153	639,974
1965	11,079,556	3,917,507	1,042,151

Data from the Spanish *Statistical Yearbooks*. Obviously the same person could enter several times during the year. The figures do not include 24-hour passes in border areas that were used by 126,111 Spaniards in 1960 and by 246,818 in 1965.
10. I use the term in a very specific sense. See Juan J. Linz "An Authoritarian Regime: Spain," in Erik Allardt and Stein Rokkan, eds., *Mass Politics: Studies in Political Sociology* (New York: Free Press, 1970), pp. 251–321, 374–81, which attempts to provide a theoretical framework for the study of the Spanish political system in comparative perspective.
11. For a more political interpretation of the failure of nineteenth-century political development, see Raymond Carr, *Spain, 1808–1939* (Oxford: Clarendon Press, 1966), p. 210. See also the interesting review by Richard Herr, *English Historical Review* 82 (July 1967): 580–85. On the post-traditional but unsuccessful modernization of Spain, see Juan J. Linz, "Tradition and Modernity," paper presented at a conference on post-traditional societies, Rome, March 1972, to be published in *Daedalus*.

evolution has been full of conflicts between the forces of change, which were often ahead of economic and social development because of the openness of the country to foreign influences, and the forces of reaction, which often had popular support. The struggle led to long and costly civil wars, overthrow of governments by military pronunciamientos, sporadic and enthusiastic (even when often ill-fated) revolutionary out-bursts, short periods of utopian reform followed by crisis or defeat, and repressive regimes sometimes succeeded by conservative ones willing to introduce important reforms with the help of moderates and administrators in periods of depolitization due to exhaustion from previous conflicts. Traditional monarchical legitimacy was undermined early. Real rather than imposed consensus, freedom with real participation, have been rare in modern Spain. The definition of a political arena with boundaries accepted by most participants, in which government and opposition compete freely for popular support, has not succeeded for long periods even when repeatedly attempted.

The failure of constitutional democracy can be attributed to a multi-tude of factors, and historians, politicians, and social scientists disagree — often violently — on which ones to emphasize.[12] A historicist perspective — frequent among both conservative and liberal intellectuals — stresses the uniqueness of Spanish history since the Middle Ages and at the onset of the modern age, shifting often into a cultural-historical determinism. Some of the arguments made could be translated easily into the language of American culture-personality theories, even when they lack the Freudian underpinnings. My own research from a more sociostructural perspective has convinced me that these approaches deserve more sys-tematic and comparative research but need to be complemented by a more socioeconomic perspective.

The key historical role of counter-reformation Catholicism in Spanish life and the destructive impact of the struggle between Carlists and Liberals in the nineteenth century led Spanish thinkers and politicians to attribute the failure of liberalism and democracy to the church. The educational and scientific backwardness of Spain at the end of the cen-tury, which hindered political development, was also blamed on the church. This simplistic view, which disregarded other dimensions of Carlism and other causes of maladjustment to the modern world, resulted in the anticlerical and antireligious policies of the Second Republic (1931–36/39), which in themselves contributed toward making the

---

12. An excellent example is Ramón Menéndez Pidal, *The Spaniards in Their History* (New York: Norton, 1966), which, while not dealing explicitly with the problem of democracy, gives the cultural, historical, and psychological background for many of the strains in the history of modern Spain.

democratic alternation of government and opposition impossible.[13] The Catholic reverse of this interpretation was to attribute the Spanish problem to the abandonment in the eighteenth and nineteenth centuries of the Catholic culture that had accompanied the days of greatness and to call for the return to a state-church alliance, if necessary, by the suppression of the dissidents.

It was even more simplistic to attribute all evils to the interference of a reactionary army,[14] ignoring the facts that a military presence in politics had been initially made necessary by the weakness of the liberal bourgeoisie when it tried to establish a constitutional regime, that the army's links with conservative interests — landed or business — are tenuous, and that the roots of the interventions in 1923 and 1936 must be found in the undeniable crises of the constitutional and democratic regimes themselves, together with the predisposition developed in the past toward military intervention.

A third culprit for the failure of democracy has been found in the land-owning aristocracy, though in this theory it is forgotten that many of the big landowners are not aristocrats and that latifundia Spain in the nineteenth century — in contrast to the Prussian Junkers — favored constitutional government, though not necessarily real democracy.[15] No one

13. The religious issue has been studied by Joan Connelly Ullman, *The Tragic Week: A Study of Anticlericalism in Spain, 1875–1912* (Cambridge, Mass.: Harvard University Press, 1968); José M. Sánchez, *The Politico-Religious Background of the Spanish Civil War* (Chapel Hill: University of North Carolina Press, 1962), and William G. Ebenstein, *Church and State in Franco Spain* (Princeton: Center of International Studies, 1960). See also Juan J. Linz, "The Party System of Spain, Past and Future," in Seymour M. Lipset and Stein Rokkan, eds., *Party Systems and Voter Alignments: Cross National Perspectives* (New York: Free Press, 1967), pp. 197–282. There is no scholarly history of the church in modern times nor of anticlericalism in Spain.

For a documented, exclusively factual study of the anticlerical policies of the Republic and the persecution suffered by the church during the Civil War, which accounts to a large extent for its overidentification with the regime, see Antonio Montero, *Historia de la persecución religiosa en España, 1936–39* (Madrid: Biblioteca de Autores Cristianos, 1961).

14. On the Spanish army, see the fundamental work of Stanley G. Payne, *Politics and the Military in Modern Spain* (Stanford: Stanford University Press, 1967), and Julio Busquets Bragulat, *El militar de carrera en España: Estudio de sociología militar* (Barcelona: Ediciones Ariel, 1967). To understand the position of the most intellectual, respected, and liberal general of the Spanish army in one of the few public statements on political issues of a high-ranking army officer, see the interview with Lieutenant-General Manuel Díez Alegría, in Salvador Paniker, *Conversaciones en Madrid* (Barcelona: Kairos, 1969), pp. 263–76. His reserved political neutrality toward the regime has some of the tone of Von Seeckt in the Weimar Republic; on the other hand, his emphasis on subordination to civilian authority and on legalism, while it bodes well for a hypothetical democratic regime, should also give pause to those who dream of an army putsch against the regime.

15. There is no academic study of the role of the nobility in 19th-century Spain, but the point is made in Jaime Vicens Vives, Jorge Nadal, and Rosa Ortega, *Historia social y económica de España y América: Burguesía, industrialización, obrerismo*

would deny that the rural social and economic structure was a decisive factor in the social and economic crisis that led to violent conflicts endangering liberal-democratic institutions and contributed decisively to the coming of the last civil war. The agrarian problem, however, is only one aspect of the economic underdevelopment of large parts of Spain which led to the bitter conflicts that constitutional regimes could neither channel nor solve. This is not the place to analyze the causes of Spanish economic backwardness, but it is appropriate to stress the difficulties this created for constitutional government. Economic underdevelopment and slow development, together with population growth, increased the pressure on the land and exacerbated rural discontent, which first under anarchosyndicalist and later socialist leadership flared up in violent local "revolutions" or outbursts of violence that often led to disproportionate repression.[16] The abject poverty of many farm laborers and farmers was and is an obstacle to their integration into society, their responsible and free participation in politics, and even their access to elementary education. Limited industrialization and the inefficiency of many enterprises made labor conflict particularly bitter, especially in the areas in which labor was under the leadership of the anarchosyndicalists, who (with some exceptions) rejected meaningful collective bargaining, parliamentary democracy, and even electoral participation for the sake of arousing a revolutionary consciousness and struggle for a utopian social order.[17] The intransigent attitude of the business bourgeoisie, particularly in Catalonia, is largely to blame for this direction the labor movement took, when in other circumstances it might have been willing to become a peaceful force defending the interests of its members. Inequalities in economic development[18] between Catalonia and the Basque provinces,

---

(Barcelona: Teide, 1959), pp. 131–40. Few of the great aristocratic families supported the Carlists, and at the turn of the century the ranks of the nobility were enlarged by ennobled financiers, industrialists, politicians, and army officers.

16. Stanley Payne, *The Spanish Revolution* (New York: Norton, 1970), is the most complete monograph on working-class protest politics in Spain. Rural social conflicts are studied in great detail by Edward E. Malefakis, *Agrarian Reform and Peasant Revolution in Spain: Origins of the Civil War* (New Haven: Yale University Press, 1970).

17. For the policies of that movement and its ideology and for basic documents, see José Peirats, *La CNT* (Confederación Nacional del Trabajo) *en la revolución española* (Buenos Aires: Ediciones C.N.T., 1955), 3 vols.

18. Juan J. Linz and Amando de Miguel, "Within-Nation Differences and Comparisons: The Eight Spains," in Richard L. Merritt and Stein Rokkan, eds., *Comparing Nations* (New Haven: Yale University Press, 1966), pp. 267–319. A basic work on internal differences in development is Amando de Miguel and Juan Salcedo, *Dinámica del desarrollo industrial de las regiones españolas* (Madrid: Tecnos, 1972). For the differing contributions of Catalonia, the Basque country, and the remainder of the country to various elites see Amando de Miguel and Juan J. Linz, "Movilidad geográfica en el empresariado español," *Revista de Estudios Geográficos* 25, no. 94 (1964): 5–29, and Juan J. Linz and Amando de Miguel, "Los

on the one hand, and the rest of the country contributed decisively to strengthening regional autonomy and even secessionist demands based on linguistic and cultural differences. These demands, particularly in the case of Catalonia, diverted the rising industrial and commercial bourgeoisie from challenging on a national level the dominance of aristocratic and middle-class landowners, bureaucrats, army officers, and professionals, mostly from the less developed parts of the country and Madrid.[19]

The unreal two-party system of Restoration Spain (1874–1923) was one consequence. Another was the substitution of ideological politics for genuine interest conflicts under the leadership of intellectuals, particularly of the coffee-house variety, and demagogic politicians representing the middle and lower middle classes of provincial Spain at the advent of the Republic in 1931. The ideological and often unreal character of political conflicts made the basic consensus between opposition and government difficult, if not impossible, and fragmented the party system.[20] Economic weakness prevented dynamic action by the government in such fields as education, public works, rural development, and social services and thereby increased the principled opposition of different sectors of the society to whatever political system was in power. The added difficulties and alienation caused by the unavoidable loss of the last remnants of empire, the exclusion of Spain from European power politics in late nineteenth and early twentieth century and particularly from the partition of Africa, and the costly and unsuccessful effort in Morocco contributed to the crisis of the Restoration, a crisis that in 1923 destroyed the most stable — and despite all its weaknesses politically most successful — regime Spain has had since the age of democratic reform: the constitutional monarchy between 1875 and 1923. Labor unrest, the Catalan question, and the unfortunate and unpopular colonial war in Morocco ultimately led to the intervention of the army and brought to a close a period in which political freedoms had become institutionalized, politicians holding different views on basic questions could live together and generally respect each other, economic expansion was taking place in a liberal-capitalist framework, intellectual life was developing in freedom, labor was be-

---

empresarios potenciales," *Revista Española de Opinión Pública* 1 (1965): 45–72. The difference in prestige assigned in those two regions to various elites is studied in an article by the same authors, "El prestigio de profesiones en el mundo empresarial," *Revista de Estudios Políticos* 128 (March-April 1968): 23–76 and 129 (May-August): 5–31 and in "La percepción del prestigio de las ocupaciones industriales y burocráticas por los jóvenes españoles," *Anales de Sociología* 1 (1966): 68–75.

19. On the ambivalences of Catalan bourgeois politics, see the study of Jordi Solé Tura, *Catalanisme i revolució burgesa: La síntesi de Prat de la Riba* (Barcelona: Edicions 62, 1967).

20. On the Spanish party sytem and its crisis in the thirties, see Juan J. Linz, "The Party System of Spain," pp. 197–282. There the reader will also find a prediction of the outcome of elections with multiple parties assuming the present Spanish social structure.

ginning to be recognized, and some minor attempts at social reform were being initiated, all in a climate of civility.

It is impossible to review here the deep crisis suffered by Spain in the thirties,[21] the failure of almost all political and social forces to make the newly born Republic a workable democratic political system, the intransigence of almost all major parties at one point or another toward oppositions, the frequent use of force and censorship against opponents, the denial of legitimacy to the aspirations and policies of almost all parties, even those using constitutional methods, that led to a political climate ripe for civil war. For many Spaniards the title of a recent book by Gil Robles, leader of the CEDA (center-right Catholic party), *Peace Was Not Possible,*[22] summarizes that period. The military uprising completed the polarization and unleashed a deep social revolution, an even bloodier counter-revolution, and almost three years of civil war.[23] The memory of that struggle and its aftermath is the basic background from which contemporary Spanish politics has to be understood. At some point, the desire for and fear of revenge may have been dominant, but the exhaustion of idealism after the struggle and the awareness of the

21. Of the large bibliography on the Spanish Republic and the coming of the Civil War we may mention, in English, Hugh Thomas, *The Spanish Civil War* (New York: Harper, 1961); Gabriel Jackson, *The Spanish Republic and the Civil War* (Princeton: Princeton University Press, 1965), which focuses more on the Republic between 1931 and 1936 than Thomas does; and Gerald Brenan, *The Spanish Labyrinth: An Account of the Social and Political Background of the Civil War* (Cambridge: Cambridge University Press, 1950). The four-volume work by Joaquín Arrarás, *Historia de la Segunda República española* (Madrid: Editora Nacional, 1956–64), is not the work of an academic scholar and does not hide its bias, but it contains a wealth of information not found elsewhere. The most heavily documented work is Ricardo de La Cierva, *Historia de la Guerra Civil española,* vol. I (1898–1936) (Madrid: San Martín, 1969). For a balanced view they should be read in conjunction with the above-mentioned liberal interpretations in English. Manuel Ramírez Jiménez, *Los grupos de presión en la Segunda República española* (Madrid: Tecnos, 1969), provides extremely useful information on the social forces at play in the Republic and the conflicts that led to its breakdown.

22. José María Gil Robles, *No fue posible la paz* (Esplugues de Lobregat, Barcelona: Ariel, 1968).

23. It is standard practice of Spaniards on both sides in the Civil War to speak of a million dead, and this is the psychologically real figure. Actually, a comparison of the number of deaths under normal circumstances with actual deaths, which would include those due to worsened sanitary conditions, reveals an excess of 246,568 (204,418 males) for the years 1936–39 (Jesús Villar Salinas, *Repercusiones demográficas de la última guerra civil española* [Madrid: Real Academia de Ciencias Morales y Políticas, 1942], p. 49). However, to the war casualties one has to add the victims of the repression at the end of the war, which are difficult to estimate. The emigration of probably 300,000 persons was another loss. However, the largest demographic loss was the drop in the number of births, which were 612,850 below the expected number (Villar Salinas, *Repercusiones,* p. 25). All of these demographic changes, including the last, lead Villar Salinas to estimate a population loss of some 1,160,000, a figure close to the myth of the million dead. In 1940 the population census gave the figure of 25,159,915 inhabitants.

madness it unleashed has left in almost half the present population, the generation that lived through those events, a deep desire: "never again."

It is this desire that makes so powerful the appeals based on "twenty-five years of peace" that the Franco regime launched and that became the central theme of the propaganda for a "yes" vote on the 1966 constitutional referendum.[24] Combined with a period of economic growth and prosperity and increased personal freedom — though without political rights — this appeal has made possible a depolitization that is the main obstacle to principled opposition to the regime. The desire for peace is well reflected in the response to a survey question: *Here I show you a series of goals for politics in Spain in the coming years. Could you please tell us which one among these possible ends you think is the most important of all?* The alternatives and the percentage of males choosing them were: justice (20%), stability (3%), things as they always have been (5%), order (9%), peace (48%), freedom (4%), development (5%), democracy (4%), no answer (2%). Among women, peace occupied an even higher rank, with 67% choosing that alternative. It is interesting to note that while 45% of the upper middle class chose peace, 59% of the working class (male and female) chose that alternative, compared to 22% and 13% respectively, mentioning justice. The preference for democracy or freedom was 10% in the first group and 6% in the second. The stability of the Franco regime today is due more to the absence of an effective opposition than to enthusiastic support, in contrast to 1939, when it was based on the enthusiastic identification with him of many Spaniards who imposed their will on others equally committed to their defeated ideals.

24. High participation could be expected given the propaganda and social pressures exercised. In a poll at the end of November, 84% of the population (92% of the males) answered that they intended to vote. The areas having the lowest figures were Catalonia, Baleares, Galicia, the underdeveloped regions of Andalucia and Extremadura, and the Basque country. The two regions with local nationalist sentiments were among the low participation areas despite their high economic and educational standards. The intention to vote "yes" was expressed by 84% of the population (85% of the males), with 69% in Catalonia, 76% in the Basque country, and 84% in Andalucia. Among the males the motives given for their votes were: because the law ensures order and peace (54%), because Franco has asked for it (22%), because it ensures the political future (15%), because it ensures economic development (5%), because it consolidates the monarchy (1%), and other (3%). Franco's request was mentioned more often by the older generations, the desire for peace as often if not more often among younger people.

A study of participation in the various types of elections taking place in Spain today—local, members of the legislature elected directly by heads of households, within corporate groups like professional associations, trade union representatives in factory councils, and so forth — would be very fruitful. See the analysis of local elections in Madrid on 20 November 1966 by José Vidal Beneyto, *Elecciones municipales y referendum* (Madrid: Cuadernos de Ciencia Social, CEISA, 1966), and the articles based on a pre-election survey in Madrid by DATA S.A. in the newspaper *Madrid* on 19, 21, 25 November, 1 and 2 December 1966.

THE PRESENT   We will deliberately formulate our analysis in fairly abstract rather than descriptive terms. Many of the problems we will touch upon are relevant, not only to the Spanish situation, but to other countries whose regimes we would also classify as authoritarian. Furthermore, where the opposition is alegal or illegal — as in Spain — a description of groups, factions, and personalities in the opposition whose strengths and future are unknown is risky or outright misleading. Their programs are either nonexistent or are found in vague formulations in interviews, scattered leaflets, or publications written in such a way as to pass the censor or judge. In addition, the remoteness from the moment of taking power, together with the intellectual or ideological character of the leaders, allows them to face key issues with broad statements — some would call them platitudes — that provide little or no insight into the solutions they would advocate to central political, economic, and social problems. To give an example: it is one thing to be progammatically "respectful toward the cultural and linguistic personality of the regions" and quite another to find a specific solution to the problem of equality of languages in the schools, the universities, the administration, and the army in areas where very different proportions of the population speak the local language, large proportions of immigrants are Castilian speaking, and so forth. To describe oppositional groups in detail can involve invidious comparisons, neglect of groups that may later become important, and emphasis on some that may soon dissolve or disintegrate. Such a study of oppositions under nondemocratic regimes can easily turn into journalism. The same can be said of detailed accounts of groups, coalitions, and personalities operating within the regime. In recent years there have been too many shifts and palace intrigues in this twilight world of semi- and pseudo-opposition to waste time describing anything but its general pattern or style rather than the actors. Therefore, references to the concrete Spanish situation will be made primarily in footnotes and should be taken as examples illustrating propositions rather than as an exhaustive descriptive account. Numerous bibliographical references will allow the reader, if he wishes, to pursue his interest.[25]

25. The most important reviews of the Spanish situation by opposition writers abroad and inside Spain, from a leftist point of view, can be found in Fernández de Castro and Martínez, *España hoy,* and in *Horizonte español, 1966* (Paris: Ruedo Ibérico, 1966) 2 vols., with contributions by 28 authors. The detailed chronology of opposition activities in the context of government actions and the international situation is particularly useful for a descriptive study of the opposition. *España hoy* includes a list of political organizations — most of them what we will call illegal rather than alegal or semiopposition — with a brief description, quotations from their programs (pp. 489–95), and a bibliography of pamphlets, manifestos, etc. (pp. 496–99).

The leading moderate opposition magazine published abroad, with considerable information on events in Spain, is *Ibérica,* published monthly under the sponsorship of Salvador de Madariaga and the late Norman Thomas in Spanish and English

OPPOSITION IN AND UNDER AN AUTHORITARIAN REGIME   My analysis is
based on a distinction between three types of modern, that is, post-
traditional, polities — totalitarian systems, authoritarian regimes, and
democratic governments — which were developed to understand better
the nature of the Spanish regime. The distinction is very similar to that
made by Robert Dahl between unified hegemonies, pluralistic hegemonies, and polyarchies.[26] Perhaps the regimes I call authoritarian are closer

---

editions. Obviously there are a number of exile antiregime publications like *El
Socialista,* published in Toulouse by the PSOE; *Mundo Obrero,* published by the
PCE; *La Batalla,* the doctrinal organ of the PCE; *España Libre,* published in New
York with a summary in English, and the publications of the Basque nationalists,
Catalanists, etc. To give detailed bibliographic references to such publications, many
of them ephemeral, would take too much space.

The most complete descriptive study of the opposition is Sergio Vilar, *Protagonistas de la España democrática: La oposición a la dictadura, 1939–1969* (Barcelona-
Paris-Madrid: Ediciones Sociales [1969]), which is based on taped interviews with
leading men from the Left, the Center, and the Right (respectively 63, 24, and 6
persons) in Madrid, Catalonia, the Basque country, Galicia, Andalucia, and Valencia,
excluding exiles. In addition to their answers to a number of questions about politics
in general, ethics and politics, the Civil War, economic organization (particularly
socialism and the Common Market), trade unions, education, the regional problem,
the monarchy, and the republic, the book includes a chronology of the activities of
the opposition, as well as brief essays on some of the movements and organizations,
such as the Comisiones Obreras, the Basque ETA, the friends of Dionisio Ridruejo.
The author describes himself as a revolutionary socialist, and in transcribing the
answers of those who diverge from his opinions he sometimes "suggests some of their
contradictions or ambiguities." He recalls the past of those who have evolved from
the regime toward the opposition and characterizes men with penetrating irony, if
not with a touch of malevolence.

Benjamin Welles, *Spain: The Gentle Anarchy* (New York: Praeger, 1965), devotes
a useful descriptive chapter to the opposition (pp. 185–228) that begins, "no aspect
of contemporary Spain is more confusing than the political opposition to Franco,"
a sentence that could have served as an epigram for this paper, which compounds
the problem by attempting to theorize on this confusing subject! The re-reading
of his account reveals the extent to which a descriptive account dates in only a few
years; main actors die, others shift their positions decisively, new groups emerge, and
events that seemed important at the time are forgotten.

Another listing and brief characterization of opposition groups can be found in
Stanley G. Payne, *Franco's Spain,* pp. 120–224.

26. He establishes this typology of political systems in *Polyarchy* (New Haven: Yale
University Press, 1971). The scalogram analysis of 114 countries by opportunities to
participate in national elections and to oppose the government, circa 1969, places
Spain in pattern 27 of 31, together with Syria, Senegal, Portugal, the USSR, and
Yugoslavia, just before Yugoslavia (see table A1, by Robert A. Dahl, Richard
Nordling, and Mary Frase Williams, which uses in part data on the opportunity to
oppose the government from the work of Banks and Textor). Except for the USSR,
I consider these countries authoritarian regimes because of the way they are ruled,
ignoring ideology and many of their policies. It would be rewarding to make a more
systematic comparison, based on intimate knowledge, of Spain and Portugal, which
as societies and regimes share so many characteristics but which have moved in the
last decades in somewhat different directions, and of Spain and Yugoslavia, which
have benefited from similar locations on the periphery of prosperous Europe, face
similar problems of regional tensions, and have similar memories of civil strife but
have regimes with different ideologies.

to Dahl's near-pluralistic than pluralistic hegemonies. My definition of authoritarian regimes as "political systems with limited, not responsible, political pluralism, without elaborate and guiding ideology (but with distinctive mentalities); without intensive or extensive political mobilization (except at some points in their development); and in which a leader (or occasionally a small group) exercises power within formally ill-defined but quite predictable limits" is based on a systematic comparison between these regimes and both totalitarian systems and the Western type of constitutional democracy with political parties competing for power within the framework of basic political freedoms.

When I speak of limited pluralism and of liberalization of the regime, I imply a tendency toward polyarchy in Dahl's sense,[27] but this does not necessarily — in the Spanish case — represent a shift from elite to mass politics. In its more totalitarian phase, the regime offered more opportunities for mass politics; political involvement at the grass roots (even when there was little or no autonomy from the leadership) was probably greater at the end of the Civil War than it is today. In the context of an authoritarian regime, liberalization does not imply increased participation. In fact, by opening the door to the hope of a change in the system, it may well lead to the withdrawal of those who would otherwise have tried to satisfy their political ambitions within the system. In this respect Spain is probably different from the Eastern European socialist countries, where the threat of intervention by the USSR destroys any hope of radical change, and a process of liberalization may result in increased participation of sectors that might otherwise be alienated.

My typology assumes that authoritarian regimes are basically different in their underlying conception and are neither totalitarian systems

27. It might be noted that in the scalogram referred to in note 26, we find many semideveloped societies in the same pattern where we find Spain, while in the preceding ones — 11 to 22 — we find almost exclusively underdeveloped African, Arab, and Asian countries. I suspect that the bunching of European socialist and pseudo-fascist countries in the later patterns may reflect the different ideological signs of the times in which they were born and perhaps more the formal aspects of government than the realities of political life. The historical heritage of Latin America may also account for the placing of all of its nondemocratic regimes (with the exception of Haiti) between patterns 10 and 16. It might also be argued that the relative modernization of semideveloped European societies accounts for the more restrictive policies they have toward opposition than are characteristic of more traditional societies and underdeveloped new states. The bunching together of Cambodia, Ethiopia, Jordan, Nepal, and Thailand is significant in this respect, as is that of new African nations. The ranking certainly suggests that some of the operational measures used have different meanings in such different societal contexts or perhaps that more exacting standards have been used by those studying Western societies. The distance of Mexico (pattern 12) from Spain (pattern 23) — despite the many similarities in culture, size, recent economic development, and some policies that would lead me to place them much closer — would make a comparative study most challenging.

diluted by inefficiency or national character nor steps toward democracy, as some of the ideologists of "guided democracy" may claim. In classifying Franco Spain today in this way I do not intend to deny the existence within it of strong tendencies toward totalitarianism, particularly in the late thirties and early forties, though I do not believe they could ever have prevailed without outside intervention or even the overthrow of Franco.[28] Certainly my definition of democracy,[29] which is the current Western one, cannot include the "organic," corporative type of democracy the regime claims to be. It would be a mistake to call it simply a traditional regime, since there is no continuity with any premodern feudal or patrimonial type of monarchical legitimacy; the system is not legitimized in these terms, and its sustaining social forces are not of this kind.[30] After over a century of intermittently successful constitutional government, which saw the introduction of universal suffrage first in 1868 and more permanently in 1890, all traditional continuity was broken with the overthrow of the monarchy in 1931.

The different types of opposition within, outside, and against the regime and their role in the political system can be understood only if we start from the assumption that Spain is not — and has not been since the middle or late forties — a totalitarian regime. Equally certain is the fact that at no time have Franco or his closest collaborators intended to return the country to what they call "inorganic democracy": free formation of political parties to compete for the votes of a national electorate, with no intermediaries, except parties, between the citizen and his elected representatives.[31] Spain is thus distinguished from most Latin American

28. This point is developed in Linz, "From Falange to Movimiento-Organización."
29. My conception of democracy is based on the works of Max Weber, Joseph Schumpeter, Seymour M. Lipset, Raymond Aron, Harry Eckstein, and other social scientists rather than the political philosophers. For a more detailed discussion of the different dimensions used in defining a regime as democratic and my conception, see "Michels e il suo contributo alla sociologia politica," an introduction to Roberto Michels, *La sociologia del partito politico nella democrazia moderna* (Bologna: Il Mulino, 1966), pp. xii–cxix, especially lxxix–cv.
30. On the difference between authoritarian regimes, like the Spanish, and traditional regimes, strictu sensu, see Linz, "An Authoritarian Regime: Spain," pp. 269–71.
31. The constitutional texts, innumerable speeches, and debates in the Cortes and the National Council of the Movimiento when the liberalization and/or democratization of the Movimiento were being discussed leave no doubt on this point. See also the texts quoted in footnote 1. For a collection of editorial comments by the Movimiento press on the antiparty character of the regime, see *Concurrencia de pareceres: Coincidencias y discrepancias en el Movimiento* (Madrid: Colección Nuevo Horizonte, Ediciones del Movimiento, 1967).
There is no formal analysis of the structure of the Spanish government in English or for that matter any recent presentation in any language. Even Spanish commentaries are scarce. The best solution is to turn to the complex legal texts, *The Fundamental Laws of the State: The Spanish Constitution*, published by the Spanish Information Service, Madrid, 1967. The Spanish edition, *Referendum 1966: Nueva constitución* (Madrid: Servicio Informativo Español, 1966), contains also the important speech of Franco presenting the bill to the legislature. For a summary-commentary

dictatorships, as well as Ataturk's Turkey. The committed partisans of a true totalitarian regime (a minority even among the members of the Falangist party after the Civil War) and the advocates of democracy therefore have constituted and still constitute a principled opposition. Some of those opponents are committed only or mainly to legal activities to challenge the system — a somewhat difficult position since the democratic alternative is essentially anticonstitutional — while others act in a limbo between legality and alegality but stop well short of conspiring to overthrow the government by a putsch or a revolution. Still others, however, are actively committed to illegal forms of protest — from political strikes to terrorism — to the extent that their limited forces and the very superior ones of the regime allow them to act. This is particularly true of the Communist party and some of the Basque nationalists.

The ideal type of totalitarian system involves monopoly of power by an organized and ideologically committed elite controlling a mass party and mass organizations that activate large segments of the population in support of the controlling group. This means, in principle, destruction or at least maximal weakening of social pluralism (what the theories of the Nazi regime called *Gleichschaltung*) and only limited tolerance of passivity toward the system, to say nothing of active opposition. Whatever pluralism exists among bureaucratic intramural cliques has no legitimacy and does not have its roots in the social structure (particularly not in the preregime structure). It has to operate within the framework of the dominant ideology. This imposes a consensus on fundamentals, on the continuity of the regime in its basic assumptions, which likens the system to the ideal of "agreement on fundamentals" so often emphasized by the students of Western democracies. The political arena tends to be well defined and entry from outside politics is difficult. The distinction between critics within and outside the system tends to be clear, and the freedom of those outside is severely if not totally limited, with few distinctions of degree and type among them. On the other hand, the importance of ideology gives an ideological character to conflicts between

---

from a Movimiento perspective, see Carlos Iglesias Selgas, *La vía española a la democracia* (Madrid: Ediciones del Movimiento, 1968). The only serious academic effort to comment on the present Constitution from a positive viewpoint is the book by Rodrigo Fernández-Carvajal, *La constitución española* (Madrid: Editora Nacional, 1969). The 1967 March-April issue of the *Revista de Estudios Políticos* (no. 152), published by the Instituto de Estudios Políticos, contains fifteen articles commenting on different aspects of the Constitution, some of them pointing toward possible evolution of the regime under it; see particularly the article by Antonio Carro Martínez, "Relaciones entre los altos órganos del Estado (Ensayo sobre el título IX de la Ley Orgánica del Estado)," pp. 7–29. Clyde L. Clark, *The Evolution of the Franco Regime* (no place, no publisher, no date, but prepared by a State Department official and declassified in April 1956), in 2 vols., with 3 vols. of appendixes, contains a wealth of information and translations (as well as the Spanish texts) of most of the important legislation between 1938 and 1950.

bureaucracies, interests within the ruling groups, and personalities. This makes for conflicts of ideas rather than of interests. As Simmel and many others have stressed, conflicts of ideas have a special bitterness in comparison with conflicts of interests.[32]

Authoritarian regimes, as I have defined them, are characterized by a legitimate limited (legal or de facto) pluralism, not only within the governing group but within institutions and social forces. This implies that some sectors of the elite, some institutional interests, and some social forces will be better represented at one point or another in the government and will have more or less influence on it. This means that ins and outs will struggle for power without deadly or grave consequences. To some extent their conflicts will be manifest or visible. The lack of all-pervasive and successful efforts at mobilization by a single organization and leadership permits attempts at penetration of the society by the pluralistic elements in the power structure. On the other hand, the legal or de facto limit on spontaneous emergence of organized groups that distinguishes the limited pluralism of such regimes from democracies restricts the opportunity for participation of large sectors of the population, either as supporters or as opposition. Within a limited pluralism, the fear of each contending group concerning any widespread activation by any other group restricts the effectiveness of even manipulated mobilization by those in power at any point in time.

A consequence is that, in contrast to totalitarian systems and the ideal democracy, the population that does not become involved in politics or withdraws from politics can be large.[33] These apathetic supporters or

32. See Lewis Coser, *The Functions of Social Conflict* (New York: Free Press, 1964), chap. 6, pp. 111–19, which develop's the ideas of Georg Simmel and other social scientists on this point.

33. On the political culture of contemporary Spain, see the articles in *Revista del Instituto de la Juventud* (Madrid, 1966) by Amando de Miguel, "Estructura social y juventud española: El modelo de la cultura política" (3:81–106), "Impacto político e interés por la política" (5:63–81), "Participación política" (6:15–37), and "Religiosidad y clericalismo en los jóvenes españoles" (8:55–84). These articles apply the Almond and Verba *Civic Culture* model to the Spanish situation, using the data from a 1960–61 national sample survey of Spanish youth (1,318 males between 16 and 21), which included many questions from their five-country study.

The low level of political interest and information can be well documented with data from national sample surveys. See, for example, the data on familiarity with the names of public figures in Fundación FOESSA (Fomento de Estudios Sociales y de Sociología Aplicada), *Informe sociológico sobre la situación social de España* (Madrid: Euramérica, 1966), p. 299. In another survey at the time of the 1966 referendum only 43% of the males knew the name of such a prominent official as the secretary general of the party.

Effectiveness of performance tends to take precedence over method of selection when Spaniards are asked to rate the importance of these two considerations in a politician, but confronted with the alternative of elected or appointed representatives the choice is overwhelmingly in favor of election. In a 1967 survey by DATA of the electorate of La Coruña province — a relatively underdeveloped area — 54% of the men (163) stressed effectiveness vs. 32% form of selection, but 75% election

apathetic alienated sectors do not enter into, but are in the background, of the conflicts between the governing group and its critics, dissidents, and opponents. The combination of limited pluralism and limited tolerance, if not encouragement, of apoliticism is the setting for the problem of government and opposition. The fact that no positive and active political or ideological identification is required for personal success in many spheres of society (sometimes even in politics itself) decreases the number of potential opponents as well as supporters.[34] It also increases the

<hr>

vs. 12% appointment. The preference for election was greater the higher the social class and education. While 41% considered that the deputies in the Cortes defended the interests of the government (vs. 36% who thought they defended those of the citizens), only 15% thought a deputy should defend the interests of the government vs. 69% who thought he should act for the citizen.

Another example of the basic democratic predispositions of important segments of the population can be found in the responses of a youth sample in 1960–61 to the following question adapted from an EMNID German youth survey:

In other countries it has often been asked whether it was preferable that (1) each and every one of us should take an interest in the politics of the country and should consider ourselves responsible for it; or (2) an outstanding man should have all the authority and decide for us.

Toward which of these alternatives are you more inclined?

The reference to other countries was included to make it slightly less explicitly linked to the Spanish situation, and a positive evaluation of the man holding all authority was provided with the word "outstanding," though this obviously could bias the question in his direction. Since the proportions of no answer vary considerably from group to group, making comparisons difficult, we shall use the ratio between the proportion choosing the authoritarian alternative and the proportion choosing the democratic alternative as an index of the "potential for submissiveness." The index among young males ranged from 1.36 (34% "one outstanding man"/27% "every one of us should take an interest") among the rural youth to 0.33 among university students. Among unskilled workers it was 1.01, skilled 0.74, lower white collar 0.72. The average for males was 0.88, for females 1.23, compared to 0.46 and 0.84, respectively, in West Germany. Emnid Institut für Meinungsforschung, *Jugend, swischen 15 und 24* (Bielefeld, 1955), 2:238. For further analysis see De Miguel, "Participación política," pp. 15–21.

34. The typology developed by Gino Germani in "Political Socialization of Youth in Fascist Regimes: Italy and Spain," in Huntington and Moore, *Authoritarian Politics*, pp. 339–79, distinguishes six types of responses to such regimes on the basis of two dimensions: first, degree of propensity for political involvement or participation, and second, degree of acceptance of the regime (see the accompanying table).

Degree of political involvement	Full acceptance	Indifference, neutrality	Partial rejection	Total rejection
High	1 active supporters ideal leaders	2 political careerists bureaucrats	3 active deviationists	4 active opponents, underground, and resistance
Low	5 passive supporters	6 apoliticals	7 passive deviationists	8 passive defeated

The reader will easily identify similar groups in our analysis. Since we deal mainly

fluidity and unpredictability of politics. While it increases the freedom of the average man, it contributes to feelings of anomie, alienation, and lack of purpose in politics, particularly in certain segments of the population like the intellectuals and the young, which are intolerant of the absence of meaning, the inconsistency, and the ludicrous frequent in such regimes.

A Spanish sociologist, Amando de Miguel, aptly summarized this problem in a paper presented at the American Sociological Association meetings in Montreal in 1964:

> The authoritarian regime either directly or indirectly contributes — in ways analyzed in great detail using the survey data in the body of the paper — to this strange picture in which passive alienates and protesting elements can express themselves so freely and we can find few participant supporters (we may specify in the population at large) which we certainly would find in a true totalitarian system. How long can protesting and defeated apathy exist without being transformed into rebellion under these circumstances is the great question mark we have to leave open. The Spanish experience of the last decades suggests a long time. Which are the mechanisms maintaining this high level of alienation, and at the same time retaining it from becoming explosive is also a virgin territory for further research. Finally how much support can the "passive supporters" with their lack of input (even mild alienation) give to sustain an effective government is another question that must remain unanswered for the time being.

The lack of institutionalization of pluralistic elements also creates unpredictability and uncertainty, contributing to crisis situations that are dangerous to the legitimacy of the system.

---

with the politically involved and/or active, our types of opposition will be found mainly in the upper half of the typology. The semioppositions are in 1 and partly in 3, the pseudo-opposition mostly in 2, mixed with some semiopposition types, the alegal opposition in 3 and with increased freedom even in 4, the illegal mainly in 4. While those in 6 and 7 might have been considered oppositionists at the high point of the totalitarian aspirations of the regime, they would probably not be considered so now. The passive defeated certainly were considered opposition by the regime and subjectively felt as such, but their political potential was neutralized by their passivity. Even the active deviationists in 3 finally became more threatening to the system, partly because they were more tolerated than the defeated in 8.

In his work on attitudes of Spanish youth, based on an extensive national sample survey in 1960–61, Amando de Miguel reached a typology (a clear case of scientific convergence) very similar to the later analysis of Germani. De Miguel also distinguished between active and passive responses and the basic acceptance or nonacceptance of the underlying assumptions and values of the regime. This allowed him to distinguish between supporters, protesters, and rebels, on the one hand, and passive supporters and passive defeated, on the other.

Semiopposition in Authoritarian Regimes
and Institutionalized Opposition in Democracies

While in democracies we have to distinguish between "loyal" or "constitutional" opposition and "disloyal" opposition, in authoritarian regimes we have to distinguish between "opponents" *within* and *outside* the system. These do not necessarily coincide with "legal" and "illegal" opponents or critics. In fact we need to distinguish between the legal semiopposition and the alegal and illegal opponents who may be more or less outside the system.[35] It is essential to distinguish what we may call *semiopposition* from "opposition" in the democracies. Equally important — but perhaps more difficult — is to distinguish such opposition from the ideological or bureaucratic cliques or factions in totalitarian systems. Semiopposition, in our sense, consists of *those groups that are not dominant or represented in the governing group but that are willing to participate in power without fundamentally challenging the regime*. This attitude involves partial criticism and some visibility and identity outside

35. My term *alegal* refers to opponents whose activities, without being strictly illegal, have no legal sanction and run counter to the spirit if not the text of the Constitution and laws of the regime. They are outside the law: alegal. The semiopposition is largely interest-based, even when it sometimes appears to be structural. Many semi-opponents claim to question the basic assumptions of the regime, to search for a way out of it, and/or to advocate basic social and economic changes, but in fact they do little or nothing of this kind. The fact that co-optation, rewards, and minor sanctions by those in power prevent any activity to achieve their professed goals leads me to speak sometimes of *pseudo-opposition*.

Obviously not all the alegal or illegal opponents of the Franco regime would belong to a loyal opposition in a democratic Spain: the PCE would continue to be a more or less disloyal opposition sometimes tempted to turn to illegality, and the same would be even more true for the extremist regional nationalists, particularly among the Basques.

See the interview by Salvador Paniker, *Conversaciones en Madrid*, for a good example of how a powerful and intelligent member of the government, Minister for Information and Tourism Manuel Fraga Iribarne, made the distinction between types of opponents deserving different treatment. He distinguishes between *hostis* and *inimicus* — to use a terminology revived by Carl Schmitt — between *enemigos* and *adversarios*, giving as examples the leader of the PCE, Santiago Carrillo, and "other persons, some of whom have been cabinet members, who are *adversarios* (opponents)." The whole interview is an interesting example of the freedom with which a competent journalist can talk with leading members of the power elite of the regime and ask questions that clearly reveal disagreement on fundamental issues. Interviews with regime politicians like Fraga, Laureano López Rodo, and Emilio Romero also show clearly the boundaries of the system.

Even the PCE does not deny a range of freedom for the opposition: "Today, thousands of Communists are known by the masses and the adversary as such, since they do not hide their ideas, even when — and it is natural — they conceal their membership in a clandestine organization. Because of this the political activity of Communists is not any more so clandestine; in some cases it borders on semilegality. It is just to proceed in this way, because following this road the party grows into the public light and will conquer one day its legality." Santiago Carrillo, *Nuevos enfoques a problemas de hoy* (n.p., n.p., n.d. but after the 1966 referendum).

the inner circle of participants in the political struggle. Those identified with such groups share some points of view, some organizational or personal loyalties, some common mentality if not ideology, and identify with some of the same symbols. These groups are visible to most if not all participants and do not require detective-like research to identify them. However, their characteristics are not fully developed, they are not institutionalized in the form of political parties, and the competition for power among them is not channeled through periodic elections. While they are not fully institutionalized, they are not illegitimate even though they may not have a legal framework in which to operate. The forms they take may be quite different from their functions (a religious association, a group editing a magazine, a veteran's association, an educational institution, a research center), and in this sense they are often alegal. Their visibility allows many citizens, but not the great mass of the population, to sympathize with one or the other of them, and those interested in entering the political arena may enter through one of them. Here the major difference from constitutional democracies is that the spontaneous growth of such groups is severely limited by law or de facto in a discriminatory way affecting large segments of the population. In democracies some groups are also outlawed or discriminated against, but this is an exceptional situation. In democracies the definition of illegality of some groups is surrounded by formal guarantees, applied only to small minorities and to groups contesting the constitutional order by force or subversion. In fact, a democracy that excluded large sectors of the population from political rights and required force to maintain that exclusion would cease to be a constitutional representative democracy.

Another great difference between the semiopposition in authoritarian regimes and opposition in democracies is that semiopposition is more like the *Opposition in der Koalition* of the FDP in postwar West Germany or of the two Austrian parties. The semiopposition groups have some share in the government or in the political power structure but oppose some aspects of it, advocating certain policies (for example, a more socially progressive legislation) or some long-range objectives (like a monarchical form of government or, after 1947, a particular candidate for the throne). There are even groups that are highly critical of the government and the institutional order but distinguish between it and the leader of the regime and thereby continue to be legitimate. Being partly "out" and partly "in" power, or even in the government, makes it difficult for the semiopposition to serve as a political alternative and to be perceived as such. Often the semiopposition is more a pseudo-opposition. The regime tends to function like a permanent coalition with shifting balances of power.

But before we go further into the conditions under which a semiopposition appears and survives and into the functions it serves, we should distinguish it from the factions or cliques in totalitarian systems. In such systems pluralism is more limited to the inner core of the elite or at least to party (and perhaps government) bureaucracies and organizations. It is unlikely that such groups antedate the regime and/or emerged out of the society rather than the political realm. It is also unlikely that they publicly advocate different basic goals for the system and make their participation contingent upon the pursuit or at least free advocacy of these goals. Generally such divergences have no legitimacy, given the emphasis on unity, homogeneity, the party line, the importance of ideology, and the seriousness of deviation from it. With a much less elaborate and precise ideology — the prevalence of mentalities rather than ideologies[36] — the legitimacy of critics and dissidents within authoritarian regimes is more difficult to question.

However, the main difference between a semiopposition in an authoritarian regime and an opposition in a democracy is the lack of accountability (through some formal mechanism like free elections) to potential, organized or unorganized, "constituencies." In fact, the free organization of potential constituents is seriously handicapped. Plural groups share power in authoritarian regimes as a result of decisions made by the leader or the inner group of the regime and their willingness to co-opt them (often in response to changing situations and/or public opinion at home and abroad). Authoritarian regimes are likely to be somewhat responsive (largely through the rule of anticipated reactions) but not accountable.[37]

TYPES OF SEMIOPPOSITION   We will list some groups in the semiopposition to get a better idea of the kind of phenomena we are discussing here.

1. *Groups advocating different emphases in policy* — for example, more statism vs. a more liberal economic policy, more welfare state measures vs. economic stabilization — without emphasizing long-run differences in the conception of the regime. Such differences range from what Skilling[38] calls specific dissent to fundamental opposition. The groups identified with such differences in outlook tend to be linked to different bureaucracies and organizations normally in a "clientele" relationship to the interests they defend. The *ins* vs. *outs* are defined by relative weight in the governing group.

2. *Dissidents within the elite* favoring different long-run policies and

---

36. On the importance of this distinction, taken from the work of the German sociologist Theodor Geiger, see Juan J. Linz, "An Authoritarian Regime: Spain," pp. 257–59.

37. On the distinction between accountability and responsiveness and its implications for the theory of democratic government, see Juan J. Linz, "Michels e il suo contributo alla sociologia politica," pp. lxxix–lxxxvii.

38. H. Gordon Skilling, "Opposition in Communist East Europe," in this volume.

institutional alternatives but accepting the top leadership — perhaps somewhat conditionally and temporarily — and willing to hold office. Sometimes this type can be called a loyal semiopposition in principle even when the differences in point of view may extend to a variety of issues. Among these dissidents we may distinguish:

a. Those aiming at the restoration of a previous regime whose over-throw was initially proclaimed as only temporary or provisional. These are the main opponents to a "commissary dictatorship," [39] which has been forced to hold on to power but has not made a clear decision about creating or institutionalizing a new regime. In some cases movements or coups initiated under restorative slogans face similar opposition on the part of those who see a prolongation of the interim period before the restoration. The pro-Franco mon-archists supporting Don Juan or the Carlist pretender were in that situation until July 1969.[40] Often the legitimacy of such op-ponents, who supported the new regime at its inception, is difficult to question. They would not have any place in a totalitarian system that has explicitly proclaimed its revolutionary character (and explicitly rejects its erstwhile allies and any return to the past).

b. Groups or personalities closely identified with the regime that advocate a more perfect realization of the ideology of the regime, that demand the continuation of the revolution, and that reject any tendencies toward compromises with the existing order. The ideo-logically pure, who see the revolution betrayed, are often found in the youth organizations, the student associations, the paramilitary organizations and similar groups affiliated to the party in a one-party regime. The weakness of these groups, even in the early phase of the Franco regime, has always limited the significance of this type of dissent in Spain. Their identification with the old leaders, their willingness to make a distinction between the "government" and the "charismatic leader," and their isolation from the mass of

39. The term *commissary dictatorship* was popularized by Carl Schmitt in his work *Die Diktatur: Von den Anfängen des modernen Souveränitatsgedankens bis zum proletarischen Klassenkampf*, 2d ed. (Munich: Duncker, 1928).
40. On the monarchical alternative until July 1969 and on the Pretender and his son and the monarchists, particularly the Unión Española party, see Benjamin Welles, *Spain: The Gentle Anarchy*, pp. 331–73. The accounts of the different meetings be-tween Franco and Don Juan are particularly interesting. Arthur P. Whitaker, *Spain and the Defense of the West: Ally and Liability* (New York: Praeger Paperbacks, 1962, first published 1961), pp. 164–76, deals extensively with the monarchists. With-out a formal renunciation of his rights by Don Juan — even an implicit one combined with a protest statement reiterating his democratic faith — and without such a renunciation by the Carlist pretender, some of whose supporters voted against the law, there is still room for a monarchist opposition, but one whose status has shifted from semilegal to alegal or even illegal after the fateful days of July 1969.

the population and traditional institutions, due to their fanaticism, seriously limit their ability to become a real threat to the system after minimum consolidation.[41] This has been the sad fate of many of the sincere fascists in the Franco regime, particularly since 1945. Such dissidents, however, transmit some of their feelings to younger generations, who, after sympathizing with them for a while, often become disillusioned by the verbal extremism and ambivalence of such unrealistic idealists (and often crackpots).[42] This type of dissident is not only found in authoritarian regimes but plays an important role in early phases of totalitarian systems, where he is often ruthlessly suppressed. In authoritarian regimes he is often manipulated after a number of years by those in power who threaten dissidents among the moderates by reviving the specter of the more radical wing among the supporters of the regime. This was the fate, for example, of the Guardia de Franco, the activists of the Escuela de Mandos de Juventudes, and other such groups in Spain, particularly in the 1956 crisis of the regime[43] and again in 1970–71.

c. A group very similar to the one just discussed that advocates closer imitation of a foreign ideological model and greater collaboration with a "friendly" country and/or party. This situation is frequent in smaller nations exhibiting economic and/or political dependency on ideological affinity with a major power. Pure idealists often become bedfellows of opportunists and even paid agents in this kind of dissidence. Such groups existed in Spain in the early forties.[44] Indirectly, the resistance to their pressure can consolidate the rule of the moderates, facilitate a certain institutionalization of pluralism,

41. The weakness of Spanish fascism, the circumstances of the Civil War, and the clear dominance of the army all contributed toward making talk of a second revolution irrelevant. There was no "night of the long knives," and only Hedilla suffered years of imprisonment. See Stanley Payne, *Falange*, passim and Linz, *From Falange to Movimiento-Organización*.

42. Minor groups, particularly several emerging from the official party youth organization and the student organization, have tried to keep alive the ideological purity of the party and its utopian goals. Among these are the Círculo Nosotros and Círculo de las Cinco Rosas, which have published magazines sometimes attacking enemies of the regime among the students at other times protesting violently against the official bureaucratized leadership of the party and its organizations, joining occasionally in protest actions of other alegal or illegal opposition groups, sometimes controlling minor party bureaucracies like the Centro de Estudios Sindicales or the cooperative of the student organization. The symbol of this frustrated small minority was the shout "Franco, traitor" in his presence in the silence of the state funeral for the founder of the party in the Valley of the Fallen.

43. For the process by which young people growing up under a regime like the Spanish turn from opposition within the system to alegal and finally subversive opposition, as well as for the generational differences within such an opposition, see the excellent and well-documented paper by Germani, "Political Socialization of Youth in Fascist Regimes: Italy and Spain."

44. See Stanley G. Payne, *Falange*, chaps. 15 and 16 passim.

and legitimate the regime as "national" resistance to foreign pressures.

d. Members of a coalition of forces installing an authoritarian regime who have not fully given up the particular goals they agreed to postpone in a national crisis or in the struggle against powerful enemies. The reassertion of long-term goals by groups that accepted pro tempore a leadership not identified with their program and its postponement in a crisis period is not uncommon. Temporary and conditional participation in the system, however, soon becomes a co-optation that weakens the commitment to ultimate goals. But the initial affirmation of the goals and their legitimacy for the future (provided there is loyalty to the leader and interest in continuing in office) justifies some external manifestations of diversity and of distinct identity, which contribute much to the pluralism of authoritarian regimes.[45] This has been the raison d'être of Carlist, monarchist, and conservative demochristian collaboration in the Spanish regime and of their almost total co-optation. The symbolic identification of such goals with certain strata or interests sometimes transforms these dissidents "in principle" into pragmatic representatives of interests within the system.

e. Supporters of the regime opposed to transforming it, to opening it up to new influences, or to liberalizing or democratizing it. An obvious example is the Stalinists (the Old Guard) in the Soviet-bloc countries, who defend the status quo. In the process, such an opposition advocates a return to more restrictive policies and turns against the new establishment of the regime. It often finds support in key sectors of the government, and even when it acts in an alegal or illegal way, it benefits from considerable connivance in high places. It can attack the present rulers by showing their weakness and their inconsistency (pointing to past statements) and can claim to represent more truly the "essence" of the regime. In a moment of crisis, it can contribute much toward a political polarization that delays or reverses the processes of liberalization of an authoritarian regime.

45. The Decreto de Unificación of parties of March 1937 in its preamble stated (my translation is literal): "Its programmatic norm is the 26 points of Falange Española, though it must be noted that since the movement which we lead is precisely that (a movement) more than a program, it will not be a rigid or static thing, but subject, in each case, to the work of revision and improvement that reality advises." Even then Franco said that after reconstruction "if the needs of the fatherland and the sentiments of the country should so advise we do not close the horizon to the possibility of installing in the nation the secular regime that will weld its unity and historical greatness," thereby legitimizing the possibility of the installation of a monarchy, though not its restoration.

In the case of Franco Spain, an active, noisy, sometimes violent opposition on the right has made its appearance in the last few years, particularly in response to the radicalization of the university students and to the Burgos trial. The magazine *Fuerza Nueva* and its editor, Blas Piñar, a member of the Cortes, have been its spokesman. Its themes are Francoism (even when his government is bitterly criticized), exaltation of the memories of the Civil War, opposition to liberalization in any field from mores to politics, some xenophobia that does not exclude the United States, hostility to the church Left and even anticlericalism as the church attempts to disengage itself from the regime, anti-intellectualism and a certain populism, appeals to the unity of Spain on Castilian terms, elements of neo-left-fascism, and glorification of the army. Like other semioppositions it has turned to organizing groups of activists, circles of sympathizers, and mass demonstrations in favor of the regime in which at the same time public criticism of the government is allowed to manifest itself. In that same movement or mood, we find groups engaging in private violence against critics of the regime, blacklisting, denunciation to the authorities, and symbolic acts like the destruction of the works of Picasso exhibited in Madrid. The links with the government, the tolerance for many of its activities, the fear of many officials of antagonizing such groups, the appeal to some sectors of the army, the willingness to go into the streets — like the mass demonstration on 19 December 1970, at the time of the Burgos trial, in support of the regime against foreign pressures and against the Basque nationalists — make this semi- (or pseudo-?) opposition a new and disturbing factor on the political scene.

3. *Dissidents among those initially identified with the system but not participating in its establishment.* Authoritarian regimes, particularly when inspired by totalitarian models, emphasize the role of youth and the need for renewal of the society. This often encourages the younger generation to become involved in youth organizations, student associations, and (when such organizations become too rigid and bureaucratic to absorb the attention of the bright young people) a large number of clubs, research seminars, editorial staffs of magazines, and so forth. The elder statesmen take a benevolent attitude, provide funds, and help to circumvent the difficulties created for these groups by "stupid" bureaucrats. A mixture of sincerity and manipulation encourages young men who think of themselves as the "young Turks" of the regime.[46] However, youthful

46. Gino Germani, "Political Socialization of Youth in Fascist Regimes," refers to Italian sources, both under and after fascism, documenting this point. See also

enthusiasm is soon subject to criticism, access to real power is closed, and the co-optation of some individuals, together with a lack of tolerance of the group, contributes to crisis in such circles. The outcome is the withdrawal into private professional life of some, co-optation of others, continued and pathetic hopes of some to gain the ear of the powerful, the beginnings of alegal activity by others. Ultimately some dissidents break with the system and turn into an illegal opposition.[47] Often these groups find themselves in a difficult and painful isolation, ostracized if not persecuted by the regime, using its ideological language and style even in attacking it, and looked upon with suspicion if not hostility by those opponents of the regime who never dreamed of it as a desirable and viable political form.

This type of dissident is frequent in the generation that succeeds those who conquered power and tends to disappear if the regime lasts a few decades, since those coming after them start in politics without any prior identification with the regime. Many young people in Spain, mainly university students, found themselves in this situation in the forties. They formed small groups, published little magazines, and organized seminars within official institutions; they were tolerated with suspicion by the regime and isolated and suspected by the Civil War exiles. Those coming after this second generation do not need to reach their position from the ideological premises of the regime nor, with increased freedom, from the protection of regime institutions. The younger opposition of today has probably not even heard of that "wasted" middle generation's incipient opposition and would probably consider it part of the regime.[48]

Other sources of generational dissidents within the system who are likely to become dissidents outside the system (under conditions of freedom of discussion, travel, and acquisition of books) include:

a. The obstacles to real political careers, which are particularly acute in those regimes — like the Spanish — that recruit most top officials from among experts, civil servants, or groups outside the single party. In such regimes the profession of politics has little to do with the ability

---

Ruggero Zangrandi, *Il lungo viaggio attraverso il Fascismo* (Milano: Feltrinelli, 1963). In Spain, Dionisio Ridruejo, *Escrito en España* (Buenos Aires: Losada, 1962), reflects some of those attempts. However the much lower rate of affiliation to the youth organization than in Italy and the relatively early depoliticization of the SEU (student organization) exposed a much smaller part of the younger generation to fascist ideology and thereby reduced the chance that they would develop critical points of view. See Linz, "From Falange to Movimiento-Organización," p. 168.

47. It would be interesting, from this perspective, to follow the subsequent careers of the collaborators on magazines like *La Hora, Alférez, Alcalá, Juventud,* and *Laye* or the cohorts of the leadership school of the Frente de Juventudes, some of whose former members, led by Manuel Cantarero del Castillo, are trying to "organize" the Left of the party. See his article in *S.P.,* no. 445.

48. The author belongs to that lost generation.

to gain support, to be a leader, commitment to an ideology, and so forth, and those young people who in other societies would enter politics have to choose other ways or give up their vocation. This might be a decisive difference between military or bureaucratic authoritarian regimes and the Eastern European socialist regimes.

b. The contrast between the success of other societies and the failures of one's own country, particularly when viewed in the light of government propaganda. The lack of critical information and the impossibility of assuming responsibility and of constructive criticism tend to make such comparisons a cause of real crises.

THE SOCIAL BASES OF THE SEMIOPPOSITION   Opposition parties within democratic regimes need considerable resources to perform their functions, as all students of party finance know. The salary of the leader of Her Majesty's Opposition is a symbol of this need to support the opposition, and recent proposals of direct or indirect public subsidies to all major parties are a logical outgrowth of that need. Parties of notables could obviously afford their limited functions with the services and funds provided by the men leading them. Labor parties can rely on a large number of small contributions by members and trade unionists.

How the critics and dissidents within an authoritarian regime and, even more, those tolerated on the fringes of the system are able to support their activities is a question that those arguing for "democracy" within a one-party state have to answer. Certainly a system permitting some factionalism and criticism will allow men out of power but susceptible to being called back to make a private living in the professions or in business. But this is likely to weaken their involvement and time for political activity. Another possibility is to allow them to hold positions in the bureaucracies of the regime: its trade unions, nationalized industries, etc. But this implies a dependency on those holding power. It limits their capacity to obtain information, to represent interests independently and effectively, and to constitute an alternative. The most effective arrangement is the growth of factionalism around particular bureaucracies closely linked with particular interests and the "colonization" of ministries and agencies by persons with similar political outlooks. However, this is personalism, particularism, nepotism, patronage politics in some of its worst forms, subverting the efficiency and the so often extolled homogeneity and unity of such regimes. It also weakens the civil service traditions of apoliticism and independence. Another not too dissimilar solution is to provide high-status positions of low power to those defeated in the struggle for power, such as ambassadorships or positions of high economic reward but little effective power, like chairmanships of boards of public corporations. In the long run, however, these rewards in income and/or status neutralize and weaken the desire to act as critics or dissidents even within the system.

The problems of opposition within an organization (very similar to those within a system) were discussed in detail by Michels.[49] His analysis shows the difficulty of dissidence when the leaders have to pay at least lip service to democracy and heterogeneity. How much more difficult it must be when ideologically they argue from an emphasis on authority and homogeneity.

Economic independence has made *Honoratioren* (the "notables") some of the most effective opponents or leadership reserve in authoritarian and even totalitarian systems. Among the notables we often find not only the men of wealth but those whose prestige and fame makes it difficult to touch them or deprive them of their chairs or their right to publish. High office holders like presidents of the supreme court or of national academies, even when appointed, have more independence than elected officials.

The existence of free professions and of business enterprises not dependent, directly or indirectly, on the government allows many dissidents at least a living, if not a base from which to maintain contacts. With increased freedom they even provide a platform for pseudo-political activities like running for office in professional associations (the official bar association typically) and pressure groups acting in their favor in case of trouble. The same can be said for some well-organized, status-conscious, integrated groups within the governmental bureaucracy arguing for the rights of their politically more outspoken colleagues in the name of professional status group privileges (limiting the threat of expulsion, threats to amobility, etc.). The cameraderie of colleagues can often surreptitiously help those being formally ostracized, as, for example, antiregime professors writing for regime-sponsored magazines, without signing their names, at the invitation of the directors, as colleagues.

One of the most independent bases of all shades of dissidence can be a church when it does not identify wholeheartedly with a regime (as it tended to do during the Spanish Civil War).[50] The unique status of a

49. Robert Michels, *Political Parties: A Sociological Study of Oligarchic Tendencies of Modern Democracy*, with an introduction by S. M. Lipset (New York: Collier Books, 1962). See also the introduction to the Italian edition by Juan J. Linz.

50. For an early overview of the currents in Spanish Catholicism, see José Luis L. Aranguren, *Catolicismo día tras día* (Barcelona: Noguer, 1955).

To understand the importance of religious issues in Spain, it should be noted that when a national sample in 1966 was asked about the relative influence of different groups and institutions the proportion saying "much" among the men was 44% for the church, 42% for the military, 35% for the banks, 31% for the Falange, 30% for the government Sindicatos (corporative organization), 16% for the entrepreneurs, 10% for the intellectuals, and 10% for the workers. The percentages denying any influence to these groups was, respectively, 2, 2, 3, 3, 3, 4, 7, and 20, with 18 for the monarchists and 24 for the Carlists, two groups for which the "no answer" was also high, while it was lowest in the case of the church and the military.

For the relationship between religion and class, see the articles in a special issue on

priest creates such a loyalty of the whole organization to any of its members that it tends to shield him from the power of the state even when his superiors identify with the governing group. However, this protection involves dependency, and in a crisis the interests of the church take precedence over everything else, and silence may be imposed (at least until the recent Vatican Council) upon critics and opponents. Leaders of lay Catholic organizations are in a somewhat similar position. They can be among the freest leaders of small nuclei of dissent. They can develop organizational skills, often dispose of mass media — or at least of some organs of opinion — and attempt to penetrate the society through specialized groups appealing to workers, students, and others. Critics, dissidents, and opponents tolerated, supported, or sponsored by a church can represent a formidable resource in case of crisis in an authoritarian regime. However, they are not likely to be a dynamic revolutionary force except under very unusual circumstances. The government is likely to neutralize and, if possible, destroy such opponents by rewards to and pressures on the hierarchy (where there is an organized hierarchy), pointing out the advantages for the church of dissociating itself from its more politically, socially, or civically conscious members. Anticlericals can easily turn into enthusiastic supporters of clericalism vs. laymen. This was the situation in Spain in the late forties and fifties, but, as we will see, in the late sixties things started to change drastically.

On the other hand, the oppositionists, whatever their misgivings about clerical dominance, will eagerly turn to the hierarchy for support against the state. Even the extreme Left does so today in Spain.[51] The polemic

Spain of *Social Compass: International Review of Socio-Religious Studies* 12 (1965); the local studies of Rogelio Duocastella, *Mataró: Estudio de sociología religiosa* (Barcelona, 1960); Duocastella, J. Lorca, and S. Miser, *Sociología pastoral de una diócesis: Vitoria* (Barcelona, 1965); I. Larrañaga and Iruretagoyena, *Hernani, 1962* (Zarauz, 1964); and the survey studies of Juan Díez Nicolás, "Status socio-económico, religiosidad y tamaño de la familia urbana," *Revista Española de Opinión Pública* 2 (1965); Pedro Negre Rigol, "La práctica religiosa obrera y sus motivaciones," *Anales de Sociología* 1 (1966): 40–55; and Amando de Miguel, "Religiosidad y clericalismo en los jóvenes españoles," *Revista del Instituto de la Juventud* 5 (1965): 55–84, based on a national youth survey. Juan Linz and José Cazorla, "Religiosidad y estructura social en Andalucía: La práctica religiosa," *Anales de Sociología* 4 (1968–1969): 74–96, show the linear relationship between class position and religiosity, not only in the cities but in the countryside, and reveal that the difference in practice between the middle and working class is appreciably greater than in France, indicating a higher overlap between religious and social conflicts.

51. The secretary general of the PCE, Santiago Carrillo, in *Nuevos enfoques a problemas de hoy*, pp. 62–75, presents "a new perspective on the relations between the progressive forces, the church and Catholicism," taking issue with the passionate anticlerical tradition of the Left, denying "the silent church" in Communist countries, analyzing "two churches" in Spanish Catholicism, and ending with a long statement on "possible coincidences in certain spheres of the ideology." On the practical level there has been cooperation between the leftist labor resistance to the regime and the clergy in strikes, protest sit-ins in churches by women of jailed leaders and workers, meetings of intellectuals in convents, etc.

between progovernment and critical clerics, in turn, introduces a lively element of controversy into political life. However, the emphasis on principles, the ethics of ultimate ends, and scholastic and casuistic thinking in such polemics and agitation introduce into it an element of unreality that contrasts with the pragmatism of clerical politics and the inevitable tendency toward compromise and middle-of-the-road policies of demo-christian politics. Again the ambivalences of opposition politics under authoritarian regimes become a difficult heritage for the future.

THE FUNCTIONS OF CRITICS AND DISSIDENTS IN AUTHORITARIAN REGIMES
The functions of the opposition in democratic multiparty constitutional regimes have been defined as interest representation, provision of information, and provision of alternatives. These functions ultimately assure the greater accountability, responsiveness and effectiveness of the political system toward majorities in the population and thereby a measure of control over the governors by the governed.[52] For a number of reasons to be specified, all these functions are imperfectly performed by critics and some of the dissidents within an authoritarian regime, but they are not completely excluded.

The critics within the system, often part of the government rather than outside it and active in professional organizations or corporative structures, have information they use in influencing policies. But their information is even less likely to be an accurate reflection of the opinions and interests of their membership than is provided by interest groups in open societies. The lack of diffusion and public discussion of their information limits its value and allows distorted information to persist at the same time that those in power have an easier time challenging it. Information-gathering mechanisms are more or less limited to government agencies or paragovernmental agencies and are affected by the trust or distrust in those agencies. The secrecy or semisecrecy surrounding such information does not contribute much to control by competing interest groups. In contrast to the situation of an opposition party, the lack of legal personality and economic means of the critics out of power or the dissidents still within the system limits their ability to gather information.

The interest representation function is also severely limited when the governing group reserves to itself the right to veto leaders, and even to propose or impose leaders, and when those representing interests are subject to rewards and sanctions not approved and imposed by their constituents but almost exclusively by one or another of the governing groups. The best way to represent the interests of their constituents is to become

---

52. Accountability to an electorate rather than responsiveness to its expectations and satisfaction of its needs, as the only viable operational criterion of democracy, is discussed in Linz, "Michels e il suo contributo alla sociologia politica," pp. lxxix–xcix.

part of the governing group (there is basically *one* such group changing by addition or attrition), but the decision is only partly if at all controlled by their members. The co-optation offer is often made to the leaders as individuals rather than as leaders in a formal sense, and they cannot ask for approval and open commitment, conditions for participation, and so forth from their constituents (which often exist informally as semipolitical, pseudopolitical, or apolitical organizations). This means that such dangers as accusations of selling out or of seeking to hold on to office when the goals cannot be achieved, which Michels noted as causing oligarchic tendencies within democratic opposition parties, are present in extreme forms. The constituency of the critics or dissidents entering into the governing group can continue in its critical position: its representatives can make demands in its name, but they cannot commit their constituents. In this way the input of information into the political process may be facilitated, but other important functions of interest representation — the commitment of constituencies and the legitimation of decisions — are weakened. The representatives may well express the interests of their constituents, but they do not necessarily have their trust,[53] and they can neither claim support nor commit their constituents. They cannot even claim the trust of a constituency, since there are no open mechanisms like fair and open elections to ascertain it. In a weak regime, where the central direction has ill-defined policy goals, such "irresponsible" interest representation may have many of the consequences of narrow interest egoism of pressure group politics in democracies, with few, if any, of the integrating consequences.

Government bureaucracies and experts, with no representation but responsive to popular needs, are often able to pass important reform legislation on the basis of a mixture of ideological and pragmatic reasons and temporary power constellations.[54] However, the absence of a visible, active, fighting opposition makes the benefits appear obvious, natural, and rightful, at no cost in sacrifices or money to other interests or the society at large. This often weakens the integrative function that can result from

53. Juan J. Linz and Amando de Miguel, *Los empresarios ante el poder público: El liderazgo y los grupos de intereses en el empresariado español* (Madrid: Instituto de Estudios Políticos, 1966).

54. Legislation like rent control for urban dwellings and farms (that have hurt strata identified with the regime), creation of national health insurance covering over 50% of the active population, creation of a public industrial sector, etc. Certainly the Spanish case suggests that the enactment of policies can be the result of ideological commitments, expert bureaucratic opinion, imitation of foreign models, etc., without the mobilization of support or pressures from the base as most input-output models of politics would assume. It would be interesting to compare the consequences of such reforms without public debate — resistance of those affected, mobilization of potential beneficiaries for the political system, and integration of the less privileged in the society — with social change through institutionalized conflict (to compare government for the people with and without the people).

struggle by the people themselves rather than from paternalistic concessions. If we add to this failures in administration and the limited participation and hostility of groups directly involved (like the medical profession in health insurance), the dysfunctions add to alienation from those who enacted the new institutions. Hostility in this case is not directed against the social forces, interests, or individuals that limit the effectiveness of the reform, since their visibility is low, but against the government. Government for the people without the people is possible, but it is not necessarily perceived by the people as for the people.

Interest representation is not impossible under authoritarian regimes; interest commitment by large groups and integration of strata by actions favoring them is, however, much more difficult. The integration into society of strata of groups not favored by the system — the negative integration[55] performed by the social democratic opposition parties of the working class in the nineteenth century and the Communist party in the West today — is obviously impossible. Their position is either that of apathetic alienates or of anomic opponents.

The function least effectively performed by the relatively autonomous groups of critics or dissidents within the system is to serve as an alternative. Critics within can serve as alternative *equipos,* "guards," collaborators, members of the team of the dictator, or oligarchic inner groups.[56] They are alternatives to him and permit a certain responsiveness to changing situations (both internal and international), but they are not perceived as alternatives by larger constituencies. There is, however, an element of hope and increased support with changes in the government, even when ultimate power is not transformed or questioned. Critics within the system do not see themselves as an alternative to the system, but dissidents within it certainly see themselves in that potential role. However, the fact that they are willing to participate in it takes credibility away from their claim. They lose prestige with their potential and actual supporters, particularly if their co-optation has been made appealing to their interests or if they honestly participate in systems of dif-

55. The concept of "negative integration" was formulated by Guenther Roth in *The Social Democrats in Imperial Germany: A Study of Working-Class Isolation and National Integration* (Totowa, N.J.: Bedminster Press, 1963).
56. The notion of *equipos* or *relevos* — the American translation *teams* does not convey the idea of successive teams, as in bicycle races, substituting for each other when exhausted — that the limited pluralism and semioppositions provide for the regime is well expressed in this 1957 statement of Franco (my translation is literal): "In Spain it is not parties that govern but *equipos* of men who accept the principles and the historical meaning of the Movimiento. These men — when natural circumstances, among them the logical wearing out that the governmental function produces, so advise — are replaced so that others continue pushing the development of common interests. Changes of the guard that do not disturb the normal course of the country, with the natural corrections that every government task, in its desire for perfection, requires" (*El Movimiento Nacional,* pp. 47–48).

ficult or impossible change with the hope of change but are unwilling to subvert them. Such collaboration can be only temporary and conditional and in any other form tends to discredit them. The alternative provided by dissidents within the system might be decisive in a crisis situation, providing a transitional way out. But dissidents are often ultimately destroyed by the lack of legitimacy that their ambivalent position involves.

THE CORTES AS AN ARENA FOR SEMI- AND PSEUDO-OPPOSITION   One of the arenas for the semi-opposition in Spain has been the Cortes (the legislature) despite the many limitations on an independent and critical role for the *procuradores* (legislators).[57] The government does not depend on a vote of confidence in the legislature, but it is quite concerned about even mild criticism and a few negative votes. There is no systematic study of legislative behavior in the Cortes, but there is no doubt that in recent years committee debates have been lively and even heated, that a number of government bills have been shelved or drastically changed, and that some legislators have raised embarrassing questions attacking one or another group within the coalition of the regime, for example on support to the University of Navarra, founded by the Opus Dei, by heads of ministries belonging to that organization. There have been public negative votes and abstentions even in plenary sessions. However, the alignments have shifted according to issues rather than represented organized and constant factions, and often those vocal in their opposition in the discussion stage vote shamelessly for the government bill. The debates both in the Cortes and in the National Council of the Movimiento — a political chamber representing the party, whose members are also procuradores in the Cortes — on the statute of the Movimiento, on the law of political associations "within the Movimiento," and on the procedures to be followed in the direct election by heads of household of part of the legislature and of the elective members of the National Council are most re-

57. On the Cortes, see the basic work by Manuel Fraga Iribarne, *El reglamento de las Cortes Españolas* (Madrid: Servicio de Información y Publicaciones de la Organización Sindical, 1959), which is unfortunately dated in some respects since the recent constitutional reforms. For a critical analysis, see "Informe sobre las nuevas Cortes: Análisis jurídico de su composición," *Cuadernos para el Diálogo* 50 (November 1967): 21–28. A research group of DATA S.A., Madrid, has completed a collective portrait of the legislators, "Quién es quién en las Cortes," which I was able to use in "From Falange to Movimiento-Organización."

On the new family representatives, see the editorial, "Representación familiar: Análisis jurídico de las normas electorales," *Cuadernos para el Diálogo* 47–48 (August-September 1968): 12–14, which discusses the many difficulties and inequities that any independent candidate would experience in running for the 102 seats (of approximately 450) open to direct election by heads of household.

For a good summary of past and present electoral laws, see the chapter "Spanien" by Dieter Nohlen in Dolf Sternberger and Bernhard Vogel, eds., *Die Wahl der Parlamente und anderer Staatsorgane* (Berlin: Walter de Gruyter, 1969), 1:1229–84.

vealing of the range of opinion and disagreement the elite can publicly display. Controversies generally end in a broad show of consensus, if not unanimity, rather than divided votes.[58] Occasionally it seems as though some legislators or Movimiento councilors form groups reflecting ideological or interest differences, as if some men might emerge as leaders, but ultimately they do not crystallize and all the activity finds almost no echo in the country even when covered by the press. It is important to note that on some issues, like a demagogic proposal to restrict multiple corporation board memberships or a bill on religious freedom for Protestants worked out with the Vatican and sponsored strongly by the minister of foreign affairs or a modest reform in favor of conscientious objectors, the legislature's amendments have been antiliberal.

The Law of Family Representation (1967) added to the legislature two representatives per province, irrespective of population, directly elected by heads of household and married women. In October 1967, elections were held for the 108 new seats, with 328 candidates running. One-fourth of those elected had already been members of previous legislatures, 48 established their eligibility on the basis of their previous membership or the signatures of at least five previous members, 31 held appointive office in national or local government and 36 were active members of the Movimiento-Organización. Even so, some of those who held no government office and established their eligibility by obtaining a thousand signatures represented new blood. They met as a group in different cities (with the consequence that the minister of interior suspended one of their meetings) and developed some esprit de corps.[59] A few have become outspoken critics: one — Eduardo Tarragona, a Barcelona businessman — demanded nominal voting on the designation of Juan Carlos as successor to Franco, and the family group provided 10 of the 19 nays to the bill and 4 of the 9 abstentions. (See table 6.1.) Even the small constitutional change creating some directly elected procuradores had important consequences, which might have been greater if more leading members of the alegal opposition had decided to run for the seats.

58. These debates and the positions advanced by different legislators are analyzed in great detail in "From Falange to Movimiento-Organización." The reader is advised to consult that paper for a better understanding of the Spanish political process and the role of semioppositions in it.
59. Lois Hecht, in an unpublished paper, has compared the legislative behavior of family representatives with that of other legislators for the period January 1968 to January 1969. Family representatives presented 12 questions compared to 11 from all other sectors of the legislature. They introduced 18 petitions compared to 14 by their colleagues, 3 interpellations requiring an oral answer by a minister compared to none, and 4 bills compared to 3.
   The publication of a speech by one of them, a Carlist representing Navarre, led to confiscation and sanctions against two newspapers. The "wandering" Cortes — that is, the caucus of the family group — meeting in Barcelona discussed the issue of extending the immunity of the deputy to the press reproducing his statements.

Table 6.1 Votes of the different sectors of the Cortes on 22 July 1969 on the bill presented by Franco, and voted on in his presence, appointing Juan Carlos de Borbón y Borbón successor as king

Sector	Voting		Absent Abstaining but present		Total	
	Yes	No				
Cabinet	18	—	—	—	18	
Appointed by Franco	22	1	—	2	25	
Appointed National Council Members	30	1	—	2	33 de jure 46	
Elected National Council Members	48	1	1	3	53 de jure 55	
Presidents of High Government Bodies	1[a]	—	—	—	1 de jure 5	
University Rectors	12	—	—	—	12	
Representatives of Cultural Institutions	6	—	—	—	6	
Representatives of Professional Organizations, Chambers of Commerce	22	—	—	—	22	
Syndical Members	135	6	4	4	149 de jure 150	
Local Government Members	106	—	1	1	108 de jure 115	
Family Representatives	86	10	4	3	103 de jure 108	
No Information on Sector	5				5	
	491	19	9	15	533	564

[a] The number of incumbencies fixed by law in each sector does not coincide with the number of actual members, since it is possible for the same person to hold seats in more than one capacity. The number of seats in the Cortes is 521, but the number of members is 491. This makes the classification of some members slightly arbitrary. In the 1968 legislature there were 14 procuradores holding de jure more than one seat; in fact one held four. This means 30 more incumbencies but not individuals. The data on the voting record have been taken from *Nuevo Diario*, 23 July 1969.

MONARCHISM: SEMIOPPOSITION OR OPPOSITION? The monarchy vs. republic issue has plagued the opposition as have few others. Originally, in 1939, all the opposition was Republican — that is, loyal to the regime founded in 1931 — or revolutionary, with the monarchists (except for some Carlists loyal to their principles and opposed to the forced unification with the Falangists) behind Franco. For the time being, the monarchists almost did not dare to be even in semiopposition to his rule. Facing the prospect of an Axis defeat that might sweep away the conservative social order Franco was protecting, some monarchists and pseudo-Falangists asked him in 1943 to restore the monarchy.[60] For some

60. See Stanley Payne, *Falange*, pp. 237-38; Clyde L. Clark, *Evolution of the Franco Regime*, pp. 415-16. The 25 members of the Cortes who signed did not suffer immediate reprisals, but six of the signataries who were members of the National Council of the party were dismissed from their seats and posts.

time pro–Don Juan monarchism appeared as an alegal opposition, with students having brawls with the Falangists. Some sectors of the army, without breaking with Franco, supported the monarchy, even when its principal supporters were banker-aristocrats (a result of the Restoration policy of raising successful businessmen to the rank of noblemen), old aristocrats, and a few intellectuals. The commitment of these groups to a constitutional and democratic monarchy was weak or ambivalent, many of them having been exposed to the ideas of Acción Española and its mixture of conservative authoritarianism and fascism.[61] However, in Lausanne in March 1945, the Pretender, sensitive to the climate of opinion in the world, issued a manifesto with a democratic slant. Some Civil War exile leaders thereupon began to negotiate with the monarchists to work together on Franco's overthrow, either considering the monarchy a transitional regime pending a referendum (as in Italy) or indifferent to forms of government but interested in democratization. The contacts between the reformist Socialist Prieto and the demochristian Gil Robles belong to that period. This divided the emigré politicians into those loyal to a "legal" government in exile and those willing to search for solutions without necessary continuity with the past.

Franco in turn, to institutionalize his regime and to fend off monarchist opposition, enacted in 1947, after a plesbiscite that served to give him a "democratic" legitimacy for life, a Succession Law that declared Spain a monarchy but obliged the future king to accept the basic principles and constitutional laws enacted by him.[62] His solution was not a restoration of the liberal constitutional monarchy that died in 1923 and whose death certificate was the 1931 municipal election but the installation of a "traditional," nonparliamentary monarchy.

Ever since, the monarchists have been divided between those willing to accept the Succession Law, with more or fewer mental reservations, and therefore favorable to a policy of pressure on Franco and of negotiations between him and the Pretender and those rejecting the Succession Law in toto. The former have been one of the key elements in the semi-opposition, even though most of the time they have turned out to be a pseudo-opposition. In the course of the years Don Juan has shifted back

61. On Acción Española, see Linz, "The Party System of Spain: Past and Future," pp. 249–51, and the literature quoted there. In the study of the ideological origins of the Franco regime this group has been relatively neglected, in comparison to the fascists, even though its ideas and leaders might have been equally if not more important for the political character of the regime. The first person to speak of installation rather then restoration of the monarchy was Calvo Sotelo, and this was a dominant theme in Franco's July 1969 speech to the Cortes proposing his successor. 62. The future head of the monarchy, Juan Carlos de Borbón, on 23 July 1969, had to swear "loyalty to his Excellency the Head of State and fidelity to the Principles of the Movimiento and other Fundamental Laws of the Kingdom," all enacted by Franco, assuring a formal continuity to his regime after his death.

and forth from negotiation to conflict with Franco, thereby alienating some of his more democratic supporters and never gaining the full trust of those favorable to continuity. In 1954 he made the fateful decision to allow his son Juan Carlos to be educated in Spain at the university and as a cadet in the three service academies. As the prince approached the age of 30 stipulated in the law as a requirement to assume power, he became, for the pro-Franco monarchists and even more for those basically hostile to the monarchy but willing to use it as a legitimizing facade for continuity, another pawn in the political game. In addition Franco, given the deliberate imprecision in the law, always had the pretenders of the Carlist branch of the Bourbon dynasty as one more card to play against noncooperative monarchists and Don Juan.

It would be tedious and unrewarding to recount here the complex dealings, intrigues, ambiguous communiqués, protests, and personalities involved in the contacts between the pretenders and Franco.[63] The semi-opposition and the moderate alegal oppositions in recent years have been equivocating on the monarchy issue. On the one hand, the restoration of the Bourbons was a legitimate aspiration in terms of the regime's laws and pronouncements. It could have been the channel for the peaceful transition everyone desired, and it might have allowed the transfer of the army's allegiance, since it would have been a "constitutional" change. On the other hand, popular interest is minimal — except for the illustrated magazine type of interest — and the openly declared monarchists are found among the most conservative if not reactionary groups: big business, an aristocracy without prestige or influence, and only a sprinkling of intellectuals, many of them in pseudo-opposition.[64] A monarchy with

63. The relations between Franco, the supporters of a monarchy (restored or installed), and the son of the last king, Juan de Borbón y Borbón, from the Civil War to the appointment of the grandson as Prince of Spain and successor to Franco on 22 July 1969 are too complex to describe here. Apparently never acceptable to the Caudillo after the prodemocratic manifesto of Lausanne in March 1945, Don Juan was unable to make his position clear enough to attract the democratic opposition, having to woo the pro-Franco monarchists while hoping to be called to the throne after Franco following the procedures of the Law of Succession, which Don Juan neither agreed to nor clearly denounced. His meetings with Franco to arrange for the education of Juan Carlos in Spain ultimately allowed the Caudillo to groom the son as successor and ignore the rights of the father. On the monarchy and Franco, see Benjamin Welles, *Spain: The Gentle Anarchy*, pp. 331–73. The marriage in 1972 of the granddaughter of Franco to Alfonso de Borbón y Dampierre, son of an elder brother of Don Juan who had renounced his right to the crown, has created further political confusion and the possibility of pressure on Juan Carlos by the advocates of continuity of the regime after Franco.

64. The Consejo Privado of the Count of Barcelona — Don Juan de Borbón y Battenberg — is a good example of a semicounterelite. The advisers of the Pretender — 92 men — overlapped only in 4 cases with members of the Cortes, but when we consider their occupations we find many similarities as well as differences. While only 3% in the Cortes are aristocrats, 18% (17 persons) are aristocrats in the council of the royal pretender. The military is represented by only 3 men in the

such a narrow base cannot be appealing, but the opportunity for "legitimate" transfer of power was before July 1969 too attractive to be foregone. Before that date the conservative character of much of the support allowed the Falangist left semiopposition (or rather pseudo-opposition) to play with the idea of a regency or a presidential republic and thereby prove its popular, modern, leftist character against more genuine oppositions willing to accept a restoration as a means of breaking out of the Franco system. The reliance of Don Juan on a private council not representative of the whole opposition and including semi- and probably pseudo-opponents made him a partisan choice that represented a heavy mortgage for a future constitutional monarch. He might have been better off rejecting such formalized support and taking an uncompromising stand as in the Lausanne manifesto. Once more semiopposition meant a loss of appeal and legitimacy and a mortgage for the future.

From Tolerated to Persecuted Opposition

In Spain in the early forties, joking about Franco or not making the fascist salute to the flag could lead to arrest or a beating by a zealot, and owning Marxist literature or even picking up Allied propaganda at Allied embassies could mean trouble. Thousands were in jail for their participation on the losing side in the Civil War and were being freed slowly into a peculiar state of insecurity called "conditional" or "supervised" free-

---

council, and 2 are there more as a consequence of their aristocratic status than of their influence in the armed forces; in contrast, military men constitute 11% of the membership of the Cortes. Lawyers, who are still such an important element in the Spanish political elite, constitute 22% of the council and 26% of the Cortes. The elite civil servants numbers 12% and 16%, respectively. Financiers and businessmen are represented by 22% in the council vs. 28% in the Cortes, and one should add that in the latter they represent medium and small business rather absent among the advisers of Villa Giralda. Contrary to expectations, there are somewhat fewer landowners in the council (3%) as compared to the Cortes (8%), with the Cortes reaching further down into rural society. As in all opposition — and semiopposition — politics, there are a larger proportion of intellectuals, notably academic intellectuals: university professors come to 18% in the council vs. 7% in the Cortes. Journalists and writers — the ideologues, together with some professors — are probably more prominent: 11% among the royal councilors. White-collar workers, lower technicians, and a few manual workers in the Cortes (13%) have no equivalent among the royal advisors: the monarchical cause had to appear to be led by men not too different from those of the regime but socially more privileged. If we turn to place of residence, 72% of the monarchical elite were residents of Madrid compared to 46% of the Cortes members, Catalonia and the Basque country were more or less evenly or slightly overrepresented in the council by comparison, as were western Andalucia and Extremadura, the traditional latifundia Spain, all to the detriment of broader geographical representativeness. See also Joaquín Bardavío, "El Consejo Privado del Conde de Barcelona," *Triunfo* (Barcelona), 24 February 1968. The council was dissolved after the designation of Juan Carlos as successor in July 1969.

dom.[65] At that point there was room for muted factionalism within the coalition that won the Civil War but no room activity on the part of those who were defeated or were neutral, and even those few who were loyal to a conservative Catholic politician like Gil Robles were made to feel like outcasts. The use of regional languages and the folklore of the dissident regions was frowned upon; associations and businesses could not have their names in Catalan or Basque; the use of these languages in public offices could lead to trouble; and neither books nor magazines could be published in them. Decades later things are very different: though there is no freedom for an organized opposition, with offices and regular meetings, opposition leaders are known to the small politically conscious segment of the population, and they and their friends can meet privately. Bookstores are full of translations of Marxists works; Hilferding, Lukacs, and even Marx, Marcuse, and Che Guevara sell well; and publishing of books in non-Castilian languages flourishes. In the press and particularly in small magazines some political issues are discussed more or less explicitly, while criticism of the social and economic system is frequent. Unfavorable comment on the Axis in the forties could lead to trouble, but criticism of Spain's ally, the United States, is commonplace today.

THE ALEGAL OPPONENTS   Let us stress the fluidity of the transition from semilegitimate criticism and dissidence within the system to alegal or even illegal opposition fearful of police persecution. The borderlines vary considerably from one authoritarian regime to another and even within the same system, depending on a great number of factors. In Spain, acts that at one point would have been severely, even cruelly, punished, today are openly tolerated, but might not be so tomorrow. However, we may note that in authoritarian regimes those dissidents who can prove that they have an initial identification with the system, or have evolved to their position out of the tendencies within the system, are likely to be treated more fairly than those emerging from among the defeated enemies of the regime. This is perhaps one of the salient differences between authoritarian and totalitarian systems.

---

65. Many of the legal texts and some statistics on the repression given in English in Clark, *Evolution of the Franco Regime.* For the legislation on political responsibilities, see volume 1, pp. 132–39, 222–32, 378–84, 418–23, 538. For the legislation on conditional freedom, also see volume 1, pp. 232–35, 305–07, 377, 384, 424–25, 426–31, 541. Luis Benítez de Lugo y Reymundo, *Responsabilidades civiles y políticas* (Barcelona: Bosch, 1940), summarizes and comments on the repressive legislation in the spirit of the time.

Dionisio Ridruejo, *Escrito en España,* pp. 92–100, describes the climate of opinion of the time, the discrimination suffered by the defeated, and their often depressing or undignified adaptation to the situation. He points out, rightly, that this additional repression was not always inspired by the regime and its authorities but has to be blamed largely on the society.

Often a "third generation," growing up under the regime after it has lost its ideological and symbolic appeal and its routinization has created greater areas of privacy and freedom, becomes politically aware and looks for channels of expression. Foreign influences and professional activities (particularly in student organizations and even in official trade unions) contribute to the growth of such opponents. They emerge without a conscious link to the ideologies, groups, organizations, and symbols of the previous regime. In a Machiavellian mood they may well use the institutions created by the regime, not to transform or improve them, but to subvert them.[66]

Sometimes institutions like the church, with a basic legitimacy and a desire for continuity after the regime, try to channel such sentiments.[67] We may surmise that the crisis in the church is depriving the regime of one basis of support, but the tensions generated are not likely to allow Spain in the seventies to base a Catholic mass party like the Italian Christian Democratic party on Catholic organizations, a fact that indirectly will weaken a moderate opposition. The split among lay Catholics has gone so far that, at the World Congress of the Lay Apostolate, Spain was represented by two delegations, one appointed by the hierarchy and another by the organizers of the congress, in which the specialized movements opposed to the existing social and political order were represented. The hierarchy itself is deeply split, largely along generational lines.

Identification with intellectual leaders of the younger generation is characteristic of the alegal opposition. In the fifties and early sixties the leadership of the alegal but tolerated opposition was almost exclusively in the hands of a number of distinguished professors. Initially a number of them could be considered a semiopposition, since they were willing to collaborate with the then minister of education, Joaquín Ruiz-Giménez, in academic politics until the ill-fated congress of young writers at the

66. The exile opposition for a long time refused, as a matter of principle, to participate in any of the organizations, elections, and other activities organized by the supporters of the regime, not even for infiltration purposes. The "third generation" in the opposition and the Communist party have opted for a different course. Gino Germani, "Political Socialization of Youth in Fascist Regimes: Italy and Spain," also notes that "until the middle thirties in Italy there was a great resistance, based on ethical reasons, against underground members of the opposition joining Fascist organizations."

67. On the church, see in English William Ebenstein, *Church and State in Franco Spain.* For a recent Spanish analysis, see Enrique Miret Magdalena, "Panorama religioso," in M. Aguilar Navarro et al., *España perspectiva, 1968* (Madrid: Guadiana de Publicaciones, 1968), pp. 173–201, and "Iglesia" in José M. Areilza et al., *España perspectiva, 1969* (Madrid: Guadiana de Publicaciones, 1969). Miret Magdalena describes well the internal crisis of Catholic Action. He also reviews the main journals of Spanish Catholicism from left to right, from conservative proregime clericalism to what he calls neoclericalism of the left of a "committed church." In the 1969 article he summarizes the issues between the regime and the Basque clergy and the positions of the hierarchy (pp. 138–39).

University of Madrid and the subsequent disorders betwen students and Falangists provoked a serious crisis in February 1956 that led to his ouster. The imprisonment of Ridruejo, who was close to that group, symbolized the break. Men like Aranguren, Tierno, and Laín Entralgo remained in the university and attracted a devoted following of many students. They became the mentors of a whole generation, particularly Aranguren, who was perhaps less explicitly political. Simultaneously innumerable professional and political organizations of students appeared outside the official student organization — the SEU — infiltrating it and asking for its reform or suppression. In February 1965 the struggles about student representation in the fourth Free Student Assembly led to a confrontation with the authorities in which a number of professors sided with the students or tried to prevent the embitterment of the conflict, an intervention that led to the ouster of five professors — among them Aranguren and Tierno — and the resignation of another in protest. Since then the influence of the professors on the student movement has been limited to some sectors, while others have turned far more radical. An important attempt to link students, particularly in the social sciences, to professors of different shades of opinion, from moderate to some radical younger staff members, in a liberal atmosphere in the Centro de Estudios e Investigaciones S.A., a private institution organized as a corporation, has been intellectually fruitful but has not achieved some of its political goals. Some of the intellectual mentors of academic protest have had second thoughts about the course it has taken.[68]

The age groups involved, the important role played in them by students, and the leadership of intellectuals make such groups opponents "in principle" rather than on pragmatic grounds. Often the deeply felt moral indignation and the lack of any channel for access to responsibility lead to an "apolitical politicism": a purely expressive politics that does not aim at assuming power but at expressing a mood and a moral position. This latent apoliticism of the intellectual is reflected in a comment by

68. The rejection of formal democracy and the risk that it will lead to positions that constitute a "left fascism," as well as the acceptance of intolerance derived from the premises of Marcuse, were noted by Aranguren in his interview in the book by Salvador Paniker, *Conversaciones en Madrid,* pp. 14–15. Adult and youthful politics seem largely to follow different directions, even when the young have exercised considerable influence on the alegal opposition to focus on structural reforms of the economy and society rather than on political change and to be open to contact with the more illegal opposition or at least unwilling to break with it. Politician-intellectuals are prominent in the semiopposition and the alegal opposition and writings of academics, particularly some economists, have considerable influence on the climate of opinion, but the more strictly intellectual types of opponents — like Laín, Tovar, even Aranguren — are not as influential as they were in the sixties. To some extent their place among the young has been taken by writers, poets, folk-singers, and artists, who offer much more romantic, simple, and easily usable ideas and symbols.

Aranguren, one of the three professors ousted from their chairs, "I cannot see how an authentic intellectual can even belong to a political party. I feel that a political party is always like a kind of straitjacket in which thought does not remain free. The intellectual has to criticize constantly, criticizing even the structure he might have created." [69]

These opponents act as spokesmen of groups that have never given them representation and whose problems they know very little about, but with whom they identify vicariously. This identification with those who have suffered and/or suffer the injustices of the political and social order is often based on a feeling of guilt on the part of the sons of the ruling elite or classes. The last names of the founders and dignitaries of the regime are noticeable. This kind of protest can become a serious threat to an authoritarian regime but tends not to provide any effective and stable alternative. As an expression of *Gesinnungsethik* (ethic of ultimate ends) full of contempt for *Verantwortungsethik* (ethic of responsibility) — using the terms in a Weberian sense — such groups can play a complex and dangerous role in the crises of authoritarian regimes.[70] They appear

69. At the same time, he recognized that "the intellectual has today a possibility for action that he did not have before: action through the university students, in the measure that the students have become a political force," as an "indirect action." See interview in Paniker, *Conversaciones en Madrid.*

70. See Max Weber's "Politics as Vocation" in H. Gerth and C. W. Mills, *From Max Weber: Essays in Sociology* (New York: Oxford University Press, 1958), pp. 77–128, especially pp. 120–21.

Personally, I feel that Ruiz-Giménez, because of his penchant for Gesinnungsethik, failed to capitalize on many unique advantages he had to be a leader of the center democratic opposition appealing to strata passively or reluctantly identified with the regime.

The rejection of compromise for pragmatic reasons in favor of Gesinnungsethik has been a constant in Spanish political life. Juan Marichal writes about Azaña, the most powerful figure in the establishment of the Republic in 1931, "for Azaña the tragedy of Spanish liberalism has been its tendency to transaction and compromise." Azaña wrote in 1923: "It will be necessary to restore doctrines in their purity and shield oneself against compromise. Intransigence will be symptomatic of integrity." He was aware of the contradiction between his principles and his "liberalism" when he said in one of his most important speeches, "The other decisive restriction that will displease the liberals" is to demand the outlawing of Catholic education: "let no one say to me that this is contrary to liberty, for it is a question of public health." The fact "that in Spain there would be millions of believers, I don't argue about: but what makes the religious essence of a country, a people, and a society is not the numerical sum of beliefs or believers, but the creative effort of its mind, the course followed by its culture." Manuel Azaña, *Obras Completas,* ed. Juan Marichal, 4 vols. (Mexico: Oasis S.A., 1966), 2:49–58, speech on art. 26 of the Constitution.

The commitment to principle and rejection of compromise finds considerable support in principle in public opinion. A poll in 1967 found 43% agreeing with the statement, "To reach a compromise with our opponents becomes dangerous, because in many cases it leads us to commit treason against our own side," while 21% disagreed and 36% were undecided. Among those with only primary education 46% agreed and 11% disagreed. Intolerance for disagreement is also reflected in 62% agreement with the statement, "A group which tolerates too many differences of

mainly among the intelligentsia, the students, and in recent times the younger clergy (perhaps as a response to the criticism the churches have undergone for their pragmatic outlook in a world full of moral dilemmas).

It would be impossible to summarize here the complex evolution of student politics — the tactical issues, the attempts of the regime to channel it (generally belated and therefore unsuccessful), the innumerable groups and coalitions of groups succeeding each other, their links and conflicts with adult political tendencies, as well as the repression some of them suffered, particularly after their activities became increasingly open and disruptive.[71]

It is interesting to note that these groups have played a similar role in democratic societies when the dominant parties have not been able to act as a channel for new demands, and the masses could not be moved to defend their own interests, for example, the civil rights struggle and opposition to the Vietnam war in the United States.

Another group of alegal opponents is composed of the passive opponents who have survived from the previous regime, maintaining personal contacts without organization. This "internal migration" often has difficulty establishing contact with the new types of dissidents and contestants.

The transition from an alegal to an illegal opponent depends fundamentally on the definition by the regime of the actions it will or will not tolerate and the type of sanctions it is willing to use. After the expansion of oppositional activities in an alegal form, their formal legal classification

---

opinion among its members cannot survive long," compared to 14% disagreeing and 24 undecided. Data reported in "Imagen del mundo en el año 2000: Perspectivas sobre el desarrollo nacional e internacional," *Revista Española de Opinión Pública,* July–September 1968, pp. 155–388, especially pp. 305–09.

71. The article by Antoliano Peña, "Veinticinco años de luchas estudiantiles," in *Horizonte español, 1966,* 2:169–212, is extremely informative even though not fully objective.

Antonio López Pina, "Notas y datos para una historia de los años sesenta: Poder y movimiento estudiantil en España (de la ley de prensa al estado de excepción)" (unpublished) has summarized different indicators (disturbances, meetings, strikes) of student protest by universities and faculties for the academic year 1967–68 and 1968 to January 1969, using the information published month by month in the Spanish press, as well as the reactions of the authorities — closing of classes, sanctions and arrests. The number of disturbances reported for 1968–69 in Madrid was 228, Barcelona 63, Bilbao 18, Seville 13, and fewer than 10 in other universities. The leading faculties in 1967–68 were disproportionately law, economics, political science, and humanities, with economics and political science outstripping all others by far in 1968–69. The arrests reached their maximum number — 152 — in November 1968, just before the announcement of the state of emergency.

In English, see Enrique Tierno Galván, "Students' Opposition in Spain," *Government and Opposition* 1, no. 4 (August 1966): 467–86. *Minerva* chronicled the university unrest in 1964–65.

For an analysis of student politics published in Spain, see Emilio Menéndez del Valle, "Casi un lustro de problema universitario," *Cuadernos para el Diálogo* 7 (extra issue) (February 1968): 30–32.

as illegal often becomes impossible. To increase the number of illegal opponents when they may be left in the state of alegality may be dangerous. The conditions under which, without having been victims of terror or real persecution, opponents themselves turn into putschists, terrorists, underground resisters, exiles, agents of hostile foreign powers, and so forth also deserve consideration.

A regime with low ideological symbolic legitimacy, either internally or externally or both, but with considerable efficiency (a rising standard of living, economic development, etc.) and efficacy (a well-organized and loyal security apparatus) may well prefer to allow an alegal opposition rather than to persecute it as illegal.

An important step in the official recognition of an alegal, but tolerated, opposition took place on the occasion of the official visit to Spain of Walter Scheel, German minister of foreign affairs, in April 1970. After informing the Spanish government and with its permission, he received in the German embassy J. M. de Areilza (democratic monarchist), J. Satrústegui (liberal monarchist), E. Tierno Galván (socialist), and J. Ruiz-Giménez (Christian democrat) to "hear the opinions of those who dissent from the government." In his press conference, reported on in Spain, he stated that "this information has filled in considerably my views on the Spanish situation" and that "he would receive through diplomatic channels a document in which they stated their opinions about the political situation." The meeting produced a hostile editorial by the director of the newspaper *ABC*, to which the four visitors answered with an open letter to which he in turn replied, and this was alluded to by the Spanish minister of foreign affairs in the farewell banquet to his colleague.

Channels of expression of the alegal opposition   Liberalization of the press law not only changed the style and content of some newspapers but allowed the publication of political essays by the legal or alegal — but not the illegal — opposition. While Ridruejo's *Escrito en España* (1962)[72] was published abroad, Gil Robles's *Cartas del pueblo español* (1966),[73] Manuel Jiménez de Parga's *Atisbos desde esta España* (1968),[74] Rafael Calvo Serer's *España ante la libertad, la democracia y el progreso* (1968),[75]

72. Dionisio Ridruejo, *Escrito en España*, the most complete and original political essay produced by the opposition. For further light on Dionisio Ridruejo, see the interview by Millán Clemente de Diego, *El futuro político de España* ([Madrid?]: n.p., 1968 but completed in 1965), pp. 123–35.
73. José María Gil Robles, *Cartas del pueblo español* (Madrid: Afrodisio Aguado, 1966).
74. Manuel Jiménez de Parga, *Atisbos desde esta España* (Madrid: Guadiana de Publicaciones, 1968).
75. Rafael Calvo Serer, *España ante la libertad, la democracia y el progreso* (Madrid: Guadiana de Publicaciones, 1968).

José María de Areilza's *Escritos políticos* (1968),[76] and the two-volume *España Perspectiva, 1968* and *1969*[77] were all published in Spain. Gil Robles, the old CEDA leader, uses the opportunity to consider some key political problems: the dangers of the flood after the present, a danger implicit in the *continuismo* of the regime and depolitization without parties; politics vs. technocratic rule; the need of parties in a democracy; monarchy and republic; presidentialism; the electoral law; the important role of the army in the maintenance of order, particularly in a transition period, and so forth. His book was seized by the government, but the judicial authority voided the administrative decision. The programmatic character of the book was stressed in a preface that stated that it had been written by a team of persons, whose names were listed alphabetically, directed by Gil Robles.

The other works, particularly that of Jiménez de Parga, are collections of newspaper articles and make more reference to current events. Spanish problems are often discussed by implication in connection with such subjects as the Greek crisis ("Ten Commandments for a [Constitutional] King"), De Gaulle, democratic Israel's success as a military might vs. authoritarian Egypt, independence of Spanish Guinea with political parties. Another constant theme is commentary on the post–Vatican Council statements of the church and papal encyclicals that serve to suggest the illegitimacy of the Spanish situation from a Catholic point of view. Debates on the constitutionalization of the party and of pluralism within the Movimiento led to even more open discussion of democracy and "legalization of the opposition." Calvo Serer's book has headings like: "The Viable Solution for Spain," "Dictatorships Are Transitory," "Neither

76. José María de Areilza, *Escritos políticos* (Madrid: Guadiana de Publicaciones, 1968).
77. Recent reviews of Spanish life from a semiopposition point of view published in Spain are M. Aguilar Navarro et al., *España perspectiva, 1968* and its follow-up for 1969 published shortly after the state of emergency, José María Areilza et al., *España perspectiva, 1969*, with a chronology of events up to March and with chapters on politics, the economy, cultural life, etc. Areilza, a liberal advisor to the senior royal pretender, Don Juan, comments on the Movimiento laws and succession politics in a good example of the range of criticism tolerated in political matters. Chapters on trade unionism, the press, the university, and the church are particularly informative and revealing, describing events and analyzing some of their implications, for example the difficulties faced by the Comisiones Obreras after a change in government policy against them. Only a reading of articles such as these can provide a sense of the degree of freedom of expression, particularly in book form, possible in Spain in 1969. See also Miguel Martínez Cuadrado, ed., *Cambio social y modernización política: Anuario político español, 1969* (Madrid: Cuadernos para el Diálogo, Edicusa, 1970), with a wealth of political information, and Juan Muñoz et al., *La economía española, 1969: Anuario de hechos, polémicas, leyes, bibliografía* (same publisher, same date), which includes a chapter on the Matesa affair that led to the indictment of three ex-cabinet members before the Supreme Court (pp. 51–257).

Freezing of the Regime nor Democratic Radicalism," "An Intermediate
Solution: A Government of Trust for the Right and of Hope for the
Left," "A Center Formula Demanded by Irreversible Democratization,"
"Reformism Is Not Utopian," "Consent, Support, and Popular Participa-
tion."

Sometimes more specific issues are discussed, like the ousted professors,
the fight on religious freedom, a bishops' attack on the large landowners,
and the incredible disproportion in representation of the directly elected
legislators (a vote in Soria weighted 28 times that of a vote in Barcelona).
It is impossible to estimate the diffusion of these articles and collections of
essays and their impact on public opinion. However, the main characteristic that should not be forgotten is that they do not come from organized
groups, and their authors do not speak for parties, organizations within
the regime, or powerful interest groups like business or labor, nor do they
make an appeal for the formulation of any organization (which would
mean moving from legality to illegality). Certainly the newspapers and
magazines that publish them are supported financially by some businessmen, and Calvo Serer is identified with the Opus Dei, but so is Carrero
Blanco (a not unlikely heir apparent) or at least many of his close collaborators, who are the most powerful men in the cabinet.[78] The limited

78. The evening newspaper *Madrid*, through its editorials and reporting, became,
under the editorship of Calvo Serer, an opposition voice. A university professor,
Calvo Serer underwent an interesting and complex ideological evolution. He was
a founder and later director of *Arbor*, the general intellectual magazine of the
Higher Council for Scientific Research, where he intended to counteract the orientation represented in the postwar years first by *Escorial*, directed by the Falangist
Dionisio Ridruejo, and later by the *Revista de Estudios Políticos*, under the direction of Javier Conde, by emphazising a Catholic traditionalist outlook critical of
many of the liberal intellectuals of the past to which those two magazines had
opened their pages. His writings — *España sin problema* (1949) and *Teoría de la
restauración* (1952) — gave expression to a line of thought shared by other Opus
intellectuals like Pérez Embid and López Amo, critical of Christian Democracy and
favorable to a traditional monarchy. An article in *Ecrits de Paris* (September 1953),
"La politique intérieure de l'Espagne de Franco," spoke of a "third force" distinct
from some of the Falangist intellectual Left and some of the Christian Democrats
who were at that point collaborating with Ruiz-Giménez, then minister of education, in a liberalizing cultural policy. In his writing Calvo Serer shares some of the
neoliberal ideas that the economic ministers of the Opus Dei implemented after the
formation of a new cabinet in 1957. However, since then, probably in part due
to his frequent travels abroad, he has evolved toward the positions reflected in the
collection of editorials quoted above. In 1969 *Madrid* was suspended for two months
and Calvo was indicted for one of his articles. In 1971 the newspaper was closed,
and he had to go into exile. On Calvo see, from a critical point of view, Daniel
Artigues (pseud.), *El Opus Dei en España, 1928–1962: Su evolución ideológica y
política* ([Paris]: Ruedo Ibérico, 1971).

(Another newspaper *Alcázar*, also linked to Opus Dei members, was forced to
change its editorial policy and staff. See Juan Luis Cebrián, "La Prensa" in
España perspectiva, 1969, pp. 93–110.) Salvador Paniker in *Conversaciones en Madrid*,
interviewing another member of the Opus Dei, Laureano López Rodó, minister for
the development plan, shows clearly the public disagreement between himself and

freedom of the last few years has allowed opposition opinion but not opposition organization. It undermines the legitimacy of the regime but does not build up an alternative. In fact, it might be argued that freedom of the pen, whose use requires time to explore the always uncertain limits and to fight the legal and alegal pressures that might endanger it, has wasted much of the energy of the opposition. The time that might have been invested in contacting men, building the foundations of an organization, working out tactics among many small groups, formulating specific policies for the day when power is assumed, even real conspiracy, went instead into endless arguments over whether this or that could be published without endangering the continued publication of a newspaper.[79] This, paradoxically, together with the professional and business activities of many opposition leaders, is one more factor limiting their effectiveness.

The cost of semifreedom   Alegal opposition, in contrast to semiopposition, aims at a basic change in the regime and in its political institutions and to a large extent a basic change in the social and economic structure. Its reluctance and/or incapacity to use illegal means is obviously a disadvantage when the regime it confronts is unwilling to give up power and

Calvo Serer. A group of men who since the middle fifties had appeared to many Spaniards to be a united and all-powerful force, who had provided the regime with men, particularly in the economic ministries, who followed a neoliberal economic policy, often conflicting with the Falangists who advocated a more social and interventionist one, and whose intellectuals had given ideological bases to a future monarchy now appears divided. Some of the men of the Opus Dei favor the continuity of the regime after Franco, while others move between semiopposition and tolerated opposition, facing a difficult situation since they had supported the candidacy of the Count of Barcelona.

   The Opus Dei, which has occupied such a central position in politics for over a decade, has been studied from a hostile point of view by Daniel Artigues, *El Opus Dei en España, 1928–1962*, and Jesús Ynfante, *La prodigiosa aventura del Opus Dei: Génesis y desarrollo de la santa mafia* (Paris: Ruedo Ibérico, 1970), with much information on its economic activities and its presence in political, intellectual, business, and other elites.

79. The press law of 1966 prepared by Manuel Fraga Iribarne, promised when he entered the government in 1962 and enacted after long debates within the regime, represented an important change, even when later legislation and its application in recent times represent steps backward. Spanish newspapers today are very different from those published under his predecessor. On the law and its impact, see Guy Hermet, "La presse espagnole depuis la suppression de la censure," *Revue française de science politique* 18, no. 1 (February 1968): 44–67, with a brief content analysis of ABC and Ya. See also the already quoted chapter by José Luis Cebrián "La prensa" for more recent developments. See Gonzalo Dueñas, *La ley de prensa de Manuel Fraga* (Paris: Ruelo Ibérico, 1969), for a hostile but very informative review of the legislation and its application. The legal texts can be found in Ministerio de Información y Turismo, Oficina de Textos Legales, *El nuevo derecho de prensa e imprenta* (Madrid, 1966). Also see Henry F. Schulte, *The Spanish Press, 1470–1966: Print, Power, and Politics* (Urbana, Ill.: University of Illinois Press, 1968).

recognizes only a semiopposition willing to be co-opted. The transition from alegal to semiopposition is obviously tempting, but so also is a shift from alegal groups to the most active illegal groups, particularly among the young, who are soon disillusioned with the inaction and basic ambivalences of their leaders. One result is high turnover in the alegal opposition and a shift toward ideological radicalism combined with inaction and ineffectiveness. It is difficult for a Spaniard abroad to describe the failures of the alegal opposition without appearing smug, particularly when writing of friends facing unpleasant, even though not too dangerous, situations. Let me stress that I make no judgment here on the intentions and idealism of members of the alegal opposition but intend only to analyze the structural and situational constraints that in my view account for their style and actions as well as for much of their incapacity to achieve their goals. It would be a mistake for any scientific observer — and for the alegal opposition itself — to attribute their lack of success only to the strength of the regime and its security apparatus.

The capacity of the alegal opposition and its leaders to provide an alternative to the regime is severely limited, but not only by the difficulties they encounter or persecution they might suffer. Even when they enjoy personal freedom and some opportunity for political activity in their homes, freedom to travel inside and outside the country, freedom to write between the lines, as it were, or to publish abroad, their capacity to appear as an alternative is greatly restricted partly because of the very freedom they enjoy. Their freedom permits their activity to be visible to the government but not necessarily to any large constituency, and this allows the government to co-opt and corrupt them, to know their weaknesses and failings. On the other hand, this freedom creates a subtle gratitude and dependence on those in power that limits their contestation activities. This in turn transforms them, in the view of many opponents of the system, into a sham opposition that weakens their legitimacy as an alternative. Furthermore, their relative freedom and the soft treatment given them in the case of repression often contrasts with harshness toward less prominent enemies of the regime[80] and the generally difficult condi-

80. Those who have lost in power struggles at the top — after the days of the Civil War, when Hedilla, then formal head of the Falange, was imprisoned and other opponents of the Gleichschaltung of parties had to choose exile — have generally suffered only economic and social disadvantages. There have been no bloody purges in the elite. Some, like Serrano Suñer, could retire into lucrative professional practice, others into private life; a few, like Ridruejo in the forties, had to go into forced residence, and those who have become leaders of the alegal opposition have been allowed more freedom than those without such a background. The most recent case is Manuel Fraga Iribarne, the minister responsible for liberalization of the press laws. After losing his cabinet post, he became an advocate of centrist reformist policy within the regime and a leading figure in the opposition within the system — the semiopposition. His position is well reflected in his essays, speeches, and interviews collected in *El desarrollo político* (Barcelona: Grijalbo,

tion of life of the masses; the contrast weakens their appeal to the common man.

The relative freedom of certain dissidents or opponents under many authoritarian regimes weakens potential moderate opponents, thereby contributing to the power vacuum that can follow the fall of such regimes and providing opportunities for extremists. In this sense it was easier for the enemies of nazism to become a legitimate alternative than for those of fascism, and easier for those of fascism, probably, than for regimes like those of less totalitarian dictatorships. Identification of the totally illegal and silent or persecuted contestants was easier to make, at least for the key positions in the new regime (since the political elite of the regime had also been more clearly defined). Only after some time, when a great number of secondary positions had to be filled and when advancement brought into important positions people outside the initial nucleus of the new democratic parties, did the issue of past activities acquire importance. But by this time people had already started to care less. In a situation such as that in the Dominican Republic, however, the lack of ideological and organizational identity of Trujillo supporters and their identification (with changing fortunes) with the social-economic, administrative-military elite of the society deprived even the murderers of the dictator of legitimacy.

The semifreedom for an alegal opposition and the fluid transitions between it and the semi- or worst pseudo-opposition have given to Spanish political life a strange and peculiar ambivalence, which extends from government to opposition, with a few exceptions. This ambivalence has been described with great insight by one of the leading figures of the intellectual opposition, the ousted professor José Luis Aranguren, in an article appropriately entitled "Real and Verbal Political Behavior in the Spanish Situation."

> Obviously, despite the outcome of the referendum, the opposition exists, and . . . everyone knows the names of its leaders. Yes, it exists.

1972). See, for example, his critique of an article attributed to Carrero Blanco (p. 42) and his allusion to the Opus Dei (p. 286). Incidentally, he clearly distinguishes between opposition *to* the system and *within* the system and suggests that the larger the second the smaller the first, placing himself explicitly in the second (p. 277).

This seems to be an important difference between authoritarian and totalitarian regimes. In this connection, the meetings with Franco of former high officeholders alienated from the regime, in which they presented their points of view quite openly (as reported by them) would be inconceivable in Nazi Germany or Stalin's USSR. See Dionisio Ridruejo, *Escrito en España*, pp. 21–22: "I was listened to with affability and irony and the uselessness of the advice did not surprise me" (1947), and Ruiz-Giménez in his interview with Salvador Paniker, *Conversaciones en Madrid*, p. 333. See also the interviews with Ridruejo and Ruiz-Giménez in Sergio Vilar, *Protagonistas de la España democrática: La oposición a la dictadura, 1939–1969*, pp. 480–95, 447–67.

What happens is that, besides being, in terms of militants, not numerous, it is completely divided to the point of atomization and consequently unable to provide serious alternative. But why this atomization? . . . The opposition cannot be *integrated* because, to a large extent, it is not an *integrated* opposition — a strong, persistent, forthright opposition knowing *what* it wants and *how* it wants it. But note that I am not blaming it for doctrinal confusion, incompetence, indecision, ineffectiveness . . . The problem is deeper. Once violence is rejected, as anyone can see it is, everyone is pushed by the force of facts to a *Situationspolitik* (I mean this in a sense close to that of *Situationsethik*) — a policy in which principles are reduced to a minimum because they are considered "abstract" and because one wants policy to be adjusted . . . to the concrete historical situation of each moment. Of each moment, because the political situation has always, during these years, been lived as transitional; and in addition to being actually changing, in greater or lesser degree, its essential ambiguity is its most characteristic trait. There is a desire to seize all the operational possibilities offered at each juncture; this accounts for the fact that no one has a firm, decided, *integral* position and explains why the simple passing of time poses the question *where* the others find themselves (the observer-actor, like the traveler on a train with another next to it, sometimes does not know which one is moving or whether both are moving).

Commenting on these attempts Aranguren writes:

Obviously *parties* are not admitted, but paradoxically *opposition* among them is admitted. Obviously, opposition always within the framework of the Movimiento (in its broad sense). Everything that is not *franquista* is thrown into outer darkness, and it is simply decreed that it does not exist (by quoting the results of the referendum-plebiscite) . . . nor is there any need for it since the regime already has its Right and its Left, its monarchists and republicans, democrats (of the organic variety) and aristocrats, liberalizers and absolutists, clericals and anticlericals (the enemies of the priests that mix into politics) . . . now almost for the first time in Spanish history, it is politics "of the Left." The roles have been carefully and exhaustively distributed.[81]

The semifreedom created by the regime has a large number of dysfunctional consequences for the opposition. One is to divert its attention away from the problem of how to achieve an evolution of the regime toward

81. José Luis Aranguren, "Comportamientos reales y verbales en la circunstancia española," *Cuadernos para el Diálogo*, no. 45–46 (June–July 1967), pp. 9–11.

democracy — or, in case this should prove impossible, how to overthrow it peacefully, or even forcefully — and toward an attack on the social and economic structure. Discussion of the *reformas de estructura* as a way of criticizing the regime that presumably defends them obviously spares the political system from direct attack, poses for its opponents a much larger task (for which they may not be prepared), and leads them to become aware of their differences of opinion (that might not exist if it came to a simple choice between democracy and continuity of the regime). It even leads them to attack — prematurely or even unnecessarily — institutions and interests that might otherwise not be hostile to them and whose partial support they may need. Whatever cracks may exist within the "Establishment" — as seen by the oppositon — are healed, and the "conservative structures" threatened by the ambitious plans of the opposition inevitably turn toward the regime. The main victims in this process are the men who could be the leaders of a democratic center-right, which could represent a serious threat to the regime. They are carried by their younger collaborators — students and intellectuals — into positions that do not fit either their own social backgrounds or the constituencies they might successfully appeal to. Their subjectively sincere positions are politically unrealistic and might even seem insincere to those not personally acquainted with them. As leaders of real organizations in a democratic context, they would not be able to take many of the vague positions they almost inevitably espouse in a situation of semifreedom and irresponsibility.

Joaquín Ruiz-Giménez and the *Cuadernos para el Diálogo*[82] exemplify this problem. Born in a family of the upper bourgeoisie of the Restoration, he is the son of a Liberal mayor of Madrid and a long-time deputy. As a young man he was the leader of the international Catholic student organization, Pax Romana. After being head of the influential Instituto de Cultura Hispánica and ambassador at the Vatican in 1951, he became minister of education. In the ministry, in spite of his background, he followed policies that incurred the displeasure of clerical forces and that were perceived as an opening to intellectual freedom. In 1956 these policies contributed toward provoking a crisis that led to his dismissal. He participated as a lay member in the second Vatican Council. As a

82. *Cuadernos para el Diálogo*, directed by Joaquín Ruiz-Giménez, initiated publication in October 1963, with a monthly circulation in February 1968 of 29,000 copies and 12,000 subscriptions. The article "4 años de línea editorial," no. 7 (February 1968), extra issue on the occasion of the 50th issue, pp. 55–78, is a selection of the 275 editorials published to date. For the program and ideology of Joaquín Ruiz-Giménez, see the so-called Manifesto of Palamós, which is the editorial in *Cuadernos para el Diálogo*, no. 47–48 (August–September 1968), pp. 3–11, entitled "Fin de Vacación: Meditación sobre España." The interview by Salvador Paniker in *Conversaciones en Madrid*, pp. 331–46, gives a brief biography and provides considerable insight into the personality of Ruiz Giménez.

lawyer and university professor, with this background and his ties with the church, he could and still can be the leader of the center faction of a European-style demochristian party and attract to the opposition middle-of-the-road sectors of opinion now passively supporting the regime. A mixture of sincere conviction derived from his interpretation of the role of the Christian in the modern world, the enthusiasm of young supporters active in the editing of *Cuadernos para el Diálogo,* a penchant for idealism rather than power politics, the intellectual climate that has made "dialogue with Marxism" popular, perhaps an unconscious wish to make the break with his Falangist-nationalist-Catholic past more explicit and believable have led to the positions of the Manifesto de Palamós (1967) and the encouragment of the Left around him, as well as to an unwillingness to work effectively with other demochristian leaders more to the right (or so perceived by his friends). The freedom publicly to question the social and economic structure of Spain rather than the political oligarchy and constitutional structure, combined with the intelligence of the regime in never openly persecuting or arresting Don Joaquín, as he is affectionately called, have contributed to this development.

Ideological ambivalence or leftist me-too-ism are one thing; building bridges to the leadership of the Left, particularly the leaders of the Comisiones Obreras, is another. The role of prominent leaders of the bourgeois opposition as lawyers of their leaders under indictment can be, from the point of view of creating trust along personal lines, one of the most positive aspects of opposition activity. This may help to create the bases of "consociational democracy" [83] in Spain as the common experiences in Nazi concentration camps did in Austria, even though there are flaws in the analogy, since the court room is not a jail and the Communist labor leadership is not the Austrian Social Democratic party leadership.

A period of prolonged opposition, without immediate hope of attaining power, will also have dysfunctional consequences when the men engaged in it face the task of ruling. Semifreedom will have allowed them to formulate many ideas and ideals without consideration of the need to find constituencies giving them support and votes. With a significant part of the electorate preempted by the Communists,[84] the search for votes and money, which any party in a democracy needs, will make inconsistencies blatant, and both the real Left and the reactionaries will have a field day

83. I use the term in the sense Arend Lijphart uses it in "Typologies of Democratic Systems," *Comparative Political Studies* 1 (April 1968):3-44, and other works by the same author.
84. See Linz, "The Party System of Spain: Past and Future," pp. 268-71, for an election prediction based on applying the Italian voting patterns by occupational classes to the Spanish social structure. Other things being equal, the continuity of the regime makes it even less likely that a democratic socialist opposition could compete successfully with the PCE given the fading memories of Civil War anti-Communism among the working class and the waning of loyalties to the PSOE.

making them obvious in an effort to discredit key men. It will also lead such men to make concessions to potential opponents, in a democratic framework, without exchange or negotiation, for example, in the thorny problem of regional nationalism and linguistic autonomy, and often without clear awareness of the practical implications of well-sounding and "in principle" legitimate concessions.

The fashionable anti-Americanism to which the regime, in spite of the bases agreement, has no objection — and which it might even tolerate if not encourage (there have been rumors of financial ties between regime figures and the magazine *Triunfo*, which has consistently held an anti-U.S.A.-imperialism position), perhaps to have a stronger hand in negotiating with Washington — may well be an obstacle to a realistic foreign policy for a Spanish democracy in the Western European framework. Similarly the constant outpouring of anticapitalism in a country that is not likely to become socialist, even though it has a mixed economy, will mortgage the future. From left-wing Falangists to academic and government economists, everyone feels free to be anticapitalist,[85] while Spanish business, like most European business but in an even more extreme form, shows its incapacity to make a capable defense of its achievements, even though they are far from small in a period of rapid economic development in the industrial sector. Many of the younger followers of the present democratic leadership faced with the inevitable moderation of their elders in the future will throw those statements in their faces and turn to those "sincerely" advocating these positions, which might well be the Communist party.

The search for an opposition stance has led to a proliferation of books on Latin America, the nondemocratic socialist countries, the failures of the United States, and Marxism, often of a semijournalistic type, and little serious literature on communism, Stalinism, or the achievements of Western-type democracies. The positive sides of the Left are overblown, and the failures of democracy exaggerated. On the other hand, the regime has not encouraged the publication of serious analysis of communism or the Soviet regime — limiting itself to bad propaganda books — while the intellectually alert opposition publishers have found it undesirable to publish serious anticommunist or social science books that give a more balanced picture, since this would be indirectly supporting the "anticommunist" regime. The stands of leftist literature that existed a few years ago under the guise of social science in the university city of Madrid could not be more to the liking of Columbia University's SDS, without

85. A reading of the official newspaper of the Sindicatos and most independent Catholic organs of opinion, the cartoons of Máximo in *Pueblo* and of Chumy Chúmez in *Madrid*, the issue of *Cuadernos para el Diálogo* on the banks, the works of economists like Juan Velarde and Ramón Tamames, and the lists of many leading publishing houses reflect this trend.

any readings in Friedrich, Brzezinski, Inkeles, or Barrington Moore to complete the image. The stupid anticommunism of the regime, combined with the pseudofreedom, helps to account for the weakness of genuine commitment to a Western type of democracy among the youngest generations. Sentiment ranges from the conviction that political democracy is neither possible nor valuable without "social and economic" democracy (rather than an instrument to achieve it) to the slogan painted in the yard of Valencia University: "Bourgeois democracy, no! Dictatorship of the proletariat, yes!"

Why are critics and dissidents within and outside the system tolerated? Why should authoritarian regimes whose explicit pronouncements and verbal "ideology" stress homogeneity, unity, consensus, if not discipline and subordination, tolerate semioppositions and alegal opponents?

Reasons given range from inability of the regime to impose unity because of the imprecision of the ideology or technological insufficiency, the cost of a thorough system, the difficulty of permanently maintaining a higher degree of mobilization, to historical factors (that is, the size of the movement or party before taking power, the strength of other social forces, and so forth). Such explanations as these ignore the different intentions of authoritarian rulers, which can include assuring temporary control, "cleaning the stable" (commissary dictatorships), and emulating or mimicking a totalitarian model (where external conformity is not sufficient but full loyalty is required of the population) without real understanding of its nature. Whatever the cause or origin of the tolerance for different degrees of criticism, if we take a functionalist perspective we can ask why its existence should be tolerated over a period of time. What does that tolerance contribute to the system?

One answer is that even when, from the point of view of the governed, the functional alternatives to the opposition in democratic political systems are inadequate to their tasks in authoritarian regimes some of the advantages of the existence of opposition in democracies apply to authoritarian regimes.

The critics, dissidents, more or less organized factions and tendencies within the system, as long as they accept the system — even for the time being — or accept the personal leadership of the dictator or head of state, give the system considerable flexibility by shifting blame, giving hope to emergent leaders, and broadening the base of recruitment. Tolerance of opposition also allows the replacement of personnel without the excessive strain of purges. It facilitates cooperation between different sectors of the elite and parts of the society. It allows postponement of basic decisions about the nature of the political system, since in the meantime participation, or the hope of participation, cuts down the contestation element.

An attempt to impose unity and homogeneity on critics and dissidents would often require coercion rather than manipulation and would alienate considerable segments of the elite and perhaps of the population generally. (This may be more true in a semideveloped society with a complex social and economic structure founded on traditional and powerful institutions, and with some constitutional-liberal-democratic experience — even though abortive — than in a really underdeveloped country, particularly one emerging from the colonial stage.) Such imposition would diminish the legitimacy of the system. Only if the regime had strong commitments to an ideology or program, rather than to power as an end in itself, would this way of operating be possible.[86] On the other hand, if the critics and dissidents in the semiopposition had stronger ideological convictions and/or personalities, it would also be more difficult for the regime to function as it does. The give and take of compromise may be an obstacle to effective, clear policies, but it does increase the regime's responsiveness to those sectors of the society whose pluralism is tolerated or institutionalized. However, without the possibility of a clear definition of responsibilities (since the alternations in power are only partial and semipublic), this responsiveness may contribute an element of *immobilisme*, like coalition government in multiparty systems.

It is not always easy to judge whether the tolerance of alegal opponents is a sign of strength or weakness in such systems. Tolerance increases the visibility of the opponents and, combined with their ineffectiveness, can contribute to weakening their prestige. Internationally this can be an asset to the regime, and the opponents serve to some extent as a safety valve, but shifts in their treatment can also become an international handicap. The limited freedom they may enjoy serves indirectly to legitimate persecution of more dangerous or "illegitimate" (in terms of class and values) opponents. The alegal opponents can also be used to check pressures from dissidents in the system on the other side of the ideological spectrum, as these in turn are used to check the moderates in the system. Most authoritarian regimes have existed in relatively small or medium-sized countries that depend considerably on world public opinion and more or less open pressures by the governments of the great powers. A number of the great powers believe in the rights of opposition, in autonomy from the state for a number of institutions, in the rights of intellectuals, and so forth and exert pressure in this direction. Only xenophobic, ultranationalistic regimes are likely to offend such sentiments consistently and on a large scale, particularly when the opponents identify themselves with the values advocated by some of these great societies.

86. This point is made by Alex Inkeles in "The Totalitarian Mystique: Some Impressions of the Dynamics of Totalitarian Society," in Carl J. Friedrich, ed. *Totalitarianism* (Cambridge, Mass.: Harvard University Press, 1954), pp. 87–108, especially p. 108.

Of course in the Western world these pressures do not benefit all political forces equally; the Communists particularly do not profit from them. Furthermore, this international linkage and support for dissidents can also backfire: they can be labeled foreign agents, and sentiments of national dignity can be aroused to support repression.[87] This is exactly what an emerging extreme right did in response to the international pressure on the government at the time of the Burgos trial.

The opponents find themselves in a particularly difficult position when they advocate the overthrow or modification of the existing regime with the support or sympathy of other countries, a policy that can negatively affect the interests of the country as well as of the regime. In fact they can hurt the country seriously without assuring the fall of the regime. Cross-pressures can be created between identification with the national interest and hostility to the regime that can easily be turned against its opponents. A campaign against the entry of Spain into the European Common Market unless there is a change of regime would be an example of this.[88] Similarly, when dissidence *within* the system is presented abroad

87. The opposition to the Franco regime is not only internal or of exiles, but liberals and leftists the world over consider it an arch-foe and, from hostile editorials in the *New York Times* to support for terrorists, act out their sympathies. This non-Spanish opposition finds itself in a complex relationship to the national opposition; its activities have a variety of impacts on the regime far from easy to know and understand. Protests in the press, letters to the authorities, and protests in front of the Spanish embassies may contribute toward softening policies toward some opponents and some situations, but in others it may well harden the regime's severity (as was probably the case in the execution of Grimau). The style, massiveness, coordinated character, names used, type of case, and so forth may account for the different reactions. An element of pride and outrage about presumed blackening of Spain's name may enter into the hard-line reactions. Liberal opposition that aims at the international isolation of Spain — from the withdrawal of ambassadors after World War II and the United Nations resolutions to the actions of liberal congressmen on U.S. bases and of European socialists against the entry into the Common Market — has not and cannot achieve the overthrow of the regime nor weaken it seriously, but it has allowed the governments of their countries to make more favorable bargains when dealing with Spain, limited economic aid for postwar reconstruction, narrowed down collaboration to the strictly military sphere (to the disadvantage of cultural exchanges and others forms of cooperation), postponed the adjustment of Spanish industry to international competition, favored the agrarian interests of other countries, and so forth. International "opposition" that is unable to overthrow a regime more often hurts the people than the regime (except perhaps in extreme cases where corruption or inequality is such that none of the advantages of international trade and cooperation trickle down to the society, which is certainly not the case in Spain).

88. One example is the reaction of the regime to the meeting organized by the European Movement in June 1962, at which opposition leaders from inside Spain — among them Gil Robles — and from exile — among them the leader of the Socialist party — met and unanimously approved a resolution favoring a return to democracy in Spain and some other broad policy statements. A giant press campaign was immediately mounted about *contubernio* (concubinage, referring to the shaking of hands of former political enemies), and mass demonstrations were held in support of Franco after he delivered a speech sounding the nationalist appeal against "pol-

as dissidence *from* the system its influence inside the country can be weakened. The proper balance naturally depends on the specific international political situation.

A peculiar problem of many authoritarian regimes is that they are often ideologically oriented in imitation of foreign models. The real power holders may not be enthusiastic about the "ideologists'" sympathies for fraternal movements in other countries, but their public image, their own phraseology, and their international relations impose a certain external acquiescence in the rhetoric. These tendencies may then achieve temporary dominance within the system, while others can subtly exploit the resentment caused in more traditional and nationalistic sectors by such "servile" elements. The ideological weakness of authoritarian regimes and the international framework in which they operate in the modern world foster an element of pluralism, legitimize it, and not infrequently provide it with encouragement and even economic support through "friendly" embassies. However, this pluralism reduces the possibility that dissident groups will express real internal differences (as loyal oppositions in democracies predominantly do) and increases the likelihood that they will have only a weak link to real social forces, if they are not outright agents of other nations.[89]

Relations between government, semiopposition, and alegal opponents
A difficult problem for dissidents *within* the system — the semiopposition — is how much contact they can and should have with opponents *outside* the system — the alegal opposition. Contacts are almost an inevitable consequence of the semifreedom, the doubts about the future of the regime, and the shared social background of both groups, at least for those not separated by deep ideological chasms. They have the advantage for each side of increasing its area of influence and the amount of information available, but they are also dysfunctional, particularly for the semiopposition. In the tolerant stages of authoritarian regimes, even high officials maintain good private relations with persons known as opponents, do favors for them, and, unconsciously perhaps, elicit information in return. These contacts in societies with some liberal tradition even increase the self-esteem of such men: they are civilized men who can separate politics from friendship or colleagueship in the professions.

luted air coming from abroad" and against "money that has no fatherland." It also led to some of the more serious sanctions — either forced residence or exile — for men who could be considered part of the alegal but respectable or, as some call it, dialoguing opposition. It also provoked the break between Don Juan de Borbón and Gil Robles. For a partial summary of the Munich meeting and some of the reactions, see Fernández de Castro and Martínez, *España hoy*, pp. 235–60.
89. That type of opposition was probably encouraged by the Germans during World War II. See Ramón Serrano Suñer, *Entre Hendaya y Gibraltar* (Madrid: EPESA, 1947), pp. 183, 258.

Politics is not the only and highest value, even when, in moments of difficulty or danger, politics wins out, and contacts are broken off. So a leading opponent of a regime talks about an officeholding "critic within" as "my intermittent friend." The opposite can also happen; personal and in-group loyalties can become so strong as to lead to political breaks. (For this reason totalitarian techniques of social isolation are much more effective and have advantages for both sides in terms of political purity.) It can be argued that it is through informal contacts that opponents have their greatest effect and best perform their liberalizing role, but their function of providing a clear alternative to the regime is endangered.

A serious problem is created by the solidarity between the collaborationist wing of parties, movements, organizations, groups, and interest groups and their erstwhile friends, colleagues, and fellow members who persist in an opposition attitude. Whatever the changing balances of influence of collaborators and dissidents in such groups may be, the survival of the groups themselves requires a certain tolerance, a certain amount of contact, collaboration, mutual aid, and use of influence that prevents either a repressive and forcibly integrationist policy by those identified with the regime or a real contestation policy by the opponents. The balance sheet of this kind of ambiguity and mixture of points of view may be favorable to those involved (and perhaps the interests they represent), but it is damaging to the ideological and political clarity of both sides. Ambivalence creates alienation and cynicism as well as a modicum of tolerance and freedom. It would be difficult to draw the balance sheet between both for the society.

THE ILLEGAL OPPOSITION   The illegal opposition has changed much in composition and tactics over the thirty-odd years of the regime. In 1939 the victorious Franco army had made the Republican army prisoners of war, the leaders of the working-class parties and the bourgeois Republicans were in jail or in exile,[90] and those who were free were cowed. The repression was bloody and those who escaped from it were clearly identified and had "conditional" or "supervised" freedom.[91] Those who

90. The total elimination of the political elite of the Left after the Civil War can be measured by these data from a pro-Franco source: José Gutiérrez-Ravé, *Las Cortes errantes del Frente Popular* (Madrid: Editora Nacional, 1953) lists deputies in exile (as well as those living in Spain) and those executed by the Republican side (but not by the Franco side). Of 99 Socialists 61 were in exile, 3 living in Spain; of 87 Izquierda Republicana the figures were 59 and 2, respectively; of 39 Unión Republicana, 27 and 1; of 36 Esquerra Catalana 25 in exile; of 10 Basque Nationalists 8; of 17 Communists 9. There are no reliable figures on how many of the remainder were shot by the Nationalists.

91. For the legislation on *libertad condicional* and its application, see Clark, *Evolution of the Franco Regime*, 1:232–33; for the 1940 law, see 1:305–06, 384–85, 423–33; for the 1942 decree, see 2:470–71, 539, 541. The figures for prisoners to whom this legislation was applied each year were: 42,305 in 1941, 23,240 in 1942, 49,060 in 1943, 15,922 in 1944, and 14,102 in 1945, with a total for this period of 144,629. These

were not exhausted by the fight, disillusioned with the conflicts among their own leaders and different ideologies in the course of the war, or critical of those who had escaped while they were in jail, put their hopes in the victory of the Allies in World War II. When that victory came in 1945 the Allied diplomatic and economic boycott was not sufficient to provoke the fall of the regime or to make possible an internal uprising against it.

A number of factors made it difficult for those remembering their bitter defeat to act successfully. The divisions and recriminations caused by defeat were too recent, the attempts to build links with the moderate or conservative anti-Franco forces — like the monarchists — were too halfhearted and partial, while the unity of the regime based on ideology, interests, and fear of reprisals was still too strong.[92] Foreign support, while too weak and halfhearted to cooperate in the overthrow of Franco, was enough to arouse some nationalist resentment adroitly manipulated by his supporters. Massive and ruthless police and military efforts defeated attempted infiltration through the border and armed insurgency in the countryside.[93] The geographical areas of greatest social unrest and those whose topography facilitated guerrilla activity did not fully coincide. When they did — as in Asturias–Leon-Galicia or the interior of Levante-Aragon or Southeast Andalusia — they were too isolated from the borders to be accessible to supplies from abroad.[94] Terror and counter-

figures may not be complete, since there is no information recorded for some months. The legislation has obvious analogies with the American parole system, but in those years probably involved tighter control and certainly served to discourage any political activity on the part of those affected.

92. The exiles maintained a formal, but legally shaky, continuity with the Republic, with a truncated legislature meeting in Mexico, a government in exile that underwent several crises — with the withdrawal of different parties — only to become finally limited to the left-bourgeois Republicans. The Basques were better able to maintain the continuity of the PNV regional government, while the Catalans were represented by two organizations, one claiming continuity with the Generalitat (regional government) dominated by the Esquerra, and a Catalan National Council founded during the war in London. It is impossible and useless to recount here the many attempts to form committees, alliances, and pacts between exile parties and trade unions and their attempts to link up with the conservative opponents of Franco over the years. A mixture of ideological rigidities, personal feuds, and disagreements about tactics and above all the staying power of Franco doomed all these efforts.

93. Tomás Cossias, *La lucha contra el "maquis" en España* (Madrid: Editora Nacional, 1956), gives a detailed account of the guerrilla effort in Levante, the factors accounting for its failure, and the reaction of the government.

94. Enrique Lister, the military chief of Spanish Communism, has published an analysis of Communist guerrilla activities for 1944–49 in "Lesson of the Spanish Guerrilla War (1939–1951)," *World Marxist Review*, February 1965, pp. 53–58, table on p. 54. The annual activity figures for 1944–49 were: 694, 783, 1085, 1317, 983, 509, that is, a total of 5371 actions. The regional distribution of the total was: Asturias and Santander 15.0%, Extremadura 12.5%, Galicia and Leon 21.0%, Levante and Aragon 15.2%, Andalucia 21.6%, and Castile 14.8%. If we calculate the ratio between the percentage of activities and the percentage of population in these regions, we obtain the following figures: 3.3, 2.5, 1.3, 1.3, 1.1, and 0.8.

terror did not appeal to the civilian population so soon after the Civil War, and there were no sympathetic moderates who could or would make their support for the insurgents felt. The students of upper- and middle-class backgrounds were too influenced by their parents, who were frightened by the prospect of a proletarian revolution or accustomed to silencing their ideas after 1939, while outside influences were excluded both by the regime and the international boycott. The defeat of the guerrillas and the onset of prosperity limited open illegal opposition. Only slowly did new generations develop their own opposition sentiments and hesitantly establish contacts with exile leaders, often to find them dated in their ideas and style.

Repression and economic insecurity made labor protest difficult before full employment. However, some of the better-paid segments of the working class — particularly the Asturian miners facing relative deprivation as a labor aristocracy, compared to other skilled workers in a dying mining district, and the workers of Bilbao's heavy industry of Guipuzcoa's quality metal manufacturing, and of the large new plants near Madrid — slowly became conscious of their power potential. Organization was facilitated when some of them, particularly the Communists — in contrast to the Socialists — decided to use the plant and local factory committee elections organized by the Sindicatos to gain respectability and co-opt the working class for the regime. This led slowly but inevitably to infiltration and, when challenged, parallel organizations.[95] The change in outlook of the church, with the emergence of a young clergy with little memory of the Civil War and more often of middle class rather than peasant origin, contributed to legitimating labor protests and opened the door to cooperation among a variety of groups in the working-class united front, for fairly specific goals but without explicit political issues, that crystal-

95. A 1958 resolution of the PCE Central Committee advocated the policy of using the channels created by the regime like the Sindicatos elections, a policy that had been initiated in October 1948 when the policy of subversion by guerrillas was given up. "There can be no doubt that our task is to develop and consolidate those legal and extralegal forms of unity of the workers, to work to raise their level, their revolutionary content. Certainly that task is not simple; on the contrary it is complicated and difficult. In those complications and difficulties lies all the difference between a policy of collaborating with the vertical Sindicatos — that is, capitulating and submitting to the dictatorship — and using for the revolutionary struggle the legal possibilities, which is the tactic advocated by our party." (See Santiago Carrillo, *Nuevos enfoques a problemas de hoy*, pp. 20–21.) In the absence of general political opposition articulated by parties, a sectoral opposition by organizations parallel to those of the regime and participation in them was advocated.

On the Spanish Communist party and Communist dissidents, the excellent monograph by Guy Hermet, *Les Communistes en Espagne: Etude d'un mouvement politique clandestin* (Paris: Armand Colin, 1971), is fundamental. Unfortunately I could not incorporate his data and analysis into this study. It also has an excellent bibliography. For a recent statement of party policy in English, see Santiago Carrillo (secretary-general of the PCE), *Problems of Socialism Today* (London: Lawrence A. Wishart, 1970).

lized in the Comisiones Obreras.[96] The Communists, after having supported the revolutionary attempts of the maquis, also turned to the Comisiones Obreas. It is hard to estimate to what extent they are composed of or controlled by party members, but the PCE makes no bones about its participation in them. Their formal apoliticism and effective pressure on employers and even the government on specific issues, particularly working conditions, allowed them to find support beyond people susceptible to political appeals. This policy, has incidentally already led to some tension between the party and some of the Comisiones Obreras leaders and might become in the future a source of conflict between a trade-union wing and the PCE leadership in exile in Prague or the party intellectuals.

The two great pre-Civil War trade union federations have tried to reorganize outside the law. In 1960 they joined with the Solidaridad de Obreros Vascos in the Alianza Sindical Obrera (ASO). Internationally, particularly the UGT, they were linked with the non-Communist labor movement, especially the German trade unions. However, some left Falangists had encouraged a base movement at the factory level, and ad hoc organizations of workers emerged — mainly in connection with the strikes of 1962 — which slowly gained permanence. Among the factors that have contributed to the emergence of the Comisiones Obreras as a new form of organization of labor, we might list the following: (1) the creation of a new working class due to industrialization and migration to the cities; (2) the emergence of Catholic lay apostolic movements like the Juventud Obrera Católica (JOC) and Hermandad Obrera de Acción Católica (HOAC); (3) the hesitation of the exiled leadership of the UGT (Union General de Trabajadores) and CNT (Confederacion Nacional del

96. There is no study of the Comisiones Obreras movement and its role in Spanish labor relations, its strength, or its leadership. Some of its leaders contributed to the issue of *Cuadernos para el Diálogo* on trade unions, but obviously this represents only a censored version of their thought. An article by Ramón Bulnes, "Del sindicalismo de represión al sindicalismo de integración," in the publication of Ruedo Ibérico, *Horizonte español, 1966*, gives some information on them and on different illegal labor organizations and also reproduces (pp. 285–325) a declaration of principles dated 31 January 1966, signed by many of the best-known leaders of the Comisiones Obreras, which emphasizes the ultimate goal of an independent, single, unified trade union organization, with closed shop, now opposed to the regime but anticapitalistic and based on acceptance of the concept of joint action by the popular masses with other social strata at certain times and for common goals. The declaration provides that the trade union "central" shall be independent of all political parties, but the signers "recognize, however, the possibility of political parties identified with the aspirations and interests of the working class."

The issue devoted by *Cuadernos para el Diálogo* (no. 11, extra issue) to *sindicalismo* — trade unionism but also corporativism, since proregime contributors understand the term in that sense — is particularly useful for an understanding of thinking on labor problems in Spain. Several leaders of the Comisiones Obreras like Marcelino Camacho and Julián Ariza contributed to the symposium around seven questions posed by the editors.

Trabajo, the anarchosyndicalist trade union federation) to use the legal opportunities offered by elections for shop stewards and grievance committees organized by the official Sindicatos. The Catholic lay movements were unable and probably unwilling to take the step to create a confessional, illegal trade union movement even though there is such a group, Unidad Sindical Obrera (US), affiliated with the ASO, but they provided the working class with new leaders. The Communists, who before the Civil War had been relatively weak among the organized workers, seized the opportunity to participate, maintaining the unitary character of the organization. Santiago Carrillo in *Nuevos enfoques a problemas de hoy*, emphasizes at great length that any worker, including a left Falangist, a traditionalist, especially the great majority without party affiliations, should participate if he has the trust of his fellow workers. However the Comisiones should not become responsible for the outside political activities of their members. They are not conceived as coordinating committees of organizations but as representatives of assemblies of workers. Carrillo warns against those who object to the emergence of a group of leaders — fearing a bureaucratization process — and argues the need for permanent leadership. The growth of the Comisiones might well have been a factor in the establishment of contacts between some members of the old CNT and the leaders of the official Sindicatos, in which the former were bargaining for some freedom as an ideological current within a Sindicatos reformed in the forthcoming new syndical law.[97]

The slow but inevitable toleration and later legalization of strikes for bargaining (economic) motives have facilitated the growth of an illegal labor movement but have also indirectly weakened the political impact of labor protest, since it is often perceived as just that and not as a threat to the regime. In fact orderly, disciplined, and justified labor unrest is increasingly acceptable to many who are not hostile to the regime. The moral legitimacy of labor's demands, even when led by Communists, will be one gain of this period if a democracy with strong non-Communist parties is born. The situation has been well described by a study commission of the International Labour Office in these words:

> The impulse for renewal in the Spanish syndical organization, however genuine and spontaneous it might have been, has been considerably stimulated by the pressure of labor movements in Spain that have to be considered separately from the official syndical organization. The core of the problem is the existence of three types of movements, which to

97. Emilio Romero, editor of the Sindicatos newspaper *Pueblo*, alludes to these contacts in his interview with Paniker. The chapter by Ramón Bulnes, "Del sindicalismo de represión al sindicalismo de integración," in *Horizonte español, 1966*, pp. 309–19, reproduces some interesting documents on these contacts. Bulnes is quite hostile to all labor organizations not identified with the movement of the Comisiones Obreras and should therefore be read with reservations.

a greater or lesser extent have a trade union character and which overlie and intertwine in an extremely complex way. Only one is not only legal but official, of national scope and influence; it plays a considerable role in labor relations and in the administration of important social services. Of the other two, one is in its origin mainly a spontaneous protest movement, and the other is the projection in Spain of the international trade union movement. These movements are not only extraofficial but illegal and have a precarious existence because of their illegal character; they have their greatest strength — there are no means to estimate it precisely — in the regions of greatest industrial importance, and they lack a comparable degree of influeuce in other parts of Spain, even when they enjoy the strong loyalty of their members.[98]

The report informs the government of a consensus on the shape the syndical law should take, including the official Organización Sindical: it should aim at "a trade union movement fully representative of its members, responsible to them, and independent of political leadership that would embrace all shades of trade union opinion within a unity freely maintained and that would cooperate in a responsible way in the direction of enterprises and play an important role in public affairs."

The willingness of the Communists to use the channels provided by the regime, in contrast to the Socialists, who for a long time refused any participation in the hated Sindicatos, combined with their organizational skills and the ambivalent admiration of the left Catholics for them, has opened the doors of labor to them. Rather than create party organizations, they have favored and placed trusted members in professional labor organizations that provide a much broader base and one more difficult to suppress, particularly in a stage of economic expansion and some scarcity

98. The report was published as International Labour Office, Report of the Study Group to Examine the Labour and Trade Union Situation in Spain, *Official Bulletin*, Second Special Supplement vol/LII, no. 4, 1969, 298 pp. The study commission visited Spain from 7 to 30 March 1969 and held conversations with over a hundred persons — government and Sindicatos officials, elected representatives of workers at the plant level, employers, labor lawyers, opposition politicians (even some of those affected by the state of emergency), and ten persons in jail for illegal labor activities. Government support for the visit reflects the desire to gain international recognition of its trade unions. The report stresses the desire for change, unity, and greater representativeness of the Sindicatos. It is an excellent review of the Spanish labor situation and of legislation as well as reality in social security, trade unions, collective labor relations, workers' participation both past and present, including movements outside the official trade union organization (pp. 179–83), criminal legislation in connection with trade union activities, and strikes. For the circulation of the first version of the report in Spain (around one million copies), see p. 21. The quotation is from the third report submitted on 3 April 1969, published in Spain in *Boletín HOAC* (Hermandad Obrera de Acción Católica), nos. 516–19 (March–April 1969), p. 14, and in ILO Conference, 53rd sess., Geneva, 1969, Provisional Record, no. 6, but, probably at the request of the Spanish Ministry of Labor, it was not included in the final published report referred to above.

of skilled labor. The unity of the working-class tradition being established through the Comisiones Obreras creates in Spain some of the conditions that in other European countries after World War II favored united labor unions, which in Italy and France were dominated by the Communists, forcing the Socialists and Catholics to abandon them years later.

The lack of open and institutionalized pluralism in the trade union field, even within the Sindicatos framework (as was vaguely advocated by one its secretaries general),[99] combined with the irreversible tolerance — despite jailings and reprisals — of the Comisiones Obreras in the large industrial centers, again may favor the less democratic sector of the opposition in the long run. On the other hand, it may well favor the less adventurist — and in that sense more moderate — sector. The process that led from the defeat of the socialist and anarchosyndicalist labor movements by brutal repression (1939–45), to sporadic guerrilla action uncoordinated with a mass base and factory organizations (1945–47), to the present factory-based semipolitical organization is an interesting chapter in the history of Spanish labor. Labor conflicts have recently become more violent wtih the deaths of several workers in Granada, the SEAT automobile plant in Barcelona, Getafe, and Ferrol. In the process, partly but not only as a result of industrialization, the focus has shifted from the countryside — where it was in the thirties — to the great new and some of the older industrial centers.[100] The large number of Spanish workers abroad becoming familiar with other societies, bosses, labor movements, political systems, and cultures is another agent of change, whose consequencees are difficult to assess.[101]

99. Giménez Torres advocated such an opening of Sindicatos at the time of the 1962 Sindicatos congress.

100. This is largely but not only the result of migration and industrialization; there remain large numbers of underprivileged farm laborers and farmers in spite of the improvements experienced by the former. The difficulty of organizing protests in a rural setting with an efficient state apparatus accounts for the few and generally unsuccessful protests and the slow penetration of the PCE in the countryside. For the mentality of farm laborers in latifundia areas see Juan Martínez Alier, *La estabilidad del latifundismo: Análisis de la interdependencia entre relaciones de producción y conciencia social en la agricultura latifundista de la Campiña de Córdoba* (Paris: Ruedo Ibérico, 1968).

101. Little is known about the activities of the opposition among Spanish workers abroad. It seems to encounter considerable difficulties among people whose main goal is to earn rapidly as much as possible, generally to return with some savings, and who want to avoid trouble in a foreign country where their legal status is insecure. They are not always impressed by the solidarity of their fellow workers in the host countries and often find support in Catholic organizations and missions. Guy Hermet, *Les Espagnols en France* (Paris: Les Editions Ouvrieres, 1967), pp. 91–92, reports a UGT (Spanish socialist trade unions) source giving the figure of 5000 members in France (400 in Paris), of which only 15% to 17% are recent immigrants; these figures can be compared to those for 18,400 immigrants in 1956, growing to 99,600 in 1960 and 170,000 in 1963. The anarchosyndicalist federation CNT is reported to have 600 members in Paris but has made few gains among new

The exiles   In 1939 the leaders of the opposition to Franco and even many of their followers were forced into exile. There many, with varying support from friendly parties and nations, kept the flame alive. The underground opposition and the "internal migration" looked to them for years for leadership. However, the failure to move the Allies to intervene to overthrow Franco, the defeat of guerrilla activities in the middle forties, the aging of the leadership, the integration of many exiles into other societies, and above all the changes in Spanish society and the turnover of generations in the course of thirty years have weakened the ties of the exiles with present opponents within Spain.

In the fifties the relationship between the exiles and the semiopposition and incipient alegal opposition emerging inside Spain posed difficult problems. There was hesitation on both sides. Those representing legitimate alternatives — within the range of the regime's own ideas about its potential evolution — like the various monarchists, obviously could not avoid contact with — their surviving leaders abroad. On the other hand, the latter started to lose contact with the realities of life in the country, while claiming to be leaders of old and sometimes new or emerging sympathizers having a similar ideology. The demands of contestation, both in terms of compromises with the existing system and/or of illegal activity, were often in conflict with the conceptions of their colleagues in Spain. Conflict between the desire for ideological or principled purity and the tendency toward broad coalitions, for example, was not infrequent, particularly in the collaboration between the democratic opposition and the Communists, but also between Republicans and monarchists. Divergent interpretations of the past contributed to the conflict that often divided the generations.

The regime itself tended to discriminate between internal opponents according to whether they did or did not have contact with leaders abroad. It generally used foreign contacts to question the legitimacy of its opponents, making them appear to be tools of exiles without contact with the reality of life in the country, embittered men of the past, perhaps even subject to foreign influences and therefore anational.

The growth of all kinds of internal opposition, the change of generations, the semifreedom within Spain, the altered international context, and the death or aging of exiled political figures in the late sixties have reduced the saliency of this problem. Except for the Spanish Communist party

arrivals. French trade unions probably do not have more than 25,000 Spanish members, and few of them are post-World War II immigrants, which Guy Hermet estimates to be 3% of the wage earners in this group. In 1966 the Spanish JOC (Catholic Workers Youth) had from 600 to 700 members in 95 groups. See also Hermet, p. 159, for data on a random sample of Spanish workers in the Paris region, which reports 18 of 82 with some trade union affiliation, but they constituted a self-selected group whose emigration was not based exclusively on economic motives.

leadership in Prague, perhaps that of the Partido Nacionalista Vasco (PNV), and a small fraction of the Socialists (the Toulouse Partido Socialista Obrero Español, PSOE), the bulk of the opposition finds its leadership and ideas today inside Spain. This is obviously more true of the alegal than the illegal opposition. Again, the Spanish situation differs a great deal from that in Italy and Germany in 1945 as a result of the authoritarian rather than totalitarian character of the regime. It also differs from the situation of authoritarian regimes that have not stayed in power for thirty years.

The Bases of Opposition

RELIGION   Through the identification of most of the church hierarchy with the Nationalist side in the Civil War in a collective letter terming it a crusade, and through its actions during and after the war, the Catholic church contributed toward legitimating the persecution and silencing the opposition. Intellectual dissent, however prudent and moderate, suffered particularly from the zeal for religious-political conformity. In its pronouncements and its legislation the regime often referred to its Catholic inspiration; Principle II of the National Movement, part of the Constitution, reads, "The nation regards as a badge of honour its respect for the Law of God according to the doctrine of the [Church] . . . which inspires the legislation of the country." [102] With winds of change blowing in the church this commitment to Catholic doctrine has inevitably legitimated much of the opposition. Since it is not in the power of the state to decide what Catholic doctrine is, since papal pronouncements are ambiguous and open to many interpretations, since most positions taken by Catholics on secular matters are not easily declared out of bounds and are legitimate until this happens, since even the power of the Spanish bishops appointed in agreement with the regime is limited in such matters and subject to reversal by Rome, a heteronomous source of ideology is introduced into the system.[103] The church that served so well to legitimate the regime has, with increased pluralism, turned into one of the bases of structural opposition. Its support is still one of the sources of the regime's strength, but the identification of the regime with Catholicism also provides one of the greatest opportunities for the opposition to challenge it "legally" or at least legitimately on the basis of its own assumptions. It is not surprising, therefore, that the opposition of priests has provoked

102. See Spanish Information Service, *Fundamental Laws of the State* (Madrid, 1967), p. 21. In his speech before the Cortes on 22 November 1966, introducing the new Organic Law of the State and modifications in other fundamental laws, Franco mentioned this principle as one of the reasons for changes in religious freedom and in the Labor Charter.
103. The notion of heteronomy is taken from Max Weber's *Economy and Society*, ed. Guenther Roth and Klaus Wittich (New York: Bedminster, 1968).

some bitter reactions at lower levels, in journalistic outbursts,[104] and even in the behavior of the police. Even further, a latent anticlericalism emerges in the face of clerical protest or in the absence of support by the church against Catholic laymen. To forestall the consequencs of that latent heteronomy, Franco himself felt obliged to say in 1968:

> We are a national and Catholic movement, and as Catholics subordinate and respectful to the principles of the church, but we do not confuse religious with political principles. In religious [matters] the hierarchy has all authority, in political, the people, which we channel and lead to greatness.[105]

Conflict between the liberal and reactionary pro regime wings of the church broke into the open in 1972 and led to direct intervention by Vatican factions and the Pope himself when a bishops' conference was confronted with the resolutions of a joint assembly of 233 of 285 invited bishops and priests. On the basis of the answers of 15,000 priests to 260 questions, and after the withdrawal of an ultraconservative minority, the assembly approved a number of resolutions questioning the identification of the church with the regime, policy toward the linguistic-national minorities, and the existence of special jurisdictions and demanding freedom of political and trade union association and assembly in a healthy and legitimate pluralism. Most significantly of all, it challenged the interpretation of the Civil War as a crusade in the 1937 collective letter of the bishops that had helped to legitimate the Franco regime. In a dramatic vote of 123 to 113, with 10 abstentions, the assembly adopted the resolution:

> We humbly recognize and ask pardon for having failed at the proper time to be ministers of reconciliation in the midst of our people, divided by a war between brothers.

The assembly also demanded the withdrawal of church representatives from bodies like the Cortes and the Council of the Realm, where they sat according to the Constitution.

The intrigues in Rome of the reactionaries provoked a sharp response on the part of the liberals, with the support of many moderates including Cardinal Tarancón, primate of Spain. The open split, however, has also strengthened the small, active ultrarightist minority of integralists who constitute today a tolerated and even supported semiopposition: *Fuerza Nueva* (under the leadership of Blas Piñar), the Guerrilleros de Cristo, and other splinter groups.

104. See the witty column of Emilio Romero in *Pueblo,* the official trade union newspaper, on the occasion of a confrontation between protesting priests and the police (reprinted in *Los "Gallos" de Emilio Romero,* Barcelona: Planeta, 1968, p. 96).
105. Statement by Franco reported in *Nuevo Diario,* 19 September 1968.

Table 6.2 Population of regions with distinctive languages and/or a historical or geographical distinctiveness and their attitudes toward nationalism or administrative autonomy (percentage of population in relation to the national total, 1970 census)

I   Regions with a tradition of local nationalism

     Catalonia   14.9, from which one should subtract the majority of the 4.1% born outside the province of residence

     Basque country (three provinces) 5.7, from which one should subtract the majority of the 1.2% born outside the province and the electorate not identified with the nationalists

II Region with a tradition of administrative and fiscal autonomy but not necessarily favorable to linguistic autonomy or local nationalism

     Navarre   1.3

III Regions susceptible to linguistic and administrative autonomy appeals but not actively committed to such demands

     Galicia   7.8
     Levante   8.6, more specifically Valencia and Castellon with 7.3%
     Balearic Islands 1.5

     (Levante and the Balearic Islands might respond to a greater Catalonia appeal)

IV Region with some tradition of local administrative autonomy but Castilian speaking and economically dependent on the central government

     Canary Islands 3.5

NOTE: These figures allow different combinations in favor of quite different political solutions to the problem of national diversity: The hard-core "non-Castilian nationalism" — Catalonia and the Basque country (ignoring for the moment the Castilian-oriented immigrants and sectors of the population) — would be 20.6%. With great effort they could rally the Galicians to their point of view. The three provinces of the Kingdom of Valencia are only partly Catalan speaking and some of these consider the local language distinct from Catalan. Despite a recently growing nationalist sentiment the region has no significant tradition of nationalism or autonomy. This is even more true of the Balearic Islands, though the use of variants of Catalan language is dominant there. If the population of these two regions, 17.9%, were added, it would raise the absolute maximum to 36.6%. The addition of regions with traditions of local administrative autonomy would bring the figure up to 43.3%, with the remainder of the country quite firmly committed to a centralistic-unitary state.

LINGUISTIC-ETHNIC SUBCULTURES: REGIONALISM, NATIONALISM, AND CULTURAL AUTONOMY   One of the most complex lines of cleavage in Spanish society lies between the dominant Castilian-speaking culture and power structure and those in the periphery who identify, in different degrees of intensity, with local languages and traditions.[106] (See table 6.2.)

106. On the conflict between center and periphery and on linguistic nationalisms, see Juan J. Linz, "Early State Building and Late Peripheral Nationalisms against the State: The Case of Spain," in S. N. Eisenstadt and Stein Rokkan, eds., *Building States and Nations: Models, Analyses, and Data across Three Worlds* (forthcoming,

On the basis of local identity, demands are formulated that go as far as secession. Opposition in these regions can range from apolitical, cultural self-affirmation to opposition to the unity of the Spanish state, whatever regime or form of government it may have. The last-mentioned sector will be a principled opposition as long as there is a Spanish state.[107] The complex relations between this kind of cultural opposition and other lines of cleavage, particularly class cleavages within each of the regions and the different ideologies from communism to bourgeois conservatism, make it almost impossible to describe the different organizations, groups, and positions. It would be even more futile to sketch the difficult relations of each of them, at different junctures, with the national-Spanish opposition, ranging from alliances to a complete break in relations. The almost inevitable opportunism of nationalist movements when it comes to relations with tactical allies, combined with the latent distrust and incomprehension of Spanish political forces toward regional politics, further complicates matters.

The Franco regime after its victory in 1939 not only reestablished the

---

1972). For data on language use and regional identification, see Fundación FOESSA (Fomento de Estudios Sociales y de Sociología Aplicada), *Informe sociológico sobre la situación social de España, 1970* (Madrid: Euramérica, 1970), based on a national survey. This basic source book on and study of Spanish society was directed by Amando de Miguel. See also the works cited in footnote 110 and see Stanley Payne, "Catalan and Basque Nationalism," *Journal of Contemporary History* 6 (November 1970): 15–51, an excellent review of the problem. There are no census data on language use.

The data from a 1967 national survey show the lack of interest in the problem among a large part of the population, as well as the great differences in response between regions, from those with strong opinions and in favor (Navarra, Catalonia, Basque country) to those uninterested but with strong minorities in favor (like Galicia), to those like Valencia where one would expect regionalist sentiments but they turn out to be weak (and not due to lack of opinion). One circumstance that might facilitate a solution of the problem is that the younger generations and the more educated seem to be more favorable to decentralization.

The answers to the question:

Do you believe that those who advocate administrative and cultural decentralization of the regions or, on the contrary, those who say that the country should be administered from Madrid are right?

show 52% of the population and 48% of the males without opinion (on the basis of a sample of 2544), with 22% and 29%, respectively (that is, 46% and 47% of those with an opinion), for decentralization. The "no opinion" was smallest (31%) in the Basque country and largest in Andalucia (70%), followed by Galicia with 65%. Among respondents with an opinion, 82% in Navarra, 75% in Catalonia, 58% in the three Basque provinces, 57% in Galicia, 50% in Baleares, 36% in Valencia, but only 33% in New Castile (including Madrid), 33% in Andalucia, and 46% in all Castile favored decentralization.

107. Few books are as revealing about the divisiveness of the regional issue, the ambivalences between autonomism and separatism, and the reaction they produce even in an opponent of the regime as Salvador de Madariaga, *Memorias de un federalista* (Buenos Aires: Editorial Sudamericana, 1967), which reproduces many documents, correspondence, and polemics with Basque and Catalan leaders in exile.

centralist state created by the Bourbons and the Liberals throughout many centuries (making some concessions to Navarra, the Carlist stronghold, and leaving to Alava some of the tax privileges it had always enjoyed[108]) but embarked on a deliberate policy of imposing the Castilian language everywhere and banning or ostracizing local languages — outlawing their use in administration, education, mass media, translations (totally until 1952 and partly until 1957), as well as making impossible almost any association that would indirectly foster nationalist sentiment. Local languages were restricted to the home. This policy has since been attenuated but not reversed.[109] Therefore in an initial stage, particularly in Catalonia, where Catalan is used by most of the nonimmigrant population and has behind it an important literature, the use of Catalan became a sign of defiance. Cultural activities, like writing novels and poetry, publishing translations, producing plays, and composing and singing popular music in Catalan, had and still have political intent. In the Catalan case, this allows many people to feel like oppositionists without having to engage in politics. It also allows politically conscious leaders to exploit innumerable events — now unexceptionable according to the laws or administrative practice — to create a climate of opinion, build organizational bases, bring together on apolitical grounds different ideological tendencies, and make a great issue of government interference with their activities.[110] This has

108. By a decree of 23 June 1937, Vizcaya and Guipúzcoa lost their special tax status and autonomous administration of many public services, which were retained by the province of Alava. Navarra also enjoys a special tax status that benefits firms domiciled there. See Juan Plaza Prieto, "Conciertos económicos," in *Notas sobre política económica española* (Madrid: Publicaciones de la Delegación Nacional de Provincias de FET y de las JONS, 1954), a collection of articles published in *Arriba*, the party newspaper, interesting for the range of opinion within the regime, pp. 395–98. A law of April 1938 abrogated the special legal status of Catalonia enacted by the Republic without restoring the status it had gained under the Restoration monarchy until 1923.

109. See for example the Orden cursada of 28 July 1940, quoted by Josep Melià, *Informe sobre la lengua catalana* (Madrid: Colección Novelas y Cuentos, Editorial Magisterio Español, 1970), threatening with dismissal municipal civil servants who used a language other than that of the state in municipal buildings and teachers who did so in their classes. Another example would be the order of 18 May, 1938, stating that family names of Spaniards could be registered only in Castilian and that the birth certificates of those with names in languages different from the official one should include the Castilian translation. See *Resumen legislativo del nuevo Estado* (Barcelona: Editora Nacional, 1939), p. 221.

110. On the growing strength of Catalan cultural nationalism, see Francesc Vallverdù, *L'escriptor català i el problema de la llengua* (Barcelona: Edicions 62, 1968), which analyzes the linguistic question and possible policies relating to bilingualism. A middle-level Catalan grammar sold 25,000 copies and one for children was printed in 40,000 copies between April 1966 and October 1967. The publishing of books has steadily increased from 183 titles in 1960 (10 of them translations) to 548 in 1966, 207 of them translations (Vallverdu, p. 103). The magazine *Tele-estel*, started in 1966, reached some 100,000 copies but then fell back to 50,000, while the monthly publication of the abbey of Montserrat, *Serra d'Or*, prints 17,000 copies and a children's magazine, *Cavall Fort*, 35,000.

There has been almost no research on cultural contact between the immigrants allowed the Catalan subcultural opposition to be widespread, basically moderate, unspecific in its demands, increasingly tolerated, and capable of building organizational elements for a future confrontation with the central power. It has, however, limited its capacity to think through the practical implications of vague nationalist demands, possible compromises with Madrid, and the need for government parties and policies in Barcelona.

Basque nationalism is in a very different position. The Basque language is a unique tongue (not related to the romance languages) without a great literary tradition, ill adapted to the modern world, difficult to learn by immigrants, and on the decline for centuries.[111] Basque nationalism has therefore inevitably been more on the defensive and therefore more aggressive and more in need of an organizational basis. In addition, in Catalonia, together with the Basque country the most industrial region of Spain, the business elite — largely composed of heads of large and medium family enterprises — has only limited personal and financial ties with business outside the region,[112] while the big investment banks and large managerial corporations particularly in Bilbao have created business and social ties outside the Basque country.[113] Whatever misgivings the Catalan

---

and the native populations in the multilinguistic areas. The thesis by Joaquín Maluquer Sostres, *L'assimilation des immigres en Catalogne* (Geneva: Droz, 1963), presents statistical data on immigration and linguistic assimilation.

The most important study of the use of the Catalan language is Antoni M. Badia i Margarit, *La llengua dels barcelonins: Resultats d'una enquesta sociològico-lingüística, volum 1, L'enquesta: La llengua i els seus condicionaments* (Barcelona: Edicions 62, 1969). A survey of the Secretariat d'Acció Católica de Promoció Social in Catalonia reported in *Serra d'Or* in May and June 1966 gives interesting information on attitudes toward language in schools.

For a more detailed analysis of linguistic diversity and its political implications, see Juan J. Linz, "A Multilingual Society with a Dominant World Language," paper presented at the Conference on Multilingual Political Systems: Problems and Solutions, Université Laval, Quebec, March 1972, to be published.

111. See the map on p. 265 in Julio Caro Baroja, *Los pueblos de España: Ensayo de etnología* (Barcelona: Barna, 1946). Alava and a large part of Navarra are Castilian speaking only.

112. The Catalan entrepreneur has been studied by E. Pinilla de las Heras, *L'empresari català* (Barcelona: Edicions 62, 1967) and within the framework of a national study by Juan J. Linz and Amando de Miguel in a large number of articles and monographic papers. For a listing of the papers see their book *Los empresarios ante el poder público* (Madrid: Instituto de Estudios Políticos, 1966), pp. 277–79.

113. On the Basque economy see José Félix de Lequerica, *La actividad económica de Vizcaya en la vida nacional* (Madrid: Real Academia de Ciencias Morales y Políticas, 1956), and Gonzalo Saenz de Buruaga, *Ordenación del territorio: El caso del País Vasco y su zona de influencia* (Madrid: Guadiana de Publicaciones, 1969), Part II. On Basque entrepreneurs, see the study by Juan J. Linz and Amando de Miguel referred to in footnote 112. An indicator of the greater integration of Basque business, particularly big business, into the national business community is the fact that in Vizcaya 54% of a sample of heads of enterprises with over 100 workers — with an oversampling of the larger ones — were born in the Basque region, compared to 71% in Catalonia among heads of enterprises in Barcelona. Among those born in Barcelona 90% direct enterprises in the region, while among the vizcainos

haute bourgeoisie may have about more radical Catalanist movements, it has a basic sympathy for cultural autonomy, if not self-government. In contrast, Basque big business is in a sense Spanish big business, and therefore the Basque nationalists appeal more exclusively to the middle and small bourgeoisie, as well as to the peasantry and the autocthonous skilled working class, particularly of recent rural background or part-time farmers.[114] In the past too, the immigrant Castilian-speaking working class in Catalonia, while not supporting local nationalism, had established uneasy ties with its left wing, the Esquerra; while the chauvinism of the Basque movement toward immigrant laborers and their identification with the centralist-socialist trade union federation, the Unión General de Trabajadores (UGT), isolated Basque nationalism. This relative isolation even within its own region has made the Basque opposition much more explicit and radical in its positions, which may account for the turn of some of its groups toward violent actions still absent in Catalonia.

In December 1970, the militant tactics of the ETA (Euzkadi Ta Azkatasuna), which included armed action against the police to obtain

the figure is 66%. See Amando de Miguel and Juan J. Linz, "Movilidad geográfica de los empresarios españoles," *Revista de Estudios Geográficos* 25, no. 94 (February 1964): 2–29. The managerial character of much of Bilbao's industry contributes to this pattern. The different responses of Barcelona and Bilboa businessmen to the crown policy of granting titles of nobility to financiers and industrialists undoubtedly contributed to the different political outlooks of the haute bourgeoisie. The links between the Basque business class and the political class under Franco are even greater.

114. The Basque opposition is analyzed from a Marxist perspective by Martín Zugasti, "El problema nacional vasco," in *Horizonte español, 1966*, 2:101–09. The author attempts to discover the social bases of different types of political mentality, distinguishing between the old working class of the industrial cities, many of whose members have liberal-democratic Spanish traditions, and the workers who have moved from the Basque countryside to the industrial cities and, feeling culturally closer to the national heritage, are therefore susceptible to the nationalist appeal. However, in both groups the higher standard of living also facilitates adaptation in the framework of a consumption society. Thirdly, there is the immigrant Castilian-speaking working class, which often encounters hostility from the native workers. While the upper bourgeoisie identifies with the central power structure and shares in it, the middle and lower bourgeoisie — the strata that in other countries turned fascist in the thirties — turned instead toward Basque nationalism. Zugasti sees today in the white-collar employees the main basis for Basque nationalism, to which he adds the more extreme chauvinist sentiment among the remaining independent farmers. However, some farmers by their dual role as farmers and as skilled industrial workers in small plants are more susceptible to leftist positions. The close contact of the clergy with this group, with the native working class, and with the local petit bourgeoisie accounts for their mixture of nationalism with anticapitalism aimed mainly at the large corporations. Other observers have called to our attention the fact that some sectors closer to the upper bourgeoisie might be shifting — in small numbers but actively — toward nationalist extremism in response to the fact that Basque big business is filling more and more managerial positions with non-Basques, who — because of the absence of universities and good technical schools in the region — may be better prepared. To this one has to add the generational conflict within the bourgeois sector of Basque nationalism.

funds and the assassination of a hated police official, provoked reprisals and led to an indictment and military court martial in Burgos, publicized by the kidnapping of a German honorary consul (who was released unharmed).[115] The court pronounced four death sentences, but after a few tense days during which enormous international and internal pressures confronted each other, Franco commuted the sentences. The trial, the difficult position in which the military judges and the army found themselves, the public protests — strikes and demonstrations — and the international outcry had a tremendous impact on Spanish political life. The giant mass demonstration initiated extraofficially by rightists groups became — after Franco agreed to appear — a symbol of support for the regime (but not necessarily the government), and since then one hears the expression, "the spirit of the seventeenth of December." The activities of the Basque separatists, the specter of violence, the way in which the court and defense conducted the trial, and the mass demonstrations and expressions of support polarized Spaniards to an unexpected degree and had a lasting effect. It was a demonstration of the way in which certain forms of opposition can contribute toward revitalizing commitments to the regime and even reversing the process of liberalization.

In both Catalonia and the Basque country, a number of problems fractionalize the opposition in a way that is not true for many other subcultural oppositions in the world, a fact that complicates any attempt to coordinate its efforts with the nonregional alegal or illegal oppositions. In contrast to many discontented subcultures the world over, Catalonia and the Basque country are highly industrial regions, with a high standard of living, rather than rural or semideveloped.[116] This means that whatever regime may be in power the central government inevitably will exact more

---

115. On the trial, the indictment, the defense, the day-by-day proceedings, the international reaction, and the political response in Spain, see Kepa Salaberri, *El proceso de Euskadi en Burgos: El sumarísimo 31/69* (Paris: Ruedo Ibérico, 1971). Somewhat less informative is Gisèle Halimi, *Le procès de Burgos* (Paris: Gallimard, 1971), with a foreword by Jean-Paul Sartre. Both works are favorable to the accused.

116. On the Catalan economy in relation to the Spanish, see J. Ros Hombravella and A. Montserrat, *L'aptitud financera de Catalunya: Balança catalana de pagaments* (Barcelona: Edicions 62, 1966), which refers to other studies of the interregional balance of payments, particularly those of Carles Pi i Sunyer, Ramón Trias Fargas, and Jordi Petit. The economically advanced regions draw income from other parts of the country in the form of profits, rents, etc. due their residents. These transfers have a positive balance and are over 1%; in the case of Madrid 13.3% in 1960, 7.5% in 1964, in Vizcaya 6.3% and 6.5%, respectively, in Barcelona 1.1% and 1.2%, and in Zaragoza 0.2% and 1.1%. These data show the dominance of Madrid over the national economy and its role as the place of residence of many landlords, but it also reveals the much greater linkage with the rest of the country of Vizcaya compared to Barcelona. It also exemplifies clearly the economically privileged position of the autonomist-secessionist regions compared to the much more frequent pattern of economic exploitation of culturally marginal regions. Data from Ramón Tamames, *Los centros de gravedad de la economía española* (Madrid: Guadiana de Publicaciones, 1968), p. 98.

taxes than it will spend there,[117] an inevitable source of conflict, while it will not have the leverage that government subsidies, investments, and patronage give central authorities elsewhere. Neglect may lead to discontent and thereby to a change in policy to head it off, but such a policy has limits when the government is dealing with a rich region. (Obviously many people in the developed area forget that without a government-protected market their industry would not have grown to its present importance and might find it difficult to sell its products, particularly since the protectionism that Catalan and Basque pressure groups imposed has slowed down the renewal of their industries and thereby limited their international competitiveness.) Inevitably the industrial character of the regions, particularly Catalonia with low birth rates, has led to a large immigration[118] of Castilian-speaking workers, who have little interest in supporting autonomy demands that might reduce them from full to second-class citizens, which they surely would become if the regional language became the official language in the administration. Some-

117. The following data from Ros Hombravella and Montserrat, *L'aptitud financera de Catalunya*, pp. 12–13, and the *Información estadística del Ministerio de Hacienda* illustrate very well the complexity of the problem of linguistic-historical nationalism in an economically developed rather than underdeveloped region: paying taxes and receiving less leads to weak feelings of identity with the state.

Government expenditures in different regions as a percentage of direct taxes collected in those regions (ignoring taxes collected in Madrid and payments made directly by the central treasury) were: Catalonia 41%, the Basque country 42%, Navarra 101%, Galicia 172%, region of Valencia 91%, and Balearic Islands 95%. For the calculations, see Linz, "Early State-Building."

For a nationalist's calculations of the economic relations between the Basque country and the Spanish government, see Fernando Sarrailh de Ihartza, *Vasconia* (Buenos Aires: Norbait [1962]), pp. 181–84. For the ideological consequences see for example on p. 204.

118. Ernest Lluch, "La minva relativa de la immigració," *Serra d'Or*, 8th year, no. 3 (March 1966), pp. (181) 21, presents the data in the accompanying table.

Population changes in Barcelona province, 1900 to 1964

	Natural increase	Growth through immigration	Immigration as percentage of total population increase
1901–10	2.74	57,111	65.5
1911–20	0.19	205,234	98.9
1921–30	4.78	376,076	83.8
1931–40 (Civil War)	0.07	129,877	99.0
1941–50	3.29	231,900	77.2
1951–60	7.68	447,513	69.4
1961–64	10.91	314,058	70.0

In the period 1962–65 alone there were 341,720 immigrants from outside Catalonia to Barcelona and 43,397 to the other three Catalan provinces, a total for all of Catalonia of 385,117 (Banco Urquijo, Servicio de Estudios en Barcelona, *Desarrollo económico de Cataluña, 1967–1970* (Barcelona: Sociedad de Ediciones y Publicaciones, 1967), 1:135.

times the idea of limiting immigration is advanced by nationalist groups,[119] but business naturally has no interest in such a policy and the Left, which wants a socioeconomic revolution in addition to a regional one, cannot easily renounce its appeal to a large part of the working class. The non-ethnic working-class parties obviously do not feel they can neglect that segment of their potential constituency, and so we find the Moviment Socialista Català (MSC) wrangling with the PSOE, in the case of recognition of the MSC as a federated party, over whether the Castilian-speaking workers should be affiliated with one or the other party. The more petit bourgeois and rural-based regional parties in turn can attack a capitalist big business class on two grounds — class and status — as well as for its limited or halfhearted identification with nationalism when it conflicts with their interests.

Opposition politics within Catalonia inevitably splits along class lines, with the haute bourgeoisie, which suffered seriously under the rule of left Catalanists and anarchosyndicalist workers (CNT) during the Civil War, hesitating about how far to oppose Franco, who saved their class interests. This split along class lines within Catalan politics had already emerged in the twenties, when the youth and intellectuals split from the Lliga, the party of the manufacturers, to form Acció Catalana, and the white collar and petit bourgeois strata plus a large part of the farmers formed the Esquerra, while others turned to Marxist parties outside the PSOE or even to a small Catalan fascist group.[120] It is not surprising that Catholicism should have appeared as a bridge between different Catalan opposition tendencies, from the Lliga elements that did not accept the regime to the new middle class.[121] The weakening of anticlericalism in

119. This is an issue on which Catalanist groups divide, with those searching for a working-class base less willing to consider restrictions on immigration of non-Catalans while others like the Unió Democrática de Catalunya speak of an "accommodation of the immigration movement to our possibilities of absorption and to incorporation into the Catalan style of life that offer immigrants the possibility of greater well-being and to our people the benefits of perfect unity."
120. On regional parties, see Linz, "The Party System of Spain: Past and Future," pp. 219–22, 257–59; for the future of such parties, see pp. 271–74. On Catalan nationalism today, see the chapter by Joan Roig in *Horizonte español, 1966,* 2:117–30 and see Oriol Pi-Sunyer, "The Maintenance of Ethnic Identity in Catalonia," in Pi-Sunyer, ed., *The Limits of Integration: Ethnicity and Nationalism in Modern Europe,* Research Reports 9 (Amherst, Mass.: Department of Anthropology, University of Massachusetts, 1971), pp. 111–13, and William A. Douglass and Milton da Silva, "Basque Nationalism," in ibid., pp. 147–86. On the case of Valencia, see Alfons Cucó, *El valencianisme polític, 1874–1936* (Valencia: Garbí 2, 1971). And on the Basque country, see Pedro González Blasco, "Modern Nationalism in Old Nations as a Consequence of Earlier State-Building: The Case of Basque-Spain," in Wendell Bell and Walter E. Freeman, eds., *Ethnicity and Nation-Building: Local and International Perspectives* (Cambridge: Schenkman, forthcoming). See also Linz, "A Multilingual Society with a Dominant World Language."
121. An important source for understanding Catalan national sentiment and its multiple manifestations is the magazine *Serra d'Or,* published monthly since 1959 in Catalan by the Benedictine monastery of Montserrat.

contemporary Europe and the actions of the Catalanist clergy,[122] particularly after the Vatican Council decrees on the use of vernacular, contributed to the emergence of a Christian democratic party in Catalonia, a force that had not emerged in the Restoration period where a compromise between Liberals and Conservatives had reduced the saliency of that issue, allowing the Lliga to show little concern with it and initially representing a wide range of Catalan sentiments. The existence of a lively Catalan-Catholic cultural tradition,[123] plus the protection the church can afford to opposition activities and the need to overcome the old Lliga's image as a "business party," have favored Christian democracy in Catalonia. It seems obvious that it might well cut into both a more conservative Catalan party and the old bases of the Esquerra.

While in Catalonia we find the emergence of a Christian opposition, in the Basque country — the most religious region of Spain — the old interclass nationalism of the Partido Nacionalista Vasco (PNV),[124] based on a mixture of religion and subcultural nationalism (not without shades of racism) and affiliated with the international of Christian Democratic parties, encounters the competition of new forces. The organizational strength of the PNV — with its rich sources of funds among successful Basque emigrants (not exiles) in Latin America, the international sympathy for a moderate non-Communist party, and its close ties with the politicians of the different Republican parties for whom the PNV's support was

122. The complex relations between regionalist-nationalist-linguistic opposition and Catholicism are reflected in the issue of the appointment of a non-Catalan bishop by the church in agreement with the Spanish government. See the collection of documents and history of the affair published by the Editions de Documentation Catalane, *Le Vatican et la Catalogne: La nomination de Mgr. González Martín à l'Archeveche de Barcelona* (Geneva, 1967) in Catalan and French. It provoked protest letters and manifestos, demonstrations, demands to resign, as well as counterdemonstrations of support from proregime and pro-Castilian opinion.

123. While Basque nationalism has been clerical, and priests have been among its most enthusiastic supporters, Catalan nationalism has many ideological sources and had its anticlerical Left. However, regionalist sentiment was fostered by outstanding bishops like Torras y Bages. One of the few who refused to sign the collective letter supporting Franco in the Civil War was the Catalan Cardinal Vidal y Barraquer, and in recent years the monastery of Montserrat and its abbot, Aureli M. Escarre, have been centers of Catalan sentiment and opposition. Escarre once said, "When the language is lost, there is also a tendency to lose religion," expressing one of the themes linking the clergy with linguistic nationalisms all over Europe. On the Basque clergy, see the semiliterary essay in *España hoy*, pp. 197–205.

124. On the PNV, see Linz, "The Party System of Spain: Past and Future," pp. 220, 279, footnote 279, for bibliographic references. See also Madariaga, *Memorias de un federalista*, for quotations and polemics with the present leaders of the PNV. *Vasconia*, by a separatist Basque nationalist, Fernando Sarrailh de Ihartza, contains a wealth of information on the history, economy, politics, constitutional proposals, and texts of the thirties, though obviously distorted by his extremist perspective. It is a source, however, for the manifestos, programmatic statements, etc. of all Basque parties and groups: the PNV since its founding days, Acción Nacionalista Vasca, GERO, and the organizations emerging in recent years.

internationally helpful — made the contrast between its strength and its inability to act visibly against Franco glaring. Even when it could maintain its ties with the Solidaridad de Trabajadores Vascos — its trade union wing — it seems to have lost its appeal to the younger generation, some of the nonreligious working class, and some white collar strata, who have turned to other organizations. The activist ETA is impressed by the militant nationalist struggles of the Irish and the Algerians and believes such tactics could be applied in Basconia.[125] The increasing turn to the left, as well as anticapitalism and socialism in the church and consequently the openness to collaboration with the Marxists, particularly the Communists, by working-class Catholic action organizations (JOC and HOAC), obviously involves strains in a highly industrial region for an interclass demochristian party that has had considerable sympathy if not support among medium and small entrepreneurs. Their sons, faced with the ineffectiveness of their parents' PVN, may be tempted to carry out their ideals in a more active way when faced with the persistence of the Franco regime. Apparently some of the ETA's supporters have been recruited from this sector.

The regional nationalist groups, particularly those of a demochristian orientation, have seen in the ideal of European unification or federalism an opportunity to modernize their appeal, to escape some of the implications of a provincial nationalism, and to search for international support.

125. The ETA defines itself as "a revolutionary Basque national liberation movement, creating patriotic resistance, independent of any other party, organization, or body." It advocates the socialization of basic sectors and planning. Internationally it speaks of European federalism, but not based on the present states and oligarchic interests, and opposes communism as antinational and dictatorial. It has turned to urban guerrillas. The praxis of the revolution already seems to have provoked a split between ETA-ZARRA — the larger and more active group — and ETA-BERRI — apparently a more intellectual group. The former accuses the latter of placing national liberation second to social liberation, while ETA-BERRI seems to attack ETA-ZARRA for its commitment to the irrationalism of Basque nationalism and its hatred of everything Spanish without consideration of the Spanish people and Spanish reaction. Another schism was apparently caused in 1967 by those who felt that the ETA, rather than a movement of different tendencies, had become Marxist-Leninist, while recently another group left to join the Communist party.

The numerical importance and the appeal of the ETA should not be overestimated, but its impact through terrorist actions and the not always discriminating response by the authorities serve, as so often with such movements, to polarize the community. The ETA's capacity to involve some clergymen in its activities, and the regime's response to them — justified or unjustified — has led to a confrontation between the church and the authorities on the issue of the rights of a clergyman in the performance of his duties, which is a legitimate issue for many who are far from feeling any sympathy with the ETA or even with Basque nationalism. For the 1962 program of the ETA see Sarrailh de Ihartza, *Vasconia*, pp. 607–08. He also reproduces a lecture by one of the ETA leaders, and in addition to the ETA program he reprints the programs of other new Basque nationalist movements — GERO, Euskal Langile-Nekazarien Alderdi Sozialista (ELNAS), and the Basque Socialist Workers and Farmers party — as well as those of French Basque nationalist groups.

They have been able to speak of a Catalonia or Basque country in a Europe reorganized by nationalities rather than along present state lines; in fact this has allowed some Basque groups (not the PNV) to speak of a new state to include two French departments. Socialist-oriented groups, ambivalent about "little" Western and neocapitalist Europe, obviously have been more hesitant. Only the Communists and the Communist-controlled PSUC (Partido Socialista Unificado de Cataluña) could not follow this line.

In the case of the Catalan nationalists, aiming at various degrees of autonomy or independence, another dividing issue has been whether to limit their aspirations to the four traditional Catalan provinces — the Principado for the maximalists, Catalonia for the moderates — or to extend them to "greater Catalonia," including other areas of Catalan language: the Balearic Islands and parts of the three provinces of the Levante (mainly Valencia), either as part of the same future political unit or with some form of association. The pre–Civil War Equerra and Lliga parties had not favored greater Catalonia, which was advocated by the Estat Català party. Among the new Catalanist political groups, the Unió Democrática de Catalunya (founded in November 1931, it seems to have displaced the Esquerra and parts of the Lliga among their middle-class clienteles, particularly the new middle classes) seems to favor greater Catalonia, while the Moviment Socialista de Catalunya, perhaps to avoid conflict and competition with the PSOE, has not advocated Gran Catalunya. Before the Civil War there was little linguistic nationalism in Valencia; even when the local organizations of both the CEDA and Radical parties were autonomous they were Castilian speaking. Recently, among students, a local nationalism seems to have gained some appeal, though there is disagreement between those who consider the local language to be Catalan and those who consider it to have a distinct identity. The former are obviously open to the appeal of a greater Catalonia. Slow economic growth and difficulties in traditional agricultural production for export are creating discontent in the area that might be channeled into regionalism or nationalism. There is no evidence of Catalanist or autonomist success in the Balearics, despite the fact that Catalan languages are spoken there more than in Valencia.

Galician autonomy and linguistic aspirations were not powerful during the Republic, and the Organización Republicana Gallega Autonomista (ORGA) was more a wing of Azaña's party than a party like the Esquerra. There are, however, indications of the growth of particularistic sentiment, mainly among the local elite, reflected in an increased use of the language. One manifestation has been the request, with 2500 signatures, for the use of Galician in the liturgy of the church and in the curriculum of teachers colleges. Economic underdevelopment, the social crisis created by the heavy emigration of the young men, and the difficulties of a mini-fundia agriculture have led to a feeling of neglect by the central author-ities. One expression of this sentiment was a petition by 120 intellectuals to the minister of agriculture. A leftist movement — Union do Povo Galego — links linguistic nationalism and the right to self-determination with anticapitalism, attacking the bourgeoisie and the middle classes not only for their exploitation but for their denationalization.[126] It is too early to tell what force such appeals may have, but certainly the stirrings in the Celtic world — Brittany, Wales, and Scotland — with which Galicians romantically identify will reinforce them.

The nationalities question is further complicated by its relationship to working-class protest movements. Catalanism was born as a bourgeois movement, supported actively by the big textile manufacturers and other businessmen who resisted trade unionism by all means, often more rigidly than the Madrid government. This attitude no doubt contributed to its turn toward anarchosyndicalism. Later Luis Companys, who defended anarchist leaders, became one of the two heads of the Esquerra and head of the regional Catalan government and tried to work with the CNT, but relations were not always easy, even when the party sometimes benefited from support given to it by CNT members in spite of their ideological apoliticism. The Socialist party and the UGT were always weak in Catalonia and therefore did not face the problem of conflict between the centralist orientation of the party and local autonomy demands. This allowed the emergence of left-Marxist Catalan parties, particularly the Communist-controlled PSUC. Recently the non-Communist Left has also formed its separate wing: the Moviment Socialista de Catalunya. In the case of Catalonia, quite in contrast with Belgium and Canada, where the parties to a large extent bridge over the national cleavages, neither the parties of the Republic nor the present opposition groups perform this role. In the Basque country they did so under the Republic,[127] but there

126. On Galician politics and national sentiment see Santiago Fernández and Maxi-mino Brocos, eds., *Galicia hoy* (Buenos Aires: Ruedo Ibérico, 1966). This book has the same ideological orientation but is much less informative than other publications of Ruedo Ibérico.

127. In the 1933 elections the PNV obtained 46% of the vote in the three Basque provinces, 58% in Vizcaya province, 45% in its industrial capital Bilbao, 46% in Guipuzcoa, and 29% in Alava. In 1936 the figures were, respectively, 51%, 30%, 37%, and 21%, with the remainder going to national parties of the Left and the Right. In 1936 the rightist national parties, which at that point were clearly anti-PNV, ob-tained in those same districts 35%, 21%, 33%, and 57% of the vote, with the re-mainder going to the Popular Front parties. In the region as a whole the national Right obtained 25% of the votes in 1933 and 32% in 1936, while the Left obtained, respectively, 29% and 33%. These figures should be kept in mind when one dis-cusses the Basque nationalist opposition, particularly since immigration has increased the non-Basque working class. On the other hand, immigration and greater economic integration into Spain might well have aroused additional support for regional nationalism.

are signs that the emergence of an ideologically and class divided opposition within Basque nationalism might allow the nationalists to gain the support of larger segments of the indigenous population.

The Communist party occupies a unique position with respect to the national question. In Catalonia it has a federated party capable of appearing to be a "Catalan" party but linked to the nationwide party and not competing wtih it locally. Using the appeals of the "nationalities policy" of the Soviet Union as ideology, it attempts to legitimate itself in the regions of subculture at the same time that it develops secret ties with the Basque Left. Obviously the ultimate and long-run success of this policy is not assured, but today it represents an advantage over the democratic opposition groups — like the Socialists and even more the demochristians — which have not found adequate organizational forms for the creation of even such federated parties as the Christian Democratic Union and Christian Social Union in Germany. This is one of the most difficult tasks for a democratic opposition and requires tact and patience as well as clear thinking in the many difficult compromises that must be made. Success or failure will be decisive not only for its activities now, but for the future of democracy in Spain. Without coordination and joint action the potential for serious opposition in the Basque country and Catalonia can easily be isolated, wasted, and even used to rally to the regime many Spaniards who feel basically hostile or indifferent to demands for linguistic equality and autonomy that might turn two of the most developed regions into politically and economically privileged regions, if not separate states.

THE JUDICIARY   Normally one would not consider the judiciary in a study of the opposition in a country, but in an authoritarian regime that to a greater or lesser extent respects the separation of powers and the autonomy of the courts and that would like to be considered a *Rechtsstaat* the courts, sheltered by a positivist interpretation of the law, can often question the decisions of the government, protect the rights of individuals, and provide opportunities to the opposition to make itself heard. In Spain the assigning of almost all political crimes to the military authorities until the recent past, and still of many of them, and now to a special tribunal of public order has limited the possibility of independent action on the part of the judiciary. However, even in these courts, known for their summary and harsh justice, trials were not used "politically" because of their positivist approach to the law, the lack of political talent of the prosecutors, and the lack of publicity surrounding most trials. The courtrooms until recently were not a political arena, even when ideologically committed and courageous opponents — particularly the Communists — could use their defense as a vehicle. The transfer from military jurisdiction has given lawyers of the opposition specializing in political and labor cases an interesting platform. In the context of some liberalization, with a tradition of judicial independence, a positivist interpretation of the law that does not consider the intent as much as the nature of the act, and competent lawyers on the side of the defendants, the government or its supporters have lost a number of cases. In matters involving freedom of the press or publishing, examples are authorization of the book by Gil Robles, *Cartas del pueblo español;* acquittal of the writer of an article in *Signo* who referred to the tragic events of Badajoz and Guernica in the Civil War, never recognized by the Franco authorities; award of damages to Gil Robles against the fascist journalist Rodrigo Royo for libel. Similarly the courts have protected against their employers the rights of workers fired for protest activities or for being absent from work because of political arrest.

The Future: Change Within the System or of the System?

Things are certainly different: the definitions of what opposition is have radically changed, but Franco is still heading the government. Many of the people who won power in 1939 — if still alive — are still there. It could lead to an inconclusive debate to argue: is the political system the same or different? Our conclusion would be: it is the same system, but things have changed within the system. The essential institutional boundaries of the political system have changed only slightly, even when many of its policies have changed decisively, the economic structure radically,[128] and the social structure considerably.[129] Power still comes from above

128. Economic change is reflected in the facts that per capita income in the period 1955–66 changed 6.2% per year, that change in the second decade of the century had been 1.3% (1% between 1920 and 1930, years of prosperity), and that the decade after the Civil War saw a drop of 0.02%. These changes are reflected in the responses of a national population sample to questions about how changes in their lives had turned out compared to their expectations when they were young, the change in the last five years, and expectations for the coming five years. See Fundación FOESSA, *Informe sociológico sobre la situación social de España* (1966).

129. A basic source for information about changes in the social and economic structure of Spain is Fundación FOESSA, *Informe sociológico sobre la situación social de España* (1966), based both on statistics and on a national sample survey taken by an independent public opinion institute, DATA S.A. The data from that survey are available for secondary analysis from the Roper Center at Williamstown, Massachusetts. See also the same institution's *Tres estudios para un sistema de indicadores sociales* (Madrid: Euramérica, 1967). Fundación FOESSA, *Informe sociológico sobre la situación social de España, 1970,* directed by Amando de Miguel, is the most important source for statistical data and research on Spanish society. In English, Stanley G. Payne, *Franco's Spain,* is an informative review with an annotated bibliography.

See Guy Hermet, "La sociologie empirique en Espagne," *Recherche méditerranéene* (Paris, Centre de Documentation Méditerranéene, 1967), 4:1–45, for an excellent annotated bibliography of Spanish sociology. See Confederación Española de Cajas de Ahorro, *Sociología española de los años setenta* (Madrid: Confederación

rather than below, ministers and most of the legislature[130] owe their position to appointment by Franco, in a crisis he or those able to gain his ear still have the final say. On the other hand, there has been a considerable renewal of the political elite. A number of cabinet members have entered the top elite relatively rapidly. The age composition of the Cortes does not differ much from the Italian lower chamber in 1967 despite the different procedure of recruitment. However, the different sectors of the Cortes are not of the same age; among the most powerful, few are not old enough to have participated in the Civil War, and only among the family representatives were the majority less than sixteen years old in 1936.[131]

If we turn to the age composition of another sector of the elite — the directors general in the ministries, a mixture between politicians and civil servants — we find the Spanish much younger than the Italian and not too different from the French. In France 55% of the directors general are under 44 years of age; in Spain 41%, thus indicating that renewal also takes place at this level. The data on 8376 mayors of almost all municipalities of Spain for 1967 show that their average age was 49 (slightly older in the largest cities), with an average age at appointment of 43. The

---

Española de Cajas de Ahorro, 1971), for a biobibliography of Spanish sociologists and selected papers.

A few figures can give the reader a sense of changes in social structure from the thirties to the present: In 1930 there were 4,627,980 persons active in agriculture (equivalent to 52% of the total active), while in 1966 the figure was 4,024,100 (equivalent to 33%) after an all-time high of 5,271,000 (equal to 49%) in 1950. The present proportion is similar to that of Italy in 1960 and the United States around 1900. In 1950 25.5% of the active males were still farm laborers, but by 1966 this had been reduced to 9.7% of the total active population, including the relatively small number (24%) of active females whose exclusion would probably raise the figure somewhat.

Another important change is the growing urbanization; while in 1930 31% of the population was living in population centers over 20,000, in 1965 the proportion had reached 50%. The proportion in centers of over 100,000 rose from 19% in 1940 to over 32% in 1965.

130. See for example the data on the Cortes in "Informe sobre las nuevas Cortes," *Cuadernos para el Diálogo* 50 (November 1967): 27, which classifies the procuradores into: appointed 155 (27%), elected within the Movimiento 55 (10%), elected indirectly through Sindicatos and local governments 246 (44%), elected directly by heads of household and married women 108 (19%).

131. In the ninth legislature (1967), 36% were freshmen — even more (74%) among the family representatives — another 35% had been members of one or two previous legislatures, while veterans of three to five legislatures numbered 19%, and above that only 11%. Of the original 419 procuradores of the first legislature of 1943, only 7% were still holding seats in the ninth legislature. The renewal rate therefore is not very different from that of other European legislatures; it is similar to the Italian and higher than the 1965 Bundestag. For detailed data on elites in the Cortes (and continuities between the present regime and previous ones), see Juan J. Linz, "Continuidad y discontinuidad en la elite política española de la Restauración al régimen actual," to be published in *Homenaje a Carlos Ollero*, Madrid, forthcoming.

average time in office is 5.9 years, somewhat longer in smaller communities, indicating again considerable renewal. There can be no doubt that there has been a substantial circulation of political personnel, even though perhaps not as much in the type of man. Certainly there has been more than we might have expected given the continuity of the regime, the absence of purges, and the absence of electoral competition. Some key groups, perhaps not at the top but very close to it, have shown considerable continuity but have allowed others to enter or have co-opted them into the elite. Not everyone in Spain might want to enter the elite of the regime, but one cannot say that it is a permanent, traditional, or closed elite at least for those sectors of society from which more than two-thirds of the elite of Western European countries is recruited. The mixture of capacity to absorb and to impose conformity with many established patterns might be one explanation of the staying power of the regime and of the difficulties of the opposition.

Basic institutional changes like the new constitutional laws of 1966–67 are enacted without any discussion or modification by the legislature after Franco proposes them, and a referendum approves them without an opportunity for opponents to present their points of view in the press, in rallies, or even less on reserved time as on French television. A free and legal choice by the defeated social strata between the official interest representation created by the regime — the Sindicatos — and any other is out of the question. Political parties are still banned (even though the founding nuclei of future parties may meet over coffee at the homes of their leaders), and any public advocacy of regional autonomy or secession is illegal whatever freedom the local cultural movement may have gained.

If we consider those basic boundaries, "the system" has not changed. However, any objective observer has to admit giant changes *within* the system. The elite has been able to renew itself more than most opponents would be willing to admit. The ideas and style of the present leadership are basically different: smooth politicians without strong ideological commitments like Solís have taken the place of men with fascist airs shouting and demanding absolute obedience to the Secretaría General of the party. Even external behavior at the Sindicatos headquarters — with discussions and bargaining going on and men in civilian garb chatting and arguing animatedly — has little to do with those entering among honor guards, making the fascist salute, and taking leave saying firmly "at thy orders" in the forties. In the ministries, modern technocrats and self-styled apolitical bureaucrats acting as politicians have replaced the self-confident autocratic victors of 1939. Visiting a cabinet member one can admit a lack of identification with the regime that in 1939 would have been dangerous even among acquaintances.

In spite of this, and perhaps in part because of it, the transformation of the regime into a true polyarchy — with free competition among groups enjoying full political freedom of association, assembly, expression, and so forth — is as far away as ever. In this, the regime has not changed. To a naïve observer it would seem that the present combination of semi-freedom and basic institutional rigidity should lead to an immediate breakdown. However, many have prophesied the end for a number of years, and it is still not in sight; in fact more people now than a few years ago seem to consider the possibility of the continuity of the regime even after Franco. This is not the result of any success of the present power holders in their belated and halfhearted efforts to "constitionalize" — rather than really institutionalize — the pluralism of social and political forces or to allow free and real participation within the framework of "organic democracy." The regime has not been able to find its functional equivalent to the Mexican Partido Revolucionario Institucional (PRI) nor does its international setting allow the party to undergo an internal democratization as has been attempted in some socialist popular democracies of Eastern Europe and might be successful in Yugoslavia. Paradoxically, liberalization of the regime — for example in matters of censorship and freedom to travel and by fewer demands for positive expressions of political conformity — make evolution of the system through change within its institutions, specifically the party, less appealing, less necessary, and therefore less likely. Without the creation of efficient channels for participation within the system — what we would call democratization — the chances for evolution are diminished. The ideological assumptions of authoritarianism — in contrast to systems based on an ideological mass movement, such as a communist or perhaps a sincerely fascist regime, with their democratic or pseudo-democratic participatory elements but lesser liberalism — make changes within the system more difficult.

It is still very doubtful that the present leadership will attempt to inaugurate democracy without conflict and discontinuity as was attempted in Turkey after World War II. The ideological assumptions of the regime, as well as the level of political, social, and economic development of Spain, would make such an attempt difficult. The potential strength of the Communist party and of the regional nationalist forces makes it hard for the regime to choose the path of Inonu and more likely to prefer the position taken at that time by Peker.[132] The transition from one type

132. See Kemal H. Karpat, *Turkey's Politics: The Transition to a Multiparty System* (Princeton: Princeton University Press, 1959), Part II.

It would be interesting to analyze why the Turkish opposition within the system was able to force the leadership of the Republican party to accept competitive politics with political parties, while the Spanish Movimiento leaders have been unwilling to take such a step. If we were to accept the thesis of social and economic prerequisites for democracy, the much greater modernity and economic development of Spain should have been more favorable. In both cases there were international pressures — to which the change in Turkey is often linked — and in the

of regime to another, from an authoritarian regime to democratic government, without discontinuity and strife — even a coup d'état — is not easy, and few models can be found.

ECONOMIC AND SOCIAL CHANGE WITHOUT POLITICAL CHANGE? EVOLUTION OR REVOLUTION? The evolution of Franco's Spain poses difficult problems to the social scientist: how can he account for the combination of basic stability and continuity in the system (if the reader accepts our description) with the important changes in policies and style we have noted? Is liberalization a process that has its limits within the system or will it ultimately, slowly and peacefully, lead to changes *of the system* like those wanted by the alegal but tolerated opposition leaders? To what extent have those changes resulted from the activities of the opposition or from needs implicit within the system — changes in outlook and composition of the elite, social changes that have found no organized expression, and external influences, if not overt pressures? Ultimately the answer to the last question touches the important problem: does political change depend on the existence of the interplay between government and opposition or are governments capable of change — and how much — without an organized and effective opposition? Are important changes in the economic structure, and with them in the social structure — from agrarian to industrial society, from poverty to relative affluence, from unemployment and paternalistic dependency to bargaining of skilled and even semiskilled workers in a modern labor market, and so forth — largely

---

case of Spain they were perhaps even greater. (Actually, this might have been an obstacle to change shortly after 1945.)

The explanation might have to be found in the different sociohistorical contexts.

TURKEY	SPAIN
Nationalist renewal against foreign enemies	Civil War
Birth of the regime in the post-WW I era of democratic ideological optimism	Birth in the antidemocratic thirties under the sign of fascist ideologies
Considerable economic and social underdevelopment that limited the mobilization of social forces outside the political class of the Ataturk regime	Complex social structure that led to the expectation of mobilization outside the existing political class of the regime
No tradition of a revolutionary or radical proletariat	Strong proletarian tradition only recently defeated
Succession of the founder of the regime consolidated in Inonu	Founder still in power
Single dissidence within the political elite	Multiple sources of cleavage latent in the political elite
No threat to nation-state unity	Fear of dangers to unity

independent of political changes? [133] Can they take place with only limited changes in the political institutional structure? These are some of the embarrassing questions the Spanish case poses. Certainly if we were Marxists we would have to ask ourselves how we could account for the persistence of a superstructure of institutions and ideologies after important changes have taken place in the infrastructure. If we were followers of the new decisionist political theory of social change, in which economic and social modernization is seen as largely dependent on government activities, how could we reconcile such changes with limited change at the top? Either our perception of the facts — socioeconomic change and relative political continuity — is false or much of our theoretical apparatus inadequate, or at least requiring further precision. It may well be that there is need for periods of lack of correspondence between changes in different sectors of social reality, and what we need is a theory of lags. How great a gap can there be between different changes and how long can it persist? Or it may well be that change in different sectors of society is relatively independent and that while a society may be successful in some it may fail in others. A relative independence between change in different sectors could account for the fact that great socioeconomic changes have not been clearly reflected in the political sphere. However, I feel that ultimately, even though with considerable delay, the modernization of the Spanish economy and society will lead to a convergence of its political institutions with those of the rest of Western Europe. [134] Even further I feel that modernization in other sectors may not be assured

133. Joan Roig, "Veinticinco años de movimiento nacional en Cataluña," *Horizonte español, 1966*, 2:125, is in accord with our analysis when he writes, "In general, the political forces of the opposition reached the sixties without seeing those changes [economic and social]. The Francoite political immobilism hid from their eyes the real changes in the socioeconomic structure, and their analyses started from the erroneous assumption that the whole society was as immobile as the political superstructure."

134. The problem of conditions for the "inauguration" and "stability" of democracy is analyzed in great detail in another paper by the author, "The Inauguration of Democratic Government and Its Prospects in Spain," presented at a conference at Bellagio in the summer of 1967. I tend to be more optimistic about the prospects for stability, compared to the 1930s, except for the problems posed by linguistic nationalisms. However, in that paper I was more pessimistic about the chances for the inauguration of democracy. Since then the May revolution in France and the changed ideological climate among youth and intellectuals, and particularly the proclamation of the Prince of Spain as successor, only reinforce my conclusion.

After the completion of this essay, Klaus von Beyme published the first and most scholarly synthesis of the political system and its evolution, *Vom Faschismus zur Entwicklungsdiktatur — Machtelite und Opposition in Spanien* (Munich: Piper, 1971). Chapter 3, pp. 83–118, deals specifically with the opposition. His excellent analysis complements mine and in some ways diverges from it. Guy Hermet, *La politique dans l'Espagne Franquiste* (Paris: Colin, 1971), has brought together with great sophistication an anthology of texts, documents, and data, adding excellent introductory remarks. For a chronicle of the history of the regime, see Jacques Georgel, *Le Franquisme: Histoire et bilan, 1939–1969* (Paris: Seuil, 1970).

without it and may even remain under the threat of revolutionary upheaval. The delay in such a process, however, may well turn the alegal opposition from an evolutionary model of political and social change to a revolutionary one and may lead to the disintegration of moderate opposition and ultimately to a political polarization that can only lead to a renewed dictatorship of one or the other side without freedom for institutionalized oppositions.

7

LATIN AMERICA: OPPOSITIONS AND DEVELOPMENT

Robert H. Dix

The twenty political systems of independent Latin America exhibit an awesome political diversity, ranging from one-party regimes to military rule to genuinely competitive politics. It is a formidable task to attempt to generalize about them in such brief compass. Yet their long experience with republican forms of government, some 150 years for most of them, almost 70 years for all, affords some distinct assets for the study of oppositions. For these nations have repeatedly and variously confronted the problem of how to institutionalize a role for legitimate, organized oppositions. By legitimate oppositions I refer essentially to those that manifest themselves in the electoral process and in constitutionally established bodies such as the legislature. In Latin America as a rule they take the organizational form of political parties, loosely defined.

We will be particularly concerned throughout with the impact of development on the emergence and nature of oppositions — in an effort both to define general trends and to account for divergences. Unless otherwise indicated, I shall use the term *development* to include economic, social, and political aspects: economic, in the sense of the adoption of technologies and institutions which promote sustained growth; social, in the sense of expanded opportunities to share in the material and psychic rewards of the society; and political, in the sense of higher levels of political participation in voting, leadership, and organizational life and of the acceptance of the national state and its government as the entities of primary political allegiance.

To what extent does development accont for changes in the roles and patterns of legitimate oppositions both in Latin America over time and,

gratefully acknowledge the support of the Center for International Affairs at Harvard University during the writing of this chapter. I also wish to thank the following for their comments and criticisms on an earlier version of the manuscript: Charles W. Anderson, Douglas A. Chalmers, Joseph S. Nye, Jr., Peter Ranis, and Robert B. Stauffer.

by inference perhaps, elsewhere tomorrow? This is an especially salient question, since the countries of Latin America may generally be classed as semideveloped. At least the major nations of the region rank well above those of the underdeveloped world at large in terms of such indicators of development as literacy, gross national product per capita, and political participation. None, however, has reached the "maturity" in these respects of the nations of northern and western Europe or of North America. The experiences of the Latin American countries may therefore have special relevance for an understanding of some of the problems and prospects of oppositions in other developing countries.

Given such a context for analysis, I propose to explore the role of oppositions in Latin America with the following aims in mind: (1) to delineate the role of legitimate oppositions in Latin America over time; (2) to examine the conditions and circumstances which in the course of development have advanced and retarded the emergence of legitimate oppositions; (3) to relate the role and performance of legitimate oppositions to those arenas of opposition not encompassed by elections, parties, and legislatures; (4) to outline and account for the broad patterns of cleavage assumed by legitimate oppositions; (5) to compare Latin American countries with regard to the status and patterns of oppositions and to account for the differences; and (6) to suggest briefly some consequences for development of the emergence of a legitimate oppositional role.

My principal focus will necessarily be on the region as a whole — on the definition and explication of broad trends. Yet in view of the considerable variation among nations with regard to the roles and patterns of oppositions it will also be a part of my purpose to inquire into the reasons for the differences. The primary concern throughout is with the implications of development for the evolution of institutionalized oppositions, and hence for constitutional democracy.

Early Oppositions

"INS" VERSUS "OUTS"   Both the North American and the Latin American wars of independence did away with monarchy and ushered in republics. But the former English colonies preserved much of the preexisting pattern of authority, in the form of a network of local and state assemblies, and reaffirmed a legitimacy based on the "inherent rights of Englishmen." The North American Revolution was in this sense a conservative one, retaining, despite the elimination of royal rule, much of the prior structure and justification of authority.

To the south, especially throughout the vast Spanish Empire, virtually all authority had emanated from the crown. Divine and natural law did constitute presumptive limits on the king's authority, as did the feasibility of translating exactly the royal will from Europe to America. But there were practically no institutionalized checks on monarchical prerogative. The end of imperial rule therefore destroyed the source of all authority and with it traditional legitimacy. Although social and economic power continued after independence to devolve on those who held extensive resources in land and servile labor, the political aspects of the Latin American revolutions were more radical. The results were therefore more disruptive than the upheaval that had created the United States a generation earlier.

Efforts were made to erect a new legitimacy in the place of monarchy. Republics modeled after the Constitution of the United States and infused with ideas from Rousseau and the Declaration of the Rights of Man were the profferred solution. Yet, despite this formal framework of republicanism, Latin American politics during the nineteenth century was marked by frequent unconstitutional changes, facilitated by the absence of institutionalized rules for determining the political succession.

The overwhelming majority were effectively excluded from the political process. The crucial political relationships centered around the alliances and rivalries of powerful families and strong men (*caudillos*) and on the nexus between patrons and their clients — between powerful landlords, merchants, and prelates, on the one hand, and their tenants, debtors, and like dependents, on the other. Both the vertical linkages between patrons and clients and the horizontal ones among persons and families of equal social standing were dyadic, that is, based on tacit or explicit arrangements of mutual aid or dependence between pairs of individuals, rather than on categorical groupings founded on common economic or occupational interests and identifications.

Such a society tended to be characterized by what Edward Banfield calls "amoral familism," [1] by a lack of trust for the "anonymous other," that is, for those not related to oneself by kinship or dyadic ties. Political identifications were likely to be closely linked to one's social and personal relationships. The cohesion of such primary groups as the family and the rural village might indeed depend on the enforcement of a kind of political discipline which inhibited, for example, marriage outside the circle of the followers of a particular *patrón* or his party.[2]

There was, too, a tendency for Latin Americans to be "allists" (*somos todos toderos*) — that is, to take a strong position on every issue, which Albert Hirschman has contrasted to a "logrolling" society like that of the United States. The former pattern occurs, according to Hirschman, where politics is controlled by a small upper class whose members are involved

---

1. Edward Banfield, *The Moral Basis of a Backward Society* (Glencoe, Ill.: Free Press, 1958).
2. See on this point Gabriel A. Almond and Sidney Verba, *The Civic Culture* (Princeton, N.J.: Princeton University Press, 1963), pp. 137–38.

in practically all issues confronting the society, or where each issue as it arises is immediately connected with some overriding political schism, or where a culture requires men to hold forth authoritatively on all subjects or to ferret out the "right" answer to all questions.[3]

Politics in such a society was likely to take on messianic overtones, even when major issues of social and political change were not at stake. Error and opposition were equated with heresy, and an intense opposition-for-opposition's sake became intrenched.[4] As one Latin American observed early in this century:

> In Colombia exalted convictions are the motives of political enmities; men abandon fortune and family as in the great religious periods of history, to hasten to the defence of a principle. These hidalgos waste the country and fall nobly, with the . . . ardor of Spanish crusaders. . . . Obedient to the logic of Jacobinism, Colombia perishes, but the truth is saved.[5]

Concurrently, with the private sector only weakly developed, government played a highly strategic role in employment and the economy. Not only did import licenses and public-works contracts depend on government favor, but the budget itself was often subject to manipulation for private purposes. In a culture where commerce and manual labor were disdained, where alternative, socially acceptable occupations were scarce, and where centralized governments controlled a relatively sizable proportion of the job market, to become a member of the group "occupying" the government seemed crucial to many.

The stakes of winning or losing in partisan competition were so high that it was difficult to acknowledge the rights of an opposition.[6] Given the importance of winning the presidency in political systems where the chief executive was almost invariably accorded a preeminent role, the rivalry between ins and outs assumed a particular intensity.[7]

At times there was electoral competition for governmental offices among rival factions or clans within a very restricted electorate. More often the clique or leader in power controlled the elections or refused to permit

3. Albert O. Hirschman, *Journeys toward Progress* (Garden City, N.Y.: Doubleday [Anchor Books], 1965), pp. 377–79.
4. The conduct of opposition with such ideological-moralistic overtones was probably also related to the fact that the economic, social, and political status of the church was often among the principal matters of controversy.
5. Francisco García Calderón, *Latin America: Its Rise and Progress*, trans. Bernard Miall (New York: Scribner's, 1917), p. 202.
6. Cf. Lucian Pye, "Party Systems and National Development in Asia," in Joseph LaPalombara and Myron Weiner, eds., *Political Parties and Political Development* (Princeton, N.J.: Princeton University Press, 1966), p. 389.
7. On this point, see James L. Payne, *Labor and Politics in Peru* (New Haven: Yale University Press, 1965), pp. 7–8.

them in the first place. For a faction or a caudillo who did not share in the government, the usual mode of opposition was resort to a coup d'état or the mobilization of a private army of one's allies and clientele to march on the capital. Almost never could the opposition expect to attain office through the ballot box. Only if the governing faction divided internally, with one segment allying itself with the opposition, might a peaceful transfer of power take place.[8] The consequence, in any case, was a repeated turnover of top government personnel, usually effected by violence or its threat.

Substantive change in social policies or political structures seldom resulted. Those succeeding to office represented the powerful and wealthy, as did their predecessors, or quickly became identified with them.[9] Conflict was intraelite in nature and not, for the most part, among persons or groups of markedly differing social status. A surface instability in government offices masked a profounder stability of the social order.

Oppositions were thus not structural in the full sense that they sought to alter fundamentally the distribution of economic and social power,[10] despite the emotional and ideological terms in which political discourse was often couched. Occasionally during the nineteenth century, victory for the advocates of federalism or centralism did result in a rather extensive reorganization of the state (for example, in Argentina and Colombia). Some of the oppositions to dictatorships by constitutionalists (and vice versa) might also be classed, then as now, as structural in the more limited political sense of that term; that is, they proposed changes in regime that went further than mere deposition of the head of government or modifications in particular policies.

But clear-cut examples of political structural oppositions in nineteenth-century Latin America were quite exceptional, centering on the few attempts to continue or reestablish monarchy following the wars of independence. Other leading instances were republican opposition to the Brazilian empire prior to its demise in 1889 and the movement led by Benito Juárez to overthrow the short-lived empire of Maximilian in Mexico in the 1860s. Oppositions going beyond reform of the political structure, or change in the status of the church, to question the basic social order were virtually unheard of.

8. An exception was Brazil before 1889, where conservative and liberal factions, or "parties," alternated in control of the congress as the result of the emperor's exercise of his "moderating power." Such alternation, however, did not affect the much more important executive.

9. Some of the caudillos were of lower-class origin, as were the armies and the street mobs that on occasion rallied to their cause. Almost never was this class difference translated into any real challenge to existing power *structures*, however.

10. For further elaboration of the meaning and significance of structural oppositions, see Robert A. Dahl, "Patterns of Opposition," in Dahl, ed., *Political Oppositions in Western Democracies* (New Haven: Yale University Press, 1966), pp. 341–44.

"CONSERVATIVES" VERSUS "LIBERALS" Personalism, and the struggle between ins and outs for whatever prestige and booty capture of the government could bring, characterized Latin American politics in the decades following independence. Yet from the beginning there were superimposed clashes of values and interests which introduced other dimensions to political contention. By midcentury, quasi-stable factions with certain ideological connotations had crystallized in many countries. Often called parties, they generally lacked the attributes of manifest organization and popular mobilization today commonly associated with that term.

Despite the periodic incidence of dictatorship and of fragmentation into multiple parties or factions, there was something of a tendency for partisan alignments to assume a roughly dualistic pattern of cleavage.[11] Conservatives were aligned against liberals, though not always under those particular designations. In essence, those families, groups, and regions which coalesced around the name *conservative* were defending the social and economic status quo as it had emerged, relatively unscathed, from the colonial period. The *liberals*, for their part, wished to sweep away those residues of privilege passed on from the "incomplete revolution" of the wars of independence. The "champions of tradition" thus faced the "soldiers of liberty" (as liberty was defined by the economic and political doctrines of nineteenth-century liberalism).[12] Often, but not always, the role of the Catholic church was at the center of the conflict.

Why the early tendency to two factions or parties? First, as Carl Landé suggests of the Philippines, in communities which are not segmented by such categorical groupings as those based on class and religion, competition among notables at the local or provincial level tends to produce two major factions, each supported by roughly one-half of the population. Any smaller group would have little chance of victory, whereas a larger faction would have difficulty satisfying all of its clientele because of limitations on its dispensable perquisites.[13] At the national level, this pattern leads to coalitions of local factions whose objective is the capture of national power (that is, the presidency).

Secondly, the major issues of nineteenth-century Latin American poli-

11. There were naturally many variations on the general pattern. Thus in Colombia the dichotomy between Liberals and Conservatives became frozen after midcentury into hereditary hatreds and irreconcilable blocs. Despite persistent factional deviations, dissidents in the Colombian case almost always returned eventually to their original parties or considered themselves in some sense loyal to Conservative or Liberal traditions. Yet in Chile, for example, an early dualistic tendency became obscured in the second half of the century by ruptures within both Liberal and Conservative ranks and by the rise of the new Radical party.

12. For an analysis of the nature of this cleavage in one country, see Robert H. Dix, *Colombia: The Political Dimensions of Change* (New Haven: Yale University Press, 1967), chap. 9.

13. See Carl H. Landé, *Leaders, Factions, and Parties*, Monograph Series, no. 6 (New Haven: Yale University Southeast Asia Studies, 1965), especially p. 18.

tics (the role of the church, centralism vs. federalism, and various socio-economic issues) evoked similar, and therefore reinforcing, political alignments. Those on one side of the religious question were, with some exceptions, on the same side with regard to others. Given the importance of the central government for the dispensation of prestige and material favors, policy cleavages at the national level fused with bifactionalism at the local and regional levels to produce a politics with noticeable bifactional tendencies.

Politics in most countries of the region came to bear the marks of a conservative-liberal dualism at some time during the nineteenth century. It nonetheless bears emphasizing that contention along such lines continued to afford but a loose framework for the perennial struggle among personal cliques, regional interests, and rivalries between those who held office and those who did not, often regardless of party labels or other issues and interests.

FORMS OF EQUILIBRIUM   The kind of political instability characteristic of the postindependence period long continued in some of the Latin American nations. Yet, by the late nineteenth or early twentieth centuries, most of the major countries had attained a relative political equilibrium, even though in none of them was the coup or the threat of forcible overthrow of the government wholly absent from political life. For a nation like Chile, such relative stability can be dated from the 1830s; for others, not until much later. In each this stability leaned toward one of two ideal type political orders, with significant and dissimilar implications for the evolution of institutionalized oppositions.

One model was that of the unifying autocracy,[14] or dictatorship. Mexico under Porfirio Díaz (1876–1911) and Venezuela under Juan Vicente Gómez (1908–35) are the archetypes. Compared to the earlier period, governmental stability and economic progress were notable. However, opposition of any kind, whether institutionalized or not, now played even less of a role. Elections and congresses were more effectively controlled then ever before, while the alternatives of the coup or regional disaffection were all but foreclosed by the overwhelming power of the unifying autocrat and by such centralizing policies as the building of railroads and the encouragement of a strong export sector in the economy.

The alternative model was that of the limited-participation aristocracy. Government was in the hands not of a dictator but of a narrow social elite, among whose members some political competition did take place.

14. This term and the term *limited-participation aristocarcy* which follows are employed by Gino Germani in his *Política y sociedad en una época de transición de la sociedad tradicional a la sociedad de masas* (Buenos Aires: Paidos, 1962), chap. 6, to represent successive stages, rather than alternative patterns, in Latin American political evolution.

Though the opposition was rarely permitted to gain control of the executive, it was allowed to organize and to win seats in the legislature; the press and other forms of verbal criticism were accorded fairly wide scope; and such constitutional rules as those relating to the presidential succession were generally observed. Leading examples of limited-participation aristocracies include Chile from about 1833 until 1920; Argentina from about the 1860s to 1916; Brazil from soon after the fall of the empire in 1889 (and in a measure even before) until the advent of Getulio Vargas in 1930; and Colombia during the four decades or so following the turn of the century.

Behind the enhanced political stability of the decades surrounding the turn of the century lay a more persistent concentration on civil pursuits on the part of Latin American elites. This was in turn related to expanding opportunities in the export sector of the economy. However, in some cases stability entailed a centralizing autocracy, in others a greater political pluralism.

The evolution of the latter type of regime appears to have depended essentially on the increasing strength and cohesiveness of the landholding-mercantile elite and on its ability to place reins on any ambitious caudillo who proposed to march to power at the head of either his own private army or the regular military forces. In certain countries, however, circumstances deflected this process. The Venezuelan elite, for example, was nearly decimated during the long struggle for independence and could never wholly curb the power of the unlettered *llaneros* (plainsmen, or cowboys) who had been called upon to man and even lead the patriot armies. In Mexico foreign intervention unleashed conflicts that weakened elite cohesion. In some of the smaller countries the civilian elite had never been strong enough or cohesive enough to keep political power from slipping back into the hands of strong men supported by the military; nor had expanding economic opportunities sufficiently absorbed the attentions of the ambitious and given them a stake in political order.

Not all Latin American countries, therefore, saw the postindependence period of rapid governmental turnover succeeded by the relative stability of either a unifying autocracy or a limited-participation aristocracy. A few remained caught in a seemingly perpetual succession of coups and rule by strong men of the earlier style. Yet in Latin America generally during the late nineteenth and early twentieth centuries, government — and with it the role of opposition — tended to settle into one or the other model or to oscillate between the two (as occurred in Peru).

The Institutionalization of Opposition

THE GROWTH OF LEGITIMATE OPPOSITIONS   By the early decades of the twentieth century, economic growth and urbanization had contributed to the rise or expansion of groups such as industrialists, the middle sectors, and urban and mining proletariats sufficiently large and articulate to have a significant impact on the politics of such countries as Uruguay, Mexico, Argentina, and Chile. The disruptions of world war and depression meanwhile induced many Latin American governments to concern themselves with economic development and planning. Communism, socialism, and fascism were exerting an influence on intellectuals and students and on some among the emerging middle sectors and labor. As a result, it became less and less feasible to confine political relationships to alliances among well-placed individuals and families and to the linkages of patron-client relationships.

Though by no means wholly replacing such traditional modes of political behavior, categorical groupings based on occupation and economic interest (unions, cooperatives, student organizations, producers' associations, chambers of commerce, and even "central committees of the middle class") became increasingly relevant for politics. Political demands were now to some degree couched in terms of general policies or programs that would benefit *groups*, thus complementing the traditional dependence on particularistic favors.

Electoral participation meanwhile expanded slowly, then markedly in most countries, as restrictions on suffrage were rescinded and as new parties sought to mobilize mass bases. By the 1960s, voting in many of the Latin American nations had attained levels comparable to those of some developed countries (see table 7.1).[15]

Together with such changes, the curve of political instability began to rise once again. Beginning in 1910, after a quarter-century of political quiescence, Mexico underwent almost two decades of civil war and upheaval. Argentina, which had had no successful coup and no major domestic violence for many decades, witnessed six coups, not to mention several depositions of military presidents by the military itself, between 1930 and 1970.[16] Chile, which had experienced only one unconstitutional change (the result of a brief civil war in 1891) since the 1830s, succumbed to almost a decade of acute instability between 1924 and 1932. Colombia's Forty-five year Peace (1904–48) was broken by a decade of rural violence accompanied by governmental instability and dictatorship.

The fundamental cause of the quickening rate of governmental overturns in a period of expanding political participation was precisely the conflict over whether new groups should be accorded access to an arena formerly restricted to a narrow elite and, if so, under what conditions.

15. In a few countries (notably Brazil, Ecuador, and Peru) literacy requirements have remained in force. Women had won the vote in most Latin American countries by the 1950s.
16. For the years 1930–65, see "U.S. Department of State Review of Illegal and Unscheduled Changes of Heads of States 1930–65," *Inter-American Economic Affairs*, Spring 1966, pp. 86–94.

Table 7.1   *Some Political, Social, and Economic Characteristics of Latin American Countries*

Country	Electorate			Literacy*		Urban Population (1965)		GNP (1966)	
	Percentage of Population Voting, 1960–65	Rank	Year	Percentage of Total Population	Rank	Percentage	Rank	Per Capita	Rank
Argentina	43	1	1963	92	1	74	1	818	2
Bolivia	27	9.5	1966	33	18	35	15.5	178	19
Brazil	18	14.5	1960	61	13.5	49	8	333	11
Chile	30	7	1964	84	4.5	69	3	576	4
Colombia	14	18.5	1966	62	12	53	7	334	10
Costa Rica	31	6	1966	84	4.5	35	15.5	406	8
Cuba	16	20	1954	88	3	57	5	511	6
Dominican Republic	32	5	1962	64	11	33	18	270	15
Ecuador	17	16	1960	68	9.5	38	13	219	18
El Salvador	15	17	1962	48	17	39	12	276	13
Guatemala	14	18.5	1958	30	19	34	17	301	12
Haiti	33	4	1961	20	20	16	20	86	20
Honduras	24	12	1965	50	15.5	23	19	230	16
Mexico	23	13	1964	71	8	55	6	493	7
Nicaragua	29	8	1963	50	15.5	42	10	349	9
Panama	27	9.5	1964	79	7	41	11	542	5
Paraguay	26	11	1968	68	9.5	36	14	220	17
Peru	18	14.5	1963	61	13.5	47	9	271	14
Uruguay	39	2.5	1966	91	2	73	2	613	3
Venezuela	39	2.5	1968	80	6	67	4	879	1

* Most recent data available, 1960–65.

SOURCES: Data for political participation and GNP per capita were obtained from *Statistical Abstract of Latin America, 1968* (Los Angeles: University of California Latin American Center, 1969), tables 50 and 83 respectively. Political participation data refer to the last presidential election for which data were available (except for Honduras, where elections chose a constituent assembly, which then named the president).

The data concerning literacy and urbanization are reported in Alexander T. Edelmann, *Latin American Government and Politics*, rev. ed. (Homewood, Ill.: Dorsey Press, 1969), pp. 93 and 52 respectively. The exception is the literacy figure for Cuba, which is the

Paradoxically, a parallel trend toward the electoral resolution of political conflict was noticeable as well, though seldom without at least an initial period of political disturbance. Thus along with a new instability which had its roots in development, there was a simultaneous, albeit irregular and uncertain, advance in the legitimation of oppositions and in the role of the legislature and the electoral process as effective oppositional sites.

One indicator of the increasing institutionalization of oppositions was the mounting frequency with which the opposition won, and the government respected, elections for the all-important presidency. Table 7.2 lists such opposition victories for the twenty-five-year period 1946–70. In most cases (Chile being the notable exception) the opposition had never before won power by the electoral route or had done so only in one or two isolated instances. That the opposition fails to win power within any given period may, of course, be a consequence of the popularity of the government party, not of any legal or other disabilities under which the opposition labors. Yet, at least in the Latin American context, electoral victories are in fact a rough indicator of the degree of institutionalization of the oppositional role. In fact, as a perusal of table 7.2 suggests, once the possibility of oppositional victory becomes institutionalized, incumbent governments tend not to survive the test of reelection.

Both in these polities and in a few where the opposition has not been able to win presidential power by legal means, or where this has occurred infrequently, there has also been a marked increase in the number of votes and congressional seats won by opposition parties. (See table 7.2 for data on opposition legislative strength in 1970.) In several cases the opposition has either gained control of the congress or been able to muster sufficient congressional strength to hamper seriously the president's program. Examples include Peru in the years 1963–68, Brazil for several years prior to 1964, and Colombia on various occasions during the 1960s. Opposition in such cases has been translated into a confrontation between the institutions of the congress and the presidency.[17]

An indicator of a quite different sort is the proliferation of constitutional and electoral devices designed to afford certain minimum guarantees for the opposition. Some of these innovations had their origins in the limited-participation aristocracies of an earlier era, but they have since been considerably extended. One such device is the so-called incomplete vote, whereby the party winning the first plurality in an electoral jurisdiction such as a province or municipality is granted two-thirds of the seats, with the second party allotted the remaining third. The best-known ex-

17. Possibly the extreme case — though it occurred in a country where the opposition has frequently won the presidency itself by electoral means — was the 1967 refusal of the Chilean Senate to permit President Eduardo Frei to travel to the United States to meet with President Johnson. The refusal was within the Senate's constitutional powers, and the decision was respected by the Chilean president.

Table 7.2 Legitimate Oppositions in Latin America

Country	Opposition Victories in Presidential Elections, 1946–70	Opposition Percentage[a] of Legislatives Seats (1970)
Argentina	1958,[b*] 1963[b*]	None (dissolved)[c]
Bolivia	None	None (dissolved)
Brazil	1950,[d*] 1955,[e*] 1960	25[f]
Chile	1952, 1958, 1964, 1970	59
Colombia	1946, 1962[g*] 1966,[g*] 1970[g*]	57
Costa Rica	1958, 1962, 1966, 1970	44
Cuba	None	None (dissolved)
Dominican Republic	1962[h*]	19
Ecuador	1952, 1956, 1960, 1968[i*]	None (dissolved)[c]
El Salvador	None	35
Guatemala	1958,[j*] 1966, 1970	35
Haiti	None	None
Honduras	None	45
Mexico	None	16
Nicaragua	None	33[f]
Panama	1948, 1960, 1969[k*]	None (dissolved)
Paraguay	None	33[f]
Peru	1956[l]	None (dissolved)[c]
Uruguay	1958, 1966	49
Venezuela	1968	72

SOURCES: Listings of presidential victories and legislative percentages were compiled by the author from sources which include Martin Needler, ed., *Political Systems of Latin America* (Princeton, N.J.: Van Nostrand, 1964), the series of *Election Factbooks* published by the Institute for the Comparative Study of Political Systems, *The New York Times, Latin America* (London), *Visión*, and the *Political Handbook and Atlas of the World, 1969–70*, ed. R. P. Stebbins (New York: Simon and Shuster, 1970).

* An asterisk following a given election year indicates that the transfer of power was, for one reason or another, not clearly from one party to another in a democratic election. Victory for the opposition was nonetheless meaningfully involved, as indicated in various of the following notes.

[a] The latest available figures are given. Percentage is of seats in the lower house, or of the single chamber in a unicameral legislature. It should be noted, however, that the line between government and opposition is not always precisely clear or stable. Percentages should therefore be treated as approximate.

[b] Elections held under military auspices with the presumed largest party, the Peronistas (under various labels), barred from running its own presidential candidates. Although the victor was not the candidate preferred by the military, he was nonetheless allowed to take office.

[c] Immediately prior to dissolution, the opposition held a majority of seats in the lower house.

[d] The victor in the 1950 election, Getúlio Vargas, had supported the election of his predecessor, General Eurico Dutra, but had subsequently broken with him.

[e] The interim regime which held office at the time of the 1955 election (following

ample was the Sáenz Peña Law, which governed Argentine elections for roughly half a century after 1912. By now, most Latin American countries have adopted one or another form of proportional representation for legislative elections, in part expressly to ensure a role for opposition candidates.

Mexico, which elects its legislators through the plurality system in single-member districts, has instituted a national electoral quotient to enable those small parties that failed to win many (or even any) seats to gain representation if they received a small percentage of the total nationwide vote.[18] In a system with one dominant party, such as the Mexican, this device was designed to accord at least a minimum of representation to the opposition, though without any intention of allowing it to gain sufficient strength to challenge the hegemony of the ruling party. So anxious is the latter to stimulate opposition in this limited sense that some parties have been granted quotas of seats, even though, by the electoral count, they have failed to earn them.

Such schemes have on occasion even affected the all-important executive. Thus Uruguay has since 1917 provided for minority-party representation throughout most of the executive branch. Between 1952 and 1966 the country experimented with a nine-man plural executive, three of whose members came constitutionally from the main opposition party.

Vargas's suicide in 1954) was generally adverse to the victor, Juscelino Kubitschek. In the end, elements of the military effected a coup to guarantee respect for the results.

[f] Indicates a more or less "official" opposition.

[g] The 1962, 1966, and 1970 elections were held under a bipartisan National Front coalition, with the presidency alternating between members of the Conservative and Liberal parties.

[h] Election held under an interim Council of State dominated by the *losing* party.

[i] Election held under auspices of a provisional government, the president of which had been chosen by a constituent assembly.

[j] Election was a rerun, held under auspices of a caretaker regime which was installed following protests of 1957 election rigging by the previous administration. The 1958 victor had lost that 1957 contest. Lacking the required majority of the popular vote in the rerun, he was chosen president by a congress dominated by adherents of the previous regime.

[k] Opposition won the election, but government was overthrown by the military twelve days after it took office.

[l] The 1963 election was also won by a candidate and party opposed to the previous constitutional administration. However, that election was held under the auspices of a military junta which had nullified the results of the 1962 election, won by the candidate favored by the government then in office. The junta favored the 1963 victor, Fernando Belaúnde Terry.

18. A minimum of 2.5 percent of the vote is necessary to gain representation (five seats). One additional seat is granted for each additional .5 percent of the vote, up to a maximum of twenty seats per party.

Perhaps the most intricate constitutional engineering of all has been the National Front arrangement initiated in Colombia in 1958, following a decade of virtual, though decentralized and sporadic civil war between partisans of the traditional Conservative and Liberal parties. The resulting plan provided for absolute equality of representation of the two parties in both the legislative and executive branches at the national, departmental, and local levels. Furthermore, the presidency was to alternate between the parties every four years for a total of four terms. "Each party," as one observer expressed it, "agreed not to try to win an election in return for a guarantee that it would not lose one." [19] One of the objects of this scheme, in the eyes of its founders, was to assure political peace and, at the same time, instill in Colombians a rooted respect for the opposition that would enable the parties to resume open competition by 1974.

DEVELOPMENT AS A FACTOR IN LEGITIMATING OPPOSITION   The impact of development on the growth of legitimate oppositions has therefore produced seemingly contradictory trends. An increasing incidence of coups beginning in the second and third decades of the twentieth century, compared to the preceding several decades, was accompanied by a proliferation of legal devices to protect the opposition, a greater frequency of respect for opposition electoral victories, and more substantial representation of oppositions in legislatures. Both trends coincided with social and economic change and the expansion of the political arena to include new political actors.

As Hans Daalder suggests, development may be conducive to a pluralistic balance among social groupings, which may in turn be a condition for the growth of a legitimated opposition.[20] The increasing complication of social and political processes, including the advent of new political actors, seems to have had some effect in making it less feasible for government to suppress oppositions and in inducing various political groups to accept as legitimate competitors those upon whose cooperation both social peace and economic growth depended.[21] The fact that material growth

19. Pat M. Holt, *Colombia Today — and Tomorrow* (New York: Praeger, 1964), p. 47. See Dix, *Colombia: The Political Dimensions of Change*, especially chap. 6, for a fuller discussion of the National Front.
20. See Hans Daalder, "Government and Opposition in the New States," *Government and Opposition* 1 (January 1966): 205–26. See also Seymour M. Lipset, *Political Man* (Garden City, N.Y.: Doubleday [Anchor Books], 1963), chap. 2, for a good analytic discussion of the effects of economic development on the growth of democracy. Among the hypotheses which Lipset sets forth are (*a*) that economic development contributes to the growth of organizations intermediate between the individual and the state and hence to political democracy, and (*b*) that the greater a country's wealth, the easier it is to accept some redistribution, so that it is less crucial for all concerned which party is in power.
21. For example, it was no coincidence that the leaders of Colombia's principal industrial region, the department of Antioquia, played one of the most important roles in forging the National Front coalition.

took place under a system closer to laissez-faire capitalism than to a state-directed economy may also have contributed, since the government lacked monopoly control over economic and other resources. It is probable, too, that higher levels of education and the increased interdependence of urban and commercial pursuits have had effects that encouraged tolerance.

Above all, with the partial shift from a personalistic politics, where power was sought for its own sake or for the particularistic perquisites it could bring, to a politics where programs and categorical groupings had relevance, opposition altered somewhat in nature. It showed less tendency to become diffuse, to challenge the government on its very incumbency, and to view political contention in terms of honor, prestige, and heresy. Instead it became more inclined to criticize specific government policies and to advance concrete demands. Governments could in turn more easily respond to such opposition by means of specific laws or administrative actions and felt less impelled to suppress opposition altogether.

Governments seem to have gradually realized that in complex, semi-developed societies, performance is necessary to renew indefinitely their hold on power. Many of their own supporters became more interested in development than in the mere prolongation of their party in office. Under such circumstances opposition was less likely to be viewed as beyond the pale, more likely to be regarded as a normal part of political life, though the political struggle could, of course, remain intense, often taking the form of rivalry among parties espousing competing developmental ideologies.

There are a variety of other factors that might be adduced to help explain the hemisphere-wide trend toward legitimation of oppositions. They include the myths of democracy, as well as the prior existence of republican constitutions. As long as the realities of social and political power conduced to the rule of the old-style caudillo or even of the later unifying autocrat, representative constitutions and the myths that had legitimated them since the onset of independence seemed innocuous enough. Yet constitutional government always remained an aspiration. As civilian elites interested in political peace and material progress gained dominance in some countries, and later as participation was expanded to new groups in much of Latin America, the myths and institutions of constitutional government stood available as something Latin Americans were in a sense already socialized to.

In certain instances historical processes, the cohesiveness of a nation, and the performance of elites or individual leaders have also played a role. However, they affect particular cases more than general trends. We will return to them subsequently when we attempt to account for variations among nations.

Rather, the most important common denominator in explaining the growth of institutionalized oppositions in Latin America appears to be development, conceived broadly in its economic, social, and political aspects. Earlier oppositions tended to be diffuse, intransigent, and narrowly based in the social structure. Only in the late nineteenth century, when export-oriented economic expansion began to challenge the capture of government as a source of economic gain and psychic reward, did some of the major countries, at least, take effective steps toward the legitimation of an oppositional role.

Subsequently, the expansion in the numbers of the politically relevant and the partial shift in the nature of political demands gave added impetus to according a place for oppositions. Indeed, as Charles Anderson has argued, normal behavior in Latin America is to admit new actors to the political system, provided they demonstrate a power capability and provided also that they do not challenge the existence of other, established power contenders.[22] When actors in the system become sufficiently numerous and various, and when enough of them define their stakes in the system in ways that permit a kind of bargaining over shares in that system, a role for organized oppositions becomes one of the feasible ways by which accommodation can be effected and the survival of the system assured.[23]

LIMITING FACTORS   When all this is said, there are nevertheless a number of limiting factors which account for the still slow pace at which the institutionalization of oppositions has progressed in most of Latin America. In several countries, including Mexico, the opposition has not once in modern times won power by the electoral route.

Of course the legal structure of the state may be molded to suppress or contain opposition, as well as to afford it guarantees. The Peronistas have for the most part been prohibited from running their own candidates in the post-Perón era in Argentina, even in those elections which have in other respects been free. Following the coup that overthrew President Goulart in 1964, the Brazilian government, by means of a series of "institutional acts," has reconstructed oppositional patterns by banning all existing parties and in effect limiting new parties to two — a government party and a loyal opposition. In Colombia the constitutional amendments which institutionalized a role for both major parties, through the expedients of parity and presidential alternation, barred other parties from access to office for the projected sixteen years of the interparty agreement.

22. Charles Anderson, "Toward a Theory of Latin American Politics," in Peter G. Snow, ed., *Government and Politics in Latin America* (New York: Holt, Rinehart and Winston, 1967).
23. It is not the only way, however, as the corporate structure of Mexico's dominant party indicates.

However, the sheer tenacity of traditional Latin American political culture, including attitudes toward oppositions, is more profound a cause. Change in the direction of industrialization, urbanization, and higher literacy rates has been significant in almost every country, but it has far from overwhelmed the past. Modern institutions and orientations often coexist with others that are traditional, sometimes in surprisingly compatible ways.

Thus something of a tendency for outs to align against ins, regardless of other considerations, is still apparent, as evidenced by the recent Peruvian oppositional coalition of two old enemies — the Apristas and the party of former dictator Manuel Odría. Moreover, though most oppositions have not sought wholesale alterations in the social structure, and though the conservative-liberal disputes of the past have lost much of their meaning, Latin American political culture continues to be rent by a series of widely divergent "views of life." Often losing much of their significance when the actual policies and programs of various parties and governments are examined, they nonetheless remain as an undercurrent that makes more difficult the full acceptance of an opposition party or movement.

Of almost equal importance, the very process of development itself has often served to limit the oppositional role. For, even as development shows a rather close association with the growth of legitimate oppositions, the pressures of political mobilization often run counter to the easy acceptance of such a role. Hence the dominant-party system in Mexico is usually justified as reflecting the unity of Mexicans in support of their Revolution and its nationalistic and modernizing goals. In multiparty states a congress controlled by local and conservative interests has frequently, during the last decade or so, partially hamstrung a president who had an implied popular mandate for "action." In such cases (Brazil under Presidents Quadros and Goulart, for example) the president, faced with a choice between strict constitutional legitimacy and the broader legitimacy of his presumed mandate, has at times felt obliged to seek devices to circumvent or stifle the opposition.[24] Quadros's dramatic resignation in 1961 after only seven months in office may have been an attempt to rally the masses in his behalf in the face of opposition both within and outside the Brazilian Congress.[25]

Similarly, political mobilization has in Latin America tended to outrun

24. See Celso Furtado, "Political Obstacles to the Economic Development of Brazil," in Claudio Veliz, ed., Obstacles to Change in Latin America (London: Oxford University Press, 1965), pp. 156–57.

25. The motives for Quadros's sudden resignation are still disputed. Any design to rally the masses was in any event unsuccessful. A parallel case was Getúlio Vargas's suicide in 1954; Vargas left a farewell note presumably aimed at arousing popular support for a movement to avenge him against his enemies

the capacity, or the willingness, of established groups and governments to adapt to the demands of new, or newly articulate, political actors. The resulting frustrations have led some to abandon any faith in reformist or electoral solutions and to seek instead, by taking up arms, to destroy the existing political order altogether. For these revolutionaries, any effects which development may have had in the direction of increased tolerance and more specific political demands have obviously been offset by the slowness with which the reformist politics of elections and bargaining have been able to bring about real changes in the lives of Latin Americans. The threat posed by rapid political mobilization has led still others to lose confidence in the ability of democratic regimes to forestall revolution. Under the circumstances they are willing to support regimes which will, at the least, exclude "dangerous" actors from the political process.

A final aspect of the continued difficulties in the way of the legitimation of oppositions in Latin America lies in the fact that elections and legislatures are not the ultimately decisive sites of political conflict, notwithstanding their increasing significance. This is a phase of Latin American politics we have not so far explicitly treated in its contemporary manifestations; its importance requires our separate attention.

Nonparty Oppositions

Latin America has never gone through that process by which those whose skills and resources are appropriate to the aggregation and mobilization of consent (for the most part, the middle class) have become dominant in society.[26] Many Latin American polities have indeed admitted to participation those who could base their claims to power on their ability to mobilize and aggregate consent. Yet those who based their claims on other grounds, such as the control of armed force, have never been eliminated from the system, as they largely have been in the developed West. Organized opposition therefore readily slips the bonds of party contention.[27]

Primary among those power contenders for whom elections are not in the end decisive is of course the military. There is really no country of Latin America where this is not the case. Costa Rica has abolished its army, but even there the militia has not wholly lost its potential political

26. See Anderson, "Toward a Theory of Latin American Politics," p. 240.
27. Though I define the term *legitimate opposition* somewhat narrowly in this chapter, there is a sense in which opposition from sources other than parties and legislatures (from the church, for example) may be considered quite legitimate. Indeed, Douglas A. Chalmers suggests in a personal communication to the author that political scientists' persistent emphasis on parties and parliaments as the major instruments for the institutionalization of oppositions and as necessary for democracy may be the product of ethnocentric bias. See in this regard the concept of "democracy by violence" in Payne, *Labor and Politics in Peru.*

significance. Chile and Uruguay, often cited as nations where the military is not a threat to the constitutional order, have not been without rumors or threats of military intervention in recent years — in Chile in 1970 when the candidate of the Marxist parties was elected to the presidency, and in Uruguay during a period of disorder and constitutional change in the mid-1960s. In many countries, in fact, the military has come to rationalize its role explicitly as that of the "guardian of the constitution" — the guarantor of public order and the protector of the state against "subversion" — over and above the authority of politicians who stake their claims to office on the aggregation of consent.[28] Military coups therefore frequently assume the functional role that elections possess in other political systems, that of determining the political succession.

It is also quite common to see political alignments develop *within* the military, with factions or cliques forming around the different military arms, around military "generations" or ranks, or around regional, ideological, or personal factions. In fact, when the military has been the dominant political force in a country, its factional disputes have largely taken the place of other forms of political conflict, as in the struggle among *azules*, *colorados*, and other cliques in the Argentine army during the early 1960s.

Aside from the military, much other organized opposition evades the channels of parties, elections, and legislatures. Some of it takes the form of direct action protest, for there is a distinct inclination among Latin American interest groups to see themselves as petitioners after the fact for the redress of government decisions that adversely affect them, rather than as bargainers over policies before they are formulated. The accent is on protest seeking the reversal of a ruling or the exception of a given group from its application. When such claims are denied, there is a tendency to take direct action in the form of a strike or by withholding products from the market.[29] Such direct action politics reflects, above all (*a*) the importance of the executive in the decision-making process; (*b*) a party system which performs ineffectively the aggregating function;

28. Whatever the rationales for intervention, it is clear from a number of recent coups that the military has frequently been spurred to action by a perceived threat to its own institutional integrity. Thus the possible victory of a party with an anti-military tradition (e.g., the APRA in Peru in 1962) or the attempt of a president or dictator to arm the workers (e.g., Perón in 1955) is often a precipitant of political action on the part of the military. See in this connection Edwin Lieuwen, *Generals vs. Presidents: Neomilitarism in Latin America* (New York: Praeger, 1964). At the same time, civilian politicians and parties may actively seek military assistance to redress a loss at the polls or to forestall an impending defeat.
29. Interest associations, notably labor unions, may also employ the threat of violence to win wage and benefit demands, as a surrogate for collective bargaining and for pressure on the legislature. According to James Payne, who has called it "political bargaining" in his *Labor and Politics in Peru,* the process has its own rules of the game and reflects a kind of "democracy of violence."

and (c) a political culture which, despite change, is still primarily "subject" in orientation and still substantially particularistic, even where group demands are involved.

Such opposition, it should be noted, is by no means necessarily intended to bring down a given government; in this sense it represents a specific rather than a diffuse style of opposition. It is also "modern" in that it is normally carried out by organized groups. Nonetheless, underlying such behavior is the implication that the threat of disruption of vital services or supplies, or the disturbance of public order, might cause the military to step in to restore domestic tranquillity. At the least, such actions are likely to produce a politically damaging impression of ineptitude on the part of the government. On exceptional occasions, however, direct action on the part of interest associations does constitute an actual attempt to overthrow the government. During the late 1950s commercial and banking interests took part, along with students and others, in "civic strikes" that helped to bring down the dictatorships of Gustavo Rojas Pinilla in Colombia and Marcos Pérez Jiménez in Venezuela.

The political behavior of Latin American student associations constitutes a special case of direct action politics. For a number of social and psychological reasons, university students are especially prone to resort to demonstrations and protest strikes. The role of university students as an oppositional force is enhanced by the tradition of the university's *fuero*, or privileged status of freedom from intervention by the police or the military.[30] In view of the upper-status background of many of the students, to arrest and torture a student may also create important political enemies, as Batista found in Cuba.

Student associations may serve as oppositional sites on those occasions when party activity in the larger society is suppressed. In several important instances, student opposition has played a leading role in efforts to overthrow a government. On occasion, too, student groups have formed the nucleus of postdictatorial political parties. Thus, along with some younger elements of the military, the Venezuelan University Student Federation was the focus in 1928 of an attempt to end the dictatorship of Juan Vicente Gómez; it was out of this student Generation of '28 that several of the main parties and some of the country's principal leaders of the current epoch emerged.[31]

Even when party opposition does flourish, student groups may be sig-

30. The tradition is occasionally abridged by the authorities, but only at the risk of augmenting both student opposition and opposition from the larger society in defense of the *fuero*. The recent incidence of the use of university grounds (e.g., the Central University in Caracas, Venezuela) as refuges, headquarters, and arms caches for non-student oppositions adds, of course, a new dimension to the matter.
31. See John D. Martz, *Acción Democrática: Evolution of a Modern Political Party in Venezuela* (Princeton N.J.: Princeton University Press, 1966).

nificant as foci of opposition. Elections for officers of student associations are usually highly competitive along national political lines. They are watched closely as indicators of broader political trends. Control of a student association by a national party constitutes an important asset in terms of potential recruits and their possible use in demonstrations for or against (usually against) the government.

Other groups, especially labor unions, may become important sites of opposition in somewhat the same sense. Thus since Perón's overthrow in 1955, while Peronista political activity has been circumscribed, Peronista-dominated labor unions have become the principal source of that movement's opposition to the incumbent regime.

Subtler than direct action, but at least as important, is the opposition originating in powerful families or economic interests. Through the ties of kinship or elite club, or through the more formalized ties of producers' associations, such persons or groups may let their opposition be known independently of any party and sometimes effectively enough to depose a government. Robert Scott notes of Peru, for example, that the presidents of some ten functional associations meet regularly to work out common policy positions.[32] Since such groups usually have excellent channels to government, since their own actions can directly affect the nation's economic performance, and since they often control the leading press organs, they loom as formidable opponents. In a country like Peru such "private governments" may set de facto limits within which any government must confine its actions or risk its downfall.

The national hierarchies of the Roman Catholic church can also be very potent foci of opposition. The church often controls or influences political parties, labor unions, or student associations. However, its most important political resource is its ability to stir the conscience or religious fervor of the faithful. George Blanksten noted some years ago of Ecuador that two blocs of voters gave elections their fundamental character: (1) government employees and those aspiring to become such, and (2) the church, including both the clergy and the lay devout. When the two blocs were arrayed against each other, there was likely to be a close contest; when they were allied, the results were usually lopsided.[33]

Traditionally, defense of the faith and of the prerogatives of the church were involked to justify the church's political intervention. Though these remain the principal motivational wellsprings, defense of church interests in the modern age has broadened in definition, at times involving the accordance of moral sanction to broadly based movements seeking the over-

32. Robert E. Scott, "Political Elites and Political Modernization: The Crisis of Transition," in Seymour M. Lipset and Aldo Solari, eds., *Elites in Latin America* (New York: Oxford University Press, 1967), p. 138.
33. George I. Blanksten, *Ecuador: Constitutions and Caudillos* (Berkeley and Los Angeles: University of California Press, 1951), p. 74.

throw of dictatorships. In the late 1950s and the early 1960s the church played a notable role in the downfall of the regimes of Perón in Argentina, Rojas Pinilla in Colombia, and Pérez Jiménez in Venezuela. It also helped to bring down the democratic regime of Juan Bosch in the Dominican Republic in 1963.

Opposition of yet another kind, also not encompassed by party alignments as such, occurs *within* governments and governing parties. Within the mass revolutionary parties that have evolved into one-party-dominant systems — notably the Mexican Partido Revolucionario Institucional (PRI) and the Bolivian Movimiento Nacionalista Revolucionario (MNR) prior to 1964 — factions polarizing on ideological disputes, on personalistic rivalries, or on competition among functional sectors of the party for their respective shares of office and other perquisites have provided a focus for intraparty competition much more important than any challenge posed by the small opposition parties permitted to exist on the fringes of such systems.

Beginning long before the advent of such modern dominant-party regimes, there have of course been many occasions on which one party or faction held the reins of power for long periods to the virtual exclusion of any effective, let alone legitimate, opposition. When this has occurred, factionalism within the government, or within the party in whose name the government has nominally ruled, has become a kind of surrogate for interparty competition. Elections with slates of candidates from opposing factions of the dominant party are not at all uncommon in Latin American history; in contemporary Colombia and Uruguay this form of opposition has actually been institutionalized. Even in genuinely competitive systems, governing parties have sometimes found their most violent opposition within their own ranks.

Another, by no means negligible, potential source of opposition may be centered in foreign capitals or in foreign enclaves within the Latin American bodies politic. Given the current sensitivity of Latin Americans to the activities of foreign capitalists — and the increasing sensitivity of the latter to Latin American sensibilities — one rarely hears any longer of foreign business enterprises directly engaged in the making and unmaking of governments, as they once reputedly were, especially in Central America. But in many Latin American countries a major element entering into the calculations of politicians has often been the likely stance of the United States with respect to their own and their parties' ambitions for office. Threats to withhold recognition and aid from regimes it does not wish to see come to power, covert encouragement and hasty recognition of others (for example, the government resulting from the Brazilian coup of 1964), prestigeful invitations to incumbents to make official visits to Washington, and efforts to unseat such governments as those of Arbenz

1 Guatemala and Castro in Cuba — these are merely a few of the kinds nd instances of United States intervention in ongoing contests between overnments and oppositions in Latin America. Nor is the United States lone in this regard, as the Cuban case, among others, demonstrates.[34] t seems clear indeed that the United States is often both able (though ot always, as the case of Chile attests) and willing, especially since the Cuban revolution, to set limits to the types of oppositions which can xpect to win power in Latin America.

Finally, organized opposition may take the form of efforts to over-hrow the government by means of revolutionary guerrilla warfare. In ontemporary Latin America, guerrilla bands are most often led by, and ometimes almost entirely composed of, urban intellectuals and middle-lass youth seeking to mobilize the campesions or the urban masses for ocial revolution.[35] Such bands have existed at one time or another in ecent years in a majority of the Latin American countries. For these evolutionaries, the electoral process is by definition unable to meet the ust demands of those on behalf of whom they claim to speak.

Parties and elections, then, constitute but one among many dimensions f opposition in Latin America. Individual countries differ substantially, f course, in terms of the respective political roles played by the military, he church, "private governments," foreign intervention, intraparty fac-ions, direct action protest, and guerrilla bands. Yet in each country, lmost all of these oppositional sites and modes have some actual or po-ential political relevance. In virtually every Latin American country lections are decisive only by leave of political actors who can, if they vish, bring to bear power resources other than the mobilization of formal opular consent.

Each arena of opposition tends to have its own principal actors, goals, nd strategies. Thus, when the military assumes an oppositional role, its bject is usually either to effect a change in the personnel of government r to alter the rules of the political game (for example, from constitutional overnment to dictatorship). Its strategy depends, of course, on the use or hreat of force. In the arena of direct action opposition by interest groups,

4. In addition to Soviet support of Fidel Castro and Castro's support in training nd material assistance for guerrilla activities in several Latin American countries, nese instances include the purported financial support of West German Christian •emocratic sources for Eduardo Frei's 1964 presidential campaign in Chile, interna-onal Communist support for Communist parties and labor movements in the hemi-ohere, and the interference of various Central American states in the internal politics f their neighbors during the 1940s and 1950s.

5. Such groups tend to deny the validity of elections per se, viewing them as *herently* unrepresentative, or fraudulent, or irrelevant. Not least among the unique spects of the Castro government in Cuba within the spectrum of Latin American olitical behavior has been its failure to give at least lip service to elections as the ltimate legitimator of government.

the goal is normally to change a policy or administrative ruling through strikes and demonstrations that threaten the government's ability to manage the public weal.

The various arenas are, of course, not wholly autonomous or disparate. For example, some nonparty groups (interest associations, "private governments," the church) may at times resort to electoral strategies. The point is rather that there are *alternative* channels of opposition and that any "decision" made via the electoral process may be disregarded or negated by a kind of veto employed by organized oppositions relying on nonelectoral methods.

Some of these extraconstitutional forms of opposition — direct action, for example — have shown a propensity to increase concomitant with the increase in legitimate oppositions. Others, such as those emanating from the military and the church, are long-standing centers of potential opposition. Yet even such traditional foci of opposition have tended to take a new view of their role. Defense of their institutional interests is still central, but those interests are now defined somewhat differently, in keeping with the changing environment in which those groups or institutions (or nations, in the case of foreign governments) must function. Even in the several nonlegitimate arenas, opposition is today less frequently than before expressed in the traditional terms of ins versus outs and as a struggle for particularistic booty and honor. It is more often viewed in the light of policy preferences and administrative performance and is often voiced in terms of the need to advance or retard change.

Nonparty oppositions, in short, tend to share with legitimate oppositions an increase in their number and variety over the last few decades, as well as a "modernizing" of their goals and of the framework within which those goals are perceived. Their continued existence and vitality, together with the lack of consensus on any one legitimate mode or arena of opposition, are critical for an understanding of the role of oppositions in Latin America. Though often important and, as we have suggested, probably increasingly so over the long term, in no Latin American political system have parties, elections, and legislatures been definitively accepted as *the* appropriate channels for the expression of organized political opposition.

The Political Cleavages of Development

TOWARD A POLITICS OF SOCIAL CLASS   Socioeconomic changes and rising levels of political participation have had their counterparts, not only in the increased incidence of legitimate oppositions and in a new variety and significance of nonparty oppositions, but also in the changing lines of cleavage along which partisan conflict is conducted.

In some countries the parties inherited from the nineteenth century faded away altogether under the challenge of different issues and emerging group alignments. In one or two instances, however, the new trends were manifested in the partial transfiguration of the traditional parties. Thus in Uruguay the Colorados (liberals) and the Blancos (nationalists or conservatives) continued their nineteenth-century rivalry while reflecting the new era. The popular base of both parties broadened considerably, with clearer ties to categorical groupings, and the focus of contention centered somewhat more explicitly on policy issues as the Colorados became the political vehicle for introducing the welfare state to Uruguay.

In still other cases, including those of Chile, Ecuador, and Argentina, one or more of the traditional parties survived and generally continued to represent elite interests, at the same time that other parties arose in response to growing social and ideological diversification. Most of the new parties established links with urban labor, peasant organizations, and similar groups, though their leadership was almost always predominantly middle-class. The themes of social justice, nationalism, and an important role for the state in economic development stood out in their programs and electoral appeals.

In general, whatever the fate of the traditional parties, there has been an increasing tendency to express political contention in class terms. The limited empirical evidence available concerning voting behavior and the social composition of government and party leaderships shows the trend rather clearly. A study of Argentine elites demonstrates a quite striking difference between the class origins of high government officials in the 1930s and those in the subsequent Perón era. The present leaderships of Chilean parties likewise show quite marked differentiations along class lines compared to half a century ago. Both survey data and ecological analyses of voting in Brazil, Argentina, and Chile indicate similar divisions among the electorate.[36]

MARXIST OPPOSITIONS   A politics rooted in the categorical distinctions of occupation and economic interest has thus partially supplanted the modes of traditional politics. The conservative-liberal dualistic cleavages of the nineteenth century have in most countries been eroded by the rise of parties grounded in new social realities and making a different kind of appeal. The political arena itself has expanded in many countries to in-

36. On Argentina, see José Luis de Imaz, *Los que mandan* (Buenos Aires: Editorial Universitaria, 1964). The statement on Chilean leaderships is based on preliminary findings of a study by the author, in progress. For divisions in the electorate, see Gláucio Ary Dillon Soares, "The Political Sociology of Uneven Development in Brazil," in Irving Louis Horowitz, *Revolution in Brazil* (New York: Dutton, 1964), pp. 164–95; Gino Germani, *Estructura social de la Argentina* (Buenos Aires: Raigal, 1955), chap. 16; and Ricardo Cruz-Coke, *Geografía electoral de Chile* (Santiago: Editorial del Pacífico, 1952).

clude, at least as voters, broad new strata of the population. Hence the proposition of a Brazilian social scientist that "the politics of development are the politics of class and ideology." [37]

Moreover, an appreciable number of political actors in Latin America, even some who are non-Marxists, see politics largely in terms of the class struggle. It might actually be contended that those countries of the region where industrialization has taken some substantial hold — this includes most of the major countries — come as close to Marx's descriptions of early industrial society as any in the modern world. The Marxian stress on the implications of the industrializing process for class conflict might, therefore, be presumed prima facie to be applicable to the Latin American situation, if it is indeed applicable anywhere.

Along with new lines of cleavage and a new multiplicity and diversity of parties, the twentieth century has in fact brought with it the advent of structural oppositions in the full, social revolutionary sense. In one or another guise, they have become an almost standard feature of modern politics in the region. Today they include the Communist parties (which exist, legally or not, in all the Latin American countries, with the possible exception of Haiti) and some Socialist parties,[38] as well as myriad Marxist-Leninist splinter groups and Castroite "armies of national liberation."

These revolutionary oppositions pursue widely divergent strategies. Some, like most of the so-called armies of national liberation and Castro's old 26th of July Movement, have preferred the immediate initiation of guerrilla warfare and terrorism. Most of the established Communist and Socialist parties advocate a more flexible approach, taking into account the "state of preparation of the masses." They may of course resort to violence, although as often in its conspiratorial as in its mass revolutionary form; but frequently they demonstrate a willingness to use the parliamentary route to power (as in Chile) or to cooperate with a dictator in the interests of survival and a relatively free hand in the labor movement (as with Communist splinter groups in Argentina, Peru, Venezuela, and Cuba in the late 1940s and early 1950s).[39] The alternative strategy of violence — and even the goal of revolution itself — may then be relegated largely to the realm of the abstract and the theoretical.[40]

37. Soares, "Political Sociology of Uneven Development," p. 193.
38. Latin American Socialist parties should not be equated with their European namesakes. Few in number in any case, and generally unimportant except in Chile, they tend to be more radical and less adherent to the gradual processes of constitutional democracy. For a good brief discussion of the Chilean Socialist party, see Ernst Halperin, *Nationalism and Communism in Chile* (Cambridge, Mass.: M.I.T. Press, 1965), chap. 4.
39. See Robert J. Alexander, *Communism in Latin America* (New Brunswick, N.J.: Rutgers University Press, 1957), pp. 13–14.
40. The best examples may be the Communist and Socialist parties of Chile, with the Socialists being rhetorically, at least, more revolutionary than the Communists. Both regularly participate in Chilean elections. The leaders of both parties sit in the Senate

Yet Marxist parties have had relatively little success in Latin America, despite apparently propitious conditions. In Cuba and Guatemala, respectively, they attained power or near-commanding influence as the tails to the kites of non-Communist nationalistic revolutions. Even in Chile, where a Marxist-dominated coalition won the presidential elections of 1970, the coalition included non-Marxist elements and at that won only some 36 percent of the total vote. To view contemporary Latin American politics, and with it the politics of development, as *essentially* one which is or might be in the foreseeable future polarized along class lines considerably oversimplifies a much more complex political reality.

THE LIMITS ON CLASS POLITICS   An obvious limitation on a full-blown class politics in any system is the series of conflicts — carryovers from an earlier political era — which were not wholly resolved prior to the advent of struggles over political participation and social justice. In Latin America one of these is the ancient conservative-liberal dichotomy, usually centering on the question of church-state relations but more broadly involving opposing views of life. Regional antagonisms also persist. Significant, too, are those continuing dyadic ties which cut vertically across economic and occupational categories. The incidence of these various cleavages varies from country to country, but nowhere is their relevance to be discounted. Indeed, in some of the less developed countries of the area these older bases of political conflict unquestionably still predominate.

Less obvious but equally crucial limitations are several that derive from, or are made evident by, the developmental process itself. These include patterns of uneven modernization, which divide social classes; the normal admission of new participants to political life via parties and governments oriented to cross-class goals; and the fusional nature of Latin American elites.

1. *Intraclass cleavages.* Classes are frequently riven by a modernist-traditionalist cleavage. The upper class may include industrial entrepreneurs and agriculturists seeking to maximize profits through mechanization and the introduction of wage labor, as well as landowners content with age-old techniques of farming and the maintenance of paternalistic relationships with their tenants and sharecroppers. The middle class is extremely diverse in its values and aspirations and in its occupations and incomes. Some of its members are downwardly mobile from the traditional elite and remain aspirants to aristocracy; their typical occupations are law and the bureaucracy. Others are more inclined to take economic risks or to enter such professions as economics and engineering.

---

and are socialized into its clublike atmosphere and its parliamentary rules of the game. Even when it was declared illegal during the period 1948–58, the Communist party directed its efforts mainly at recovering its legal status and political offices, rather than at revolution. In 1970 a Socialist, Salvador Allende, was elected president of Chile.

The dichotomy between modernists and traditionalists within the lower, or "popular," classes is likewise pronounced. Superficially it might appear to be an urban-rural cleavage, and it is true that the most traditional segments of Latin American society are generally those engaged in subsistence agriculture. Yet in most countries the farming population has exceedingly varied relationships to the land and to landowning. In certain Latin American countries (for example, on some Central American banana plantations and on some of the sugar plantations of pre-Castro Cuba) there have existed veritable "factories on the land," characterized by wage payments, a relationship of impersonality between owner and worker, and an emphasis on productive efficiency. Their workers form a "rural proletariat" more akin in outlook to the industrial worker than to the typical campesino.

Striking, too, is the division of the urban lower class into those employed in industry and mining (and comprising an industrial proletariat) and the marginals living in the jerry-built slums that surround many of the large urban centers. Though the distinction is not always clear-cut, the latter tend to be but occasionally employed or to be engaged in such economically marginal jobs as lottery-ticket selling, shoeshining, domestic service, and unskilled construction work.

For in much of Latin America, urbanization has far outrun industrialization and the capacity of the metropolitan centers productively to absorb the in-migrants from the smaller cities and towns and rural areas. In both its rapidity and its extent, the pace of urbanization contrasts markedly with the earlier experience of Europe and North America. Socially mobilized, politically available, and even participant (at least to the extent of voting), but remaining unintegrated into modern industrial life and without having shed most of their traditional value orientations, Latin America's urban marginals come closer to Marx's lumpenproletariat than to his conception of a working class. They have been less interested in class solidarity against the factory-owning bourgeoisie than in acquiring a piece of land on which to build a dwelling and in securing such amenities as sewers, potable water, and transportation for their barrios.

There is evidence that the voting behavior of the urban marginal diverges, at least initially, from that of the industrial worker — that he is less prone to support Marxist parties and more likely to vote for parties whose image or orientation is somewhat more traditional or which are led by charismatic figures. Later, however, if the migrant's aspirations are frustrated and as he becomes more fully aware of the inequities of his urban environment, it may be that he will turn to more radical politics.[41]

41. See, on this point, Soares, "Political Sociology of Uneven Development," pp. 191–95; see also Glaucio Soares and Robert Hamblin, "Socio-Economic Variables and Voting for the Radical Left: Chile, 1952," *American Political Science Review* 56, no. 4 (December 1967): 1962.

The industrial worker, meanwhile, tends to gain earlier and fuller access to the political system and to the benefits of social welfare legislation. He also earns higher wages than others among the lower social strata in what are real economies of scarcity. Industrial workers (and some miners, such as the Chilean copper workers) thus come to comprise a kind of labor aristocracy. Their interests lie in protecting their special niche, rather than in advancing the causes of the urban marginals or the campesinos. Though sometimes supporting ideologically class-oriented parties, they are seldom really revolutionary. In the aggregate they show much more interest in wage levels than in the class struggle.[42]

The alignment of modernist versus traditionalist also turns on sex and age. Both factors seem to have particular elevance to the politics of Latin America. There is clear evidence, at least from Chile, that women vote in a markedly different way than men, notably when a Marxist choice is arrayed against a Christian Democratic one.[43] Usually attributed to the differential influence of religion on women in a Catholic society, the causes may well be broader. Women's traditional isolation from the "men's world" of politics and regular employment, though diminishing, still persists in some degree. It may also be that for the woman of the lower-class "culture of poverty," where she is the stable center of the household and perhaps the breadwinner as well, defense of the home against the presumed threat of Marxism is as much of an influence as any effected directly by religion or the church.

As for age: in societies undergoing rapid internal change, the political experiences and goals of one generation are especially likely to be distinct from those of another. It was the emphasis on youth and its claimed ability to regenerate Cuba, rather than the theme of class struggle, which was the hallmark of Castro's rise to power. Similarly, internal rifts in such parties as Venezuela's Acción Democrática and Peru's APRA during the past decade have centered on a youthful impatience with traditional structures (as well as with frustrated opportunities for advancement) more than on any other discernible ground of social differentiation.

2. *Vertical incorporation of the lower classes.* Further mitigating the class-conflict potential of Latin American societies has been the manner of admission of new groups into a participant political role. The common sequence in Latin America has been for the lower classes first to be extensively incorporated into the political system through the agency of government itself or of a party-in-government having elite or middle-class leadership. Though these are by no means entirely unresponsive to

---

42. See, for example, the chapters by Osvaldo Sunkel, Celso Furtado, and Hélio Jaguaribe in Veliz, *Obstacles to Change in Latin America*, and the chapter by Henry Landsberger in Lipset and Solari, *Elites in Latin America*.
43. In the 1964 presidential election, the female vote was 63 percent for the Christian Democratic candidate, 32 percent for the Marxist candidate. Among men the vote, while favoring the Christian Democrat, was only 50 versus 45 percent.

their clienteles, the relevant structures and communication patterns have tended above all to fulfill a mobilization and control function with respect to the lower classes. In a sense they reflect adaptations of the traditional patron-client relationship to mass politics. Leading examples include Perón's Argentina, Mexico under the PRI, and the quasi-corporate state initiated by Vargas in Brazil in the late 1930s.

An alternative vehicle has been the mass-oriented party which had its origins external to government and only subsequently won power. Such were Venezuela's AD and Bolivia's MNR. More responsive to demands from their memberships and less manipulative than in the Argentine, Mexican, and Brazilian cases, they have nonetheless manifested elements of the latters' mobilizing and paternalistic characteristics.

Such vertical incorporation of the lower classes into a role in the polity tends to link them organically with segments of other classes in coalition parties or governments and to give them common allegiances (for example, to a charismatic leader) or common objectives of national development (for example, industrialization). At the same time that they gain access, they evolve a dependence — at least for a key initial period — on a government or a political party which they do not themselves, in the main, direct. The lower classes are thereby harnessed to the goals of development without becoming alienated or threatening to destroy the positions of those with established status.[44]

3. *Fusional elites.* A final factor blurring the class lines of political conflict is that an outright challenge to the traditional landed elite by a rising industrial bourgeoisie has not quite materialized in much of Latin America, despite industrial growth. Economically, the real spur to Latin American industrialization came from the imperatives of import substitution during the depression and two world wars. Although industry and agriculture might compete for governmental favor (over tariff policy, for example), industry did not have to grow at the expense of agriculture to the extent that this occurred elsewhere.[45]

Reinforcing such circumstances of economics has been the marked tendency for members of traditional landowning families to link themselves with modern industry or its financing, and for rising industrialists to buy up land, marry into traditional families, or otherwise fuse with the aristocracy of *abolengo* (ancestry, or lineage). Furthermore, since mass politicization has generally preceded sustained economic development in Latin America, it has behooved potentially competing sectors within the elite to cooperate in promoting growth while restricting as much as possible its social and political consequences.[46]

44. See on this point Lipset, *Political Man*, pp. 66–67.
45. See Furtado, "Political Obstacles to the Economic Development of Brazil."
46. Cf. the concept of "syncratism" in A. F. K. Organski, *The Stages of Political Development* (New York: Knopf, 1965).

It seems arguable that if (in Louis Hartz's terms) socialism emerges only in those societies where feudalism has existed prior to the rise of industrial society,[47] working-class socialism can emerge only with difficulty in the presence of an industrial establishment which takes on many of the values and identifications of the traditional aristocracy and fails to generate within itself a full-fledged class consciousness.

THE MODERNIZING COALITION   Interclass linkages of various kinds, reinforcing those cleavages that inhere in modernist-traditionalist distinctions rather than in class lines, provide the bases for a type of party not readily subsumed into a polarization between left and right. As a rule this so-called modernizing coalition has a leadership core of professional men and intellectuals of middle-class origin, who gather to their support a substantial number of the newer and smaller industrialists, portions of the middle class, much of organized labor, and other presumptive modernists. Most such parties have a disproportionate initial appeal to youth, although this support may fall away as the party attains power or becomes bureaucratized and as new generations come to the fore. Sometimes, too, such parties receive support from the younger and more modern strata of the military and church hierarchies.

Characteristically, however, modernizing coalitions are not restricted to the modernists in the polity. Some have effectively mobilized previously inarticulate urban strata. Others (for example, Mexico's PRI, Venezuela's AD, Bolivia's MNR, and Chile's Christian Democrats) have been able to mobilize a large proportion of the peasantry as well, partly through policies of agrarian reform and partly through grassroots organizational efforts. Some, including Chile's PDC, have proved quite effective among women.

Central to the ideology of these coalitions are usually a nationalism which supersedes class and other categorical groupings and a broad program of development with which a wide range of groups can identify. Though sometimes originating as highly ideological parties (as did Peru's APRA), they tend to be quite pragmatic, especially once in power. Meaningful correlations with class-based support can usually be made, but the more striking characteristics of these parties are their broad, pragmatically implemented developmental goals, their multiclass composition, and their mobilization of premoderns. Their emergence is an indication that the stakes of development may to some extent override those of more parochially defined group interests in late-modernizing societies.

Although occasional modernizing coalitions have at some point in time

47. Louis Hartz, *The Liberal Tradition in America* (New York: Harcourt, Brace, 1955).

been revolutionary (for example, Bolivia's MNR), most have been reformist. They do not really seek to destroy one structure of power more
or less totally and to erect another in its stead. Rather, what is normally
aimed at (as confirmed by the behavior of such parties once they are in
the government) is an augmented share of power for newly mobilized
social sectors, without destroying the essential outlines of the existing system. Their agrarian reform programs, for example, typically include substantial compensation for expropriated land and are seldom extensive
enough to transform radically the structure of power in the countryside.
Political movements of this sort do seek significant change and are in a
sense, therefore, structural oppositions; but they are not, in the meaning
of the word used here, really revolutionary.

The majority of modernizing coalitions have evolved within competitive systems. Such parties have expressly sought to strengthen constitutional democracy. Most of the social democratic or so-called Aprista
parties, as well as the Christian Democratic parties, are of this type.[48]
Their emergence has clearly contributed to the perceptible advance in the
institutionalization of oppositions in Latin America.

Some modernizing coalitions, however, have taken an authoritarian
form and indeed have been organized by governments in power. They
include populistic, authoritarian parties and regimes led by caudillos like
Perón[49] and Vargas, as well as the broad-based "national revolutionary"
party in the one-party-dominant system of Mexico. Yet even these
coalitions have sometimes retained important elements of pluralism in
their internal structures. Thus the Mexican PRI is divided into three
separate sectors for labor, *ejido* (communal) peasants, and a bevy of
mainly middle-class associations dominated by government employees.
Each sector has an institutionalized voice in party affairs. At the same
time, big business is integrated into the political system by other organizational devices.

In a number of countries, modernizing coalitions represent the principal
axis around which political conflict revolves. Though products of an era
of class and group politics, their multiclass composition and their relatively pragmatic, reformist approach to change clearly differentiate them
from explicitly class-based, highly ideological parties and from those
parties which are primarily elite- and tradition-centered. They differ

48. Parties considered Aprista-type — referring to the American Popular Revolutionary Alliance (APRA) of Peru — include the AD of Venezuela, the National
Liberation party (PLN) of Costa Rica, and the Dominican Revolutionary party
(PRD). The most important Christian Democratic parties in Latin America are those
of Chile and Venezuela.
49. Although the Peronistas were particularly strong in the urban labor movement,
much of the movement's direction and support came from segments of the middle
class, from industrialists, from rural workers, and from the army.

from Kirchheimer's "catch-all" parties[50] in being oriented to development, rather than to the problems of postindustrial society, and in their function of incorporating premoderns into the political system. Moreover, in most cases they have evolved, not out of previous class-mass parties, but out of modernizing segments of the middle class seeking to unite various groups behind a program of change.

Marked changes in the patterns of political cleavage have therefore accompanied such trends as economic growth, social change, and increased political participation in at least the major Latin American countries. At the same time, certain attributes of the developmental process itself have considerably modified any overriding tendency for political conflict to become structured along class lines. Even the myriad revolutionary "fronts of national liberation" are not really class movements in the Marxian sense, being comprised as a rule primarily of youth of middle-sector origin. Not least, some of the political parties that have emerged as a reflection of the new, complex lines of cleavage have been among the leading vehicles for the institutionalization of a legitimate oppositional role.

Conclusion

VARIANCES IN THE LEGITIMATING OF OPPOSITIONS   If certain broad trends relating to the emergence of oppositions are discernible for Latin America as a whole, some sharp contrasts are notable as well. A few countries, like Uruguay and Chile, have afforded oppositions virtually maximum scope, while in others, such as Paraguay and Haiti, the opposition role has been minimal.

Table 7.3 gives the author's ranking of Latin American countries according to the degree of legitimacy accorded to oppositions during the last quarter-century (1946–70). The ranking is necessarily somewhat subjective and even almost arbitrary. It says nothing about the degree of popular participation, nor even about political stability (since coups have at times changed governments without materially affecting the functioning of oppositions). The ranking also fails to distinguish between those nations (for example, Argentina) where oppositions have occasionally flourished and have occasionally been obliterated and those (for example, Mexico) where oppositions, while never really wholly illegitimate, have remained consistently quite token in national politics. Nonetheless, the ranking may provide a takeoff point for a comparison of the status of legitimate oppositions in the Latin American nations.

50. See Otto Kirchheimer, "The Transformation of Western European Party Systems," in LaPalombara and Weiner, *Political Parties and Political Development*, pp. 177–200.

Table 7.3 Oppositional Legitimacy in Latin America: A Ranking

Rank	Country	25-Year Ratings[a]
1, 2	Chile	75
	Uruguay	75
3	Costa Rica	70
4	Ecuador	66
5	Brazil	61
6	Venezuela	45
7	Peru	46
8	Colombia	43
9	Honduras	41
10	Panama	38
11	Guatemala	36
12	El Salvador	32
13, 14	Argentina	28
	Bolivia	28
15	Mexico	25
16	Cuba	19
17	Dominican Republic	18
18	Nicaragua	15
19	Haiti	12
20	Paraguay	8

[a] These ratings are the end result of a year-by-year evaluation of each of the twenty countries during the quarter-century 1946–70. For each year, each country was assigned a score on the following scale: 3 (opposition substantially unfettered), 2 (opposition limited), 1 (opposition token or severely limited), 0 (opposition suppressed or virtually absent). The total of 75 ascribed to Chile and Uruguay is thus the maximum possible on this scale.

The annual scoring was based on a variety of sources, including Needler, *Political Systems of Latin America,* and the series of *Election Factbooks* published by the Institute for the Comparative Study of Political Systems. Where oppositions were free to function but where an important contender was barred, de facto or de jure, from contesting the presidency (e.g., the Peronistas in Argentina and the Apristas in Peru), the score assigned was 2. Illegalization of minor parties or Communist parties was not, however, taken into account in this manner.

Why does the role of oppositions differ so markedly among them? A measure of correlation with social and economic indices offers one possible line of explanation, in keeping with our earlier analysis of the impact of development. Those nations which confer the highest level of legitimacy on oppositions tend to rank considerably higher than the others in gross national product per capita, literacy, and urbanization (see table 7.1). This suggests, for example, that relative abundance somewhat eases the struggle over distribution of society's limited rewards and thus encourages tolerance. Yet there are contradictions. The correlation is quite rough between these indices and our ranking of oppositional legitimacy.

Argentina and Cuba, particularly, place lower — and countries like Ecuador, Guatemala, and Honduras rather higher — than would be expected. The institutionalization of oppositions may require certain minimal levels of economic and social development, but such an explanation seems insufficient to account for the differences among nations.

It is noteworthy that the three countries that have gone farthest in legitimating the role of organized oppositions are among those that have shown the highest degree of national integration and social cohesion. Costa Rica and Uruguay are small in physical size; in terms of their effective polities they might almost be deemed city-states.[51] Chile, while considerably larger, consisted throughout its formative years of a core (the central valley) from which it subsequently expanded both north and south. The majority of the Chilean population and the bulk of its economic, political, and cultural life still center in that area. Thus in terms of social size, all three are small countries. Although class divisions remain important, especially in Chile, racial and regional divisions are minor. Moreover, internal communication within the heart of these polities is good. The other small nations of Latin America either lack such cohesion or are at a much lower level of social and economic development and thus fall short of that presumptive threshold for the growth of legitimate oppositions.[52] The implication is that it is much easier to accept a political opponent as legitimate if he is part of one's perceived social family.

Historical processes — especially as they relate to the timing and manner of resolution of the crisis of participation and the initial role accorded to intraelite competition — must also be taken into account in explaining contemporary oppositional roles. In some countries, traditional elites proved flexible enough to accord a place in the system, gradually and sequentially, to such groups as the middle sectors and urban labor by extending to them — at an early point in their rise to strength and self-consciousness — the franchise, the right to organize, and certain minimum social benefits. Established political actors were thus not unduly threatened, while the newer aspirants found it difficult (or unnecessary) to unite for a massive assault on the existing power structure. In such cases the rules of the political game evolved under limited-participation aristocracies were fairly readily extended to new groups.

51. In Costa Rica the central *meseta* of less than two thousand square miles (roughly one-tenth of the total area of the country) contains more than half the nation's population. Almost all the principal towns are located there, within short distances of one another. Montevideo, the capital of Uruguay, and its environs contain about half of that country's population.

52. Paraguay and El Salvador may be cases in point. Not only have their levels of economic and social development been low; their cohesion seems somewhat more questionable than that of Uruguay, Costa Rica, or Chile.

At the same time, several countries that rank fairly high for legitimation of oppositions (for example, Panama and Ecuador) do so, even in 1970, under the aegis of limited-participation aristocracies whose bases have broadened somewhat but which have not yet really accepted the effective participation of new groups in the direction of their societies. The degree of acceptance of the opposition role in these countries may well reflect the ability of their respective elites so far to forestall, rather than resolve, their nations' crises of participation.

Finally, the Latin American experience has shown that the close relationship between development and the growth of a genuinely competitive politics still leaves a margin for individual leadership. Politicians who have become established in office through coups, civil wars, or the internal co-optative processes of an incumbent party and who have had the personal following or other political resources to maintain themselves indefinitely in power have, nonetheless, gone out of their way at times to enhance the status of the opposition and even smooth the way for its victory. Thus José Batlle y Ordóñez, caudillo of the Uruguayan Colorado party during the early decades of the twentieth century, was the chief proponent of the idea of a collegiate executive in that country. José Figueres, leader of the victorious forces in a brief civil war in Costa Rica in 1948, gave way to the duly elected president within a year. As chief executive several years later, he presided over elections in which the opposition won the presidency and was permitted to assume power, notwithstanding pressures from within his own party to nullify the results. In this sense personalism has occasionally been used to mobilize traditional-style political loyalties for the support of new institutional patterns, thus helping to effect a transfer from a charismatic to a rational pattern of legitimacy which includes respect for an opposition.

The emergence of institutionalized oppositions in the developing countries may be substantially dependent on a variety of economic and social preconditions. Yet the fact that some countries appear to run politically ahead of such preconditions and others behind them — and that there have been both advances and retreats in most countries in the process — suggests a creative role of some significance for such factors as individual leadership and the behavior of elites.

VARIANCES IN PARTY SYSTEMS   Comparative delineation of the cleavage patterns that legitimate party oppositions have assumed in Latin America is made difficult by the instability of parties and of constitutional governments. None of the currently legal Guatemalan parties existed prior to 1955, for example, while in Brazil the military government abolished the old parties in 1965 and decreed the creation of new ones in their stead. It is nonetheless evident that, whereas the nineteenth-century norm tended to be two parties (or factions or tendencies), today it is a multiplicity of parties. (For a classification of Latin American party systems, see table 7.4.) At the same time, the traditional intraelite cleavages have been replaced or complicated by interclass conflicts and by coalitions that cut across social classes to unite around broadly defined goals of development.

The principal exceptions to the multiparty system in Latin America are broadly of three types, constituting for the most part merely apparent or artificial deviations from the norm. The first occurs where all parties have been abolished or suspended (Argentina since 1966, though before that time the country had many legal parties) or where party life is so rudimentary as to comprise a de facto no-party system (Haiti). The second group of exceptions is made up of the surviving traditional two-party systems of Uruguay, Colombia, Honduras, and Nicaragua. Yet, especially in the first two countries, parties have often been characterized by a myriad of semiautonomous, competing factions; and in both nations a series of constitutional provisions has been largely responsible for freezing the party system into a formally dualistic mold. Brazil, too, has today a two-party system, but virtually by governmental dictate.

Lastly, there are the one-party systems that have emerged out of social revolutions (Cuba under Castro, Mexico since 1929, and Bolivia between 1952 and 1964 under the aegis of the MNR). In at least the Mexican and Bolivian cases, the dominant parties have been in an important sense pluralistic, for they have incorporated explicit voices for categorical groupings such as workers and peasants, with the single party serving as a framework for bargaining over patronage, policy, and other benefits. In both cases there have continued to exist several minor parties which have been permitted to win a few legislative seats, though never effectively to challenge the incumbency of the dominant party.

Although constitutional and electoral arrangements have helped to preserve the facade of two-party systems in such countries as Uruguay and Colombia, similar factors are insufficient to explain such diversity as does exist elsewhere in the number of parties. In fact, most Latin American countries have plurality elections for the presidency and some version of proportional representation elections for the legislature.[53] Ethnic and linguistic subcultures likewise have little relevance as causal factors, since the large Indian minorities in several countries lack discrete political organization. Even when deep-seated social revolutions (such as the Bolivian and Mexican) have involved the Indian, the primary issue has been land, not ethnic or cultural conflict.

53. The result is often a proliferation of party lists in legislative elections, combined with a marked reduction in the number of presidential candidates. Two- or three-candidate presidential elections, with each candidate supported by several parties, are quite common.

Table 7.4 Political Party Systems in Latin America (1970)

Country	Number of Parties*	Remarks
Argentina	0	Parties abolished 1966. Previously multiparty.
Bolivia	Multi	Nominally multiparty, though military now dominant. Ruled 1952–64 by a single official party, which effected the Revolution of 1952.
Brazil	2	Made two-party, in effect by government fiat, in 1965. Prior to that, multiparty.
Chile	Multi	Five parties with over 10 percent of vote. Multiparty since late nineteenth century.
Colombia	2	Nominally two-party, but various factions operate virtually as independent parties.
Costa Rica	Multi	Three principal parties, with tendency to bipolarity in presidential elections.
Cuba	1	Single party a fusion of old Communist party and various newer movements supporting the Castro Revolution.
Dominican Republic	Multi	Party system fragmented, though with some underlying tendency toward bipolarity.
Ecuador	Multi	Party system in flux: includes remnants of traditional parties and various ad hoc parties and coalitions.
El Salvador	Multi	Until about 1964 dominated by single official party. Latter now has fairly strong competition from other parties, with an incipient tendency to bipolarity.
Guatemala	Multi	Individual parties have been notably short-lived. Three main parties at present.
Haiti	0	In effect a no-party system.
Honduras	2	Occasional splits within major parties lead to temporary multiparty situations.
Mexico	1	An official party, an outgrowth of the Revolution, dominates system.
Nicaragua	2	Splinters (formed when both traditional parties split in two during the 1930s and 1940s) are currently of little importance.
Panama	0	Currently under military rule. Formerly multiparty, characterized by shifting party alliances and coalitions.
Paraguay	1	Formally multiparty, but one party rules in alliance with military to exclusion of effective opposition.
Peru	0	Parties suspended since October 1968. Formerly three major parties, two of which form congressional coalition to oppose government.
Uruguay	2	Several virtually autonomous factions nominally operate under rubric of each major party.
Venezuela	Multi	Four or five main parties, with cabinet normally a coalition of two or more.

* Classifications are the author's, based on a wide variety of sources. They say nothing, of course, of the relative importance of the respective party systems in carrying out such political functions as interest aggregation and decision making.

Differences in party systems seem to be accounted for, rather, by such things as the timing and nature of the impact of the newer categorical groupings, the tenacity of traditional bifactionalism and of the particular cleavages which evoked and sustained it, and by the presence or absence of a social revolution seeking simultaneously to mobilize a mass base and restrict or eliminate opposition.

Meanwhile, the emergence of class-based parties and of modernizing coalitions is rather closely correlated with such indicators of development as GNP per capita, literacy, and voter participation. In most of the Central American countries, Haiti, Paraguay, and Ecuador, such parties either have not appeared at all or have played but minor or fleeting roles. The categorical groupings that elsewhere have served as the bases for such parties are in these countries so far fairly rudimentary. By the same token, their party systems have been unable to pose much of a counterweight to such nonparty oppositions as "private governments" and the military. In Colombia the deep hold on the national psyche of loyalties to the two traditional parties, the artificial restrictions of the National Front, and the Tory reformism of the elite have forestalled the emergence of parties of a newer style and preserved the dominance of the Liberals and Conservatives. However, the nearly successful campaign for the presidency in 1970 of Gustavo Rojas Pinilla, the former dictator, at the head of a populistic political movement suggests that Colombia, too, may be changing in this respect.

Of course underlying such differences as those in the number of parties, in the specific configuration of political cleavages, or even in the form which oppositions take — that is, whether or not they assume the guise of political parties in the first place — are the nature of oppositional goals and demands and in particular their positions concerning the rapidity and degree of change.

Three broadly defined orientations may be discerned. One looks to the promotion of economic growth, usually by creating favorable conditions for private entrepreneurship, while seeking to confine to the minimum necessary the redistribution of social rewards, the expansion of effective political participation, and those manifestations of nationalism that may alienate foreign aid and foreign investment. Colombia's traditional parties and, in many Latin American countries, such nonparty oppositions as "private governments" and the military adhere to this position. A second set of goals is reformist. It propounds an increased economic role for the state, more rapid social change, expanded political participation, and a more explicit nationalism — but at rates, and by means, that will bring the agreement and cooperation of as many as possible within the system. Christian democratic and social democratic parties fall in this category, which is also the most frequently associated with demands for a legitimate role for oppositions. The third, revolutionary, approach seeks rapid and wholesale change in all areas, as well as the elimination altogether of the power of established elites. These are the objectives of the numerous, but as yet small and relatively unsuccessful, urban and rural guerrilla movements.

These several approaches have many of the concerns of development in common. They differ in the extent and speed of change which they seek and in their posture toward the established system. The distinctions among them, painted here in admittedly very broad strokes, play a large part in shaping the other dimensions of political contention in contemporary Latin America.

THE FUTURE   There is as yet no Latin American country where an institutionalized role for the political opposition has been definitively accepted. Moreover, the posited long-term trend toward the increasing importance of an arena of legitimate opposition has been subject to some striking lapses. Notably, in several of Latin America's major countries, Argentina, Brazil, and Peru, the military has within the last few years stepped in to abolish or drastically modify existing patterns of opposition. In these and similar cases, incumbent politicians have been charged with sponsoring unacceptable social and political changes, with sheer ineffectiveness in promoting national development, or with undermining the national interest or dignity. In yet other instances, as in Cuba, it is social revolution that has proved destructive of the legitimate oppositional role.

It is possible that the strains of development, with their implied threat to important actors in the current system, on the one hand, and with their stimulus to still other actors to drastically revise the existing social and political order, on the other, will lead to periods of authoritarianism that will indefinitely hold back the process of the institutionalization of oppositions. In fact, there seemed a discernible tendency during the 1960s for Latin American politics to polarize between an authoritarianism of the right — seeking to minimize social and political change — and an authoritarianism of the left — seeking to maximize it.

Throughout Latin American history, development, broadly defined, has often had contradictory effects. Thus in the nineteenth century the early stages of development witnessed the creation of centralizing autocracies in some nations, the emergence of semicompetitive regimes in others. The twentieth century has seen the growth of electoral and legislative oppositions, on the one hand, and of various forms of noninstitutionalized oppositions on the other.

Nevertheless, taking Latin America as a whole, the expansion in levels of political participation and the complication of social and economic processes seem, so far at least, to have on balance spurred the evolution of a legitimate oppositional role. The increased tolerance, pluralism, participation, and interdependence presumably resulting from development may thus be promotive of institutionalized competition over the long pull, even while there is a continued propensity to resort to authoritarianism at particular junctures of crisis in the developmental process. More typical of Latin America, in any event, than a gradual, essentially uninterrupted, progression from autocracy or absolute monarchy to full-fledged constitutional democracy (or constitutional monarchy), as in the European case, has been the alternation of periods of constitutional rule with periods of dictatorship. Cyclical patterns are clearly in evidence, along with the long-term trend-line.[54]

In this connection it is perhaps worth noting that even oppositions within military dictatorships seem generally to be accorded wider scope than was the case in the days of Porfirio Díaz and Juan Vicente Gómez. A certain, albeit strictly limited, criticism of the regime is often tolerated, while a relatively wide spectrum of organized groups is able to present demands or to resist the implementation of government policies (as has been the case with labor in contemporary Argentina). On occasion, such opposition is institutionalized, as with the token opposition party in post-1964 Brazil.

Moreover, successful social revolution has been the exception in Latin America and will probably continue to be so, despite the proliferation of revolutionary groups during the decade of the 1960s. Again, where new political actors (labor unions, the peasantry, and various middle-sector organizations) are admitted to the political system as they demonstrate a power capability but where the old actors remain very much on stage,[55] the likely pattern is a political process which, amid the new diversity, advances in its respect for political oppositions. At the same time, the system can be expected to confront crises which will lead some political actors at times to employ violence to resolve them.

Development has also altered the patterns of cleavage according to which party oppositions were previously aligned, with the modernizing coalition tending to become a major element of Latin American politics at the expense not only of traditional political alignments but of the growth of a strictly class-based politics as well. It must be recognized that this could be a passing phase, characteristic of a brief transitional period prior to the full participative impact of sectors such as the campesinos and the urban marginals. A more advanced stage of economic and social modernization, plus the failure of modernizing coalitions to accomplish

54. For the incidence of "unequivocally dictatorial" governments over the period 1935–64, see Martin Needler, *Political Development in Latin Amercia: Instability, Violence, and Evolutionary Change* (New York: Random House, 1968), p. 41.
55. Charles Anderson has in this connection referred to Latin American political systems as "museums." See his "Toward a Theory of Latin American Politics."

their developmental tasks, might bring sharper divisions along class lines, accompanied by an increase in structural oppositions of the revolutionary variety. This might indeed be one interpretation of what happened in Chile, and certainly there are more active and vocal advocates of thoroughgoing social revolution than at any time in Latin American history.

Yet the experience of midtwentieth-century development in Latin America seems to indicate otherwise — that the political need to harness the wills and capacities of many groups behind broadly common goals of development, as well as the nature of the intraclass cleavages and interclass linkages forged in the developmental process, will tend to produce a political pattern centered on one or more modernizing coalitions. These in turn may be expected to compete with residual traditional parties; with more strictly middle-class parties, like the Radicals of Argentina and Chile; with usually small revolutionary parties directing their appeals primarily to slumdwellers or to the campesinos; and with occasional ad hoc, personalistic movements having no real programs and few effective ties with the categorical groupings of the modern age. In many instances modernizing coalitions will be the chief proponents of tolerance for other parties; in yet others they may well be the instruments through which authoritarianism provides itself with a mass base.

Finally, there is one aspect of the relationship between oppositions and development that we have so far ignored: how have openly competitive polities with organized oppositions fared as vehicles for development? Lucian Pye has suggested that competitive politics may in the end be the most effective road to development, despite the superficial attractions of authoritarian solutions.[56] In the Latin American context, the quite successful and largely authoritarian Mexican experience seems to suggest otherwise. Yet the importance of involving a variety of social groups in the decision-making process is not really gainsaid by the Mexican case. Indeed, the Mexicans themselves seem to be moving very timidly in the direction of more openly competitive politics. The persistent failure of Latin American military regimes to resolve their countries' problems of development, or even to provide very effective government except for short transitional periods, suggests that a political system which in some way reflects the increasing social pluralism and the new levels of participation and social mobilization may be essential for sustained development in "semideveloped" societies like those of Latin America.

At the same time, cases such as Chile and Uruguay, as well as Argentina

56. Pye, "Party Systems and National Development in Asia," especially pp. 394–96. For a similar view with particular reference to Latin America, see Charles W. Anderson, *Politics and Economic Change in Latin America* (Princeton, N.J.: Van Nostrand, 1967).

between 1916 and 1930, are reminders that increased political democracy does not ensure that a country will engage in a sustained march toward development. The existence of a competitive politics may serve merely to institutionalize a share in the system for the most articulate groups, while simultaneously preventing real structural change through the need to take into account politically those who stand to lose by change. Development may stop short of economic takeoff and the full integration of the lower classes into the social and political systems. The Venezuelan case, on the other hand, suggests that rapid development and organized opposition are by no means incompatible, given the presence of certain other conditions.[57]

The proposition that political democracy is the surest way to rapid development is thus even more problematic than our argument that development has in Latin America thus far been accompanied by the gradual, though erratic, emergence of legitimate oppositions.

57. One of those conditions may be the availability of sufficient economic surplus to enable the polity to satisfy new claimants without materially damaging established interests. In Venezuela's case, rich petroleum resources seem to have played such a role.

8

INDIA: OPPOSITIONS IN A CONSENSUAL POLITY

Rajni Kothari

In India there are many oppositions — of different types and at various levels — representing among them a majority of the people. At the same time, the need for consensus and cooperation is affirmed by all. A nation-building ethos emphasizes the need for integration and gets alarmed at centrifugal forces, especially with the forceful reminder of a long history of political fragmentation and disunity. The emphasis on economic development as a barometer of national well-being further stresses the need for integration and a pooling of talents and resources; and the growing politicization of regional and linguistic diversities and sectarian loyalties reinforces the feeling that oppositional trends must somehow be held in bounds. At the same time, the uninhibited development of competitive party politics and its penetration at so many levels of the social and administrative hierarchy have articulated a differentiated, highly varied structure of competition and dissent, which expresses itself in ever new forms and leads to changing organizational strategies from a variety of oppositional sites. All of this results in a unique style of nation building — a constant search for unanimity amid a shifting structure of factions — which is in many ways a continuation of the long Indian tradition of unity in diversity.

The characteristic lines along which the various oppositions have expressed themselves and the resulting patterns of consensus and dissensus may first be crudely stated.

1. It was from a very small and homogeneous (upper-class, English-educated) elite that the ruling class of India was formed, and it was from this ruling class that oppositional elements emerged. This gave a striking similarity of social background, general outlook, and predispositions among those who occupied positions of authority and those who opposed them. This situation has been perpetuated to the present day by (a) the

length of dominance of the Congress party and the fact that the more effective oppositions were carried out *within* the fold of the Congress and of the governmental and patronage structure to which it gave rise, (b) the process of selective assimilation in the Congress, through which leaders from other social groups have been coopted into the framework of dominance, and (c) the socialization within the Congress of the men who challenged its dominance.

2. Barring some extremist fringe movements, there has been no challenge to the basic values and goals of the democratic system.[1] There has, indeed, been a considerable agreement on procedural matters too.

3. There is much ambiguity and lack of precise differentiation in the government-opposition continuum and in the competing patterns of coalition that have emerged at various levels. There is in Indian politics a constant tendency toward accommodation by agglomerating various subgroups into a loose and amorphous organizational structure, reflecting the cultural style of traditional Indian society.[2] The result is a fragmented and amorphous structure of authority that breeds even more fragmented oppositions, which are often hard to distinguish from the coalitions in power. This makes it difficult to identify positions and demarcations; all entities seem to dissolve into "the ruling class." [3]

4. The oppositional forces, organized as well as unorganized, have proved more effective in pressing their differences on matters of policy and implementation where the structure of authority is stable and continuous than where its margin of preponderance is either negligible or shifting. The former condition has enabled a process of bargaining and alignment between different kinds of opposition, on the one hand, and groups within the ruling party, on the other, thus leading to a differenti-

1. The positions of these fringe movements within the parties on the extreme ends of the tradition-modern continuum have varied with the parliamentary fortunes of the opposition parties, a majority of whom have by now had a taste of governmental power somewhere in the country. With the exception of the Dravida Munnetra Kazhagam (DMK) in Tamilnadu (formerly called Madras), however, none of these have remained in power for long.

2. The concept of *agglomeration* of a large variety of groups into a common cultural stream, as distinct from *aggregation,* emphasizes the assimilative and additive components of organization over against open confrontation and polarization. For an insightful treatment of this theme in the context of Hindu society, see Iravati Karve, *Hindu Society: An Interpretation* (Poona, India: Deccan College, 1961).

3. In party politics itself, the long period of Congress rule has led to a gross differentiation between "government" and "opposition," so much so that even when other parties have formed a government, as they did after the fourth general elections in 1967, the tendency to brand them as "opposition" persisted, even among the leaders of the non-Congress parties. However, apart from this gross Congress/non-Congress (or Congress/opposition) differentiation, no distinctions are clear; and the shifting patterns of coalition across this nominal boundary make it difficult to identify the different elements except in an ad hoc fashion. The situation is even more blurred in regard to the nonparty oppositions.

ated and varied representation of dissenting opinion and conflicts of interest. The latter condition lacks the necessary stability for sustained bargaining and precipitates a situation in which the representative and dissenting aims of the oppositions give place to a general preoccupation with the seizure of power.

5. Similarly, the rules of the game have worked more smoothly — and generally in keeping with democratic conventions — when the margin that divides authority from opposition is comfortable than when it is not, for the latter case provides scope to dissident forces to challenge the apparently established conventions.

6. There is an increase in the tendency of the opposition to subordinate other goals to the simple aim of displacing those who happen to be in power. As a result, while there is considerable consensus on fundamentals, there is great structural and organizational fluidity, with a consequent erosion of political authority and a decline of its "majesty." The ambiguous concept of democracy lends justification to a shifting structure of loyalties and the recurring phenomenon of defection from parties and coalitions on grounds of presumed injustice. As democracy entails both representative and plebiscitary connotations, it lends justification to populist strands (including mob actions) and weakens the authority of governments and of constitutional techniques of protest. Frustration in the struggle for power — or in maintaining a coalition intact — has often led to populist pressures as against the legitimacy of legislative majorities. This has made the pursuit of normal channels of opposition and defection vulnerable to defeat by extremist politics, and it has put a special premium on skills that distract from the normal pursuit of parliamentary politics and administrative programs.

7. The structure of various oppositions and of alignments among them tends to be highly personalized and badly organized. There is a continuing tendency toward factionalism and the maintenance of the various personalized and factional identities, thus preventing amalgamations and larger, stronger organizations. When such amalgamations or alliances are tried, they remain short-lived and exhibit a lack of sustained and purposive institution building among opposition groups. The result is a wide spread of oppositional activity which, however, fails to aggregate into an effective force, thus often giving rise to frustration and anomic behavior. The general consequence is fragmentation in the ranks of opposition and its inability to challenge the dominance of the Congress party.

8. There is a wide range in the strategies of opposition and the sites in which they are carried out — from friendly persuasion of the prime minister and reasoned advocacy on the floor of Parliament to organized mob violence and general strikes. The overall thrust, however, is toward making greater demands on the government and toward a wider distribu-

tion of political goods, both within and outside the framework of the dominant party.

9. The simultaneous vertical and lateral structuring of power in the context of a federal polity gives rise to alternative targets of oppositional activity, including opposition from one level of government against another level (where another party is in power), which provides an easy scapegoat for one's own failures and inadequacies. The same party, operating as government at one level and as opposition at another, should normally gain a heightened sense of realism and responsibility. Under circumstances of instability of power, however, this can also lead to a diminution of accountability and competition at faultfinding. Both tendencies are at work in India.

10. Adult franchise has led to an incremental involvement of traditional structures of caste and class in the national framework of political mobilization. This has meant increasing demands by a wide variety of groups vis-à-vis the government and a further fragmentation of the structure, variety, and sites of oppositions. The Indian strategy of integration through politicization of a highly differentiated social system inevitably makes the transition to stable, institutionalized politics full of ambivalence and fluidity.[4] Under such conditions, oppositions thrive but without acquiring a clear identity and an organized character.

11. Such a thriving and proliferation of oppositional activity in the functioning of national and regional politics has led to another kind of opposition, especially from the intellectual elements in the country, and more particularly from the economic developmentalists. This group calls for an end to excessive competition in the system and sees a need for a more authoritarian system, with a view to pushing through a faster rate of economic growth. The fact that the social base from which these intellectual elements come, namely the urbanized middle classes, has provided a traditional source of opposition rather than loyalty to the Congress, counter-posed by the facts that most intellectuals still consider the expression of dissent and freedom of opinion as values worth preserving and that they know that only the Congress is capable of bringing about the necessary changes, has of course led to further ambivalence in the relationship between intellectual opinion in India and the political system it is trying to develop. But such opinion is an important strand in the fabric of oppositions found in India.

All in all, then, there is a great variety of oppositions in India, considerable tolerance of each kind, and much ambivalence in regard to their value.

4. For a theoretical statement of the strategy of integration through politicization, see "A Theory of Indian Politics" in "Working Paper on Electoral Behaviour in India," *Party System and Election Studies*, Occasional Papers of the Centre for the Study of Developing Societies, no. 1 (New Delhi: Allied Publishers, 1967).

A Tradition of Pluralism

Before discussing these trends in the context of recent and contemporary Indian history, it seems worthwhile to look briefly at the elements in India's tradition that inform such a pattern of political alignments and oppositions. Are there any elements in India's history and culture which help to explain such a ready and willing acceptance of political opposition as a legitimate activity? If so, in what way do they condition the present structure and style of dissensus and consensus? Or is this an entirely new phase in Indian history?

The striking thing about India's historical culture is the great variety and heterogeneity that it has encompassed and preserved. This is owing to many reasons — the diversity of ethnic and religious groups that have come in succession and settled down; the eclectic rather than proselytizing style of spiritual integration characteristic of Hinduism; the absence of either a unifying theology or a unifying and continuous secular tradition; and above all, a highly differentiated social system that has brought functional hierarchies, spatial distinctions, and ritual distances into a manifold frame of identifications and interdependence. The result of all this has been a continuous pattern of coexistence between diverse systems and life styles; persistence of local subcultures and primary loyalties; an intermittent, unstable, and discontinuous political center; and an essentially apolitical social tradition.

These pluralistic structures and life styles were woven into a common fabric through patterns of dominance that were institutionalized in a legitimized status hierarchy. It was through a privileged elite (of Brahmins), drawn from a very narrow social base and commanding institutionalized charisma and authoritative pedagogic and arbitrational roles, that the heterogeneity of Hindu society was contained within a common social structure, mythology, and tradition. What united the elite itself was neither a theology nor any other kind of uniform doctrine but rather their status in society as providers of authority and wisdom — a status they enjoyed by virtue of birth, privileged training, and the deference due those who were so born and trained. The skills they deployed were essentially sophistic and arbitrational; there was considerable scope for dissent, ambiguity, and reinterpretation; and both their status and their function epitomized society's structural differentiation and its autonomy from political encroachment by the kings and their administrators.

Thus by long experience India has learned to be tolerant of pluralism, dissent, and opposition. It has also displayed a high tolerance of ambiguity. At the same time, through the centuries it has developed what may be called a consensual style in dealing with problems and issues. Important components of this consensual style are respect for status hierarchies, resort to arbitration in disputes arising from ambivalence in the status system, accent on unanimity and on talking out a point of difference instead of forcing a decision, a tendency toward segmentation of issues and their resolution rather than their cumulation, and a generally high legitimacy for institutionalized roles at various points in the authority structure of society. This style is further buttressed by a dispersed, fragmented, and intermittent system of authority and a long-standing cynicism in regard to the use and abuse of power. Over the centuries Indians have also been used to wide disparities in material comforts and in their access to positions of influence and power, and they have shown a marked tolerance of deprivation and humiliation. All these characteristics of Indian tradition — tolerance of dissent and ambiguity, tolerance of deprivation, and a consensual style operating through intermittent structures of arbitration and institutionalized roles — inform the patterns of opposition in contemporary India, characterize its structures, strategies, styles, and sites, and account for its wide diffusion and relative lack of aggregation.

Many of these patterns are, of course, new and have been crystallized through various political structures in India's modern constitution: the party and electoral systems, the federal system of politics and administration (down to the districts, blocks, and *panchayats*), the legislative forums, and the caste and communal configuration underlying politics. But, although the modern forms of opposition are relatively recent in India, whose democratic constitution is only a little more than twenty years old, the fact that they have become so quickly legitimated and in a measure institutionalized can be explained only by reference to its long traditions. As many of these traditions were both reflected and given a concrete shape in the movement for national independence, it is instructive to look briefly at this powerful background of contemporary Indian politics.

The Nationalist Movement

The Congress movement for independence was itself in the nature of an opposition, a protest movement against the regime. Its function was not limited to ousting the alien government from power and succeeding it; the movement also fulfilled the other functions of opposition — criticism of policies, competition for popular support, ventilation of sectional and national grievances, noncooperation and nonviolent protest within the framework of accepted norms of a liberal democracy, and participation and even willing cooperation at lower levels of the government for short periods. Furthermore, the Congress was more than mere opposition against the British rule. It also constituted a massive, stubborn opposition to several features of traditional Hindu society. Social reform was as much at the heart of its program as national independence, emphatically till the 1920s and then in a more complicated form during the Gandhian phase of the movement. Gandhi provided a powerful symbolism to his drive for national regeneration. He called the untouchables the "sons of God"; he made the cottage industry of homespun *khadi* prescribed clothing for everyone who claimed to be a nationalist; he implored educated urban youth to accept austere living and engage in "village uplift" and the eradication of age-old social evils. Expression of dissent against certain traditional practices and concerted movements for their eradication, without repudiating the total framework of Hindu social ethic — indeed, preserving it by reinterpreting it — constituted an important part of the Congress program of mobilization and socialized its cadres in the conventions of constructive opposition.

Furthermore, like any broad oppositional movement, the Congress permitted within its fold several splinter groups with differing emphases of ideology and strategy; and it tolerated defecting groups which set up other parties, either regionally or nationally.[5] Other groups also arose outside its fold and contested its claims to represent the interests of this or that section of the people.[6] Finally, ideological groups with distinctive programs and constitutions of their own were allowed to continue within the Congress until the coming of independence. Notable among these were the Congress Socialist party and the Congress Communist party, both of which ultimately left the Congress and set themselves up as discrete political parties. The Congress all along strove to secure the cooperation of these groups and parties; in the case of the Muslim League, it entered into a coalition in 1946, when the first national government constituted wholly of Indians was set up in Delhi, a year before the British finally left the subcontinent. Thus the traditions of oppositional politics and of

5. Thus a group of liberals, differing from the majority opinion in the Congress, established the Swaraj party in 1923. Similarly, the socialists within the Congress set up the Congress Socialist party in 1934. This party was to be the basis of a whole line of socialist parties that were formed after independence.

6. The Justice party was formed in Madras in 1917 on a difference of strategy among Congressmen and with a view to mobilizing non-Brahmin sections in Madras. A Unionist party was formed in Punjab in 1936; the Congress merged with it in the 1944 elections. The Hindu Mahasabha arose in 1925, partly no doubt to protect the rights of the Hindus, but also as a Maharashtrian splinter group from the Hindi-speaking majority in Central and West India. The Communist party of India was set up in 1924, and the Forward Block, consisting of defecting Congressmen under the leadership of an outstanding former Congress president, was formed in 1940. Other more intellectual types of parties, like the Radical Democratic party under M. N. Roy, were set up by men who had at one time belonged to the Congress. Above all, the Muslim League was formed in 1905 and, after a long period of mild constitutional activity, became an active contestant of the Congress in its claim to represent the interests of the Muslims. Similarly, under Dr. B. N. Ambedkar, a well-known jurist and scholar, the Scheduled Caste Federation was set up to serve the interests of the downtrodden castes of untouchables and to contest the claim of the Congress to serve their cause.

tolerance and accommodation of contesting groups were already part of the Congress ethos before it came to power, quite apart from its general commitment to a secular, democratic constitution and liberal political values.

It should also be remembered that in India even under colonialism there had been a steady expansion of electoral franchise. Several elections were held, though under a very restricted franchise, and different parties prospered as a result, not the least being the Congress itself, which held the reins of government at the provincial level from 1937 to 1939.[7] Congressmen as well as other distinguished men of affairs ran for election to the Central Assembly. They also held positions in agencies of local self-government and various district boards and municipalities, where they acquired considerable patronage and administrative experience. These elections to local and provincial assemblies — and in a lesser degree to the Central Assembly — exposed a generation of Indian politicians to parliamentary procedures and decorum. Some of these men were to lend advice and impart dignity to the functioning of India's full-fledged parliamentary system after independence.

More important than all this, however, was the continuous ideological commitment to liberal democracy which India sustained for more than sixty years, with almost total consensus on all sides. This commitment laid the essential foundation of its political culture, in which opposition and dissent were as important ingredients as consensus and unanimity. Indeed, the latter very subtly included the former, as we shall see when we examine the party system. On the other hand, it should be emphasized that opposition as a strategic ingredient of India's political culture functioned in diffuse and varied ways — indeed, in far too varied ways to allow for any effective consolidation in the form of strong and viable opposition parties. It is this fact that shapes the more prominent features of postindependence oppositional politics.

Independence and the Development of Non-Congress Fronts

Independent India inherited two considerable frameworks of authority, one represented by the network of bureaucracy, the other by the organization of the Congress movement. The introduction of adult franchise as a means of building a national political community provided the dynamic core of a wide variety of institutional innovations, competitive trends, and problems of adjustment in the functioning of both these frameworks of authority.

The process crystallized through the party system. It was a party

7. In 1939 Congressmen resigned from office, protesting against the British government's associating India with the war effort without consulting the Congress.

system with a difference, oriented toward building an authoritative structure of political affiliations throughout the nation and weaving these into the framework of organization inherited from a nationalist mass movement, rather than toward extending two or more parliamentary groups into the constituencies in the wake of an extended franchise, as happened in some Western countries. The consequence of directing political mobilization through the movement's organizational network, which now assumed the role of the ruling party, while at the same time permitting dissenting elements to organize themselves into oppositional and factional pressures, was the rise of a pattern of dominance and dissent that determined the framework of subsequent changes in the party system. This system also provided a mechanism for involving traditional as well as modern elites in the processes of planned economic development.

The system was crystallized through three general elections, which established the dominance of the Congress party and its command of vast resources and commitments as an integral feature of the developing political system. It was this system of one-party dominance, providing a somewhat different framework of competition from those of Western democracies, which enabled the nation to grapple with simultaneous problems of integration and development.[8] This type of party system led to political consolidation at various levels, provided substantial cushioning through the mobilization of rural support, and — for the first time in Indian history — enabled the government to reach out into the villages.

Responding to this system, there emerged a very large number of social and political organizations at all levels, pressing upon the government and the dominant party for participation, resources, and recognition, as well as for specific policy changes and administrative actions. As the authority and legitimacy of the system spread, these demands and aspirations crystallized and found their place in the framework of one-party dominance, either as part of the factional network within the Congress party or as pressures from outside, exerted individually or through other political parties.

This factional structure within the Congress party aggregated at the state level through ad hoc, intermittent polarizations between the ministerial and organizational wings of the party, the organizational group

8. For a discussion of this model, see the series by Rajni Kothari, "Form and Substance in Indian Politics," especially the article "Party System," *Economic Weekly* 13, no. 22 (3 June 1961):847–54. A more recent and detailed account is given in Rajni Kothari, "The Congress System in India," *Asian Survey* 4, no. 12 (December 1964):1161–73, reprinted in *Party System and Election Studies* (note 4). See also W. H. Morris-Jones, "Parliament and Dominant Party: Indian Experience," *Parliamentary Affairs* 17, no. 3 (Summer 1964):296–307, and his "Dominance and Dissent," *Government and Opposition* 1, no. 4 (July 1966):451–66. For a detailed trend analysis of the system, see Gopal Krishna, "One Party Dominance — Development and Trends," in *Party System and Election Studies.*

performing the representative role of opposition and often leading to a turnover of governmental elites. Furthermore, as the elaborate group structure of the Congress party reflected almost all shades of opinion and interest, there quickly developed a series of structural relationships between oppositional groups outside the party and corresponding factions within it. Issues, regional and sectarian loyalties, and an increasing determination to make demands on the government were found to cut across party identifications and make for more comprehensive communication channels.

This role of the opposition in structuring the internal operation of the ruling party was a peculiar feature of the Indian system for a long time. It enabled the Congress to remain in power because the party was periodically undergoing change and alternation in parliamentary and governmental personnel.[9] It also led to a sense of efficacy among opposition parties, despite their thin chances of assuming governmental power for almost twenty years. At the same time, dissidence within the dominant party continued and often found easy outlets because of the multiparty nature of the opposition outside the Congress. It was the availability of such dissidence that ultimately crystallized the anti-Congress coalitions in various states after the fourth general elections, held in February 1967.

Starting sometime before the death of Nehru in 1964, the competitive arena within the Congress began expanding around both persons and issues, and after 1967 it began to spill over outside the Congress. The Congress was never a united party, nor could it be expected to be so, given the fact that the more significant political competition had to be waged within the Congress at different levels, with the opposition parties playing a catalytic role from outside the "margin of pressure." [10] Nehru's contribution in the consolidation of the Congress party's authority was immense, but the manner in which he operated the system suffered from two disadvantages. Because of his dominant personality, the national party organization was not allowed to perform its strategic role in the system, with the result that the large number of conflicts that took place at both governmental and organizational levels in different states did not articulate into aggregate structures of competing elites and policy groups. In a developing society, party organizations have to play an important role in building channels of communication between the people and the government. On the other hand, there is an equally pressing need to maintain and stabilize the government's authority to pursue secular, national goals and to withstand the demands and pressures emanating from various factional groups with some firmness. Nehru's style, though it inevitably

9. Kothari, "Party System," and Morris-Jones, "Dominance and Dissent." For turnover of elites even while the Congress held the monopoly of power, see table 8.2.
10. "Congress System in India," p. 1162.

sought a balance between these two needs of the system, tended to emphasize the latter.

The second disadvantage came from the nature of the elite over which Nehru presided. As the functioning of the system rested so much on personal relationships between the prime minister and various factional leaders in the states, it limited the articulation of interests and the growth of public opinion on the basis of specific differences of policies and programs. Such articulation took more informal forms, with the result that an understanding of the system was limited to just a few among the nation's decision makers. Toward the end of Nehru's life, with his own grip weakening and with powerful new forces emerging from the state level — symbolized in a dramatic manner in the Kamaraj Plan[11] — the real drawback of such an elite structure was exposed. Instead of senior leaders relinquishing government positions and attending to party building at the grass roots, as stipulated in the Kamaraj Plan, what took place was that, with the death of Nehru, Congress bosses aggregated at the national level and a new kind of conflict developed right at the center of the system, in the form of governmental versus organizational groups, the latter taking on the form of a coalition of regional leaders. Two quick successions and the struggle over nominations of Congress candidates to the various legislatures in the fourth general elections in 1967 crystallized this conflict within the Congress, contributed to a decline in its cohesion, and encouraged large numbers of Congressmen to defect from the party. This benefited the various non-Congress parties, which were able successfully to challenge the dominance of the Congress in many states in 1967 and to form united fronts of these parties with a view to installing non-Congress coalition governments in these states.[12]

---

11. The Kamaraj Plan was adopted by the All India Congress Committee on 10 August 1963. The resolution incorporating it was moved by K. Kamaraj, who was then the chief minister of Madras (now renamed Tamilnadu). The main idea of the plan was to secure the voluntary relinquishment of their ministerial posts by senior Congressmen to enable them to devote all their time to the organizational work of the party, so that the "unhealthy trend" noticeable in the formation of groups and factions in the party and the consequent "loosening of the Congress organization" could be arrested.

Following the unanimous adoption of the resolution, all ministers at the center and in the states submitted their resignations to the Working Committee, which authorized Prime Minister Nehru to decide which of the resignations would be accepted. On 24 August, Nehru submitted to the committee the names of six central cabinet ministers and six chief ministers who should be asked to take up organizational work. The committee accepted his suggestions and the resignations of the twelve senior leaders were duly forwarded to the Union president and state governors for acceptance.

12. The term *united fronts* covers all the non-Congress coalition fronts that were formed after the 1967 elections. The exact names differ from state to state. We shall use the generic term in order to avoid confusion and the need to translate local nomenclatures.

The outcome of the 1967 elections was a considerable diminution of the Congress party's hold on governmental power, although it left undisturbed the policy priorities, the ideological balance, and the coalition style of politics initiated by the Congress.[13] When the Congress returned to a dominant position once again in 1971–72, it found that not much had changed in the intervening period. As already indicated, the important consequence of the organization of party politics around the Congress for a generation was that the post-1967 political developments have found their major stimuli in the fragmentation and consolidation of the Congress itself, rather than in the emergence of any viable alternative to it, although alternatives have emerged in one or two states (Tamilnadu — and of course Kerala, where a Communist government had provided an alternative to the Congress as early as 1957).

The emergence of united fronts against the Congress in 1967 broke the monopoly of the Congress, essentially by a greater convergence between votes polled and seats won (see table 8.1), thus reducing the traditional advantage of the Congress accruing from a simple majority, single-constituency electoral system. On the other hand, the fragmentation of the Congress extended to a fragmentation of the party system as a whole. Thus not only did there come into being more than one Congress party in many states;[14] there have also been two (in some states three) Communist parties and two (in some states three or four) Socialist parties.[15] There are also extremist and moderate wings within the Jan Sangh, ex-Congress and non-Congress groups within the Swatantra party, and several fronts among the depressed sections, the scheduled castes, and the tribals — not to speak of the numerous splinter groups at the state level and the legion of independents, who constitute the largest single non-Congress bloc.

Above all, the coalitional pattern in the non-Congress states after 1967 consisted of a much more amorphous and heterogeneous assortment of

13. Six out of eight non-Congress coalition governments were headed by Congress dissidents. The "minimum programs" adopted by these governments were essentially restatements of traditional Congress policies of economic and social change. On the whole, 1967 represented greater continuity than change, a greater consolidation than dissipation of Congress consensus. For a more detailed analysis on these lines, see Rajni Kothari, "India's Political Transition," *Economic and Political Weekly*, Special Number, August 1967, pp. 1489–97.
14. In Kerala the dissidents formed a Kerala Congress and in West Bengal a Bangla Congress. In several other states a Jan Congress ("People's Congress") was set up against the official Congress party. In 1969 the parent organization was itself split, resulting in two congress parties known as the Ruling Congress, abbreviated as Congress (R), and the Organization Congress, abbreviated as Congress (O).
15. In 1971 the two main socialist factions, the Praja Socialist party (PSP) and the Samyukta Socialist party (SSP), both of which were at one time in a single party, were reunited to form the Socialist party of India. The new party, however, is still full of fissures.

Table 8.1 Congress Performance in Elections, 1952–1972

	1952		1957		1962		1967		1968/69[a]		1971/72[b]	
	Votes	Seats	Votes	Seats	Votes	Seats	Votes	Seats	Votes	Seats	Votes	Seats
Andhra Pradesh	31.51	34.33	41.72	61.75	47.25	59.00	45.42	57.49			52.11	76.31
Assam	43.91	72.38	52.35	67.62	48.25	75.24	43.60	57.94			53.19	83.33
Bihar	41.92	74.13	41.91	66.04	41.35	58.18	33.09	40.25	30.30	37.11	34.12	52.52
Gujarat	55.93	90.38	56.40	74.24	50.84	73.38	45.96	55.36			50.56	83.23
Haryana	40.31	83.60	45.85	70.91	40.42	57.41	41.33	59.26	43.88	59.26	46.90	64.20
Himachal Pradesh[c]							42.19	56.67			50.75	78.56
Jammu & Kashmir[d]							53.02	73.58			55.62	77.03
Kerala	35.75	38.28	37.85	34.13	34.42	50.00	35.43	6.77			17.70	22.56
Madhya Pradesh	44.53	76.56	49.83	80.56	38.54	49.31	40.67	56.42			48.14	74.32
Maharashtra	47.14	80.79	45.31	51.52	51.23	81.44	47.03	75.19			56.32	82.22
Mysore	51.28	77.10	52.08	72.60	50.22	66.35	48.43	58.33			53.56	76.39
Orissa	38.85	47.86	38.26	40.00	43.28	58.57	30.62	22.14			28.13	36.43
Punjab	30.73	53.64	48.51	82.56	45.74	56.98	37.74	45.19	39.19	36.54	42.84	63.46
Rajasthan	39.71	53.68	45.13	67.61	39.98	50.00	41.42	48.37			51.01	78.80
Tamilnadu[e]	38.41	47.83	45.34	73.66	46.14	67.48	41.38	21.37				
Uttar Pradesh	47.93	90.70	42.42	66.52	36.33	57.90	32.20	46.82	33.98	49.65		
West Bengal[f]	38.42	61.75	46.14	60.32	47.29	62.30	41.13	45.36	41.31	19.64	49.44	77.14
Lok Sabha	44.99	74.44	47.78	75.10	44.72	73.08	40.78	54.62			43.69	67.95

[a] Mid-term elections were held only in the states of Bihar, Punjab, Uttar Pradesh, and West Bengal in 1969 and in the state of Haryana in 1968.

[b] The fifth general elections were split, the Lok Sabha elections being held in 1971 and most of the assembly elections in 1972. However, elections to a few of the state assemblies (in Orissa, West Bengal, and Tamilnadu) were held in 1971 along with the Lok Sabha election. In 1972, all the states except Orissa, Tamilnadu, Uttar Pradesh, and Kerala (in each of which a mid-term election had already taken place and a stable government was in office) went to the polls.

[c] The Himachal Pradesh assembly started functioning from 1967.

[d] Prior to 1967 the Congress party did not directly contest the election in Jammu & Kashmir.

[e] In 1971, following an electoral understanding with DMK, the Congress party did not directly contest the assembly election in Tamilnadu.

[f] Assembly elections were held in West Bengal in 1971, but a stable government was not possible and President's Rule had to be imposed. Elections were held again in 1972 along with the other states. The data given in the table are from the 1972 election. In the 1971 election to the West Bengal assembly, the Congress party polled 37.91% of the votes and 29.25% of the seats, respectively.

groups and policy positions than had been the case in the factional coalitions within the Congress before 1967. The result has been that whereas
the process of defections from the Congress party led to a toppling of
Congress governments soon after the 1967 elections, several united front
governments were similarly toppled in only a few months.[16] This led to a
further fragmentation of party positions and a disenchantment with the
simple posture of anti-Congressism as a basis for uniting the opposition.
Parties like the Jan Sangh, which aspired to an all-India status, or the
Praja Socialist party (PSP), which was in principle opposed to being
associated with extremist parties, were increasingly found to part com-
pany with other groups in the united front.

In its attempt to break the hegemony of the Congress, the anti-Congress
united fronts in 1967 sought to develop an all-inclusive, or catchall,
strategy of coalition making. The Congress had all along been a characteristic catchall party, trying to encompass all the more relevant segments
of political reality, including a great many oppositional segments. It was
like Hindu society in miniature, accommodative and agglomerative, trying
to accomplish little but absorb a great deal, given less to specificity and
differentiation and more to consensus and catholicism. The Congress was
a grand coalition with great historical antecedents and represented the
Indian nation in all its essentials. The opposition parties, while they played
their minority roles in such a system, saw clearly that they could not
come into their own unless all the minorities came together and challenged the hegemony of the dominant party — which, anyway, at no
time enjoyed more than 45 percent of the votes in the country.

The high priest of such a strategy was the late Ram Manohar Lohia,
the socialist leader and founder of the SSP. He himself was a leader in the
art of defecting from established parties, but he soon realized the folly
of the enterprise and devoted himself assiduously to the mission of destroying the Congress monopoly of power by uniting all anti-Congress
forces in the country. Lohia was fairly successful in his mission: he
polarized the country along Congress versus anti-Congress lines and in the
process took on whoever was prepared to oppose the Congress. The immediate goal of dislodging the Congress from its position of dominance
was accomplished, but the results were hardly enduring, as Lohia himself
was to admit very soon. In the 1971 election to the Lok Sabha (the lower
house of the national Parliament), another attempt was made to evolve a
strong anti-Congress bloc, known as the "grand alliance," made up of the
Jan Sangh, the Swatantra, the Organization Congress, and the SSP,
but this too failed miserably.

16. The Congress lost power in five states as a result of the election. In three other
states it was toppled after the election as a result of "crossing the floor" by dissidents.
United front governments fell in five states in less than three months, from December
1967 to February 1968.

What is interesting is that when the all-inclusive style of the opposition confronted the hitherto all-inclusive style of the Congress, it was the latter that began to reform itself. Since 1967 the Congress has allowed dissidents to leave the party, and in 1969 it went through a major split, on the initiative of Mrs. Indira Gandhi, which has given to it a more cohesive character. It is now talking of developing a more disciplined party so that it can return to perform its historic task of transforming Indian society and removing the poverty of the masses with greater efficiency.

The changes brought about in the Congress party by Mrs. Gandhi reflect the nature of India's party system and the manner in which it responds to changes in both the political structure and the larger shifts that take place in the social and attitudinal characteristics of the people. The 1967 elections highlighted both the fact that the Indian voter had come of age and could not be manipulated by existing boss structures and vote banks based on caste and communal loyalties[17] and the fact that the Congress leadership, in its preoccupation with factional quarrels, had failed to measure up to people's expectations.[18] The lesson struck home and the Congress party began to respond to its defeat through an internal struggle for power that ended in a decisive win for the prime minister, Mrs. Gandhi, who had based her appeal on a forward-looking, progressive platform aimed at the much needed economic reforms. This led to a split in the Congress party in August 1969, the majority faction going with Mrs. Gandhi and the minority faction, the Organization Congress, joining hands with opposition parties like the Jan Sangh, Swatantra, and, later on, the SSP. In December 1970 Mrs. Gandhi, now heading a government which no longer enjoyed an absolute majority, decided to dissolve the Lok Sabha and appeal to the people, through a general election to the Lok Sabha in March 1971, for a mandate for the ruling party based on a left of center program of economic reconstruction. The ruling Congress was returned to power with an overwhelming majority, securing two-thirds of the Lok Sabha seats. A year later, in March 1972, elections to 16 (out of a total of 20) state assemblies were held, soon after the prolonged crisis in Bangla Desh and India's decisive victory in the war with Pakistan had led to a soaring popularity for Mrs. Gandhi and her party. The Congress was returned to power with sweeping majorities, capturing 14 out of 16 states. The two elections marked a return of the Congress party to dominance and to political stability throughout the country, following a five-year spell of instability in large parts of the country.

17. See D. L. Sheth, "Political Development of Indian Electorate," *Economic and Political Weekly*, Annual Number, 1970, pp. 137–48.
18. A national sample study of the Indian electorate at the time of the 1967 elections showed that the voters had grown highly critical of the performance of the Congress governments. See Rajni Kothari, *Politics in India* (Boston: Little Brown, and New Delhi: Orient Longmans, 1970), pp. 203–04.

The two elections not only reduced the opposition parties to their earlier position (they still got a sizable proportion of the votes cast but, thanks to fragmentation in their ranks, were unable to convert these into an adequate number of seats), but also settled the factional conflicts within the erstwhile Congress and reestablished a more cohesive center.

Smarting under the successful realignment of factional positions in the Congress and their own failure to make the most of the opportunity they were given in 1967, the opposition parties gave up their earlier approach to composite coalition making and, except for some local adjustments, faced the electorate once again (as was the case before 1967) as so many parties. Looking back, it appears that if the opposition parties had only continued on the path laid out by Lohia — resolved their differences and maintained an alliance platform on a sustained basis — they stood a good chance of providing an effective opposition to the Congress and, in a few states, even dislodging it from power. They appear, however, to lack the stamina for such sustained effort.

The Role of the Dominant Center

To describe or interpret any system that is still undergoing changes in structure and orientation may be a doubtful exercise, but it is still worthwhile to try. The institutionalization of a stable party system in India is likely to take quite some time, and in the meantime pressures for basic institutional changes are likely to be exerted increasingly by those who are keen on governmental performance and economic development, especially since the return to Congress dominance in 1971–72 was made possible by an accent on these factors. However, certain broad features of the party system and of government-opposition relationships can be discerned.

It is a system in which a historically dominant party is opposed by a large number of opposition parties and factional groupings that are dispersed throughout the country. The role of the dominant party has been to evolve a consensus on both normative and procedural matters, as well as on major policy issues. In such a system the dominant party becomes a norm-setter for all other parties, and the model set by the Congress has in fact been spreading, both in terms of policies and programs and in terms of coalition styles and consensus making. In this system it is the dominant party that acts as an aggregator by developing into a comprehensive, representative mechanism: it represents all shades of opinion, all major interest groups in the society, and indeed all other parties as well.

It is a system in which one set of coalitions is opposed by another set of coalitions. The dominant party itself is a coalition of factional and ideological groupings. So were the multiparty, anti-Congress coalitions that came to power in 1967. Whenever the other coalitions cease to be viable, the dominant party steps in and either develops another kind of coalition — by cooperating with other parties or defecting groups, or sometimes by backing a minority government formed by one of these groups, as has been the case in Kerala since 1970 — or uses its authority at the center in the form of President's Rule in the state or supersession of the functions of the state legislature by the national Parliament, as happened in a number of states throughout 1967–72. The upshot of all this is the continuance of a party system and of patterns of dominance and dissent that derive their characteristics from a polycentric opposition to a dominant center.

Oppositions in India emerge out of a pluralistic social and regional base and a long tradition and habit of reducing social organization to its fragments. Diverse kinds of oppositions are therefore natural constellations. At the same time it is the need to develop mechanisms of consensus making and focal centers of authority that has led to consolidations between the dominant party and various of the coalitions that oppose it. It should not be forgotten that it was the factional fragmentation of the dominant party and its failure to contain all the fragments that led to the mounting of the anti-Congress consolidations, which were further exercises in consensus making. They in turn were found to be even more fragmented and faction-ridden and ultimately succumbed to pressures from the dominant party when the latter sought to restore the status quo ante. All of this underlines the continuing importance of the consensus represented by the dominant party. The patterns that emerge form a cross between these twin tendencies of factionalism and consensus making. What the dominant party does is to provide a model organization around which each of these tendencies gravitates.

It is necessary to emphasize these characteristics at some length, as they bring out an important aspect of oppositions in developing democracies such as India. The crucial parameter in the building of a new nation is to build authoritative structures and procedures and to legitimate them in the eyes of various subsystems in the society. Oppositional activity within this developing framework, while it undoubtedly legitimates the framework and the consensus it represents, can also prove dysfunctional in carrying out its goals if it does not take place around the structures, personnel, and symbols of a dominant partner in the system. It is this establishment of a dominant center around which all kinds of oppositions are clustered that characterizes the system that India has been trying to operate for the past generation.

There are several historical-institutional features that have informed the development of the system. First, the Congress, when it came to power, assigned a positive and overwhelming role to government and politics in the development of society. Secondly, it made the power of the central authority the chief condition of natural survival. This power was not only consolidated but greatly augmented. Thirdly, it made legitimacy the principal issue of politics and gave to the government and the ruling party an importance of great symbolic value. "Only the Congress can be trusted": this is why only the Congress was the party of consensus. The political system was legitimated through identification with a particular leadership and its agents and heirs, in whom the symbolism of the Congress was concrete and manifest. Fourthly, the Congress in power had a concentration of resources, a monopoly of patronage, and a control of economic power which crystallized the structure of its power and made competition with it a difficult proposition. Fifthly, by adopting a competitive model of development, the Congress made mobilization and public cooperation a function of political participation rather than a bureaucratic control and police surveillance. With the passage of time this model opened up, brought new groups and parties into positions of power, led to a widening of the national consensus and a chastening of ideological and extremist sections within all parties, and made power the great moderator in politics. It is this system that still operates in India, despite periodical strains.

Relations between the Center and the States

The federal structuring of both dominance and dissent provides an important key to the process of consensus and competition within the Indian system. All non-Congress parties are essentially state-based, and the different patterns of opposition have found their optimum expression in the states. However, the more important non-Congress parties, such as the Jan Sangh, aspire to emerge at the national level and acquire an all-India image, even at the risk of affecting pockets of concentration of their strength in the regions. This has led to continuous center-state interactions, both within individual non-Congress parties and between them and the Congress. Because of the essentially regional standing of most of the parties and because of their increasing interaction with the national level following the decline of Congress predominance, the issue of a national consensus has in many respects become a federal question.

Here an important development is the emergence of a consensus system between the center and the states which cuts across party loyalties and identities — a consensus system which has considerable possibilities but which is also exposed to important strains. Soon after the formation of Congress and non-Congress governments in the different states in 1967, the prime minister of India, Mrs. Gandhi, and her close associates were able to develop a comfortable quid pro quo with the chief ministers in the states, including the non-Congress chief ministers. Indeed, it was found that managing some of the non-Congress chief ministers was easier, since they were no more than chief ministers, whereas the chief ministers who belonged to the Congress tended also to be party regional bosses, holding important positions in the party's central high command.

At the same time, this effort at developing a strategy of coalition between the center and the states which cuts across party lines has been exposed to important pressures, growing partly out of the amorphousness of the party system and partly out of the Congressmen's habituation to a monopoly of power for a long period of time. As has already been mentioned, it was largely through defections from the Congress that the various united fronts could come to power. Soon after they came to power by a small margin, however, the attempt of the different parties constituting each united front to implement their "minimum program" found them pulling in different directions and behaving like so many factions, without a common framework of a single party, such as had unified the earlier coalition of factions that the Congress party represented. This led to a reverse process of defections from the united fronts back to the Congress and tempted the Congress leaders in the states to topple the united front governments from power. Two new types of coalition thus emerged in the states: (a) a coalition between the Congress legislative party and one or more defecting groups from the united front, and (b) formation of a minority government by a defecting group backed by Congress support. Once this happened in one or two states, pressures from the other state Congress parties for forming coalitions with such dissident groups mounted, and the hitherto successful attempt of the central Congress leadership to establish a working relationship with non-Congress united fronts came partly to a halt. Then, with Mrs. Gandhi's attempt to wrest power from organizational bosses within the Congress through an open split in 1969, a further realignment of Congress-opposition forces took place, leading, as we have seen, to the return of the Congress to its traditional position as the central and dominating force in Indian party politics.

In this return of the Congress to a dominant position, however, there can be found a tension between two different approaches. One was to bring the Congress back to power in as many states as possible by whatever means.[19] The other was to pursue a more eclectic sharing of power,

19. It is important to stress the problem of means in this process. It is a problem that is rather new in Indian politics; it did not occur so long as the Congress held power by virtue of its numerical strength almost everywhere. Since 1967, however, in the game of toppling governmental coalitions from power, constitutional conventions that were supposed to have been firmly established have been called into question. Important among these are the power of a state governor to interpret political conditions in the state and decide whether or not constitutional government has broken down, the extent to which a governor should listen to a chief minister

come to terms with a more fragmented party system, establish a working
relationship between the Congress leadership at the central level and the
non-Congress governments in the states, and push ahead with the implementation of urgent tasks of government. Tension between these two
strands of thinking in the Congress party underlined the continuing
importance of its party caucus, made up essentially of state leaders and
regional bosses, as against the governmental leadership at the center.
This too provided the background to Mrs. Gandhi's initiative in 1969.

Corresponding to the differences in approach of the organizational and
governmental wings of the Congress party were similar differences in
the functioning of other parties and coalitions after 1967. Thus in various
non-Congress states after 1967 the united fronts had set up coordination
committees consisting of leaders of different parties as well as ministers.
All important policies and major governmental crises were discussed in
the coordination committees, whose approach was often at variance with
that of the chief minister and his close associates. The governmental-
organizational disputes in the functioning of these parties and coalitions
after 1967 were in many ways reminiscent of similar disputes in the
Congress in the period of exclusive Congress domination.

The instability and the continuing conflict found in the non-Congress
states were, of course, partly a result of the more heterogeneous group
structure of the coalition governments and their coordination committees,
which the dissident Congressmen (without whom these coalitions would
not have been possible in the first instance) were at loggerheads with
representatives of the other constituent parties. The other parties —
which sometimes ranged all the way from the conservative Jan Sangh to
the two Communist parties — had also very little in common and no
history of working together. They tended to fall out on the smallest
of issues. On the other hand, there has taken place a noticeable increase
in the cohesion of the Congress party, due mainly to the split in the
party and the emergence once again of a dominant leader bent on maintaining unity and attending to urgent tasks facing the country. As this
happened, the earlier tendency of the Congress party to absorb smaller
local parties and splinter groups that stood for the interests of certain
neglected strata of the population by accommodating these interests in
the Congress party was also resumed.

The federal axis also functions at levels below the state, through the
various districts and their lower units, each district representing a fairly
large and homogeneous population (1.5 million on an average). The

---

who is alleged to have lost a majority in the legislature, the power of the center to
impose President's Rule in a state, and the power of a Speaker of a state legislature
to convene and adjourn the house under conditions in which a government has been
dismissed from office by the governor.

national movement's approach of political mobilization, continued and further consolidated by the Congress after independence, consisted in penetrating the entire country by setting up units of self-government at various levels (districts, blocks, and panchayats) and giving them various developmental, political, and resource mobilization functions. The system got a considerable organizational boost through the remarkable initiative of the central Congress leadership, which committed itself to a policy of democratic decentralization (better known as *panchayati raj*) which involved considerable devolution of power, establishment of representative institutions at the district and lower levels, and mobilization of these in the functioning of the national and state schemes of economic development and political participation. Such mobilization and participation have also proved vehicles for diffusion of the egalitarian ideology and have led to a challenge to traditional social elites and their replacement by new-style political elites.

Partisan and oppositional tendencies thus tend to penetrate down to the bottom of the society. Although the Congress, as well as the other parties, continues to pay lip service to the desirability of keeping local institutions such as panchayats, cooperatives, and credit and educational institutions out of party politics, and although there are pressures for unanimous elections and nonparty elections, the fact remains that the Congress has gained considerably from its control of these institutions and the patronage they command, and other parties are slowly beginning to compete with the Congress for such control. Again, as between the state and the center, the strengths of the parties differ considerably between the districts and the states. Thus in states where the Congress lost power in 1967, it continued to dominate a majority of district councils. On the other hand, the factional oppositions within the Congress in the districts (for example, between the Congress organizational committees and the district panchayats) have been successfully exploited by opposition candidates in organizing their electoral support at the time of district as well as state and national elections.

The crystallization of electoral politics at these lower levels of the federal hierarchy has increased the pressures upon the state party organizations and state governments; it has also contributed to the aggregation of factional relationships between the organizational and governmental wings of the Congress, and gradually of the other parties as well. The importance of the Congress party caucuses — and the various coordination committees of other parties and coalitions — in the functioning of the governmental system derives to a considerable extent from the pressures that build up from the districts. Thus the decentralization of political and administrative functions provides an important framework within which oppositional patterns are found to operate.

There are demands for greater state autonomy and, within states, for district autonomy in certain spheres (as over certain revenues or over food procurement); but this is a symptom of greater interplay of confidence between the center, the states, and the districts, rather than of weakness on the part of central or state leaderships or of the Congress leadership in general. (The Congress states demand these concessions almost as much as the non-Congress states.) The time factor here is very important. If these same demands had come ten years ago, when certain givens of the situation were not understood and when the system had not acquired certain roots, they could have proved debilitating. Now they may well provide a design for a more rational allocation of functions and a more efficient pattern of mobilization and participation.

The Growth of Agitational Politics

Such a wide-open system of competition and representation necessarily politicizes and brings to the surface opposite trends of a plural society undergoing rapid modernization in so many spheres. Secular and sectarian, national and parochial, institutionalized and extrainstitutional forms of political behavior tend to confront each other in the context of a pluralistic political system. There are different sites at which these confrontations between opposite styles are found to operate. Thus in the operation of the party system two very different styles of opposition are to be found.

On the one hand, there are parties that aim at being all-India parties, want to project an all-India image, and increasingly try to contest the Congress in more and more areas, around more and more issues, and essentially through secular identities. The most important among these parties is the Jan Sangh, traditionally a right-wing party devoted to a militant brand of Hinduism, but which has lately — following its success at the polls, which has increased its sense of efficacy — been turning away from its militant posture. It has begun to realize that to have an all-India image, it must offer a more secular, national identity and commit itself to operating within the framework of parliamentary politics. At the same time, it is making a determined effort to organize itself in more and more constituencies in more and more states, thus developing a structure in which different types of parochial identities are brought together in a common organizational framework. It is interested less in maintaining acquired strength in this constituency or that district and more in spreading out and acquiring a national dimension, even if this might affect its earlier position and identity in certain regions. In striking such a balance between organizational and ideological identities (along parochial lines) and in cultivating a national, secular identity at the higher level, the Jan Sangh is likely to become very much like the Congress, though for a long time still limited in the number of states in which it can hope to make an impact.

The Swatantra party and the PSP have all along aimed at being national parties, as evidenced by the fact that they lay more stress on elections to the national Parliament than to the state legislatures. Unlike the Jan Sangh and the Congress, however, they have by and large failed to penetrate a large number of constituencies through their own organizational strength. All the same, these parties do represent a secular and essentially parliamentary, national thrust in their opposition to the Congress; and in many states, as well as in the national Parliament, they provide important bulwarks to the functioning of democratic politics.[20]

On the other side are parties like the two Communist parties and the SSP (which, even after the 1970 merger, continues to dominate the Socialist party), whose style of operation seems directed to consolidating their strength in the regions where they are already strong, rather than to looking out and spreading to larger parts of the country. Of course, within the Communist and Socialist parties there are deep differences over the importance they should attach to parliamentary as against extra-parliamentary types of opposition — differences that have become acute as a result of the accession of these parties to power in the non-Congress states. The Right Communist party as a whole, the parliamentary wing of the Left Communist party, and an important faction in the SSP would like to follow a more secular, parliamentary approach. The extremists among the Left Communists and the Socialist party, as well as a large number of left splinter parties, on the other hand, lay more store by other techniques of opposition. On the whole, however, the style of such parties provides an edge to the extremist wings over the moderate wings, and appeals for ideological purity continue to be relevant in their search for power.

Similar differences in approach and style are to be found in the operation of the legislative system. We have already noted the division between those who would emphasize implementation of national priorities and governmental performance in things like economic development and those whose main emphasis is on the power struggle and the ousting of those who are in power. The existence of a Congress-dominated national Parliament and three different types of state legislature — one set under the Congress or Congress-supported coalitions, another set under non-Congress coalitions, and a third set where lack of a majority on either side has led to the temporary imposition of President's Rule — has given rise to patterns of opposition in which state leaderships work against

20. As mentioned in note 15, the PSP merged with the SSP in 1970 to form a united party.

central leaderships, the legislatures are turned into platforms of regional and parochial interests, continuous changes in legislative opposition parties affect governmental stability, and the national Parliament itself turns into a forum of regional interests as much as of policy confrontations between the nationally oriented parties.

There are other sites in which this confrontation between secular, parliamentary forms of opposition and more parochial, extraparliamentary forms is found to occur. An important development in the crystallization of oppositional strength is the increasing use made of demonstrations, mass rallies, and strikes. To these are added new Indian versions of protest against authority, some of which had gained legitimacy during the nationalist movement. These are hunger strikes, *bandhs* (closures, that is, general strikes in whole states or cities), *gheraos* (the cordoning off and virtual imprisonment of managements or ministers), and *dharnas* (sit-in strikes before secretariats or homes of public officials). Such extraparliamentary opposition is sometimes directed against state governments but has more often been employed against the central government, frequently with a view to discrediting the Congress and obliging the national leadership to make concessions to certain demands. There have been occasions when the non-Congress united front governments have themselves given a call for such demonstrations of protest and ministers have participated in them. With the decline of the overwhelming authority of the Congress in the 1967 elections and the slight taste of power that they accorded to various parties — and also with the increasing need of the government at all levels to accommodate more and more pressures — the temptation to resort to such agitational tactics is on the increase, although almost always within the bounds set by the coercive powers of state authority and the antipathy of India's masses to too much agitational politics.[21] This antipathy is now spreading to the leadership of a number of opposition parties, which have found agitations and the violence to which they lead a double-edged weapon. There has been a return to more institutionalized forms of opposition, and opposition parties have in fact cooperated with the Congress and the central government in rooting out political violence, notably in West Bengal.

On the other hand, such agitational politics are an inevitable concomitant of the growing diffusion of political functions and the increasing

21. The deployment of force to curb mob violence has been a subject of considerable public interest and controversy in India. By and large it is realized that angry demonstrations and even mob violence have a place in a democracy; and although the instruments of state authority, such as the police, are frequently employed to check violence, they are also expected to behave in a responsible manner. By experience, the Indian police have acquired considerable skill in handling mob situations. At any rate, the contrast with the rather amateurish and crude handling of mobs in the United States is striking.

aspiration for political participation by a variety of political and social groups. Agitational politics is not entirely the making of a few political parties. Agitations have their own infrastructure in society,[22] and in a democracy they are often the symptom of a growing involvement of more and more strata of society in the processes of political participation. Such involvement leads, on the one hand, to a broadening of the institutional consensus and a development among the hitherto excluded classes of a stake in the system. It also leads, on the other hand, to a growth of self-confidence among these classes, an increasing visibility of disparities, and an accelerating sense of injustice, together with a feeling of powerlessness before machine politics and an urge to get around it. Out of all this comes a growing challenge to the hegemony of the upper-class elite which dominated the political structure for so long in the style of an oligarchy.

Agitational politics are thus legitimate politics: they follow necessarily from oppositional activity seeking channels of expression in the context of a changing political structure. In order adequately to grasp the significance of such changes, it is useful to look into this infrastructure of caste and class conflict, which underlies the shifts taking place in government-opposition relationships.

Political Pragmatism and the Secularization of Castes

One way of considering these changes is to examine the changing patterns of political mobilization and recruitment. The Congress movement for independence was sustained and diffused through a band of idealistic, Gandhian workers, drawn from the professional classes in the urban areas, whose involvement in the villages took place under Gandhi's call for constructive work in the countryside. Soon after independence, however, the Congress undertook the task of integrating various social groups that had remained uninvolved in the movement for independence but commanded considerable influence and power in the rural areas. The Congress tried to consolidate its electoral base essentially by coming to terms with entrenched social interests and important individuals who controlled sizable vote banks in the rural areas. These new recruits into the Congress electoral machine and into the leadership of the new institutions still came from the upper castes, were by and large English-educated, and understood the idiom of modern politics without much difficulty. Thus, although stratified by differential skills at different levels

22. For an analysis of the significance of agitational politics and its relationship to formal democracy, with a case study of one such movement, see Rajni Kothari, "Direct Action: A Pattern of Political Behaviour," *Quest* (an Indian quarterly), no. 24, 1960, pp. 22–35.

of the polity, the ruling class still continued to be remarkably small and homogeneous.

As the electoral process crystallized further, however, the authority of these upper-caste elites was challenged by leaders from the middle and lower social strata, which were numerically preponderant. Thanks to the pluralistic caste structure of Indian society and its low vulnerability to classlike conflicts for a long time, there did not take place any clear-cut polarization of interests. Rather there developed a multigroup, multifactional structure of support to which the contending candidates, factions, and parties had to appeal. The Congress tried to deal with this emergence of new caste groups into politics essentially by co-opting important leaders of different castes and communities into the power nexus of the party. Caste lobbies emerged within the Congress, federated with a view to mobilizing sufficient numerical strength, and provided the dynamics of interest articulation within the Congress, and later on between the Congress and its opponents. In this process almost all social groups carried some weight. In fact, the marginal groups (like the scheduled castes), religious minorities (like the Muslims and Christians), and "backward classes" attained an importance out of proportion to their numbers.[23] Whenever the Congress was unable to accommodate such social groups, other parties stepped in. Often the role of these parties was to organize the ignored sections of society, agitate for their demands, make their weight felt, and finally gain them accommodation within the Congress system of power.

This process of elite mobilization and co-optation was greatly facilitated by the Congress party's initiative at penetrating lower levels of the national hierarchy through democratic decentralization (panchayati raj) and access to a variety of local institutions. It was soon realized that real power came not so much from legislative seats or from belonging to somebody's group as from the control of local institutions; it lay not so much in charisma as in organization.

While this approach to political mobilization has facilitated the continuing authority of higher-level leadership in the various parties and the socialization of new recruits into the relatively homogeneous ruling class, three other trends indicate a more substantial transformation. First, the ascendancy of men with pragmatic and manipulative skills but without strong party identities or ideological commitments has given rise to a new style of politics, while the idiom of politics continues to be moralistic. This has led to feelings of disillusionment among the middle

23. For an analytical statement of this process and a case study of it, see Rajni Kothari and Rushikesh Maru, "Caste and Secularism in India: Case Study of a Caste Federation," *Journal of Asian Studies* 25, no. 1 (November 1965):33–50. For the growing importance of the marginal groups, see André Beteille, *Caste, Class and Power* (Berkeley: University of California Press, 1966).

classes. A low rate of governmental performance and an increasing gap between promise and fulfillment have augmented this feeling. Together these factors have led to a growing oppositional sentiment among the middle classes, who have been dislodged from their earlier commanding positions in the polity. As these classes still control the channels of communication and the skills of pedagogy and rhetoric, there has developed in public discussion a disproportionate emphasis on problems of corruption and loss of integrity in politics, which has given rise to a general lowering of political morale.

Second, this very growth of pragmatic politics has increased the number and volume of power contests and has in turn led to considerable frustration among those who are denied party tickets or fail to win elections. In the absence of alternative opportunities in other spheres, which is characteristic of an underemployed economy, this has led to a search for ever new causes around which the frustrated politicians can mobilize support and make themselves felt.

Third, and more important than the first two trends, economic development and social legislation have contributed considerably to a secularization of caste cleavages and their activization in politics. The undisturbed growth in prosperity and power of the upper peasantry, which for a long time commanded the allegiance of the lower castes through a network of patron-client relationships, is slowly giving place to a visibility of disparities and a reaction against the "kulaks" on the part of the small farmers, sharecroppers, and landless laborers. The visibility is heightened by the fact that the benefits of both redistributive social legislation and planned development have accrued to the newly rich who come from the upwardly mobile castes. The rural masses are used to the privileges of the traditional upper castes, which used their wealth and position along known ways. They are not used to the new-style prosperity of the "upstarts," whose style of life and display of wealth cause resentment among both the upper and lower castes. Moreover, the new rich happen to be aggressive in their political attitudes; in most places they have replaced the traditional elites and have at the same time amassed remarkable concentrations of wealth and political power. They also have no regard for traditional notions of patronage and trusteeship and are found to be callous and self-righteous in their attitudes toward the deprived sections of the community. Yet to a great extent they owe their power to access to government and political parties. When others try to avail themselves of the same opportunities — such as permits for agricultural inputs like new seeds or fertilizers or other scarce commodities — their demands are blocked by the "upstarts." All of this accentuates the feeling among the lower castes that they are being denied their legitimate rights. At the same time, they are beginning to realize the power of their vote and the importance of organizing themselves at state and higher levels.[24]

An awareness of their separate identity and interests is still developing among the lower castes, and it will take some time to get fully articulated. But the trends are clear. The growth of several political groups and dissident parties drawn from the lower peasantry — cutting across traditional party identities — is a symptom of the political importance of emerging cleavages in rural politics. In Bihar a new party of the "backward castes," the Soshit Dal ("Party of the Oppressed"), emerged in early 1968, withdrew from and toppled the anti-Congress united front government, and assumed power with the backing of the Congress party.[25] In Madhya Pradesh the formation of a similar party led both the chief minister of the united front government (from which it threatened to defect) and the leader of the Congress opposition to pledge their support in case it wanted to form the government. In Tamilnadu, the scheduled-caste lobby is acquiring the position of a strategic bargaining force and is likely to provide an important lever to the Congress in its desperate struggle for revival against the powerful DMK, which is in power.[26] The Communists in Tamilnadu have also started mobilizing the grievances of these and other backward sections, mainly through trade union activity. On the other hand, in states like Kerala and Andhra Pradesh, where the CPI(M) drew its support by closely identifying with particular castes, the upward mobility of important sections of these castes, following their prosperity in agriculture, has created important gaps in its support base, and its strength has begun to dwindle in some areas. In West Bengal, however, the extremist wing of the same party organized in 1967 a rebellion among the landless laborers and engaged in widespread lawlessness until the united front government, dominated by the Left Communists, had itself to take repressive action against the extremists.[27]

24. Some of these lower castes, besides organizing themselves politically, are claiming the status of one of the traditional *varnas*, such as the warrior class of Kshatriyas. Throughout Indian history many low-placed castes have taken this route to social mobility. See Kothari and Maru, "Caste and Secularism in India." See also M. S. A. Rao, "Caste and the Indian Army," *Economic Weekly* 16, no. 35 (29 August 1964): 1639–43. The Ahirs are demanding the formation of an Ahir regiment in the Indian army.

25. Later in the year, however, this government lost its majority and resigned after a no-confidence motion was carried against it.

26. The DMK is the only non-Congress party to be able to form a government on its own. It captured 138 seats out of a total of 234 in the Madras legislative assembly in 1967; the Congress trailed behind with a mere 50. It has held on to a dominant position despite the revival of the Congress under Mrs. Gandhi in most other states since the 1971 Lok Sabha election. It is so dominant that in that election the Congress entered into an "understanding" with the DMK — leaving most of the seats to the PMK — which virtually established the latter's monopoly in Tamilnadu.

27. The latter were called the Naxalbari group after the area in which they had for

Other kinds of caste platforms are also emerging and cutting across party identities. Thus the following of Charan Singh, the powerful chief minister of Uttar Pradesh in the united front government in 1967–68, consisted of intermediate castes in the ranks of all the parties in the united front. This caste appeal by the chief minister alienated the traditional leadership of parties like the Jan Sangh and the SSP, polarized each of them, and ultimately led to a head-on clash between the chief minister and the organizational leaders of the constituent parties. (Later, the Congress party absorbed these elements, and this led to a collapse of Charan Singh's party, including defeat of Charan Singh himself in the 1971 election.) Similar splits are found in other states. The secularization of caste identities by federating them into political alignments along upper, middle, and lower caste lines is a peculiarly Indian version of class cleavages. All of this is taking place alongside the continuing urban-rural conflicts, which are now sharpening because of the flow of urban savings and educated people into rural areas. This flow followed the agricultural breakthrough of the late 1960s and is encouraged by the difficulty, which all political parties face, of taxing agricultural incomes or lowering procurement prices of agricultural produce.

Thus a changing agricultural scene and increasing caste and class cleavages in the rural areas, on the one hand, and a relatively low rate of industrial growth and employment opportunities in the urban areas, on the other, are leading to a growing sense of deprivation and inequity. Together they are likely to produce a fragmentation of political structures and loyalties and put to the test the assimilative capability of India's social and political systems. Mrs. Gandhi's emergence as a champion of these deprived groups has, for the time being, arrested this fragmentation. But much is going to depend on her ability to implement the "mandate" she has held out to these sections. Their loyalties cannot be taken for granted for long.

The articulation of these various trends at the governmental level is to be found in a growing turnover of political elites and the emergence of new political groups and dissident parties. The twenty-year dominance of the Congress before 1967 did not prevent such a turnover, as will be seen from table 8.2. When the Congress held power in most of the states, the function of the opposition was internalized. The result was a pluralistic factional structure within the Congress in which dissident groups, as well as other political parties, were involved and different kinds of interests

---

a time seized control, captured land from the large owners, and redistributed it among the landless. Later the movement spread, and the Naxalites were very active in Calcutta and its surroundings, spreading violence in the name of revolution and accepting Mao Tse-tung as their leader. The movement had also spread to some parts of Andhra Pradesh and Punjab. It has now been practically wiped out, following strong police measures.

Table 8.2   *Ministerial Turnover under Congress Dominance, 1952–1966*

Changes in Incumbents[a]

	Chief Minister	Cabinet Ministers	Other Ministers
Andhra Pradesh	3	26	1
Assam	1	9	10
Bihar	2	15	21
Gujarat	5	19	26
Jammu & Kashmir	3	16	12
Kerala[b]	4	26	[c]
Madhya Pradesh	3	17	22
Madras	2	12	[c]
Maharashtra	3	29	30
Mysore	2	30	8
Orissa	4	20	5
Punjab	2	18	24
Rajasthan	1	18	18
Uttar Pradesh	3	15	33
West Bengal	1	16	34

SOURCE: *Times of India Yearbooks,* 1952–66.
[a] A chief minister or minister who was returned to the same position after being replaced for some time is not counted as a change.
[b] The turnover in Kerala includes other parties as well as the Congress.
[c] No such position in these states.

were accommodated. On the whole, however, political competition was carried on within an elite that was socially and politically homogeneous. The increase in dissidence and defection from the Congress consequent upon the growing number of aspirants for office coming from different strata of society, and the resulting gains by other parties, have further broadened the institutional base through which different caste associations and federations are being mobilized into the governmental process.[28] The process of defection was also to be found in the functioning of non-Congress parties and coalitions that came into being in 1967. They found it difficult to satisfy the demands of the different social groups they had sought to accommodate. From such defections the Congress has in turn benefited. But the price of its gains is the promise to take up the cause of the weak and the downtrodden. This circulation of Congress and anti-Congress forces has provided channels of representation to hitherto ignored social groups,[29] which can now make themselves felt within the

28. For a series of case studies, as well as an analytical statement on these processes of caste-politics interaction, see Rajni Kothari, ed., *Caste in Indian Politics* (New Delhi: Orient Longmans, 1970). See also Lloyd I. Rudolph, "The Modernity of Tradition: The Democratic Incarnation of Caste in India," *American Political Science Review* 59, no. 4 (December 1965): 975–89.
29. The opening out of political recruitment and the availability of alternative choices have also provided new opportunities to other social groups, such as the urban

established parties. In this way the dominance of a homogeneous ruling class is slowly coming to an end.

The Issue of Legitimacy

In addition to caste and party, India has many other pluralities, and each of these turns into a source of opposition. This characteristic of oppositions in India — namely, that they derive their extent and diffusion from a pluralist social organization — is important to bear in mind. It underscores the fact that India is still far from becoming a mass society; its pluralism also is of a different kind from that in Western democracies. It is less a confrontation between aggregated subsystems and more a coexistence between historically autonomous diversities and identities. Hence the great variety and diffusion of oppositions and their lack of clear-cut boundaries. Hence also the absence of a highly organized and strong system of institutionalized opposition.

The problem of linguistic diversity, which figured prominently in the years after independence and gave rise to a number of agitations, was dealt with by regrouping the states along linguistic lines. Although there is a small section of opinion in India which is not yet reconciled to this step, and although foreign observers have raised an alarmist voice at the likely displacement of the English-educated class by linguistic elites,[30] there is little doubt that the creation of linguistic states was an important step in the direction of creating more homogeneous, natural units of government and removing an important source of almost interminable tension.

Language as a source of tension, however, reemerged on the question of what should take the place of English as a medium of instruction. The issue sharply divided the Hindi-speaking region of North India from the Dravidian language belt of South India. In the process, the DMK, a powerful opposition party, emerged in the South; the Congress paid a

---

lower-middle and professional classes and the intellectuals, especially in the smaller towns. Mrs. Gandhi's campaign for ousting the old guard both from her own party and later, during the 1971 and 1972 elections, the conservative opposition parties, led to a massive mobilization of these elements. Earlier, they virtually withdrew from the political process and felt powerless about it. There is some analogy here with students in the United States — as well as a section of the academic community — who were mobilized by Senator Eugene McCarthy during the 1968 campaign for nomination as presidential candidate of the Democratic party and later by Senator McGovern in the 1972 campaign. On balance, however, the remobilization of the urban middle-class professionals in India is not as prominent as the mobilization of the peripheral lower classes in the rural sector.

30. The most agitated of these accounts is to be found in Selig Harrison, *India: The Most Dangerous Decades* (Princeton: Princeton University Press, 1960). See also Karl W. Deutsch, *Nationalism and Social Communication* (New York: Wiley, 1953), chap. 6.

heavy price by losing Tamilnadu, which was one of its strongholds; militant students moved by linguistic sentiment emerged as a powerful political force in both South and North India; and the legislative assembly of Tamilnadu repudiated the national Parliament's resolution favoring a three-language formula (Hindi, the regional language, and English as a "link language") as a way out of the language impasse. Following the language riots in Madras city and other parts of Tamilnadu, however, a concerted effort at reconciliation was made, and the extremist feelings on both sides have been brought under control. There has also been a steady spread of both Hindi and English, and there is nearly universal consensus on adopting regional languages as media of instruction in schools and colleges.

A disturbing outgrowth of linguistic identities has been the sporadic outburst of militant chauvinist movements in certain areas directed against minority language groups in the region and pressing for reservation of the bulk of the jobs for the "sons of the soil." The most prominent among these is the Shiv Sena (*Sena* means "army") in Maharashtra, directed against the employment of South Indians in Maharashtra. There are similar movements in other states, though they are not as powerful as the Shiv Sena. Slowly, however, as the real grievances voiced by these organizations have been accommodated and as the appeal of the Congress under Mrs. Gandhi has shifted toward a more socialistic and welfare orientation, the popularity of these movements has gone down and their more objectionable and violent activities have been arrested. With this, parties like the Shiv Sena are likely to become part of the general mosaic of oppositional sites.

A positive aspect of the language problem in India is the modification of extremist positions on the part of the more important parties of both the North and the South, following their success at the polls. Thus, whereas at one time the DMK held out a threat of secession of the southern states, or at any rate of Madras, from the Indian Union, it is now one of the most ordered and moderate among the non-Congress parties and is committed to operating within the system.[31] Similarly the Jan Sangh, at one time an extremist party in the cause of Hindi, has mellowed considerably; it has officially accepted an equal status for regional languages and Hindi and is willing to accept English as a link language for a long time to come. Its aspiration to become an all-India party has contributed to this important change in its position. In both cases, success in elections

31. Even when it sponsored a resolution in the Tamilnadu legislative assembly against the national Parliament's three-language formula, it did so more to anticipate and contain the violent mood of the students and the people of Madras in general than deliberately to flout the wishes of the Parliament. In fact, Chief Minister Annadurai soon hastened to make amends and find a way out of the deadlock created by the positions taken by the two legislatures.

and proximity to governmental positions have played a major role. Once again power is found to be the great moderator.

Language is not the only source of regional identities and tensions. Whereas secessionist threats vis-à-vis the Indian Union as a whole have been arrested, similar threats vis-à-vis the individual states have found expression. Thus the hilly and tribal populations in East India asked for autonomy and demanded separate states for themselves (as was the case with the All Party Hill Leaders Conference in Assam and with the Nagas, the Mizos, and other tribal areas). Such demands, as well as the growth of highly articulate and local groups with regional identities, were seen by the modernist elements in India as threats to national integrity. The national government, however, took a more pragmatic line: it suppressed violent and secessionist movements but at the same time experimented with new forms of federal relationship (for example, sub-federations within states as a transition to full statehood, as in the case of Meghalaya, and regional coordination of small states for purposes of planning and administrative coordination). On the whole this willingness to allow legitimate forms of self-government and autonomy has produced workable solutions in an otherwise volatile region.

Religious diversities have also been activated as a result of the increasing plurality of electoral support, the ability of cohesive minorities to influence political decisions, and the consequent awareness of the strength of communal identities among religious minorities, especially the Muslims. For a long time the Muslims found their security under the Congress umbrella and were integrated with the mainstream of electoral and political trends in the country.[32] More recently, however, they have become aware of their bargaining position and have gained considerable confidence in operating through their own organizations, in demanding a greater share in jobs and other opportunities, and in agitating for their rights and for justice vis-à-vis the majority community. All this has led, on the one hand, to a greater participation of this dominant minority in the system. On the other hand, it has led to sporadic tension at the local political level, wherever ethnic cleavages are not amicably resolved and where either the majority or the minority community acts belligerently out of a feeling of insecurity and animosity.

It is important to note, however, that these are sporadic events and that neither the Hindu nor the Muslim political groups or parties put forward their demands in purely religious or ethnic terms. Rather, the demands are made within the system, and social animosities take on the form of political

32. See Gopal Krishna, "Electoral Participation and National Integration," *Economic and Political Weekly*, Annual Number, February 1967, pp. 179–90. For a case study of mobilization of the Muslim communal vote, see Bashiruddin Ahmed's study of an Amroha by-election, "Congress Defeat in Amroha: A Case Study in One Party Dominance," in *Party System and Election Studies*.

oppositions. The Jan Sangh has opened up to include Muslims in its fold and has in fact fielded Muslim candidates on its ticket: the Muslim League operates in a few southern states, but it is forced to avow its loyalty to the country and to the principle of secularism; and in the North, although the authority of the nationalist Jamiat-ul-Ulema has been challenged by the more radical parties, such as the Jamat-e-Islami and the Majlis-e-Mushawarat, the challenge is couched in essentially political terms, the chief aim being to articulate the demands of the Muslims and not just to be taken for granted by the Congress and other parties.

Other more secular kinds of diversities also provide sources of oppositional activity. At least two of these are very important — trade unions (including associations of teachers and administrative ranks) and student bodies. On the whole, both these fronts have maintained close liaison with political parties and have in the process been greatly fragmented in their organization. Each major party has its own labor, student, and youth wings, and the national and state governments have actively pursued policies of arbitration in disputes. With the general fluidity of the party positions following the fourth general elections, however, and even more since the appeal of Mrs. Gandhi's radical image to these groups, there have been indications of more autonomous centers of student and labor activity. The immediate result has been further disunity in both movements and more numerous contests for status and recognition. At the same time, there have been more spontaneous local outbursts of industrial and student unrest, with the result that the leadership of political parties, which formerly provided counsel to these movements, has been lagging behind in initiative and policy. Although in the past these Western-type associational activities[33] have been less autonomous and effective than caste associations and political parties, they are likely to grow with increasing urbanization and education and with a decline in the average age of the Indian population.

The increasing politicization of all these diversities of Indian social life has increased the load on the coercive and arbitrational structures of government, which are often found wanting in their ability to deal with successive challenges. As this happened simultaneously with the increase in fluidity and instability of the party and governmental systems following the 1967 elections, doubts were raised as to the viability of a parliamentary democracy based on adult franchise in the face of pressing problems of national integration and economic development. Lately, these voices are on the decline, following the Congress party's dramatic comeback to power and the increased confidence of the nation following the crisis in Bangla Desh and the decisive victory of India, all leading to both greater integration in the country and increased legitimacy of the

33. For a pressure-group analysis of various kinds of associations in India, see Myron Weiner, *The Politics of Scarcity* (Chicago: University of Chicago Press, 1962).

democratic system. There are, of course, still a few who talk of more viable alternatives and some kind of system change, such as adoption of a presidential form of executive or some form of authoritarian inter-regnum.[34]

More representative of this general kind of opposition and discontent is a slow and muttered disenchantment with a Western type of political system and with party politics as a whole. There has always been a small section in India, highly educated and generally greatly committed to the values of a free society, who have asked for a partyless democracy, for a national government of merits, and for unanimously selected or nominated, rather than popularly elected, governments. Essentially involved in a romantic search for institutional solutions that will "fit the Indian genius," these leaders of opinion have found new material for their plea in the growing instability and greater incidence of agitational politics since 1967. The appeal for the type of politics that will transcend party and sectarian loyalties is essentially directed to the central leadership of the Congress party, enlightened parliamentarians, and national leaders of other demo-cratic parties. For example, when faced with the tension between a central government leadership keen on economic development and industrial peace, on the one hand, and a state party caucus keen on establishing the Congress hegemony, on the other, it is demanded that the prime minister rise above party and develop a truly national consensus.

Quite apart from such appeals for clean politics from idealistic sections, there is a growing opinion among professional, middle-class circles that some of the conflicts have been inherent in India's constitutional and ter-ritorial system. It is noticeable that while the pace of national consensus is spreading through the involvement of more and more political groups and social strata, this is not necessarily an unmixed blessing, at any rate not in the short run — and in politics the long run cannot be allowed to supersede the short run. There has been a considerable lack of institu-tionalization of the structure and distribution of power, some deinstitu-tionalization of earlier structures, a growing fragmentation of coalitional structures, and hence a precarious base for institutional legitimacy. Such conditions leave much scope for doubt and can give rise to some funda-mental questioning about the viability of competitive politics, in spite of considerable consensus on the values of democracy and freedom. Indeed, these questions are very often raised in the name of accepted goals, such as economic development and egalitarianism.

India thus presents the picture of a consensual political culture that has yet to achieve a basic consensus on institutional fundamentals and

34. It is interesting to note that in a large number of developing countries, the in-tellectuals desire a system change in the abstract and generally conceive it in di-chotomous terms. Where the regime is authoritarian, they would like to introduce a democracy. Where it is a democracy, they are fascinated by the authoritarian model.

an unambiguous commitment to, and a sense of sacredness of, its constitutional and political system. At this stage of political consciousness, a pluralistic system of power necessarily gives rise to a large residue of uninstitutionalized forms of political opposition. The result, as we have seen, is that oppositions are at once highly widespread and lacking in institutional strength and cohesion.

The caste system, a consensual culture, an agglomerative rather than aggregative tradition of social organization, a high tolerance of ambiguity and fragmentation, a generally low temperature of political conflict, and at the same time a high degree of autonomy and potency of central political authority — all this has given India a long period of overall stability, despite a wide arena of social change and considerable institutional fluidity. The resilience of these factors may well be the main reason for the present legitimacy of political democracy and the high tolerance of opposition and dissidence. But it is only by proving the efficacy of such a system in the performance of modern tasks that its authority will be firmly established.

A high frequency and wide diffusion of oppositional activity are not necessarily signs of strength. It is equally important to develop frameworks of consensus and centers of dominance around which disagreements of opinion or interest can be organized. India has been trying to evolve, through the Congress system, a unique kind of mix between these contrary tendencies of consensus and dissent — a mix that issues out of its immediate historical antecedents, on the one hand, and the essential and enduring plurality of its culture, on the other. It has enabled the country to adopt an incremental approach to political mobilization, one that strives to accommodate the traditional pluralities, rather than to reject them in the fashion of doctrinaire modernism. At the same time it has shown that major changes in the substance of the consensus can be effected through a highly open system of one-party dominance — perhaps much better than is the case in systems of alternating parties such as the Anglo-Saxon democracies have. This combination of rejection of the politics of confrontation, on the one hand, and absorption of far-reaching changes through sensitivity of the politics of consensus, on the other, has given India its peculiar political style and its overriding openness. It is, no doubt, a difficult system to operate. The combination of curious fascination and anxious concern for the system voiced by many observers is only a symptom of the ambivalent response that most Indian institutions arouse in the onlooker. The next decade, by testing Indian democracy in terms of the most vital tasks of politics everywhere (viz. the creation of a truly just social order), is likely to provide a more definite answer. Meanwhile, it provides a most interesting alternative to other existing systems of government and opposition.

9

POLITICAL OPPOSITION
AND POLITICAL DEVELOPMENT
IN JAPAN

Michael Leiserson

In 1850 the Japanese people had been living on farms or in isolated hamlets under a semifeudal regime for almost 250 years. The major provincial lords were sovereign within their fiefs, but relations between the lords were strictly regulated, and peace was maintained by the Tokugawa lords, most powerful of all, who governed the land from Tokyo. Tokugawa society was organized into hierarchies of status, and the Togugawa's own top status was legitimated by the authority of the Emperor. Nine-tenths of the people were farmers, living in traditional agrarian poverty, although there was relative comfort for the farmer-landlords and for the traders and merchants in the large cities. Access to the government (to say nothing of political opposition) was closed off for all except the Tokugawa and their vassals. The country was also closed off from the rest of the world: not only trade, but almost all foreign religious, economic, and intellectual influences were screened out. Although there were some gradual changes — along with the rise of a commercial economy, the movement of the landed nobility to the cities and the transformation of feudal knights into fief officials were especially important for later developments — in general the society which the first Tokugawa rulers had designed in the years after 1615 was still a going concern.

By 1890 the Tokugawa regime was gone. Japan's closed doors had been burst open by the Western powers. A coalition of the most powerful feudal lords had overthrown the Tokugawa and obtained the support of

I wish to thank Donald C. Hellman and Kurt Steiner for their helpful comments on an earlier version of the manuscript. The chapter was written in 1968 and has not been revised since, except stylistically, but a brief postscript has been added.

341

the Emperor for a new regime, only to lose their own positions when the new, highly centralized Imperial government abolished the feudal land-owning system. Intense study and activity by the Imperial bureaucrats had produced a modern army and navy, a fledgling industrial economy, a constitutional government, and continued national independence. If the peasants were still poor and the new urban workers even poorer, on a national scale there was much more abundance. Cities had grown and an industrial bourgeoisie had emerged. Foreign influences were everywhere, and political activity was reported daily in the new newspapers.

In 1930 Japan was in many ways a modern nation. Industrial and military prowess had produced, in the fashion of the day, overseas colonies and worldwide admiration. Japan's predominant naval strength in the western Pacific had been recognized by international treaty, and membership in the League of Nations symbolized acceptance by the nations of the West. The modern educational system had created a nation literate and skilled enough to staff the growing economy, dutiful and consensual enough to participate in universal manhood suffrage without sinking the rapidly moving ship of state. Constitutional government was a well-established tradition, and party competition and interest-group activity were vigorous. Traditional social practices had combined with modern political and industrial activities in economic and governmental institutions which were therefore stable, if not satisfactorily rationalized. Grievances of the growing tenant farmer and urban worker classes were being championed by small but growing left-wing political parties. Social democracy never appealed to the economic and social elites, however, who preferred no parties or else supported the moderate and conservative parties which dominated the National Assembly during this period.

Today Japan has a consumer-oriented, highly modern society. The effects of domestic repression and foreign expansion before and during World War II were canceled or even reversed by the Allied military Occupation. The "Prussian" Imperial Constitution was replaced with the "Anglo-American" present constitution, farm tenancy was nearly abolished, industrial workers were organized in unions, the military and nobility were eliminated as participants in domestic politics, the influence of giant economic cartels was weakened, the Emperor system was disbanded — these and many other reforms of the Occupation have helped make contemporary Japan seem more an extension of 1930 Japan than of 1940 Japan. Economic growth has continued rapidly, and some of the national abundance is now shared in by most people. Political participation and open expression of political opposition have continued to expand. The descendants of prewar moderates and conservatives now obtain the voting allegiance of only half the population, and more progressive and radical parties are important actors on the political stage. Internationally, as a full member of the Organization for Economic Cooperation and Development (OECD) and as the strongest industrial power in the Far East, Japan appears to be overcoming the legacy of hostility left from the war and is playing an increasingly important role in the politics and economics of the region.

This brief account of Japan's past 120 tumultuous years shows that, by any reasonable definitions of the terms, Japan has industrialized, modernized, and developed during this period.[1] How are the patterns of and changes in Japanese political oppositions related to these economic, social, and political processes?

In my view, the evolving structure of political opposition in a nation is a part of the processes of modernization and development. That is, political opposition is reciprocally related to (and not only a consequence of) broader historical conditions and changes. This relation involves two interrelated levels: the specific issues and policies called into question by an opposition and the more-or-less stable pattern of oppositional action. More specifically: (*a*) socioeconomic and political conditions and changes help to shape both the pattern of political opposition and the issues upon which opposition occurs; (*b*) conversely, the pattern of political opposition and the demands made by oppositions help to shape (via governmental policy or otherwise) socioeconomic and political institutions and developments; and (*c*) there is clearly a relation between the pattern of political opposition and the issues focused upon by the oppositions.[2]

To see political opposition as a part of the process of development in this way is quite natural, if one recognizes that politics — particularly governmental policy — is intimately involved in development. Indeed, one could begin by observing that the evolving structure of politics and government in a nation is a part of the processes of modernization and development, and then deduce the place of political opposition in these processes by noting the interrelatedness of government and opposition. To understand the significance and evolution of political opposition and of modernization and development, it is necessary to consider them in their interrelationships.

Unfortunately, because of space limitations, it is not possible here to

---

1. By *industrialization* I mean the familiar technological and economic changes which occurred in the West during the nineteenth century. By *modernization* I mean the social changes which are supposed to accompany industrialization: rationalization (differentiation, secularization) and mobilization. By *development* I mean improvement in the quality of a community's public life, particularly increased opportunities to participate and/or increased social responsibility on the part of those who do participate.

2. Points (*a*) and (*c*) were argued by Robert Dahl in the "Explanations" and "Patterns" chapters of Dahl, ed., *Political Oppositions in Western Democracies* (New Haven: Yale University Press, 1966), respectively. Point (*b*) was ignored there but will be emphasized here.

give equally detailed consideration to these matters in all the stages of Japanese history over the past 120 years. Consequently, in the following section I shall deal primarily with what appear (at least in retrospect) to be turning points in Japanese history and omit more than a cursory discussion of the normal patterns of opposition and development between these epoch-making events. I shall then describe in some detail the structure of opposition in contemporary Japan. This disparity of treatment is regrettable, both for the Japanophile and for the student of the Third World today, who can probably find more interesting parallels between his subject and prewar Japan than postwar Japan. But there are grounds for speculating that the description of government and opposition in postwar Japan, properly generalized, would also hold for the prewar period between historical turning points.

JAPANESE POLITICAL THOUGHT AND POLITICAL OPPOSITION   Before embarking upon this chronological survey, however — in order to provide some of the cultural and intellectual context and thus, hopefully, more of the meaning of the events to be described — a brief discussion of Japanese views of politics and of opposition is essential. Whereas in the West the mainstream of political theory for three hundred years has emphasized individualism, equality, and amoral (secular) government, in Japan the emphasis has been on community, the inequality of men, and the interdependence of politics and ethics. Of course, defeat in World War II discredited many of the institutional manifestations of Japanese political theory, and the Occupation did its best to destroy the heritage of prewar "mystical nationalism" and "Emperor worship." But even today, when a Japanese intellectual, worker, businessman, or farmer looks at his government, shakes his head, and says, "That's not real politics," he is agreeing in some important ways with the statesmen of a hundred years ago about the nature of government. Granted that there is much less ideological unity today than in prewar Japan, still some assumptions and categories of thought remain widely shared. It is these enduring and so presumably basic ideas about politics which I want to define here, stressing content ("myth") rather than form ("doctrine") and ignoring the question of the spread of political consciousness in the population.

The cornerstone of Japanese political thinking seems to be the notion of community. (This "tribal" orientation surely stems from the "tribal" nature of the society: a single race, with one language, geographically isolated, with common customs and religious beliefs, under the authority of a single Imperial family since prehistory, and with an economy devoted until recently only to rice growing and fishing.) Since an individual can scarcely be said to exist in the absence of human relationships, an individual's interests cannot be separated from his interest in social relationships. Hence good social relations, based upon a felt mutuality or reciprocity, are a goal of every sensible person. The leaders of a community, similarly, work to maintain harmonious social relations because that — along with solutions of external problems — is what people need. Clearly, there is no inherent conflict between governors and governed, no division between public and private interests.

Similarly, since the duties of the governors are clear, they can make decisions calmly and harmoniously, without open strife and competition. It is part of the natural order of things to have governors, since someone must suppress selfish actions and maintain the integrity of the community as a whole; this is ample justification for government. What might appear to an outsider to be the servility or subservience of one class toward another can be seen correctly as a natural acceptance of the natural inequality within any community — jut as the hand accepts direction from the head, without feeling demeaned and without insisting that since there are two hands and only one head, the hands should outvote the head. But it goes without saying that the head does not treat the hand unreasonably, and similarly the governors should ensure that everyone can live in a way appropriate to his station. Likewise, in this sort of community, everyone should obey his duty to cooperate with the governors to achieve the public good. These principles can easily be seen to hold for any level of community, from the family to the state; indeed the state is best comprehended as national household. (Kokka, "state," is written with the two ideographs meaning "nation" or "country" and "house." [3])

In the context of such a political theory, stressing social harmony, the morality of the governors, the place of each person in society, and endless mutual obligations, is there any basis for a notion of political action which

3. As an extremely oversimplified account, this may be accurate for both pre- and postwar Japan, but in practice this theory worked out very differently in the two periods because of the different position of the Imperial institution. Before the war, the existence of the Emperor "guaranteed" that the implicit and explicit moral imperatives enjoined upon the governors were being obeyed. Since the war, the changed status of the Emperor provides no such guarantee; and so contemporary political criticism begins and ends with the argument that the governors and politicians are not living up to their calling. Moreover, because this sketch is of the enduring (and hence traditional) basic political theory, it would of course be rejected by many postwar Japanese who have consciously rejected prewar traditions. Nevertheless, I believe there are few people for whom any set of beliefs has come to *replace* the ones described here. And contemporary Japanese surely respond more positively to these ideas than do, say, Americans. For example, it is striking for an American, accustomed to a political culture that regularly sees "trouble-makers" behind every disturbance of the civic peace, that the mere existence of social unrest is for Japanese even today evidence that the governors are somehow inadequate. When the head of the highly prestigious University of Kyoto resigned in the wake of treatment by student demonstrators far more personally offensive than anything the American Students for Democratic Action ever did, he explained "If students behave in such a way to me, their teacher, then I must have failed to educate them properly, so I must take some responsibility for their actions."

is separate from or opposed to the government? There is such a basis — indeed, there are several — but it should not be surprising that the sort of opposition which can be justified within this intellectual tradition does not closely resemble the opposition of Western political theory. In fact, there is no word in Japanese which expresses adequately the meaning of the English word *opposition*.[4] This fact should help to avoid an obvious pitfall: just because one can observe opposition occurring does *not* mean that the people being observed understand their actions as oppositional. When, in the following pages, Japanese political oppositions are described, it is essential not to impute to these men or to their rivals the attitudes and motivations of more familiar political opponents.

Various kinds of opposition can be justified, depending upon which parts of this basic theory are emphasized and upon the generally agreed-upon fit between the theory and a given situation. For example, there is a place for a loyal opposition: "The government is operating pretty much as it should, but it may be helpful for the government to have some additional points of view made known, so I will try to help out with this." There is also a place for an incorrigible opposition: "The present governors are corrupt and unjust and are not living up to their responsibilities, so they must be replaced with better men." There can be, too, another type of opposition which asserts: "The people have been confused and misled; they need education and firm guidance." These sorts of political opposition, it should be noted, share the quality of sincerity and also the inability to justify partisan demands. There is no room for opposition for opposition's sake, for a politician who opposes simply to put himself in the place of the current powerholder. (Such behavior may occur, of course, but it is not recognized as responsible political action.) The business of government is too serious, and the governors are too likely to be as worthy and as competent as the opponents, for the country to have to put up with partisan or selfish interest-seeking. Rather, an opposition gains in stature and moral force to the extent that its leaders can be seen to be

4. *Yatō* means simply "opposition party," literally "a party which has left the capital and gone back to the country." It was used originally to describe the oligarchs who left the Meiji government in 1873 and returned to their fiefs to organize opposition. *Tairitsu* is better translated as "confrontation," while *teikō* and *hankō* connote resistance and defiance, as in a mutiny or a refusal to go along with a command. *Hantai* is the dictionary translation; it means "against," "opposite from," and many other related ideas, but it is never used in contemporary political discussion in the sense of political opposition. As these translations may suggest, to speak of, say, "the opposition dissolving into the system" in Japanese would be meaningless, because there is no familiar concept of opposition occurring apart from the political party or the defiant struggle through which opposition is expressed, because, that is, of the absence of the Western notion that opposition is an intrinsic part of politics. The lack of such a concept is consistent, it should be noted, with the political theory outlined above.

acting sincerely from deep inner conviction and without thought of personal advantage.[5]

With these sorts of expectations, it follows that the Japanese are not looking for an opposition which is pragmatic ("opportunistic"), which focuses primarily upon replacing the incumbent governors ("selfish office-seeking") or upon criticizing specific policies ("obstructionism," "irrelevance"). The last thing a Japanese opposition should do is allow the impression that it is *primarily* interested in winning power and prestige for itself, through elections or otherwise. Rather, it should be sincere, principled, uncompromising. It should not appear by its nature or volition to violate the national unity; rather, it should be able to show that it is more concerned for the community's integrity than even the governors are.

From Feudalism to Constitutional Government, 1853–1912

THE MEIJI RESTORATION 1868 in Japan is 1776 in the United States, 1789 in France, or 1917 in the Soviet Union. It symbolizes the birth of a modern Japanese nation. In that year the governing structure of centralized feudalism presided over by the Tokugawa was abolished, and full power and authority were nominally restored to the Emperor, who took the reign name Meiji (meaning "Enlightened Rule"). Whether this political change was cause or symptom has been debated, but no one has denied that vast changes of all kinds accompanied and rapidly followed this emergence of a new government. What happened in the Meiji Restoration and why? What part did political opposition play?

The coup d'état of 3 January 1868 climaxed fifteen years of increasingly violent struggle between provincial feudal lords and the Tokugawa government. Historians are fairly unanimous in locating two main sources of this struggle: long-run socioeconomic changes which undermined the structure of Tokugawa society and the ability of the Tokugawa to rule, and the demands made by the Western maritime powers beginning with and following Commodore Perry's arrival in 1853. The socioeconomic changes created classes of discontented people, weakened the relative power of the Tokugawa government vis-à-vis some fiefs, and unbalanced the rough equality between power and privilege for social classes which a

---

5. Not surprisingly, a difficult barrier to the development of peaceful, parliamentary opposition in Japan has always lain in the fact that such opposition by its nature appears to be less sincere and more opportunistic and self-serving than violent, structural opposition. Thus, in Japanese political mythology, Saigō is revered while Itagaki is viewed cynically; the political parties of the 1920s and 1930s are criticized or dismissed entirely, while the assassins are respected and have art films made about them (Mishima's *Yūkoku*); and today's Communists morally outshine the Socialists, who in turn outshine the Democratic Socialists.

stable society must maintain.[6] And thus the demands made by the United States, Britain, Russia, and the Netherlands — and the power behind those demands — constituted an unavoidable, momentous challenge for Japan, at a time when the rulers were unable to find any way of responding without further weakening their own position.

In the context of unrest, discontent, and Tokugawa weakness, the question of how to respond to the Western threat was inextricably linked with the domestic political — that is, constitutional — question of who should organize that response. Essentially, three different "constitutions" were the conflicting goals which motivated the struggles during the fifteen-year period of political uncertainty between 1853 and 1868. The Tokugawa lords and their close vassals generally preferred to continue the existing government while adopting a radically changed foreign policy. Many provincial lords, on the other hand, wanted to end the Tokugawa dictatorship. But the anti-Tokugawa forces differed on the alternative to the status quo. Each lord wanted to increase his own fief's influence in the government, and each anticipated a restoration of the Emperor's authority; but some envisioned a kind of collegial rule or congress of nobles which would include the Tokugawa, while others (the more powerful) hoped to replace Tokugawa power with their own.

Eventually, in November 1867, after a humiliating military defeat the previous year, the Tokugawa ruler formally returned his governing authority to the Emperor in an attempt to salvage as much power as possible under a system of collegial rule. But this prompted the most anti-Tokugawa lords, who held a slight military advantage and who had formed an alliance shortly before with some nobles of the court, to stage their coup d'état. By "gaining possession" of the Emperor and by defeating the Tokugawa forces in a short civil war, this alliance succeeded in replacing the Tokugawa as the governors of Japan.[7]

---

6. Cf. Gerhard Lenski, *Power and Privilege* (New York: McGraw-Hill, 1966). Concretely, the discontented classes included most members of Tokugawa society, though the sources of the discontent varied (declassé feudal knights were numerous, starving farmers were prone to riot). But most ominous for the status quo, rural landowners and urban merchants had more real social power than the official status system gave them prestige, while many former knights performed no function, and had no skill, to justify their high social prestige.

7. The strongly anti-Tokugawa coalition consisted of the four fiefs of Satsuma (located at the southern tip of the southern island of Kyūshū), Chōshū (at the extreme western end of Honshū), Tosa (on the southern side of the island of Shikoku), and Hizen (near Nagasaki in northwestern Kyūshū). Within one year after the Restoration, these four fiefs had openly taken control of the government, filling all but one of the critical posts of councillor (*sangi*) with their own men. No more appointments were made; and except for death, retirement, and resignation over policy clashes, these men never left their posts. The remaining seven took over the key ministerships when the cabinet system replaced the *sangi* in 1885. These seven

Described in this way (that is, deemphasizing the underlying socio-economic causes and emphasizing the political events), the Meiji Restoration appears — properly, in my opinion — as a successful movement of political opposition carried out by a part of the traditional ruling class with the support of some of the people, mainly wealthy merchants and landowners. Because the Tokugawa system of government did not allow for any opposition, the Restoration had to be a political revolution; but the victorious feudal lords and court nobles did not form their coalition on the basis of an agreement about what they should do with their newly won power, let alone to modernize or lead a social revolution. Nevertheless, the Restoration did have some features which gave it a revolutionary impact far beyond that of a simple change of political officeholders. For one thing, the victorious fiefs' armies were financed largely by the wealthy merchant houses of the great trading cities; it could be expected that the new rulers would not institute a system of government which would impede the growth of commerce as had the Tokugawa system. Moreover, among the leaders of the victorious fiefs there were many men who were firmly committed to making Japan into a nation equal in strength to the Western nations, so that the latter could not do in Japan what they were doing in China. The Restoration gave these men entry into the highest levels of government, whereas the Tokugawa system of government had prevented them from exercising much influence.

Viewed from one angle (the development of capitalism), the Meiji Restoration can be seen as a mere symptom of a more basic socioeconomic process: the rise of the merchant class. But viewed from another angle (Japan's response to the West), the Restoration, as a successful oppositional movement, brought into positions of authority men with ideas about what the country should do which were radically different from the policies of the previous rulers. In this sense, the Restoration is an excellent example of the principle of the autonomy of politics and, more narrowly, of the significance of political opposition for national development. Suppose, for instance, that the extremist, victorious opposition had not succeeded and that the moderate feudal lords and the Tokugawa had allied and formed a government centered on some sort of congress of nobles. Various possibilities, different from what actually followed the Imperial Restoration, can be imagined: civil war, or the emergence of indigenous parliamentarism via some sort of estates general, or (most

---

men also became the *genrō* (see pp. oo–oo). Of the nine men who served as prime ministers between 1885 and 1918, eight were from these four fiefs (seven were from Satsuma and Chōshū), and the ninth was a court noble allied with these fiefs. See R. K. Reischauer, *Japan Government-Politics* (New York: Nelson, 1939), pp. 64–65, 107; and Roger F. Hackett, "The Meiji Genrō," in Robert E. Ward, ed., *Political Development in Modern Japan* (Princeton: Princeton University Press, 1968), pp. 69–71.

likely) subordination to the Western colonial powers. That none of
these possibilities did occur must, I think, be seen largely as the result of
the victory of the extremist opposition in the Meiji Restoration.

THE EMERGENCE OF OPPOSITIONS   The coalition of feudal lords and
knights and Imperial courtiers who engineered the Meiji Restoration lost
little time in implementing the policy of strengthening Japan vis-à-vis the
West. Their goal was not revolution, nor was it modernization in the
broad sense in which the word is understood today. Rather, the victorious
coalition aimed at building a strong nation economically and militarily
(*fukoku kyōhei*); political and social changes were made only in order to
reach that goal. In this sense Japan's modernization began conservatively:
the goal was economic and military development and national security,
and the strategy was to conserve existing institutions, customs, and social
class relations as much as possible. Gradually, of course, it became necessary to make some changes in political and social institutions, but wherever
possible the Meiji leaders preferred to renovate existing institutions, so
as to be able to use them in the pursuit of economic and military goals.

Ample evidence of these priorities lies in the timing and phasing of
Meiji modernization. First of all, the new regime was to be formally led
by the Emperor. A centralized administration was called for in an Imperial
Rescript of 1868 and was established rapidly thereafter. The feudal lords'
fiefs were confiscated by the central government in 1871,[8] and payment
of taxes in kind was replaced by money payment of taxes the following
year. Thus in three years the new government had assured itself of an
adequate financial base and had established an administrative structure to
collect revenues and to implement further policies. To strengthen the new
government at home as well as overseas, a conscription law was decreed
in 1870 and rigidly enforced in the following years. Strategic industries
such as mines and iron foundries (the latter having been set up for military
reasons in the two decades prior to 1868) were taken over by the new

---

8. How could the new government "abolish" feudalism in three years? The answer
lies partly in the very generous treatment meted out — at first — to the feudal lords;
although some retainers and knights felt the squeeze, the lords were well cared for.
More importantly, the four lords who had nominally led the Restoration coalition
were persuaded by their "advisors" (who were really running the government) to
make a present of their lands to the emperor in 1869; with this as a model, it was
possible for the new government to get the other lords "voluntarily" to "return"
their lands to the Emperor. At first this exchange was in name only: the central
government sent an official to each fief, but he acted only as its representative, and
the former lord was called governor. Gradually the government's policy became
more clearly antifeudal (e.g., in 1871 the government promised to pay both lords
and knights a permanent pension, but a few years later the pension, especially for the
knights, was sharply reduced and was converted into a lump sum payable in government bonds). But this policy had dire effects only on former knights, while former
lords were able to survive the transition relatively comfortably.

central government and given the highest priority. The first railroad was in operation by 1872. Foreign trade doubled in the decade following 1868, and a system of national banks was established in 1872 to facilitate exchange and credit. A system of universal elementary education was also established in 1872, and by 1880 41 percent of the school-age population was already enrolled.

But these changes were not intended to — nor did they — accompany equivalently radical political changes. First and foremost, the countryside was held constant. It was necessary to keep the peasants (who made up over four-fifths of the population) on the land and powerless, enmeshed in traditional social relations and without local self-government, because the peasants were to finance economic growth through the land tax. Second, individuals' rights were made clearly subordinate to the policies of the Imperial government. The absence of any desire for a modern system of legally guaranteed rights was implicitly demonstrated when the Meiji leaders established their bureaucracy (which was to exercise judicial as well as administrative tasks, at first) before giving any thought to governmental structures which would allow for popular representation or for the protection of private rights. Later, the constitution made the priority of government over subjects explicit. Third, the government established a new peerage system, not so much to create new vested interests in the regime as to give existing influential groups (former feudal lords and knights, wealthy merchants, the Imperial court) a stake in the new system. Other examples of the lack of enthusiasm among the rulers for democratic political and social change were the conscious use of the army and the schools to make the people into loyal, obedient subjects of the Emperor and the absence for twenty-two years of *any* mechanism to allow for popular participation in national policy making. During this entire period, the structure of the government was simply that of a bureaucracy, adorned at the top with ineffectual councils representing only the former feudal elite.

But even under this strategy of conservative modernization, plenty of change did occur in Meiji Japan. Stability and national integration were achieved in spite of the changes taking place — thanks to the linguistic, ethnic, and religious homogeneity of the people, the institution of the emperor, and especially the continuity in the leadership of the government.[9] The great feudal lords and court nobles of the Restoration coalition first held the top positions in the government, but policy was largely in the hands of the nominally subordinate officials who had really carried out the Restoration. These "lieutenant colonels" of the Restoration — men such as Kidō, Ōkubo, Itagaki, Ōkuma, and Saigō — quickly became

9. See note 7 above.

the "generals" of the government after 1868, to be gradually replaced by the "majors" and "lieutenants" who had worked with them in forming the victorious Restoration coalition and in founding the new government. This last group (which was later called the *genrō* and will be discussed below) remained in power until well after the turn of the century and the establishment of constitutional government — a continuity in leadership which modernizing nations today may well envy (in inverse proportion to the value they place on democracy).

But of course the oligarchy did not simply replace older leaders with younger ones. Political disagreements and conflicts spawned the mutations on which the evolution of the oligarchy turned. The first serious split among the rulers came in 1873 over the question whether to engage Korea in war or to focus on economic growth. Out of this split emerged two oppositional movements, which appear in retrospect as the beginning of the two basic traditions of Japanese political opposition (see figure 9.1).

One of these movements, personified by Saigō Takamori, the knight who had led the coup d'état in 1868, is usually called reactionary because

Figure 9.1   Traditional Lines of Japanese Political Opposition

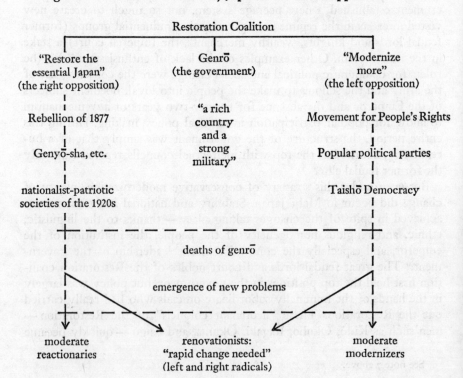

of its opposition to the government's increasingly antifeudal economic and social policies. This movement expressed itself in several armed uprisings during the 1870s, culminating in the abortive Satsuma Rebellion of 1877, in which Saigō's knights were defeated in battle by the conscription-based army of peasants which the modernizing government had recently established. This defeat signaled the end of armed resistance to the new government. The other oppositional movement of the 1870s organized itself not in feudal armies but in political societies which called for greater popular participation in government. (It must be remembered that at this time "popular" participation was conceived as involving, not the masses, but only the former feudal ruling class and the wealthy merchants and landlords.) This movement was fed by grievances among the farmers at the taxation and military service being forced on them, as well as by the spread of Western political ideas, which made the open expression of antigovernment attitudes less illegitimate. The establishment of provincial assemblies in 1878 gave this opposition a forum for debate, though certainly not yet for participation in policy making.

THE MOVEMENT FOR PEOPLE'S RIGHTS   The development of the latter movement — from the founding of the short-lived Society for Fixing One's Aim in Life in 1874 through the establishment of political parties seven years later and up to the promulgation of the Constitution in 1889 — is usually called the Movement for People's Rights. This was the first nonmilitary, organized political opposition in modern Japan. Organizationally, the Movement was never coherent: there were scores of local societies as well as ambitious "national" parties, but effective coordination between the capital and the countryside, let alone a hierarchical unity, was never achieved. Ideologically, the Movement gained momentum by demanding constitutional, representative government; but as it gained strength, many other interests came to be reflected in the actions and statements of the leaders. These leaders were drawn largely from the former feudal ruling class, though wealthy farmers and landowners exercised influence in their local societies, and men affiliated with commercial and industrial interests were also prominent among the leaders of urban groupings.

The Movement peaked in 1881, when most of the local societies joined one of two new national parties, the Liberals and the Progressives. The Liberal party, descendant of several relatively radical political societies of the previous decade, was led by Itagaki Taisuke, a "lieutenant colonel" of the Meiji Restoration who had left the government in protest over its cautious foreign policy in 1873. The party was strong in the countryside and often dominated the prefectural assemblies, although this rural base contained the seeds of a later split between tenant farmers and landowners.

(By 1890, as we shall see below, the party had shorn itself of the more radical elements.) The Progressive party was founded by another dissident oligarch, Ōkuma Shigenobu, when he left the government in the Crisis of 1881. In comparison with the early Liberals, the Progressives were rather moderate, urban, and close to the business community, though the Liberals too had some business support.

After 1877, the Movement for People's Rights was the only fundamental political challenge to the oligarchs' strategy of conservative modernization. It had grown out of the near-universal feeling that some sort of constitutional government was desirable for Japan. Accordingly, the Emperor's promise in 1881 that there would be a constitution greatly weakened the motive force behind the popular political movements. At the same time, the radical activities of some tenant farmers, who were suffering under the Imperial government's fiscal policies and an economic depression, began to attract more attention. Riots and prison sentences for sedition followed rural uprisings in several prefectures. To meet these disturbances and perhaps to lure party leaders away from their grassroots following, the government enforced a number of repressive laws during the 1880s, culminating in the so-called Peace Preservation Regulations in 1887, the immediate consequence of which was that nearly six hundred persons, including almost all important opponents of the government, were exiled from the capital. The upshot of these developments and of the establishment in 1885 of a cabinet form of government, in preparation for promulgation of the Constitution four years later, was that opposition to the government split in two. The "responsible" oppositions prepared to enter the elections and confront the government in the new Diet. The "irresponsible" oppositions in the provinces formed organizations with such names as Debtors' party, Tenants' party, and Oriental Socialist party before succumbing to the authorities. By 1889 the government's skillful carrot-and-stick policy had borne fruit: there was no opposition to the new Constitution.

Historians are not unanimous in their evaluation of the significance and consequences of the Movement for People's Rights, although its educational importance is unquestioned. It may be that the Movement forced the oligarchy to promise in 1881 that a constitution providing for a representative assembly would shortly be written. It may be, however, that the Movement merely strengthened the hand of those within the oligarchy who themselves desired the establishment of a constitutional, representative form of government. In spite of this uncertainty, or rather because of it, the Movement for People's Rights is a classic instance of structural political opposition in Japan: articulate public opinion was strongly in favor of some constitutional changes, a segment of the ruling group was (autonomously or not) in favor of this demand, and this *combination* of pressure and power was sufficient to establish new broad guidelines within which policy would subsequently evolve. To put the point somewhat differently, the Movement alone, in opposition (as it was in the 1870s), could neither overthrow the government nor persuade it to make basic constitutional changes. But the Movement did not act alone; eventually some of the oligarchs came to share its goal of constitutional, representative government. Together, as a coalition, the Movement and the more progressive oligarchs were able to determine the government's decision, namely, to have a constitution and a representative national assembly. This decision, implemented in the Constitution which was promulgated in 1889, was tremendously important, as it shaped the context within which political conflicts were to be worked out during the following generation.

CONSTITUTIONAL GOVERNMENT, 1890–1912   The two decades following 1890, the year in which the first Imperial Diet met, were characterized by several important trends. The Imperial Constitution was accepted by all political actors. The political necessity of having the support of a majority of the Diet's Lower House for a cabinet came to be recognized by the oligarchs (*genrō*) who "advised" the Emperor on whom to appoint in the cabinet. Even if political parties were selfish, grasping, and thoroughly undesirable as partners in governing — and most of the *genrō* thought so — political party support was needed. Both because of the Constitution and because of pre-Constitutional forces and traditions, there was no possibility that a political party or even a coalition of parties could effectively control the government without the support of several other power groups. The House of Peers in the Diet, the Privy Council, the personal followings of individual *genrō* and the institution of *genrō* council meetings, the institution of an "appeal to the Throne," and the autonomous Army and Navy General Staffs were loci of power and authority into which the parties could not enter. Structural opposition, in the form of socialist study groups, weakly raised its head. The government's technique for dealing with such opposition was illustrated in measures like the draconian Public Police Law of 1900, which replaced the 1887 law and added a clause prohibiting labor unions. Any incentive the parties might have had to broaden their popular base and the types of interests they were representing was removed by the restrictive tax qualifications on the suffrage.[10] In the first election, according to government figures, only 450,000 males out of a total population of over forty million were eligible to vote, and as late as 1920 the eligible voters

10. Moreover, the open, often violent intervention of the Home Ministry in elections raised serious questions about whether a party could succeed at all at the polls if it became too mistrusted by the government. Official reports show that 25 persons were killed and 388 wounded in the 1892 election; Liberal candidates were arrested and their property was burned.

composed less than 6 percent of the total population. The fact that all the political parties were elite groups, composed of landowners, industrialists, bureaucrats, and a few professional politicians, resulted in a style of party conflict that stressed policy differences rather than ideological confrontation, though policy differences involving the rural-urban cleavage could get fierce. Finally, in the realm of policy, the successful wars with China and Russia and the long-sought abrogation of the "unequal treaties" which the Western powers had obtained from Japan shortly after they opened the country[11] helped to create a substantial consensus in Japan on the broad outlines of desirable national policy. The *fukoku kyōhei* policy was vindicated. There was general agreement that the emphasis on national development and international recognition was beneficial and should continue.

One result of these trends was that by 1910 political opposition in Japan had "dissolved" into the ruling system. *Genrō* and bureaucrats had entered the political parties, while party men were entering into compromises with the oligarchs. The parties did not remain on the outside, in opposition, waiting for a ground swell of popular sentiment to sweep them into undisputed control of the government and enable them to enact some new program. Electoral restrictions made such a ground swell unlikely; diffusion of power in the government made undisputed control and enactment of a program impossible. Rather, the parties accepted the system as it was and attempted to gain as much power as possible within it. That the road to power wound through the Imperial Palace and the offices of big business and the bureaucracy, rather than through working-class quarters and peasant districts, was simply a fact of political life — albeit a fact which the political parties were quite willing to accept. In short, once having made the decision not to oppose the constitutional settlement of 1890, and given their power-seeking orientation, the parties came to find that the institutional and political realities of the Meiji ruling system left them with little chance to be an opposition at all. The only way to exercise ruling power, which was the party leaders' goal, lay in coalition with other power groups. In order to be eligible for membership in such coalitions, it was necessary not to be too far distant — in aims, tactics, and style — from those groups and individuals who could become one's future coalition partners.

This description of politics in the late Meiji period emphasizes the "modern" nature of the major political oppositions of the time. There was also another kind of political opposition, which can be traced back to the founding of the Dark Ocean Society (*Genyō-sha*) in 1881 and even

11. These treaties contained humiliating provisions (such as extraterritoriality) and economically damaging provisions (such as that Japan could not set her own tariffs and customs duties).

to the assassination of Ōkubo Toshimichi, one of the key leaders of the Meiji Restoration, in 1878. This opposition — a continuation of the traditionalistic reaction, which had been defeated in battle in 1877, to the Meiji oligarchs' policy of modernization — still called for a greater emphasis on the "strong military" half of the oligarchs' goal, "a rich country and a strong military." Popular resentment at the Triple Intervention (by Western powers, preventing Japan from reaping the full fruits of military victory over China in 1895), overwhelming popular support for revision of the "unequal treaties," and widespread criticism of the Treaty of Portsmouth (for not recognizing sufficiently Japan's victory over Russia in 1905) were sufficient to make all political groups somewhat chauvinistic, but societies like the Dark Ocean Society and the Amur River Association were especially expansionist.[12]

It was with regard to tactics, however, that these groups distinguished themselves more clearly from other oppositional groups. Indeed, their preference for tradition produced contempt and disdain for political parties and elections. In place of such Western methods for expressing opposition and influencing rulers, the ultranationalists used intimidation, physical violence, and various kinds of threats against even the most highly placed leaders. By virtue of their personal ties and good relations with several members of the nobility and oligarchy, and thanks to their strong-arm bullies or "goons" (*sōshi*) who were used at election time, these right-wing groups were able to exert pressure on the rulers and at the mass level out of proportion to their numerical membership. But during this period their opposition was expressed primarily as hostility to the political parties and as pressure regarding governmental policies. They were not yet opposed to the political system as a whole.

Taishō Democracy and Shōwa Fascism, 1912–45

PASSING OF THE GENRŌ   The Meiji Emperor died in 1912. His son, who took the reign name Taishō, reigned from 1912 to 1926; his grandson, who took the reign name Shōwa, has been Emperor since 1926. Since it was the Taishō period that saw the first commoner become prime minister and the first cabinets dominated by the political parties, this flowering of liberal democratic trends is often called Taishō Democracy. Similarly, since militaristic and nativistic groups and policies came to dominate the government after around 1931 — and since it provides a neat contrast with the potentialities visible in the earlier period — scholars have labeled the post-1931 developments Shōwa Fascism. These labels can be very

12. The name of the Amur River Association, founded in 1901 as an offshoot of the Dark Ocean Society, referred to the geographical boundary its members were willing to accept on Japan's manifest destiny.

misleading, without being entirely inaccurate, as an examination of political oppositions during the two periods will show.

In later years, the Meiji period came to have the aura of a golden age, when political giants strode the earth, smiting the forces of foreign intervention and domestic reaction and instability, forging a modern economy and state which compelled respect from the whole world. And it is true that the *genrō* were remarkably successful nation-builders and modernizers. But their very successes created conditions which, once the steadying hand of the masters was removed, posed serious problems for the next generation of leaders. It was this situation — the demise of the Meiji oligarchy and the emergence of political, economic, social, and international dislocations which were unavoidably liked with earlier successes — rather than any sudden changes in the body politic, which provided the base for both Taishō Democracy and Shōwa Fascism.

Robert Scalapino has pointed out that the "two-party democracy" in late Meiji and Taishō Japan was in reality not very different from the system of rule in one-party states in much of the Third World today.[13] There was serious electoral competition in Japan during this time, and its significance should not be underestimated. But electoral competition had no effect upon policy making and cabinet formation, partly because of the nature of electoral politics and partly because of the power of the *genrō*. The leading *genrō*, such as Itō Hirobumi and Yamagata Aritomo, did not exercise their influence by participating in the hurly-burly of cabinet-government politics. Instead, after the turn of the century, they were represented in cabinet politics by their protégés, men such as Katsura Tarō and Saionji Kimmochi, while they retired to the Privy Council.

From such "transcendental" positions, working through networks of acquaintanceships and loyalties built up during twenty-five years of wielding power, the *genrō* were able to coordinate the actions of many different powerholders who otherwise would have quarreled endlessly. Coordination may have appeared to be accomplished by an invisible hand, but the forces producing coordination were not at all disembodied. Saionji and Katsura could peaceably alternate control over the prime ministership from 1901 through 1912,[14] thanks to such networks of friendly relations as those between Itō and the bureaucracy, Yamagata and the armed services and the Privy Council, and Itō and the majority Seiyūkai party, which Saionji and Katsura could rely upon their mentors to use in case of trouble. When a cabinet crisis or a serious dispute on policy arose,

13. Robert Scalapino, "Elections and Political Modernization in Prewar Japan," in Ward, *Political Development in Modern Japan*, chap. 8.
14. During this twelve-year period there were four cabinets, headed by these two men, with an average lifespan of three years. This contrasts with the average lifespan for the entire period 1885–1945 of 1.4 years per cabinet. Even more striking, in the ten years of "party government" following Yamagata's death, 1922–32, cabinets lasted an average of only *one* year.

the seven *genrō* would hold a conference and then "advise" the Emperor (that is, they would make the decision) on what to do. This power to advise the Emperor, which the *genrō* nearly monopolized, was of course the key to their authority.

However, these aging elder statesmen did not produce any successors. Prince Saionji, the youngest, served as prime minister for the last time in 1912 and thereafter failed to exercise remote control as effectively as Itō and Yamagata. Gradually death took its toll, and by 1924 all of the *genrō* but Saionji had died. Thus the main stabilizing, coordinating mechanism within the Japanese government was lost. Whereas in 1914–15 the "militarist" Yamagata could effectively restrain those generals in the army who were calling for action on the Chinese mainland, there was no such restraining force in 1928 or 1931.[15]

TAISHŌ DEMOCRACY   While the influence of the *genrō* was disappearing, three developments were combining to confront Japan's new leaders with some nearly insoluble problems. These developments concerned popular participation in politics, the various effects of economic growth and social mobilization, and the international situation in the western Pacific, Siberia, and China.

Japan's growth during the period 1913–30 was remarkable. Population increased by 25 percent; the national income more than doubled, even when measured in real (constant) money terms; the number of people living in towns over 10,000 increased by 50 percent; and it has been estimated that the real wages of industrial workers rose during the same period by over 50 percent. This growth was possible because of the infrastructure (transportation, banking, communications, etc.) and high level of investment built up during the Meiji period, and it was further stimulated by World War I. The war boom was consolidated and extended during the following decade. Nevertheless, serious instabilities, especially in farm prices and the banking and currency system, remained to plague the economy. In the late 1920s near-disaster was the result of a domestic deflationary policy, an attempt to return to the gold standard, and the onset of the Great Depression. From 1925 to 1930 real income for farmers is estimated to have dropped by one-third, and foreign trade dropped 50 percent in value terms, while the government's retrenchment policy earned the enmity of the armed services.

The significance of these developments lies in their connections with political events. In the early 1920s, workers' and farm tenants' unions were formed; in 1925 universal manhood suffrage was enacted into law; and in 1926 the first serious socialist parties were formed. As a result, there were now means available for the growing urban working class and the

15. In 1928 Japanese officers in Manchuria arranged the murder of a powerful Chinese warlord. In 1931 came the notorious Manchurian Incident.

increasingly oppressed tenant farmers to articulate their grievances and demands to the government. The first election under the new system was held in 1928, and the social democratic parties won 5 percent of a total vote of almost ten million (but this was so badly distributed that they won only 8 out of 458 seats in the Lower House). Three elections later, in 1936, the Left's vote had risen to 6 percent, and in 1937 10 percent of the electorate voted for social democratic parties. In the latter year, 38 out of 466 seats were held by social democrats.

These social democratic parties were deeply opposed to the entire ruling system, including the bourgeois parties, but their tactics were on the whole those of a loyal opposition. Except for May Day rallies and petition campaigns, the non-Communist Left concentrated in practice on electoral and parliamentary opposition to overthrow the capitalist system. This was doubtless due in large part to the repressive Peace Preservation Law of 1925 (the same year that universal suffrage was enacted!) and its enforcement by a police force which did not hesitate to use boots and sabers to break up demonstrations. The Socialists' goal really was to do away with the existing system, and in the 1930s many socialists joined forces with the rightist national socialists in opposing the bourgeois government.

Other political developments also followed the increasing industrialization and embourgeoisement after the Russo-Japanese War (1905). On the center, the major parties became increasingly tied financially to the large industrial-financial combines, called *zaibatsu*, which were coming to control more and more of the economy. Scandals involving bribery and corruption were not rare, but more important perhaps was the general and continued reliance of the parties for election campaign funds upon the largest economic groupings. Since these parties, descendants of the earlier Liberals and Progressives, were led primarily by ex-bureaucrats and ex-military men plus some rural gentry — and since votes, at least in rural areas, were delivered in blocs by local notables and election bosses — the social interests represented by these parties had tended from the beginning (1890) to be the interests of the political elite (that is, "a rich country and a strong military") and of the landowners. The *zaibatsu* could enter this coalition because of their key role in Japan's economic growth and their personal ties and financial contributions to the politicians, but they hardly made the parties into representatives of the broad middle class.[16] Small independent farmers, shopowners, people in service

16. It is important not to impute to Japanese capitalists *any* of the ideology of capitalism in the West. The virtues of competition and the need for as little government as possible were not apparent to "the community-centered entrepreneur," as Gustav Ranis describes the early Japanese capitalist. See his "The Community-Centered Entrepreneur in Japanese Development," *Explorations in Entrepreneurial History* 8 (1955).

occupations, schoolteachers, and so on, to say nothing of workers and tenant farmers, could not expect the major parties and parliamentary politics to solve their problems.[17] Because the major parties were thus so clearly tied to special interests (big business and the landowning and absentee landlord classes), their increasing power was easily attacked as illegitimate, whether from the right, the left, or in general from below.

Of course, the major parties did have programs. (The Seiyūkai, for example, was for a "positive" — that is, expansionist — foreign policy and continued economic expansion.) But given their landlord-dominated memberships, the types of connections it was necessary to cultivate with the bureaucracy in order to exercise power, and their reliance upon big business for operating funds, the parties would have found it difficult to sponsor legislation favoring tenant farmers and urban workers even had they wished to do so. Moreover, in a political culture which stressed national unity, devotion to duty, and self-sacrifice, it was difficult to overlook the corrupt, self-serving nature of the parties or to find any reason to be patient with them when they proved unable to cope with increasingly difficult problems, at home and abroad, after 1925.

Electoral politics during Taishō Democracy also undermined the parties' legitimacy, even while superficially increasing their parliamentary power. The institutionalized pattern was for a party to gain control of the government by some parliamentary maneuver (for example, a ruling party would split and some factions would support the opposition party on a vote overthrowing the cabinet), and then call for elections. The new ruling party would put an "election specialist" into the powerful Ministry of Home Affairs, under whose authority were not only the police but also the (nonelected) prefectural governors. Each governor would be charged with ensuring that the new ruling party did well in his prefecture, and given the power of the governorship and personal ties with key local notables, most governors could satisfy the demand. Money was needed in this process to help persuade the notables and election bosses to deliver their machine votes to the ruling party.[18]

Finally, a number of structural oppositions emerged during the period of Taishō Democracy. Most were akin, in style and aims, to the Dark Ocean Society and the Amur River Association, the nationalist and military expansionist societies of the Meiji period. These groups were incensed by the government's failure to obtain full satisfaction from the Western powers at Versailles (1919) and Washington (1921) and were determined

17. These elements of the middle class were the main source of support for the fascist movement in the 1930s. See Maruyama Masao, *Thought and Behavior in Japanese Politics* (New York: Oxford University Press, 1963).

18. This system worked. Professor Scalapino has pointed out that a party in control of the government *never* lost an election in prewar Japan (see his "Elections and Political Modernization in Prewar Japan").

to push further the expansion on the mainland which, after doing well in the Shantung Peninsula in 1914, had gotten stuck in the Siberian campaign of 1918–20.[19] Others, often more like appendages of the ruling class than oppositional groups, were formed to "protect the essence of Japan from communism." Several of these groups were actually headed by prominent members of the military and the nobility, such as the *kokuhonsha*, founded in 1924 by Baron Hiranuma, vice president of the Privy Council. If such groups were too close to the establishment to be considered truly opposed to the government, the same could not be said of the groups headed by such men as Kita Ikki and Ōkawa Shūmei, who by 1920 were advocating a form of national socialism for Japan. Kita's *Outline Plan for the Reconstruction of Japan* (1919) was banned by the police, but its influence spread anyway. His call was for a revolution, led by the military, which would socialize Japanese capitalism and prepare Japan to lead an anticolonial revolution in Asia. Other revolutionaries, such as Gondō Seikyo, called for the destruction of urban capitalism and a return to an agrarian-centered economy. None of these revolutionaries, however, was opposed to the Emperor system.

There was also a structural opposition on the left — the Communists — but it was illegal and severely harassed by the police, so that its influence was extremely limited. However, this "illegal Left" did play some part in splitting the social democrats (the "legal Left"), who were divided in their attitudes toward the Communists. Moreover, one tactic for controlling the entire Left, after passage of the repressive Peace Preservation Law of 1925, was to redefine the content of "legal" socialism more and more narrowly each year, with the effect that there was some migration to the banned side of the line of legality from the other. Nevertheless, the significance of the Communist structural opposition lies in the weakness of the entire Left, rather than in any positive effects which the

19. This new oppositional movement cannot be understood without recalling the international situation after World War I and the foreign policies of the party governments from 1918 to 1932. It was generally agreed in Japan that Manchuria and northern China should naturally come more and more within the Japanese sphere of influence; but except for supporting continued economic penetration, Japanese foreign policy in the decade after 1919 was highly conciliatory. There were successes: the Washington Four Power Treaty of 1921 recognized Japan's naval superiority in the western Pacific, and in return for leaving Siberia in 1920, Japan took all of the island of Sakhalin. But in the context — the Soviet Union could only get stronger in the future, threatening Japan's position in Manchuria and even in Korea, and there were clearly more economic benefits to be gotten from China than Japan was currently getting — there was reason to doubt the judgment of men like Foreign Minister Shidehara, who argued that caution and negotiations were the wisest means toward success in Manchuria. When, in the late 1920s, policies of economic retrenchment led to actual reductions in levels of army strength, it began to look as though party government meant a betrayal of the fundamental policy, held since the Meiji era, of building "a rich country and a strong military."

proletarian opposition was able to produce. The threat of revolution came from the right, much more than from the left.

To summarize these complex developments, the deaths of the *genrō* meant the demise of the only institution in Japan capable of getting all elite groups to agree (or acquiesce) on policy. This occurred at a time when economic growth, social mobilization, and Japan's international situation were generating intense and ever more conflicting demands upon the government. The conflicting positions of the various political actors as of 1930 are very crudely described in figure 9.2. There were basically two dimensions of cleavage: (1) between those who saw the answers to

Figure 9.2   Political Issues and Actors in Japan, 1930

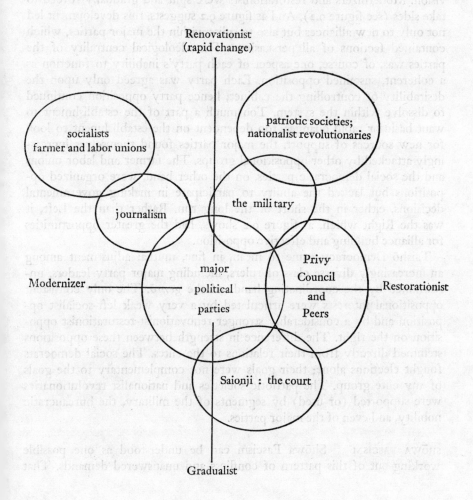

Japan's problems in further modernization and those who looked for some sort of restoration of what was fundamentally Japanese, and (2) between those who believed that the existing politico-economic system had to be rapidly renovated and those who hoped to change as gradually as possible. The difficulty of building a stable ruling coalition lay in the fact that each actor could look in two directions for allies. A renovationist could find himself in sympathy at times with modernizers, at other times with restorationists; a modernizer might be drawn to a renovationist or to a gradualist, and so on. A cabinet of modernizers — for example the Hamaguchi Cabinet of 1929–30 — could be riven in two when renovationist-modernizers and gradualist-modernizers failed to agree on policy.

In very oversimplified terms, the major ideological development during this period was the increasing salience of the renovationist-gradualist division. Modernizers and restorationists were split and gradually forced to take sides (see figure 9.2). And as figure 9.2 suggests, this development led not only to new alliances but also to splits within the major parties, which contained factions of all persuasions. The ideological centrality of the parties was, of course, one aspect of each party's inability to function as a coherent, sustained opposition. Each party was agreed only upon the desirability of controlling the cabinet; hence party opposition continued to dissolve within the system. Too much a part of the establishment to want basic or rapid changes, too dependent on the establishment to look for new sources of support, the major parties found themselves increasingly attacked by other oppositional groups. The farmer and labor unions and the social democratic parties, on the other hand, were organized oppositions but lacked the ability to participate in making governmental decisions, either in the short or the long run. Rather than the Left, it was the Right which, as figure 9.2 shows, had the greater opportunities for alliance building and effective opposition.

Taishō Democracy came to mean, in fine, mutual adjustment among an increasingly diverse class of rulers, including major party leaders, unrestrained by the coordinating hands of the *genrō*. The only consistent oppositional interests were articulated by a very weak left-socialist opposition and by a considerably stronger renovationist-restorationist opposition on the right. The difference in strength between these oppositions stemmed directly from their relations to the elites. The social democrats fought elections alone; their goals were not complementary to the goals of any elite group. The patriotic societies and nationalist revolutionaries were supported (or used) by segments of the military, the bureaucratic nobility, and even of the major parties.

SHŌWA FASCISM   Shōwa Fascism can be understood as one possible working-out of this pattern of conflicts and unanswered demands. That is, the government leaders and their policies after 1932 increasingly reflected the successes, in the interelites struggles, of some of the elites and their oppositional cohorts. Shōwa Fascism was thus a new constitutional settlement, directed by a de facto coalition of the military, some of the peerage, some of the political parties, and the right-wing patriotic societies. This coalition cannot be described primarily as a mass movement, any more than the success of the Movement for People's Rights during the Meiji period can be understood without considering the leadership of dissident oligarchs such as Itagaki and Ōkuma. Without the leadership of the military — without its *constitutional* power and its authority as the Emperor's personal sword, and without the tactical support of its friends in the government — the movement might have produced only a few assassinations.

Indeed, the successes of the "fascist" movement, aside from the demise of the political parties and a change in symbols, were almost entirely successes of the military elite: increased power for the services in national policy making, increased governmental-military control over the economy, increased military activity abroad. Revolutionaries like Kita Ikki were executed; right-wing social reformers saw the benefits of increased economic growth go not to poor farmers but to increased military procurements; conservatives saw the Emperor's prerogative used increasingly to justify a radically new type of government-directed and -planned economy; and patriotic societies found that they were no longer wanted after they had helped to remove the party politicians from the seats of paramount power. This is not to say that such developments were consciously planned by the military elite ahead of time, though within the Army General Staff there were such planners. But the partial successes and eventual conclusion of the "fascist" opposition of the 1930s can be comprehended only in light of the connection between the patriotic societies and a segment (the military and some others) of the ruling class and against the background of oppositions among the ruling elites.

In summary, the interpretation of Shōwa Fascism offered here is that it was a typical successful Japanese oppositional movement. It was similar to the Meiji Restoration, the Movement for People's Rights, and the events of the 1950s in terms of its organization, its tactics, and the nature of its success. Organizationally, it combined popular support, structural oppositions, and a segment of the ruling class. Tactically, elections were relatively unimportant; the creation of a national mood, demonstrations, and extralegal pressures supplemented the decisive struggles which occurred between ruling elites. Success meant, not a sudden replacement of one set of rulers by another, but the gradual emergence between 1931 and 1937 of a new coalition which enforced a new constitutional order. Finally, the "fascist" oppositional movement was typical in that it grew out of a conflict between the governing system and the demands of the society which the governing system could not resolve. Its success was no more inevitable than the success of any oppositional movement at any time in any country, but it certainly did not constitute a deviation from some normal path of politics in Japan.

Postwar Democracy

Japan's commitment to the forms of constitutional government was revealed even at the height of the period of Shōwa Fascism. The cabinet government system remained in use during the entire wartime period; elections were held even at the height of the Pacific War; and even under the circumstances of the time, some candidates ran for and were elected to the Diet who were not approved by the government. However, regardless of the form which Shōwa Fascism took, the content did not allow for any organized opposition. The collapse of oppositions may be partially explained as the result of wartime pressures which began with the China War in 1937 and never let up. But the "voluntary" dissolution of political parties in 1940 and the formation of a quasi-totalitarian one-party system must be recognized as, at the very least, marking the temporary closing of Japan's experiment with organized political opposition.

The profusion of political groups which burst into the open as soon as the wartime straitjacket had been removed showed that the eclipse of oppositions had been only temporary. (Indeed, some prewar party leaders had even met secretly during the war to plan for a new political party which would surface when the opportunity should come.) Moreover, the government itself, once the tight grasp of the military was loosened, quickly began to recover its prewar appearance. There is no reason to doubt that military defeat alone, without an Allied Occupation of the country, would have been sufficient to return to the moderate conservatives and to the political parties the power and influence which had been theirs before the rise of the military. But the United States and its allies had other plans for Japan than a complete return to the prewar situation.[20]

THE CONSTITUTION OF 1947   In retrospect, it is clear that the Occupation made four fundamental decisions which have stood the test of twenty years' time: (1) It decided not to destroy the Emperor's position as head of state but only to downgrade it. (2) It decided to establish a new constitutional framework to restructure policy making and the settlement of conflicts. Extraparliamentary loci of authority — the Privy Council, the

20. In the following paragraphs, *Occupation* and *United States* are used interchangeably, as the Occupation was an American operation.

Imperial Household, the House of Peers, the military General Staffs — were abolished. (3) It decided to reform the landowning system radically, so as nearly to abolish farm tenancy. (4) It decided to establish labor unionism on a solid footing.

The effect of the new Constitution, promulgated on 3 May 1947, has been to make Japanese national politics into parliamentary, cabinet government politics along Western European lines and to abolish the legitimacy of antiparliamentary groups. The political parties in the Diet choose the country's top political leaders and basic policies, subject merely to the sort of pressure-group politics which is taken for granted in industrialized Western nations. The political effect of the land reform has been to create a huge class of basically satisfied farmer-owners, who vote regularly for the conservative parties. The political effect of the institutionalization of labor unions, linked in large national federations, has been to extend permanently the range of the political spectrum, giving the organized laboring class a political voice and guaranteeing that the Socialist parties will continue to obtain a respectable share of the vote in nationwide elections.[21]

To understand the basic political structure when the Occupation left Japan, it is necessary to know what the Occupation tried to do before it left. The reforms noted above were all enacted in its early "democratization and demilitarization" stage. After 1947 its goals changed to economic reconstruction and remilitarization. (This change was due to the evolution of United States' strategic thinking about the Far East in the light of the Cold War and Communist victories in China.) The crucial 1949 general election in Japan, by providing the Liberal (conservative) party with an absolute majority in the Lower House of the Diet, assured that there would be no more coalition governments containing Socialists and no more minority conservative governments for the duration of the Occupation. The Liberal (conservative) government, headed by Prime Minister Yoshida Shigeru, worked closely with the Occupation to rebuild the economy and strengthen the state. This revised version of the *fukoku kyōhei* ("rich country–strong military") policy consisted of four goals:

21. Of course, the Occupation did many more things. Female suffrage; the purge of all people politically active during the fascist period, *except* the bureaucracy; the attempt to break up the *zaibatsu* (economic combines); the local government, education, and police reforms; Article IX of the Constitution, renouncing war; the Japan–United States Security Treaty; an impressive "bill of rights"; and changes in the legal status of the family system — these and other measures were part of the "new deal" which the Occupation gave to Japan.

These reforms and the other policies of the Occupation were not promulgated by a formal Allied Military Government, for there was none. The Occupation ruled through the men and institutions of the Japanese government. Ironically, "democracy" came to Japan via a most traditional political structure, the bureaucracy, which thereby preserved its independence and power.

diplomatically, alliance with the West; militarily, gradual rearmament; economically, rapid reconstruction and growth; and politically, a stable government unshaken by attacks from the Left. After the end of the Occupation, Prime Minister Yoshida pursued this last goal somewhat further, in the direction of making the Left less able to attack at all — a policy that was tagged as a "reverse course" (in contrast to the early years of the Occupation) and stirred up serious controversies.

The policy of economic reconstruction and growth was eventually highly successful. However, because it was a policy of austerity (wages and consumer goods lagged behind rises in productivity) and because it was so closely tied with the Korean War and the American alliance, it deepened the cleavage between business and the conservative parties, on the one hand, and labor and the Left, on the other.[22] As the economy boomed, the *zaikai* (the top financial, industrial, and business community) regained and even amplified its prewar voice in politics. The prewar story of personal ties between businessmen and politicians, of financial dependence of the conservative parties on large businesses, and so on, repeated itself. On the other hand, the Socialists and the labor unions became more and more strongly opposed to the conservative, business-oriented regime. Although the Occupation had helped to form Sōhyō, the major union federation, in order to destroy Communist influence in the labor unions, by 1952 Sōhyō and many of the Socialists were in violent opposition to all the policies of the Yoshida government.

By 1952 it was also clear that several other actors would play some role in the post-Occupation political stage. The ultraright, though greatly weakened by the Occupation purge, was still capable of some organization. The Communist party, driven underground during the Korean War, was prepared to continue its opposition. Offstage, the United States continued to play an important part in Japanese politics — often as a whipping boy, but not infrequently as an active influence. And an important addition to the nonconservative camp came from the reemergence of the mass media, especially the newspapers, as an autonomous political force. This development was probably tied with another — the politicization of the intelligentsia. With a "never again" zeal, these two groups played an active if mainly critical role in the opposition to some of Prime Minister Yoshida's policies.

Finally, the political parties were important actors on the political scene

22. There were many individual politicians who were liberal conservatives and moderates (that is, between socialists and conservatives) during the Occupation; but they were either independent of any political party, or in some small party, or merely followers in the conservative party of Yoshida. It is striking — and should be counted a missed opportunity for the eager reformers in the Occupation — that no nonsocialist, genuinely progressive *party* survived the Occupation. Cf. the fate of the younger Progressives, described below. Of course this "failure" was hardly accidental.

during and after the Occupation. In 1952 there were four major parties in the Diet: a left and a right Socialist grouping, the governing Liberals, and the Progressive party. This last had two wings, corresponding to the two generations represented among the party leaders. The prewar politicians and bureaucrats (many of them depurgees) were relatively conservative, while the postwar generation included a number of moderates, "humanist socialists," and so on.

THE "CONSTITUTION OF 1955" [23]   Figure 9.3 describes the relative positions of the important political actors with regard to what I consider the two basic issues at the close of the occupation. Although the Occupation had of course significantly shaped the postwar constitutional order, some fundamental questions remained to be resolved after independence. One of these basic issues involved the extent to which Occupation-enforced sociopolitical reforms would be nullified, in fact or in law. The other basic issue involved the directions in which national resources and energies would be allocated. In concrete terms, these two issues came down to rough dichotomies:

1. Should the government extend and protect the Occupation's democratic reforms, or should it "correct the excesses" of the Occupation (as the conservatives explained their goal)?

2. Given that the Occupation's trust-busting program was misguided, should government planning and economic consolidation be aimed at producing high levels of economic growth, or at distributing social welfare as fairly as possible? Related to this, should resources be allocated to defense industries or not?

These questions remained to be answered before the basic constitutional order of postwar Japan would be settled.

The late-Occupation and immediate post-Occupation ruling coalition consisted of the Yoshida Liberals (who had an absolute majority in the Diet after 1949), the bureaucracy, the economic elite, or *zaikai*, and the United States. This coalition's disposition on the two basic constitutional issues can easily be inferred from its members' location in figure 9.3. But when the Liberals lost their absolute majority in 1954, this coalition was overthrown by a coalition of Progressives plus some Liberals whose desire for power or distaste for the United States led them to oppose Prime Minister Yoshida. The new coalition had the support of only part of the bureaucracy and the *zaikai*, but it enjoyed the tolerance and occasional

23. This is a loose translation of the title of an article by Professor Masumi Junnosuke, "1955 Nen no Seiji Taisei," *Shisō*, no. 480 (June 1964), pp. 55–72.

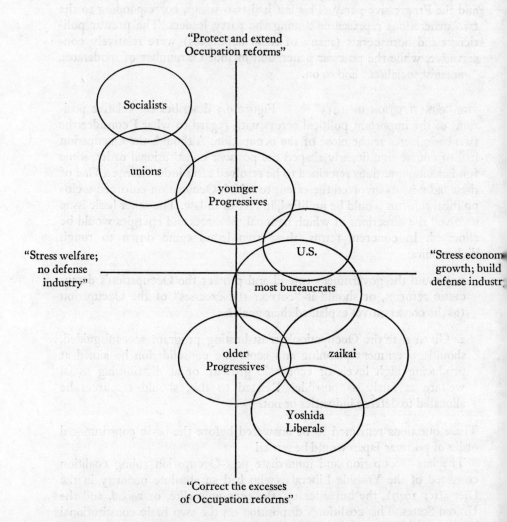

Figure 9.3   Major Political Issues and Actors in Japan, 1952–54

"Protect and extend
Occupation reforms"

Socialists

unions

younger
Progressives

U.S.

"Stress welfare;
no defense
industry"

most bureaucrats

"Stress economic
growth; build
defense industry"

older
Progressives

zaikai

Yoshida
Liberals

"Correct the excesses
of Occupation reforms"

NOTE: The positions regarding the major issue of foreign affairs — Japan's tie with the United States — are also indicated by this figure. The continuum runs from top left (least pro–United States) to bottom right (most pro–United States).

support of the Socialists and the unions. (In figure 9.3 this coalition can be seen to be leftward and upward from the Yoshida coalition.) This was the ruling coalition which set out to restore relations with the Soviet Union in late 1954. But its leader, Prime Minister Hatoyama, found that he would have a very hard time pushing through to his diplomatic goals unless he could strengthen his coalition. Although he could muster voting majorities in the Diet, he was faced with vociferous opposition from the Foreign Ministry, The Yoshida Liberals, parts of the *zaikai* (who were concerned about the American reaction to Hatoyama's "pro-Communist" foreign policy), and even elements within his own party. In order to rule effectively, it was necessary to expand his coalition of supporters.

This was the context in which the 1955 merger of conservatives and moderates to form the Liberal-Democratic party (LDP) took place. Prime Minister Hatoyama's lieutenants were trying to decrease the opposition to his policies from the conservative establishment. Some Liberal party members were anxious not to be frozen out of the political arena by a coalition of Progressives and Socialists. The *zaikai* and the Yoshida Liberals were extremely concerned over visible tendencies toward *immobilisme* (such as budget bills not being acted upon in time) and greater participation in policy making by the Socialists — both of which appeared to threaten the goal of rapid economic growth. The two Socialist parties had just merged, achieving greater bargaining strength in parliamentary negotiations.

The coalition which formed as the LDP was centered upon the older Progressives, the bureaucracy, the *zaikai*, and the bulk of the Liberal party. The younger Progressives and a few extreme Liberals were presented with a tacit ultimatum: join on our terms or starve to death. The younger Progressives, less well-off and less well-attached, joined quickly; a few Liberals held out somewhat longer. The United States supported the merger but apparently did not play an active role. In figure 9.3 this LDP coalition is located downward and rightward from the Hatoyama coalition, in the bottom-right part of the graph.

The terms upon which the LDP-forming coalition agreed dealt with both power and policy. Political leadership would henceforth be exercised solely by LDP members. The tie with the United States would not be broken. Economic policy would aim at rapid growth, and the defense industry would be built up. Some of the "excesses" in the Occupation's democratic reforms would be "corrected," especially in the areas of education, law enforcement (police), labor unions, and the antiwar provisions of the Constitution.[24] Within these basic constraints, policies

24. The LDP coalition did not succeed with this final part of its program, but the failure should not be taken as an indication of any lack of desire. Rather, the causes of the failure seem to lie in three interrelated considerations. The elections of 1955

would be worked out in a consensual fashion, with cooperation among the LDP politicians, the bureaucrats, and the *zaikai*. Governments would be formed only by the LDP, which would also take over the organization and direction of the Diet. The coercive authority in this contract was the ability of the *zaikai* to withhold funds from any politician who should violate the agreed-upon terms. Speaking more generally, the 1955 constitutional settlement determined the rules and sources of political recruitment and the basic policy constraints within which a pluralistic, interest-group-centered process of partisan mutual adjustment would produce specific policies.

THE MAJOR POLITICAL PARTIES, 1952–68 Figure 9.4 describes summarily the evolution of the Japanese party system after independence. Following the two mergers in 1955, the basic outline of the party system changed only gradually. The Socialists split again in 1959, a small group forming the Democratic Socialist party (DSP) and the majority remaining in the more radical Japan Socialist party (JSP). The LDP and the Socialists continued to share the vote only with the minuscule Japan Communist party (JCP) until 1967, when a new party called the Kōmeitō (officially the "Clean Government party"; literally, the "Bright Public party") came to rival the Democratic Socialists as the third largest party in the Diet. All during this time the LDP held an absolute majority, but the size of this majority declined from 65 percent to 54 percent over four general elections. Given the strict party discipline which holds on Diet voting (for all parties), the LDP's majority has of course kept it the perennial ruling party.[25]

The ruling LDP is a mixed bag. It combines the internal bureaucracy of a left-wing mass-based party, the nearly self-destructive free-for-all of an American party presidential nominating convention, and the lack of organized grassroots support of a French grouping of *ministrables*. There is

and 1958 made it clear that the conservatives could not gain the two-thirds majority in the Diet necessary to amend the Constitution. The Socialists were prepared to resort to physical obstruction in the Diet and massive popular demonstrations in the streets to oppose the conservatives' efforts to "repeal" the Occupation. And, perhaps most importantly, whenever the prime minister and his supporting coalition became involved in some imbroglio, the oppositional factions within the LDP did not hesitate to turn the situation to their advantage in their pursuit of political power.
25. To give some feel of what these parties are like, comparison with better-known Western party systems may be helpful. Superficially, the closest similarity is with Germany: the LDP is somewhat stronger than the Christian Democrats but roughly similar in outlook and socioeconomic backing, while the JSP (at least before the DSP split away) was like the Social Democratic party. A good parallel would exist with Italy, if the Christian Democrats did not contain a labor wing and did contain the small center and right-wing parties. The JSP lacks the mass base of the Italian Nenni Socialists and Communists but overlaps them ideologically, while the Japanese DSP closely resembles the Saragat Socialists.

Figure 9.4   *Parties' Diet Seats and Popular Vote,*
1952–67

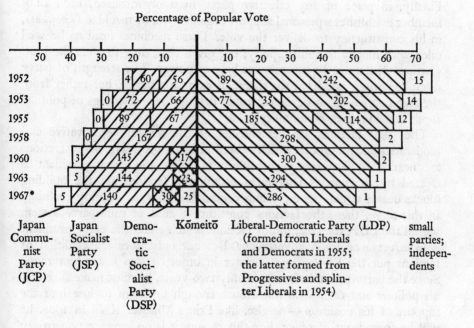

Percentage of Popular Vote

NOTE: The *length* of each segment of a horizontal bar shows the party's percentage of the popular vote. The *numbers within* the bars show the number of Diet seats held by each party.

*In 1967 the total number of seats increased to 486 from 467.

an LDP Policy Research Council subcommittee corresponding to nearly every standing committee in the Diet and to each government ministry. These party subcommittees work interdependently with their legislative and bureaucratic counterparts in the process of formulating policy proposals. The Policy Research Council itself reviews its subcommittees' work and, if favorably disposed, passes the ideas to the party's General Council, which makes final decisions on policy for the party. On the other hand, when it comes to choosing the party president (who is naturally the prime minister and who makes the appointments to the party's internal organs), discipline and order disappear in wild factional struggles. The factions, it should be noted, do not fight directly for control over the organs of the party bureaucracy (that is, over party policy making); rather, they concentrate on determining the leadership of the party itself. Finally, in place of any effective party mass organization, each LDP member establishes a personal support organization, or machine (*kōenkai*), in his constituency to deliver the vote. These machines need to be well oiled with money to run properly; but given that, they provide the LDP dietman with a nearly autonomous base of power. The strength of party discipline arises, not from the threat of expulsion per se, but rather from the fear that too great deviance would dry up the wellsprings of political funds in the business community.

The LDP factions are descendants of the several conservative and moderate political groups which existed prior to 1955. The major factions are headed by aspiring prime ministers. Since the party president is elected by the party's Diet membership, the factions are the building blocks out of which the victorious candidate builds his winning coalition. In this sense, then, the factions constitute a kind of multiparty system within the LDP; the coalition of factions which elects the party president is in effect a coalition government. But not only does the coalition of factions put the LDP prime minister in office; it also keeps him there. Since the party president's term is only two years, he must make sure that his policies and tactics do not arouse enough criticism to lose him the support of his coalition — or else, like Prime Minister Kishi in 1960, he will be forced out of office. For this reason, it is no exaggeration to say that dissident LDP factions are the major intraelite opposition in Japan today.

The JSP, on the other hand, is the major opposition party. Of course, since such "socialist" measures as the nationalization of the railroads, the establishment of a national health system, and economic planning have been carried out by the conservatives, in the absence of major sociopolitical changes the possible scope of new Socialist programs is somewhat limited. Nevertheless, the JSP promises to draw Japan away from its close relationship with the United States, to institute a far-reaching program of social welfare, and to rationalize the economic system. But regardless of such programs, there is no doubt that the impact of a Socialist government would be significant, simply by undermining the close relationships between LDP and such "apolitical" organizations as the agricultural cooperatives, the associations of prefectural and local government officials, and such parts of the bureaucracy as the Ministries of Education, Welfare, Labor, and Justice.

Like the LDP, the Socialists lack internal unity and grassroots organization. In place of a mass membership, the JSP can rely on the support, funds, and votes of most of organized labor, especially of the giant union federation, Sōhyō. But the weakness of its mass organization is perplexing, since the JSP has long been committed to achieving power through electoral and parliamentary means. Its extraparliamentary tactics are limited to staging demonstrations, supporting strikes, and occasionally engaging in physical obstruction of Diet proceedings. Otherwise, the JSP's strategy and tactics mark it as a loyal opposition.[26]

The Democratic Socialists were, until 1959, the most right-wing faction within the JSP. They have never gone much beyond that stage, in terms of Diet strength, although the continued support of the second largest labor federation promises that they will not disappear altogether. At the time of its formation, the DSP stressed that it was a socialist party which was committed primarily to preserving and strengthening true parliamentary democracy in Japan, thus earning distinction as a classical opposition in the British tradition. There seems to be no chance that the DSP will substantially increase its Diet strength; but should the LDP lose its absolute majority, the Democratic Socialists apparently hope to stand first in the line of potential coalition partners. Until such a time, the DSP is continuing to play the role of a responsible opposition, between the ruling party and the "irresponsible" JSP. Generally the DSP refuses to participate in joint struggles with the JSP if the Communists are included, but on most significant clashes in the Diet the DSP does not side with the government.

The Communist party's fortunes have varied considerably in the past two decades. Its respectable image during the Occupation, before the onset of the Cold War, led to some electoral success in 1949, but the Cold War and the Occupation's anti-Communist purges during the Korean War period destroyed both the JCP's influence and most of its mass following. Since it reemerged in 1955, there has been a steady, slow increase in voting support, but in 1967 the JCP still won only five seats in the Lower House of the Diet. The sources of JCP strength lie less in Diet seats than in the party's strong organization; in the sympathetic support of much of the intelligentsia, many students, and a few labor unions; and in the cooperative attitude which some elements of the JSP hold toward the Communists. The worsening relations between the Soviet Union and Communist China have affected the JCP, but since 1965 the party has adopted a neutral stance between the two — a development welcomed by many Japanese, especially in the large cities, where support for the JCP as a "pure" opposition is relatively strong.

The Kōmeitō is a fascinating puzzle. It is the political expression of an evangelical Buddhist sect called the Sōka-gakkai, a group which claims to embody the spirit of a famous thirteenth-century Buddhist priest and which has gained adherents rapidly in the postwar period. The Sōka-

26. Indeed, widespread rumors to the effect that the ruling party has on occasion bought JSP cooperation in the Diet with money raise the possibility that the JSP is already becoming essentially an opposition within the system.

gakkai has a strong, cell-type, mass organization which allows considerable central coordination, and it is generally believed that Kōmeitō votes in elections come almost entirely from families belonging to the religious order. As religion and politics have traditionally been linked in Japan, the growing strength of the Sōka-gakkai in the late 1950s and early 1960s was naturally paralleled by increasing political activity. After electing some members to local and prefectural assemblies and then to the Upper House of the Diet, the Kōmeitō finally ran thirty-two candidates in the 1967 general election, of whom twenty-five were elected. Even now, nevertheless, it is difficult to appraise the political tendencies of this religious-political partnership.

Kōmeitō spokesmen stress that the party is an opposition dedicated to improving the quality of politics and of the people's life, to preserving parliamentary democracy and the "peace Constitution." Such sentiments place the Kōmeitō very close to the Democratic Socialists; and in the short run, indeed, the Kōmeitō's strategy seems to be the same as the DSP's, namely, to be an available coalition government partner when the hoped-for multiparty era arrives. However, it is clear that the Kōmeitō is not an autonomous agent; its highest leaders are appointed and replaced at the direction of the Sōka-gakkai. And the absolutist nature of Sōka-gakkai religion, plus its hierarchical organization and the bullying tactics of conversion often used, suggest that preserving parliamentary democracy may be more of a temporary tactic than a basic goal.[27] Further, since the bulk of the Sōka-gakkai's members seem to be either lower middle class —the "noncommissioned officers of Japanese fascism," in Professor Maruyama's phrase[28]— or workers outside the labor unions, the movement tends to arouse fear in the middle and upper classes and the established political parties, who labeled the Sōka-gakkai as "neofascist" in the days before it became too influential to affront. A final appraisal of the Sōka-gakkai/Kōmeitō is not possible on the basis of ideology and social support alone, however; the crucial question is whether membership will continue to expand. As a small party, the Kōmeitō is playing the role of a responsible opposition, and there is no reason to doubt that, given this level of strength, this role will continue.

Oppositions and Elections

Since 1955 the constitutional order in Japan has been stable, with only minor fluctuations and gradual long-run changes. The Liberal-Democratic

27. This is not an unreasonable interpretation in context. When Japanese opposition parties speak of preserving parliamentary democracy, they usually mean, concretely, keeping the LDP from running the entire Diet show unilaterally.
28. Maruyama, *Thought and Behavior in Japanese Politics.*

party has maintained an absolute majority in the Diet, with all the left and center parties in opposition. The basic policy guidelines are those determined by the "constitution" of 1955; within those constraints, specific policies are arrived at by bargaining and mutual adjustment among LDP politicians, interest groups, and bureaucrats. The leadership of the government always consists of LDP faction leaders and their lieutenants; the prime minister is put in office by a coalition of LDP factions. It is the workings of that system which this and the two following sections try to describe and explain, looking first at how the LDP maintains its Diet majority, then at how governments are made, and then at how policy is made — stressing, in each case, the role of oppositions. (As explained above, pp. 346–47, this way of speaking of oppositions does not readily make sense in Japanese. This is a fact that cannot be overemphasized.)

The rhetoric of Japanese election campaigns emphasizes opposition between the ruling party and the other parties, but a closer examination of the electoral system in action suggests that here may be a good example of opposition dissolving into the system. A typical dietman does not win an election by attracting the votes of citizens who might have voted for another party's candidate; rather, he wins by turning out his own party's fairly stable vote in his district. Thus the hardest campaigning an LDP candidate must do is usually directed, not against his oppositional rivals, but against other LDP candidates in the same district. A party's candidate may, in his campaign, repudiate the statements or actions of his party leaders almost as often as he criticizes the other parties. And, of course, elections have not yet resulted in replacing the majority party with a different majority party. So an accounting of oppositions and elections in post-1955 Japan must involve an explanation of why, in the midst of all the strident rhetoric of confrontation, there has been only gradual, secular change.

The history of the parties' electoral fortunes described in figure 9.4 can be accounted for by four factors: voters' attitudes, the legal electoral system, the parties' electoral strategies, and their vote-delivering mechanisms. With regard to voters' attitudes, the impression given by the figure — that there are stable party loyalties in the population — is corroborated by public opinion polls.[29] The LDP has the regular support of roughly 40 percent of the population, and the Socialists (JSP) can claim the loyalties of about 25 percent. The Kōmeitō and the Democratic Socialists (DSP) are each currently supported by about 5 percent of the people. A large part of the "don't know" respondents in such polls are rural women, who can be expected to vote for the LDP; urban "don't knows" are fewer, but they partly constitute a floating vote which can

29. Each of the three major newspapers in Japan conducts a reliable nationwide survey once a year in which party-support questions are always asked.

go to the opposition parties. The Communists' voting support probably comes out of this last group; people hesitate to tell pollsters of their Communist affiliations.[30] In short, a fairly stable base of party loyalties helps to explain why the votes gained by the parties in general elections show only fairly slight and gradual changes.

These gradual changes consist of a long-run decrease in conservative support and a long-run increase in support for the opposition parties. One key to this change is the steady numerical decline of the farm population as industrialization progresses. Both aggregate voting results and opinion surveys regularly show that votes in rural areas are predominantly conservative, while the Left gets the bulk of its support from more urban, industrialized areas. Rural popular attitudes and social institutions have made it "a truism that in Japan the foundations of conservative political strength lie in the countryside." [31] Thus it is not surprising that village-to-city migration and farm-to-factory job changes are strongly associated with the decrease in conservative support. By 1967 this trend had already gone so far that the LDP for the first time received less than half the popular vote.

But of course party identification alone cannot account for election results. There is also the question of why people vote so consistently for candidates of the party they support. Do election campaigns matter so little — are the issues raised in elections so irrelevant to partisan choice — that the act of voting means nothing more than an indication of relative party preference? No ultimately satisfactory answers to this question can be given, but empirical studies of voting behavior do suggest some general conclusions.[32] First, in the rural areas of Japan, containing one-third of the population, people still tend to vote as the hamlet or village notables

30. Perhaps a better indicator of Communist support is the circulation of the party newspaper, *Red Flag*, which has a Sunday circulation of over four million in a nation of roughly one hundred million people.
31. Robert E. Ward, "Urban-Rural Differences and the Process of Political Modernization in Japan," *Economic Development and Cultural Change* 9 (October 1960): part 2, p. 148. A recent survey of Japan's four major metropolitan areas showed that urbanites support the Socialists just as much as the LDP, while urban people younger than forty markedly prefer the socialists (*Asahi Shimbun*, 20 November 1965).
32. See Ward, "Urban-Rural Differences." Most of these studies have been conducted by Japanese social scientists and are not available in English, but there are partial summaries in Allan B. Cole, *Japanese Society and Politics: The Impact of Social Stratification and Mobility on Politics*, Boston University Studies in Political Science, no. 1 (Boston, 1956); Douglas Mendel, *The Japanese People and Foreign Policy* (Berkeley and Los Angeles: University of California Press, 1961); Masumi Junnosuke, "A Profile of the Japanese Conservative Party," *Asian Survey* 3 (August 1963): 390–401; and Warren Tsuneishi, *Japanese Political Style* (New York: Harper and Row, 1966). A good recent set of studies is contained in Nihon Seiji Gakkai (Japan Political Science Association), ed., *Seiji-gaku Nempō* [Political Science Annual] *1965: Seiji Ishiki no Riron to Chōsa* [Political Consciousness: Theory and Research] (Tokyo: Iwanami Press).

suggest they vote. The national political struggle simply does not intrude into most of the countryside. Vote brokers who deliver all the votes of an area en bloc in exchange for favors are still around, but more important are the personal ties of the rural elite with prefectural or county politicians. Here, in the traditional, parochial countryside social structure, lies the base of conservative strength. Second, for many Japanese the tiny subcommunity within which they work, eat, and play determines how they will vote. The three or four employees in a barbershop will probably vote as their employer votes; the coal miners in most mines will vote as their union leaders suggest.[33] Third, for the attentive public — the politically informed voters — the basic electoral choice is not so much between parties as for or against the "constitution" of 1955, though the issue may not be posed consciously in these terms. This choice does not vary from election to election. A stereotypical university professor may switch from voting Communist to voting Socialist, but he will not seriously consider voting for the LDP; a stereotypical banker might vote for an unknown LDP nominee in disgust with some recent scandal involving the LDP incumbent, but he will not be likely to vote for one of the opposition parties' candidates.

These three types of political consciousness all contribute to electoral stability because they make it almost impossible for voters to switch from one side of the government-opposition confrontation to the other. This is why the total figures on party identification and on vote outcome are almost identical. If a voter supports the LDP because his hamlet chief and everyone in the hamlet supports the LDP, or because his peers and employer support the LDP, or because he is basically in agreement with the "constitution" of 1955, he is clearly not in a mental state to consider voting, say, Socialist. Of course, it is important to recognize the difference between a voter who cannot change his vote because he does not see his vote as a conscious political act and a voter who cannot change because he is committed to or against the ruling system. But either type of voter — and together they clearly constitute the bulk of the Japanese electorate — creates electoral stability.

But the popular vote is not converted directly into Diet seats. The electoral system for the Lower House plays an important screening role between the vote and election outcomes.[34] There are 123 constituencies,

33. The prevalence of these two types of political (un)consciousness suggests that the trend to the left among in-migrants may be due to a shift in the source of social pressures (e.g., breaking the social relationships which bind one to the people in some LDP dietman's support organization, when one leaves the farm), rather than to some radicalization of the newly urban ex-farmer.
34. See Nathaniel B. Thayer, *How the Conservatives Rule Japan* (Princeton, N.J.: Princeton University Press, 1969), chap. 5. The great importance of the electoral system was illustrated when the Socialist- and Communist-backed candidate, Professor

somewhat arbitrarily drawn (in a manner similar to the U.S. House of Representatives). Each electoral district sends either three, four, or five representatives to the Lower House, depending on the district's population; but the voters within a district cast only one vote each. Of the several candidates, those (three, four, or five) with the most votes are declared elected. For example, in the 1967 general election, each voter in the Second District of Hiroshima Prefecture, which sends four representatives to the Lower House, had to cast his ballot for one of seven candidates. The results were (asterisks indicate winners):

Candidate	Party	No. of Votes	Status
*Masuoka	LDP	61,235	new
*Hamada	JSP	55,752	new
*Tanigawa	LDP	51,901	incumbent
*Nakagawa	LDP	50,995	incumbent
Matsumoto	LDP	49,616	former incumbent
Kato	Indep.	43,568	new
Harada	JCP	9,588	new

The crucial feature of such a middle-sized-district electoral system — that is, one in which the districts elect more representatives than a single-member district system (as in the United States) but fewer than a multi-member proportional representation system — is that the parties not only fight each other but also fight within themselves, as the four LDP candidates obviously did in this example. Also, the mere existence of groups in the population loyal to a party does not guarantee success at the polls, since a party must get its supporters to distribute their votes among its candidates with maximum efficiency.

The two parties large enough to run more than one candidate in an electoral district, the LDP and JSP, face this latter problem often. Within any district there is a given number of sure party votes, and there are usually only a few floating voters. The party wants to elect as many candidates as possible, but if it nominates too many men, they may divide the available vote into such small pieces that several of them lose. For example, two LDP candidates with 100,000 votes to share between them may well be defeated by a JSP candidate with only 60,000 votes, whereas a single LDP candidate would win. The problem is compounded by intra-party rivalries, for in such a situation the two LDP candidates are almost

Minobe, won the election for governor (mayor) of Tokyo in 1967. In this constituency, containing over ten million people and thus by far the largest constituency anywhere and at any level of government in Japan, there is only *one* person who can be elected (in contrast to the districts which elect representatives to the Diet). Almost everything about this election was different from the elections for the national legislature — but particularly the emphasis on opposition and the outcome.

always backed by different factions in the national party, neither of which wants to withdraw its candidate. On the other hand, once the decision about which candidates to recognize has been made, the factions play a vital role. Wherever a party has more than one candidate running in a district, there is naturally competition among them to appeal to that party's fairly stable number of voters. In such cases (which are very common for the LDP and not rare for the JSP), the candidates rely upon their factions, much more than upon the party, for money and support in the campaign. Thus, in a district which has elected three LDP representatives, the three men generally belong to three different LDP factions. This critical role which a faction plays in the electoral process assures it of the continuing allegiance of its members between elections, which in turn gives the faction its strength as an intraparty opposition, should it choose to oppose the party leadership.

The mechanisms which the parties use to deliver votes vary. The Communists run only one candidate in a district, so their problem is to turn out their vote; they do this by means of the party organization. Both Socialist parties rely heavily upon their associated labor unions to deliver the vote; further, each candidate cultivates his own support organization, or personal political machine (*kōenkai*), within his district. The Kōmeitō appears to rely entirely upon the Sōka-gakkai for votes, although now that there are Kōmeitō members in the Lower House, they may begin to build up individual support organizations too. The LDP uses interest associations when it can (for example, candidates frequently get the support of the local Medical Association, the local Small and Medium Businesses Association, the local Sake Brewers Association, and so on), but it relies primarily upon the support organizations of its members. With the exception of the well-organized parties (JCP and Kōmeitō), then, candidates generally rely on local interest groups, especially in the cities, and on individual support organizations, especially in the countryside.[35]

These support organizations vary in cohesiveness. Some are merely networks of loose personal connections between a dietman and important prefectural politicians and notables; others are elaborate hierarchical structures stretching from Tokyo through several levels of government all the way to the grass roots. Some are geographically concentrated within a district (obtaining 80 percent of the vote, say, in a few towns and villages), while others cover an entire district (obtaining 35 percent of the vote, say, from all over the district). The support organizations vary, too, in the extent to which they are personalized or institutionalized; some depend entirely upon the ties and friendships of the dietman, while others

---

35. The connection between these two vote-delivering mechanisms and the determination of individual voters' attitudes by village or subcommunity attitudes, as described above, should be clear.

can be transferred from one dietman to his successor. These support organizations, which have been used by the LDP and its predecessors since the earliest elections in the 1890s, are a major reason for the persistence of overwhelming conservative strength in the countryside.

But the parties' electoral strategies do not devolve entirely into individual races. Party headquarters' decisions are important for all parties (though the impact is somewhat weakened by factional struggles in the LDP and JSP), especially regarding the number of candidates to be run, which candidates are to receive official party recognition, where and how the party's top leaders will campaign, and the sorts of issues which national party propaganda will emphasize. In general, the LDP, DSP, and Kōmeitō campaign relatively more on bread-and-butter issues and local issues, while the JSP places relatively greater emphasis on ideological and foreign policy issues — and thus appears to pick up fewer floating votes than might otherwise be possible. The JSP's reply to this implied criticism is twofold. Officially, they point out that the JSP is trying not only to win an election but also to educate the Japanese people politically, to raise their level of political consciousness, and that to campaign on bread-and-butter issues and local issues would be to submit to just those traditions in Japan which support the conservatives.[36] They also claim that a stress on ideology is helpful to motivate the party and union officials who work to get out the vote; while a few floating votes might be gained by dropping the emphasis on ideology, as many or more party loyalists might also be lost. Nevertheless, the stunning success of the relatively unideological, folksy campaign waged by Professor Minobe, who was elected the first Socialist mayor of Tokyo in 1967, will probably have some influence on the JSP's campaign style in the future.

In summary, then, the parties' electoral successes can be accounted for in broad terms by the distribution of, and trends in, partisan loyalties in the population, plus the existence of efficient vote-getting mechanisms for turning these loyalties into votes on election day. Short-term fluctuations can be accounted for by the nature of the electoral system, plus the parties' electoral strategies.

Oppositions and the Formation of Governments[37]

As in any multiparty, parliamentary system, electoral decisions in Japan determine only the framework within which the parliamentary actors

36. Although, in fact, many Socialists, when campaigning in their districts and out of the hearing of the mass media, do drop the emphasis on ideology and foreign policy.

37. References for the assertions made in this section may be found in Michael Leiserson, "Coalition Government in Japan," in Sven Groennings, W. E. Kelley, and Leiserson, eds. *The Study of Coalition Behavior* (New York: Holt, Rinehart and Winston, 1970).

must function. Between 1952 and 1955 the actors who participated in forming cabinet coalitions were the two Socialist parties and the conservative parties. Since 1955, however, the actors who have participated in cabinet formation have been the factions within the Liberal-Democratic party.

During the immediate post-Occupation period, a genuine multiparty system seemed to be emerging. Governments were, it is true, formed only by the conservative parties, but the Socialists on occasion did enter into coalitions with one wing of the conservatives to topple and to install conservative governments. The first Hatoyama Cabinet (1954), for example, was invested by the anti-Yoshida conservatives and the Socialists; in return, Prime Minister Hatoyama shortly dissolved the Lower House and held a general election, as he had promised the Socialists. But the party mergers in 1955 put an end to these developments. The new, conservative LDP held 64 percent of the Lower House seats, and a period of one-party rule began. The effect — which had been the purpose — of the formation of the LDP was to make it impossible for Socialists to participate in choosing the leaders of government and in making policy.

Instead of interparty coalition government, then, Japan since 1955 has had intra-LDP, interfaction coalition government. The role of opposition has been played at different times by each of the LDP factions. Conversely, each faction has at some time been in the ruling coalition. Table 9.1 shows these changes, along with the sizes of the factions from the LDP's formation through 1967. The shifting alliances recorded there reflect or foreshadow several of the most important political decisions made in post-1952 Japan. Prime Minister Hatoyama, with his mixed Socialist-conservative support, pushed through the normalization of diplomatic relations with the Soviet Union (1955–56) in the teeth of fierce opposition from the pro-United States Yoshida conservatives, some of the business community, and part of the Foreign Ministry. Prime Minister Ishibashi, victorious over the front-runner, well-connected Kishi Nobusuke, began his term of office in 1956 amid great personal popularity and widespread hopes for improvement of relations with mainland China, only to be stricken with a severe illness only two months later. He was replaced by Kishi and a resurgence of conservative, pro-United States policy. Prime Minister Kishi almost fell from office early in 1959 in the uproar over his Police Duties Law revisions (which would have restored to the police some prewar powers stripped from them by the Occupation), but by adroitly dropping both his program and his key coalition partners, he was able to escape relatively unscathed from the melee. In 1960, on the other hand, he could not: opposition to the Security Treaty and to Kishi's handling of it in the Diet was so intense that Ikeda was able to make his faction's support for Kishi contingent upon the latter's immediate resignation and support for Ikeda as successor.

Table 9.1   Contested LDP Presidential Elections,
Prime Ministers, Coalitions, and Factions' Strengths, 1956–66

Date of LDP Presidential Election	Victor, i.e., Prime Minister	Mainstream Coalition (in Addition to Prime Minister's Faction)	Neutrals and Oppositional Factions
Situation before 1956[a]	Hatoyama	Kono, Kishi, Ono, Ishii	Miki (the younger Progressives), Ikeda, Sato (the Yoshida Liberals)
1956 (December)[b]	Ishibashi (2)	Ikeda (7), Ishii (11), Miki (10), Ono (9)	Kishi-Sato (30), Kono (8)
1957 (February)	Kishi (33)	Sato,[c] Kono (13), Ono (10)	Miki (14), Ikeda (9), Ishii (8), Ishibashi (6)
		1958 General Election	
1959 (January)	Kishi (36)	Sato,[c] Kono (9), Ono (11)	Ikeda (15), Miki (9), Ishii (9), Ishibashi (4)
1960 (July)	Ikeda (16)	Kishi-Sato (42)	Kono (9), Ono (9), Miki (8), Ishibashi (3), Ishii (8)
		1963 General Election[d]	
1964 (July)	Ikeda (13)	Kono (15), Ono (10), Miki (10), Kawashima (5)	Kishi-Sato (27), Fujiyama (7), Ishii (7)
1966 (December)	Sato (36)	Kishi,[c] Miki (10), Kawashima (4), Ishii (5)	Ikeda (Maeo) (14), Funada (5), Nakasone (9), Fujiyama (7)

NOTE: Figures represent the percentage of all LDP Diet members (both houses) affiliated with a faction and are taken from Leiserson, "Coalition Government Japan" (cited in note 37).

[a] Before the election of December 1956, faction memberships were not unambiguous enough to enable a precise statement of faction strength.

[b] Twenty-three percent of the LDP Diet members were not in factions at this time but most of them had entered factions by February 1957.

[c] The figure given for one of the Kishi-Sato brothers includes the strength of the other's faction.

[d] After the 1960 general election, Kishi "retired" from politics. His faction divided among three of his lieutenants and so became three factions: the Kishi-Fukuda, Kawashima, and Fujiyama factions. In 1964–65, Ono, Ikeda, and Kono died. The Ikeda faction stayed together under Maeo's leadership, but the Ono and Kono factions split: some members became satellites of the Kishi-Sato bloc, and the others joined with Funada and Nakasone (subleaders of the original factions).

Ikeda began his term as prime minister with continued right-wing backing, but he shifted his coalition in order to pursue policies which were opposed by his erstwhile friends, such as rapprochement with the Socialists and a normalization of Diet politics. In spite of right-wing strength within the LDP, Prime Minister Ikeda's coalition was able to re-elect him three times, the last (1964) in the face of strong opposition by Kishi and the candidacy of Kishi's younger brother, Sato Eisaku, himself a strong faction leader. Ikeda's death shortly after his victory resulted in the prime ministership passing to his rival, who proceeded to pursue several of the policies on which Ikeda had delayed action in order not to arouse the Socialists to violent opposition, such as the restoration of relations with South Korea (1965), the revision of domestic labor laws, and the choice of a date for National Foundation Day. (This last issue was controversial because the conservatives wanted the date to be the same as the prewar "Fourth of July.")

It is clear that many important issues have arisen, have been formulated in a particular way, and have been resolved by the LDP leaders in a manner determined to a large extent by the exigencies of coalition government politics within the LDP. This curious multi-party-system-within-a-party was built into the LDP from the start. The party began as a union of several quite disparate groups of dietmen, each of which naturally wanted to gain control over the new party. As part of the tactical struggle for control, some factions were able to write into the party rules the provision that the party president would be elected every two years by a party convention, delegates to which would be the LDP Lower and Upper House dietmen (plus a nominal prefectural representation).[38] Given this system of choosing the LDP leader — who, of course, automatically becomes the prime minister — the factions existing at the start had to strengthen their internal organization and discipline, so that in the party convention the faction leader would have as many votes as possible. But at the time (and ever since) no faction controlled a majority of the party's dietmen. Coalitions between factions were necessary, and the system of intra-LDP coalition government was born.

The system has persisted, as table 9.1 shows. The reasons for the factions' persistence are fairly clear: their crucial role in the general elections; their importance to the individual dietmen as a source of friendship, information, and protection; the characteristics of the business community and its relations with conservative politicians, which enable the factions to obtain funds independently of the party organization; the continued absolute majority of the LDP in the Diet; the existence of policy-making

38. This arrangement would be equivalent to the American party convention system, if the Republicans always won every election and if about 90 percent of the Republican convention delegates were the Republican senators and congressmen.

mechanisms within the party which resolve conflict without involving the factions; and the rewards obtained by the faction leaders for their followers. As a result of the persistence of the factions and of the party presidential convention system, LDP prime ministers have continued to be put in office by coalitions of factions, opposed by the other intraparty factions. So it is necessary to inquire into the nature of these factions and of their styles of opposition.

A major LDP faction has from twenty-five to forty-five or fifty members in the Lower House and a following of ten to twenty in the Upper House. It has a single leader, who has been in the Diet (or else very closely affiliated with the party — as, for example, the chief fund raiser) for well over a decade. There is a faction office with a one- or two-man staff and perhaps a faction newsletter. The informal hierarchy within the faction is fairly clearly known to all; it is measured by the degree of trust the leader places upon a follower and by the number of followers who look to one of their number as a subleader (because he is older, wise in the ways of party warfare, and respected; or because he helps them raise money for their election campaigns; or because he is related to them by a distant marriage; or for any other reason). These subleaders are veterans of several terms' service in the Diet who have already served in the cabinet and who may have hopes of leading the faction, or a part of it, after the leader retires or dies.

The faction's members gather once a month for informal meetings, where they exchange gossip, discuss developments in the political situation, and listen to any instructions which the leader or his lieutenants might have. There may be other meetings for specific purposes, and a subgroup of the faction might also attend the meetings of one of the various suprafactional LDP policy study groups, where open criticism or support for the prime minister's policy allows the participants to size up the strength and direction of political currents. At the higher levels of power, factional leaders and subleaders meet to discuss possible cooperation and to share their respective interpretations of recent moves, possibly in the party's luxurious new headquarters building but more probably in an elegant tea house in the entertainment district not far from the Diet Building. When election time comes around, the faction leader, as a member of the party's Election Strategy Committee, will fight to get all his followers renominated and to get official party recognition for as many new candidates who are already under his wing as possible, in order to increase the size of his faction.[39]

39. This committee is — or has been, at any rate — a significant arena of opposition under the "constitution" of 1955. If a faction in opposition to the prime minister is able, somehow, greatly to increase its strength within the party (see, in table 9.1, Ikeda's jump from 9 to 15 percent of the party's Diet membership in the 1958 election and Kono's jump from 9 to 15 percent in the 1963 election), then that faction is in a

An LDP faction can choose a variety of oppositional strategies. In full opposition it will criticize the party leadership publicly; attack leadership proposals in intraparty policy-making organs if there is a chance of embarrassing the leadersip; campaign against the party leaders if they are losing popularity; and form an alliance with other oppositional factions. It certainly will not vote for the incumbent party president in his bid for reelection. In return, an opposition faction will not be well treated in the allocation of posts in party policy-making organs or the cabinet, nor get many new candidates officially recognized by the party in a general election, and it may have difficulty raising funds in the business community. Depending upon the faction leader's ambitions and estimation of where the main chances lie, an opposition faction may or may not enter the cabinet, and may or may not establish good relations with the moderate socialists and Kōmeitō.

To a very great extent, the decision to oppose the party leadership depends on three factors. First, there is the faction's size and internal discipline; small or incohesive factions may disintegrate if the faction goes into opposition. Second, there is the sort of treatment the faction receives at the hands of the party leaders; failure to get its members into the cabinet and the top party posts will almost always drive a faction into opposition. Third, there is the faction leader's estimate of whether opposition or cooperation is more likely to assist him with his long-run goal of becoming prime minister. Ideology and policy considerations, personal reputation, and connections with the bureaucracy and the business community are all relevant when a faction leader makes this estimate.

Although there are differences between the factions on policy, these differences do not appear to influence decisively the faction leaders' decisions about supporting or opposing the prime minister — except when such ideological struggles have clearly desirable power consequences. Table 9.2 gives some evidence of these different policy dispositions, though the data also show that most factions include differing views within themselves. But these and similar differences between factions do not seem decisive in the factional struggle for power. Rather, factions already in opposition will use or create a policy issue to attack the prime minister, as happened to Kishi in 1958 and 1960, Ikeda in 1963–64, and Sato in 1966–67. There has been *no* instance of a faction leaving the ruling coalition because of policy disagreement with the government.[40]

Of course the LDP factions are not the only elements of opposition in contemporary Japan. The important role played by other oppositions in

---

much stronger position from which either to oppose or to bargain its way into the cabinet.

40. At least no faction has ever claimed such a reason, which is perhaps more important than whether policy was *really* the cause of a defection.

Table 9.2 Percentage of Oppositional Attitudes Within Each LDP Faction, Spring 1966

	Kono	Funada	Ikeda	Kawa-shima	Miki	Fuji-yama	Sato	Kishi-Fukuda	Ishii
Small-electoral-district system: "Opposed"	84	42	89	84	64	55	60	7	0
Security Treaty with the U.S.: "Don't extend on long-term basis"	64	*	60	30	67	*	25	0	10
Foreign affairs, esp. relations with China: "Am a member of the 'Africa-Asia Policy Study Group' within LDP"	70	55	35	35	30	28	15	7	0

NOTE: The percentages given show, of those members of each faction who took some stand on the issue, the proportion whose position was opposed to that of the prime minister and the government. (This poll appeared in the magazine *Gendai no Me,* June 1966, before the Kono faction split and Nakasone took leadership of the larger wing, as indicated in table 9.1.)

* Too many members refused to answer to indicate a meaningful percentage.

some kinds of policymaking is noted in the following section. But with regard to choosing governments, during the period of the LDP's absolute majority, the factions have been the only significant agents of opposition.[41]

Oppositions and Policy Making

If government making in Japan is a curiously isolated, "purely political" process, the same is certainly not true of policy making. Here one

41. To the extent that the *zaikai,* or business community, participates in the choice of the LDP leader, it exerts its influence through the factions — by financial backing, electoral support, advice to the factions' leaders, and so on. Although many well-informed observers view the factions as mere puppets dancing on strings held by the *zaikai,* this view is not entirely persuasive, for two reasons. *After* the fact, it is always possible to find elements of the business community which supported the winner, but predictions made before elections have not always been correct or even unambiguous. Also, it is known that the business community assists *each* major candidate at a party presidential convention (presumably out of a desire to have a friend in power), a fact which suggests either that the business community cannot be said to determine the choice *between* candidates or else that the business community is not unified enough to be considered a single actor with a single desired outcome.

The business community's influence consists, as was shown above, in having shaped the constitutional order and policy guidelines within which the LDP factions' struggle for power takes place. Its influence also is apparent in policy making (in contrast to government making), as the next section shows.

:an see all the social, cultural, and economic cleavages which Japan can
nuster — between farm and factory, village and city, prewar and postwar,
wealthy and poor, and so on. But speaking in broad terms of fundamental
policy differences, there are three major dimensions or cleavages dividing
he Japanese body politic. Not surprisingly, these are roughly the same
limensions of conflict in terms of which the "constitution" of 1955 was
analyzed earlier (see figure 9.3).

First, there is the cleavage opened late in the Occupation and continu-
ng under Prime Ministers Yoshida and Kishi concerning the "reverse
course," that is, whether to "correct the excesses" of the Occupation reforms. Specific issues which have arisen in this area include constitutional
revision, rearmament, the antimonopoly law, revision of the educational
nd police systems, the autonomy of local government, and the date on
which to celebrate National Foundation Day (analogous to the Fourth of
uly in the United States.) In general, the conservatives have supported
uch "reverse course" policies and have been opposed by all the other
political parties, much of the mass media and intelligentsia, the labor
nions, and younger people generally. Aside from specific groups and
institutions which could benefit by such issues (e.g., on rearmament, the
idustries hoping to gain defense contracts; on restricting the autonomy of
ocal self-government, the central government bureaucracy), support for
he "reverse course" has come largely from the more traditionalistic
ectors of society, especially rural areas and older people.

Second, there is a deep division in the politically attentive public over
foreign policy. Regarding the overall relationship with the West and
he United States, the business-LDP establishment is much more united
an on "reverse course" policies (the economic benefits from these ties
eing impossible not to see), and the opposition is relatively weaker. In
his area opposition comes from the JSP, the JCP, some labor unions, and
ome of the intelligentsia. The policies which have brought this opposition
ut on the streets include the Security Treaty with the United States[42]
nd relations with South Korea. The same cleavage has been apparent
egarding the restoration of relations with the Soviet Union, the establish-
ent of the Asian Development Bank, and the question of relations with
hina and Taiwan.

Third, there is a dimension of policy disagreement relating to social
welfare and the distribution of the national abundance. This dimension of
onflict becomes visible on such issues as setting the government-fixed
ce price for producers, regulating business and labor unions, and making
idget policy. On such bread-and-butter issues there is not so much op-

. In 1960 opposition was especially strong because Prime Minister Kishi was al-
ady suspect for his "reverse course" tendencies and because his Diet tactics were
fensive to many opinion makers, especially the newspapers and intelligentsia.

position as pressure-group politics. The parties simply reflect the views of their supporters or, if their supporters disagree, of their more important supporters.

The atmosphere which surrounds issues on these three dimensions varies strikingly. Even where the same actor is involved (as the JSP was involved in the revisions of domestic labor laws, as well as in disputes over foreign policy and the "reverse course"), its tactics and its style of behavior change markedly from one dimension to another. A new initiative by the government along the "reverse course" or in foreign policy will produce a major political crisis — refusals to participate in investigatory commissions; demonstrations and strikes; physical violence in the Diet — but bread-and-butter policies are disposed of fairly calmly. Also, the influence of the oppositions varies widely among these three issue-dimensions. The oppositions (that is, pressure groups) use different tactics on bread-and-butter policies than on "reverse course" and foreign policy questions. But although successful tactics for the opposition in the latter areas are the same, oppositions have been able to implement these winning tactics more often in the "reverse course" area than with regard to foreign policy.

Why is there so little organized, sustained, ideological opposition regarding domestic socioeconomic issues? Why does opposition here dissolve into the system? Three major explanatory factors can be suggested. For one thing, conservatives in Japan, in contrast to the United States, have not opposed social welfare. Nationalized railroads, a national health insurance system, economic planning, agricultural cooperatives, and similar programs were implemented under conservative governments. Paternalistic — and selective — though the attitude may be, Japanese conservative ideology has always been closer to state socialism than to laissez-faire liberalism. This ideology has its roots in traditional Japanese political thought, which also provides a second explanation: since a partisan, sectional, or group-specific interest is very difficult to legitimate, it would be foolish, if not psychologically impossible, for any political organization which desires national stature (such as a political party) to focus its programs and activities upon such "selfish" demands.

But these explanations for the absence of a programmatic socioeconomic opposition would be incomplete without considering the nature of policy making in contemporary Japan. It is apparent to all political actors that there is some possibility of getting one's concrete interests reflected in government policy by engaging in consultations and negotiations with the ministerial bureaucrats and LDP politicians who are writing the bills, formulating the new policy initiatives, and implementing the broadly drawn legislative acts. Conversely, it has been clear to everyone since

1955 that for an opposition party to draw up a comprehensive program of economic reform and social welfare and to present it to the LDP government would be futile as far as policy goes — although it could be useful electorally, or to harass the government in the Diet, as the socialists have done on occasion with their own budget proposals. Only when an interested group is not aware of some impending decision, or when the government refuses to engage in negotiations (as, for example, has happened to the radical Japan Teachers Union, which at least parts of the Ministry of Education and some members of the LDP have long wished to destroy), does visible, public opposition need to emerge out of the more typical patterns of pressure-group politics. With the exception of annual demonstrations which are really festivities, such as the arrival in Tokyo each summer of thousands of farmers who want higher rice price supports, there have been very few instances of overt oppositions on bread-and-butter issues. Today even labor unions appear to prefer to take their case to the negotiating table rather than to risk their chances by serious strikes or demonstrations, and most of the time such negotiations are possible.[43]

On bread-and-butter issues, then, not to negotiate simply guarantees that the worst possible outcome (from the point of view of the interested group) will occur. On "reverse course" and foreign policy issues, however, this is not necessarily the case at all. Since in these areas it is usually the government that takes an initiative, while the oppositions prefer inaction (preserving the Occupation reforms, not tying Japan still closer to United States foreign policy), the outcome "do nothing" is often *most* preferred by the opposition. Nevertheless, simply being uncooperative does not bring success to the opposition, since the government, if united, can almost always legislate its preferences into policy. Thus the opposition in these areas of policy must also succeed in allying with a part of the government or the ruling party in order to veto or check the government's policy proposal.

A successful opposition strategy on "reverse course" and foreign policy issues thus involves, first, bringing many people and groups into active, public disagreement with the government and, second, having a part of the ruling group take up and support the oppositional position within government councils.[44] This winning strategy has never been possible on foreign policy issues, but it has been used on "reverse course" issues. A

43. Once one is negotiating — i.e., participating in decision making — the requirement in the traditional political culture that leaders behave harmoniously and uncompetitively prevents open, uncompromising opposition.
44. Recall the pattern of successful opposition in the Meiji Restoration, the Movement for People's Rights, and the Shōwa Fascism of the 1930s.

few examples may be helpful to clarify this general picture of oppositional strategies and successes in the three areas of conflict.[45]

"Reverse course" issue 1: The Police Duties Law revision bill (1958).
With little advance warning, Prime Minister Kishi introduced into the
Diet a bill designed to return to the police some of the powers which the
Occupation had taken from them, namely, to stop and search and to
enter buildings virtually at will. Almost immediately a deluge of criticism
descended — from newspapers, left-wing parties, intelligentsia, labor unions, and so on. When it became apparent that the prime minister intended to push the bill through the Diet fairly rapidly in the face of all
this opposition, even some of the business community began to raise voices
of caution. At the time there was a strong oppositional alliance within the
LDP, composed of three factions which hoped to defeat Kishi in his race
for reelection as party president a few months later. Some of the members
of this alliance were genuinely opposed to the content of Kishi's bill, as
well as to his handling of it in the Diet. As it became clear that the cost
of passing the bill might well be to lose the coming election, the prime
minister weakened. Eventually the bill was left to languish and die without
final action. (Kishi was reelected as LDP president.)

"Reverse course" issue 2: Rearmament (perennial). Japan has completed her third Five Year Defense Plan, and every year the budget
contains the appropriations necessary to finance the increasing expenditures on military equipment and personnel. The Socialists and Communists and some of the intelligentsia strongly oppose the trend. They
argue that the policy is unconstitutional (forbidden by Article IX, which
renounces war as an instrument of national policy) and dangerous in its
implications for the country's economic system and foreign policy. The
left parties attack the armaments program every year in the Budget Committee of the Diet, producing information on defense contingency plans
which outline how Japan should attack North Korea in certain situations,
claiming that these plans are actually the ones being used by the government. But no one in the LDP–business community establishment takes
these objections seriously, the newspapers refrain from much criticism,
and even the labor unions merely go through the motions of verbal opposition. The policy of increasing military strength each year continues.

45. The following case studies are based upon the vernacular press of the time, plus
D. C. S. Sissons, "The Dispute over Japan's Police Law," *Pacific Affairs* 32 (March
1959):34–45; Donald C. Hellman, *Japanese Foreign Policy and Domestic Politics*
(Berkeley: University of California Press, 1969); Hans H. Baerwald, "The Ratification
of the Japan-Korea Normalization Treaty" (mimeographed 1967); Taguchi Fukuji,
"Nō-sei o meguru Tō Shunō-bu to Jingasa Giin" (Party Leadership and Backbenchers
on Agricultural Policy), *Ekonomisto*, 10 April 1964, pp. 18–27; and Ehud Harari, "The
Politics of Labor Legislation in Japan" (Ph.D. dissertation, University of California,
1968).

Foreign policy issue 1: Restoration of diplomatic relations with the Soviet Union (1955–56). Prime Minister Hatoyama wanted very much to end the existing state of war between Japan and its powerful northern neighbor, but an influential group within the Foreign Ministry was opposed, and the Yoshida Liberals fought bitterly against the government's initiative. If the Socialists had not supported the government, it would have fallen; but even with a voting majority, the government was severely shaken by the conflicts within the conservative camp and had to expand its coalition. Though the opposition was conservative on this issue, rather than left-wing, the tactics were typical. Public opinion was agitated; Diet and intraconservative camp proceedings became extremely difficult in the face of endless delaying actions; and all potential weaknesses in the unity of the ruling party were explored with an eye to bringing about some defection from the prime minister's majority and overthrowing the cabinet. It became impossible for the prime minister to make any concessions to the Russians because of the public opinion campaign being waged by the opposition, and since the Russians would not yield either, a peace treaty was impossible. Nevertheless, as has been the custom in this area of conflict, by adroit political maneuvering the prime minister did succeed in normalizing diplomatic relations, in spite of the unusually strong opposition.

Foreign policy issue 2: The Japan-Korea Treaty (1965). After several years of negotiations, the treaty to establish relations with the Republic of Korea and make reparations for forty years of colonialization was initialed and taken home for public inspection. The left parties opposed the treaty violently, charging that it was designed to pull Japan into a United States-dominated "Northeast Asia Treaty Organization" and that it was unfair to the Korean people who had suffered under Japanese colonialism in the past. Labor unions, students, and some of the mass media were critical of the treaty, and large-scale demonstrations occurred daily around the Diet Building. But the LDP was united and had the backing of the business community (which was already looking forward to the investment opportunities being opened up by the treaty). In a series of moves recalling Prime Minister Kishi's steamroller tactics in the 1960 crisis over the Security Treaty with the United States, the government forced the treaty through the Diet and received the needed ratification (though in the absence of all the opposition parties' representatives).

Socioeconomic issue 1: Setting the government's rice price (annual). Every year the government sets the price at which it guarantees that farmers will be able to sell their rice. The Finance Ministry's Budget Bureau tries to keep the rice support price the same as the previous year's, and each year LDP and other parties' representatives from rural areas petition the Ministry for a higher support price. The finance minister usually ends up having a talk with the other leaders of the LDP, in which political considerations override economy. The LDP simply cannot afford to offend its rural backers too sharply, so the farmers win a small victory over the haughty bureaucrats in the powerful Finance Ministry.

Socioeconomic issue 2: Ratification of ILO Convention 87 (1967). As early as 1959, the Foreign and Labor Ministries suggested ratifying the International Labour Organization's declaration of Labor's right to organize in unions. Negotiations on whether Japan should ratify were carried out during Prime Minister Ikeda's tenure between an LDP Special Committee, some JSP members, and representatives of the labor federations. Labor and the JSP were naturally in favor of ratification. The negotiations were difficult, and on at least one occasion a tentative agreement was reached only to be vetoed by certain groups in the LDP. Amid much name-calling, however, the negotiations did continue, and a special government commission was set up on which labor representatives participated. A compromise was reached on a package which combined ratification of the ILO Convention with revisions of domestic labor laws in such a way as actually to weaken certain unions (those of the local government workers and teachers) which are especially repugnant to many conservatives.

In summary, for the opposition to succeed in checking or changing some government policy, it is necessary either for the opposition to organize into a pressure group or for some part of the governing elite to take up the opposition's cause (autonomously or responsively). In either case, clearly, success depends upon access and power resources, but the most effective resource seems to be a believable threat that makes the rulers fear for their jobs. Otherwise, in the short run, an opposition cannot effectively influence government policy. Over time, of course, the most effective way to change government policy would be to change the leaders of the government; but at present such a change is handled entirely by the within-the-system opposition, the LDP factions.

Conclusions and Speculations

The pattern of political opposition in Japan during the past hundred years can be described as follows:

1. There are two basic forms or styles of political opposition: opposition within the system, and opposition outside the system.[46]

2. Opposition within the system is pragmatic, bargaining opposition over governmental policies and leadership. It is not recognized as real

---

46. The terms *within the system* and *outside the system* are translations of the Japanese *taisei-gai* and *taisei-nai*, but they are of course familiar in contemporary American idiom. Points 2 and 3 define these notions *as applied to oppositions*.

opposition in Japan because it accepts the existing pattern of interests and power ("constitution") and attempts to exercise influence within it.

3. Opposition outside the system is principled, uncompromising opposition to basic aspects of the existing structure of power and authority. It may be expressed within the parliament, in elections, or in extra-parliamentary actions. It may be legal or illegal, revolutionary or peaceful.

4. Either type of opposition may appear to act as an opposition according to the classical (British) model. However, this appearance is a tactic: within-the-system opposition is not seriously interested in changing basic national policies, and opposition outside the system wants to change the basic constitution as well as basic policies.

5. A party or group cannot be both types of opposition at once, of course, but over time shifts are possible.

6. Changes in national governmental policies and leadership, to the extent that they are due to oppositions at all, are due to within-the-system opposition. There is one important exception: outside-the-system opposition can succeed in forcing changes in policies and leadership if, and only if, it forms an alliance with some of the within-the-system opposition. (Each turning point chronicled here resulted from such an alliance.)

7. Partly because of this condition, there is a tendency over time for oppositions to be incorporated into the system; that is, outside-the-system oppositions tend to become within-the-system oppositions.

8. The alliance which is required for an outside-the-system opposition to be effective usually has radical, unanticipated, constitutional effects. (For example, in the four turning points discussed here, an elite partner in the alliance did not expect: modernization, party government, a fascist politico-economic system, or an intraparty, cabinet government system.) Major political changes occur as these effects of oppositional alliances work themselves out.

9. Whether an outside-the-system opposition and a within-the-system opposition exist, and whether an alliance between them is possible, depend broadly speaking on two sorts of conditions: socioeconomic developments and intraelite relationships. (Much of the present chapter is a documentation of this fact.)

These summary generalizations suggest, in light of current electoral trends, that Japan is due for some political changes in the near future in the wake of an opposition-elite alliance. At the end of the 1960s political commentators in Japan were describing the present period as one of multiparty politics. Three months after the general election of 1967, in which the Liberal-Democrats for the first time won fewer than half the votes, the LDP joined forces with the Democratic Socialists in support of a common candidate for the governorship of Tokyo — and this moderate-conserva-

tive lost to Professor Minobe, an independent Socialist backed by th
Communist and Socialist parties. (The Kōmeitō ran its own candidate
taking away badly needed votes from the LDP.) In the Tokyo Metropoli
tan Assembly, the LDP had not been the largest party bloc since 1965
when the Socialists took over first place. Since then the assembly ha
had three major party groupings — Socialists, LDP, and Kōmeitō — an
coalition politics has been the rule. The same trend can be observed i
the prefectural assemblies, where the declining share of the LDP's vot
has followed roughly the same course as at the national Diet level (se
figure 9.4) and the four opposition parties have gradually increased thei
representation. This general trend at the prefectural level is both slowe
and less significant than at the national level, but in some prefectures th
LDP has lost both its legislative majority and the governorship.

Thus the outlook for the future in Japan is for multiparty politics an
genuine coalition governments. (It is quite likely, although not immedi
ately germane here, that the ruling LDP will split if it loses its absolut
majority.) This outlook raises two questions: Will the "constitution" o
1955 be "rewritten"? And will the style or content of political oppositio
change?

Whether the breakup of the system of 1955, if it occurs, will involve
complete reconsideration of the "constitutional" settlement made at tha
time depends clearly upon what happens to the coalition which enforce
that system. If the business community and the political bureaucracy (an
the mass media) remain allied with a considerable group of conservative
the new coalition government may simply involve the replacement o
some conservatives with a group of moderates (from the Democrati
Socialists or Kōmeitō). In that case, it does not seem likely that there wi
be immediate radical changes in the policy guidelines set up in 1955. O
the other hand, should the bureaucracy and the mass media, plus a part o
the business community, be willing to support a moderate-left coalition o
labor unions, Socialists, Democratic Socialists, and the Kōmeitō, one migl
expect radical policy changes to be forthcoming. (Of course, even in th
former case, significant though unpredictable long-run changes are likely.
Essentially, the political choice comes down to a grand coalition (Socia
ists and LDP), or a minor coalition of the Right (LDP plus DSP and/c
Kōmeitō), or a minor coalition of the Left (JSP, DSP, and Kōmeito
Should the LDP split, other possibilities might emerge, perhaps even
coalition of the center (left-LDP, Kōmeitō, and DSP). If any of thes
possible coalitions were to form, excluding the LDP (or the right win
of the LDP), it would be a major political change in Japan.

If there is no major political change, it seems reasonable to specula
that the style and content of political oppositions will continue more o

less unaltered. But the emergence of *inter*party coalition government would entail a considerable increase in electoral opposition and certainly in the influence of nonconservative parties in government making. These developments, in turn, aided by the trend toward urbanization, should erode the political unconsciousness of many voters. Since political apathy, indifference, and ignorance are much greater among conservative voters than among other groups of voters, the emergence of multiparty politics promises to lead to a decrease in conservative voter support in Japan. For this reason the LDP, since the multiparty trend became apparent, has again begun serious consideration of revisions in the electoral system; but incumbent LDP dietmen are too wedded to the existing system to welcome any change, and the opposition parties are unanimous in their complete hostility to any change yet proposed. With regard to electoral opposition, then, available evidence suggests that the 1970s will see heightened political consciousness among voters, more stress upon opposition-government confrontation in elections, and increasing successes for the present opposition parties.

But what will happen if the LDP loses power — say, to a center-left coalition of Socialists, Democratic Socialists, and Kōmeitō? Presumably most or all of the present generation of LDP politicians will act as a within-the-system opposition, but some doubt may be raised about the extreme-right groups, both within and outside the LDP's circle of influence. Will the tradition of violent opposition, with roots as far back as Saigō's Rebellion of 1877 and suppressed only twenty-five years ago by a military occupation, spring back with assassinations, virulent nationalist public-opinion campaigns, and "revere the Emperor" slogans? It must be admitted that there is little indication of any such possibility. There is not, surely, much more of a social base for a right-wing radical movement than for a left-wing radical movement (the minuscule voting support for right-wing extremists suggests that there may be even less), and the very slow progress of the Communist party shows how small that base is. Japan's economic progress and, though to a lesser extent, political development — to say nothing of the wartime defeat and the antimilitaristic, even pacifist sentiments of much of the population — have made most Japanese, if not supporters of the current regime, then at least incapable of imagining a return to the prewar system.

Does this mean that the dialectical pattern of outside-the-system oppositions allying with within-the-system oppositions to produce political change has ended? No such conclusion seems warranted. Rather, the appropriate anticipation is that the next such alliance will involve some sort of opening to the left. There seem to be promising opportunities for Japan's political development.

Postscript 1972

Four years' perspective permits two conclusions to emerge from a close scrutiny of the parts of this chapter covering the postwar era. First, the focus is too narrow and the treatment too abstract or formalistic. This narrowness and formalism has two characteristics. First, there is too little explanation of the *sources* of the issues that generate opposition, beyond the observation that the major dimensions of opposition have been the issues that the "constitution of 1955" attempted to resolve. If it is fair to assume that significant opposition can occur only on significant issues, and that significant political issues are those that emerge from unresolved constitutional-level tensions, the absence in this chapter of a thorough analysis of the sources of significant oppositions indicates that the chapter has not lain bare these constitutional problems and therefore has not adequately analyzed the dynamics of postwar Japanese politics. Even more seriously, no consideration has been given to *noninstitutionalized* or unconventional political opposition — for example, of the antiwar movement, the struggles between students and university administrations and government officials, the paramilitary organizations of the right wing, the increasingly violent youthful left-wing opposition, or the dogged four-year resistance by farmers and segments of the Left to the government's attempts to build a new international airport. A serious discussion of such oppositions would be essential in any adequate account of the potentialities of politics in Japan and would also reveal aspects of the importance of the opposition political parties that are not visible in the above discussion of oppositions and elections, government formation, and policy making.

On the other hand, it appears that the treatment of postwar oppositions is essentially accurate on the subjects dealt with. Particularly, the end of the regime of Sato Eisaku and the election in July 1972 of Prime Minister Tanaka Kakuei, who both defeated Prime Minister Sato's own chosen successor and is committed to improving Japan's relations with China (in contrast to Sato's policies), seems to be virtually a replaying of the pattern of coalition government and intra-LDP opposition described above. Since the LDP has continued to hold on to its majority in the Diet, Tanaka's victory has not been the result of an open split in the party. But in the tactics that Tanaka used to win the prime ministership, in the immediate policy effects that his victory is expected to produce, and in the possibility that his victory may lead to the sort of moderate-center coalition envisaged in the conclusion above and thence to a renegotiation of the "constitution of 1955" — in these facts one can easily discern the pattern of political opposition described here.

INDEX